Learning Disabilities
From Theory Toward Practice

Lawrence J. O'Shea
Intermediate Unit I: Special Education Services
Coal Center, Pennsylvania

Dorothy J. O'Shea
Slippery Rock University of Pennsylvania

Robert Algozzine
University of North Carolina at Charlotte

MERRILL,
an imprint of Prentice Hall
Upper Saddle River, New Jersey   Columbus, Ohio

Library of Congress Cataloging-in-Publication Data

O'Shea, Lawrence J.
    Learning disabilities : from theory toward practice / Lawrence J.
O'Shea, Dorothy J. O'Shea, Bob Algozzine.
      p.   cm.
    Includes bibliographical references and index.
    ISBN 0-02-389321-4
    1. Learning disabilities—United States.   2. Learning disabled
children—Education—United States.   I. O'Shea, Dorothy J.
II. Algozzine, Robert.   III. Title.
LC4705.085   1998
371.92'6—dc21   97-28717
                                            CIP

Cover art: Ashley Marcum, West Central School, Columbus, Ohio, © Franklin County Board
  of Mental Retardation/Developmental Disabilities
Editor: Ann Castel Davis
Production Editor: Linda Hillis Bayma
Design Coordinator: Karrie M. Converse
Production Coordination: WordCrafters Editorial Services, Inc.
Photo Researcher: Nancy Harre Ritz
Cover Designer: RMD Marketing, Advertising
Production Manager: Deidra M. Schwartz
Director of Marketing: Kevin Flanagan
Marketing Manager: Suzanne Stanton
Advertising/Marketing Coordinator: Julie Shough

This book was set in Garamond Light by Maryland Composition Company, Inc., and was
printed and bound by Courier/Westford, Inc. The cover was printed by Phoenix Color Corp.

 © 1998 by Prentice-Hall, Inc.
Simon & Schuster/A Viacom Company
Upper Saddle River, New Jersey 07458

Photo Credits

pp. 2, 37, 154, 282, 295, 320, and 416: Scott Cunningham/Merrill; pp. 17, 184, 214, 256, 298,
360, 389, and 429: Anne Vega/Merrill; pp. 28 and 223: Tom Watson/Merrill; pp. 56, 83, 98,
200, 263, and 332: Anthony Magnacca/Merrill; p. 116: Barbara Schwartz/Merrill; p. 138: Cour-
tesy of Riverside Hospital

Printed in the United States of America

10 9 8 7 6 5 4 3 2 1

ISBN 0-02-389321-4

Prentice-Hall International (UK) Limited, *London*
Prentice-Hall of Australia Pty. Limited, *Sydney*
Prentice-Hall Canada Inc., *Toronto*
Prentice-Hall Hispanoamericana, S. A., *Mexico*
Prentice-Hall of India Private Limited, *New Delhi*
Prentice-Hall of Japan, Inc., *Tokyo*
Simon & Schuster Asia Pte. Ltd., *Singapore*
Editora Prentice-Hall do Brasil, Ltda., *Rio de Janeiro*

This book is dedicated to our parents:
William S. O'Shea, Sr., and Mary Jane O'Shea
Joseph C. Ley, M.D., and Dorothy A. Ley
Nicholas J. Algozzine and Jennie E. Algozzine

practices used with their students, evolved.

Preface

This textbook is for use in course work dealing with a survey of learning disabilities. Its focus on explanatory theories of learning disabilities and, within each theoretical model, the assessment and instructional/treatment programs generated set this book apart from other current textbooks and allow for a broad overview of the field. Our contextual approach indicates how theories and practices emerged over the past 100 years and the developmental links between various theories and practices. We believe it important that teachers who today are working with students with learning disabilities be cognizant of how their field, and the assessment and instructional practices used with their students, evolved.

Chapters are arranged in a chronological sequence reflecting the evolution of different models and paradigmatic shifts within the field of learning disabilities. The rationale for such a format is to present an overview of the field in the context of the theories and practices as generated, rather than using the more prominent and popular format of providing an overview of the field, including a chapter on characteristics, theories, and issues, and then discussing specific learning disabilities by content area (i.e., reading, mathematics, oral and written language, and so forth). We have chosen our particular format because we believe that reflective teachers should be familiar with the historical sequence of their field. Current and future teachers should be able to provide a sound rationale for assessment and instructional or treatment programs provided to individuals with learning problems based upon theoretical models. They should be aware that even though various models may not be influencing current classroom applications (e.g., a psychoneurological and biological model), a variety of theoretical forces, in tandem with educational, familial, and social developments, helped to shape what we know as "learning disabilities."

Our content includes discussions of the sociopolitical context, characteristics, historical developments, and the models flourishing during the development and establishment of the learning disabilities field. Additionally, we approach assessment and instructional issues within each model from an effectiveness explanation of the theory's translation into practice. We examine an evolutionary sequencing from varied perspectives: (1) the role of theories in assessment and programming decision making; (2) the use of theoretical models to evaluate effectiveness of assessment and curriculum practices during the course of the theory's predominance; and (3) the basis for current and future trends and issues in the learning disabilities field.

Our purposes are to review influential explanations for learning disabilities teacher practices. Accordingly, in Chapter 1 we discuss the sociopolitical context of the learning disabilities field, including legal mandates. We also include content on legislation initiatives and litigation and on the environmental influences of parent and professional groups who have helped shape educational policy. Issues related to the definition of learning disabilities and the characteristics of individuals with learning disabilities highlight Chapter 2. Also in this chapter we encourage teachers to use their experience, their reflective teaching practices, and their own beliefs as the driving forces in making educational decisions when they design programs for students with learning disabilities. Further, in Chapter 3 we emphasize that the field evolved due to broad, rich understandings of learning and behavior, pedagogy, curricula, assessment, and materials usage in ways that currently allow teachers to function as instructional decision makers. As instructional decision makers, teachers become reflective. Reflectivity is what distinguishes master teachers from more narrowly focused technicians. Our distinction reflects the differences between experienced teachers who analyze what they do in a social, historical, and theoretical context, and experienced teachers who can implement instructional procedures, but without considering why or how implementation affects, and is affected by, systems outside of the classroom.

Chapters 4 through 9 present an overview of the theoretical models from which assessment and instructional practices have evolved. We firmly believe that theoretical models played major roles in shaping the learning disabilities field and in shifting attention to predominant instructional practices. When teachers of individuals with learning disabilities recognize and gain a respect for the broader application of the theories shaping the field over the past 100 years, they will be better able to function as systematic decision makers.

The final part of our textbook focuses on a changing educational scenario, as teachers increasingly work in collaborative roles with family members and other professionals. We emphasize that education is a lifelong process. As outlined in Chapter 10, today there is greater emphasis on teachers functioning as consultants to parents and other teachers, because the traditional role of teachers working with students with learning disabilities continues to evolve. Many teachers increasingly provide educational services to students with parents and other teachers in inclusive settings. Consequently, their skills in collaboration underscore how reflective teachers function in the contexts of shared decision making, parent conferences, and consultation with general education teachers.

In Chapter 11, we include work on teachers' historical and current roles with family members. The roles of parents and professional advocacy groups in changing public policy influenced the sociopolitical process in the development of the current educational environment. However, teachers' roles with families evolved as students' acquisition and generalization of organizational and self-management strategies applied to studying, employment, family life, and independent living. Today's teachers working in the context of a changing educational scenario need to be cognizant of the importance of family members in working with teachers and in students' long-term school survival and success.

Finally, in Chapter 12 we extrapolate into the future, using developments in current theories and trends. We project emerging views of learning disabilities and present controversial issues dealing with the types of services that may be available within an increasingly diverse student population. We end our text reiterating the theme that important changes taking place in providing services to students with learning disabilities have evolved from the philosophical, moral, ethical, sociological, medical, and educational underpinnings of our society, and from models for understanding and treating learning disabilities. Teachers who understand that the learning disabilities field is based on the interaction of society, schools, and families are in the best position to serve their students' strengths and needs.

Acknowledgments

We wish to acknowledge our families, Lindsay, Chris, Kathryn, Mike, and Kate, for their support and patience, and the contributing authors for their excellent work. We also appreciate the invaluable feedback provided by reviewers: Jean C. Faieta, Edinboro University of Pennsylvania; Helen Hammond, University of Texas at El Paso; Synnove J. Heggoy, Georgia Southern University; Gayle Hosek-Mayer, University of Texas at El Paso; Judith J. Ivarie, Eastern Illinois University; Ronald C. Martella, Eastern Washington University; and Gary Sigler, Eastern Washington University. We are grateful to Ann Davis and Pat Grogg at Merrill/Prentice Hall for their efforts in leading us through the review and production process. Finally, we thank the children and youth with whom we work, who enable us to keep everything in perspective.

Contents

PART ONE

The Context and Population of Learning Disabilities

The LD field is based on the interaction of society, schools, and families.

CHAPTER 1

Sociopolitical Context for Educational Services to Students with Learning Disabilities

In this chapter we will . . .

- Discuss the foundations that professionals and other members of society have accepted as a basis for developing services for students with learning disabilities.
- Review the historical development of the field that serves as background for understanding current practices.
- Examine the legal underpinnings that shape contemporary practice.
- Examine persisting dilemmas and practical concerns that make delivering services a continuing challenge.

A fairy tale about special education might begin like this:

> Once upon a time, there were no special education classes for students with disabilities. And so for many years, students who learned differently spent many wasted and miserable years in regular classrooms, without the provision of special services. They were taught by teachers whose instructional methods did not meet their special learning needs. Then, one day, people decided that this was wrong, and special classes for students with disabilities were born.

A science fiction story about special education in the future might begin like this:

> It is the year 3020. We are in a school where there are no people with disabilities. In fact, the terms handicap and disabilities have not been a part of civilization's vocabulary for quite some time. This troubles some inhabitants of the planet. There is a nagging suspicion that some people are not like others. There is a growing concern that people may be passing inferior genetic structures to their offspring in a vile plot to stop progress and bring civilization to former levels of banality.

There was a time when disability labels were not as widely used or popularly recognized as they are today and, hence, *learning disabilities* (LD) was not a prominent term in the educational literature. The nature of the LD field did not take shape until the term was formally recognized. As noted in at least one textbook about students with LD:

> The authors of special education textbooks written before 1965 make no reference at all to the term learning disabilities. This is hardly surprising; it was only after that date that learning disabilities began to be accepted as the generic label under which a variety of syndromes affecting learning, language, and communication could be grouped. Before 1965, local, state, and federal education agencies did not officially recognize learning disabled as a category of handicapped individuals, that is, as a defined group of individuals whose special education or other treatment needs could be paid for with public money. As a result, there were few classes for learning disabled children, fewer remedial or habilitation facilities for youths and adults, and almost no college teacher preparation programs in the learning disabilities area. (Myers & Hammill, 1990, p. 3)

Today, more than a million students with LD are provided special education services by teachers specifically certified to teach them in a variety of instructional environments designed to meet their unique learning needs [U.S. Department of Education (USDE), 1995a]. These students represent approximately half of all students receiving special education services, and they are the largest group of students with special learning needs (Ysseldyke & Algozzine, 1994).

Schools were first established for a very specific reason: to prepare the young to assume their responsibilities to society. Although both the methods for achieving this noble goal and conceptions of the responsibilities have changed over time, the goal itself is still considered valid. This book is about people who experience difficulties in school, and this chapter focuses on philosophical, sociological, educational, and legal foundations guiding provision of services to some of these people.

SOCIAL AND POLITICAL BASES OF SPECIAL EDUCATION

The very first schools in this country were secondary schools established in Massachusetts in the early 17th century. The first of these schools, called Latin grammar schools largely because of their curricula, was established in Boston in 1635. The sole purpose of the Latin grammar schools was to prepare students to enter Harvard College, America's first institution of higher education, which was established in 1636. The pattern of schooling followed that established in Europe, where higher education in general was reserved for the top two classes in society—the landed nobility and the landed gentry. When John Adams attended Harvard, the students were ranked according to social standing, not academic achievement. He was near the bottom. The curricula of the Latin grammar schools consisted almost entirely of the study of Latin and Greek, an emphasis that had its historical roots in the early religious basis of education: to train youth to read the Old and New Testaments.

Between 1634 and 1638, the first laws were enacted for the public support of education in America—laws enabling the Commonwealth of Massachusetts to tax its populace and to assume responsibility for schooling. It is important to recognize that the commonwealth took on the responsibility of public education because parents were allegedly doing an inadequate job of educating their children at home. These first laws establishing public support of education also had a religious basis.

Virtually the only kind of public secondary school in America until the middle of the 18th century was the Latin grammar school. However, a significant change occurred in 1750 when Benjamin Franklin opened his academy (later the University of Pennsylvania). Franklin believed that students should be educated in modern languages, especially English, and in practical subject matter like navigation, surveying, and kite flying. Franklin's school also included instruction in history, geography, rhetoric, logic, astronomy, geometry, and algebra.

Past laws establishing education in America have been and continue to be enacted by the states. No provision in the United States Constitution ever established federal responsibility for education, and eventually the Tenth Amendment allocated such responsibility to the states. Objectives for education, thus, may vary from state to state, as do regulations specifying the kinds of educational services to be provided to students with disabilities. The fact that education is the responsibility of the states becomes especially interesting and important when we look at litigation and legislation relevant to the education of children and youth with disabilities. Federal courts have intervened in the affairs of schools when constitutional or legal rights have been at issue, and the federal government has intervened by providing funding contingent on the states' ensuring specific educational services for specific populations of students (for example, those with LD).

By law, education in the United States is compulsory. In 1840 Rhode Island passed the first compulsory education law, and in 1852 Massachusetts passed the second such law. By 1918 compulsory education was legally effective in all states. Movement toward publicly funded compulsory education in Canada followed such assignment and acceptance of responsibilities in the United States. All U.S. states and all Canadian provinces except Quebec and Newfoundland, passed compulsory attendance laws between 1842 and 1918 (Ysseldyke, Algozzine, & Thurlow, 1992).

Since significant decisions with widespread implications bear greatly on what goes on in education, the movement of children from their homes to public educational settings had considerable impact on the nature and characteristics of schooling. As the diversity of students attending schools increased, the expectations and behaviors of teachers and administrators also changed. Methods for meeting the needs of increasingly diverse groups of students were developed, and modern educational methods (e.g., graded classes, ability groups, and special education classes) became prominent. Schools are responsive to societal needs, and, hence, the characteristics of society, the schools, and families continually interact to produce contemporary educational practices. The field of learning disabilities is the product of such interaction (Sleeter, 1986).

How well has it all worked? Are students better off today? Who attends school? Have enrollment trends changed over time? Have students' basic skill performances improved? Has public opinion about education changed? How are the schools doing in meeting broad mandates and goals related to student achievement?

Consistent progress through school is a characteristic of academic success. Relative to modal grade, that is, the grade in which most students of a certain age are enrolled, which is used as an indicator of educational progress (USDE, 1995b):

- Overall, Black and Hispanic 13-year-old males have the highest average percentage of individuals below modal grade (more than 40% for 1995). This has been the general pattern since 1970.

- Since 1980, all ethnic groups have experienced consistent increases of individuals below modal grade.

- More male students are below modal grade than females.

Dropping out is sometimes a consequence of failing to make satisfactory progress in school. Recent statistics have given cause for concern about dropouts at all levels of education (USDE, 1995b):

- Black male dropout rates (among 16- to 24-year-olds) have fallen from 22% in 1972 to 11 to 14% in the 1990s; however,

- Hispanic dropout rates have not declined, and are much higher than Black or White rates (e.g., 30% higher in 1990).

- While the proportion of dropouts for all races was 11% for the sophomore class of 1990, more than 35% returned to receive a high school diploma or an equivalency certificate by 1994.

- The overall number of high school graduates as a percentage of the 17-year-old population has remained the same (i.e., 70 to 75%) for the past 25 years.

Reading and writing are essential for school success. In recent years, these academic skills have been measured as part of the National Assessment of Educational Progress (NAEP). Overall, American students have demonstrated continued low levels of performance in these important basic skill areas. For example, no group at any age level has achieved an average score in either the adept (can find, understand, summarize, and explain relatively complicated information) or advanced (can synthesize and learn from specialized reading materials) levels. About 42% of 17-year-olds are adept readers, but scores of both Blacks and Hispanics are well below those of their White classmates. Results for writing were similar; few students demonstrated performance at the highest levels of the scale (USDE, 1995b).

Relative to critical math and science skills, results from the recent NAEP assessments are similar to those from reading and writing assessments. Mathematics proficiency was about the same as it was in 1978, and science proficiency, for 13- to 17-year-olds, was lower in 1992 than it was in 1970. Overall, levels of mathematics and science performance remain low; most students, even at age 17, are unable to perform at the upper levels of proficiency (USDE, 1995b).

Content and Context of Schooling

Public school enrollment in kindergarten through grade eight rose from 27.0 million in fall 1985 to an estimated 32.3 million in fall 1995. Enrollment in the upper grades declined from 12.4 million to 11.3 million in 1990, before showing increases in the early 1990s. Public elementary enrollment is projected to grow by 9%, while public secondary school enrollment is expected to rise by 12%. Moreover, by 1997 public school enrollment is projected to pass the previous high set in 1971 and to continue to increase into the next century.

Who attends school and what goes on there is changing (U.S. Department of Education, 1995a). In recent years, preschool enrollment has doubled for White children 3 to 4 years old. About 5% of the total population of 3- to 5-year-olds were attending preprimary programs on a full-day basis in 1969; by 1990, the figure had more than tripled. Average kindergarten enrollment rates for White children increased from 74.1% in 1972 to 80.4% in 1986; rates for Black children increased from 67.1 to 82.1% during the same time period. Total public school enrollments fluctuated between 39 and 43 million students from 1979 to 1993, and special education enrollments rose more than 40 percent during the same period (see Figure 1.1), largely due to increases in numbers of students classified with learning disabilities (USDE, 1995a).

Total minority enrollment in elementary and secondary schools rose from 24% in 1977 to almost 34% in 1993. The figures for Hispanic student enrollments increased from 6.4 to 12.7% during the same time period, and Asian/Pacific Islander student enrollments rose from 1.2 to 3.6% of the public school enrollment. During this same time, the percentage of Black and Hispanic children attending school and living below poverty levels was about three times higher than that of their White classmates.

There is a reciprocal relationship between environmental conditions and children's attitudes toward school, learning, and other behaviors exhibited in schools. Recent reports indicate that about 16% of Black students and about 14% of Hispanic students do not feel safe in their schools; about 12% of White students feel unsafe in their schools. Students from private schools express generally more positive atti-

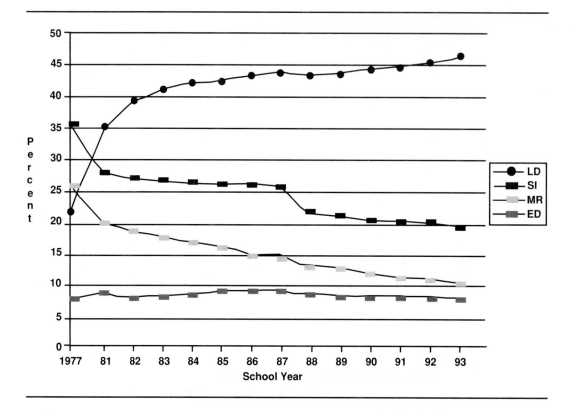

Figure 1.1

Growth in students served in learning disabilities programs.

(From data provided in U.S. Department of Education, Office of Special Education and Rehabilitative Services. *Annual Report to Congress on the Implementation of the Individuals with Disabilities Act.* Washington, DC, various years.)

tudes toward school, and 91 to 95% of them believe teachers are interested in the students at the school (about 80% of students in public school share this view). Eighty percent of eighth and 10th graders believe the teaching they are receiving is "good." About 40% of students surveyed in public schools indicated that disruptions interfered with their abilities to learn, and the numbers of students reportedly using drugs and alcohol remain high (USDE, 1995a).

Problems that affect public schools have been well documented. Teen pregnancy, drug abuse, vandalism, and student disruptions are among the problems identified by professional and lay analyses (USDE, 1995b). Teachers believe that lack of parent support or interest is the biggest problem in the schools. People in the general public disagree; they believe drug use is the most serious problem facing the schools. Teachers believe students' lack of interest is a serious problem, but a very small percentage of the general public agrees (USDE, 1995b).

Foundations of Learning Disabilities

On April 6, 1963, the field of LD was born. At a conference sponsored by the Fund for Perceptually Handicapped Children, Samuel Kirk mentioned that he used the term learning disabilities to refer to a group of children with developmental disorders that were different from then contemporary areas of childhood disabilities (e.g., deafness, blindness, mental retardation). The Association for Children with Learning Disabilities (ACLD) was formed in response to concerns parents and other professionals had for students exhibiting developmental disorders of spoken and written language (Myers & Hammill, 1990). Today, ACLD has changed its name to the Learning Disabilities Association of America (LDA); it has more than 50,000 members and is known to be a strong advocate for parental concerns and issues.

The LDA is only one of several professional groups that deal exclusively with interests of people with learning disabilities. The Council for Learning Disabilities (CLD) was formed in 1968 as a division of the Council for Exceptional Children (CEC). The purpose of this subgroup was to promote the education and general welfare of people with LD, much as the other divisions of the CEC promoted the education and general welfare of other groups of exceptional children and adults. In 1982, the membership voted to become independent of CEC, but its goals and many of its professional activities remain the same as the original organization. The Division for Learning Disabilities (DLD) was formed by the CEC to replace the CLD; it currently has more than 13,000 members and regularly publishes research and practical articles in its professional journals. Both professional groups work to improve services to individuals with learning disabilities.

The presence of these and other organizations gives the LD field a political base that contributes greatly to its professional identity and effectiveness. Through journals, newsletters, conferences, and sociopolitical networks, these groups shape the direction of identification and teaching practices. Members of these groups contribute to the knowledge base and lobby governmental agencies for better services. Differences in historical influences in any field are reflected in the perspectives of key people responsible for theories and practices. This is especially true in a field like LD, which has its origins in the theories and practices of physicians and clinicians working with individuals with brain injury (Lerner, 1994; Myers & Hammill, 1990; Wiederholt, 1974).

Origins of the Field of Learning Disabilities

Speculations about the origins of fundamental theories and practices in LD have been traced to physicians and other professionals who studied brain injury and its effects on language and other functioning of adults (Wiederholt, 1974). Key people linked with the early development of the LD field are illustrated in Table 1.1.

The various assumptions associated with early explanations of learning problems centered on what was known about brain damage and brain diseases. An initial focus on understanding learning problems related to the role of the hemispheric processing of the brain in encoding information. Medical researchers attributed specific functions to each hemisphere. The left hemisphere was associated with lin-

Table 1.1

Foundations of Learning Disabilities

Key Person	Time Period	Area of Study
Gall	1802	Spoken-language disorders
Bouillaud	1825	Spoken-language disorders
Broca	1861	Spoken-language disorders
Wernicke	1881	Spoken-language disorders
Dejerine	1887	Written-language disorders
Head	1906	Spoken-language disorders
Hinshelwood	1917	Written-language disorders
Goldstein	1927	Perceptual-motor processing
Strauss & Werner	1933	Perceptual-motor processing
Gillingham	1934	Written-language disorders
Orton	1937	Written-language disorders
Fernald	1943	Written-language disorders
Lehtinen	1947	Perceptual-motor processing
Osgood	1953	Spoken-language disorders
Myklebust	1954	Spoken-language disorders
Kephart	1955	Perceptual-motor processing
Wepman	1960	Spoken-language disorders
Kirk	1961	Spoken-language disorders
Cruickshank	1961	Perceptual-motor processing
Frostig	1961	Perceptual-motor processing
Barsch	1962	Perceptual-motor processing
Getman	1962	Perceptual-motor processing
Fitzgerald	1966	Spoken-language disorders

guistic, analytic, and abstract sequential processing or mediation. Nonlinguistic, spatial and holistic processing, or manual pattern recognition, were attributed to right hemispheric functioning. Some physicians held that brain hemispheres had specialized functions useful in explaining patients' inabilities to read, speak, or write appropriately. Others reasoned about location areas pertaining to brain damage and atypical brain development. For example, Gall represented early physicians when espousing that vital sources of movement and sensation were located in the brain stem (Lerner, 1994; Wiederholt, 1974). Bouillaud argued that localization of specific damage was due to lesions in the different brain areas. Some physicians hypothesized brain diseases in the form of physical insult to the brain (Wiederholt, 1974).

Beginning in the early part of the twentieth century and continuing thereafter, researchers focused on prenatal, perinatal, and postnatal events associated with brain anomalies. The most prominent implication resulting from early-20th-century research is that learning difficulties were thought to be caused by some neurological damage or other difference that resulted in the diagnosis and treatment of brain injury or minimal brain dysfunction. As Sleeter (1986) pointed out, during the course of the mid-20th-century, hypothesized organic causes of LD included suggestions of a failure of the brain to establish cerebral dominance, minimal brain damage, a failure to achieve certain stages of neurological development, or maturational lags in general neurological development. These areas of brain dysfunctioning were later represented in efforts to define LD (cf. Lerner, 1994; Myers & Hammill, 1990; Wiederholt, 1974).

Specifications of organic brain involvement and neurological influences, in addition to psychoeducational programming for individuals with brain injury, dominated much of the mid century research and practices (Sleeter, 1986; Wiederholt, 1974). Current investigators suggested that during this time period, medically trained, psychoeducational researchers began formal clinical studies of problem learning and applications to learning processes. Primarily because of the influx and support of behavioral underpinnings and learning applications, medically trained researchers, influenced by behavioral assumptions, studied the learning process in adults and children with brain injuries (cf. Lerner, 1994; Wiederholt, 1974). Many psychological-assessment and remedial-educational practices appeared in clinical research. For example, some researchers analyzed practices related to disorders of written language or spoken language; others analyzed disorders of perception and motor processes (Ysseldyke & Algozzine, 1994).

By the 1970s, educational, psychological, and medical researchers began to address inherent problems in brain injury etiologies and their relationships to problem learning or behavior and appropriate performance measures (Sleeter, 1986). The focus of the 1970s was on the difficulty of using medical analogies to deal with educational problems. Criticism of medical or clinical assumptions and their lack of relations to classroom practices dominated research journals, with the effect that medical researchers could not demonstrate, then, that individuals with learning problems have brain injury or brain damage (Lerner, 1994). Further, medical data provided little new or concrete direction to educational assessment and intervention practices (Ysseldyke et al., 1992). Critics reiterated researchers' and practitioners' attention to competing theoretical tenets, such as in the form of behavioral and cognitive-behavioral challenges to psychoneurological views (Lerner, 1994; Sleeter, 1986; Wiederholt, 1974).

Because of direct challenges by competing theorists and the resulting definitional dilemmas of the 1970s, researchers advocating psychoneurological views continued to influence thinking on learning. The terminology shifted from use of "brain damaged" to "Minimal Brain Dysfunction Syndrome" (MBDS) (Lerner, 1994) and recently "Attention Deficit Disorder (ADD)" has captured the interest of professionals and parents searching for an internal cause for serious problems in school.

In the 1970s, several forces merged to create the birth of LD as a field in special education. Forces included (a) parents seeking ways to focus greater attention on their children's learning strengths and needs, such as what children need to learn, and how to best teach; and (b) professionals advocating appropriateness of a systematic, direct approach to instruct students with problem learning within a broad range of service delivery options. Professionals also sought modified teaching methods and settings to accommodate learning abilities and styles. Sleeter (1986) characterized the modern LD field as one represented by advances made by psychologists, neurologists, and physicians studying children and youth who displayed difficulties acquiring language and reading skills, and by educators who experimented with methods for teaching them. Once sufficient research had been conducted and publicized, parents, educators, and physicians began to organize and together press for appropriate assessment and educational services.

In 1975, the United States Office of Education, through Public Law No. 94–142 (i.e., later amended in 1990 to the Individuals with Disabilities Education Act) and earlier amendments to the Elementary and Secondary Education Act (i.e., Children with Specific Learning Disabilities Act of 1969) provided support and direction for the LD field. Early efforts bear witness to the historical origins of the field. For example, the federal LD definition includes terms such as *perceptual handicaps, brain injury, minimal brain dysfunction, dyslexia, and developmental aphasia*. Recent efforts continue to emphasize the importance of multidisciplinary assessment and educational interventions to help children and youth learn (Lerner, 1994; Sleeter, 1986).

During the past 200 years, medical, psychological, and educational professionals have assumed the interaction of numerous psychological and neurological variables, thus helping researchers to explain, assess, and treat individuals with learning problems. For example, 19th-century investigators researched the nature of brain damage and brain diseases, early-20th-century professionals initiated the clinical study of atypical learning patterns and brain anomalies or brain injuries, and mid-20th-century researchers sought to refine brain-injury etiologies, organic brain problems, and clinical applications of assessment and intervention practices. Current researchers focus on multidisciplinary collaborations and integration of medical and educational technology into appropriate school practices for individuals with assumed central nervous system (CNS) dysfunctions. And the complex system that has evolved in efforts to provide services to all students with disabilities has always shared the weight of federal law as evidence of the value assigned to special education by parents, teachers, and other members of society. Today, the legal foundations of special education are more clearly articulated than at any other time in history. Challenges that have arisen from implementing the laws have become the bases for continuing changes in special education. Challenges arising from implementing recent special education laws are the basis for continuing changes in the field of LD.

LEGAL BASIS FOR SPECIAL EDUCATION

The first piece of legislation containing specific provisions related to people with disabilities was an 1827 act setting aside land for the Kentucky location of an asylum for the deaf and speech-impaired. The first substantive law establishing a government hospital for people with mental disabilities was not passed until 1857. The facility, located in Washington, D. C., and later named St. Elizabeth's Hospital, was designed primarily for delivery of services to members of the army and navy who became "insane." Also in 1857, Congress passed an act to establish an institution for the people with hearing, speech, and sight impairments in Washington, DC. Almost one hundred years later, in 1954, this institution became known as Gallaudet College, a school that continues today to provide higher education to students who are deaf or hearing impaired (Ysseldyke & Algozzine, 1994).

In 1858, Congress provided the first funds for education of students with disabilities when $3,000 per year for 5 years was appropriated for maintenance and student tuition at the Columbia Institution for the Instruction of the Deaf and Dumb and Blind. In 1879, Congress appropriated $250,000 for the purchase of supplies and materials for education of blind students throughout the United States. Such supplies and materials were to be provided by the American Printing House for the Blind, another organization that still exists today.

For the next 40 years, there was very little legislation specifically relevant to individuals with disabilities. Following World War I, however, Congress passed a law, called the Soldiers' Rehabilitation Act (1918), enabling vocational rehabilitation of disabled veterans of World War I. That act was restricted to services for veterans, as Congress said specifically that rehabilitation of disabled citizens other than veterans was not a federal responsibility. Then 2 years later, Congress passed the Citizens Vocational Rehabilitation Act, providing for "counseling, job training, job placement, supplying of artificial limbs and other prosthetic devices" (Ysseldyke & Algozzine, 1994). World War II provided a different kind of impetus for provision of services to individuals with disabilities. As large numbers of men entered the armed services, a manpower shortage developed in industry. Congress passed legislation providing job training and rehabilitation for individuals with disabilities to enable them to fill positions in industry.

During the late 1950s and early 1960s, there was a significant increase in federal legislation for exceptional persons. Some of the laws were enacted after advocacy groups put pressure on Congress to meet their group's needs. Yet it is important to recognize that much of the legislation came as a result of personal commitments by a president and a vice president of the United States, John F. Kennedy and Hubert H. Humphrey. As LaVor (1979) notes:

> Possibly the biggest assist that the handicapped received in terms of public acceptability, the stimulus for further legislation, was the fact that President Kennedy had a retarded sister and Vice President Humphrey had a retarded grandchild. As a result of personal commitments on the part of both men, in 1961 the President appointed the "President's Panel on Mental Retardation" with a mandate to develop a national plan to combat mental retardation. Two years later legislation was passed that implemented several of the panel's recommendations.
>
> In the years that followed, legislation was passed providing funds for states to develop state and community programs and to construct facilities to serve the mentally retarded. Funding was also made available to establish community mental health centers and research, to provide demonstration centers for the education of the handicapped, and to train personnel to work with the handicapped. (p. 99)

In 1958, following the Russian launching of *Sputnik*, Congress passed the National Defense Education Act, a defense-oriented legislation designed to increase education of mathematicians and scientists. The law implied that gifted students should receive extra educational services. In 1961, Congress passed legislation to support training for teachers of individuals who were deaf and, in 1963, amended the legislation to provide for training of teachers for students with hearing, speech, and/or visual impairments; serious emotional disturbance; physical disabilities; and other health impairments.

Beginning in 1963, there was a significant increase in legislation relevant to education of students with disabilities. At that time, funds were provided to states to enable the provision of vocational education, and in 1965, Congress passed the Elementary and Secondary Education Act (ESEA). In the same year, Title I of ESEA was amended to establish grants to state agencies to enable them to provide a free, appropriate public education to students with disabilities. In 1967, ESEA was amended again to provide even more services for students with disabilities. Regional resource centers were established for testing these students, as were service centers for people with hearing and sight impairments. Funds were authorized to facilitate both personnel recruitment and information dissemination of special education services. In 1968, the Handicapped Children's Early Education Act was passed, funding model-demonstration programs for preschool students with disabilities. On April 13, 1970, provisions related to gifted and talented children were included as amendments to ESEA.

In 1972, the Vocational Rehabilitation Act was extended, and state rehabilitation agencies were required to give first service priorities to those with the most severe disabilities. During the late 1960s and early 1970s, there was a dramatic increase in court cases directly related to the education of students with disabilities. This litigation led eventually to passage in November 1975 of the Education for All Handicapped Children Act, Public Law No. 94-142. Legislation providing special education has increased significantly. Major practices today (ranging from the inclusion of severely handicapped individuals in educational programs to barrier-free architecture) might not have occurred without legislative action.

 People with disabilities now have legal rights that are similar to the legal rights of nondisabled people. Though this is how it should be, this is not how it has always been. Today, the rights of people with disabilities are guaranteed by federal laws grounded in principles embodied in Section 504 of the Rehabilitation Act of 1973:

> No otherwise qualified individual with handicaps . . . shall solely by reason of his handicap, be excluded from the participation in, be denied the benefits of, or be subjected to discrimination under any program or activity receiving Federal financial assistance.

In 1975, the Education for All Handicapped Children Act (Pub. L. No. 94-142) was passed and a "free, appropriate education" became an expected and established right for people with disabilities (Ysseldyke, et al., 1992). For the first time in history, a law established principles and guidelines for the delivery of special education services. Its important amendments (Pub. L. No. 99-457) and reauthorization (Pub. L. No. 101-476), revision, and renaming [Individuals with Disabilities Education Act (IDEA)] in October of 1990 reaffirmed a national intent to support alternative education for students with special learning needs. Prior to passage of these laws, students with disabilities had no guarantee that they would be accepted in public school classrooms. Exclusionary practices, refusal to provide services, special charges for services provided free to others, and segregationist practices all were commonplace and documented during hearings that led to enactment of the first "compulsory special education attendance" act (Pub. L. No. 94-142). The social and political action that led to and continues from this profound development grew out of parents' and professionals' dissatisfaction with the kinds of services being provided to students with disabilities (Rothstein, 1995; Torgesen & Wong, 1986; Ysseldyke, Algozzine, & Thurlow, 1992).

Changes in laws have brought about changes in special education. Sometimes legal action is necessary to bring about social, political, and educational change. For example, in the 19th century, legislation was enacted to provide care for people with physical and mental disabilities. Early in this century, federal acts were passed to provide support for vocational rehabilitation of war veterans, and during the 1950s and 1960s, legislation was passed to develop programs designed to improve education (Ysseldyke et al., 1992). A summary of legal developments that influenced contemporary special education is presented in Table 1.2.

The right to education for students with handicaps and disabilities did not become a comprehensive program until 1975 with the passage of the Education for All Handicapped Children Act (EAHCA). This legal action (Pub. L. No. 94-142) put forth provisions designed to alleviate social, political, and educational problems identified by parents and other professionals prior to passage of this monumental legal action (Ysseldyke & Algozzine, 1990, 1994). Due process (DP) provisions and protection in evaluation procedures (PEP) provisions focused on problems identified in the process of determining eligibility and classifying students for special education. Least restrictive environment (LRE) and individualized education program (IEP) provisions focused on problems associated with placement and special education programming.

Due Process Provisions

Without procedural safeguards mandated by Public Law No. 94-142, the concept of—and right to—a free, appropriate education would be an empty promise for individuals with disabilities and their families (Rothstein, 1995). One of the major features of these procedural protections is the opportunity for participation in all decision making affecting the education of a child considered eligible for special education (i.e., DP provisions). The law provides that parents, guardians, or parent surrogates of children with disabilities have the right to examine all pupil records and the right to independent evaluations in all decisions affecting educational placement and programs.

A key element in procedural DP is notice. Whenever a school proposes or refuses to initiate or change the identification, evaluation, or placement of a child, the parents must be given prior written notice in their native language, unless this is not feasible. Parents have a right to object at the time they are notified, and those who object have the right to an impartial DP hearing where they may challenge the school's decision. Parents who are not satisfied with the findings of the DP hearing may (in most states) appeal the decision to the state education agency. Either party not satisfied with actions taken by the state education agency may appeal the decision to the civil courts. When DP hearings are held, parents have several rights: the right to be accompanied by counsel and experts in the education of students with disabilities; the right to present evidence, cross-examine, and compel the attendance of witnesses; and the right to a written or electronic verbatim recording of the hearing.

Table 1.2
Summary of Legal Developments
Influencing Special Education

Date	Development
1954	*Brown v. Board of Education:* Court held that separate but equal is not equal for purposes of education in a case involving racial segregation.
1966	Elementary and Secondary Education Act: Title VI amendment established the Bureau of Education for the Handicapped, to provide leadership in special education programmaing.
1970	Elementary and Secondary Education Act: Title VI repealed, and the Education of the Handicapped Act passed; Part B provided grants to states to support special education programming.
1972	*Pennsylvania Association for Retarded Children v. Commonwealth of Pennsylvania:* District courts approved consent decrees that enjoined states from denying education without due process to students classified as mentally retarded.
1972	*Miles v. Board of Education:* Set framework for due process guidelines that schools must follow before excluding students with handicaps from school.
1973	Rehabilitation Act: Section 504 prohibited discrimination on the basis of handicap. (Pub. L. No. 93-112)
1975	Education for All Handicapped Children Act: Established timetable for funding states and provided a framework for special education programming and due process protection for students with handicaps. (Pub. L. No. 94-142)
1983	Education of the Handicapped Act Amendments: Reauthorized discretionary programs and established services to facilitate transition from school to work. (Pub. L. No. 98-199)
1986	Handicapped Children's Protection Act: Provided for reasonable attorney's fees and cost recovery for parents in disputes with school districts over rights to free, appropriate education. (Pub. L. No. 99-372) Education of the Handicapped Act Amendments: Reauthorized discretionary programs and mandated services for preschoolers with disabilities. (Pub. L. No. 99-457)
1990	Individuals with Disabilities Education Act: Reauthorized Education for All Handicapped Children Act, with modifications to reflect contemporary perspectives and concerns. (Pub. L. No. 101-476)

Continuing Challenges.   Due process provisions create opportunities for parental participation in all decision making affecting the education of a child eligible for special education services. For DP requirements to be effective, they must be implemented at critical points in the decision-making process (Rothstein, 1995).

A continuing question related to DP is deciding when an action constitutes a change in placement. In general, minor changes such as moving classrooms or changing transportation schedules do not constitute changes sufficient to trigger DP requirements.

While administrative or judicial proceedings are taking place, students are expected to remain in current educational placement. This "stay-put provision" has given rise to a significant amount of litigation subsequent to the passage of Public Law No. 94-142 (Rothstein, 1995). Disciplinary removal and temporary removal due to emergencies have been central concerns that courts have resolved.

For example, when officials of the San Francisco Unified School District (cf. *Honig v. Doe*, 1988) tried to expel from school indefinitely two students classified as emotionally disturbed, legal actions were filed claiming that such actions were in violation of the DP guarantees of EAHCA. In the legal decision, the Court held that a removal for more than 10 days constitutes a change in placement and triggers DP

Today, more than a million students with learning disabilities are provided special education services. These students represent approximately half of all students receiving special education services, and they are the largest group of students with special learning needs.

protections. Language addressing this concern will likely be included in the legislative reauthorization of the Individuals with Disabilities Education Act. Details will be available from the Council for Exceptional Children.

Least Restrictive Environment (LRE) Provisions

Another key component of Public Law No. 94-142 is the concept of providing education for students with disabilities in programs that are as much as possible like those provided for nondisabled children (i.e., LRE provisions). States were mandated to have in place policies and procedures to ensure that

> to the maximum extent appropriate, handicapped children, including children in public or private institutions or other care facilities, are educated with children who are not handicapped, and that separate schooling, or other removal of handicapped children from the regular educational environment occurs only when the nature or severity of the handicap is such that education in regular classes with the use of supplementary aids and services cannot be achieved satisfactorily.

While the practices embodied in this provision are often referred to as *mainstreaming*, the term is not found anywhere in the statutory or regulatory language of the Education for All Handicapped Children Act (Rothstein, 1995).

The philosophy underlying concern for providing education in an LRE is based on several principles. First, it is generally agreed that any form of segregation in education is fundamentally wrong and inherently stigmatizing. Similarly, placement in separate (and potentially unequal) programs creates a situation in which self-fulfilling prophecies exert significant (and negative) influence on educational progress. Placing students in separate special classes also does not make sense in light of all that is known about the positive values of peer interactions for students with disabilities and their nondisabled peers (Rothstein, 1995; Ysseldyke, et al., 1992).

Continuing Challenges.   A key underlying principle of the EAHCA is that special education is to be provided to the maximum extent appropriate with students without disabilities. Judicial interpretation of this principle has added the element of age appropriateness as an interpretive concern (Rothstein, 1995). Broader issues relate to "mainstreaming," as application of the LRE provisions is often called.

The provision of LRE education does not require that every student be educated in general education classrooms. The law and related guidelines specify that restrictive placements may sometimes be necessary and that schools should provide a continuum of services to meet students' special education needs. Courts have looked at the stigma associated with separate placement and the benefits of positive peer modeling when deciding the appropriateness of placements. Controversy over where students with LD should receive special education will likely continue. Currently, most students with LD are served in resource rooms, separate special classes, or regular classes for most of the school day (USDE, 1995a).

Protection in Evaluation Procedures (PEP) Provisions

Before a child can receive special education, professionals must determine eligibility and make decisions about appropriate placement. The PEP provisions of the EAHCA address fairness in assessment and decision making. The law specifies the procedures that state and local education agencies are expected to develop and follow.

> Procedures to assure that testing and evaluation materials and procedures utilized for the purposes of evaluation and placement of handicapped children will be selected and administered so as not to be racially or culturally discriminatory. Such materials or procedures shall be provided and administered in the child's native language or mode of communication, unless it clearly is not feasible to do so, and no single procedure shall be the sole criterion for determining an appropriate educational program for a child. (Section 615-5C)

Specific rules and regulations for the implementation of the PEP provisions were published in the *Federal Register*, August 23, 1977 (U.S. Office of Education, 1977). These rules and regulations are as follows:

1. A "full and individual evaluation" of a child's needs must be made prior to initial placement of that child in a special educational program.

2. Tests used must be administered in the child's native language or other mode of communication.

3. Tests that are used must have been validated for the specific purpose for which they are used.

4. Tests are administered by "trained personnel" in conformance with instructions provided by their producer.

5. Tests and other evaluation materials must include those intended to assess specific areas of educational needs and not merely those designed to yield a single general IQ.

6. When tests are administered to students who have impaired sensory, manual, or speaking skills, the results must reflect aptitude or achievement rather than the impairment.

7. No single procedure is to be the sole criterion on which special education placement is determined.

8. Evaluations for special education placement are made by a multi-disciplinary team, including at least one teacher or other specialist with "knowledge in the area of suspected disability."

9. Children are to be assessed in all areas related to a suspected disability, including, when appropriate, health, vision, hearing, socioemotional functioning, general intelligence, motor abilities, academic performance, and communicative status. (20 U.S.C. 1415(b) (2) (B) 121a.532a-f)

Continuing Challenges.   Before they are declared eligible for LD services, students must receive a diagnostic assessment of their educational needs. Because of the stigma associated with this process and the biased practices uncovered prior to passage of EAHCA, parents must receive notice of and consent to this assessment before the process can be completed. Parents have a right not to participate in this process and to have an independent evaluation done if they disagree with the outcomes.

Issues related to payment for independent evaluations have not been completely resolved. When schools request, conduct, or arrange for individual evaluations, they bear the burden of any expense associated with the process. If parents are successful in challenging a decision reached during a school-district evaluation, they may recover the costs of the independent assessment used to support their challenge (Rothstein, 1995).

Bias in testing has taken center stage in litigation surrounding the PEP provisions (Ysseldyke et al., 1992). The use of testing procedures (e.g., IQ testing) has been challenged in major court cases claiming discrimination and bias on the basis of race (cf. *Larry P. v. Riles*, 1984; *Lora v. Board of Education*, 1984; *PASE v. Hannon*, 1980). The general outcome has been the continuing recommendation that a test score should not be the sole criterion in making eligibility decisions. Efforts to make unbiased decisions in LD will continue to be driven by guidelines developed as a result of this seminal litigation.

Individualized Education Program (IEP) Provisions

The requirement of a written individualized education program is the central idea driving efforts to provide free, appropriate education for students receiving special education. Members of Congress reasoned that if students with disabilities were to be provided with an appropriate public education designed to meet their individual needs, a mechanism for keeping track of the special education received by those students was necessary. An IEP is a written document that includes (a) a statement of the student's present levels of functioning, (b) a statement of annual goals and short-term objectives for achieving those goals, (c) a statement of services to be provided and the extent of regular programming (d) the starting date and expected duration of those services, and (e) evaluation procedures and criteria for use to monitor progress on at least an annual basis.

Continuing Challenges.   To qualify for federal support under the EAHCA, states must have policies in place that assure "all handicapped children the right to a free appropriate public education." The first Supreme Court case to address any issue of the EAHCA was concerned with what the term "appropriate" means in providing educational services (Rothstein, 1995). In *Board of Education v. Rowley* (1982), the Court held that a free appropriate public education consists of instruction specifically designed to meet the unique needs of students with disabilities, supported by services necessary to permit benefits from the instruction to be realized (Rothstein, 1995; Ysseldyke et al., 1992). Despite the specificity of the language used to interpret questions about the individualized education programs provided to students with disabilities, related controversies will likely continue on the appropriateness of special education for individual children.

The EAHCA required that a free, appropriate education be made available to all students with disabilities, ages 3 to 21, by September 1980. Subsequent amendments and revisions have extended and reauthorized the intent and actions initiated by this monumental legal action. As a result, schools are prohibited from excluding students with disabilities, and federal funds are made available only to those school districts that comply with the provisions of the law. Assurances protecting students with LD and their parents or guardians are stated in due process (DP), protection in evaluation procedures (PEP), least restrictive environment (LRE), and individualized education program (IEP) provisions. The rights to DP and PEP procedures are attempts to deal with problems in eligibility for, and classification in, special education. The LRE and IEP provisions focus on decisions concerning placement of classified students and how learning will differ from that of the regular curriculum. All provisions of Public Law No. 94-142 (reauthorized in 1990 in the Individuals with Disabilities Education Act) affect aspects of decisions made about progress in special education programs, and addressing them has profoundly changed special education. Despite all the progress in social and political arenas this legal action has engendered, continuing dilemmas and concerns create significant problems for professionals concerned with students classified with LD.

Practical Classroom Applications

As this chapter has highlighted, professionals and other members of society have laid many foundations as bases for developing services for students with LD. The historical development of the field has served, and will continue to serve, as background for understanding current practices and many of the legal underpinnings shaping contemporary practice. While there are persisting dilemmas and practical concerns that make delivering services a continuing challenge, there are many practicalities that help to place knowledge of LD into perspective, including the considerations described below.

1. *Students with mild disabilities are those typically placed in special education categories called learning disabled, educable mentally retarded, or emotionally disturbed.* The term *mild disabilities* is not used to imply that these students do not have serious problems learning or that their problems are less important than those of any other students. The term has come to be used for this group of students because many of their individual characteristics overlap and many of these students can be served in general education classroom environments or resource rooms, with assistance from special educa-

tion teachers (USDE, 1989; Ysseldyke & Algozzine, 1990).

As we discuss in detail in Chapter 2 of our text, students with learning disabilities exhibit a disorder in one or more of the basic psychological processes involved in understanding or using spoken or written language. These may manifest in disorders of listening, thinking, talking, reading, writing, spelling, or arithmetic. Learning disabilities include conditions which have been referred to as perceptual impairments, brain injury, minimal brain dysfunction, dyslexia, and developmental aphasia. They do not include learning problems which are due primarily to visual, hearing, or motor handicaps; to mental retardation; emotional disabilities; or environmental disadvantage. Students with mental retardation are those with impaired intellectual and adaptive behaviors and whose development reflects a reduced rate of learning. A student with emotional disabilities or behavioral disorders is one who exhibits persistent and consistent severe behavioral disabilities which consequently disrupt the student's or others' learning processes. In children classified with emotional disabilities, their inability to achieve aca-

(continued)

Practical Classroom Applications (continued)

demic progress or satisfactory interpersonal relationships cannot be attributed to physical, sensory, or intellectual impairments.

Students classified as learning disabled, mentally retarded, or emotionally disturbed account for more than two-thirds of all students with disabilities (USDE, 1989), and they share many characteristics (Hallahan, Kauffman, & Lloyd, 1996). For example, students with LD often have problems with reading comprehension, language development, interpersonal relations, and/or classroom behavioral control (Lerner, 1994). These same characteristics are presented in descriptions of students called mentally retarded and emotionally disturbed and many students who are nondisabled (Ysseldyke & Algozzine, 1990). Because many of their characteristics are not severe and because they overlap in conditions with different names, students with LD, mental retardation, and emotional disturbance are sometimes grouped together and called "mildly disabled."

2. *Social, political, and economic factors change what happens in special education.* When society's attitudes toward education of students with disabilities change, laws may be written or revised, and funding patterns may change. When funding patterns change, social attitudes may change, and so on. The interrelationships between the factors influencing special education are illustrated by looking at the impact of passage of Public Law No. 94–142. That law, and the mandates included in it, have caused many changes in educational practice, though the effects of those changes probably won't be known for some time.

For decades, special education existed as a separate, parallel system to regular educa-

tion. With passage of Public Law No. 94–142 and the requirement that students with disabilities be educated in the least restrictive environment, special education is best seen as part of a continuum of delivering services to these students. With passage of the act in 1975 and its 1990 update, a new kind of partnership had to be forged between special and general education. Schools were confronted for the first time with educating new populations of individuals with disabilities (e.g., students ages 3 to 5 and 18 to 21). School systems were required to enter into cooperative arrangements with other agencies for provision of related services (e.g., social services, physical therapy) and to bear the expense of paying for them.

One major area affected by this massive legislation was the training of personnel. To provide services to new populations of students, schools needed appropriately trained teachers. Accordingly, general education teachers, charged with the task of educating any students with disabilities in regular classroom settings, need in-service education. However, this has created huge problems; schools do not have resources to provide such training. Preservice teacher preparation programs are now only beginning to examine this issue.

3. *Many teachers of students with LD are vulnerable to stress and burnout.* When teachers are faced with the task of providing services that they believe they are not trained to provide, they develop considerable job-related stress. Many shift jobs, and others leave the profession. Stress and burnout are variables influencing success with students with disabilities, whether teachers are working in special education or general education, when teachers perceive role conflicts

(continued)

and role ambiguities with other professionals, or when they perceive ineffective working conditions and environmental factors. Certain special education conditions are very stressful and often lead to burnout and eventual attrition. In other words, teachers often leave their jobs when stress takes over their lives (Billingsley, 1993; Billingsley & Cross, 1992; Brownell & Smith, 1992).

Cooley & Yovanoff (1996) identified potential interventions aimed at reducing or alleviating burnout and improving retention among all personnel dealing with special needs students. Short-term interventions include professionals' individual responses to the stressors they encounter, the quantity and quality of collegial interactions available to them, and access to appropriate alternatives to administrative support when such support is lacking. There are factors over which teachers themselves have some control, or which fall within administrators' purview to address. Other strategies are to equip teachers with coping skills and to reduce collegial isolation that all educators commonly experience. Opportunities for teaming and work-related problem solving are useful. Support and constructive, collaborative dialogue between professional peers can help to reduce stress and burnout.

4. *The placement of students with learning and other disabilities into general education services creates many burdens on schools.* The enrollment of increasing numbers of students with disabilities in public education programs has also placed a large financial burden on the schools. Buildings and equipment must be modified and new equipment and facilities must be purchased. Because schools must provide education and related services, they end up paying for special curriculum materials and other necessary aides

and devices. As the financial burden increases, people begin to question the extent to which provision of services to so many students is worthwhile.

5. *Major questions arise regarding limits of responsibility.* Even though the mandates appear relatively clear, school personnel often have difficulty in deciding and defining responsibilities for students' services. For example, as schools are required to serve new age ranges of students with disabilities, there is little provision for enabling school personnel to meet age-related needs. The mandate for service is present, but the technology for provision of service is not. What usually happens is that schools simply expand their curriculum upward or downward in efforts to educate these new populations of students. However, without concerted effort by dedicated professionals and families, students with disabilities *can* be overlooked.

It is important to recognize that educational challenges in the form of technological advances, changing family and community diversity, and economic realities will continue to set parameters for students' lifelong learning in the next century. These and other challenges require concerted efforts by professionals and families to face the next century using sharing processes and joint problem-solving skills. Effective services for students at risk for learning difficulties and with LD rely on using our understanding about what we believe is effective.

There are important changes taking place in efforts to provide services to students with LD. As we discuss throughout this textbook, efforts are grounded in the philosophical, moral, ethical, sociological, medical, and educational underpinnings of our society. We believe substantive reform will evolve as foundational changes occur in the educa-
(continued)

Practical Classroom Applications (continued)

tional infrastructure. Issues that will have an impact directly on reform efforts for students with LD address students' learning needs and strengths. What we know about students' needs and strengths has evolved from societal underpinnings and models in assessing and instructing students. Accordingly, we believe understanding the foundations of contemporary practice will go a long way in helping us move forward in making education for students with LD better in the future.

SUMMARY

- Learning disabilities was not a prominent term in the educational literature, and the nature of the field did not take shape until it was formally recognized.

- There are philosophical, sociological, and educational foundations guiding provision of services to individuals with learning disabilities.

- No provision in the United States Constitution establishes federal responsibility for education. Objectives for education may vary from state to state, as do regulations specifying the kinds of educational services to be provided to students with LD.

- The LD field is based on the interaction of society, schools, and families.

- Enrollments, attitudes, and problems that affect public schools and services to students with learning problems have been well documented.

- There are several professional groups dealing exclusively with interests of people with LD.

- The LD field is represented by advances made by many, including psychologists, neurologists, physicians, educators, and families.

- Legal changes brought about changes in special education and LD services.

- People with disabilities now have legal rights that are similar to the legal rights of other people.

- Without procedural safeguards, the concept of and right to a free, appropriate education would be an empty promise for individuals with disabilities and their families.

- There are continuing challenges and concerns that shape professionals providing services to individuals with LD, including issues related to definitions, classification, programming, and categorical integrity.

DISCUSSION QUESTIONS

To help extend your understanding of the context in which services for students with LD are provided, reflect on and discuss the following questions:

1. Why do you think the term *learning disabilities* was not used until the 1960s to describe students having learning problems?

2. Do you think current conditions in schools advance or inhibit the development of LD as a category in special education?

3. If you were responsible for rewriting the legislation that guarantees a free, appropriate education for students with disabilities, what key components would you include in it?

4. Do you think individualized education programs should be available to all students or just students with disabilities?

5. Under what conditions would you permit a student with a disability to be educated completely in a general education classroom, with his or her natural neighbors and peers?

CASES AND STATUTORY MATERIALS

Board of Education v. Rowley, 458 U.S. 176 (1982).

Brown v. Board of Education, 347 U.S. 483 (1954).

Honig v. Doe, 108 S. Ct. 592 (1988).

Larry P. v. Riles, 343 F. Supp. 1306 (N.D. Cal. 1972), aff'd 502 F. 2. 963 (9th Cir. 174) (1984).

Lora v. Board of Education, 587 F. Supp. 1572 (E.D. NY 1984).

Miles v. Board of Education, 348 F. Supp. 866, 880 (D.D.C. 1972).

PASE v. Hannon, 74C3586, (N.D. Ill. 1980).

Pennsylvania Association for Retarded Children v. Commonwealth of Pennsylvania, 334 F. Supp. 1257 (E.D. Pa. 1971); 343 F. Supp. 279 (E.D. Pa. 1972).

REFERENCES

Billingsley, B. S. (1993). Teacher retention and attrition in special and general education: A critical review of the literature. *The Journal of Special Education, 72*(2), 137–174.

Billingsley, B. S., & Cross, L. H. (1992). Predictors of commitment, job satisfaction, and intent to stay in teaching. A comparison of general and special education. *The Journal of Special Education, 25*(4), 453–471.

Brownell, M. T., & Smith, S. W. (1992). Attrition/retention of special education teachers: Critique of current research and recommendations for retention efforts. *Teacher Education and Special Education, 15*(4), 229–248.

Cooley, E., & Yovanoff, P. (1996). Supporting professionals-at-risk: Evaluating interventions to reduce burnout and improve retention of special educators. *Exceptional Children, 62*(4), 336–355.

Hallahan, D. P., Kauffman, J. M., & Lloyd, J. W. (1996). *Introduction to learning disabilities.* Boston: Allyn and Bacon.

LaVor, M. (1979). Federal legislation for exceptional persons: A history. In F. Weintraub, A. Abeson, J. Ballard, & M. LaVor, *Public policy and the education of exceptional children.* Reston, VA: Council for Exceptional Children.

Lerner, J. (1994). *Learning disabilities.* Boston: Houghton Mifflin.

Myers, P., & Hammill, D. (1990). *Learning disabilities.* Austin, TX: PRO-ED.

Rothstein, L. F. (1995). *Special education law.* New York: Longman.

Sleeter, C. E. (1986). Learning disabilities: The social construction of a special education category. *Exceptional Children, 53,* 46–54.

Torgesen, J. K., & Wong, B. Y. L. (Eds.). (1986). *Psychological and educational perspectives on learning disabilities.* San Diego, CA: Academic Press.

U.S. Department of Education. (1989). *Eleventh annual report to Congress.* Washington, DC: U.S. Department of Education.

U.S. Department of Education. (1995a). *Seventeenth annual report to Congress.* Washington, DC: U.S. Department of Education.

U.S. Department of Education, National Center for Education Statistics (1995b). *Digest of Education Statistics—1995.* Washington, DC: U.S. Department of Education, Office of Educational Research and Improvement.

U.S. Office of Education. (1977). Education of handicapped children: Implementation of Part B of the Education of the Handicapped Act. *Federal Register, 42*(163), August 23.

Wiederholt, L. (1974). Historical perspectives on the education of the learning disabled. In L. Mann & D. A. Sabatino (Eds.), *The second review of special education* (pp. 103–152). Austin, TX: PRO-ED.

Ysseldyke, J. E., & Algozzine, B. (1990). *Introduction to special education* (2nd ed.). Boston: Houghton Mifflin.

Ysseldyke, J. E., & Algozzine, B. (1994). *Introduction to special education* (3rd ed.). Boston: Houghton Mifflin.

Ysseldyke, J. E., & Algozzine, B., & Thurlow, M. L. (1992). *Critical issues in special education* (2nd ed.). Boston: Houghton Mifflin.

Many individuals with learning disabilities often experience lifelong difficulties in early childhood, elementary/middle school years, adolescent, and adult stages of life.

CHAPTER 2

Contemporary Characteristics of Learning Disabilities

In this chapter we will . . .

- Discuss the prevalence of students identified as having LD.
- Provide an historical explanation of definitions and characteristics.
- Describe the use of definitions in conceptualizing, identifying, and characterizing specific components in defining LD.
- Discuss controversy generated by various LD definitions.
- Provide a chronological overview of the dominant theories and forces shaping the LD field.
- Analyze various definitions of LD and the influence of different disciplines, research, and sociopolitical factors.
- Define a *severe discrepancy* between achievement and potential.
- Identify four major methodological approaches in a discrepancy: grade level deviations, comparisons of standard scores, regression analyses, and expectancy formulas.
- Discuss problems in using discrepancy data.
- Examine the use of intelligence scores.
- Identify the debate generated from use of intelligence scores.
- Operationalize the definition of LD and its effect on prevalence figures and funding.
- Synthesize the need for a well-articulated definition and its importance for research purposes.
- Identify early childhood issues surrounding children with mild disabilities.

- Describe a variety of characteristics that interfere with the ability to learn successfully in the elementary or middle school years.
- Examine adolescence as an adjustment to academic and social expectations of the high school setting.
- Discuss adulthood and how many academic, social, and emotional problems encountered in adolescence persist into adulthood.
- Discuss peculiar traits or qualities typically observed in individuals who are known to have LD.
- Describe heterogeneous grouping and empirically valid subgroups of LD.
- Examine the discrepancy factor; academic problems; motivation, memory, attention and hyperactivity; social skills; cognitive and metacognitive skills; and perceptual skills.

Individuals with LD comprise the most popular category of special education (Algozzine, 1991). Ten years ago, 47% of all students receiving special education services were classified as having learning disabilities [U.S. Department of Education (USDE), 1990]; today, more than half of all children with disabilities have LD. Approximately 5% of all school-age students are identified currently as learning disabled and, to have their individual needs met, are receiving services in various educational environments (Smith & Luckasson, 1995).

According to Ysseldyke and Algozzine (1990), figures of the prevalence of students identified as learning disabled relative to all students with disabilities have ranged in recent years from 28 to 64%. Rapid growth and expansion in the LD field since the 1970s (see chapter 1) has resulted from the efforts of professionals and parents to define, identify, and characterize a *heterogeneous* group of individuals who together display a variety of learning and behavioral characteristics, have normal intelligence, and yet are not achieving commensurate with their typical peers.

Definitions, identification procedures, and characteristics of LD have been and continue to be influenced by prevailing theoretical orientations, research findings, and sociopolitical forces. Today, the challenge remains to define and diagnostically characterize individuals with LD who demonstrate unique academic and behavioral problems and who require differential educational programming (Torgesen, 1991).

The purpose of this chapter is to describe the characteristics exhibited by individuals with LD. The description is explained from three perspectives: an historical explanation of definitions and characteristics showing how sociopolitical forces and theories have shaped the conceptualization of LD; a description of the LD condition as a life-long disability; and a discussion of the contemporary academic, behavioral, and cognitive characteristics.

CONTEMPORARY CHARACTERISTICS OF LEARNING DISABILITIES

Definitions and Characteristics

Definitions are important. They bring order to the way we interpret our surroundings and interact with others. Definitions are useful because they assist in conceptualizing, identifying, and characterizing what it is we are defining.

In the field of LD, like other special education categories, it is crucial that the term learning disabilities be conceptualized and defined precisely. This is important for generating governmental funding and enabling professionals to "identify, diagnose, prescribe treatment for, teach or remediate, motivate, or generally improve the life of a person who has a learning disability" (Hammill, 1990, p. 74).

Attempts to define learning disabilities have been made by different groups of individuals (e.g., Kirk, 1962; National Advisory Committee on Handicapped Children (NACHC), 1968; National Joint Committee on Learning Disabilities (NJCLD), 1981, 1988). The definitions have consisted of specific components, some of which have changed while others have remained intact. These components include reference to neurology, psychological processes, academic performance, language, cognition, discrepancy, intelligence, exclusion, life span, and other disabilities (Hammill, 1990; Mercer, 1991). Table 2-1 lists the conceptual components of the definitions, and the components are defined in Table 2-2.

The various definitions of LD continue to be major sources of controversy in the field (Adelman & Taylor, 1983; Hammill, Leigh, McNutt, & Larsen, 1987; Siegel, 1989). The controversy is rooted in the evolution of a field that has been dominated and plagued by varying theoretical influences and prevailing sociopolitical forces. What follows is a chronological overview of the dominant theories and forces that have shaped the development of various definitions and characteristics of LD. Popular definitions are discussed, and current issues surrounding LD definitions conclude this section.

The 1940s and 1950s.   Historically, since the 1800s, different groups of individuals from different disciplines have sought to describe and define a group of adults and

Table 2.1
Conceptual Components of Learning Disabilities Definitions

Strauss & Lehtinen (1947)	Kirk (1962)	Bateman (1965)	NACHC (1968)
neurological	neurological	neurological	neurological
process	process	process	process
cognition	academics	discrepancy	academics
discrepancy	language	exclusion	language
other disabilities	exclusion		cognition
(emotional behavior)	discrepancy		discrepancy
			exclusion

USOE (1976)	USOE (1977)	NJCLD (1988)
academics	neurological	neurological
language	process	academics
discrepancy	academics	language
	language	cognition
	discrepancy	discrepancy
	exclusion	exclusion
		life span
		other disabilities

Table 2.2
Definitional Characteristics in LD

Neurological   Refers to a suspected central nervous system dysfunction.

Process   Suggests learning problems are due to disorders in basic psychological processes.

Academics   Includes listening, reading, writing, and mathematics.

Language   Includes speech and oral language proficiency.

Cognition   Refers to thinking or reasoning ability.

Discrepancy   Indicates a difference between a person's achievement and potential or intelligence. Suggests intraindividual strengths and weaknesses.

Exclusion   Means that learning disabilities are not caused by other disabilities. Implies normal intelligence in students with learning disabilities.

Life Span   Recognizes that learning disabilities may occur across a person's entire life, including early childhood, elementary/middle-school age, adolescence, and adulthood.

Other Disabilities   Recognizes that persons with other disabilities may also have a learning disability.

children who exhibit a variety of behavioral and learning characteristics that have interfered with their ability to read, write, compute, and reason. In the 1940s and 1950s, neuropsychological models provided a medical explanation for learning problems. The belief was that children's learning problems were rooted in cerebral damage, and that a diagnostic/prescriptive approach could be taken for remediation. As a result of extensive clinical research, Strauss and Lehtinen (1947) defined a child with learning problems as:

> the brain-injured child . . . who before, during or after birth has received an injury to or suffered an infection of the brain. As a result of such organic impairment, defects of the neuro-motor system may be present or absent; however, such a child may show disturbances in perception, thinking, and emotional behavior, either separately or in combination. This disturbance can be demonstrated by specific tests. These disturbances prevent or impede a normal learning process. Special educational methods have been devised to remedy these specific handicaps. (p. 4)

Thus, children were characterized as having brain damage resulting from exogenous factors (i.e., not genetically linked). Furthermore, a variety of characteristics were cited including disorders with perception, cognition, behavior, and neurology (Mercer, 1991). Strauss and Lehtinen's definition has been criticized because of the medically based emphasis on etiology, and the lack of educational relevance (MacMillan, 1973).

In the late 1950s and early 1960s, events were occurring—both socially and politically—that would have significant effects on the development of the LD field. Nationally, this country was reacting to the advancement of Russia's space program and the launching of *Sputnik* in 1957 (Sleeter, 1986), a development seen as posing a serious threat to the United States's reputation of excellence and achievement. Schools became the target of national concern and were charged to produce more academically advanced students. Recommendations were made to improve reading instruction, examine graduation requirements, and implement a national examination to measure student mastery levels ("Back to the 3 R's?," 1957). Proposals were made to raise achievement standards and establish ability groups to allow brighter students more academic opportunities (Woodring, 1957). These proposals paved the way for the development of special education categories and the establishment of procedures to determine who "fit" where.

The 1960s. "By the early 1960s, children who failed in reading were divided into five categories; differentiated by whether the cause of the problem was presumed to be organic, emotional, or environmental; and whether the child was deemed intellectually normal or subnormal. They were called slow learners, mentally retarded, emotionally disturbed, culturally deprived, and learning disabled" (Sleeter, 1986, p. 49). Thus, instructional categories were determined based on academic and intellectual abilities (Sleeter, 1986). Students with LD, as we know the term today, were defined as having normal intelligence and learning problems due to cerebral dysfunction. Evidence showed that the majority of students in LD classes were White and from middle-class families (Franks, 1971; White & Charry, 1966), and that Educable Mentally Retarded (EMR) classes contained mostly minority children from families of lower socioeconomic status (Franks, 1971).

During the 1960s, the psychological process model gained prominence as the theoretical explanation for learning problems and was the focus of subsequent educational assessment instruments and remedial techniques (Bender, 1992). This model was "based on the premise that specific abilities serve as the foundation for learning and performance and that attention to deficits in these specific abilities should provide the basis for intervention efforts" (Mercer, 1991, p. 272). Children with LD were defined as having academic problems resulting from basic psychological process deficits that could be identified and remediated. By remediating the process deficits, teachers could then expect to see concurrent improvement in reading, mathematics, and so forth.

Several definitions were proposed during the 1960s to reflect more accurately the academic nature of student learning problems. Difficulties stemming from the neuropsychological model in proving brain damage coupled with parental dislike of the brain-injury label influenced professionals to find more educationally relevant explanations for learning problems.

Three definitions (i.e., those offered by Bateman, 1965; Kirk, 1962; NACHC, 1968) were popular during the 1960s. (See Hammill, 1990 for further discussion of other definitions.) In 1963, Kirk (1962) introduced the term learning disabilities, which was accepted by the Association for Children with Learning Disabilities at their organizational meeting. According to Kirk:

A learning disability refers to a retardation, disorder, or delayed development in one or more of the processes of speech, language, reading, writing, arithmetic, or other school subjects resulting from a psychological handicap caused by a possible cerebral dysfunction and/or emotional behavioral disturbances. It is not the result of mental retardation, sensory deprivation, or cultural and instructional factors. (1962, p. 263)

The significance of this definition was in the use of the educational term *learning disabilities* to describe the problem more accurately than had previous medically oriented terms, such as *brain-injured* or *perceptually impaired.* Kirk (1962) stressed the academic (e.g., language, reading, writing, arithmetic) nature of LD; included reference to a neurological or emotional cause; and excluded other disability conditions. Students with LD were viewed as having at least normal intelligence.

In 1965, Bateman offered the idea of "significant discrepancy" as part of her definition of LD. The assumption was that these students had normal intelligence (i.e., learning potential) and yet were not achieving commensurate with their potential. According to Bateman:

> Children who have learning disorders are those who manifest an educationally significant discrepancy between their estimated intellectual potential and actual level of performance related to basic disorders in the learning process, which may or may not be accompanied by demonstrable central nervous dysfunction, and which are not secondary to generalized mental retardation, educational or cultural deprivation, severe emotional disturbance, or sensory loss. (p. 220)

The gap between potential and performance has since become known as an aptitude-achievement discrepancy; this concept was probably the most significant component of Bateman's definition. Curiously, no reference was made to specific *types* of LD.

Because of the need to fund services for this group of students, the federal government became interested in students who exhibited learning problems. Therefore, definition and identification criteria became important to determine who was eligible for services under Public Law No. 91-230 (passed in 1971), Children with Specific Learning Disabilities Act (Mercer, 1991).

Earlier, the NACHC (1968), chaired by Kirk and funded by the U.S. Office of Education (USOE), proposed the following definition, which became the basis for future USOE committee work (Hammill, 1990):

> Children with special (specific) learning disabilities exhibit a disorder in one or more of the basic psychological processes involved in understanding or in using spoken and written language. These may be manifested in disorders of listening, thinking, talking, reading, writing, spelling or arithmetic. They include conditions which have been referred to as perceptual handicaps, brain injury, minimal brain dysfunction, dyslexia, developmental aphasia, etc. They do not include learning problems that are due primarily to visual, hearing, or motor handicaps, to mental retardation, emotional disturbance, or to environmental disadvantage. (p. 34)

The writing of the three definitions proposed by Bateman, Kirk, and NACHC was influenced by the conceptualization of LD at the time. The definitions reflect the academic nature of the learning problem and the influence of the psychological processing problems in the theoretical explanation of learning disabilities. Thus, children characteristically were seen as demonstrating a variety of academic problems (heterogeneity of LD) resulting from disorders in basic psychological processes.

The 1970s.   The 1970s brought significant changes to special education. The changes stemmed from strong, influential social and political forces advocating for the civil rights of all children. First, spurred by strong parent advocacy groups and legal decisions that favored children and families, legislation (e.g., Pub. L. No. 94-142) was passed requiring professionals to develop unbiased assessment instruments for identifying children with exceptionalities. One intent was to stop the overidentification of minority children as having mental retardation. Second, the definition of mental retardation was amended with the lowering of the maximum IQ score to two standard deviations below the mean (Sleeter, 1986). Thus, fewer children qualified for special education services as EMR, and more children were labeled as LD. The challenge for the school system was to establish LD programs for all of these students and to have qualified teachers to remediate students' deficits.

The psychological process model of learning disabilities was challenged when researchers questioned the validity and reliability of assessment instruments and remedial techniques (Hammil & Larsen, 1974). When the psychological process model was discredited, professionals looked to other orientations to fill the theoretical void. Behaviorists advanced their philosophy by providing a plausible theoretical orientation and basis for academic instruction. Students were viewed as lacking in specific isolated academic skills. Therefore, instructional techniques became academically oriented rather than rooted in attempts to remediate hypothetical psychological processes. Although evidence of basic psychological-process deficits was still required to identify students as having LD, discrepancy formulas (i.e., mathematical computations that identified significant differences between achievement and intelligence test scores) became the primary method for identifying these students.

During the 1970s two definitions were generated by the USOE. The first definition stated:

> A specific learning disability may be found if a child has a severe discrepancy between achievement and intellectual ability in one or more of several areas: oral expression, written expression, listening comprehension or reading comprehension, basic reading skills, mathematics calculation, mathematics reasoning, or spelling. A "severe discrepancy" is defined to exist when achievement in one or more of the areas falls at or below 50% of the child's expected achievement level, when age and previous educational experiences are taken into consideration. (USOE, 1976, p. 52405)

The severe discrepancy clause sparked further controversy as efforts were made to operationalize the definition. Hallahan, Kauffman, and Lloyd (1985) cited 17 ways to identify a significant discrepancy. Quantifying what constituted a severe discrepancy should have facilitated the process of identifying children with "true" LD. In reality, the heated arguments surrounding the use of various proposed discrepancy formulas caused the USOE to drop the clause from the definition. (The discrepancy issue is discussed elsewhere in this chapter.)

When Public Law No. 94-142 was signed by President Ford in 1975, the legislation guaranteed a free appropriate public education for all students with disabilities. It was then necessary to have definitions for all of the exceptionalities, for funding and identification purposes. Thus, the 1968 NACHC definition of LD was modified and adopted as the federal government's LD definition for inclusion in Pub. L. No. 94-142. In 1977, the USOE published the following definition in the *Federal Register*:

The term "specific learning disability" means a disorder in one or more of the basic psychological processes involved in understanding or in using language, spoken or written, which may manifest itself in an imperfect ability to listen, speak, read, write, spell, or to do mathematical calculations. The term includes such conditions as perceptual handicaps, brain injury, minimal brain dysfunction, dyslexia, and developmental aphasia. The term does not include children who have learning disabilities which are primarily the result of visual, hearing, or motor handicaps, or mental retardation, or emotional disturbance, or of environmental, cultural, or economic disadvantage. (p. 65083)

Students with LD continued to be defined as possessing a "basic psychological process disorder" (i.e., processing problem) that was evident in academic problems. The definition included a language and neurological element, and it excluded children who displayed characteristics indicative of other disabilities (e.g., mental retardation, emotional disturbance) or sociocultural disadvantages.

An important component of this 1977 USOE definition was the effort to operationalize it. Accordingly, students could then be identified as learning disabled if (a) there is a "severe discrepancy" between academic ability (i.e., achievement) and potential (i.e., intelligence) in reading, mathematics, listening, speaking, or writing; and (b) the "severe discrepancy" is not the result of another disability (e.g., mental retardation, sensory impairments, emotional disturbance, cultural or economic disadvantage). Thus, the discrepancy factor (i.e., significant discrepancy between academics or language and intelligence) coupled with the exclusion factor (i.e., learning disability not caused by other disability conditions) served to operationalize the definition and thereby assist states in identifying students as having LD (Mercer, 1991). Mercer, King-Sears, and Mercer (1990) found, after surveying state departments of education, that the majority of states use the academics, exclusion, and discrepancy components when identifying students with LD.

The 1980s and 1990s.   Social and political forces have continued to have an impact on the field of LD throughout the 1980s and now into the 1990s. Schools have undergone restructuring with more emphasis on school-based management. The "back to basics" movement has regained momentum, resulting in higher academic standards, more minimum competency testing, and stricter graduation requirements. And the "inclusion movement" has generated a variety of service-delivery models, including full-time placement of students with LD in general education classrooms. Consequently, the challenge for educators who teach students with LD is to monitor the ramifications of these educational changes on programs and services, and to ensure that students with LD are indeed mastering their educational objectives (NJCLD, 1990).

During the 1980s and into the 1990s, students with LD have been characterized as inactive, passive learners (Torgesen, 1977) who lack cognitive and metacognitive strategies (Deshler, Schumaker, & Lenz, 1984; Wong & Wong, 1986), and who have difficulty generalizing knowledge across settings, people, and materials (Ellis, Lenz, & Sabornie, 1987). Thus, the cognitive-metacognitive (Brown & Campione, 1986) and cognitive behavior modification (Meichenbaum, 1980) models for explaining LD and structuring instruction have gained wide acceptance. Such acceptance is due in part to the strong empirically valid research base associated with these theoretical

Various groups of individuals from various disciplines have sought to describe and define a group of adults and children who exhibit a variety of behavioral and learning characteristics that have interfered with their ability to read, write, compute, and reason.

approaches, the reliability and validity issues associated with psychological-process testing and treatment (See Hammill & Larsen, 1974; Kavale, 1981; Larsen, Parker, & Hammill, 1982), and the issues of generalization and the teaching of isolated skills surrounding the behavioral approach.

Though the definition of LD continues to generate debate, Hammill (1990) has suggested that the most current influential definitions *agree* more than disagree with each other. The 1977 *Federal Register* definition remains popular and influential. According to Mercer et al. (1990), 57% of the states still use this definition, in its original or modified form, for identification purposes.

The other popular definition was written by the NJCLD (1981, 1988). This definition was an attempt to clarify terminology and conceptual thinking of the 1977 *Federal Register* definition. (The NJCLD wrote its first draft of a definition in 1981; the 1988 version had several revisions, thus the 1988 definition is presented here.) The definition reads:

Learning disabilities is a general term that refers to a heterogeneous group of disorders manifested by significant difficulties in the acquisition and use of listening, speaking, reading, writing, reasoning, or mathematical abilities. These disorders are intrinsic to

the individual, presumed to be due to central nervous system dysfunction, and may occur across the life span. Problems in self-regulatory behaviors, social perception, and
social interaction may exist with learning disabilities but do not by themselves constitute a learning disability. Although learning disabilities may occur concomitantly with
other handicapping conditions (for example, sensory impairment, mental retardation,
serious emotional disturbance) or with extrinsic influences (such as cultural differences,
insufficient or inappropriate instruction), they are not the result of those conditions or
influences. (p. 1)

The member organizations of the NJCLD have accepted the 1988 definition because
it (a) includes recognition of the life-span view of LD, (b) deletes the controversial
term psychological processes, (c) supports the notion that LD can exist with other
disabilities that are not causal agents, (d) and includes *spelling* under *writing*.

In 1987, the Interagency Committee on Learning Disabilities (ICLD), representing the Department of Health and Human Services and the Department of Education, presented their effort to improve upon the 1981 NJCLD definition. The major
recommendation was to add social skills as a primary learning disability; this recommendation sparked controversy in the field. Gresham and Elliott (1989) responded to the ICLD's definition by stating "the evidence for social skills deficits as
a primary learning disability is inconclusive. Many, if not most, children classified as
learning disabled show significant deficits in social skills and peer acceptance.
Whether or not this represents a specific learning disability remains an unanswered
question" (p. 123). NJCLD objected to the inclusion of social skills as a primary disability yet acknowledged that LD can have negative social ramifications. The Department of Education expressed concern about identification criteria and prevalence figures if social skills were included as a primary learning disability. Thus, due
to the controversy surrounding the social-skills factor, the ICLD's definition is not
widely endorsed.

The definition of LD has evolved from the influences of different disciplines, research, and sociopolitical factors. The effect of these influences has been evident in
the use of various components to define LD. Although the 1977 *Federal Register* and
the 1988 NJCLD definition of LD are accepted today, several issues discussed below
remain unresolved.

Discrepancy Formulas

One definition issue is the use of discrepancy formulas to define and identify LD.
The discrepancy component contained in the 1977 *Federal Register* definition was
designed to be used in identifying students as learning disabled. The challenge to
states has been to determine how to define and quantify a "severe discrepancy" between achievement and potential.

According to Cone and Wilson (1981), four major methodological approaches
have been used to document a discrepancy: grade level deviations, comparisons of
standard scores, regression analyses, and expectancy formulas. Much criticism has
been directed at the use of some of these approaches. Hanna, Dyck, and Holen
(1979) cited statistical and conceptual weaknesses when using deviation and expectancy formulas. NJCLD (1986) issued a position statement opposing the use of
various formulas for identification purposes. They claimed that (a) assessment in-

struments were not available for all age groups to measure achievement levels; (b) some assessment instruments used to identify a discrepancy were psychometrically inadequate; (c) some students would not be identified as learning disabled due to depressed intelligence scores, and thus a "severe discrepancy" would not be obtained; and (d) significant discrepancies did not always indicate a specific learning disability, thus the danger of misdiagnosing students as learning disabled. Ysseldyke, Algozzine, and Epps (1983) conducted studies on students who were considered to be typical, low-achieving, and learning disabled to determine the percentage of students who could be identified as learning disabled, based on discrepancy formulas, low-achievement cutoffs, or intelligence test scatter. Ysseldyke et al. (1983) found that by using one of the identification formulas (a) 1 to 78% of the students already classified as learning disabled could be identified with such a label, (b) 0 to 71% of the low-achieving students would qualify as learning disabled, and (c) 2 to 65% of the typical population could be identified with a learning disability. Therefore, not only could students be labeled as learning disabled who were not, students who were labeled as learning disabled did not qualify when the identification criterion formula was changed (Hallahan et al., 1985).

Furthermore, researchers supported the notion that discrepancy data are not used consistently by multidisciplinary teams when deciding the eligibility of students as learning disabled (McLeskey, 1989). Rather the persuasive input from team members, and existing sociopolitical factors, held more weight in the decision-making process (Ysseldyke, Algozzine, Shinn, & McGue, 1982).

Intelligence Scores

A second definition issue pertains to intelligence test scores. Students with LD are frequently cited as having normal or above average intelligence (Smith & Luckasson, 1995). Yet, the use of intelligence scores as a definitional component has generated great debate. Arguments focus on (a) psychometric inadequacies of instruments that purport to measure intelligence (Siegel, 1989), (b) the use of intelligence and achievement scores to determine a "severe discrepancy" (Graham & Harris, 1989; Stanovich, 1989), and (c) the connection between intelligence and LD (Baldwin & Vaughn, 1989).

Other Definition Issues

Several other definition issues continue to plague the field. First, operationalizing the definition (e.g., validating discrepancy formulas; developing valid and reliable assessment instruments to measure neurological dysfunctions) remains a challenge. It is important that the definition and identification of LD distinguishes this particular group of students from other disability categories and from students who are low achievers as a result of factors not related to LD. Furthermore, how the definition is operationalized will affect prevalence figures, which in turn affects funding dollars for LD services.

Second, a well-articulated definition is important for research purposes. A clearly defined group of students will promote better generalization and replication of research findings. According to Torgesen (1991), it is important to the integrity of the

LD field that we examine definition and identification practices and scrutinize sociopolitical forces that influence how we assess, label, and place students in LD programs.

LEARNING DISABILITIES AS A LIFELONG CONDITION

It is well recognized that individuals with LD experience lifelong difficulties stemming from their specific disability (Mercer, 1991; NJCLD, 1988; Smith & Luckasson, 1995). As Keogh and Sears (1991) have noted, "learning disabilities may not be limited to a particular age group or to a particular setting. LD are no longer thought to be school-specific or to be the exclusive province of elementary-aged children" (p. 486). It is evident that LD are prevalent throughout life and must be addressed accordingly. This section will discuss LD as a lifelong condition by examining the characteristics associated with early childhood, elementary/middle school years, adolescence, and adult stages of life. Table 2-3 summarizes the characteristics associated with each of these areas.

Early Childhood

With the enactment of Public Law No. 99-457 in 1986, states must provide services for children from birth to 5 years old. Therefore, states must have procedures for identifying, assessing, and instructing children and the qualified personnel to do so.

Table 2.3
Possible Problematic Areas (by stage of life)

Early Childhood (birth–5 years)	School-Age (Kindergarten–8th grade)	Adolescence (9th–12th grade)	Adulthood (postsecondary)
Motor	Motor	Academics	Academics
	Readiness	Reading	Reading
	Language	Mathematics	Mathematics
		Writing	Spelling
		Spelling	Writing
Reception	Academics	Language	Social and
Visual	Reading		Emotional Skills
Auditory	Mathematics		
	Writing		
	Spelling		
Language		Cognitive Skills	Cognitive Skills
Cognition Skills	Cognitive Skills	Reasoning and	Career and
		Problem Solving	Vocational skills
Social	Attending	Social and	Independent
		Emotional Skills	Living Skills
	Reasoning and Problem Solving		
	Social and Emotional Skills		

Typically, children who display obvious language, cognitive, physical, and sensory disabilities are easily identifiable. Children who display mild developmental disabilities are harder to pinpoint. Because a learning disability is associated with academic problems and is identified as a discrepancy between potential and achievement, a categorical learning disabilities label may not be appropriate for children ages birth through 5 years (Smith & Luckasson, 1995). Rather, a child's disability is usually described according to developmental delays; that is, it might be determined that the child is exhibiting a language or motor delay as measured by normal developmental scales.

Certain characteristics displayed by children usually signal that early intervention is warranted. Children might be targeted for services if they exhibit the following characteristics: excessive motor activity, problems producing speech sounds, difficulty with language production and comprehension, memory and discrimination difficulties, and cognitive delays. Some of these children go on to be identified as having learning disabilities during the school-age years, because of the continued presence of early childhood anomalies. This scenario is common for children with early language disorders (Mallory & Kerns, 1988).

It should be noted that many issues surround early identification of children with mild disabilities, which will be discussed elsewhere in this book. Some of these issues include labeling at an early age, identifying the least restrictive environment (U.S. Department of Education, 1990), being sensitive to developmental milestones and developmental rates, and defining "developmentally delayed." An additional concern involves determining developmentally appropriate behaviors, as many children, for example, exhibit problems that later disappear, such as reversing letters and articulating certain sounds.

Elementary and Middle-School Years

Many students are diagnosed with LD during the elementary (i.e., kindergarten through fifth) or middle-school years (i.e., sixth through eighth grade). Ability-achievement discrepancies are identified as a result of student difficulty in meeting increasingly more complex academic, social, and behavioral expectations. For example, students must demonstrate ability in the areas of oral and written language. They must be able to follow directions, attend to tasks, complete activities independently, and utilize effective cognitive strategies in the academic and social realms.

As seen in Table 2.3, school-age students with LD exhibit a variety of characteristics that interfere with their ability to learn successfully. The challenge for teachers is to provide a structured, supportive environment that promotes academic, social, and behavioral success. Teachers must work closely with a variety of professionals and the families of their students, selecting materials and curricula that meet the needs of each child.

Adolescence

Adolescence is a period of time marked by changes in physical, emotional, and cognitive growth. In addition to adjusting to the normal developmental changes associated with adolescence, students with LD also must adjust to academic and social expectations of the high school setting. Such expectations include being capable of comprehending content-area reading, studying effectively, using mathematical skills to compute and reason, communicating both in oral and written forms, engaging appropriately in social interactions, and preparing for the transition from adolescence and high school to adulthood and postsecondary stage, and the accompanying adjustments.

Clearly, students with LD at the high school level continue to struggle academically and socially, as evidenced by the characteristics in Table 2.3. According to Schumaker, Deshler, Alley, and Warner (1983), the academic skills of many students with LD plateau by the 10th grade. Very often the skill development remains at an elementary level. Some students continue to be plagued by social skill deficiencies as well (Bryan, 1976). Inappropriate social skills interfere with satisfying peer relationships and may prove problematic in vocational preparation settings.

The net effect is that an alarming number of students with LD are dropping out of high school (Levin, Zigmond, & Birch, 1985). According to the U.S. Department of Education, Office of Special Education Programs (OSEP) (1989), almost 27% of students with LD who were 14 years of age or older dropped out of high school during the 1987–88 school year. Although efforts have been made to tailor secondary curricular models (e.g., Deshler & Schumaker, 1986) to specific student characteristics, many of these students leave high school by the 9th grade (deBettencourt, Zigmond, & Thornton, 1989) and, not surprisingly, are underemployed compared to their peers who graduated with a diploma (Edgar, 1987). Thus, the challenge remains to motivate adolescent students with LD to remain in school by providing meaningful educational models, services, and transition plans that offer students alternatives to traditional instruction and career opportunities.

Adulthood

Adulthood is marked by continued intellectual development, social and emotional maturity, and career attainment (Havighurst, 1972). Adults are challenged to manage the increasing responsibilities that accompany marriage, purchase of a home, new career, birth of a child, and so forth, attempting to cope successfully with the many stressors and decisions of everyday living.

For some adults, dealing successfully with typical adulthood demands is hindered by the continued presence and impact of their learning disability. Researchers have shown that many of the academic, social, and emotional problems encountered in adolescence persist into adulthood and influence successful adult adjustment and independent living (Blalock, 1997; Gerber et al., 1990; Johnson & Blalock, 1987). For example, Smith (1988) stated that adults with LD reported survival-skills difficulties (e.g., managing money) that reflect basic academic deficiencies. Other researchers have shown that both career satisfaction and adjustment for persons with LD were less satisfactory than those of nondisabled adult peers (Chelser, 1982; Humes & Brammer, 1985). Furthermore, although adults with LD may choose to pursue postsecondary education (Dalke & Franzene, 1988; Sitlington & Frank, 1990), success depends upon the availability of higher education support systems and the abilities of the individual to compensate for the learning disability.

Research interest in the area of adults with LD continues to grow. It is imperative that empirically sound follow-up studies are devised to learn more about the needs of this population, including recommendations for better secondary instruction, transition programs, and postsecondary support systems.

CHARACTERISTICS OF LEARNING DISABILITIES

According to Myers and Hammill (1990), "the term characteristics refers to those peculiar traits or qualities typically observed in individuals who are known to have learning disabilities" (p. 25). In 1966, Clements identified a variety of characteristics theoretically resulting from minimal brain dysfunction. Some of those characteristics included soft neurological signs, emotional problems, and disabilities in communication, attention, academics, thinking, and perception. Smith and Luckasson (1995) offered a list of various characteristics that added to Clement's characteristics and reflected a more contemporary theoretical viewpoint. Judging from the number of characteristics, it is not surprising that learning disabilities are frequently viewed as a *heterogeneous* group; that is, LD is an umbrella term referring to a variety of disorders (Keller & Hallahan, 1987; Wallace & McLoughlin, 1988).

In light of the heterogeneous nature of LD, researchers have sought to identify empirically valid subgroups of LD (Caldwell, Recht, & Newby, 1987; Lovett, Ransby, Hardwick, & Johnson, 1989; Lyon, & Flynn, 1990; Lyon & Watson, 1981), subgroups that would benefit from different interventions (Lyon, Newby, Recht, & Caldwell, 1991). Researchers have initially revealed language, visual, and behavioral subgroups (McKinney, 1988), and the importance of memory factors in identifying the various subgroups (Swanson, 1983; Torgesen, 1988). Preliminary results of attempts to define unique subgroups that are responsive to differential treatments have been mixed, partly because this line of research has been plagued by methodological limitations. However, such research is promising and intuitively appealing (Kavale & Forness, 1987). Thus, further subgroup and intervention research is warranted.

Following are characteristics cited most frequently in the LD literature (e.g., Lerner, 1988; Lovitt, 1989; Mercer, 1991; Smith & Luckasson, 1995), and thus represent current thinking regarding the conceptualization of learning disabilities. It is important to keep in mind that individuals with LD may not possess all of the following characteristics. It is through the assessment process that specific characteristics are identified for each individual. Thus, professionals must approach each student individually when designing appropriate educational services.

Discrepancy between Aptitude and Achievement

The discrepancy factor remains a prominent defining characteristic of LD and is used widely by states in identifying students as learning disabled (Mercer et al., 1990). As previously noted, a discrepancy exists if a student's performance on achievement tests (e.g., oral language, written language) is significantly discrepant from (as defined by individual states) his or her intelligence test scores.

Academic Deficiencies

It is well recognized (e.g., NJCLD, 1988; USOE, 1977) that academic problems are a major characteristic of LD. Although with LD, academic disabilities are noted in reading, oral language, written language, and mathematics, reading problems are the primary disability among these individuals (Lovitt, 1989; McLeod & Armstrong, 1982).

A variety of academic problems have been documented within specific skill areas. In reading, for example, researchers have shown that (a) many elementary-age students experience difficulty acquiring phonological skills that are necessary for successful word recognition and comprehension (e.g., Stanovich, 1988; Torgesen, 1988; Vellutino & Scanlon, 1986), (b) oral reading fluency is problematic (e.g., Shinn & Marston, 1985), and (c) students at all grade levels experience problems with comprehension skills.

In oral language, students with LD may possess disorders in syntax, semantics, morphology, phonology, articulation, and/or pragmatics (Gibbs & Cooper, 1989; Wiig & Semel, 1984). These oral language difficulties can interfere with a student's ability to comprehend language related to the curriculum, instruction, or interactions with other students (Gruenewald & Pollack, 1984; Wallach & Miller, 1988).

Written-language skills include handwriting, spelling, punctuation, capitalization, and composition. Students with LD exhibit difficulties with the mechanical, cognitive, and metacognitive elements of writing (Graham, Harris, MacArthur, & Schwartz, 1991). Such difficulties appear in their written work in the form of spelling errors, lack of appropriate punctuation, and syntax (Anderson, 1982; Poplin, Gray, Larsen, Banikowski, & Mehring, 1980), as well as lack of coherence and story development (Englert, Raphael, Fear, & Anderson, 1988; Montague, Maddux, & Dereshiwsky, 1988; Wong, Wong, & Blenkinsop, 1989).

Mathematical difficulties for students with learning problems are also diverse, spanning the mathematics curriculum across the grade levels (Cawley & Miller, 1989). Difficulties may stem from slowness in operation execution (Kirby & Becker, 1988), developmental delays (Cawley, Fitzmaurice-Hayes, & Shaw, 1988), memory deficiencies (Bley & Thornton, 1995), language problems (Cawley, 1970), lack of effective cognitive and metacognitive strategies (Cherkes-Julkowski, 1985), difficulty with generalization (Rivera & Smith, 1987), and procedural errors (Russell & Ginsburg, 1984). Such difficulties can interfere with the successful acquisition of mathematical concepts and skills in areas such as computation, problem-solving, geometry, mental calculations, estimation, probability, statistics, decimals, measurement, and fractions.

Motivation

According to Smith and Luckasson (1995), "motivation is usually defined as the inner stimulus that causes people to be energized and directed in their behavior" (p. 228). Motivation exists when an individual has some interest or drive toward a particular condition. In the classroom, some degree of success and interest must accompany learning in order for students to pursue academic tasks willingly.

Researchers have shown that some students with LD lack the necessary motivation to produce success (Adelman & Taylor, 1983; Schumaker & Hazel, 1984; Torgesen, 1977). Students may attribute unsuccessful experiences to their own inabilities (Golumbia & Hillman, 1990; Smith & Luckasson, 1995) or successful ones to luck, rather than viewing their abilities and efforts as contributing factors to success (Pearl, 1982; Pearl, Bryan, & Donahue, 1980). *Learned helplessness* may be a characteristic of this group of students, as they expect to fail and are dependent on other people to solve their problems (Smith & Luckasson, 1995). Torgesen and Licht (1983) and Wong (1980) found that these students were *passive* or *inactive learners;* that is, they did not interact with the material, possess effective learning strategies, or seek assistance when necessary.

Memory

Swanson and Cooney (1991) defined memory as "the ability to encode, process, and retrieve information that one has been exposed to" (p. 104). According to these researchers, students with LD exhibit memory abilities comparable to younger students who are not learning disabled. Research on short-term memory (limited storage of information) and long-term memory (permanent storage of information) has shown that students with LD (a) lack effective strategies, such as rehearsal or organization, to assist in memorizing information (Swanson, 1983; Torgesen & Goldman, 1977; Vellutino & Scanlon, 1987); (b) lack effective metacognitive skills to facilitate recall (Wong, 1982); and (c) possess limited semantic memory capabilities (Swanson, 1983).

Attention and Hyperactivity

Research findings support the notion that many students with LD have more difficulties with attention than do their typical peers (Hallahan, 1975). In some studies, researchers found that students with LD exhibited problems with selective attention abilities, such as selecting relevant aspects of a task (Keogh & Margolis, 1976; Tarnowski, Prinz, & Nay, 1986), and with sustained attention abilities, such as focusing on and maintaining task behavior (Hallahan, Kauffman, & Lloyd, 1996).

Attention and hyperactivity have been linked by the American Psychiatric Association (APA) in its *Diagnostic and Statistical Manual of Mental Disorders* (DSM-IV) (1994). *Attention Deficit Hyperactivity Disorder* (ADHD) is a term describing students who display developmentally inappropriate characteristics of inattention, hyperactivity, and impulsivity (Reeve, 1990). Mannerisms associated with ADHD include fidgety behavior, distractibility, impulsivity, problems staying in seat, as well as task-completion problems, cause-and-effect difficulties, and poor communication and/or social skills such as interrupting and not listening (APA, 1994).

Approximately one-third of students with LD are thought to have ADHD (Hallahan, 1989). However, this is a controversial area in need of continued research. Issues such as the interaction of LD and ADHD, the unique characteristics of LD and ADHD, treatment for students with LD/ADHD, medication, and whether the LD causes the ADHD, or vice versa, all warrant further study.

Social Skills

McIntosh, Vaughn, and Zaragoza (1991) stated that "many students with learning disabilities are not well accepted by their peers, have social skills deficits, and have difficulties making and maintaining friends" (p. 451). The extent of social-skills deficits among students with LD was given definitional attention when the Interagency Committee on Learning Disabilities (1987) attempted to include problems with social skills as a specific learning disability. Although the recommendation to include social skills as a type of learning disability has met with disfavor by many professionals, social deficits are recognized as a characteristic of many students with learning problems (Gresham & Elliot, 1989).

Bryan (1991) noted social-skills deficits in four areas, including how students with LD (a) view themselves, (b) are viewed as socially competent by others, (c) communicate using the rules and language of social interactions, and (d) behave in social situations. In each area, evidence suggests that students experience difficulties coping effectively with social interactions. For example, studies support the notion that students with LD view themselves as less academically able than their typical peer group (Chapman, 1985; Kistner & Osborne, 1987). In other studies (e.g., Bryan & Sonnefeld, 1981), students were found to possess appropriate social cognition regarding how to respond to situations but were more prone than their typical peers to succumb to peer pressure.

Ellis and Friend (1991) reported that adolescent students with LD may lack appropriate social skills or may possess the skills but lack generalization abilities (i.e., be cognitively aware of an appropriate social skill, such as conversational turn taking, but not transfer this knowledge to different situations). Blalock (1981) found that social skills deficiencies continued into adulthood as individuals with LD participated in fewer leisure activities and had problems making and keeping friends. Thus, social-skills deficits must be identified and remediated as part of the curriculum at all grade levels.

Cognitive and Metacognitive Skills

Cognitive skills enable individuals to perform tasks by acquiring, storing, or retrieving information (Scheid, 1989). Metacognitive skills involve knowing what techniques are necessary to accomplish tasks, and employing self-regulatory strategies to monitor task completion (Baker & Brown, 1984). Studies have shown that students with LD lack effective, sophisticated cognitive and metacognitive strategies to promote successful academic performance (Hallahan, Kneedler, & Lloyd, 1983; Wong & Jones, 1982; Wong & Wong, 1986). However, students with LD can be taught how to (a) approach tasks, (b) use strategies to facilitate learning, and (c) monitor their own performance to determine if effective learning is occurring (Brown & Palincsar, 1987; Reid & Borkowski, 1987; Schumaker, Deshler, Alley, Warner, & Denton, 1982).

Perceptual Skills

Perceptual development skills usually refer to visual and auditory abilities to receive and integrate neurological messages. Terms such as *visual discrimination, auditory reception,* and *visual-motor integration* are typically used to refer to various perceptual abilities (Mercer, 1991). Various assessment instruments and training programs emerged during the 1960s and 1970s purporting to identify, test, and remediate deficits in perceptual skills. Furthermore, it was believed that remediation of such deficiencies would result in academic improvements, usually in reading performance.

Perceptual deficiencies have been associated with LD (see earlier definitions) but, due to the controversy have been deleted from current definitions (e.g., Hammill & Larsen, 1974; Hammill, Goodman, & Wiederholt, 1974) that surround assessment and treatment of these hypothetical constructs. In light of this, though students may exhibit difficulties with discrimination tasks, it is wise to focus on specific academic activities (e.g., discriminating between *b* and *p* or *was* and *saw*) rather than activities that are nonacademic in nature.

Practical Classroom Applications

Characteristic knowledge and skills help all professionals make informed decisions that significantly affect their students' survival and success. Researchers and teachers will continue to work side by side in identifying students' typical and atypical behaviors. Teachers will be involved in determining both the etiologies and theoretical perspectives of students' learning problems and the characteristics of individuals at risk for problems with learning. Further, teachers will help to define the effects learning problems may have on one's life. Finally, classroom knowledge will be used as a basis to compare and contrast the cultural and environmental milieu of the child and the family.

Teachers may consider the following implications of the contemporary characteristics of LD to classroom instruction. Application suggestions presented relate to the definitions, lifelong perspective, and characteristics of LD.

1. *Review the psychoeducational assessment data for your students who have been identified as having LD.* Given the assessment information, identify the specific LD (e.g., mathematics, reading, written expression) as presented in the USOE and NJCLD definitions. Consider the students' classroom performance in the areas identified as discrepant from their potential. Examine curriculum-based assessment information, which relates to the specific learning disabilities, for potential strengths as well as weaknesses.

2. *Consider the learning characteristics associated with specific LD.* Relate this information to your students with LD by identifying their specific difficulties that are attributable to their disability. For example, if a student has a learning disability in written expression, identify the learning characteristics presented by this student (e.g., problems with spelling, handwriting, composition development.)

3. *Examine your students' Individualized Education Programs (IEPs).* Identify the goals and objectives specified for instruction, as related to the students' specific learning disabilities. Include cognitive and metacognitive strategy instruction as part of the students' instructional programs. Teach students to generalize strategies across settings, people, and materials.

4. *Collaborate with other professionals who can assist in providing interventions to address your students' specific LD.* For example, you may need to team with the speech/language pathologist to address oral language problems.

5. *Provide instructional adaptations as necessary to address specific LD.* For instance, if a student has a reading disability, then you may need to adapt textbook instruction so that the student can access and comprehend the material.

6. *Provide instruction that relates to the lifelong condition of LD. A strong academic remedial program is vital during the elementary grades.* As students move into middle

(continued)

Practical Classroom Applications (continued)

school, content area and study skills become critical and transition planning is imperative to prepare students for postsecondary opportunities. In high school, students with LD can benefit from a curriculum tailored to their adulthood goals, life-skills instruction, career preparation, further transition planning, and, in some cases, work experiences.

7. *Provide support groups for students with LD.* Help them come to understand what is meant by a learning disability, the characteristics, and the ways LD may be manifested as students mature. Teach students self-advocacy skills and their legal rights.

8. *Help families develop an understanding of the concept of learning disabilities by* *providing support groups and awareness information.* Acquaint families with organizations in their community that provide services to people with LD (e.g., Learning Disabilities Association of America).

9. *Provide in-service training to faculty members in your school.* Acquaint them with the definition of learning disabilities, the characteristics and heterogeneity of the disability, and the lifelong aspects.

10. *Provide varied instructional arrangements.* For example, using a variety of small groups and pairs helps students with LD have opportunities to work with typical classmates to complete activities and assignments.

SUMMARY

- Individuals with LD comprise the most popular category of special education.

- Professionals and parents have sought to define, identify, and characterize a *heterogeneous* group of individuals who display a variety of learning and behavioral characteristics, have normal intelligence, and yet are not achieving commensurate with their typical peers.

- Different groups' attempts to define learning disabilities result from the influence of different disciplines, research, and sociopolitical factors.

- Past instructional categories were determined based on academic and intellectual abilities. Students with learning disabilities were thought to be those having academic problems resulting from basic psychological process deficits that could be identified and remediated.

- Difficulties of the neuropsychological model in proving brain damage, coupled with parent dislike of the brain-injury label, influenced professionals to find more educationally relevant explanations for learning problems.

- The federal government became interested in students who exhibited learning problems as a result of its need to fund services for this group of students.

- The psychological process model of learning disabilities was challenged when researchers questioned the validity and reliability of assessment instruments and remedial techniques.

- Discrepancy formulas (i.e., mathematical computations that identified significant differences between achievement and intelligence test scores) became the primary method for identifying students with LD.

- Controversy in LD relates to concern over a "severe discrepancy" between achievement and potential and the use of intelligence scores as definition components.
- Many individuals with LD often experience lifelong difficulties in early childhood, elementary/middle-school years, adolescence, and adulthood.
- Characteristics of individuals with LD may include the display of a discrepancy between aptitude and achievement; academic difficulties; and problems in motivation, memory, attention and hyperactivity, cognitive and metacognitive skills, or perceptual skills.

DISCUSSION QUESTIONS

To help extend your understanding, reflect on and discuss the following questions:

1. What impact do family members have in moving forward our understanding of classification and labels in LD?
2. In reflecting on your own beliefs regarding students' characteristics and classroom behaviors, are your assessment and instructional practices congruent with local, state, and federal recommendations?
3. Are you familiar with your local written school board policies on assurances and due process rights related to identification and assessments of students with LD?
4. What impact do local school and community services agencies, including the library, advocacy centers, or legal aid offices have on ensuring identification rights to students with LD, and their families?
5. How do these above agencies affect services in your area?
6. What are your local school district's prereferral policies on at-risk students with learning problems?
7. What are specific steps in local assessment and placement practices for students with identified LD?

REFERENCES

Adelman, H. S., & Taylor, L. (1983). Enhancing motivation for overcoming learning and behavior problems. *Journal of Learning Disabilities, 16,* 384–392.

Algozzine, B. (1991). Decision making and curriculum-based assessment. In B. Y. L. Wong (Ed.), *Learning about learning disabilities* (pp. 39–58). NY: Academic Press.

American Psychiatric Association. (1994). *Diagnostic and statistical manual of mental disorders—DSM-IV* (4th ed.). Washington, DC: Author.

Anderson, P. L. (1982). A preliminary study of syntax in the written expression of learning disabled children. *Journal of Learning Disabilities, 15,* 359–362.

Back to the 3 R's? (1957, March 15). *U.S. News and World Report,* 38–44.

Baker, L., & Brown, A. L. (1984). Cognitive monitoring in reading. In J. Flood (Ed.), *Understanding reading comprehension* (pp. 21–44). Newark, DE: International Reading Association.

Baldwin, R. S., & Vaughn, S. (1989). Why Siegel's arguments are irrelevant to the definition of learning disabilities. *Journal of Learning Disabilities, 22*(8), 513–514.

Bateman, B. (1965). An educational view of a diagnostic approach to learning disorders. In J. Hellmuth (Ed.), *Learning disorders* (Vol. 1, pp. 219–239). Seattle, WA: Special Child Publications.

Bender, W. N. (1992). *Learning disabilities: Characteristics, identification, and teaching strategies.* Boston: Allyn and Bacon.

Blalock, G. (1997). Transition education. In D. P. Rivera & D. D. Smith (Eds.), *Teaching students with learning and behavior problems* (3rd ed.). Boston: Allyn and Bacon.

Blalock, J. W. (1981). Persistent problems and concerns of young adults with learning disabilities. In W. Cruickshank & A. Silver (Eds.), *Bridges to tomorrow, Vol. 2, The best of ACLD* (pp. 35–55). Syracuse, NY: Syracuse University Press.

Bley, N., & Thornton, C. (1995). *Teaching mathematics to students with learning disabilities* (3rd ed.). Austin, TX: PRO-ED.

Brown, A. L., & Campione, J. (1986). Psychological theory and the study of learning disabilities. *American Psychologists, 41*, 1059–1068.

Brown, A. L., & Palincsar, A. S. (1987). Reciprocal teaching of comprehension strategies: A natural history of one program for enhancing learning. In J. Day & J. Borkowski (Eds.), *Intelligence and exceptionality: New directions in theory, assessment, and instructional practices* (pp. 81–132). Norwood, NJ: Ablex.

Bryan, T. H. (1976). Peer popularity of learning disabled children: A replication. *Journal of Learning Disabilities, 9*, 307–311.

Bryan, T. H. (1991). Social problems and learning disabilities. In B. Y. L. Wong (Ed.), *Learning about learning disabilities* (pp. 195–231). NY: Academic Press.

Bryan, T. H., & Sonnefeld, J. (1981). Children's social ratings of ingratiation tactics. *Journal of Learning Disabilities, 5*, 605–609.

Caldwell, J., Recht, D. R., & Newby, R. F. (1987). *Improving the reading comprehension of dysphonetic and dyseidetic dyslexics using story grammar.* Paper presented at the Third World Congress on Dyslexia (June 1987), Chania, Greece.

Cawley, J. (1970). Teaching arithmetic to mentally handicapped children. *Focus on Exceptional Children, 2*(4), 1–8.

Cawley, J., Fitzmaurice-Hayes, A., & Shaw, R. (1988). *Mathematics for the mildly handicapped—A guide to curriculum and instruction.* Boston: Allyn and Bacon.

Cawley, J., & Miller, J. (1989). Cross-sectional comparisons of the mathematical performance of children with learning disabilities: Are we on the right track toward comprehensive programming? *Journal of Learning Disabilities, 22*, 250–254, 259.

Chapman, J. W. (1985). *Self-perceptions of ability, learned helplessness and academic achievement expectations of children with learning disabilities.* Massey, New Zealand: Massey University, Education Department.

Chelser, B. (1982). ACLD vocational committee completes survey on LD adult. *ACLD Newsbriefs (No. 146), 5*, 20–23.

Cherkes-Julkowski, M. (1985). Metacognitive considerations in mathematics instruction for the learning disabled. In J. Cawley (Ed.), *Cognitive strategies and mathematics for the learning disabled* (pp. 99–116). Rockville, MD: Aspen.

Clements, S. D. (1966). *Minimal brain dysfunction in children: Terminology and identification.* Washington, DC: Cosponsored by the Easter Seal Research Foundation of the National Society for Crippled Children and Adults, and the National Institute of Neurological Diseases and Blindness Public Health Service.

Cone, T. E., & Wilson, L. R. (1981). Quantifying a severe discrepancy: A critical analysis. *Learning Disability Quarterly, 4*, 359–371.

Dalke, C., & Franzene, J. (1988). Secondary-postsecondary collaboration: A model of shared responsibility. *Learning Disabilities Focus, 4*(1), 38–45.

deBettencourt, L. U., Zigmond, N., & Thornton, H. S. (1989). Follow-up of post-secondary age rural learning disabled graduates and dropouts. *Exceptional Children, 56*, 40–49.

Deshler, D., & Schumaker, J. (1986). Learning strategies: An instructional alternative for low-achieving adolescents. *Exceptional Children, 52*, 583–590.

Deshler, D., Schumaker, J., & Lenz, B. K. (1984). Academic and cognitive interventions for LD adolescents: Part I. *Journal of Learning Disabilities, 17*, 108–117.

Edgar, E. (1987). Secondary programs in special education: Are many of them justifiable? *Exceptional Children, 53*(6), 555–562.

Ellis, E. S., & Friend, P. (1991). Adolescents with learning disabilities. In B. Y. L. Wong (Ed.), *Learning about learning disabilities.* NY: Academic Press.

Ellis, E. S., Lenz, B. K., & Sabornie, E. J. (1987). Generalization and adaptation of learning strategies to natural environments: Part 1: Critical Agents. *Remedial and Special Education, 8*(1), 6–20.

Englert, C. S., Raphael, T. E., Fear, K. L., & Anderson, L. M. (1988). Student's metacognitive knowledge about how to write informational texts. *Learning Disability Quarterly, 11*, 18–46.

Franks, D. J. (1971). Ethnic and social status characteristics of children in EMR and LD classes. *Exceptional Children, 37*, 537–538.

Gerber, P. J., Schnieders, C. A., Paradise, L. V., Reiff, H. B., Ginsberg, R. J., & Popp, P. A. (1990). Persisting problems of adults with learning disabilities: Self-reported comparisons from their school-age and adult years. *Journal of Learning Disabilities, 23* (9), 570–573.

Gibbs, D. P., & Cooper, E. B. (1989). Prevalence of communication disorders in students with learning disabilities. *Journal of Learning Disabilities, 22* (1), 60–63.

Golumbia, L. R., & Hillman, S. B. (August 1990). *A comparison of learning disabled and nondisabled adolescent motivational processes.* Paper presented at the Annual Meeting of the American Psychological Association, Boston.

Graham, S., & Harris, K. R. (1989). The relevance of IQ in the determination of learning disabilities: Abandoning scores as decision makers. *Journal of Learning Disabilities, 22* (8), 500–503.

Graham, S., Harris, K. R., MacArthur, C., & Schwartz, S. (1991). Writing instruction. In B. Y. L. Wong (Ed.), *Learning about learning disabilities.* NY: Academic Press.

Gresham, F. M., & Elliott, S. N. (1989). Social skills deficits as a primary learning disability. *Journal of Learning Disabilities, 22* (2), 20–124.

Gruenewald, L., & Pollack, S. (1984). *Language interaction in teaching and learning.* Austin, TX: PRO-ED.

Hallahan, D. P. (1975). Distractibility in the learning disabled child. In W. M. Cruickshank & D. P. Hal-

lahan (Eds.), *Perceptual and learning disabilities in children, Vol. 2: Research and theory* (pp. 195–218). Syracuse, NY: Syracuse University Press.

Hallahan, D. P. (1989). Attention disorders: Specific learning disabilities. In T. Husen & N. Postlethwaite (Eds.), *The international encyclopedia of education: Research and studies* (Suppl. Vol. 1, pp. 98–100). NY: Pergamon.

Hallahan, D. P., Kauffman, J. M., & Lloyd, J. W. (1985). *Introduction to learning disabilities* (2nd ed.). Upper Saddle River, NJ: Prentice Hall.

Hallahan, D. P., Kauffman, J. M., & Lloyd, J. W. (1996). *Introduction to learning disabilities.* Boston: Allyn and Bacon.

Hallahan, D. P., Kneedler, R. D., & Lloyd, J. W. (1983). Cognitive behavior modification techniques for learning disabled children: Self-instruction and self-monitoring. In J. D. McKinney & L. Feagan (Eds.), *Current topics in learning disabilities* (Vol. 1). NY: Ablex.

Hammill, D. D. (1990). On defining learning disabilities: An emerging consensus. *Journal of Learning Disabilities, 23*(2), 74–84.

Hammill, D. D., Goodman, L., & Wiederholt, J. L. (1974). Visual-motor processes: What success have we had in training them? *The Reading Teacher, 27*, 469–478.

Hammill, D. D., & Larsen, S. (1974). The effectiveness of psycholinguistic training. *Exceptional Children, 41*, 5–15.

Hammill, D. D., Leigh, J. E., McNutt, G., & Larsen, S. (1987). A new definition of learning disabilities. *Journal of Learning Disabilities, 20*(2), 109–113.

Hanna, G. S., Dyck, N. J., & Holen, M. C. (1979). Objective analysis of achievement-aptitude discrepancies in LD classification. *Learning Disability Quarterly, 2*, 32–38.

Havighurst, R. J. (1972). *Developmental tasks and education.* NY: Longman.

Humes, C., & Brammer, G. (1985). LD career success after high school. *Academic Therapy, 21*, 171–176.

Interagency Committee on Learning Disabilities. (1987). *Learning disabilities: A report to the U.S. Congress.* Bethesda, MD: National Institutes of Health.

Johnson, D. L., & Blalock, J. W. (1987). *Adults with learning disabilities: Clinical studies.* Orlando, FL: Grune & Stratton.

Kavale, K. A. (1981). The relationship between auditory perceptual skills and reading ability: A meta-analysis. *Journal of Learning Disabilities, 14*, 539–546.

Kavale, K. A., & Forness, S. (1987). The far side of heterogeneity: A critical analysis of empirical subtyping research in learning disabilities. *Journal of Learning Disabilities, 20*(6), 374–382.

Keller, C. E., & Hallahan, D. P. (1987). *Learning disabilities: Issues and instructional interventions. What research says to the teacher.* Washington, DC: National Education Association.

Keogh, B. K., & Margolis, J. (1976). Learn to labor and wait: Attentional problems of children with learning disorders. *Journal of Learning Disabilities, 9*, 276–286.

Keogh, B. K., & Sears, S. (1991). Learning disabilities from a developmental perspective: Early identification and prediction. In B. Y. L. Wong (Ed.), *Learning about learning disabilities.* NY: Academic Press.

Kirby, J. R., & Becker, L. D. (1988). Cognitive components of learning problems in arithmetic. *Remedial and Special Education, 9*(5), 7–15.

Kirk, S. A. (1962). *Educating exceptional children.* Boston: Houghton Mifflin.

Kistner, J. A., & Osborne, M. (1987). A longitudinal study of LD children's self evaluations. *Learning Disability Quarterly, 10*, 258–266.

Larsen, S. C., Parker, R. R., & Hammill, D. D. (1982). Effectiveness of psycholinguistic training: A response to Kavale. *Exceptional Children, 49*, 60–66.

Lerner, J. W. (1988). Learning disabilities: Theories, diagnosis, and teaching strategies. Boston: Houghton Mifflin.

Levin, E. K., Zigmond, N., & Birch, J. W. (1985). A follow-up study of 52 learning disabled adolescents. *Journal of Learning Disabilities, 18*, 2–7.

Lovett, M. W., Ransby, M. J., Hardwick, N., & Johnson, M. S. (1989). Can dyslexia be treated? Treatment-specific and generalized treatment effects in dyslexic children's response to remediation. *Brain Language, 37*, 90–121.

Lovitt, T. C. (1989). *Introduction to learning disabilities.* Boston: Allyn and Bacon.

Lyon, G. R., & Flynn, J. (1990). Assessing subtypes of learning abilities. In H. L. Swanson (Ed.), *Handbook on the assessment of learning disabilities: Theory, research, and practice* (pp. 59–74). San Diego, CA: College-Hill.

Lyon, G. R., Newby, R. E., Recht, D., & Caldwell, J. (1991). Neuropsychology and learning disabilities. In B. Y. L. Wong (Ed.), *Learning about learning disabilities.* NY: Academic Press.

Lyon, G. R., & Watson, B. L. (1981). Empirically derived subgroups of learning disabled readers: Diagnostic characteristics. *Journal of Learning Disabilities, 14*, 256–261.

MacMillan, D. L. (1973). *Behavior modification in education.* NY: Macmillan.

Mallory, B. L., & Kerns, G. M. (1988). Consequences of categorical labeling of preschool children. *Topics in Early Childhood Special Education, 8*, 39–50.

McIntosh, R., Vaughn, S., & Zaragoza, N. (1991). A review of social interventions for students with disabilities. *Journal of Learning Disabilities, 24*(8), 451–458.

McKinney, J. D. (1988). Empirically derived subtypes of specific learning disabilities. In M. C. Wang, H. J. Walberg, & M. C. Reynolds (Eds.), *The handbook of special education: Research and practice.* Oxford, England: Pergamon.

McLeod, T., & Armstrong, S. (1982). Learning disabilities in mathematics—Skill deficits and remedial approaches. *Learning Disability Quarterly, 5*, 305–311.

McLeskey, J. (1989). The influence of level of discrepancy on the identification of students with learning disabilities. *Journal of Learning Disabilities, 22* (7), 435–438.

Meichenbaum, D. (1980). Cognitive behavior modification with exceptional children: A promise yet unfulfilled. *Exceptional Education Quarterly, 1* (1), 83–88.

Mercer, C. D. (1991). *Students with learning disabilities* (4th ed.). NY: Merrill.

Mercer, C. D., King-Sears, P., & Mercer, A. R. (1990). Learning disabilities definitions and criteria used by state education departments. *Learning Disability Quarterly, 13*, 141–152.

Montague, M., Maddux, C., & Dereshiwsky, M. (1988). Story grammar and comprehension and production of narrative prose by students with learning disabilities. *Journal of Learning Disabilities, 23*, 190–197.

Myers, P. L., & Hammill, D. D. (1990). *Learning disabilities: Basic concepts, assessment practices, and instructional strategies* (4th ed.). Austin, TX: PRO-ED.

National Advisory Committee on Handicapped Children. (1968). *Special education for handicapped children (First Annual Report)*. Washington, DC: Department of Health, Education, and Welfare.

National Joint Committee on Learning Disabilities. (1981). *Learning disabilities: Issues on definition*. Unpublished manuscript. (Available from the Orton Dyslexia Society, 724 York Road, Baltimore, MD 21204. Reprinted in *Journal of Learning Disabilities, 20*, 107–108.)

National Joint Committee on Learning Disabilities. (1986). Use of discrepancy formulas in the identification of learning disabled individuals. *Learning Disability Quarterly, 9*, 245.

National Joint Committee on Learning Disabilities. (1988). [*Letter to NJCLD member organizations*].

National Joint Committee on Learning Disabilities. (1990). *Providing appropriate education for students with learning disabilities in regular education classrooms*. Position Paper.

Pearl, R. (1982). LD children's attributions for success and failure: A replication with a labeled LD sample. *Learning Disability Quarterly, 5*, 173–176.

Pearl, R., Bryan, T. H., & Donahue, M. (1980). Learning disabled children's attributions for success and failure. *Learning Disability Quarterly, 3* (1), 3–9.

Poplin, M., Gray, R., Larsen, S., Banikowski, A., & Mehring, T. (1980). A comparison of components of written expression abilities in learning disabled and non-learning disabled children at three grade levels. *Learning Disability Quarterly, 3*, 46–53.

Reeve, R. E. (1990). ADHD: Facts and fallacies. *Intervention in School and Clinic, 26* (2), 70–77.

Reid, M. K., & Borkowski, J. G. (1987). Causal attributions of hyperactive children: Implications for training strategies and self-control. *Journal of Educational Psychology, 76*, 225–235.

Rivera, D., & Smith, D. D. (1987). Influence of modeling on acquisition and generalization of computational skills: A summary of research from three sites. *Learning Disability Quarterly, 10*, 69–80.

Russell, R., & Ginsburg, H. (1984). Cognitive analysis of children's mathematical difficulties. *Cognition and Instruction, 1*, 217–244.

Scheid, K. (1989). Cognitive and metacognitive learning strategies—Their role in the instruction of special education students. *The Instructional Methods Report Series*, Columbus, OH: LINC Resources.

Schumaker, J., Deshler, D., Alley, G., & Warner, M. (1983). Toward the development of an intervention model for learning disabled adolescents: The University of Kansas Institute. *Exceptional Education Quarterly, 4*, 45–74.

Schumaker, J., Deshler, D., Alley G., Warner, M., & Denton, P. (1982). Multipass: A learning strategy for improving reading comprehension. *Learning Disability Quarterly, 15*, 295–304.

Schumaker, J., & Hazel, J. S. (1984). Social skills assessment and training for the learning disabled: Who's on first and what's on second? Part 1. *Journal of Learning Disabilities, 17*, 422–431.

Shinn, M., & Marston, D. (1985). Differentiating mildly handicapped, low-achieving, and regular education: A curriculum-based approach. *Remedial and Special Education, 6* (2), 31–38.

Siegel, L. S. (1989). Why we do not need intelligence test scores in the definition and analyses of learning disabilities. *Journal of Learning Disabilities, 22* (8), 514–518.

Sitlington, P. L., & Frank, A. R. (1990). Are adolescents with learning disabilities successfully crossing the bridge into adult life? *Learning Disability Quarterly, 13*, 97–111.

Sleeter, C. E. (1986). Learning disabilities: The social construction of a special education category. *Exceptional Children, 53* (1), 46–54.

Smith, J. O. (1988). Social and vocational problems of adults with learning disabilities: A review of the literature. *Learning Disabilities Focus, 4* (1), 46–58.

Smith, D. D., & Luckasson, R. (1995). *Introduction to special education: Teaching in an age of challenge* (2nd ed.). Boston: Allyn and Bacon.

Stanovich, K. E. (1988). Explaining the differences between the dyslexic and the garden-variety poor reader: The phonological-core variable-difference model. *Journal of Learning Disabilities, 21* (10), 590–604.

Stanovich, K. E. (1989). Has the learning disabilities field lost its intelligence? *Journal of Learning Disabilities, 22* (8), 487–492.

Strauss, A. A., & Lehtinen, L. E. (1947). *Psychopathology and education of brain-injured children* (Vol. 1). NY: Grune & Stratton.

Swanson, H. L. (1983). Relations among metamemory, rehearsal activity and word recall in learning disabled and nondisabled readers. *British Journal of Educational Psychology, 53*, 186–194.

Swanson, H. L., & Cooney, J. B. (1991). Learning disabilities and memory. In B. Y. L. Wong (Ed.), *Learning about learning disabilities*. NY: Academic Press.

Tarnowski, K. J., Prinz, R. J., & Nay, S. M. (1986). Comparative analysis of attentional deficits in hyperactive and learning-disabled children. *Journal of Abnormal Psychology, 95*, 341–345.

Torgesen, J. K. (1977). The role of nonspecific factors in the task performance of learning-disabled children: A theoretical assessment. *Journal of Learning Disabilities, 10*, 27–34.

Torgesen, J. K. (1988). Studies of children with learning disabilities who perform poorly on memory span tasks. *Journal of Learning Disabilities, 21* (10), 605–612.

Torgesen, J. K. (1991). Learning disabilities: Historical and conceptual issues. In B. Y. L. Wong (Ed.), *Learning about learning disabilities* (pp. 3–37). NY: Academic Press.

Torgesen, J. K., & Goldman, T. (1977). Rehearsal and short-term memory in second grade reading disabled children. *Child Development, 48*, 56–61.

Torgesen, J. K., & Licht, B. G. (1983). The learning disabled child as an inactive learner: Retrospect and prospects. In J. D. McKinney & L. Feagans (Eds.), *Current topics in learning disabilities* (Vol. 1, pp. 3–31). Norwood, NJ: Ablex.

U.S. Office of Education. (1976). Education of handicapped children: Assistance to states: Proposed rulemaking. *Federal Register, 41*, 52404–52407. Washington, DC: U.S. Government Printing Office.

U.S. Office of Education. (1977). Definition and criteria for defining students as learning disabled. *Federal Register, 42:250*, 65083. Washington, DC: U.S. Government Printing Office.

U.S. Department of Education. (1989). *Eleventh annual report to Congress on the Implementation of The Education of the Handicapped Act*. Washington, DC: Office of Special Education Programs.

U.S. Department of Education. (1990). *Twelfth annual report to Congress on the Implementation of The Education of the Handicapped Act*. Washington, DC: Office of Special Education Programs.

Vellutino, F. R., & Scanlon, D. M. (1986). Experimental evidence for the effects of instructional bias on word identification. *Exceptional Children, 53*, 145–155.

Vellutino, F. R., & Scanlon, D. M. (1987). Linguistic coding and reading ability. In S. Rosenberg (Ed.), *Advances in applied psycholinguistics* (pp. 71–69). NY: Cambridge University Press.

Wallace, G., & McLoughlin, J. A. (1988). *Learning disabilities: Concepts and characteristics* (3rd ed.). Upper Saddle River, NJ: Prentice Hall/Merrill.

Wallach, G. P., & Miller, L. (1988). *Language intervention and academic success*. Boston: College-Hill.

White, M. A., & Charry, J. (1966). *School disorder, intelligence, and social class*. NY: Teachers College Press.

Wiig, E., & Semel, E. (1984). *Language assessment and intervention for the learning disabled*. Upper Saddle River, NJ: Prentice Hall/Merrill.

Wong, B. Y. L. (1980). Activating the inactive learner: Use of questions/prompts to enhance comprehension and retention of implied information in learning disabled children. *Learning Disability Quarterly, 3*(1), 29–37.

Wong, B. Y. L. (1982). Strategic behaviors in selecting retrieval cues in gifted, normal achieving and learning disabled children. *Journal of Learning Disabilities, 15*, 33–37.

Wong, B. Y. L., & Jones, W. (1982). Increasing metacomprehension in learning-disabled and normally-achieving students through self-questioning training. *Learning Disability Quarterly, 5*, 228–240.

Wong, B. Y. L., & Wong, R. (1986). Study behavior as a function of metacognitive knowledge about critical task variables: An investigation of above average, average and learning-disabled readers. *Learning Disability Research, 1*, 101–111.

Wong, B. Y. L., Wong, R., & Blenkinsop, J. (1989). Cognitive and metacognitive aspects of learning disabled adolescents' composing problems. *Learning Disability Quarterly, 12*, 300–322.

Woodring, P. (1957, Sept. 2). Reform plan for schools. *Life*, 123–136.

Ysseldyke, J., & Algozzine, B. (1990). *Introduction to special education (2nd ed.)*. Boston: Houghton Mifflin.

Ysseldyke, J., Algozzine, B., & Epps, S. (1983). A logical and empirical analysis of current practice in classifying students as handicapped. *Exceptional Children, 50*, 160–165.

Ysseldyke, J., Algozzine, B., Shinn, M. R., & McGue, M. (1982). Similarities and differences between low achievers and students classified as learning disabled. *The Journal of Special Education, 16*, 73–85.

PART TWO

The Evolution of Theories and Practices

A fundamental assumption is that theory and practice are not in conflict with each other.

CHAPTER 3

The Use of Theories to Guide Practices

In this chapter we will . . .

- Rationalize the use of theories in practice.
- Describe paradigms embodying scientific inquiry.
- Summarize the evolution of model development in LD.
- Present a case for the development of a super structure tying together the knowledge gained from research.
- Argue for both the importance of theories as guiding principles for educational practice and the need for comingling of the traditionally separate roles of researcher and practitioner.

Professionals at all levels (i.e., from teachers in classrooms to administrators in schools to teacher trainers and researchers in universities) benefit from a sound understanding of the array of theories that have been formulated to explain LD. As Lewin (cited in Polansky, 1986) professes, "there is nothing so practical as a good theory" (p. 3). Theory-driven professionals are at the core of the "best" in LD practices.

THEORY-DRIVEN PROFESSIONALS

Educators at all levels need to reflect continuously on their beliefs and convictions, vis-à-vis theoretical frameworks. This is at the core of their functioning as professionals: Their understanding of scientific theory impacts how they direct their own influence on the philosophical, social, and political forces that shape practices in the field. In their reflection, educators consciously shape their belief structure around a theoretical framework, adopt the language of the theories, and know the literature that provides a supportive base for their beliefs. If professionals can explain their views from a scientific base that values standardized procedures (rationalistic or naturalistic) for making a case for a set of beliefs, then they are thereby empowered with knowledge of their own professionalism and are able to impact the beliefs and structures of the educational system in which they function (Anderson & Barreara, 1995).

For instance, teachers who embrace a behavioral explanation of LD can use the works of Lovitt (1989), White and Haring (1980), and Englemann and Carnine (1982) that focus on shaping the learning environment rather than treating some inherent physiological or psychological anomaly. The theoretical and empirical research base of behaviorism (i.e., the relationships between antecedents, behaviors, and consequences) has a language, set of guiding principles, and rationale for arguing its explanation of behavior. The structures of the theory enable teachers to examine their own manipulation of classroom variables in a rational manner instead of in a hit-or-miss, haphazard, way. In addition, firm understanding of the theory empowers a teacher to make the case for solving school-based and district-based problems from a behavioral perspective.

Professionals embrace theoretical orientations in different ways. Some hold to a single paradigm (e.g., reductionist or social constructivist) or theoretical framework (e.g., behaviorist, cognitivist) with an uncompromising zeal. Others take a more eclectic stance, adapting different paradigms or theories to different problems and situations. If professionals are to accept a "paradigmatic pluralism" where practices are derived from a mix of assumptions that reflect differing, but complementary, views of the phenomenon called learning disabilities, then they may use a variety of theories selectively based upon the variables associated with individual cases or problems (Speigel, 1992, Dixon & Carnine, 1994). An example may be the use of direct-instruction methods to teach students the acquisition of metacognitive strategies; behavioral principles are melded with principles of cognitive psychology in the formulation of teaching practices.

In this text we acknowledge the existence of multiple factors in shaping the field of LD, including philosophical, social, political, and theoretical frames of reference (see Senf, 1986; Smyth, 1989). However, our primary focus is on the development and evolution of theories from the perspective of a scientific search for understanding. Implicit is the recognition that philosophical, social, and political forces also shape theories and practices much like the model explicated by Mercer (1992) and the anecdotes used by Medawar (1984, pp. 18–21). We do not discount the effects of these forces, as summarized in chapter 1, we simply believe that the evolution of the field of LD is best served by using theory development as the primary driving force (Kavale & Forness, 1985a; Stanovich, 1988; Swanson, 1988).

A fundamental assumption is that theory and practice are not in conflict with each other. Theorists should not be housed in the ivory towers of universities, and practitioners should not be housed exclusively in classrooms. Additionally, there is not a one-way flow of information that originates from theorists and moves in a downward fashion to the domain of practice. Professionals from all dimensions of the field, especially reflective teachers, have the opportunity to provide critical insights into the relationships between phenomena associated with learning disabilities (Scruggs & Mastropieri, 1988). By their systematic approaches to solving problems and explaining LD, professionals shape existing—and construct new— perspectives and procedures for studying and treating LD. Teachers are the most prominent element of the profession and are in closest contact with our constituency. We believe that the advancement of the field as a science and a practice must come in large part from the theories and practices developed by teachers in classrooms (see Smyth, 1989).

THE CASE FOR THEORY DEVELOPMENT: FROM QUACKERY TO PERSONALISTIC VIEWS TO SCIENTIFIC EXPLANATIONS

The study of and practice of educational treatments for individuals with LD cannot be conducted in some isolated vacuum. The phenomenon of LD must be studied in the general context in which it is manifested—the classroom. Consequently, the role of teachers is absolutely primary. Their practices must be sound, systematic, and logical in order that we go beyond simply providing day-to-day services to individuals with LD and move toward understanding what works and what doesn't, as well as the underlying principles that characterize effective practices. As Stanovich (1988) laments, "Nothing has retarded the cumulative growth of knowledge in both learning disabilities and the psychology of reading more than the failure to deal with problems in a scientific manner" (p. 210).

Quackery

Unfortunately, a preponderance of quackery and personalistic views of LD have diverted attention away from scientific explanations of LD. In the first case, there is a tendency for professionals and parents to gravitate toward theories or practices that deviate from mainstream scientific evidence. As desperation for finding a "cure" increases, parents and professionals seek out more radical treatments that are often clouded by the mysticism of pseudoscience. Frequently, radical treatments are derived from a neurophysiological framework. Theories derived from highly technical, hard sciences are perceived as carrying greater explanatory power than those that are derived from softer sciences such as psychology. The explanations are based on logical, but unproved, assumptions. Individuals unfamiliar with the technical aspects of biology and physiology can be easily duped by misinformation that is twisted into some apparently logical theory. Many parents and professionals appear to believe that theories and treatments derived from respectable sciences by individuals with academic degrees could not possibly engage in fraud or deception. The principle of caveat emptor is subordinated by a compelling desire to remediate the learning disability (Worrall, 1990).

Silver's (1987) review of controversial approaches to the treatment of LD provides examples of the quackery or pseudoscience that has been used to explain and treat learning disabilities. Perhaps the most infamous theory and techniques are those developed by Doman and Delacato (1968). According to their theory, an individual's failure to pass successfully through various developmental stages in mobility and language, along with failure to achieve competence in the sensory modalities (i.e., visual, auditory, tactile, and kinesthetic) results in immature brain development below the cortical level and problems in "neurological organization." Doman and Delacato's stages of development are based upon the principle that ontogeny recapitulates phylogeny. That is, a child progresses through stages equivalent to the evolutionary stages of development of the species from fish to reptile to primate to manhood. Treatments are targeted at remediating the brain by having children engage in activities related to developmental stages such as patterning, crawling, and creeping (Hallahan & Kauffman, 1976; Wallace & McLoughlin, 1988).

Although the theory is a radical departure from more commonly accepted theories and principles (Wong, 1979), the treatments and techniques are used throughout the world. This occurs even in light of the long-standing criticisms lodged by the scientific community and the American Academy of Pediatrics (1982) conclusion that the patterning treatment has no merit.

A second example is a chiropractic approach to curing learning disabilities based upon the theory and treatment presented in a book by Ferrerei and Wainwright (1985). The authors theorize that damage to two cranial bones and an ocular muscle imbalance are the cause of learning disabilities. Displacement of the sphenoid and temporal bones causes neurological problems due to unequal pressure on the brain. With "an almost infinitesimal bony manipulation the disability will be corrected" (Ferreri & Wainwright, 1985, p. 16). Despite the fact that the theory and treatment have not been tested using scientific experimentation, the authors claim a supportive research base that really does not exist. Additionally, the theory is based on anatomical concepts unaccepted by most anatomists, yet chiropractic clinics across the United States advertise this "cure" for LD (Silver, 1987).

Personalistic Views

A second problem exists when knowledge is conceptualized as personalized—residing within the individuals who dispense it to others (Stanovich, 1988). For example, knowledge in quackery may be personalized, that is, the exclusive domain of the quack. Quacks claim to have made "scientific" breakthroughs in the discovery of cures to what ails us. They allege that they and they alone can provide treatments that will provide dramatic effects. They can dispense the medicine or show us how to implement the treatment, but they will not allow a truly independent scientific study of their cure. On the other hand, legitimate science is not immune to personalistic views. Without an attempt to deceive or commit fraud, scientists may protect their work and restrict others to the details of their procedures. They become recognized as the authorities regarding a particular phenomenon. Their judgments about other work in the area are viewed as godlike, and they in essence control the acceptance and rejection of alternative views. In either the case of the quack or the unquestioned scientist, personalistic views lead to fads, gurus, and uncritical acceptance of expert authorities (Stanovich, 1988).

In good science, knowledge is shared, is publicly available, and is verifiable. The ethics of scientific experimentation require that research reports be constructed with a solid theoretical basis, a description of the methods and treatments that allows replication by others, and an honest analysis of the experimenter's results. The report is published in journals or other media for public review and evaluation. This democratization of knowledge reduces the exclusivity of information. It allows the community of interested theorists and practitioners the opportunity to consume information and refute or accept the efficacy of treatments or the explanation of phenomena. Public discussions result, and consensual decisions are derived regarding the validity of the experimentation. A less authoritarian community is maintained because all members can access and scrutinize pertinent information.

Scientific Explanations

The purpose of science is to identify truth in nature. Through our observations of nature, we note phenomena and attempt to explain logically the relationships between phenomena. This act is one of discovering what already exists in truth and is not the creation of new phenomena or structures of nature: "Deduction only makes explicit information that is already there" (Medawar, 1984, p.80). Scientists seek only to discover and ultimately to understand the relationships between phenomena. They are looking to find out the parameters of nature. Scientists, in their initial observations of nature, look for the rules of nature in order to determine what is possible and not possible by controlling some variable associated with a phenomenon. This process is like learning to play soccer without knowing the rules (and not having access to a rule book) and, therefore, the possible strategies for scoring goals. Through observation of what can be done with the ball and through experimenting with the placement and movement of players on the field, a coach can learn about the relationships between important aspects of the game such as ball control, passing, speed, and so on.

What distinguishes scientific explanations from quackery or pseudoscientific principles are the laws themselves—and even more so, the rigorous testing process. Scientists test and retest laws against experimentally or naturally observed data to confirm the explanatory power of a law or principle. With confirmation of laws comes the capability to predict in novel or untested situations the effects of causal variables. Thus, scientific laws enable scientists to generalize relationships between variables with relative certainty that the law will account for what occurs in other situations in nature.

The attempt by cognitive psychologists to understand the parameters of various cognitive processes used by students displaying learning problems is an example of the rigorous confirmatory process. Torgesen (1977) found that students with LD seemed to demonstrate the same cognitive capacities as peers without LD, but failed to apply various metacognitive strategies that aid in the use of cognitive faculties. Further research has led to the suggestion that these children are deficient in cognitions about cognitions or in executive planning to carry out cognitive operations and monitor their own progress. Consequently, researchers have attempted to define these metacognitive processes. Jacobs and Paris (1987) defined metacognitive strategies as those mental activities that entail self-appraisal of cognition and self-management of thinking. Brown, Day, and Jones (1983) characterized metacognition as the planning, monitoring, revising, and repairing activities used for information processing. Other theorists (Dansereau, 1978; 1985; Jones, Amiran, & Katims, 1985; Sternberg, 1977, 1979, 1983) have conceptualized metacognitive training in various taxonomies in order to delineate how learners can be taught to use metacognitive processes.

An array of studies has been conducted to test whether or not students' metacognitive processes could be manipulated through instruction. Generally, the results have been very positive; that is, students' performance on academic and social tasks improves following instruction in the use of various metacognitive strategies related to those tasks. With this apparent link between metacognitive, or learning, strategies and student performance, researchers have established an apparent causal link or explanation for some students' learning problems. However, the linkage does not in and of itself explain why some students appear to learn and use metacognitive strategies without explicit instruction and others do not. Nor is it clear that students are capable of learning higher order executive strategy functions or have generalized thinking capabilities that allow one to select the situationally relevant learning strategies (Gagne, 1980, 1985). Consequently, inquiry into the casual nature of metacognition skills continues, and researchers delve further into the complex of variables that seem to play a role in metacognition and, ultimately, knowledge acquisition.

Cognitive research exemplifies the rigor of scientific study that provides a system of checks and balances through the democratization of information. If truth is the honest representation of what occurs in nature, then systematic, shared inquiry is necessary in order to identify the characteristics of nature and our ability to manipulate critical elements to achieve some desired change. This research provides us with greater certainty about what is really happening in nature, not only in an esoteric sense, but more practically it provides us with a guard against unscrupulous quackery and pseudoscience.

To provide this guard, communities of scientists agree on assumptions or views of how nature works and then establish a set of general procedures for studying phenomena. Some have argued that these sets of assumptions and procedures can be divided into two broad paradigms: reductionism and holism.

TWO PARADIGMS FOR INQUIRY

Paradigms, or views of the world, are used as a framework for inquiry into the nature of phenomena. Torgesen (1986) summarizes Kuhn's (1970) classic definition of a paradigm: "When a group of scientists within a discipline come to share similar ideas about the basic assumptions of their field, important questions to be addressed, the kind of explanatory concepts that are preferred, and the methodologies that are appropriate, they are said to share a scientific paradigm" (p. 400). Heshusius (1989) describes paradigms as broadly based world views comprising our philosophies and beliefs about the foundational structure of phenomena and the procedures to study them. Paradigms represent how we think about how we think. Theories, on the other hand, are statements that attempt to describe the relationships between variables associated with some phenomenon. They are much more narrow in scope and are developed within a set of assumptions about inquiry.

For this discussion, we have followed Heshusius' categorization of paradigms and theories. Accordingly, there exist two fundamental scientific world views: reductionistic and social constructivistic. Within these broad frameworks, a series of theoretical models have developed that seeks to explain the nature of the phenomenon we call learning disabilities.

The Reductionistic Paradigm

The traditional framework for inquiry is the "scientific method" associated with the assumptions and procedures espoused by Newton and applied to the natural sciences. The assumptions are that nature can be observed from a detached, objective point of view. Reality or truth can be discerned by the scientist in essence removing himself from participation in nature and playing the role of observer (i.e., nonparticipant observer). Within a reductionistic paradigm, scientists attempt to reduce complex phenomena into their component parts. Variables of interest are isolated and controlled in order to either observe their characteristics as separate parts of a phenomenon or to manipulate a variable to ascertain the effects of such on other dependent variables. Within a line of research, theories are built by observing that which occurs naturally in the environment, in order to identify salient components of some phenomenon. Then investigators try to identify whether or not any of the component variables are related to each other and, if so, how strong a relationship there is. Next, scientists may observe different levels of a variable as they occur naturally in the environment, to determine if these levels affect some dependent variable differentially. In other cases, scientists may contrive a replication of nature in a laboratory study and actually create the different levels of the variable and measure the effects of the levels of a variable on some dependent variable. Based upon their findings, scientists formulate principles or rules that explain how variables associated with some phenomenon interact. These rules are further used to make predictions or generalizations about what might happen in future events if these relationships are observed (Borg & Gall, 1989; Heshusius, 1989; Phillips, 1976; Reid, Robinson, & Bunsen, 1995; Smith & Heshusius, 1986).

Theories about the phenomenon of study and the relationships between its component parts are shaped as a series of studies progress through this deductive process. The teacher effectiveness research literature provides an example of this process. Early work by Anderson, Evertson, and Brophy (1979); Fisher, et al. (1980); Good and Brophy (1986, 1987); Rosenshine (1976, 1978); and Rosenshine and Stevens (1986) began by observing the behaviors of teachers in their classrooms, in order to determine what effective teachers do. Observers went into classrooms to note salient patterns of teacher behavior. Notable patterns were used to operationally define component teacher behaviors (e.g., asks varying types of questions, conducts reviews, uses advanced organizers, uses instructional time efficiently, and provides opportunities for practice). Further investigations sought to establish whether teacher behaviors were correlated with each other and with student achievement. Where strong relationships existed, researchers began to focus on specific teacher behaviors and observe them at different levels of performance. For instance, Good and Grouws (1977) studied the instructional behaviors of 40 effective and ineffective fourth-grade mathematics teachers. In this naturalistic study, they observed the frequency and regularity of teachers' behaviors (i.e., different levels of the review, seat work, and homework variables) and found significant correlations between teacher behavior and student outcomes. That is, when teachers use content reviews more frequently, student achievement is significantly higher. In a later study, Good and Grouws (1979) integrated the use of reviews, seat work, and homework in an experimental design in order to establish a causal link between these specific behaviors and changes in student performance. They trained a set of teachers in the use of reviews, seat work, and homework based on the results of their earlier study. A control group that did not receive the training was used to compare the effectiveness of the training. Therefore, the use of reviews, seat work, and homework was controlled to test the effects of their differential use on quantifiable measures of student achievement (i.e., number of questions answered correctly on achievement tests). Based upon their results, Good and Grouws concluded that the treatment did affect the teacher behaviors, which in turn lead to higher gains for the experimental group.

Similarly, other teacher behaviors have been studied. Through the compilation of data from a series of studies, theories about teacher effectiveness and the nature of the act of teaching continue to be shaped and reshaped. Predictions about student achievement are made based upon knowledge of teachers' instructional behavior. This rigorous process of scientific investigation is used to establish an empirical base for our assumptions and theories about some phenomenon in nature (e.g., teacher effectiveness). Due to the careful control, the systematic process of identifying and testing variables, and the replication of investigations, we establish a level of certainty that what we have objectively observed reflects accurately the reality of teacher behaviors and their affect on student performance. By studying the relationship between variables and demonstrating that changes in one set of variables (e.g., teacher behaviors) affects changes in some other variables (e.g., student performance measures), we establish principles of causality that enable us to predict similar occurrences under similar conditions.

The scientific method has characterized most of the research conducted in the study of LD. Reductionistic-oriented theories were developed, but empirical support has not been totally convincing. Poplin (1988) and Heshusius (1989; 1994), critics of the paradigm, have claimed the shortcomings of individuals with LD may have been compounded by the reductionistic theories and practices used over the past several decades. They have argued for the proliferation of a new paradigm to guide inquiries into the LD phenomenon.

The Social Constructivistic Paradigm

Unlike the scientific method, social constructivism is centered around the philosopher Hegel's theory of internal relations; that is, entities are necessarily altered by the relations in which they enter (McPhail, 1995; Phillips, 1976). The nature of a phenomenon is represented by the relationship of the whole to its parts and the relationships between its parts (i.e., holism). The whole cannot be represented simply by the addition of its components; it must be viewed as more than the sum of its parts. The whole determines the nature of its parts and the parts cannot be understood if considered in isolation from the whole because the parts are dynamically interrelated or interdependent (Phillips, 1976). Consequently, to reduce a phenomenon into its parts in order to isolate a component and then observe it is a futile exercise because in isolation, the component variable is different from when it is viewed in the context of its relationship with other parts and the whole.

A second foundational characteristic of social constructionism deals with epistomology, the nature and origins of knowledge (Denzin 1988; Geertz, 1973; Harris & Graham, 1994, 1996; Poplin, 1988; Reid et al., 1995). Knowledge is viewed as being shaped by contextual conditions and meanings as well as scientists' interests and purposes. The latter phrase refers to the acceptance of subjectivity inherent in the act of inquiry. Where reductionists reject subjectivity and view it as a personalized bias that subverts some independent truth, social constructivists view subjectivity as a natural, valued, and inseparable part of social phenomena (Heshusius, 1989, 1994; Jacob, 1988; Mercer, 1992). For instance, in the study of teacher behavior, scientists enter a social environment to observe classroom interactions between teacher and students. The presence of the observer alters the reality of the classroom, and, thus, objectivity is compromised. Social constructivists forego attempts to be purely objective. Instead subjectivity is viewed as unalterable. Social constructivists often encourage scientists to interact with teachers and students in various ways, to act as a participant observer, and to report interpretations of the emotional, philosophical, and social elements of the classroom. These elements are viewed as a necessary and integral part of the whole classroom phenomenon. Without accounting for these parts, the whole is not accurately represented.

Social constructivistic procedures used to study phenomena have a different emphasis, but they parallel the procedures used in the scientific method (Kronick, 1990; Lincoln & Guba, 1985; Rist, 1977). For reductionists the truth value is a function of *internal validity*, the degree to which the experimenter controls for extraneous variables that may compete with the independent variable as the cause of some change in the dependent variable. Social constructivists on the other hand view truth as a function of the *credibility* of the interpretation of events made by an observer.

Similarly, parallels between reductionistic and social constructivistic methodology exist for other procedural aspects. The degree to which the findings in one study of some population sample are applicable to other people outside the sample is referred to as *external validity* in scientific methodology. The same fundamental concept is referred to as *transferability* in holism. Consistency in data patterns is referred to as *reliability* by reductionists and *dependability* by social constructivists; neutrality is synonymous with *objectivity* by reductionists and *confirmability* by social constructivists.

The most salient procedural distinction in social constructivistic research is the use of qualitative methods to study phenomena and collect data. Accordingly, descriptive accounts or running records of the events within some context are recorded rather than quantifying data into some numerical form. In some disciplines, such as Human Ethology, the accounts may be very sterile, involving the anecdotal recording of low inference events with little or no interpretative commentary by a non-participant observer. In other disciplines, such as holistic ethnography, scientists study social phenomena in an attempt to describe cultures. They document events and the meaning of the events as parts of an integrated whole. They use participant observation and informal interviews in collecting data and use triangulation procedures to affirm and verify patterns in their data. Depending on the specific discipline, the subjective interpretations of events and interactions carry varying degrees of value. Typically though, the subjectivity is valued as long as the descriptions are credible (Anderson & Barreara, 1995; Jacob, 1988).

The debate over the merits of these two world views will continue. Both sets of assumptions and procedures will be critiqued, reshaped, and elaborated in a necessary attempt to refine the process of scientific inquiry. The debate over paradigms, conducted and reported in an open forum, provides a foundational basis for making value judgments about the legitimacy of the field of LD as a science. Continued research into the dynamics of LD—research that follows agreed-upon rules for conducting investigations that involve truthfulness, applicability, consistency, and neutrality—helps to assure information consumers that explanations are based on science not quackery.

LD AS A SCIENCE: THE CHRONOLOGY OF MODEL DEVELOPMENT

Normal science is defined by Kuhn (1970) as "research that is based upon one or more past achievements, achievements that some particular scientific community acknowledges for a time as supplying the foundation for further practice" (p. 10). Swanson (1988) makes the argument that the field of LD is a normal science, albeit immature in its development. Unlike more mature sciences, LD research has not been fostered by basic research or theory development. Kavale and Forness (1985b) conclude that there is a thin theoretical foundation and little agreement over an encompassing research paradigm. The field of LD has moved forward due to sociopolitical forces that have shaped the definition, practices, and theories (Torgesen, 1986). As discussed earlier there has not been a shortage of quackery or personalistic pseudoscientific explanations for the phenomenon of LD.

Nonetheless, an historical review of the field of LD provides evidence of emerging theoretical and paradigmatic frameworks. Although the theoretical developments in the field of LD are often criticized for their loosely knit framework, these developments are consistent with Kuhn's (1970) conceptualization of the developmental nature of science; that is, early investigations of phenomena are characterized by a lack of any organized research agenda. No consensus exists regarding research methods and assumptions. As diversely oriented research programs provide information about the nature of phenomena, groups of scientists begin to find agreement about their perspective of phenomena. However, there are invariably characteristics of phenomena that are incongruent with the explanatory principles of a theory. Scientists seek to account for anomalous data through further research. New data lead to modifications in the theory or abandonment of a theory and the adoption of some competing theoretical explanation.

Over the past few decades, this developmental progression in theory and paradigm building has occurred in the field of LD, beginning with a psychoneurological view and culminating most recently with a social constructivistic perspective. The outcome on LD research is beneficial in the sense of providing insights as to what LD isn't rather than what it is, and to provide a clearer understanding of the limitations of scientific methodology. The development of LD as a science has been an effortful, painful, and frustrating process.

Psychoneurological Model

An early focus on learning problems involved the perceptual aspects of reading and the role of hemispheric processes in encoding visual information. Researchers attributed specific functions to each hemisphere (i.e., left—linguistic, analytic, abstract sequential processing, or mediation; right—nonlinguistic, spatial and holistic processing, or manual pattern recognition) and geared their remedial treatments toward overcoming some hypothesized physical insult to the brain by developing the neurolinguistic capacity of the left hemisphere (Blau & Loveless, 1982; van den Honert, 1977).

Orton (1925), credited with many of the early developments in hemispheric dominance theories of learning, assumed sensory impulses were received by both hemispheres simultaneously forming memory traces in the form of mirrored images. If dominance did not exist because of some impairment to the brain, perceptions would be confusing and inconsistent, resulting in reading difficulties.

Accordingly, Gillingham and Stillman (1965) devised an instructional method to increase the contribution of the auditory channel (e.g., phonics element) by employing a multisensory synthetic phonics approach involving a tracing (i.e., tactile-kinesthetic) technique for teaching single letters and their sound equivalents. Phonemic-graphemic relationships are taught through left hemisphere mediation using the logical, temporal, and analytic functions (Orton & Gillingham, 1968).

Fernald developed a similar technique, using the tactile and kinesthetic modalities to help remediate students' reading and spelling problems (Lovitt, 1989). She combined a whole-word, language-experience approach, with emphasis on the _vi_sual, _a_uditory, _k_inesthetic, and _t_actile senses resulting in the VAKT models of learning (Fernald, 1943; Miccinati, 1979; Myers, 1978). The approach is based on the theory that multisensory experiences with stimuli provide redundant cues about the stimuli, which then assist readers in accurate perception (Hallahan, Kauffman, & Lloyd, 1985).

Kephart's (1960, 1971) theoretical model regarding the relationship between perception and motor development is one of the most widely recognized. The core of his model deals with the developmental match between perception and motor functioning, which allows perceptual information to guide motor responses. In stage one, the hand is used to lead eyes in generating visual perceptions as a young child explores his environment. In stage two, the tactile and kinesthetic sensations from the hand are used only to confirm the visual information or to solve complex problems in perception. Finally, the match between perception and motor activity is refined enough that the child explores his environment with his eyes in the same way he once explored with his hands (Kephart, 1971).

Frostig and Horne (Frostig & Maslow, 1973) developed a series of activities designed to assist readers having visual perceptual difficulties. The activities entail development of: (a) the eye-hand coordination in a way consistent with Kephart's models, (b) visual discrimination skills through exercises involving readers finding embedded figures and identifying the same object presented in varying forms, and (c) spatial relations by observing the relationships between objects.

Myklebust (1978), on the other hand, proposed stimulus overloading as an explanation for perceptual problems. He believed that when two or more types of information are delivered to the brain, a breakdown occurs, resulting in confusion, poor recall, or even seizures. Luchow and Shepherd (1981) provided supportive evidence for the overload theory. They found that input from the auditory and tactile channels does not aid perception and in some cases actually interferes with performance on matching tasks.

Blau and Loveless (1982) similarly followed the overload theory but challenged the benefits of the visual modality in assisting in multisensory programs. Their theoretical model is designed to provide for the most direct hemispheric input; it involves using the left hand to tap the specialization of the right hemisphere for spatial arrangement and manual patterns, and eliminating visual interference by blackened goggles. The theory and training differ from those of Orton and Gillingham (1968) and Witelson (cited in Blau & Loveless, 1982) because emphasis is on using the right hemisphere and holistic, manual recognition abilities rather than the analytic, spatial, and sequential processing abilities of the left hemisphere.

Continuing Challenges.   The models that exemplify psychoneurological theory help demonstrate the extensiveness and complexity of theory related to LD. The models assume an underlying physical anomaly or dysfunction that is potentially applicable to a wide range of learning problems. However, the empirical validity of the theory is debatable. For instance, the argument that the benefit of multisensory reading programs is a function of the increased attention to task—and not to cerebral dominance—has considerable surface validity and has not been dismissed as a competing hypothesis (Koenigsberg, 1973; Thorpe & Borden, 1985). Programs such as the Frostig and Horne require students to develop visual-discrimination skills ostensibly parallel to those needed in decoding written words. However, there is no evidence that such programs using nonalphabet stimuli result in a generalized improvement in perceptual skills, that is, produce any better effect than more traditional reading programs that use letter and word stimuli.

Although the neurological basis of some reading and cognitive problems can be documented, location of anomalies, as suggested by psychoneurological theorists, is not supported by data (Hynd, Marshall, & Gonzalez, 1991; Hynd & Semrud-Clikeman, 1989). Hynd and Semrud-Clikeman (1989) maintain that research findings do warrant the conclusion that the perceptual and cognitive processes normally associated with the left hemisphere are often deficient, but they emphasize that to suggest a localized nature of the anomaly is to overstate the case. Even with recent developments of new technologies to study the brain (e.g., magnetic resonance imaging, positron emission tomography, computerized tomography scanning, and regional cerebral blood flow), the use of diagnostic technology to identify the nature of the relationship between neurologistic functions and reading skills is still surrounded by significant problems (Hynd & Semrud-Clikeman, 1989; Obrzut, 1989). How such anomalies can be remediated is even more uncertain and appears to involve methods outside the traditional teacher realm. Ultimately, the psychoneurological basis for learning problems may attain strong explanatory power, but to date it has fallen short.

Biological Model

Biological explanations for learning disabilities have centered on the impact of prenatal, perinatal, and postnatal events on learning. Early physicians assumed a connection between general biological patterns and observed learning problems; they associated an individual's behaviors and developmental skills to those of other family members (Fisher, 1905; Hinshelwood, 1911; Thomas, 1905). Eventually, mid-20th-century researchers integrated findings from biological and learning studies suggesting further evidence of aberrant family-learning patterns and intraindividual difficulties in offspring (e.g., Eustis, 1947; Marshall & Ferguson, 1939). Mid-twentieth-century researchers began documenting familial learning difficulties that purportedly passed down from one generation to the next (Coles, 1987). Relying on family, twin, and siblings studies and data, researchers often focused on genetic and environmental issues. By the late 20th century, researchers suggested many biological influences on individuals' learning, behavior, and development. For example, researchers considered biological influences on word blindness (Hallgren, 1950), the role of familial patterns in reading disabilities (Hermann, 1959), and genetic and environmental variables affecting learning (Jost & Sontag, 1944; Morrison & Stewart, 1973; Nichols & Chen, 1981; Vandenberg, 1966).

Researchers have examined the genetic makeup of individuals with learning problems in order to determine the potential role of genes as a causal agent in LD. Such a link would explain the characteristic familial learning problems that early researchers reported. Genetic alterations, including those presumably associated with LD, may result from one of three general inherited mechanisms: (a) inheritance of an altered gene or group of genes from one parent that produces an abnormal effect in the child and is also present to some extent in the parent; (b) inheritance of abnormal genes from each parent, which have produced no abnormality in either parent, but which, in combination in the child, produce an abnormal effect; and finally, (c) a change or mutation, occurring in a gene or group of genes as it is being transmitted to the child through the fertilization process. In the latter mechanism, parents do not have an abnormality in their own genetic composition (Patton, Beirne-Smith, & Payne, 1990; Westman, 1990).

One specific area that researchers have examined is the link between genetics and prenatal brain development and the maturation process. Geschwind and Behan (1982) advanced the embryological theory linking individuals' handedness, immune-system diseases, and LD. They suggested that before the twenty-first gestational week, neurons of the cerebral cortex develop in a central area of the brain, then migrate to final positions in the cortex. Geschwind and Behan contended that in the normal brain the right hemisphere develops 1 to 2 weeks earlier than the left. For individuals with learning difficulties, however, a developmental asymmetry causes the right temporal region to develop earlier and the left hemisphere to become larger. Accordingly, they reasoned an unusual surge of the hormone testosterone, before the thirty-first gestational week, influences the fetal brain of individuals with LD. Testosterone would occur more frequently in males, based on fetal testes secretions. Hence, due to excess testosterone, left hemisphere growth could be delayed while the right hemisphere remained unaffected (Geschwind & Behan, 1982; Lovitt, 1989; Smith, 1991). The migration of immature neurons in the left hemisphere would be arrested, causing the abnormalities observed in brains of individuals with LD (Lovitt, 1989).

Hynd, Marshall, and Gonzalez (1991) reported some unidentified factor appears to be altering both the normal process of cellular migration and placement of neurons during fetal development and brain asymmetry. Other researchers also suggested brain asymmetry establishes prenatally (Witelson & Kigar, 1988; Witelson & Pallie, 1973). While currently there is no evidence suggesting that the brains of individuals with LD are characterized by brain damage or lesions associated with the postnatal period, there appears to be a relationship existing between deviations in neurological development, neurological anomalies, and the specific symptoms shared by divergent behavioral syndromes (Hynd et al., 1991).

Other researchers have suggested that during each developmental phase, genetic messages result in chemicals that attach to specific brain receptors, stimulating growth in that particular area (Hynd et al., 1991; Hynd & Semrud-Clikeman, 1989; Pennington & Smith, 1988; Smith, 1991; Westman, 1990). Genetics researchers have also theorized that different brain structures, diverse patterns of brain maturation, biochemical irregularities, or susceptibility to diseases impairing brain functioning may be transmitted genetically (e.g., Hynd et al., 1991; Hynd & Semrud-Clikeman, 1989; Witelson & Kigar, 1988).

From another line of research, data on intraindividual growth and development emanating from biological discoveries has pointed to effects of teratogenic factors. Researchers have highlighted the importance of prenatal exposure to teratogenics, such as the maternal ingestion of toxins (e.g., alcohol, drugs), and to learning or behavioral development (Abel, 1984.; Butler, Goldstein, & Ross, 1972; Hanson, Streissguth, & Smith, 1978; Lovitt, 1989; Office of Policy Research and Improvement,

1990; Rosett, 1980; Sparks, 1984; Wilson, 1975). During critical points of intrauterine development, toxins pass through the placenta to the fetus and may effect gene or cell development. For instance, a mother's ingestion of alcohol during pregnancy can result in a reduced number of cells produced and a consequential growth deficiency (Sparks, 1984). Two crucial factors affecting the likelihood of some deleterious effect of teratogens are the developmental period when the fetus is exposed and the threshold level at which a birth defect will result.

Recent researchers indicate pessimistic outlooks for children exposed prenatally to substance abuse factors (Smith, 1991; Westman, 1990). Children exposed prenatally to teratogenic influences have increased risks academically, behaviorally, medically, and socially. Many face potential failures in the home, school, and community.

A second set of biological factors that have been investigated are postnatal conditions associated with individuals' school-related difficulties. For example, children's infections and diseases, head or body injuries, and biochemical responses (e.g., effects of psychostimulants, diets, vitamins) have been associated with various learning problems (Adler, 1979; Brenner, 1982; Cott, 1972; Feingold, 1975). Biological and environmental interactions analyzed traditionally include psychosocial deprivation; sensory deprivation; severe neglect; malnutrition; infections and diseases (e.g., allergies, encephalitis, meningitis, Reye's syndrome, infections, tumors); head or body injuries (e.g., brain insults or trauma, serious concussions, circulation problems, strokes, high fever); or environmental-biological forces (e.g., psychostimulants/biochemicals; dietary influences including vitamins, malnutrition, dehydration; carbon monoxide; or accidents) (Smith, 1991; Westman, 1990; Ysseldyke & Algozzine, 1990).

Early researchers focused on the effects of medications such as psychostimulants to inhibit an individuals' inappropriate behaviors and thereby increase the opportunity for them to behave appropriately (Coles, 1987; Silver, 1987; Westman, 1990). However, mid-twentieth-century investigators began to recognize not only the benefits of medication, but also the harmful side effects. Researchers conducted extensive investigations focusing on drug effectiveness, teachers' roles in drug monitoring, and drug relationships to students' academic skills and attention (e.g., Kavale, 1982; Lovitt, 1989; Silver, 1987). Recent studies included the relationships between stimulant medications, students' school achievement, and students' attributions to their individual learning abilities (e.g., Cooley & Ayres, 1988; Gadow, 1983; Jacobsen, Lowrey, & Cucette, 1986; Kistner, Haskett, White, & Robbins, 1985; Silver, 1987).

In addition to medication, researchers began to investigate the relationship between other postnatal biological factors and behavior. Feingold (1975) proposed an association between dietary conditions and hyperactivity, suggesting the elimination of all foods containing artificial colors and flavors, as well as salicylates and certain other additives. More recently, researchers explored the role of neurotransmitters on brain functioning, for example, viewing the role of biochemicals in relation to memory, learning ability, and motor coordination (Peters & Levine, 1977; Snyder, 1984). Fishbein and Meduski (1987) noted dietary effects on behavioral control in neurotransmitters, also describing implications to learning and memory problems. Megavitamin treatments have been tested for their effectiveness in controlling suspected hypoglycemia and LD. According to theorists, the bloodstream's inability to synthesize normal vitamin amounts may be the cause of learning problems (e.g., Cott, 1972; Lerner, 1988; Silver, 1987). Researchers have provided controversial evidence on massive vitamin doses and their benefits to the treatment of LD. Improper levels of trace elements, such as copper, zinc, magnesium, manganese, and chromium, and more common elements, such as calcium, sodium, and iron, have also been identified as possible causal factors in LD. Their presence is essential for the maintenance of normal physiological function (Silver, 1987). Researchers have viewed the effects of high dosages of lead and toxic effects, although relationships to LD are not clear.

Continuing Challenges.   Individuals' genetic endowment studies continue to evoke professional controversies and interests (e.g., Coles, 1987; Hynd et al., 1991; Kelly, 1975; Lovitt, 1989; McKusick, 1969; Patton et al., 1990; Pennington & Smith, 1988; Westman, 1990). However, biological data traditionally generated controversy such that many proposed hypotheses often failed to provide comprehensive and definitive answers regarding hereditary or familial roles and precise genetic influences on LD (Coles, 1987; Lovitt, 1989; Smith, 1991; Westman, 1990). Likewise, a genetic or environmental basis to LD is likely to be controversial for some years to come. Importantly, researchers have not yet identified the LD cause(s). They have neither been able to predict nor explain adequately LD hereditary or familial patterns. Like their historical counterparts, biological theorists can only assume potential causal, predictive, and explanatory processes; clear and specific biological links to learning are not yet available. As research continues, some of these controversies may be cleared up with modern, scientific data.

Similar concerns have been expressed regarding the relationship between postnatal biological factors and LD. Investigators have challenged theories regarding the effectiveness of psychostimulants to control hyperactivity and increase academic performance (Aman, 1978). The critics pointed to poor methodology, and in studies that met the requirements of valid scientific inquiry, they pointed out the lack of effectiveness to alter academic performance (Coles, 1987). Criticism has also been lodged against Feingold's findings (Kavale & Forness, 1983; Mattes & Gittelman, 1983), the claims made by proponents of megavitamin treatment for LD (Lovitt, 1989; Silver, 1987), and the role of trace elements in LD (Silver, 1987).

Psychological Processing Model

The failure of psychoneurological and biological models to generate consistent and effective remedial learning programs led to a shift in the field toward a psychological processing explanation. Spearheaded by Samuel Kirk and his colleagues' development of the *Illinois Test of Psycholinguistic Abilities* (ITPA) in the late 1960s, researchers began to focus on psychological processes as causal factors. During the previous decades, psychoneurological testing and programming had failed as a system to differentiate learners with and without brain dysfunction. Additionally, a shift occurred in responsibility for treating students with suspected learning problems. With teachers facing students who apparently had normal intellectual ability and yet were underachieving in academic areas, researchers began to explore other explanations of learning problems. Many began to analyze the psychological processes thought to play key roles in school-related learning activities. On the hypothesis that the underlying psychological processes used in academic learning could be identified, treatment programs were designed by researchers to remediate these processes. With the underlying psychological processes "fixed," academic problems would be ameliorated (Minskoff, 1975).

In the 1960s Kirk, McCarthy, and Kirk began to develop the ITPA. Samuel Kirk and his colleagues believed that language and the psychological processes used by speakers to emit signals or symbols, and those used by listeners to interpret signals, were the root of reading and other language problems (Hammill & Larsen, 1974). Additionally, they assumed that discrete elements of language behavior are identifiable and measurable and provide the underpinnings for learning how to read. Thus, it was believed that if language processes are defective, they may be the cause of readers' learning failures and can be remediated. With this hypothesis, ultimately, classroom learning could then be improved by strengthening weak areas through psycholinguistic-based instruction.

Kirk, McCarthy, and Kirk (1968) adapted Osgood's (1957) model of the intellect as the organizational base for the ITPA. Accordingly, the instrument is structured around three components: communication channels, psycholinguistic processes, and levels of organization. The communication channels include the visual and auditory modalities, the two primary channels for receiving and expressing information. The psycholinguistic processes include reception, organization (i.e., manipulation of concepts and linguistic skills), and expression. The levels of organization are representational (i.e., symbolic behavior) and automatic (i.e., chains of habit).

The ITPA was used as a diagnostic instrument to determine students' specific weaknesses that later become the targets of remedial programs. Remedial programs designed to overcome general psycholinguistic processing problems (i.e., *Peabody Language Development Kit, The MWM Program for Developing Language Abilities,* and *The GOAL Program: Language Development*) are purported to improve language and reading performance. Hegge, Kirk, and Kirk (cited in Lovitt, 1989) specified procedures that are very similar to those used in the Orton-Gillingham method. Specifically, students are taught sound-symbol relationships and skills in sound blending moving from individual letters to single syllable words (Logan & Calarusso, 1978; Mercer & Mercer, 1989).

Continuing Challenges.   A stormy debate within the field of LD arose over the efficacy of psycholinguistic training programs to improve children's performance on skills as measured by the ITPA. Based on an analysis of the ITPA training programs' effectiveness, Hammill and Larsen (1974) concluded that psycholinguistic training programs were generally ineffective in developing ITPA skills. According to Hammill and Larsen, the apparent ineffectiveness of the training could be attributed to various factors. Specifically, these authors noted that the programs seemed to emphasize associative and expressive abilities at the expense of receptive and automatic skills. However, such skills may simply be unteachable using the activities designed for psycholinguistic programs, or the constructs may not be measured appropriately by the ITPA. According to Hammill and Larsen (1974), "efficacy of training psycholinguistic functionings has not been conclusively demonstrated" (p.12).

Kavale (1981) criticized the primitive techniques used in Hammill and Larsen's analysis and replicated the analysis using a meta-analysis technique developed by Glass (1977). By means of this more statistically sophisticated technique, Kavale found an effect size of 0.40 standard deviations above the mean in favor of psycholinguistically trained groups as measured by the ITPA. Kavale concluded, therefore, that psycholinguistic training programs are valid for improving psycholinguistic skills. A rebuttal to Kavale's meta-analysis was later presented by Larsen, Parker, and Hammill (1982) and Sternberg and Taylor (1982), in which the authors pointed out flaws in the meta-analysis and criticized the practical importance of the differences between groups.

Given the debatable data on the effectiveness of some aspects of the models, it is necessary to evaluate the goals and purposes individual programs are purported to achieve, and whether methods used in certain programs are designed to promote designated skills specified by model developers. For instance, in both the Hammill and Larsen and the Kavale studies, one key link is missing: The basic premise for identifying and remediating underlying psycholinguistic skills is to aid students in school-related activities, reading being the central skill. However, in these two analyses, only the training program's effectiveness to change psycholinguistic skills is addressed. Thus, the effects of change in psycholinguistic skills on learning have not been examined. Therefore, teachers selecting psycholinguistically based training programs must make the highly questionable assumptions that psycholinguistic skills can be taught and that these skills, indeed, have a direct bearing on learning.

Behavioral Model

Theorists' failure to support the assumption of an internal physical or psychological dysfunction that can be remediated through specific instructional activities led to application of behavioral theory to the field of LD. Application of behaviorism to educationally related behaviors caused the focus in the field to shift to investigating the interactions between the learner and the learning environment. Specifically, behaviorists have approached learning disabilities from a perspective of ineffective interactions between learners and various instructional variables external to students. The assumption is that academic behaviors are learned through a history of learning facilitated by associations of antecedents, behaviors, and consequences (Wolery, Bailey, & Sugai, 1988). The hypothesized cause of learning problems, therefore, is poor instruction instead of some internal physical or psychological anomaly.

The *sine qua non* of this theory is the precise structuring of instruction by manipulating instructional antecedents and consequences. The effectiveness of these manipulations is judged by observed changes in overt behavioral responses (not cognition). Classroom variables are manipulated to provide appropriate physical facilities, promote engagement, use functional and interesting materials and activities, pace lessons briskly, employ contingent management techniques, structure effective transitions from one activity to another, provide multiple opportunities for learning (e.g., massed and distributed opportunities to practice responses), capitalize on naturally occurring events and routines, and communicate expectations. Teachers are taught to use a diagnostic approach by first identifying curricular goals, then collecting baseline data to determine readers' present educational levels, and distinguishing the configuration of environmental variables affecting instruction. Based upon these data, teachers specify the learning objective and subsequently plan and implement intervention programs. Finally, progress is monitored and evaluated on a formative basis (White & Haring, 1980; Wolery et al., 1988).

Early behavioral scientists contributed to the application of behaviorism to learning disabilities through their work with children exhibiting other disabilities. For example, Whelan's work with children demonstrating severe emotional disturbances involved experimenting with the use of highly structured classroom environments in order to modify academic, as well as social, behaviors (Hallahan & Kauffman, 1976). Influenced by Whelan's work, Haring and Phillips (1962) compared the relative efficacy of three programs for students having emotional disturbances that varied in structure and placement. Based on a comparison between a structured special classroom program, a nondirective, nonstructured special classroom, and a regular classroom program with consultative assistance to the teacher, Haring and Phillips concluded that the structured special education classroom was most effective.

Later work by O. R. Lindsley (1964) at the University of Kansas produced a set of structured procedures for academic learning, termed "precision teaching" (Lovitt, 1989). These procedures are characterized by systematic monitoring of academic progress through a set of highly structured sequential objectives. Emphasis is placed not only on students' accurate responses, but on *fast* and accurate responses, thus ensuring mastery and maintenance of the responses (White & Haring, 1980).

One of the more controversial developments to emerge from behavioral theory is the direct instruction (DI) procedure and curriculum developed by Englemann and his associates at the University of Oregon. Engelmann's theoretical framework is based on the belief that effective instruction requires a behavioral analysis of criterial responses (e.g., sounding out words, writing sums to addition problems), analysis of the knowledge systems (i.e., structuring classes and subclasses of information based on interrelationships), and analysis of communications systems (i.e., faultless communications through scripted lessons prevent the acquisition of misrules, erroneous concepts, or use of under- and overgeneralizations) (Englemann & Carnine, 1982; Tarver, 1986). This framework is operationalized by teachers first modeling the response for students, then leading them in making the response with the teacher, and finally testing students by having them make the response without the teacher (Englemann & Bruner, 1984).

As behavioral scientists began to focus on antecedent events in shaping behaviors (e.g., curriculum materials and teacher behaviors), the influences of developments in cognitive psychology began to be felt. The blend of behavioral learning principles with an emphasis on monitoring overt behavioral responses and the verbal mediation strategies devised by cognitive psychologists led to a hybrid of the two models, called *cognitive behavior modification* (CBM). CBM procedures require students to act as their own instructor, using self-guiding verbalizations to complete a series of steps to demonstrate appropriate social or academic behavior (Meichenbaum, 1980). The primary objective of CBM, as applied to academic areas, has been in helping students generalize their responses over time and across settings. CBM techniques enable students to become less dependent on others, to control their behaviors (Wolery et al., 1988).

Early CBM procedures were developed to train students to control behaviors that

interfered with performing academic tasks (e.g., impulsivity) through self-verbaliza-
tions (Douglas, Parry, Marton, & Garson, 1976; Lloyd, 1980). Later developments in
CBM training took the form of self-instructional procedures focusing on completing
specific academic tasks (Lloyd, 1980).

Continuing Challenges.   Although models based on behavioral principles have
been influential in the field of LD, many researchers have questioned the theoretical
model's ability to explain and predict developments in the learning process (Poplin,
1987, 1988). Other researchers have emphasized the lateness of a concerted recognition of the role played by cognition, an over-reliance on adult interventions, and
learners' activeness in the learning process (Heshusius, 1986, 1994; Poplin, 1988).

Nonetheless, because of the widespread application of behavioral and cognitive
behavioral models to academic instruction, and the high rate of the effectiveness of
practitioners employing the theoretical orientation, the basic teaching procedures
developed from these models continue to be used by teachers. This trend is evident
in the adoption of the direct instruction methods to teach metacognitive learning-
strategies curricula (Deshler, Schumaker, Alley, Warner, & Clark, 1982; Deshler &
Schumaker, 1986) and cognitive and developmental curricula (Reid, 1988; Reid &
Stone, 1991).

Cognitive/Metacognitive Model

While behaviorists have continued to develop the CBM technologies, learning disabilities researchers with a cognitive-model orientation have continued to develop
technologies that address generalization of task-appropriate behaviors (Flavell,
1985). Their focus, however, has been on how students with learning problems use
various cognitive processes. Cognitive theorists believe that these children, when
presented with some mental tasks, do not think about or attempt to use their cognitive processes in planning, carrying out, or monitoring their own progress (Jacobs &
Paris, 1987; Wong, 1986). These processes are linked to the child's awareness and
use of declarative knowledge (i.e., what information is important), procedural
knowledge (i.e., how to do tasks), conditional knowledge (i.e., when to do tasks),
and metacognitive knowledge (i.e., knowing about cognitive processes and self-
management) (Jacobs & Paris, 1987).

Theorists hypothesize that metacognitive skills are teachable and therefore have
devised training programs for different levels of metacognitive skills. Sternberg (1977,
1979, 1983) delineated three forms of training: Microcomponent training focuses on
information processing skills related to specific curricular content (e.g., math facts);
macrocomponent training entails the development of complex processing systems,
such as note taking and outlining study skills; and metacomponent training involves
engineering executive control mechanisms that can be applied flexibly and with a degree of speed to specific problem-solving situations (Derry & Murphy, 1986). Danser-
reau's (1978, 1985) metacognition levels comprise primary and support strategies in
the instruction process. *Primary strategies,* involving information retention, include:
paraphrase imagery, networking, and key idea analysis; *support strategies,* used to
maintain a mind set for learning, include: goal setting and scheduling, concentration
management, self-monitoring, and diagnosing to check understanding, concentration,

and mood. Jones, Amiran, and Katims (1985) categorized strategies as either encoding strategies, involving naming, rehearsing, and elaborating key ideas; generative strategies (i.e., using prior knowledge to determine the meaning conveyed in the written text), including paraphrasing, visualization, elaborating with analogies, inferencing, and summarizing; and constructive strategies including reasoning, transformation, and synthesis, all of which are used when information is being derived from multiple sources that are ambiguous or inadequate to the reader.

The most widely applied example of metacognitive-based strategies in learning disabilities is the Strategies Intervention Model (SIM) conceptualized at the University of Kansas (Deshler, Schumaker, Lenz, & Ellis, 1984). Early research by Alley and Deshler (1979) was based on the theory that educational delivery systems and curriculum at the secondary level were ineffective because they failed to address the underlying needs of students with LD. They held that students could succeed in high school if the delivery system and curriculum focused on teaching students learning strategies—"techniques, principles, or rules that will facilitate the acquisition, manipulation, integration, storage, and retrieval of information across situations and settings" (p. 13). For instance, RAP, a three-step strategy helps students summarize what they have read by following the mnemonic: *R*ead paragraph; *A*sk self questions; and *P*ut it in own words (Schumaker, Denton, & Deshler, 1984).

The SIM includes structures for how to teach and what to teach. Specifically, the "how to teach" component is based upon the behaviorally oriented DI model involving teachers modeling, leading, and testing students through the acquisition stage of learning. The "what to teach" component draws from the metacognitive needs of adolescents with learning disabilities; that is, teachers promote awareness and regulation of the information-processing demands of the secondary school setting. Generalization of strategy use is facilitated by various procedures. For example, antecedent steps encourage generalization by changing negative student attitudes that might affect students' efforts to generalize. During strategy acquisition, concurrent steps facilitate generalization by having students learn strategies well enough for them to become generalized. After students have demonstrated mastery of strategy use in controlled materials, they are taught to apply the strategy to various contexts, situations, and settings. Ultimately, independence (i.e., executive functioning) is generated by teaching students to use self-instruction procedures to mediate generalization (Ellis, Lenz, & Sabornie, 1987).

Continuing Challenges.   Strategy use by students with LD has generated a great deal of discussion over the past decade. The question is whether good information processors possess a set of strategies that they employ, whereas poor information processors (e.g., students with LD) do not. For instance, Rohwer (1980) argued that a developmental-strategy hypothesis may explain the effect of memory strategies and the level of instruction needed, that is, strategy training triggers the use of processing capabilities that have developed over time. Flavell (1985), in turn, proposed a production-deficiency hypothesis: Young children fail to produce verbal mediation strategies spontaneously but once introduced to such strategies are able to use them to improve performance. Some authors have misinterpreted Flavell's hypothesis to mean that students with LD have such strategies, but do not use them.

Another question is whether good information processors demonstrate good executive control (i.e., awareness of purpose) to tap learning strategies, while poor information processors possess the strategies, but not the executive control to call them up. Gagne' (1980, 1985) contended that executive-strategy functions cannot be taught through direct instruction in the same manner as learning strategies can. He suggested that, instead, the overall cognitive function is dependent more on long-term exposure and practice, as well as intelligence.

Social Constructivism Model

A more radical shift in viewing the concept of LD has been proposed by advocates of social constructivistic thought and procedures in the field of LD. Proponents of social constructivism (Heshusius, 1986, 1989, 1994; Poplin, 1987, 1988; Smith & Heshusius, 1986) have argued that positivistic and empiricist traditions underlying earlier theoretical models (i.e., psychoneurological, behavioral, and cognitive) are not adequate to understand human behavior. Thus, these models are based upon a methodology originally designed in the natural sciences to analyze component parts of inanimate objects in isolation from the whole. The reductionistic approach to studying LD is most clearly evident in the use of task-analysis and behavioral objectives, especially when academic behaviors are reduced to extremely minute units (e.g., instruction that emphasizes recognition of words-in-isolation tasks). Social constructivists, in contrast, argue that the study of human behavior must focus on the complex whole, because of the interdependence of the elements of behavior (i.e., social, cognitive, motivational, and pragmatic dimensions of the learning process). Therefore, in a classroom setting, students must be viewed in the context of what is meaningful and functional to them both inside and outside the classroom (Dithey, 1988).

The basic tenets of the social constructivistic view are derived from phenomenological thought, which "sets forth the importance of understanding a person's direct experience of her world, irrespective of how she conceptualizes and categorizes it" (Heshusius, 1986, p. 30). Researchers and teachers, therefore, seek to determine how children make their own reality, based on the assumption that students are self-directed, meaning-constructing, meaning-seeking individuals who act upon their environments accordingly (Palincsar & Klenk, 1993). Students' knowledge bases are shaped by contextual conditions and meaningfulness, as well as by their individual interests and purposes. Self-directed learning is more motivating than teacher-directed learning that imposes the problem and the solution. Academic programs designed for students with LD (as well as for other students) without considering the context of purpose, use, and desired social relations fail to provide motivating and meaningful environments conducive to self-directed learning (McPhail, 1995).

Teaching procedures are based on the concepts of proleptic teaching (i.e., anticipation of competence) and expert scaffolding (i.e., support structures for learning). Specifically, the teacher provides a model of a strategy or skill being taught through a natural dialogue with students and gradually allows the student to take over the steps and procedures involved in applying the strategy or skill (Paris & Winograd, 1990; Pressley, Hogan, Wharton-McDonald, Mistretta, & Ettenberger, 1996; Rosenshine & Meister, 1992). This concept is closely related to Goodman's

(1989) conceptualization of child-centered learning, whereby teachers "lead from behind." That is, as students demonstrate needs and seek out assistance, the teacher provides the guidance and support structures to allow the students to learn what they need to complete a particular task. Teachers do not establish and follow a preset curriculum sequence. They follow the sequence dictated by each student's naturally developing needs.

The most prominent example of the social constructivistic paradigm in education is the whole language, or literacy, approach. The principles of holism are applied to reading and language arts instruction by having students engage in activities that are purposeful to them, such as story reading and journal writing. The unit of meaning is a whole story rather than some smaller part (e.g., letter sounds or isolated words), and meaning is constructed from stories that are rich in language forms. Writing skills are encouraged through language-experience activities whereby a student dictates a story while others or the teacher write it down. Through constant exposure to literature and writing, children begin to use different language forms that, in essence, mimic what is presented in books. They start to speak using expression and vocabulary that they would find in books and stories they have heard (i.e., proleptic learning). Children's intonation is very vigorous and very expressive as they tell stories, create, and convey information (Holdaway, 1979).

The primary system for identifying words lies in the semantic relationships expressed through meaningful stories and children's experiences (Smith, 1971), whereas syntax and morphology serve as a secondary system that supplements semantic elements. Processing written language requires such strategies as self-regulating operations involving self-monitoring of meaning construction, confirmation, and self-correction. The pleasure and enjoyment of literature is developed through positive experiences with books. Young children acquire an intrinsic reinforcement system that is illustrated in the amount of time that they spend independently interacting with books. They enjoy being read to and enjoy pretending to be reading or just interacting and telling stories with the aid of a book.

Continuing Challenges.   The instructional practices derived from the social constructivistic model have a strong intuitive appeal. Thus, the focus on meaningful learning experiences that take into account the terminal goal (e.g., reading to gain information and to derive pleasurable vicarious experience) and the social role of learning (i.e., a primary channel for communication of ideas) is attractive to many teachers. However, critics argue that the assumption that the cause of students' learning problems is the fragmentation of the curriculum, the associated meaningless activities, and the teacher's control of the curriculum is incomplete. Social constructivists understate the fact that whole language programs do involve curriculum fragmentation in the form of "mini lessons." Students are taught discrete component skills directly and separately from the whole. While acknowledging the merits of such assumptions for internally motivated students, critics point out that many students are not self-directed and require externally regulated motivational techniques.

A related criticism is that social constructivists have not presented a workable format for evaluating students' academic progress. For example, Ulman and Rosenberg (1986) argued that without measurable objectives (fragmented pieces of curriculum) to monitor incremental progress, teachers compromise the need for accountability. Formative assessment is central to making instructional decisions that decrease the likelihood of students floundering for extended periods of time, making no progress. Furthermore, Licht and Torgesen (1989) suggested that other forms of student evaluation that entail children's subjective views of their own skills are not necessarily ignored in reductionistic programs (e.g., attribution theory).

DEVELOPING A METATHEORY

These theoretical models have generated myriad assumptions and facts about the phenomenon called LD. They have been characterized as a "patchwork" approach to the development of viable explanations (Kavale & Forness, 1985b), that is, a haphazard compilation of data without a systematic approach to explaining the phenomenon called LD (Swanson, 1988). There is a deficiency of guiding principles or law-like propositions derived from specific factual information from which to make generalizations about the nature of LD and its treatment. Kavale (1987) argues that the lack of theory is a primary reason why we have not experienced any monumental breakthroughs in the field. Although we have accumulated hoards of data, we have failed to discover any new facts.

Kavale (1987) points to the argument that to take a natural science orientation toward the study of LD means that we have to break the total into fragmented parts and try to analyze them separately. However, human behavior is not conducive to this kind of study; it involves a much more complex set of interdependent variables. But by taking this position, there is an implication that some deeper understanding exists that we could really never communicate. In an attempt to be scientific, we have tried to dictate what we study—or allowed the research method to—and in so doing we have looked at somewhat trivial questions and problems. In abiding by the rules of scientific procedure, however, researchers have failed to address more important and prominent problems because of the difficulties of applying methodology (Bogdan & Luftfiyya, 1992). This is a wrong step for the field to take. The reason this is done comes back to the attempt to elevate the study of LD to a plane that is akin to the biological or physical sciences. We have established specific procedures for studying the phenomena, procedures that are systematic and logical, but are also restrictive.

A related problem is the heterogeneity of the group of scholars that examine the field of LD (Kavale, 1987; Wong, 1979). While there are those individuals that would want to study LD from a hard scientific methodological view (Kavale & Forness, 1985a; Fuchs & Fuchs, 1992), others would like to look at it from a more phenomenological perspective (Heshusius, 1989; McPhail, 1995; Poplin, 1987). An emerging group of scholars is applying qualitative research methods to the study of disabilities in an attempt to answer questions that are difficult to address using traditional quantitative methods (Bogdan & Kugelmauss, 1984; Iano, 1986; Poplin, 1987; Stainback & Stainback, 1989). The different theories and explanations that come into play are all very diverse, and as a result we have a very heterogeneous group of individuals to investigate and explain the nature of LD.

In order to derive some cohesiveness to the multidirectional, multidimensional research thrusts, researchers and practitioners have to seek out a connective web that bonds various theories. Awareness and the discussions of the need for metatheory are major steps forward in the maturation of LD as a science. Instead of focusing within the narrow confines of a single theoretical model, we are beginning to step back and examine the bigger picture—how do all of these different research thrusts and theories connect? The generation of macro-level theories provides a suprastructure that connects theories within a paradigm (Kavale, 1987). Within the superstructure there should be subordinate theories that explain components of the macro theories. The theories would be explained by a system of laws that exists between theoretical entities and some set of observable indicators. This suprastructure can better establish clear lawlike principles or relationships that would permit us to make some explicit generalizations. Facts would be used to explain lawlike generalizations in a hierarchical fashion, and reference would be made to more general rather than specific cases of the LD phenomena. Laws are explained by theories, and the theories give the justifications and explanation for the laws. The connection between the theories and the macro theories would be explanations that come through principals which subsume whatever is to be explained into this higher-order macro theory. Oscillation between macro- and micro-level perspectives is necessary to achieve the depth and breadth of understanding needed for our knowledge base to mature (Phillips, 1976).

We believe Kavale's (1987) critique of the haphazard nature of LD research is somewhat overstated (cf., Scruggs & Mastropieri, 1988), but his call for the development of a metatheory is nonetheless sound. The developments within the field of LD are traceable with notable discoveries of the characteristics of the LD phenomenon. There are distinctive lines of research that have provided solid information about causality and effective treatments. Torgesen (1987) argues that in fact LD research programs have and do exist and have and do provide new facts and insights into the relationships between facts. He classifies five theoretical models reviewed here, into three scientific paradigms: information processing, neuropsychology, and applied behavioral analysis. The organization of these lines of research has been less than ideal. But, that is the nature of a laisse faire research environment. The benefit is the creative variety of research; the drawbacks are the creation of pseudoscience and somewhat chaotic science.

Torgesen (1987) argues that acceptance of these different paradigms as frameworks for studying the field may create some confusion from time to time. But different points of view are compatible with the complexity of the phenomena and the development of the field at this stage in time. Kronick (1990) has conveyed the same message in arguing the complementary nature of reductionistic and social constructivistic paradigms in LD research. Simpson (1992) characterizes this issue by arguing that qualitative and quantitative methodologies should be viewed on a continuum rather than as one being superior to the other. By accepting the complimentary coexistence of different paradigms, we can direct efforts toward work at the theory level through the integrated use of inquiry procedures from both paradigms. Tighter and better structured assumptions and methods regarding problems and the variables chosen for evaluation can evolve by our beginning at the theory level and moving toward the connective suprastructure.

What is needed is the continuation of the dialogue initiated by Kavale, Forness, Swanson, Poplin, Heshusius, Bogdan, and Kronich about this higher structural level that some call paradigm and others call metatheory. In a democratic research environment, there can be no effective dogmatic research agenda dictated by the epistomologically privileged. Proponents of a methatheory can only guide others to thinking in terms of a larger structure and hope that their arguments will compel grass-roots researchers and practitioners to frame their own research within some suprastructure. The dialogue should also include discussion of the importance of practitioners in the development of theory and superstructures. They should not be the docile recipients of knowledge generated from research institutions. Instead they should play a more fundamental role than is currently the case in driving various efforts in theory development and practical applications.

THEORY-DRIVEN TEACHERS

Practitioners and researchers alike benefit from theory and paradigm development in that a structure for understanding why LD students function as they do and how instructional procedures can address deficiencies in students' learning (Wansart, 1995). Researchers reflecting on views of the complex systems that are involved in the learning process leads to examining assumptions of the nature of LD.

The development of the field of LD and the study of effective practices of teachers dealing with learning problems are both relatively new. Since no one knows precisely why or how learning problems develop, a multitude of explanations are possible, leading to varied etiologies and prescriptions. As such, theories provide a general rationale for a variety of events or patterns associated with teacher operations and student development. Theories are based upon a set of assumptions that are evaluated and tested within a given context over time. Theoretical models, in turn, help teachers to fit research and clinical impressions into comprehensive and convincing accounts of the learning process. Teachers may use and develop theoretical models to explain causes of learning problems by organizing their knowledge of the learning process. Knowledge of the governing concepts and principles of theoretical models can guide teachers to determine whether instructional practices are used to the advantage of learners, and to select appropriate instructional materials based upon knowledge of their theoretical framework.

Theoretical frameworks and theory building are traditionally looked down upon by practitioners whose primary concern is how they instruct, not why to instruct a certain way. Despite its reputation as esoteric and too lofty for practitioners within the field, theory building is, in reality, a very practical and useful activity.

Polansky (1986) provides a number of justifications for the practicality of theories. First, theory mobilizes professionals' energies by providing a more clear understanding of why they operate the way they do. In turn, individuals who share a theory come together and collaborate on problems and help shape in others further understanding of what they do. Second, theory helps individuals to selectively attend to critical matters. Theory provides the guiding principles that are used to as-

Theory structures enable the teacher to examine his or her own manipulation of classroom variables in a rational manner instead
of in a hit-or-miss haphazard way.

sist the development of our perspective about the salient and unimportant characteristics of a problem. Third, theory infuses a dynamic that leads to predictions about
future events that have similar characteristics to past events. If the theory enables an
individual to predict future events with a higher than chance probability, then the
theory is maintained. If not, it is discarded or modified. The ongoing change in theory is the dynamic that allows for knowledge and understanding to be systematically
extended or elaborated. Fourth, theory allows individuals to go beyond known facts.
Theory provides an individual with the procedures for exploring the cause and effects of misunderstood phenomenon. The procedures provide a methodology and
rationale for following a logical deductive sequence. Fifth, theory provides a parsi-
mony that condenses what is known and has been tested into a set of guiding principles. It simplifies thinking by consolidating knowledge, assumptions, and propositions into some orderly whole. All of these attributes allow teachers to make sound
judgments about why students interact the way they do and how teachers can respond. They liberate teachers from dependence on nonadaptable "cookbook" approaches to instruction. Thereby, teachers function more as decision-making professionals than as drone-like technicians.

Teacher Roles and Reflectivity

Teachers of students with LD are greatly influenced by the way their roles in the instructional process are defined. Teachers may be viewed in a narrow context as classroom technicians (Cruickshank, 1987) or in a broader context as empowered, reflective decision makers (Ross, 1989; Ross, Bony, & Kyle, 1993; Smyth, 1989; Wansart, 1995). According to the former, teachers focus on their instructional and behavior-management skills, while in the latter, they focus on their skills as reflective decision makers seeking to frame experiential-based problems and identify possible solutions in the context of the social, historical, theoretical, ethical, and political systems in schools (Smyth, 1989). Reflective decision making generally entails "active, persistent, and careful consideration of any belief or supposed form of knowledge in the light of the grounds that support it and further conclusions to which it tends" (Dewey, 1993, p. 9).

The more narrow scope of reflectivity emanates form the traditional top-down hierarchical conceptualization of the field of LD. Practitioners are viewed as "cogs in a self-perpetuating machine" that is driven by an elite corp of decision makers (Tom, 1985). Teachers are characterized by a narrow perspective of acquiring or maintaining skills to practice their craft (e.g., planning a logical method to manage instructional groups; scheduling activities), while implementing their instructional and management techniques in the classroom setting with little regard for broader policy concerns. Researchers are viewed as being epistomologically privileged, owning the exclusive rights to truth and knowledge regarding pedagogy. They affect the service delivery systems through their consultative roles to the upper administrative and supervisory levels of school districts. District administrators are the czars of broader policy and procedural decisions that are dictated to teachers. Decision making is conducted with little or no input from the teachers and other direct service personnel.

The flaw of this scenario is that the decision-making base is too restrictive. It excludes representation by professionals who are most immediately involved in service delivery. Additionally, the breadth of decision makers often excludes ancillary-support service providers or service providers outside of the educational system (i.e., physicians, therapists, etc.). Consequently, questions are asked and answers are provided that have little bearing on service providers' primary concerns or the operations of their classrooms or clinics.

An alternative conceptualization of how the field of LD could be driven is from a reflective, inquiry-oriented approach (Ross, 1989; Ross, Bony, & Kyle, 1993; Smyth, 1989; Wansart, 1995). Accordingly, school-district-wide decision making would be more a bottom-up process much like that advocated in Total Quality Management programs (Schmoker & Wilson, 1993). Teachers and other professionals on the front line of the service-delivery system would be viewed as an essential part of the policy-and-procedures decision-making system. They would be empowered with the responsibility and authority to identify and solve delivery, curriculum, and management problems at the classroom, school, and district levels. Further, the active involvement of teachers would facilitate a sense of ownership for programs. Teachers would be motivated to work together in a forum of collective decision making

(Schmoker, 1996). A commitment would also be placed on respecting, valuing, and sharing the opinions expressed by those in a working group. The resulting egalitarian work environment would encourage cooperation toward common goals, replacing hierarchical control with more self-direction, loyalty, and motivation (Chandler, 1982).

To shift to a participatory decision-making system, teachers and other direct-line service providers would have to take into consideration social, historical, theoretical, ethical, and political systems in schools, that is, the broader perspective of the reflective professional. The central underlying force in decision making in a profession such as education should be the theoretical framework or paradigm adopted by a group of decision makers. Consideration of social, historical, and political forces is necessary, but these considerations should be secondary to the logical application of theory into practice. Reflection on theory would entail identifying real system problems and deducing what instructional practices should be employed and why their employment makes sense in light of the groups' assumptions about the etiology and treatment of LD. Answering the *why* question is the most critical aspect of moving from a haphazard pseudoscientific process to a scientific and professional one.

Smyth (1989) proposes a four-step process of reflection that can be used by groups of empowered educators to inquiry about their practices and the rationale for them. The first step is to *describe* what it is the group does. They account for the daily operations of instruction at the classroom, school, and school-district levels, and in the field of LD. The second and third steps involve *informing* the group through self-analysis of the descriptions of what the group does and *confronting* the reasons for doing what they do. This process should lead to the identification of the principles that underlie instruction. For instance, do teachers use direct-instruction approaches because their instructional materials dictate that, or because they believe the methods to be effective? Do the teachers know and understand the theoretical explanation for why the materials are supposed to work? Does the theoretical model fit their personal theory and belief structure about effective instruction? Are there social, historical, and political forces that have shaped practices and beliefs? The fourth step is to *reconstruct* the groups' practices, theories, and beliefs. Issues of theory should be primary in considerations of how the group can function differently, with supplemental consideration given to other potentially opposing forces.

To facilitate the reflective, inquiry-oriented approach, teachers and other professional educators will have to be well grounded in their understanding of the evolutional nature of theories. As described earlier in the chapter there are varied explanations of LD that implicate equally varied sources and types of treatment. The application of the informing and confronting steps of Smyth's model require an understanding of the phenomenon of LD well beyond simply knowing about different treatments. An understanding of both how the theories were developed and why they gained and lost broad acceptance by the field is necessary for reconstructing one's personal theories, beliefs, and practices. As members of an educational programming team, service providers have to believe that their services can be assistive to individuals with LD.

With reflectivity occurring in the broader sense, teachers empower themselves as primary change agents and problem solvers. Their roles change, not only in terms of their impact on shaping school and district-wide policies and procedures, but in the way in which they engage their students (Ross et al., 1993). It would be contradictory for teachers to embody the empowerment concept so central to social constructionism without examining how they either facilitate or thwart their own students' empowerment. The implications of being empowered are that one facilitates empowerment in others. It would be very difficult for reflective teachers to avoid the question of how much control they exert on their students' learning and to what extent they facilitate self-directed learning and independent functioning. In thinking about their work, they would have to confront their use of highly structured teaching strategies such as direct instruction or precision teaching, versus the use of child-centered strategies such as proleptic teaching or discovery learning and their effects on learning. This would create conditions conducive to further reflection and empowerment.

Another context variable that implicates the need for reflective, theory-driven teachers is the conceptualization of the setting demands for children and adults in the twenty-first century. The most common perspective is that of students attacking real-life problems using problem-solving strategies and tactics. Teams of culturally diverse students cooperatively work together in identifying problems and seeking out information through various sources, using electronic databases. Correspondingly, teachers function less as lecturers and providers of information and more as coaches or guides to assist students in identifying problems, developing possible solutions, and monitoring attempts to resolve problems (Florida Commission on Reform and Accountability, 1992). Again, teachers face questions regarding how they interact with students, and what theoretical base drives what guiding principles, that implicate what practices.

With the increasing scope of factors that affect the operational description of a professional educator, there is a need to have some guiding principles to help organize and make sense of these factors. Teachers are burdened with having to account for the myriad variables associated with their students' physical, psychological, intellectual, and emotional makeups; the educational resources made available to them, and the demands ascribed by the public. Theories are the most practical means of bringing order and reason to a complex of variables. They not only assist in making sense of the present, but through careful testing of their explanatory power, they assist in delineating which guiding principles will survive the test of future utility. The result is further development of a valid and reliable body of knowledge regarding the phenomenon of LD.

The closer teachers and other front-line practitioners are to theory and theory development, the faster they can discard disproven theories and employ emerging principles. The closer they are, the better able they will be to ward off charlatans of pseudoscience. Further, they will be better able to communicate their practices and the rationale for their practices to other professionals, parents, students, and the general public. The extent these things can be accomplished determines the degree of credibility the field of LD enjoys.

Practical Classroom Applications

The following implications regard the use of various theoretical explanations of LD. The suggestions reflect ways to use theories to improve practices for students with LD.

1. *The field of LD has a traceable path of theory development and application.* Researchers and practitioners have pursued investigations of the causes and treatments for LD from a wide range of theoretical perspectives. Arguably, there has been a loose structure to guide the development of theory within and across theoretical frameworks. The dysfunctional effects of this lose structure have been the development and perpetuation of theories and treatments that have little scientific validity or practical utility. Awareness of the nature of theory development helps to guard against unscrupulous pseudoscience. Traditionally, the victims of quackery and pseudoscience have been practitioners and parents who either are unfamiliar with the rigors of scientific investigation and validation or who are blinded by their legitimate desire to ameliorate the effects of LD.

By developing a rich understanding and use of theory and the practices that emanate from them, practitioners can be more effective in serving the needs of individuals with LD. They can develop a level of reflectivity that transcends their central role as technicians, to become decision-making professionals. Practitioners may use their understanding of theories and the relationships between theories to consolidate their knowledge of effective treatments and formulate their own personal theories that serve as guiding principles for their practices. In their development, they are able to communicate to other professionals and parents not only what they are doing, but why they are doing

it. And they can provide a rationale for using one treatment instead of another, as well as more effectively argue for changes within educational systems with a knowledge base that is thorough and persuasive.

Additionally, practitioners' participation in theory and treatment development has been overlooked. These are the people who work directly with individuals with LD daily, gaining invaluable insights to the intricacy of the LD phenomenon, yet, little effort is made to tap their wealth of knowledge. The traditional barriers that seem to separate theorists from practitioners—and theories from practices—can be disassembled. One step is to erode the barriers in the knowledge base and construct teaching practices from it.

2. *University researchers need to open up their protection of epistemology, and practitioners must open up their protection of their hands-on experiences.* Researchers protect epistemology by creating value systems that only allow for the most technical methods for validating theory and practice. An example is the over-reliance and overstated value of intricate statistical procedures. The opening of epistemology can occur through the acceptance and support of research methodologies that are less technical and more available to practitioners (e.g., use of simple teaching or experimental, single-case, time-series designs or anecdotal running records used in qualitative research).

Practitioners can open up their knowledge base by accepting the practicality of good theory development. Too often the blanket criticism of researchers is that they are removed from direct contact and are unsophisticated in their understanding of the logistics of running a classroom. For example, practitioners criticize universities for teach-

(continued)

Practical Classroom Applications (continued)

ing about theories underlying metacognition and argue that training should be focused on how teacher trainees should teach specific learning strategies. Such shortsightedness relegates teaching to a "cookbook" enterprise. Effective practitioners need to know why they are implementing the treatments they use, if they are going to be able to function as effective decision makers and make adaptations to fit students' individual needs.

One simple and fundamental step that may facilitate the breakdown of barriers is through the physical integration of university- and school-based professionals. Proposals emanating from the school renewal literature call for the establishment of professional development and research centers. Existing schools would be designated as places where professional educators would assist students in gaining an education, train teachers, and conduct research, all in one facility. Under such a system, theories and practices of pedagogy and andragogy would go hand in hand. Those who traditionally were practitioners would now share in research and theory development, and those who were university researchers would assist in modeling effective teaching practices in real classrooms. The result would be fluent dialogue and exchange of roles leading to the disassembling of protected knowledge bases. Theory and practices are merged as complimentary parts of a whole. Through the merger of theory and practice, the respect for scientific inquiry, and the development of a metatheory superstructure that reflects the relationships between theoretical models, the field of LD can mature and progress in its conceptualization of the LD phenomenon.

SUMMARY

- Educators at all levels need to reflect continuously on their beliefs and convictions, vis-à-vis theoretical frameworks.

- Theory structures enable the teacher to examine his or her own manipulation of classroom variables in a rational manner instead of in a hit-or-miss, haphazard, way.

- Professionals embrace theoretical orientations in different ways.

- The evolution of the LD field is best served by using theory development as the primary driving force.

- A fundamental assumption is that theory and practice are not in conflict with each other.

- The phenomenon of LD must be studied in the general context in which it is manifested—the classroom. Consequently, the role of teachers is absolutely primary.

- Pseudoscience has been used to explain and treat LD.

- In good science, knowledge is shared, publicly available, and verified.

- Paradigms, or views of the world, are used as a framework for inquiry into the nature of phenomena.

- *Theories* are statements that attempt to describe the relationships between variables associated with some phenomenon. They are much more narrow in scope and are developed within a set of assumptions about inquiry.

- There exist two fundamental scientific world views: reductionistic and social constructivistic.

- An historical review of the field of LD provides evidence of emerging theoretical and paradigmatic frameworks.

- Theoretical models (i.e., Psychoneurological Theory, Biological Theory, Psychological Processing Theory, Behavioral Theory, Cognitive/Metacognitive Theory, Social Constructivistic Theory) have generated myriad assumptions and facts about the phenomenon called LD.

- Awareness of—and the discussions of the need for—metatheory are major steps forward in the maturation of LD as a science.

DISCUSSION QUESTIONS

This chapter has developed the case for the practical importance of theories. Accordingly, we urge contemplation in order to examine your own perspective on causes of LD. To help extend your understanding, reflect on and discuss the following questions:

1. What are my perceptions regarding the credibility of popular theories of LD?

2. Which theory or theories do I believe best reflect the guiding principles that I use as a teacher?

3. Does paradigmatic pluralism allow for a strengthening of guiding principles by taking the best of different paradigms, or does it dilute the integrity of individual paradigms?

4. Has there been sufficient scientific inquiry to consider LD as a scientific field of study?

5. How aware am I of my own beliefs regarding LD, and how do they affect the way I teach?

6. To what extent should teachers focus their reflectivity on technical matters versus on more global issues regarding their roles in shaping the field of LD?

7. Is it plausible to have a coordination of efforts between theorists and practitioners?

8. Can teachers conduct research in their classrooms, and is there sufficient benefit to justify the effort?

9. Are theories really practical to teachers?

10. What would be the logistical and philosophical problems associated with the integration of university- and school-based professionals in teacher training and research?

REFERENCES

Abel, E. L. (1984). *Fetal alcohol syndrome and fetal alcohol effects*. New York: Plenum.

Adler, S. (1979). Megavitamin treatment for behaviorally disturbed and learning disabled children. *Journal of Learning Disabilities, 12*, 678–681.

Alley, G. R., & Deshler, D. D. (1979). *Teaching the learning disabled adolescent: Strategies and methods*. Denver, CO: Love.

Aman, M. G. (1978). Drugs, learning, and the psychotherapies. In J. S. Werry (Ed.), *Pediatric psychopharmacology: The use of behavior modifying drugs in children*. New York: Brunner/Mazel.

American Academy of Pediatrics (1982). The Doman-Delacato treatment of neurologically handicapped children. A policy statement by the American Academy of Pediatrics. *Pediatrics, 70*, 810–812.

Anderson, G. L., & Barreara, I. (1995). Critical constructivist research and special education. *Remedial and Special Education, 16*, 142–149.

Anderson, L. M., Evertson, C. M., & Brophy, J. E. (1979). An experimental study of effective teaching in first-grade reading groups. *Elementary School Journal, 79*, 193–222.

Blau, H., & Loveless, E. J. (1982). Specific hemispheric-routing-TAK/v to teach spelling to dyslexics: VAK and VAKT challenged. *Journal of Learning Disabilities, 15*, 461–466.

Bogdan, R, & Kugelmauss, J. (1984). Case studies of mainstreaming: A symbolic interactionist approach to special education. In L. Barton and Tomlison (Eds.), *Special education and social interests*. London: Croom Helm.

Bogdan, R., & Lutfiyya, Z. M. (1992). Standing on its own: Qualitative research in special education. In W. Stainback and S. Stainback (Eds.), *Controversial issues confronting special education: Divergent perspectives* (pp. 243–251). Boston: Allyn and Bacon.

Borg, W. R., and Gall, M. D. (1989). *Educational research* (5th ed.). New York: Longman.

Brenner, A. (1982). The effects of megadoses of selected B complex vitamins on children with hyperkinesis: Controlled studies with long-term follow-up. *Journal of Learning Disabilities, 15*, 258–264.

Brown, A. L., Day, J. D., & Jones, R. S. (1983). The development of plans for summarizing texts. *Child Development, 54*, 968–979.

Butler, N. R., Goldstein, H., & Ross, E. M. (1972). Cigarette smoking in pregnancy: Its influence on birth weight and perinatal mortality. *British Medical Journal, 2*, 127–130.

Chandler, T. A. (1982). Can Theory Z be applied to the public schools? *Education, 104*, 343–345.

Coles, G. S. (1987). *The learning mystique: A critical look at "learning disabilities."* New York: Pantheon.

Cooley, E. J., & Ayres, R. R. (1988). Self-concept and success-failure attributions of nonhandicapped students and students with learning disabilities. *Journal of Learning Disabilities, 21*, 174–178.

Cott, A. (1972). Megavitamins: The orthomolecular approach to behavioral disorders and learning disabilities. *Academic Therapy, 7*, 245–258.

Cruickshank, D. R. (1987). *Reflective teaching: The preparation of students of teaching*. Reston, VA: Association of Teacher Educators.

Dansereau, D. F. (1978). The development of a learning strategy curriculum. In H. F. O'Neill, Jr. (Ed.), *Learning strategies* (pp. 1–29). New York: Academic Press.

Dansereau, D. F. (1985). Learning strategy research. In J. W. Segal, S. F. Chipman, & R. Glaser (Eds.), *Thinking and learning skills* (Vol. 1, pp. 209–240). Hillsdale, NJ: Erlbaum.

Denzin, N. (1988). *The research act*. New York: McGraw-Hill.

Derry, S. J., & Murphy, D. A. (1986). Designing systems that train learning ability: From theory to practice. *Review of Educational Research, 56* (1), 1–39.

Deshler, D. D., & Schumaker, J. B. (1986). Learning strategies: An instructional alternative for low-achieving adolescents. *Exceptional Children, 52*, 583–590.

Deshler, D. D., Schumaker, J. B., Alley, G. R., Warner, M. M., & Clark, F. L. (1982). Learning disabilities in adolescent and young adult populations: Research implications (Part I). *Focus on Exceptional Children, 15* (1), 1–12.

Deshler, D. D., Schumaker, J. B., Lenz, B. K., & Ellis,

E. S. (1984). Academic and cognitive interventions for LD adolescents (Part II). *Journal of Learning Disabilities, 17* (3), 170–187.

Dewey, J. (1933). *How we think.* Chicago: Henry Regnery.

Dithey, W. (1988). *Introduction to the human sciences.* Detroit, MI: Wayne State University Press. (Original work published 1923.)

Dixon, R., & Carnine, D. (1994). Ideologies, practices and their implications for special education. *Journal of Special Education, 28,* 356–367.

Doman, G., & Delacato, C. (1968). Doman-Delacato philosophy. *Human Potential, 1,* 113–116.

Douglas, V. I., Parry, P., Marton, P., & Garson, C. (1976). Assessment of a cognitive training program for hyperactive children. *Journal of Abnormal Child Psychology, 4,* 389–410.

Ellis, E. E., Lenz, B. K., & Sabornie, E. J. (1987). Generalization and adaptation of learning strategies to natural environments: Part 1: Critical agents. *Remedial and Special Education, 8,* 6–20.

Englemann, S., & Bruner, E. (1984). *DISTAR reading I.* Chicago: Science Research Associates.

Englemann, S., & Carnine, D. (1982). *Theory of instruction: Principles and applications.* New York: Irvington.

Eustis, R. S. (1947). Specific reading disability. A familial syndrome associated with ambidexterity and speech defects and a frequent cause of problem behavior. *New England Journal of Medicine, 237,* 243–249.

Feingold, B. F. (1975). Hyperkinesis and learning disabilities linked to artificial food flavors and colors. *American Journal of Nursing, 75,* 797–803.

Fernald, G. M. (1943). *Remedial techniques in basic school subjects.* New York: McGraw-Hill.

Ferreri, C. A. & Wainwright, R. B. (1985). *Breakthrough for dyslexia and learning disabilities.* Pompano Beach: Exposition Press of Florida, Inc.

Fishbein, D., & Meduski, J. (1987). Nutritional biochemistry and behavioral disabilities. *Journal of Learning Disabilities, 20,* 505–512.

Fisher, C., Berliner, D., Filby, N., Marliave, R., Cahen, L. and Dishaw, M. (1980). Teaching behaviors, academic learning time, and student achievement: An overview. In C. Denham and A. Lieberman (Eds.), *Time to learn.* Washington DC: the National Institute of Education, U.S. Department of Education.

Fisher, J. H. (1905). Case of congenital word-blindness (Inability to learn to read). *Ophthalmic Review, 24,* 315–318.

Flavell, J. H. (1985). *Cognitive development.* Upper Saddle River, NJ: Prentice Hall.

Florida Commission on Reform and Accountability (1992). *Blueprint 2000: Initial recommendations for a system of school improvement and accountability.* Tallahassee: Florida Department of State.

Frostig, M., & Maslow, P. (1973). *Learning problems in the classroom.* New York: Grune & Stratton.

Fuchs, D., & Fuchs, L. (1992). Special education research and the scientific method. In W. Stainback and S. Stainback (Eds.), *Controversial issues confronting special education: Divergent perspectives* (pp. 315–322). Boston: Allyn and Bacon.

Gadow, K. D. (1983). Effects of stimulant drugs on academic performance in hyperactive and learning disabled children. *Journal of Learning Disabilities, 16,* 290–299.

Gagne', R. M. (1980). Learnable aspects of problem solving. *Educational Psychologist, 15,* 84–92.

Gagne', R. M. (1985). *The conditions of learning and theory of instruction.* New York: Holt, Rinehart & Winston.

Geertz, C. (1973). *The interpretation of cultures.* New York: Basic.

Geschwind, N., & Behan, P. (1982). Left-handedness: Association with immune disease, migraine, and developmental learning disorder. *Proceedings of the National Academy of Sciences (USA), 79,* 5097–5100.

Gillingham, A., & Stillman, B. (1965). *Remedial training for children with specific disability in reading, spelling, and penmanship* (7th ed.). Cambridge, MA: Educators Publishing Service.

Glass, G. V. (1977). Integrating findings: The meta-analysis of research. *Review of Research in Education, 5,* 351–379.

Good, T., & Grouws, D. A. (1977). Teaching effects: A process-product study of fourth grade mathematics classrooms. *Journal of Teacher Education, 28,* 49–54.

Good, T., & Grouws, D. A. (1979). The Missouri Mathematics Effectiveness Project: An experimental study in fourth grade classrooms. *Journal of Educational Psychology, 74,* 355–362.

Good, T. L., and Brophy, J. E. (1987). *Looking in classrooms* (4th ed.). New York: Harper & Row.

Good, T. L., and Brophy, J. E. (1986). School effects. In M. C. Wittrock (Ed.), *Handbook of research on teaching* (3rd ed.). New York: Macmillan.

Goodman, Y., (1989). Roots of the whole-language movement. *The Elementary School Journal, 90,* 113–127.

Hallahan, D. P., & Kauffman, J. M. (1976). *Introduction to learning disabilities: A psycho-behavioral approach.* Upper Saddle River, NJ: Prentice Hall.

Hallahan, D. P., Kauffman, J. M., & Lloyd, J. W. (1985). *Introduction to learning disabilities* (2nd ed.). Upper Saddle River, NJ: Prentice Hall.

Hallgren, B. (1950). Specific dyslexia ("congenital word blindness"). A clinical and genetic study. *Acta Psychiatric et Neurologia,* Scandinavica, Suppl. 65-1-287.

Hammill, D. D., & Larsen, S. (1974). The efficacy of psycholinguistic training. *Exceptional Children, 41,* 5–14.

Hanson, J. W., Streissguth, A. P., & Smith, D. W. (1978). The effects of moderate alcohol consumption during pregnancy on fetal growth and morphogenesis. *The Journal of Pediatrics, 92,* (3), 457–460.

Haring, H. G., & Phillips, E. L. (1962). *Educating emotionally disturbed children.* New York: Mc-Graw-Hill.

Harris, K. R., & Graham, S. (1994). Constructivism: Principles, paradigms, and integration. *Journal of Special Education, 28,* 233–247.

Harris, K. R., & Graham, S. (1996). Constructivism and students with special needs: Issues in the classroom. *Learning Disabilities Research and Practice, 11,* 134–137.

Hermann, K. (1959). *Reading disability: A medical study of word-blindness and related handicaps.* Springfield, IL: Charles C. Thomas.

Heshusius, L. (1986). Pedagogy, special education, and the lives of young children: A critical and futuristic perspective. *Journal of Education, 168* (3), 25–38.

Heshusius, L. (1989). The Newtonian mechanistic paradigm, special education, and contours of alternatives: An overview. *Journal of Learning Disabilities, 22,* 403–415.

Heshusius, L. (1994). Freeing ourselves from objec-tivity: Managing subjectivity or turning toward a participatory mode of consciousness? *Educational Researcher, 23* (3), 15–22.

Hinshelwood, J. (1911). Two cases of hereditary congenital word-blindness. *British Medical Journal, 1,* 608–609.

Holdaway, D. (1979). *The foundations of literacy.* Sydney, Australia: Ashton Scholastic.

Hynd, G. W., & Semrud-Clikeman, M. (1989). Dyslexia and neurodevelopmental pathology: Relationships to cognition, intelligence, and reading skill acquisition. *Journal of Learning Disabilities, 22,* 204–216.

Hynd, G. W., Marshall, R., & Gonzalez, J. (1991). Learning disabilities and presumed central nervous system dysfunction. *Learning Disability Quarterly, 14* (4), 283–296.

Iano, R. P. (1986). The study and development of teaching: With implications for the advancement of special education. *Remedial and Special Education, 7* (5), 50–61.

Jacob, E. (1988). Clarifying qualitative research: A focus on traditions. *Educational Researcher,* 16–24.

Jacobs, J. E., & Paris, S. G. (1987). Children's metacognition about reading: Issues in definition, measurement, and instruction. *Educational Psychologist, 22,* 255–278.

Jacobsen, B., Lowery, B., & CuCette, J. (1986). Attributions of learning disabled children. *Journal of Educational Psychology, 78,* 59–64.

Jones, B. F., Amiran, M., & Katims, M. (1985). Teaching cognitive strategies and text structures within language arts programs. In J. W. Segal, S. F. Chipman, & R. Glaser (Eds.), *Thinking and learning skills* (Vol. 1, pp. 259–297). Hillsdale, NJ: Erlbaum.

Jost, H., & Sontag, L. W. (1944). The genetic factor in autonomic nervous system function. *Psychosomatic Medicine, 6,* 308–310.

Kavale, K. (1981). Functions of the Illinois Test of Psycholinguistic Abilities (ITPA): Are they trainable? *Exceptional Children, 47* (7), 496–510.

Kavale, K. (1987). Theoretical quandaries in Learning Disabilities (pp. 19–34). In S. Vaughn and C. Boss (Eds.), *Research in learning disabilities: Issues and future directions.* Boston: College-Hill.

Kavale, K. A. (1982). The efficacy of stimulant drug treatment for hyperactivity: A meta-analysis. *Journal of Learning Disabilities, 15,* 280–289.

Kavale, K. A., & Forness, S. R. (1983). Hyperactivity and diet-treatment: A meta-analysis of the Feingold hypothesis. *Journal of Learning Disabilities, 16,* 324–330.

Kavale, K. A. & Forness S. R. (1985a). The science of learning disabilities. San Diego, CA: College-Hill.

Kavale, K. A. & Forness S. R. (1985b). Learning disability and the history of science: Paradigm or paradox? *Remedial and Special Education, 6* (4), 12–23.

Kelly, T. E. (1975). The role of genetic mechanisms in childhood handicaps. In R. H. A. Haslam & P. J. Valletutti (Eds.), *Medical problems in the classroom* (pp. 193–216). New York: Academic Press.

Kephart, N. C. (1960). *The slow learner in the classroom.* Upper Saddle River, NJ: Prentice Hall/Merrill.

Kephart, N. C. (1971). *The slow learner in the classroom* (2nd ed.). Upper Saddle River, NJ: Prentice Hall/Merrill.

Kirk, S. A., McCarthy, J. J., & Kirk, W. D. (1968). *The Illinois Test of Psycholinguistic Abilities.* (rev. ed.). Urbana: University of Illinois Press.

Kistner, J., Haskett, M., White, K., & Robbins, F. (1987). Perceived competence and self-worth of LD and normally achieving students. *Learning Disability Quarterly, 10,* 258–266.

Koenigsberg, R. S. (1973). An evaluation of visual versus sensorimotor methods for improving orientation discrimination of letter reversals by preschool children. *Child Development, 44,* 764–769.

Kronick, D. (1990). Holism and empiricism as complementary paradigms. *Journal of Learning Disabilities, 23,* 5–10.

Kuhn, T. (1970). *The structure of scientific revolutions* (2nd ed.). Chicago: University of Chicago Press.

Larsen, S. C., Parker, R. M., & Hammill, D. D. (1982). Effectiveness of psycholinguistic training: A response to Kavale. *Exceptional Children, 49,* 60–66.

Lerner, J. (1988). *Learning disabilities. Theories, diagnosis and teaching strategies* (5th Ed.). Boston: Houghton Mifflin.

Licht, B. G., & Torgesen, J. K. (1989). Natural science approaches to questions of subjectivity. *Journal of Learning Disabilities, 22,* 418–421.

Lincoln, Y. & Guba, E. (1985). *Naturalistic inquiry.* Beverly Hills, CA: Sage.

Lindsley, O. R. (1964). Direct measurement and prosthesis of retarded children. *Journal of Education, 147,* 62–81.

Lloyd, J. (1980). Academic instruction and cognitive behavior modification: The need for attack strategy training. *Exceptional Education Quarterly, 1,* 53–63.

Logan, R., & Colarusso, R. (1978). The effectiveness of the MWM and GOAL programs in developing general language abilities. *Learning Disability Quarterly, 1,* 33–38.

Lovitt, T. C. (1989). *Introduction to learning disabilities.* Boston: Allyn and Bacon.

Luchow, J. P., & Shepherd, M. J. (1981). Effects of multisensory training in perceptual learning. *Learning Disability Quarterly, 4,* 38–43.

Marshall, W., & Ferguson, J. H. (1939). Hereditary word-blindness as a defect of selective association. *Journal of Nervous and Mental Diseases, 89,* 164–173.

Mattes, J. A., & Gittelman, R. (1983). Growth of hyperactive children on maintenance of regimen of methylphenidate. *Archives of General Psychiatry, 40,* 317–321.

McKusick, V. A. (1969). *Human genetics.* (2nd Ed.). Upper Saddle River, NJ: Prentice Hall.

McPhail, J. C. (1995). Phenomenology as philosophy and method: Applications to ways of doing special education. *Remedial and Special Education, 16,* 159–165.

Medawar, P. B. (1984). *The limits of science.* New York: Harper & Row.

Meichenbaum, D. (1980). Cognitive behavior modification with exceptional children: A promise yet unfulfilled. *Exceptional Education Quarterly, 1,* 83–88.

Mercer, J. (1992). The impact of changing paradigms of disability on mental retardation in the year 2000. In L. Rowitz (Ed.), *Mental retardation in the year 2000* (pp. 15–38). New York: Springer.

Mercer, C. D. & Mercer, A. R. (1989). *Teaching students with learning problems* (3rd ed.), Upper Saddle River, NJ: Prentice Hall/Merrill.

Miccinati, J. (1979). The Fernald technique: Modification increases the probability of success. *Journal of Learning Disabilities, 12,* (3), 139–142.

Minskoff, E. (1975). Research on psycholinguistic training: Critique and guidelines. *Exceptional Children, 42,* 136–144.

Morrison, J. P., & Stewart, M. A. (1973). The psychiatric status of the legal families of adopted hyperactive children. *Archives of General Psychiatry, 28*, 888–891.

Myers, C. A. (1978). Reviewing the literature on Fernald's technique of remedial reading. *The Reading Teacher, 31*, 614–617.

Mykelbust, H. R. (1978). *Progress in learning disabilities* (Vol. IV). New York: Grune & Stratton.

Nichols, P., & Chen, T. (1981). Minimal brain dysfunction: A prospective study. Hillsdale, NJ: Erlbaum.

Obrzut, J. E. (1989). Dyslexia and neurodevelopmental pathology: Is diagnostic technology ahead of the psychoeducational technology? *Journal of Learning Disabilities, 22*, 217–218.

Office of Policy Research and Improvement. (1990). Cocaine babies: Florida's substance exposed youth. Tallahassee: Florida Department of Education.

Orton, S. T. (1925). "Word blindness" in school children. *Archives of Neurology and Psychiatry, 14*, 581–615.

Orton, S. T., & Gillingham, A. (1968). Special disability in writing. In S. B. Childs (Ed.), *Education in specific language disability* (pp. 79–110). Pomfret, CT: Orton Society.

Osgood, C. E. (1957). Motivational dynamics of language behavior. In M. R. Jones (Ed.), *Nebraska symposium of motivation* (pp. 348–424). Lincoln: University of Nebraska Press.

Palincsar, A. S., & Klenk, L. (1993). Broader visions encompassing literacy, learners, and contexts. *Remedial and Special Education, 14* (4), 19–25.

Paris, S. G., & Winograd, P. (1990). Promoting metacognition and motivation of exceptional children. *Remedial and Special Education, 11* (6), 7–15.

Patton, J. R., Beirne-Smith, M., & Payne, J. S. (1990). *Mental retardation* (3rd ed.). New York: Merrill.

Pennington, B. F., & Smith, S. D. (1988). Genetic influences on learning disabilities: An update. *Journal of Consulting and Clinical Psychology, 56* (6), 817–823.

Peters, B. H., & Levine, H. S. (1977). Memory enhancement after physostigmine in the amnesic syndrome. *Archives of Neurology, 34*, 215–219.

Phillips, D. C. (1976). *Holistic thought in social science.* Stanford, CA: Stanford University Press.

Polansky, N. A. (1986). There is nothing so practical as a good theory. *Child Welfare, 65* (1), 3–15.

Poplin, M. (1987). Self-imposed blindness: the scientific method in education. *RASE, 8,* (6), 31–37.

Poplin, M. (1988). The reductionistic fallacy in learning disabilities: Replicating the past by reducing the present. *Journal of Learning Disabilities, 21,* 389–400.

Pressley, M., Hogan, K., Wharton-McDonald, R., Mistretta, J., & Ettenberger, S. (1996). The challenges of instructional scaffolding: The challenges of instruction that supports student thinking. *Learning Disabilities Research and Practice, 11,* 138–146.

Reid, D. K. (1988). *Teaching the learning disabled: A cognitive approach.* Needham, MA: Allyn and Bacon.

Reid, D. K., Robinson, S. J., & Bunsen, T. D. (1995). Empiricism and beyond: Expanding the boundaries of special education. *Remedial and Special Education, 16,* 131–141.

Reid, D. K. & Stone, C. A. (1991). Why is cognitive instruction effective? Underlying learning mechanisms. *Remedial and Special Education, 2* (3), 8–19.

Rist, R. (1977). On the relations among educational paradigms: From disdain to detente. *Anthropology and Education Quarterly, 8,* 42–49.

Rohwer, W. D., (1980). An elaborative conception of learner differences. In R. E. Snow, P. A. Federico, & W. E. Montague (Eds.), *Aptitude, learning and instruction* (pp. 23–43). Hillsdale, NJ: Erlbaum.

Rosenshine, B. (1976). Classroom instruction. In N. L. Gagne (Ed.), *Psychology of teaching: The 77th yearbook of the National Society for the Study of Education.* Chicago: National Society for the Study of Education.

Rosenshine, B. (1978). The third cycle of research on teacher effects: Content covered, academic engagement time, and quality of instruction. *The 78th yearbook of the National Society for the Study of Education.* Chicago: University of Chicago Press.

Rosenshine, B., & Meister, C. (1992). The use of scaffolds for teaching higher-level cognitive strategies. *Educational Leadership, 49* (7), 26–33.

Rosenshine, B. & Stevens, R. (1986). Teaching functions. In M. C. Wittrock (Ed.), *Handbook of Research on Teaching* (3rd ed., pp. 376–391). New York: Macmillan.

Rosett, H. L. (1980). A clinical perspective of the fetal alcohol syndrome. *Alcoholism: Clinical and Experimental Research, 4,* 119.

Ross, D. D., Bony, E. & Kyle, D. W. (1993). *Reflective teaching for student empowerment: Elementary curriculum and methods.* New York: Macmillan.

Ross, D. D. (1989). First steps in developing a reflective approach. *Journal of Teacher Education, 39,* 22–30.

Schmoker, M. J., & Wilson, R. (1993). *Total quality education: Profiles of schools that demonstrate the power of Deming's management principles.* Bloomington, IN: Phi Delta Kappa.

Schmoker, M. (1996). *Results: The key to continuous school improvement.* Alexandria, VA: Association for Supervision and Curriculum Development.

Schumaker, J. B., Denton, P. H., & Deshler, D. D. (1984). *Learning strategies curriculum: The paraphrasing strategy.* Lawrence: University of Kansas.

Scruggs, T. E., & Mastropieri, M. A. (1988). Legitimizing the field of learning disabilities: Does research orientation matter? *Journal of Learning Disabilities, 21,* 219–222.

Senf, G. M. (1986). LD research in sociological and scientific perspective. In J. K. Torgesen & B. Y. L. Wong (Eds.), *Psychological and educational perspectives on learning disabilities* (pp. 27–54). Orlando, FL: Academic Press.

Silver, L. B. (1987). The "magic cure": A review of the current controversial approaches for treating learning disabilities. *Journal of Learning Disabilities, 20* (8), 498–504.

Simpson, R. G. (1992). Quantitative research methods as the method of choice within a continuum model. In W. Stainback and S. Stainback (Eds.), *Controversial issues confronting special education: Divergent perspectives* (pp. 235–242). Boston: Allyn and Bacon.

Smith, J. K., & Heshusius, L. (1986). Closing down the conversation: The end of the quantitative/qualitative debate among educational inquirers. *Educational Researcher, 15,* 4–12.

Smith, C. R. (1991). *Learning disabilities. The interaction of learner, task, and setting* (2nd ed.). Boston: Allyn and Bacon.

Smith, F. (1971). *Understanding reading: A psycholinguistic analysis of reading and learning to read.* New York: Holt, Rinehart & Winston.

Smyth, J. (1989). Developing and sustaining critical reflection in teacher education. *Journal of Teacher Education, 39* 22–30.

Snyder, S. H. (1984). Drug and neurotransmitter receptors in the brain. *Science, 224,* 22–31.

Sparks, S. (1984). *Birth defects and speech-language disorders.* San Diego, CA: College-Hill.

Speigel, D. (1992). Blending whole language and systematic direct instruction. *The Reading Teacher, 46,* 38–44.

Stainback, W., & Stainback, S. (1989). Using qualitative data collection procedures to investigate supported education issues. *Journal of the Association for Persons With Severe Handicaps, 14,* 271–277.

Stanovich, K. E. (1988). Science and learning disabilities. *Journal of Learning Disabilities, 21,* 210–214.

Sternberg, L., & Taylor, R. L. (1982). The insignificance of psycholinguistic training: A reply to Kavale. *Exceptional Children, 49,* 254–255.

Sternberg, R. J. (1977). *Intelligence, information processing and analogical reasoning: The componential analysis of human abilities.* Hillsdale, NJ: Erlbaum.

Sternberg, R. J. (1979). The nature of mental abilities. *American Psychologist, 34,* 214–230.

Sternberg, R. J. (1983). Criteria for intellectual skills training. *Educational Researcher, 12,* 6–12.

Swanson, H. L. (1988). Toward a metatheory of learning disabilities. *Journal of Learning Disabilities, 21,* 196–209.

Tarver, S. G. (1986). Cognitive behavior modification, direct instruction and holistic approaches to the education of students with learning disabilities. *Journal of Learning Disabilities, 19,* 368–375.

Thomas, C. J. (1905). Congenital "word blindness" and its treatment. *Ophthalmoscope, 3,* 80–385.

Thorpe, H. W., & Borden, K. S. (1985). The effect of multisensory instruction upon the on-task behaviors and word reading accuracy of learning disabled children. *Journal of Learning Disabilities, 18,* 279–286.

Tom, A. (1985). Inquiring into inquiry-oriented teacher education. *Journal of Teacher Education, 36* (5), 35–44.

Torgesen, J. K. (1977). The role of non-specific factors in the task of performance of learning disabled children: A theoretical assessment. *Journal of Learning Disabilities, 10,* 27–35.

Torgesen, J. K. (1986). Learning disabilities theory: Its current state and future prospects. *Journal of Learning Disabilities, 19*, 399–407.

Torgesen, J. K. (1987). Response: Theoretical quandaries in learning disabilities. In S. Vaughn and C. Boss (Eds.), *Research in learning disabilities: Issues and future directions* (pp. 30–31). Boston: College-Hill.

Ulman, J. D. & Rosenberg, M. S. (1986). Science and superstition in science education. *Exceptional Children, 52*, 459–460.

van den Honert, D. (1977). A neuropsychological technique for training dyslexics. *Journal of Learning Disabilities, 10*, 15–27.

Vandenberg, S. G. (1966). Contributions of twin research to psychology. *Psychological Bulletin, 56*, 327–352.

Wallace, G. and McLoughlin, J. A. (1988). *Learning disabilities: Concepts and characteristics* (3rd ed.). Upper Saddle River, NJ: Prentice Hall/Merrill.

Wansart, W. L. (1995). Teaching as a way of knowing: Observing and responding to students abilities. *Remedial and Special Education, 16*, 166–177.

Westman, J. C. (1990). *Handbook of learning disabilities.* Boston: Allyn and Bacon.

White, O. R., & Haring, N. G. (1980). *Exceptional teaching.* Upper Saddle River, NJ: Prentice Hall/Merrill.

Wilson, E. O. (1975). *Sociobiology: The new synthesis.* Cambridge, MA: Harvard University Press.

Witelson, S. F., & Kigar, D. L. (1988). Asymmetry in brain function follows asymmetry in anatomical form: Gross, microscopic, postmortem and imaging studies. In F. Bollar & J. Grafman (Eds.), *Handbook of neuropsychology* (Vol. 1, pp. 111–142). New York: Elsevier Science.

Witelson, S. F., & Pallie, W. (1973). Left hemisphere specialization for language in the newborn. *Brain, 96*, 641–646.

Wolery, M., Bailey, D. B., & Sugai, G. M. (1988). *Effective teaching. Principles and procedures of applied behavior analysis with exceptional students.* Boston: Allyn and Bacon.

Wong, B. (1979). The role of theory in learning disabilities research: Part I, An analysis of problems. *Journal of Learning Disabilities, 12*, 19–29.

Wong, B. Y. L. (1986). Metacognition and special education: A review of a view. *Journal of Special Education, 20*, 9–29.

Worrall, R. S. (1990). Detecting health fraud in the field of learning disabilities. *Journal of Learning Disabilities, 23*, 207–212.

Ysseldyke, J., & Algozzine, B. (1990). *Introduction to special education* (2nd ed.). Boston: Houghton Mifflin.

The study of neurological processes and brain functions has been influential in advancing understanding concerning learning modes and learning problems.

Chapter 4

The Psychoneurological Model

In this chapter we will . . .

- Trace historical events leading to the study of the brain's structure, function, and relationship to oral and written language processes and sensory perception.

- Identify insights on the brain's involvement on language development, atypical language patterns, assessments, and interventions.

- Discuss the early beginnings of the psychoneurological model, including nineteenth-century developments reflecting how and why individuals with language and perception problems have been presumed to have neurological difficulties.

- Note changes in terminology (e.g., *brain disease, brain anomaly; brain damaged, minimal brain dysfunction, psychoneurological learning disorder*) and research issues (e.g., *brain localizations; specific abilities orientation.*)

- Identify brain hemispheric functions including the processes associated with the left hemisphere and those associated with the right hemisphere.

- Outline Broca's and Wernicke's early work on the connection between language function and the localization of those functions within the brain.

- Summarize the theories forwarded by Broadbent, Hinshelwood, and others regarding perception and "word blindness."

- Discuss twentieth-century developments, including the behavioral characteristics identified by Goldstein, Strauss, and Lehtinen that formed the basis for a presumed connection between brain dysfunction and learning problems.

- Review the multisensory instructional practices developed by Fernald (VAKT), Orton, and Gillingham, and the perceptual-oriented activities developed by Frostig.

- Discuss modern controversies, including Irlen's Scotopic Sensitivity Syndrome and its treatment through the use of colorized lenses, Doman and Delacato's patterning treatment, Ayer's sensory integration, and applied kinesiology treatment.

- Outline recent advances in brain morphology brought about through technologies (e.g., electroencephalography, magnetic resonance imaging, and CAT scanning.)

The psychoneurological model surfaced over 200 years ago, beginning with learning problems viewed as *brain diseases*. An initial focus related to the role of the brain's hemispheric processes in encoding information. Brain hemispheric functions included *left hemisphere*: linguistic, analytic, abstract sequential processing, or mediation, and *right hemisphere*: nonlinguistic, spatial and holistic processing, or manual pattern recognition. Physicians held that the brain hemispheres had specialized functions useful in explaining patients' inabilities to read, speak, or write appropriately (Broca, 1861; Marie, cited in Wiederholt, 1974). Some physicians hypothesized brain diseases in the form of physical insult to the brain's function (Jackson, 1870; Wernicke, 1908). Eventually, physicians described patients' sensory, perceptual, motor, and language capacities relative to assumed brain functions and then correlated their descriptions with medical and learning data acquired through autopsies at patients' deaths. Many reasoned location areas pertaining to brain dysfunction and atypical brain development such as movement and sensation in the brain stem. *Brain diseases defined learning research in the period beginning in the early 19th century* (Wiederholt, 1974).

Figure 4.1 illustrates the brain's left and right hemispheres and function areas involved in early controversies. The brain's functional units include the state-regulating, information-processing, and programming modes in the left and right hemispheres.

Early 20th-century physicians analyzed brain areas affected by assumed brain lesions, brain disease, brain tumors, and/or brain function-location-structure hypotheses underlying *brain anomalies* or *brain damage*. Physicians began documenting behavioral effects of brain damage. Some began observing and recording behaviors of both children (Still, 1902; Tredgold, circa 1908, cited in Westman, 1990) and adults with brain damage (Goldstein, 1936).

By the mid-twentieth century, professionals assumed atypical learning etiologies. For example, researchers suggested that learning problems were the result of the brain's failure to establish cerebral dominance (e.g., Orton, 1937); some unobservable minimal damage (e.g., Strauss & Kephart, 1955); the brain's failure to achieve certain stages of neurological development (e.g., Delacato, 1959); or maturational lags in neurology (e.g., Bender, 1963; Rabinovitch, 1962).

Medically trained, psychoeducational researchers then began formal *clinical study of problem learning and applications to learning processes*. Researchers trained in medical orientations, but influenced by behavioral assumptions, studied the learning process in adults and children with assumed brain injuries (e.g., Bender, 1963; Cruickshank, 1967; Delacato, 1959; Frostig, 1972; Orton, 1937; Osgood, 1953; Rabi-

Figure 4.1
Brain hemisphere and function areas.

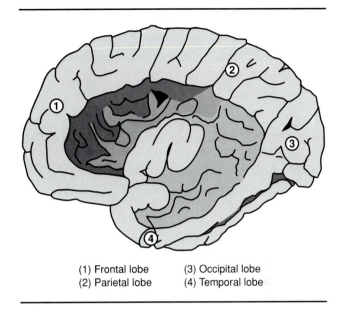

(1) Frontal lobe   (3) Occipital lobe
(2) Parietal lobe   (4) Temporal lobe

novitch, 1962; Strauss & Kephart, 1955; Strauss & Werner, 1942; Wepman, 1967). Many psychological assessment and remedial educational practices appeared in clinical research (e.g., Cruickshank, 1967; Frostig, 1972; Kephart, 1971; Strauss & Werner, 1942; Werner & Strauss, 1941). Studies related to disorders of written language (e.g., Gillingham & Stillman, 1965; Spalding & Spalding, 1962), or spoken language (e.g., Osgood, 1953; Wepman, 1967). Others targeted disorders of perception and motor processes (e.g., Cruickshank, 1967; Frostig, 1972). Psychoeducational researchers sought to refine assessment and intervention practices in clinical settings. Table 4.1. lists examples of researchers, their focus on brain-injury etiologies, target populations, and assumed brain injury effects on individuals' behaviors.

Late-twentieth-century researchers began to address inherent problems in brain-injury etiologies, relationships to problem learning or behaviors, and appropriate performance measures (Hallahan, Kauffman, & Lloyd, 1985; Sleeter, 1986; Smith, 1991). A focus was on the difficulty of using medical analogies to deal with educational problems. *Criticism of medical, clinical assumptions to classroom practices dominated research journals.* Medical researchers could not prove that individuals with learning problems demonstrated brain injury or brain damage. Medical data provided little new or concrete direction to educational assessment and intervention practices. Competing theories (such as behavioral and cognitive-behavioral views) challenged psychoneurological thinking.

Because of direct challenges by competing theorists and resulting definitional dilemmas in the late 1970s, researchers advocating psychoneurological views continued to influence learning study directions. However, their terminology shifted from "brain damaged" to *Minimal Brain Dysfunction Syndrome* (MBDS). Ross (1976) suggested that the term *minimal* surfaced because brain damage could not

Table 4.1

Twentieth-Century Researchers Interested in the Study of Brain-Injury Etiologies and Resulting Behaviors

Time	Researchers	Brain-Injury Etiology	Target Population	Behaviors
1900–1910	Still	Tumors, infectious diseases, or head injuries	Children with "defects of moral control"	Temper tantrums; disobedience; impulsivity
1905–1915	Tredgold	Mild brain injuries at birth	Children	Hyperkinesis; impulsivity
1915–1940	Goldstein	Acquired brain injuries as a result of war	Adult soldiers	Stimulus bound; perseveration; unable to deal with abstractions; figure and ground problems; prone to emotional reactions; catastrophic reactions
1920–1930	Hohman; Ebaugh	Encephalitis	Children	Restlessness; insomnia; irritability; antisocial; impulsiveness; distractibility; emotional lability
1930–1935	Kahn; Cohen	Inadequate cortical inhibition of subcortical responses	Children with "No known brain damage"	"Organic driveness;" antisocial; irritable; impulsive; hyperkinetic
1935–1940	Bender	Influenza	Children	Irritability; impulsiveness; hyperkinesis
1935–1940	Bradley	Brain injury	Children with brain injuries	Overactivity; hyperkinesis
1935–1950	Wener; Strauss; Lehtinen	Prenatal, perinatal, postnatal injury; infection	Children with mental disabilities	Impulsivity; repetitiveness; task fixation; hyperactivity; figure-ground confusion; use of nonessential elements when categorizing; inability to integrate parts into whole
1950–1955	Eisenson	Lag in cerebral maturations	Children with acquired aphasia	Behavioral difficulties; articulation, fluency, comprehension, and language problems
1955–1960	Osgood	Ineffectiveness of behavioral development; processing problems in integrating and representing knowledge	Children with normal and atypical language difficulties	Atypical language problems including decoding and encoding; processing difficulties

(continued)

Table 4.1 *continued*

Time	Researchers	Brain-Injury Etiology	Target Population	Behaviors
1955–1960	Doman; Delacato	Failure to achieve certain stages of neurological development	Children with mental disabilities; children with neurophysical difficulties	"Poor neurological organization;" difficulties in muscle development, sensory stimulation; problems in manual, visual, auditory, and tactile actions
1955–1960	Kephart	Perception and motor dysfunctions	Children with brain injuries and normal intelligence	Difficulties in perception, motor, language, behavior, and conceptual learning; academic difficulties
1960–1970	Frostig	Neurological dysfunctions; perception and motor dysfunctions	Children with neurological impairments	Visual-perception difficulties; gross motor difficulties; academic difficulties
1955–1970	Pasamanick; Knobloch	Maternal diseases and maternal infections; prematurity	Children	Difficulties at birth; problems in developmental milestones; academic difficulties
1955–1980	Cruickshank	Cerebral diseases	Children with cerebral palsy	Forced responsiveness to stimuli; repetitiveness; fixation on task and thought; visual motor difficulties; figure ground confusion; stimulus bound behavior; difficulties in abstractions; perseveration
1960–1970	Kirk	Processing malfunctions	Children with learning and language difficulties; children with mental disabilities	Expressive and receptive language difficulties
1960–1970	Bakwin; Bakwin	Minimal cerebral injury	Children with constitutional developmental lags	Speech difficulties; problems in developmental milestones; academic difficulties

(continued)

Table 4.1 *continued*

Time	Researchers	Brain-Injury Etiology	Target Population	Behaviors
1970–1980	Gesell	Minimal cerebral injury; brain cell mutations/lags during gestation	Children with "maturational lags"	Speech difficulties; poorly defined cerebral dominance; motor difficulties; perception difficulties; reading difficulties
1970–1980	Laufer; Wender	Prenatal and postnatal difficulties; malformation, prenatal malfunctions; reticular activating system malfunctions; diencephalic dysfunctions	Children	Dysfunctions in motor activity, attention, cognition, impulse control, motor coordination, physical development, langauge development, emotional lability, thought, and self-identity
1975–1985	Coletti	Perinatal factors (e.g., shortage of oxygen; prolonged or precipitous labor; premature separation of the placenta; difficult delivery)	Newborns with low birth weights and gestational ages	Poorer general helath; mild to severe problems at birth; greater length of hospitalization; labor complications
1985–1990	Touwen; Huisjes	Prenatal factors	Premature newborns with low birth weights and gestational ages	Nervous system difficulties
1985–1990	Als, Rossetti	Prenatal factors	Premature newborns with low birth weights and gestational ages	Subsequent academic and behavioral difficulties in school

be demonstrated. *Dysfunction* evolved because the term implied nothing about the brain's structure, only that the brain was not working correctly. Further, *syndrome* rationalized a cluster of problems or symptoms that together formed the LD entity.

New definitional and classification issues in the LD field (e.g., assessments, service delivery, and school program entrance criteria, as detailed in chapters 1 and 2) contributed to growing confusion about the medical nature of learning problems in seemingly "normal" individuals with presumed MBDS. While it was seen as useful in drawing attention to a heterogeneous group of developmental disorders, the continuing usage of the term *MBDS* had little empirical validity. It assumed a homogeneous symptomatology and implied a known etiology. MBDS supporters linked too many behaviors to implied brain damage, either as an escape from making a diagnosis or as a "neuromythology" to cover ignorance (Westman, 1990).

Sleeter (1986) characterized the modern LD field as one represented by advances made by psychologists, neurologists, and physicians studying children and youth with difficulties acquiring language and reading skills, and by educators experimenting with methods for teaching them. Once sufficient research had been conducted and publicized, parents, educators, and physicians began to organize and together press for appropriate *assessment and educational services*. Modern LD forces include: (a) parents seeking ways to focus greater attention on their children's learning strengths and needs, what children need to learn, and how they are best taught; and (b) professionals advocating appropriateness of a systematic, direct approach to instructing students. Professionals also desire modified teaching methods and settings to accommodate learning abilities and styles (Smith, 1991).

Medical and educational integration evolved into a late-1980s view of *LD as subtle malfunctions in the most complex element of the human body, the central nervous system* (CNS) (e.g., Galaburda, 1985; Hynd, Marshall, & Gonzalez, 1991; Richardson, 1992; Westman, 1990). Hynd et al. (1991) reported that while it cannot be concluded that all LD are due to CNS dysfunction, recently researchers have pointed to neurological evidence of the developmental origins to LD. Extended studies entailing this budding focus on living and postmortem brain analyses of individuals with LD promise forthcoming educational implications. Current medical technology (e.g., electroencephalography, magnetic resonance imaging, brain autopsies, positron emission tomography, computerized tomography scanning, and regional cerebral blood flow), offer visible data on CNS function, location, and structure. While many efforts are still necessary in analyzing any teaching-learning implications from CNS research, medical technology now is enabling researchers to empirically test psychoneurological assumptions. As the twenty-first century advances, educators may be using modern medical data to help children and youth with LD learn most effectively.

Today, psychoneurological research may be conceptualized as directed efforts toward *collaboration and integration of medical and educational data into the teaching and learning processes*. The United States Office of Education, through Public Law No. 94-142 (and 1990 amendment, the Individuals with Disabilities Education Act) provided support to continuing psychoneurological influences on the direction of the LD field. The federal LD definition included terms such as *perceptual handicaps, brain injury, minimal brain dysfunction, dyslexia, and developmental*

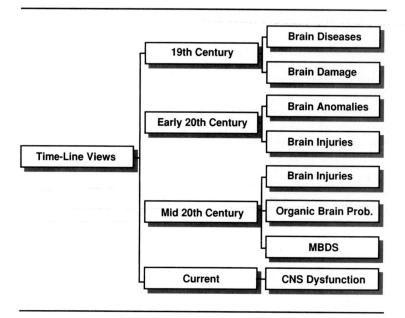

Figure 4.2
Historical links in psychoneurological theory.

aphasia. Current school professionals continue to seek appropriate services to students with LD. A resulting focus in applied research entails *multidisciplinary assessment and educational interventions to help children and youth learn.* Figure 4.2 presents a time line visually representing historical links in psychoneurological theory.

THE EVOLUTION OF PSYCHONEUROLOGICAL-BASED THEORIES AND PRACTICES

At the beginning of the 19th century, medical researchers began to analyze brain functions within both cerebral hemispheres, while assessing an assortment of problems in spoken and written language, perception, and behavioral responses. Some assumed that the brain's two hemispheres functioned as a whole, while others contended that there was specific brain-function localization. Eventually, by the early twentieth century, researchers focused on children's and adults' observed behaviors thought to be associated with language and perception difficulties originating in cerebral hemispheres. Mid-20th-century researchers continued to address clinical assessment and intervention issues related to individuals' difficulties using the various senses. However, current investigators interested in perception-multisensory data continue to generate controversies concerning methodological issues (e.g., validity and reliability of process training) and intersensory assessment and instructional practices.

NINETEENTH-CENTURY DEVELOPMENTS

Manifestations in Language

Medical themes in the 1800s centered on determining hemispheric roles manifesting in problem language (Hinshelwood, 1917; Taylor, Holmes, & Walshe, 1931). Neuroanatomist Franz Gall in approximately 1810, advocated the notion of brain-function localization, initiating the debate on hemispheric functions. Gall is best known for associating localized brain damage to *aphasia* (i.e., the inability to speak). His work suffered when he promoted *phrenology,* the study of the mind and character traits by examination of the bumps on a person's head. His belief in phrenology caused him in later years to be labeled a "charlatan" (Wiederholt, 1974). However, by 1861, Broca offered support to Gall's views by positing that brain hemispheres had specialized functions (cited in Hinshelwood, 1917). Broca made the first attempt to localize expressive speech to a function of a rather restricted brain area. As a physician, he observed and described a patient who had once had and later lost the ability to speak (i.e., *acquired aphasia*). This patient, at autopsy, showed a lesion in the posterior part of the third frontal lobe in the brain's left hemisphere. This area became known as *Broca's area* and the expressive aphasia described was called *Broca's aphasia* (Hinshelwood, 1917).

Jackson, around the mid-1870s, criticized Broca's localization theory, arguing that human brain parts linked intimately. Jackson contended that damage to one brain part would reduce overall general functioning. Jackson discussed his observations on localized movements in the cerebral hemispheres, as revealed by his detailed accounts of convulsion, chorea, and aphasia. He reasoned that ". . . convulsions, chorea movements, affections of speech, and other motor movements, are not only to be thought of as 'symptoms of disease,' but can also be considered as results of experiments made by disease revealing in the rough the functions of cerebral convolutions . . ." (Jackson, cited in Taylor et al., 1931, p. 77). Jackson coined the word "verbalizing" and associated the brain's left hemisphere to major control of the propositional aspects of language (Hinshelwood, 1917; Taylor et al., 1931).

Wernicke, in approximately 1874, attempted to discriminate and detail other brain functions and locations. Wernicke postulated that the cause of aphasia was related to connecting auditory and motor speech areas of the brain. Wernicke located the auditory speech area in the superior temporal convolution on the left while reporting that the anterior half of the brain entailed movement function. The posterior, including the temporal lobe, was found to involve sensory impressions. Wernicke's brain work centered on discriminating the general auditory and auditory speech areas. He proposed four centers for speech disorders: (a) motor aphasia, (b) conduction aphasia, (c) sensory aphasia, and (d) total aphasia. He assumed that a lesion in the temporal lobe would produce loss of understanding of speech, as well as difficulty in naming and speaking. According to his assumptions, without the ability to understand, one would be unable to correct mistakes. In addition, the individual might lose the ability to read and write.

Wernicke (1908) redressed the debate over cerebral dominance and influence when he presented his *schema of language conceptualization* in 1885. He contended that simple activities were specialized in the brain's cortex, but higher functions were dependent on the interconnections of these areas (Hinshelwood, 1917).

Manifestations in Perception and Reading

Perception and multisensory research, and the relationship to learning, began in the 1890s. This research resulted directly from an early focus on studying brain damage. Bastian (1898) and Morgan (1896) postulated that some developmental damage existed in the region of the left parietal-occipital cortex, in the brains of individuals with learning problems. This postulated deficit was believed to disrupt the functioning of the cortical pathways important in learning. Of particular historical importance were assumptions that: (a) the learning deficit was related to some visual-perception system disruption, and (b) the neurodevelopmental deficit was localized in the left hemisphere, specifically at the juncture of the left parietal-occipital cortex (Hynd et al., 1991).

Further medical research was conducted to study the impact of suspected brain diseases on the processing of written discourse. Broadbent's (1872) patients who were unable to read printed or written words thus demonstrated *verbal aphasia* (i.e., the inability to verbalize and/or conceptualize what they saw in print). In these cases, the inability to read was accompanied by speech disturbances and amnesia. Broadbent assumed that reading, as an outlet for expression, was connected to thought location within brain components. He concluded that words, as remembered sounds, are represented by cell groups "at the summit of the receptive side of the nervous system . . . from cell-groups, words are employed as symbols for the resulting ideas of objects. The outlet for intellectual expression in spoken words, which are motor acts, is the left third frontal gyrus of the brain" (Broadbent, 1872, pp. 193–194).

Kussmaul furthered Broadbent's views by contending that *word blindness* could be located clinically as an isolated condition (Hinshelwood, 1917). Kussmaul invented the term "word blindness" for the condition in which the patient, with normal vision and therefore seeing the letters and words distinctly, was unable to interpret written or printed language. Kussmaul believed that word blindness was a pathological condition—with complete text blindness possible—even though the individual demonstrated sight, intelligence, and speech. Berlin, a German ophthalmologist, introduced the term *dyslexia* in 1887, suggesting individuals had difficulty in reading due to cerebral disease. Berlin argued dyslexia was an acquired condition imposing lifelong ramifications. Similarly, Morgan (1896) described his highly intelligent teenage patient who could read figures and complete mathematical operations while also displaying *word blindness.*

TWENTIETH-CENTURY DEVELOPMENTS

Manifestations in Language

Based on research by early pioneers, 20th-century researchers began viewing language development, language difficulties, and problem language effects on individuals' behaviors. Early investigators continued to argue brain functions associated

with brain anomalies and brain injuries. For example, Marie questioned clinical observational reporting, while rejecting then current views concerning the cerebral localization of specific brain functions (Wiederholt, 1974). Marie introduced the term
anarthria in approximately 1906, arguing against the belief that aphasia was of ne-
cessity associated with a lesion of the third frontal convolution of the brain. He concluded there was no separate center in the brain for visual and auditory aspects of
words.

Head, in the mid-1920s, objected to Marie's attack on the nature and causes of
aphasia by countering Marie's dispute. He was critical of Broca's and Wernicke's
oversimplifications of the neural connections between different brain components.
Head connected brain-function research to language specifications and detailed
aphasia. After his many clinical observations, he developed a data collection system
and diagnostic method for assessing aphasia. Head reasoned that individuals with
aphasia did not suffer from generalized impairment of intellectual ability, even
though they often sustained brain damage evidenced by language difficulties. He believed that the motor correlates of learning disorders were not due to high-level processing. Head further argued that disorders in language could not be classified as
motor (i.e., expressive) or sensory (i.e., receptive). He reported that many of his patients with brain anomalies could carry out simple recognition tasks including finding object similarities, but could neither form symbolic relationships nor verbally express these relationships (Wiederholt, 1974).

Head posited that the more the brain damage destroys the lower portion of the
pre- and postcentral convolutions and the parts which lie beneath them, the more
likely are the defects to assume a "verbal" form. He postulated that a lesion near the
upper temporal lobe tends to produce "syntactical" speech disorders. Semantic defects tend to center around the brain's supremarginal gyrus. A lesion in the angular
gyrus portion seems to disturb the power to discover, to understand, and to employ
names or other nominal expressions (Sleeter, 1986).

Head's research opened the way for addressing the relationship of intellectual
ability to language acquisition. He indicated that abstract conceptual ability is affected greatly by aphasia, thus promoting his argument that atypical language
lessens one's reasoning skills. He also helped to refine language components including *phonology* (i.e., sound system), *syntax* (i.e., grammatical structure), *morphology* (i.e., expression), *semantics* (i.e., meaning), and *pragmatics* (i.e., usage).
Additionally, he influenced modern views on individuals with LD, including: (a) children and youth may have intellectual potential that shows up only through specific
sensory modalities and on certain types of tasks; (b) behavioral descriptions often
provide more discrete information than diagnoses of brain lesion locations; and (c)
if language and ability are synonymous in society, then early language intervention
is critical (Richardson, 1992; Smith, 1991).

By the mid-twentieth century, other prominent researchers advocated behavioral views that began competing with psychoneurological explanations for language acquisition and problem language. For example, based on the work of noted
learning theorists such as Watson, (1913) and Skinner (1959), researchers began supporting behavioral explanations. Classical conditioning entailed a form of learning in
which an initially neutral stimulus became paired with a stimulus to elicit a reflex;

after repeated pairings, the neutral stimulus alone elicited the reflexive response (Watson, 1913). Operant conditioning, also a form of learning, entailed an increase in the response frequency if followed by a reward or reinforcement and a less frequent response frequency if followed by punishment (Skinner, 1938). Early work centered on animals, but by midcentury, efforts were directed toward applying classical and operant conditioning techniques to treatment of many human problems, including learning difficulties. (See chapter 7 for more details on behavioral theories.)

Behavioral language theorists argued language acquisition and problem language occur as the result of the environment shaping an individual with a given ability (i.e., an innate general learning potential) (Lindsfor, 1980). The behavioral view holding that individuals are reinforced for responses to various stimuli became a highly controversial explanation in general psychology and language research. Skinner (1959) and Staats (1971) represented behavioral researchers challenging basic psychoneurological language assumptions (e.g., innate abilities and aberrant brain involvement). Many ensuing 20th-century researchers reported a high success rate with behavioral procedures (e.g., behavior modification or behavior therapy). Learning-based approaches began to replace psychoneurological assumptions as researchers' treatments of choice. Behavioral theorists also competed with psychoneurological theorists in explaining general learning.

In many ways, the competing behavioral concepts forced midcentury medical researchers to promote greater insights into the complexity and subtlety of language, language acquisition, and problem language behaviors. For example, Eisenson (1954) viewed behavioral aspects of problem communications in his work with children with acquired aphasia. *Organic brain problems* occurring either prenatally, perinatally, or postnatally were associated with cerebral dysfunctions and maturational lags. Eisenson documented that children with acquired aphasia displayed irregular brain patterns on the left cerebral hemisphere and further reasoned a corresponding slower development of receptive and expressive language. He suggested that slower language development would manifest in problem language behaviors, such as in children's articulation difficulties, small vocabulary, poor grammar, short sentence length, poor comprehension, inconsistent responses to noises, memory difficulties, perseveration, and emotional lability.

Psychoneurological views continued to flourish during the 1950s and 1960s, but many medically oriented researchers and language practitioners considered behavioral-environmental aspects to language processes. They called for psychoeducational interventions into problem language and other academic difficulties. For example, the mid-twentieth century had influential psychoneurological researchers, including Strauss and Kephart (1955); Johnson and Myklebust (1967); Myklebust (1978); Kirk, McCarthy, and Kirk, (1968); and Sperry (1968), viewing (a) normal and atypical language development, (b) organic brain problems, and (c) assessment and instructional strategies.

Language Learning Researchers.   Many language learning researchers became influential during the 1960s and 1970s. Myklebust (1978) suggested a developmental sequence of auditory language acquisition, an experiential hierarchy leading from concrete to abstract thinking, and instructional strategies geared toward remediating language and perception deficits. Myklebust maintained that for those without an intact central nervous system, a learning disorder in perception disturbance, imagery disturbance, symbolic process disorders, or conceptualizing disturbances may result (Johnston, 1975; Myklebust, 1978; Myklebust & Boshes, 1969). Myklebust attributed students' atypical learning to neurological impairment, coining the term *psychoneurological learning disorder* (Myklebust & Boshes, 1969). The term had great appeal to school practitioners because it identified the learning problem as the common thread among children. It also emphasized the role in handling the problem, while supporting a psychological and neurological component. Finally, the term allowed educators and speech clinicians to deal with the problem without medical intervention (Johnston, 1975).

Johnson and Myklebust (1967) extended psychoneurological learning research into auditory language disorders, dyslexia, written problem language, speaking difficulties, and nonverbal disorders of learning. They provided assessment suggestions and general instructional considerations promoting individualized teaching based on students' language levels. They based assessment and instructional procedures on students' readiness for balanced language programs. Johnson and Myklebust argued students should be actively involved in their own learning. Accordingly, educators then should use *multisensory instruction blending a reliance on students' senses and perceptions*; work toward control of attention, rate, proximity, and size while developing both the verbal and nonverbal areas of students' experiences; and finally, provide instruction guided by assessment of students' *behavioral, psychoneurological, and language considerations*.

Researchers greatly influenced the study of language instruction and brain-structure–function relationships. For example, Sperry (1968) suggested that the brain's right hemisphere can comprehend simple written and spoken words when this comprehension is expressed nonverbally. The right hemisphere is superior to the left in analyzing complex spatial relations and sound reception (Sperry, 1968). Importantly, psychoeducational researchers assumed that instructional strategies geared toward *correct hemispheric programming could aid language development and usage* (e.g., Lindsfor, 1980; Smith, 1991; Westman, 1990). Table 4.2 summarizes specifics of language-based assessments and instructional approaches in the work of noted mid-20th-century language researchers.

Finally, psychoneurological theory on the study of problem language still generates controversy. For examples, recent holistic arguments continue to challenge traditional psychoneurological assumptions. Table 4.3 identifies a 200-year language chronology, pinpointing examples of major language research.

Manifestations in Perception

Early-20th-century British researchers conducted perception and behavior investigations. Still (1902) linked hyperkinetic and impulsive behavior to brain lesions. He viewed brain dysfunction as a *result of tumors, infectious disease, or head injuries while associating temper tantrums, disobedience, and impulsivity to moral control defects*. Observing and recording children's behaviors consumed much of Still's research efforts. Around 1908, Tredgold (cited in Westman, 1990) viewed the etiology of hyperkinetic children as the result of mild brain injuries at birth.

Table 4.2
Language-Based Assessments and Instructional Approaches
from the Work of Noted Mid-Twentieth-Century Language Researchers

Approximate Period	Researchers	Focus
1950–1960	Osgood	Receptive and expressive language skills; stimulus-response variables in communication; assessment and remedial teaching skills, based on decoding and encoding communication behaviors
1950–1975	Myklebust Mykelbust & Boshes Myklebust & Johnson	Language behaviors associated with dysfunctions of sensory systems, nervous systems, mental abilities, or emotional interactions; psychoneurological learning disorders; language acquisition and psychoeducational interventions; learning problems and neurological adjustments
1955–1975	Sperry	Hemisphere deconnection and awareness; split-brain studies isolating the function of one brain hemisphere from another; study of individuals whose severe seizures ended when the brain's corpus callosum was severed; language functioning controlled by the brain's hemispheres; visual-tactile associations and brain hemispheres

Many of the major historical perception events occurred in the mid-20th-century, with work centering on observing and understanding individuals with *brain injury* (e.g., Goldstein, 1939, 1942, 1954; Werner & Strauss, 1941). Goldstein, a primary influence on documenting the existence of brain injury in adults, analyzed brain injuries linked to neurological and perception functions. Goldstein was a physician treating soldiers with brain-injuries during World War I. He was able to observe these soldiers' behavioral characteristics and documented that the men displayed atypical reading, spelling, mathematics, and writing (even though many had normal achievement prior to their brain assault). Goldstein labeled *perception difficulties* as: (a) hyperactivity and attention to unimportant objects (i.e., being distracted by numerous external stimuli), (b) perseveration (i.e., being locked into repeated action), (c) impulsivity (i.e., acting without thinking), and (d) visual perception (i.e., figure-ground difficulties).

Much of what Goldstein learned about his brain-injured soldiers, whom he described as "traumatic dements," formed the basis of his work *The Organism*, setting forth his gestalt theory of brain injury (Goldstein, 1939). The completion of his book marked Goldstein's integration of then current perception assumptions and observed problem behaviors. Goldstein extended his brain-injury research on adults to children.

Strauss and Werner, beginning in the 1930s, also worked with children, many of

Table 4.3.
Examples of Researchers Involved in a Language Chronology, Their Focus on Language-Hemispheric Influences, and Language Themes

Period	Researchers	Language-Cerebral Influences	Themes
19th Century	Gall	Brain disease	Phrenology; brain-function localization
	Broca	Specialized functions	Acquired aphasia
	Jackson	Localized hemispheres	Verbalizing
	Wernicke	Auditory speech functions	Speech centers; schema of language conceptualization
Early 20th Century	Marie	Brain-function localization	Anarthria
	Head	Localized brain injuries	Brain injuries and specialized langauge deficits; aphasia
Mid-20th Century	Osgood	Specific organic language deficits; hemispheric influences	Spoken language problems; etiologies
	Wepman	Specific organic language deficits; hemispheric influences	Auditory-multisensory problems
	Gillingham	Specific organic language deficits; specific hemispheric influences	Written language problems
	Eisenson	Irregular brain patterns; maturation lags	Behavior; acquired aphasia
	Osgood	Normal language	Receptive and expressive language acquisition; development
Current	Dunn & Smith	General language learning processes	General psychoneurological language training
	Kirk & peers Minskoff & peers Karnes & peers	Specific psycholinguistic processes	Training in psychoneurological langauge (i.e., for expressive and receptive skills)
	Wiig & Semel	General psycholinguistic processes	General language behaviors; language usage disorders; language training
	Chaney Goodman Crais	Comprehension disorders; holistic influences	Whole language problems; language comprehension; language interventions based on students' interests and skills levels

whom displayed similar brain assaults and perception disturbances to those observed in Goldstein's adult soldiers (Werner & Strauss, 1941). However, Strauss and peers also studied brain damage in children with mental disabilities, focusing specifically on distractibility. Additionally, they were interested in the instability of perception between figure and ground.

Brain Injury Effects on Behavior, Perceptions, and Senses.   Goldstein influenced other studies of neurological-perception difficulties resulting from traumatic brain insults. Accordingly, mid-20th-century researchers began to assess brain injury implications, organic difficulties, and assessment and instructional means of remediating individuals' behaviors in clinical settings. Fernald and Keller (1921) and Strauss and Lehtinen (1947) specified assessment and instructional methods to overcome students' brain injuries and academic achievements. Fernald and Keller (1921) designed what later became known as a *visual-auditory-kinesthetic-tactile (VAKT)* approach to instruction for students with brain injury. They encouraged the use of students' multiple senses during instruction.

Strauss and Lehtinen (1947) developed a set of instructional practices for students with brain injury, practices based on environmental manipulation and educator control. Accordingly, these researchers developed a 1940s assessment system for the *Strauss-Lehtinen syndrome,* a behavioral profile manifested by children having organically based cerebral dysfunction (Capute, 1975). Children displayed behaviors including (a) *hyperactivity,* a spectrum of attentional peculiarities with short attention span on one side and perseverance on the other; (b) *emotional lability; (c) low frustration tolerance; and (d) distractibility.* Strauss and Lehtinen offered many assessment and instructional suggestions addressing perception readiness activities and academic skills. Linking students' perception and multisensory difficulties to MBDS, Strauss and Lehtinen detailed the need for development of multisensory (i.e., visual, auditory, and kinesthetic) perceptions before students could progress to basic academic skills (e.g., reading, writing, spelling, and mathematics).

In many ways, due to their prominence and influence, Strauss and Lehtinen's instructional recommendations set the stage for educators' adoption of the brain focus in assessing and intervening in students' atypical learning patterns. For example, Strauss and Lehtinen's instructional recommendations influenced other researchers in the late 1940s and 1950s including Blau (1946), Eustis (1947), Goldstein (1954), Hallgren (1950), and Kawi and Pasamanick (1959). These 1940s and 1950s researchers investigated perception problems, the nature of specific disabilities, and basic academic instructions based on Strauss and peers' recommendations. The Strauss-Lehtinen syndrome and the means for diagnosing and treating it were still in vogue by the 1970s (Capute, 1975).

Specific Training and Academic Difficulties.   During the time period of the 1960s and early 1970s, psychoneurological researchers extended instructional training into specific perception and academic difficulties (e.g., Frostig & Horne, 1964; Gillingham & Stillman, 1960; Kephart, 1971). Gillingham and Stillman (1960) provided extended multimodal practice to remediate visual-spatial weaknesses in reading, spelling, and writing. Frostig and Horne (1964) developed activities designed to assist students having visual perception difficulties by encouraging students' development of eye-hand coordination, visual discriminations, and spatial relations training entailing object relationships. Frostig and peers developed a visual-perception assessment device and detailed worksheets for remediating specific visual motor and visual perception difficulties. Kephart's (1971) efforts included matching students' perception development and motor functioning, allowing perception information to guide motor responses. Motor responses, in turn, acted as feedback mechanisms pertaining to perception accuracy and physical development. Kephart studied (a) *laterality* (i.e., discriminating left and right), (b) *directionality* (i.e., movement), and (c) accurate *body image*. Kephart also compared students with mental disabilities and brain injuries to children with average intelligence and brain injuries. These comparisons resulted in a perception survey rating system he developed to help to assess children's perception and motor functioning.

Cruickshank (1967, 1977, 1979) continued the perception theoretical line, maintaining that LD were the result of neurological impairment and perception deficits. Reiterating students' MBDS involvement, Cruickshank applied Strauss and Lehtinen's instructional suggestions to his work with students with cerebral palsy but of normal (IQ = 85–115) intelligence. Cruickshank reiterated the importance of instructing students on readiness and perception tasks before teaching them basic academic skills. He also argued that students with mild mental disabilities should be included in the LD categorical definition, noting similarities between behaviors of students with mild intelligence deviations, and the behavior of their peers with normal intelligence and learning problems (Cruickshank, 1979).

Other themes focused on training issues. For example, many researchers and practitioners began to associate specific brain functions, perception difficulties, and multisensory integration with academic achievement (e.g., Bakker, 1979, 1992; Calanchini & Trout, 1971; Levinson, 1980; Vellutino, 1979; Willeford & Burleigh, 1985). Accordingly, a focus on *intersensory modality integration training* resulted (Westman, 1990). For example, Calanchini and Trout (1971) viewed problems in visual perception disabilities linking disturbed functions to the brain's frontal lobe. They associated impaired voluntary oculomotor function to the sensorimotor cortical level. They also linked problems in auditory intensity and tonal discriminations to the superior temporal gyrus. Based on brain involvement knowledge and multisensory problems, other researchers attempted to correlate academic achievement to these visual perception or auditory perception disabilities, especially as the disabilities associated with reading (e.g., Bakker, 1979, 1992; Vellutino, 1979) or listening skills (e.g., Willeford & Burleigh, 1985).

Researchers also studied the vestibular system in distortions of spatial perception (e.g., Levinson, 1980; Polatajiko, 1985) fueling a growing debate on intersensory integration training, perception problems, and academic gains (Westman, 1990). Larsen and Hammill (1975) reviewed 60 mid-1970s studies relating academic attainment in reading, writing, spelling, and mathematics to visual discrimination, spatial relations, visual memory, and auditory-visual integration. They found that none of the studies actually produced significant correlations. Larsen and Hammill questioned intersensory integration training. They urged that measured intersensory modality integration was not sufficiently related to academic achievement to be diagnostically useful.

Modern LD researchers pioneered the use of brain morphology to identify aberrant physiology in much of the four cortical regions usually involved in reading and spelling.

Over the course of the ensuing years, researchers continued to assume brain-channel processing, perception difficulties, and the relationship of multisensory training to instructional interventions (e.g., Blau & Loveless, 1982; Luchow & Shepard, 1981; Myklebust, 1978; van de Honert, 1977). However, behaviorism influenced many researchers. For example, Myklebust (1978) proposed *stimulus overloading* as an explanation for students' perception problems in academics. He believed that when two or more data reach the brain, a breakdown occurs resulting in confusion, poor recall, or even seizures. Luchow and Shepard (1981) provided supportive evidence for the overload theory. They found that input from the auditory and tactile channels does not aid perception and in some cases actually interferes with academic tasks requiring students to match and process data.

Following the precepts of perception overload, van de Honert (1977) trained junior high readers to lateralize, that is, to use the left hemisphere to develop phonic decoding skills by channeling input to the left hemisphere. This use reportedly forced the brain's left side to process incoming information. Although she found a considerable improvement (after blocking students' left eyes to minimize visual stimulation through the right hemisphere), van de Honert discovered that the eye charts, from which she had assumed that information presented to the left eye was being lateralized to the left hemisphere, were drawn inaccurately. Therefore, the explanation for the improvement was invalid.

Blau and Loveless (1982) similarly followed the overload theory, but challenged visual modality benefits in assisting multisensory programs. Affected programs entailed visual, auditory, and kinesthetic senses (i.e., VAK) and VAKT (VAK and tactile) in their application to spelling instruction. The researchers' model provided the most direct hemispheric input, using the left hand to tap the specialization of the right hemisphere for spatial arrangement and manual patterns (i.e., *routing stimulation*), where modality is "deflected" through the use of blackened goggles to eliminate visual interference. They emphasized using the right hemisphere's holistic, manual recognition abilities rather than the left hemisphere's analytic, spatial, and sequential processing abilities. Blau and Loveless assumed that perception problems were due to a lack of intervention strategies for using hemispheric specializations and interactions.

Table 4.4 illustrates an historical overview of research on perception-multisensory problems and the focus of diagnosis and treatment.

Manifestations in Reading

Hinshelwood (1917) extended Berlin's work and began studying and writing about *congenital dyslexia*. Hinshelwood attempted to analyze and explain the condition in order to diagnose it scientifically. He sought to show how to teach students with this condition. Hinshelwood, an ophthalmologist, identified a brain component (i.e., the angular gyrus) as the brain area related to congenital dyslexia.

Hinshelwood described a patient who had lost visual memory of all the printed and written characters previously recognizable to that patient. Hinshelwood reported that the patient could speak clearly and write fluently from dictation, although afterwards he could not read what he had written himself. Upon autopsy, an anatomist and pathologist examined the patient, reporting a lesion of the cerebral cortex. Hinshelwood likened the observation to a form of *mind blindness*. In his view, mind blindness was simply loss of visual memory while *word blindness* was a simple form of mind blindness due to loss of a special group of visual memories, those of words and letters (Hinshelwood, 1917).

Hinshelwood's landmark publication offered the first major attempt to present the etiology of disorders of written language (i.e., reading, writing, spelling) and to describe educational intervention techniques. Hinshelwood's three-stage method of teaching children to read (i.e., first, teaching children to store up in the visual-memory part of the brain the individual alphabet letters; second, teaching children to read words by spelling them aloud; and third, teaching children strategies for gradual acquisition and storage of visual memory of words) is rarely identified with his name. However, his work in reading research influenced other physicians studying their patients' difficulties in language and reading (e.g., Dearborn, 1933; Orton, 1925, 1937).

Table 4.4

Overview of Perception-Multisensory Problems and Diagnostic Focuses

Time Period	Researcher(s)	Problem	Diagnostic Focus
19th Century	Bastian	Brain disease; observations	Patient's difficulties in responses; autopsies
	Hinshelwood	Brain disease	Left hemisphere involvement; visual-perception; autopsies
	Morgan	Brain disease	Patient observation; autopsies
Early 20th Century	Still	Brain diseases/brain anomalies	Children's behaviors
	Tredgold	Brain diseases/brain anomalies	Children's behaviors
	Goldstein	Brain injuries adults	Behaviors: perception, hyperactivity, perseveration, impulsivity, visual perception
Mid-20th Century	Strauss and Peers	Brain injuries children	Clinical assessments; instructional strategies
	Fernald	Brain injuries children	Perceptions and senses; VAKT instruction
	Blau & Peers	Brain injuries children	Perception specific disabilities; basic academic instruction
	Gillingham & Stillman	Brain injuries children	Multimodal practice; visual-spatial weakness; academic readiness
	Frostig & Peers	Brain injuries children	Visual perception difficulties; eye-hand development; instructional strategies
	Kephart	Brain injuries children	Perception difficulties; motor matches; laterality—directionality—body image
	Cruickshank	MBDS link children	Cerebral palsy; perception readiness; academic tasks
	Calanchini & Trout	MBDS link children	Intersensory difficulties; modality integration; academic gains
Late-20th Century (Current)	Bakker & Peers	MBDS link children	Perception difficulties; multisensory integration; academic gains
	Levinson	MBDS link children	Intersensory difficulties; modality integration; academic gains
	Blaus & Loveless	MBDS link children	Hemispheric stimulation; routing, deflected modality; lack of strategies use
	Myklebust	Psycholinguistic link children	Overload theory stimulus overload; auditory-tactile strategies

Early-20th-century reading professionals relied on Orton's work for their bases in planning, implementing, and analyzing reading instruction. Orton (1925, 1937), focusing on early developments in hemispheric dominance theories, first addressed word blindness in school children. Orton assumed that sensory impulses were received by both hemispheres simultaneously forming memory traces in the form of mirrored images. Orton believed that location, not extent of brain damage, was the overriding factor in reading ability. He believed that reading, as a language component, was centered in one brain hemisphere. According to his assumptions, if cerebral dominance existed, the memory traces in the nondominant hemisphere would be suppressed and normal perception would occur. If dominance did not exist because of some brain impairment, perceptions would be confusing and inconsistent, resulting in reading difficulties.

Orton offered suggestions for overcoming reading problems by special training. For example, he believed "logical training for these children would be that of extremely thorough repetitive drill on the fundamentals of phonic association with letter forms, both visually presented and produced in writing, until the correct associations were built up and the permanent elision of the reversed images and reversals in direction was assured . . ." (1925, p. 614). Orton (1937) preferred to use the term *developmental* when referring to word blindness (rather than *congenital*) because the former could include both an individual's hereditary tendencies and environmental factors. Orton was the first medical scientist to stress the unity of the language system and its sensorimotor connections. Orton viewed listening, speaking, reading, and writing as all interrelated functions of the communication system. Orton (1937) later developed remedial techniques for strephosymbolia, a form of reading disability.

Table 4.5
The Developmental Dyslexias

Type	Mechanism	Manifestations
Vestibulo-Cerebellar Dysmetria	Incoordination of range of oculomotor movements interferes with visual perception (extrapyramidal tremors)	Blurring of words Jumping around page Omission of words Loses place in paragraph
Visual-Spatial Dysgnosia	Interference with recognition of visual-spatial stimuli patterns	Cannot recognize familiar words Can sound out and recognize words Phonetic spelling errors Mislocates and reverses letters May be dyscalculia
Auditory-Linguistic Dysphasia	Interference with comprehension and expression of written language in addition to visual symbol-sound integration	Can recognize familiar words Cannot recall meaning Cannot sound out words Confuses small abstract words Bizarre spelling errors History of delayed speech
Articulo-Graphic Dyspraxia	Interference with exposition of written language	Can read silently but not orally Dysgraphia, omission, and perseveration of letters in spelling Motor incoordination

Note. From *Handbook of Learning Disabilities: A Multisystem Approach* by J. Westman p. 497. Copyright, 1990 by Allyn and Bacon, Boston. Reproduced with permission.

Table 4.6
Characteristics of Dyslexia Subgroups

	Vestibulo-Cerebellar	Visual-Spatial	Auditory-Linguistic	Articulo-Graphic
Reading				
Familiar Word		X		
cannot recognize				
cannot name			X	
cannot pronounce				X
Unfamiliar Word				
can sound out	X	X		
cannot sound out			X	X
Errors				
omit letters and syllables				X
omit words	X	X		
mutilate words			X	
alter sequence of letters		X		
confuse similar words		X		
confuse small words			X	
lose place in line	X	X		
words blur	X			
perseveration of syllables and words				X
grammatical errors			X	
Handwriting				
legibility impaired				X
spatial orientation errors		X		
spontaneous writing impaired			X	X
copy inaccurately	X	X		
Spelling				
alter letter sequences		X		
spell phonetically		X		
nonphonetic spelling errors			X	
letter omission and perseveration				X
Arithmetic Problems		X		
Visual-Spatial Problems		X		
Auditory Discrimination and Memory Problems			X	
Oculomotor Problems	X			
Primitive Neck-righting Response	X			
Motor Coordination Problems				X

Note. From *Handbook of Learning Disabilities: A Multisystem Approach* by J. Westman p. 499. Copyright, 1990 by Allyn and Bacon, Boston.

Influenced by Orton's reading research, Dearborn (1933) proposed a motor-response–based hypothesis for reading. Dearborn hypothesized that without hemispheric dominance, motor functions would be affected. When an individual is not hemispherically one sided, then competing motor tendencies appear and inconsistent eye movements and confusing visual perception result. Accordingly, reading problems relate to eye coordination difficulties and limited visual-perception skills.

Based on an outgrowth of Orton's (1937) work in studying the relationship of cerebral dominance to reading and language disorders, and Dearborn's (1933) motor-based views, Gillingham and Stillman (1965) devised an assessment-instructional method to increase auditory channel contributions (e.g., phonics element) to reading. Their studies resulted in the *Orton-Gillingham Method*, a multisensory synthetic phonics approach (i.e., auditory) employing a tracing (i.e., tactile-kinesthetic) technique for teaching single letters and their sound equivalents. Accordingly, phoneme-grapheme relationships, acquired through left hemisphere mediation, use the logical, temporal, and analytic functions (Orton & Gillingham, 1968).

Fernald (1943) developed a similar reading technique using the tactile and kinesthetic modalities. Her clinic assessment analyses were to help in remediating students' reading, writing, and spelling problems. She combined a whole-word, language-experience technique emphasizing visual, auditory, kinesthetic, and tactile senses, resulting in the *VAKT* models of learning (Fernald, 1943; Miccinati, 1979). Followers assumed that multisensory experiences and stimuli provide redundant cues about the stimuli assisting readers' accurate perceptions. Accordingly, Fernald's reading approach included tracing and writing from memory individually presented words, writing from memory individually presented words, writing from memory words found in the text, and learning sight words presented in the text (Fernald, 1943).

Reading investigators in the 1950s through the mid-1970s sought to define characteristics of LD subgroups and relationship to problem reading. For example, researchers sought to define and classify specific reading disabilities, resulting in the term *developmental dyslexias*. Perception and multisensory researchers offering training suggestions continued to influence reading practices. Developmental dyslexias subgrouped into such "processing" developmental dyslexia categories as: *vestibulo-cerebellar dysmetria* (i.e., incoordination of range of oculomotor movements interfering with visual perception), *visual-spatial dysgnosia* (i.e., interference with recognition of visual-spatial stimuli patterns), *auditory-linguistic dysphasia* (i.e., interference with comprehension and expression of written language, in addition to visual symbol-sound integration), and *articulo-graphic dyspraxia* (interference with exposition of written language) (Westman, 1990). Tables 4.5 & 4.6 illustrate the developmental dyslexias, including the types, mechanisms, and behavioral manifestations.

REACTIONS TO "PROCESSING INSTRUCTIONAL MODELS" IN READING RESEARCH

Some behaviorally oriented researchers reacted to researchers promoting psychoneurological orientations in reading instruction. For example, criticism surfaced within the LD field concerning the validity and reliability of psychoneurological

Table 4.7
Psychoneurological Themes in Math and Reading Investigations, from the Late 1880s

Time	Researcher(s)	Themes
1872	Broadbent	Documented patient observations; described mathematical and reading skills; labeled "mechanism of thought" and "mechanism of speech"; conducted autopsies
Circa late 1880s	Kussmaul	Defined *word blindness*
1887	Berlin	Introduced term *dyslexia;* related dyslexia to cerebral disease
1897	Morgan	Used patient observations; described mathematical and reading skills
1917	Hinshelwood	Illustrated psychological reporting by Binet on patients' mathematical skills; described congenital dyslexia; described educational intervention techniques
Late 1920s	Orton	Described childrens' word blindness; viewed cerebral dominance and reading skills; described educational intervention techniques
1933	Dearborn	Viewed motor-response base to reading; reasoned reading problems related to eye coordination difficulties and limited visual perception skills
1943	Fernald	Viewed tactile and kinesthetic modalities in reading; devised VAKT approaches
1947	Strauss & Lehtinen	Focused on students' acquisition of basic numerical operations and concepts; offered clinical assessment and instructional methods in academics
1950s	Brownell; Piaget	Viewed mathematical skills and perception readiness
1961	Cruickshank	Reasoned perception difficulties and mathematical or reading difficulties; offered educational intervention methods

models and resulting "processing approaches." Importantly, theoretical complexities reportedly limited psychoneurological reading models' classroom applications (e.g., Koenigsberg, 1973; Thorpe & Borden, 1985), resulting in practitioners' minimal use (O'Shea & O'Shea, 1990). For educators reading programs such as the *Orton-Gillingham method, Fernald's VAKT methods, and Blau and Loveless' hemispheric routing* were shown to have relatively low efficiency ratios; that is, they required extensive amounts of instructional time and effort to achieve incremental gains in students' achievement (Koenigsberg, 1973; Thorpe & Borden, 1985). Additionally, benefits of multisensory reading programs as a function of the increased attention to task (i.e., and not due to cerebral dominance) had considerable surface validity. These explanations to identified benefits of process-oriented reading programs could not be dismissed as competing hypotheses (Koenigsberg, 1973; Thorpe & Borden, 1985).

Psychoneurological reading programs, (e.g., Frostig & Horne) require students' visual discrimination skills ostensibly parallel to those needed in decoding, but researchers often used nonalphabet stimuli to produce some generalized improvement in visual discrimination skills. However, critics argued data were lacking that such programs resulted in a generalized perception improvement producing any better effects than more traditional reading programs using letter and word stimuli (Koenigsberg, 1973; Thorpe & Borden, 1985). Table 4.7 illustrates psychoneurological research themes in the area of mathematics and reading instruction.

MODERN CONTROVERSIAL PSYCHONEUROLOGICAL RESEARCH

Recent supporters of psychoneurological explanations for LD continue to offer further evidence of the existence of LD linked to developmental disabilities (e.g., Galaburda, 1985; Hynd et al., 1991). However, some assessment and treatment approaches remain more controversial than others (Hynd, 1992; Silver, 1987). For example, many professionals trained in medically related fields (e.g., physical therapists, optometrists, neurophysiologists, chiropractors) continue to address students' learning difficulties while promoting controversial LD assessments and treatments of neurological and brain dysfunctions (Hynd et al., 1991; Irlen, 1991; Obrzut, 1989). Many educators and parents continue to be influenced by atypical assessment and instructional practices (Silver, 1987).

Modern Controversial Views

When researchers reviewed the benefits of optical treatments to correct reading difficulties recently, *optical approaches* (e.g., Irlen, 1991) surfaced as the latest bandwagon approach to interest parents and professionals. Advocates reported that dyslexia may involve an abnormality that slows down one of two major visual pathways in the brain, so that two kinds of visual information are not received in the right sequence by individuals with dyslexia. One visual pathway, the magnocellular system, has large cells that carry out fast processes for receiving position, motion, shape, and low contrast. The smaller parvo cells in the brain carry out slower processes for perceiving still images, color, detail, and high contrasts. Irlen reading advocates assume light strikes photoreceptors in the retina; the information is then processed by magno cells and parvo cells in midbrain regions labeled *the lateral geniculate bodies.* Then the signal travels to the visual cortex for further processing. In studies done on individuals with dyslexia, the magno cells were found to be smaller than normal. Readers' low-contrast information processing was found to be slower than normal. Figure 4.3 illustrates brain abnormalities that reportedly slow down one of two major visual pathways in the brain, resulting in two kinds of visual information sequenced inappropriately by individuals with dyslexia.

Visual training remains a popular, but highly controversial instructional ap-

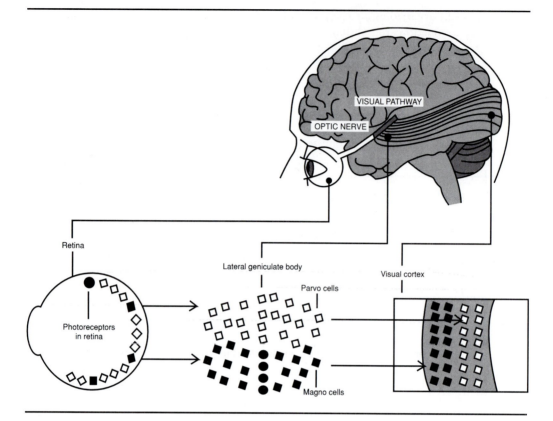

Figure 4.3

In reading, light strikes photoreceptors in the retina, the information is then processed by magno cells and parvo cells in midbrain regions called the lateral geniculate bodies. Then the signal travels to the visual cortex for further processing. In a study of dyslexics, the magno cells were found to be smaller than normal, and low-contrast information processing was found to be slower than normal.

Note: Copyright © 1991 by the New York Times Company. Reprinted by permission.

proach to treating dyslexia. Investigators suggested using *colored lenses as light filters* to overcome reader's difficulties with images, color, detail, and high contrasts (Irlen, 1991). Irlen and peers claimed that colored lenses filter specific light frequencies while removing a range of perception disorders that adversely affect mathematical, reading, or related learning performance. Irlen labeled the condition *Scotopic Sensitivity Syndrome* (SSS). She suggested a perceptual dysfunction affecting principally reading- and writing-based activities. Accordingly, individuals with SSS require more effort in reading because they see the printed page differently from other readers. Constant adaptation to distortions from print or from the white background on paper causes readers fatigue and discomfort. SSS is said to limit the length of time individuals can read and maintain comprehension.

Claiming SSS as a significant factor in a high percentage of people with LD, Irlen and Lass (1989) reported that about 50% of individuals with reading disabilities have the condition. Using *Irlen lenses*, proponents suggested light filters help in improving reading performance and eliminating reading discomfort (Howell & Stanley, 1988; O'Connor, Sofo, Kendall, & Olsen, 1990; Robinson & Conway, 1990; Robinson & Miles, 1987).

Irlen lenses treatment is not without critics (Howell & Stanley, 1988; Hoyt, 1990; Solan, 1990; Winter, 1987). Critics argued significant findings in SSS studies, and, therefore, colored lenses should be scrutinized carefully. Users need to consider higher instructor expectations, placebo effects, and oculomotor problems in any reported reading gains. Other critics questioned the efficacy of visual training and methodological inconsistencies in reported findings (e.g., Blaskey, Scheiman, Parisi, Ciner, Gallaway, & Selznick, 1990; Stanley, 1987).

Neurophysiological Retraining

Silver (1987) described the controversy involving *neurophysiological retraining*, a group of approaches based on the concept that by stimulating specific sensory inputs or exercising specific motor patterns one can retrain, recircuit, or in some way improve the functioning of a part of the CNS. Doman and Delacato (1968) developed *patterning*. This treatment approach followed the principle that failure to pass correctly through a certain sequence of developmental stages in mobility, language, and competence in the manual, visual, auditory, and tactile areas reflected poor "neurological organization." Failure indicates potential brain damage. Doman and Delacato suggested treatments involving muscle manipulation, sensory stimulation, rebreathing of expired air with a plastic face mask (e.g., to increase vital capacity and to stimulate cerebral blood flow), and restriction of fluid, salt, and sugar intake (e.g., to decrease cerebral spinal fluid production and cortical irritability). Per Silver (1987), patterning results are unproven, and demands on families are so great that in some cases families may be harmed through patterning continuation. Despite warnings from medical professionals, (i.e., American Academy of Pediatrics, 1982) patterning is still advocated by some physical therapists, physicians, parents of individuals with LD, and educators (Silver, 1987).

An additional neurophysiological retraining entails *vestibular dysfunction procedures* (e.g., methods reducing ocular muscle imbalances; chiropractic massages). These procedures continue to generate controversy. The vestibular system's role in the higher cortical functions required for academic performance is not known (Silver, 1987). However, earlier medical researchers suggested the importance of the vestibular system in academic learning, claiming a causal relationship between vestibular disorders and poor academic performance (e.g., written language in children with LD) (Ayres, 1972; Levinson, 1980; Polatajiko, 1985). Other researchers have argued that many children and youth with LD require specialized vestibular therapy before they can benefit from academic input. Still others, such as deQuiros (1971) and Levinson (1980) have argued that evidence of vestibular disorder is predictive of LD, and that therapy aimed at correcting dysfunctions can prevent LD.

Accordingly, Ferreri and Wainwright (1987) proposed an *applied kinesiology* treatment entailing chiropractic massaging and specific body manipulations to cor-

Table 4.8

Modern and Controversial Themes in Assessment and Treatment Practices Related to Problem Learning and LD

Neurological Disorganization (e.g., Doman & Delacato, 1968)

Controversial Behaviors/Symptoms of Neurological Disorganization: Failures to pass through certain developmental sequences in mobility, language, and competence in the manual, visual, auditory, and tactile areas. Individuals display poor cerebral blood flow, high cerebrospinal fluid production, and cortical irritability.

Controversial Assessments/Interventions of Neurological Disorganization: Patterning techniques, sensory stimulation, rebreathing exercises, and restriction of fluid, salt, and sugar intake.

Brain Retraining (e.g., Gazzaniga, 1972, and others)

Controversial Behaviors/Symptoms of Individuals Needing Brain Retraining: Limited speech, symbol, and sound centers on the brain's right side, to the exclusion of those on the left, or supplemental to the defects on the left.

Controversial Assessments/Interventions of Brain Retraining: Zaidel (1975) used contact lenses to direct information to one or another hemisphere. Zihl (1981) used lights to restore visual field and related functions. Bakker (1984) and Bakker and Vinke (1985) retrained reading achievement through weaker cerebral hemisphere's skills, using EEG and achievement measures. Earlier, Claiborne (1906) suggested directing individuals with dyslexia to be left-handed in order to cultivate speech, symbol, and sound centers on the brain's right side, to the exclusion of those on the left, or supplemental to the defects on the left.

Vestibular and Vestibular-Cerebral Systems Dysfunctions (e.g., Levinson, 1980)

Controversial Behaviors/Symptoms of Vestibular Dysfunction: Individuals display faulty eye movements, poor postural coordination, poor balance, and poor spatial nystagmus. No data provide conclusive evidence for vestibular dysfunction in children with LD.

Controversial Assessments/Interventions of Vestibular Dysfunction: Included examination of spontaneous and gaze nystagmus and vestibular and optokinetic testing. Levinson (1980, 1984) proposed the treatment of dyslexia with anti-motion-sickness medication; vestibular nystagmus was induced by a rotating chair.

Cloacal Reflexes and Ocular Locks (e.g., Ferreri & Wainwright, 1987)

Controversial Behaviors/Symptoms of Cloacal Reflexes and Ocular Locks: Individuals have assumed damage to two specific cranial bones, the sphenoid and the temporal, (cloacal reflexes) and an ocular muscle imbalance (ocular lock). Problem learning is assumed to be caused by damage to two specific cranial bones, the sphenoid and the temporal, by what are called "cloacal reflexes," and by an ocular muscle imbalance they term an "ocular lock." The displacement of the sphenoid and temporal bones causes neurological problems by creating unequal pressure areas on the brain. *Ocular lock:* a neural problem created when the eyes move in certain directions *include* weakened muscles, heavy eyes, irregular motion, difficulties in coordinating lines of printed read materials).

Controversial Assessments/Interventions of Cloacal Reflexes and Ocular Locks: Specific body manipulations will correct difficulty with cranial faults, cloacal reflex functioning, and ocular muscle imbalance through the use of applied kinesiology. Because of automical connections, movement of the cranium adversely affects brain functions. Restoring the cranial bone to its correct position corrects brain malfunctions. *Cloacal reflexes trainings* center on manipulating the pelvis and coordinating with "visual righting," and "tonic neck reflectors" to the center of the head and neck with the lower part of the body. Correction of *ocular lock* by cranial bones manipulation into the correct position.

Scotopic Sensitivity Syndrome (e.g., Irlen, 1991)

Controversial Behaviors/Symptoms of Scotopic Sensitivity Syndrome: Individuals with problem reading often have difficulties with light source, luminance, intensity, wavelength, and color contrast. They also experience: headaches, eyestrain, excessive blinking, loss of place, skipping lines, excessive rubbing of eyes, squinting, opening eyes wide while reading, intermittent blur, double vision, movement of words, attention and concentration problems, rereading the same lines, and confusing similar words and letters.

Controversial Assessments/Interventions of Scotopic Sensitivity Syndrome: Use of light filters and visual retraining to improve comfort when reading. Using light filters or colored lenses for improving reading performance. Providing traditional optometric intervention for relieving behaviors commonly reported by people seeking help.

rect the difficulty with cranial faults, cloaca reflex functioning, and ocular muscle imbalance. Silver (1987) detailed the history of applied kinesiology, finding that proponents, especially many chiropractors, associate problems in the brain and the
body's muscular system with learning difficulties. Silver (1987) offered data refuting
Ferreri and Wainwright's theory.

Despite the reported absence of supportive data, followers continue to support
unorthodox assessment and treatment practices. For example, many optometrists
continue to believe that visual deficits underlie etiologies of reading disabilities;
some chiropractors advocate muscle and massage therapies as learning aids. School
professionals, especially educators working with students with LD and their families,
need to be wise consumers concerning many academic assessments and interventions that purportedly "cure LD" (Silver, 1987). Table 4.8 illustrates modern and controversial themes in assessment and treatment practices related to problem learning
and LD.

RECENT PSYCHONEUROLOGICAL ADVANCES

There are recent advances in psychoneurological undertakings providing provoca-
tive evidence of a neurological conceptualization to LD (Hynd et al., 1991; Hynd &
Semrud-Clikeman, 1989; Obrzut, 1989). Although not without controversy, many recent investigators have used the advantage of computers and medical technology.
For example, Hynd et al. (1991) addressed brain morphology revealing aberrant
physiology in much of the four cortical regions usually involved in reading and
spelling. The left hemisphere is more relevant than the right (Smith, 1991). Although
relatively few in number, data suggest that significant advances may be forthcoming
in integrating psychoneurological evidence of the deficits that characterize various
LD subtypes. Technological advances in brain research may reveal a more accurate
understanding of the neurological basis to LD (Hynd et al., 1991; Hynd & Semrud-
Clikeman, 1989).

Recent empirical support includes the benefits of modern medical techniques
analyzing postmortem and living brains. Hynd and colleagues (1991) reported that
decades of behavioral-psychometric research documenting psychoneurological
problems justify examination of brain morphology of individuals with LD. However,
in their view, it cannot be concluded that all LD are due to CNS dysfunction. Many
more data are required to integrate medical advances and learning research. While
they agree the postmortem and neuroimaging literature is complex and sometimes
fraught with technical and methodological challenges (Hynd et al., 1991), nonetheless, recent data demonstrate the potential for more technically sophisticated investigations with other forms of LD (Galaburda, 1985; Hynd & Semrud-Clikeman, 1989;
Pennington & Smith, 1988). Hynd et al. (1991) argued that future postmortem and
neuroimaging studies can be used to support the idea that severe disabilities are indeed due to neurological factors of developmental origin.

It should be noted, however, that other researchers argued that even with more
recent advances in new technologies (e.g., electroencephalography, magnetic resonance imaging, and so forth), significant problems remain in using diagnostic tech-

Table 4.9
Recent Medical Advances Providing Controversial Future Medical-Learning Research in the LD Field

An Anatomical Basis for Reading Disorders

Results of Processes Underlying Dyslexia

As reported by Richardson (1992), there has been a marked resurgence of interest in dyslexia since Geschwind's (1962) reintroduction of an anatomical basis for reading disorders. Geschwind (1982) has documented other observations made by Orton in the 1920s, such as a higher frequency of concomitant left-handedness, normal visual perception, clumsiness, and stuttering; a history of delay in the acquisition and use of spoken language; and that dyslexia tends to be familial. Geschwind concurs with Orton, who pointed out that these characteristics may coexist with dyslexia, but they are not causal; more likely, they are the *results of processes that underlie the dyslexia.*

Hemispheric Asymmetry

Although *gross hemispheric asymmetry* has been recognized for 100 years, Geschwind demonstrated that the left planum temporale (a triangular area behind the auditory association cortex) often is larger than the right. Other asymmetries also were documented. Geschwind reasoned that Orton's neurological analyses of the disorder of the brain places it in the exact site in which his great neurological predecessors in the latter part of the 19th and the beginning of the 20th centuries had localized the major area for reading ability. Geschwind further reasoned that, using modern medical technological techniques, he had found brain changes in the same locations.

Galaburda and Kemper (1979), in an analysis of the brain of a 20-year-old, left-handed male with dyslexia, found that the white matter of his left hemisphere was larger than the right and contained islands of ectopic neurons; there were also numerous heterotopias within the cortex, especially in the perisylvian areas. The left planum temporale was equal in size to the right, with absence of the asymmetry usually found there. Since that first study, similar findings have been observed in the brains of other individuals with dyslexia. It is believed that these *distortions of cortical architecture* probably date back to the period of *neuromigration occurring between the 16th and 24th week of gestation.*

Postmortem and Neuroimaging Research Documents Specific Brain Variations

Hynd, Marshall, and Gonzalez (1991) discussed contemporary attempts to explain how the brains of individuals with LD might differ from those without LD. While most of the evidence differentiating the two has been correlative and inferential (i.e., children with LD do poorly on some cognitive-behavioral measures, similar to the way children with more severe brain damage do; therefore, they must suffer minimal brain dysfunction (MBD). Because of the serious inferential problems associated with this literature (see Hynd, 1988), Hynd and peers (1991) focused on the postmortem and neuroimaging research that documents specific variations found in the brains of children and adults with LD. They suggested that alterations in fetal development may result in aberrations in neurological development, and postmortem studies of the brains of individuals with significant LD could be particularly useful for establishing a direct relationship between brain morphology and severe reading disability.

nology to identify the nature of the relationship between neurological functions and academic skills (Coles, 1987; Smith, 1991). For example, Coles (1987) argued that it is true that many of the technological advances contribute to other valid medical diagnoses. These could contribute more insights into LD if the focus of the research were not as limited and circumscribed as it has been. According to Coles, medical research technology has failed to provide scientific confirmation. Due to its seemingly formidable nature, advanced technology has nonetheless silenced dissent and in this way works to validate a medical LD explanation.

Many hypotheses about brain functioning are now becoming observable and testable; however, *it is not yet known how to relate neural findings to valid educational interventions* (Smith, 1991). Current methodological variations and technological limitations cause inconsistent results. Unfortunately, current measures tap a different autonomic, electrophysiological, or behavioral substrata of LD. The neurodevelopmental variables underlying a specific LD are hard to isolate or translate into educational intervention plans. However, recent neurobiological and postmortem evidence links the role of developmental variations in brain involvement and lateralization to certain forms of reading difficulties (e.g., Hynd et al., 1991), promising exciting future research avenues. Table 4.9 identifies recent medical advances providing promising future research avenues in the LD field. Ongoing efforts involve physician, educator, student, and parent cooperation.

Practical Classroom Applications

As this chapter has highlighted, the psychoneurological model contributed many historical data, especially readiness aids and assessment or instructional training devices. While unable to prove a direct relationship between brain and learning interactions or to cure problem learning, theory adherents have sensitized most professionals to the importance of neural interactions permeating students' learning and behaviors. Thus, benefits of psychoneurological theory have helped to explain the evolution of LD knowledge known currently. In our historical chronology, it is apparent that psychoneurological theory has proved both useful and controversial. Some considerations to reflect on the benefits of the psychoneurological model follow.

1. *Teachers benefit from psychoneurological research.* Psychoneurological research provided a base and structure to guide teachers' understanding of the human complexities involved in problem learning. By contributing early information on the brain's structure, function, and relationship to oral and written language processes and sensory perception, researchers advancing the psychoneurological model helped to move science and teaching forward. As we have discussed throughout this chapter, researchers provided many insights into the brain's involvement on language development, atypical language patterns, assessments, and interventions. While psychoneurological views do not hold as strong an influence today as in earlier days, current teachers who understand the rationale for psychoneurological research gain a broader understanding—scientifically, medically, and behaviorally—of students' learning processes.

(continued)

Practical Classroom Applications (continued)

2. *Learners gain from the psychoneurological model.* Researchers have provided many advances in students' perceptions, senses, and learning conditions. Today we know a great deal about learning processes, LD, and brain hemispheric functions associated with the left hemisphere and right hemisphere. Continual brain research in the structures and functions of thinking processes has assisted our understanding of how learners learn. However, researchers have not been able to establish a connection between educational treatments and psychoneurological etiologies.

3. *The multisensory approaches to reading and spelling instruction continue to influence classroom instructional methodologies.* The Orton and Gillingham (1968) visual, auditory, and kinesthetic (VAK) approach to reading instruction combines multisensory stimulation with a synthetic phonics approach. Teachers using a variety of combinations of students seeing printed letters or words and saying the sounds and/or writing the graphemes, help students learn though a variety of sensory channels. Fernald's (1943) visual, auditory, kinesthetic, and tactile (VAKT) approach is a similar technique, but employs a whole word rather than a phonic approach to teaching decoding skills. Remnants of both approaches, with the emphasis on hands-on instruction can be seen in modern classrooms. The ongoing controversy is not so much about the effectiveness of these methods, but on the instructional time it takes to use them and the explanation for their effectiveness. Researchers are unclear about why these approaches are effective. Some argue that the multisensory stimulation

provides redundant cues that enable the learner to remember and discriminate sound symbol relationships. Others argue that the kinesthetic and tactile activities are more interesting to learners so that they attend to the task better and, therefore, learn the associations more readily. Whatever the reason, the techniques used in part or in whole can be useful to teachers and students.

4. *The learning disabilities field is richer due to the psychoneurological model.* The study of neurological processes and brain functions has been and continues to be very influential in advancing understandings concerning learning modes and learning problems. Because many brain hypotheses may become observable, testable, and supported in the very near future, professionals in schools, hospitals, and clinics have been and will be importantly affected by the model. For example, as the population ages and more geriatric researchers continue to study brain functions and neurological problems affecting the elderly, (e.g., Alzheimer's disease and Parkinson's disease), many professionals in the LD field may gain in such areas as how and why neurological difficulties affect individuals with language and perception problems seen earlier in life.

There are no easy answers to the complex issues involved in learning and learning difficulties. Nonetheless, while not prominent today, a psychoneurological model may continue to influence the LD field. Most likely, and as history has evidenced, as we continue to learn more about the human neurology, psychoneurological assumptions will continue to shape and mold practitioners' futures.

SUMMARY

- Historical medical, psychological, and educational professionals assumed the interaction of numerous psychological and neurological variables in order to assess, treat, and explain problem learning. Nineteenth-century investigators researched the nature of brain damage and brain diseases.

- Hemispheric functions of the brain included *left hemisphere*: linguistic, analytic, abstract sequential processing, or mediation and *right hemisphere*: nonlinguistic, spatial and holistic processing, or manual pattern recognition.

- Broca made the first attempt to localize expressive speech to a function of a rather restricted brain area. Wernicke contended that simple activities were specialized in the brain's cortex but higher functions were dependent on the interconnections of these areas.

- Kussmaul invented the term *word blindness* for the condition in which the patient, with normal vision and therefore seeing the letters and words distinctly, was unable to interpret written or printed language. Berlin, a German ophthalmologist, introduced the term *dyslexia* in 1887 suggesting that individuals had difficulty in reading due to cerebral disease.

- Head posited that the more brain damage destroys the lower portion of the pre- and postcentral convolutions and the parts which lie beneath them, the more likely are the defects to assume a "verbal" form.

- Goldstein labeled *perception difficulties* as: (a) hyperactivity and attention to unimportant objects (i.e., being distracted by numerous external stimuli), (b) perseveration (i.e., being locked into repeated action), (c) impulsivity (i.e., acting without thinking), and (d) visual perception (i.e., figure-ground difficulties).

- Strauss and Lehtinen's instructional recommendations set the stage for educators' adoption of the brain focus in assessing and intervening in students' atypical learning patterns.

- Gillingham and Stillman (1965) provided extended multimodal practice to remediate visual-spatial weaknesses in reading, spelling, and writing. Frostig and Horne (1964) developed activities designed to assist students having visual perception difficulties by encouraging students' development of eye-hand coordination, visual discriminations, and spatial relations training entailing object relationships.

- Kephart's (1971) efforts included matching students' perception development and motor functioning allowing perception information to guide motor responses. Motor responses, in turn, acted as feedback mechanisms pertaining to perception accuracy and physical activity.

- Cruickshank, maintaining that LD were the result of neurological impairments and perception deficits, reiterated the importance of instructing students on readiness and perception tasks before teaching them basic academic skills.

- Hinshelwood, an ophthalmologist, identified a brain component (i.e., the angular gyrus) as the brain area related to congenital dyslexia.

- Orton was the first medical scientist to stress the unity of the language system and its sensorimotor connections. Orton viewed listening, speaking, reading, and writing all as interrelated functions of the communication system.

- Gillingham and Stillman (1965) devised an assessment-instructional method to increase auditory channel contributions (e.g., phonics elements) to reading. Their studies resulted in the *Orton-Gillingham Method*, a multisensory synthetic phonics approach (i.e., auditory), employing a tracing (i.e., tactile-kinesthetic) technique for teaching single letters and their sound equivalents. Fernald combined a whole-word, language-experience technique emphasizing visual, auditory, kinesthetic, and tactile senses, resulting in the *VAKT* models of learning.

- Irlen suggested that SSS, a perceptual dysfunction affecting principally reading- and writing-based activities, requires readers to make constant adaptation to distortions from print or from the white background on paper, which causes readers' fatigue and discomfort.

- Silver (1987) described the controversy involving neurophysiological retraining, a group of approaches based on the concept that by stimulating specific sensory inputs or exercising specific motor patterns one can retrain, recircuit, or in some way improve the functioning of a part of the CNS.

- Hynd et al. (1991) pioneered the use of brain morphology to identify aberrant physiology in much of the four cortical regions usually involved in reading and spelling. Significant advances may be forthcoming in integrating psychoneurological evidence of the deficits that characterize various LD subtypes. Technological advances in brain research may reveal a more accurate understanding of the neurological basis to LD.

DISCUSSION QUESTIONS

To help extend your understanding, reflect on and discuss the following questions:

1. What are the fundamental contributions of the psychoneurological model regarding learning?

2. To what extent might current academic areas be taught differently if historic researchers did not provide direction to begin the process of unlocking neural development and the learning process?

3. How would teachers practice today if early researchers had not associated brain-function and structure relationships to academic skills and behaviors?

4. How is a psychoneurological influence evident in traditional learning materials, curricula, teaching methods, and management procedures? Is there an influence in current learning materials, curricula, teaching methods, and management procedures?

5. How will medical advances in neurology influence the future learning materials, curricula, teaching methods, and management procedures?

6. How will educators' specific roles and responsibilities in classrooms change as more medical data become validated?

REFERENCES

American Academy of Pediatrics (1982). The Doman-Delacato treatment of neurologically handicapped children. A policy statement by the American Academy of Pediatrics. *Pediatrics, 70,* 810–812.

Ayres, A. J. (1972). *Sensory integration and learning disabilities.* Los Angeles: Western Psychological Services.

Bakker, D. J. (1979). Hemispheric differences and reading strategies: Two dyslexias? *Bulletin of the Orton Society 29,* Reprint no. 82.

Bakker, D. J. (1992). Neuropsychological classification and treatment of dyslexia. *Journal of Learning Disabilities, 25,* 102–109.

Bastian H. C. (1898). *Aphasia and other speech defects.* London: H. K. Lewis.

Bender, L. (1963). Specific reading disability as a maturational lag. *Bulletin of the Orton Society, 13,* 25–44.

Blaskey, P., Scheiman, M., Parisi, M., Ciner, E. B., Gallaway, M., & Selznick, R. (1990). The effectiveness of Irlen filters for improving reading performance: A pilot study. *Journal of Learning Disabilities, 23,* 604–610.

Blau, A. (1946). The master hand: A study of the origin and meaning of right and left sideness and its relation to personality and language. *Research Monograph No. 5.* New York: American Orthopsychiatric Association.

Blau, H., & Loveless, E. J. (1982). Specific hemispheric-routing-TAK/v to teach spelling to dyslexics: VAK and VAKT challenged. *Journal of Learning Disabilities, 15,* 461–466.

Broadbent, W. H. (1872). On the cerebral mechanism of speech and thought. *Transactions of the Royal Medical and Chirugical Society, 15,* 145–194.

Broca, L. (1861). Remarques sur le siege de la faculte du langage articule suivie d'une observation d'aphemie. *Bulletin Societé Antoropologia, 2,* 330–357.

Calanchini, P. R. & Trout, S. S. (1971). The neurology of learning disabilities. In L. Tarnopol (Ed.), *Learning disorders in children: Diagnosis, Medication and Education.* Boston: Little, Brown.

Capute, A. J. (1975). Cerebral palsy and associated dysfunctions. In R. H. A. Haslam and P. J. Valletutti (Eds.), *Medical problems in the classroom. The teacher's role in diagnosis and management* (pp. 149–164). Baltimore: University Park Press.

Coles, G. S. (1987). *The learning mystique: A critical look at "learning disabilities."* New York: Pantheon.

Cruickshank, W. M. (1967). *Teaching the brain-injured child.* Syracuse, NY: Syracuse University Press.

Cruickshank, W. M. (1977). *Learning disabilities in home, school, and community.* Syracuse, NY: Syracuse University Press.

Cruickshank, W. M. (1979). Learning disabilities: A definitional statement. In E. Polka (Ed.), *Issues and initiatives in learning disabilities: Selected papers from the first national conference on learning disabilities.* Ottawa, Canada: Canadian Association for Children With Learning Disabilities.

Dearborn, W. F. (1933). Structural factors which condition special disability in reading. *Proceedings of the American Association for Mental Deficiency, 38,* 266–283.

Delacato, C. H. (1959). *The treatment and prevention of reading problems.* Springfield, IL: Charles C. Thomas.

deQuiros, J. B. (1971). Diagnostic diferencial de la dislexia especifica. *Fonoaudiologica Buenos Aires, 17,* 117–123.

Doman, G., & Delacato, C. (1968). Doman-Delacato philosophy. *Human Potential, 1,* 113–116.

Eisenson, J. (1954). *Examining for aphasia.* New York: The Psychological Corporation.

Eustis, R. S. (1947). Specific reading disability. A familial syndrome associated with ambidexterity and speech defects and a frequent cause of problem behavior. *New England Journal of Medicine, 237,* 243–249.

Fernald, G. M. (1943). *Remedial techniques in basic school subjects.* New York: McGraw-Hill.

Fernald, G. M. & Keller, H. (1921). The effect of kinesthetic factors in the development of word recognition in the case of the nonreader. *Journal of Educational Research, 4,* 355–377.

Ferreri, C. A. & Wainwright, R. B. (1987). *Breakthrough for dyslexia and learning disabilities.* Pompano Beach: Exposition Press of Florida, Inc.

Frostig, M. (1972). Visual perception, integrative function and academic learning. *Journal of Learning Disabilities, 5,* 1–15.

Frostig, M., & Horne, D. (1964). *The Frostig program for the development of visual perception.* Chicago: Follett.

Galaburda, A. M. (1985). Developmental dyslexia: A review of biological interactions. *Annals of Dyslexia, 35,* 21–33.

Gazzaniga, M. S. (1972). One brain—two minds? *American Science, 60,* 311—317.

Gillingham, A., & Stillman, B. (1965). *Remedial training for children with specific disability in reading, spelling, and penmanship* (7th ed.). Cambridge, MA: Educators Publishing Service.

Goldstein, K. (1936). The modifications of behavior consequent to cerebral lesions. *Psychiatric Quarterly, 10,* 586–610.

Goldstein, K. (1939). *The organism.* New York: American Book.

Goldstein, K. (1942). *Aftereffects of brain injuries in war.* New York: Grune & Stratton.

Goldstein, K. (1954). The brain injured child. In H. Michael-Smith (Ed.), *Pediatric problems in clinical practice.* New York: Grune & Stratton.

Hallahan, D. P., Kauffman, J. M., & Lloyd, J. W. (1985). *Introduction to learning disabilities* (2nd ed.). Upper Saddle River, NJ: Prentice Hall.

Hallgren, B. (1950). Specific dyslexia (congenital word blindness). A clinical and genetic study. *Acta Psychiatric et Neurologia,* Scandinavica, Suppl. 65-1-287.

Hinshelwood, J. (1917). *Congenital word-blindness.* London: H. K. Lewis.

Howell, E., & Stanley, G. (1988). Colour and learning disability. *Clinical and Experimental Optometry, 71 (2),* 66–71.

Hoyt, C. S. (1990). Irlen lenses and reading difficulties. *Journal of Learning Disabilities, 23,* 624–626.

Hynd, G. W. (1992). Neurological aspects of dyslexia: Comment on the Balance Model. *Journal of Learning Disabilities, 25,* 110–112.

Hynd, G. W., Marshall, R., & Gonzalez, J. (1991). Learning disabilities and presumed central nervous system dysfunction. *Learning Disability Quarterly, 14 (4),* 283–296.

Hynd, G. W., & Semrud-Clikeman, M. (1989). Dyslexia and brain morphology. *Psychological Bulletin, 106,* 447–482.

Irlen, H. (1991). *Reading by the colors: Overcoming dyslexia and other reading disabilities through the Irlen method.* Garden City Park, NY: Avery.

Jackson, J. H. (1870). Evolution and dissolution of the nervous system. In J. Taylor, G. Holmes, & F. M. R. Walshe, (Eds.), (1931), *Selected writings of John Hughlings Jackson.* London: Hodder and Stoughton.

Johnson, D., & Myklebust, H. (1967). *Learning disabilities: Educational principles and practices.* New York: Grune & Stratton.

Johnston, R. B. (1975). Minimal cerebral dysfunction: Nature and implications for therapy. In R. H. A. Haslam and P. J. Valletutti (Eds.), *Medical problems in the classroom. The teacher's role in diagnosis and management* (pp. 281–304). Baltimore: University Park Press.

Kawi, A. A. & Pasamanick, B. (1959). Prenatal and paranatal factors in the development of childhood reading disorders. *Monograph of the Society for Research in Child Development, 24,* (4).

Kephart, N. C. (1971). *The slow learner in the classroom* (2nd ed.). Upper Saddle River, NJ: Prentice Hall/Merrill.

Kirk, S. A., McCarthy, J. J., & Kirk, W. D. (1968). *The Illinois Test of Psycholinguistic Abilities* (Rev. ed.). Urbana: University of Illinois Press.

Koenigsberg, R. S. (1973). An evaluation of visual versus sensorimotor methods for improving orientation discrimination of letter reversals by preschool children. *Child Development, 44,* 764–769.

Larsen, S. C., & Hammill, D. D. (1975). The relationship of selected visual-perceptual abilities to school learning. *Journal of Special Education, 9,* 281–291.

Levinson, H. N. (1980). *A solution to the riddle of dyslexia.* New York: Springer-Verlag.

Lindsfor, J. W. (1980). *Children's language and learning.* Upper Saddle River, NJ: Prentice Hall.

Luchow, J. P. & Shepherd, M. J. (1981). Effects of multisensory training in perceptual learning. *Learning Disabilities Quarterly, 4,* 38–43.

Miccinati, J. (1979). The Fernald technique: Modifications increase the probability of success. *Journal of Learning Disabilities, 12*(3), 139–142.

Morgan, W. P., (1896). A case of congenital word blindness. *The British Medical Journal, 3,* 1378–1380.

Mykelbust, H. R. (1978). *Progress in learning disabilities* (Vol. IV). New York: Grune & Stratton.

Mykelbust, H. R. & Boshes, B. (1969). *Minimal brain damage in children.* Washington, DC: Neurological and Sensory Disease Control Program, Department of Health, Education, and Welfare.

Obrzut, J. E. (1989). Dyslexia and neurodevelopmental pathology: Is diagnostic technology ahead of the psychoeducational technology? *Journal of Learning Disabilities, 22,* 217–218.

O'Connor, P. D., Sofo, F., Kendall, L., & Olsen, G. (1990). Reading disabilities and the effects of colored filters. *Journal of Learning Disabilities, 23,* 597–603.

Orton, S. T. (1925). "Word blindness" in school children. *Archives of Neurology and Psychiatry, 14,* 581–615.

Orton, S. T. (1937). *Reading, writing and speech problems in children.* New York: Norton.

Orton, S. T., & Gillingham, A. (1968). Special disability in writing. In S. B. Childs (Ed.), *Education in specific language disability* (pp. 79–110). Pomfret, CT: Orton Society.

O'Shea, D. J., & O'Shea, L. J. (1990). Theory-driven teachers: Reflecting on developments in reading instruction. *Learning Disabilities Forum, 16*(1), 80–91.

Osgood, C. E. (1953). A behavioralistic analysis of perception and language as cognitive phenomena. In S. J. Bruner (Ed.), *Contemporary approaches to cognition.* Cambridge, MA: Harvard University Press.

Pennington, B. F. & Smith, S. D. (1988). Genetic influences on learning disabilities: An update. *Journal of Consulting and Clinical Psychology, 56*(6), 817–823.

Polatajiko, H. J. (1985). A critical look at vestibular dysfunction in learning disabled children. *Developmental medicine and child neurology, 27,* 283–292.

Rabinovitch, R. D. (1962). Dyslexia: Psychiatric considerations. In J. Money (Ed.)., *Reading disability: Progress and research needs in dyslexia.* Baltimore: Johns Hopkins Press.

Richardson, S. O. (1992). Historical perspectives on dyslexia. *Journal of Learning Disabilities. 25*(1), 40–47.

Robinson, G. L., & Conway, R. N. (1990). The effects of Irlen colored lenses on students' specific reading skills and their perception of ability: A 12-month validity study. *Journal of Learning Disabilities, 23,* 589–596.

Robinson, G. L., & Miles, J. (1987). The use of coloured overlays to improve visual processing: A preliminary survey. *The Exceptional Child, 34,* 65–70.

Ross, A. O. (1976). *Psychological aspects of learning disabilities and reading disorders.* New York: McGraw-Hill.

Silver, L. B. (1987). The "magic cure": A review of the current controversial approaches for treating learning disabilities. *Journal of Learning Disabilities, 20*(8), 498–504.

Skinner, B. F. (1938). *The behavior of organisms: An experimental analysis.* New York: Appleton-Century-Crofts.

Skinner, B. F. (1959). *Verbal behavior.* New York: Appleton-Century-Crofts.

Sleeter, C. E. (1986). Learning disabilities: The social construction of a special education category. *Exceptional Children, 53*(1), 46–54.

Smith, C. R. (1991). *Learning disabilities. The interaction of learner, task, and setting* (2nd ed.). Boston: Allyn and Bacon.

Solan, H. A. (1990). An appraisal of the Irlen technique of correcting reading disorders using tinted overlays and tinted lenses. *Journal of Learning Disabilities, 23,* 621–623.

Spalding, R. B., & Spalding, W. (1962). *The writing road to reading.* New York: Morrow.

Sperry, R. W. (1968). Hemisphere deconnection and unity in conscious awareness. *American Psychologist, 23,* 723–733.

Staats, A. (1971). Linguistic-mentalistic theory versus an explanatory S-R learning theory of language development. In D. I. Slobin (Ed.), *The ontogenesis of grammar.* New York: Academic Press.

Stanley, G. (1987). Coloured filters and dyslexia. *Australian Journal of Remedial Education, 19,* 8–9.

Still, G. F. (1902). The coulstonian lectures on some abnormal psychical conditions in children. *Lancet, 1,* pp. 1008–1012, 1077–1082, 1163–1168.

Strauss, A. A., & Kephart, N. C. (1955). *Psychopathol-*

ogy and education of the brain-injured child: Vol. 2, Progress in theory and clinic. New York: Grune & Stratton.

Strauss, A. A., & Lehtinen, L. E. (1947). Psychopathology and education of the brain-injuried child. New York: Grune & Stratton.

Strauss, A. A., & Werner, H. (1942). Disorders of conceptual thinking in the brain injured child. Journal of Nervous and Mental Disease, 96, 153–172.

Taylor, J., Holmes, G., & Walshe, F. M. R. (1931). Selected writings of John Hughlings Jackson. London: Hodder and Stoughton.

Thorpe, H. W., & Borden, K. S. (1985). The effect of multisensory instruction upon the on-task behaviors and word reading accuracy of learning disabled children. Journal of Learning Disabilities, 18, 279–286.

Van den Honert, D. (1977). A neuropsychological technique for training dyslexics. Journal of Learning Disabilities, 10, 15–27.

Vellutino, F. R. (1979). Dyslexia: Theory and research. Cambridge, MA: MIT Press.

Watson, J. B. (1913). Psychology as the behaviorist views it. Psychological Review, 20, 158–177.

Wepman, J. (1967). The perceptual basis for learning. In E. C. Frieson & W. B. Barbe (Eds.), Educating children with learning disabilities. New York: Appleton-Century-Crofts.

Werner, H., & Strauss, A. A. (1941). Pathology of figure-background-relationship in the child. Journal of Abnormal and Social Psychology, 36, 236–248.

Wernicke, C. (1908). The symptom-complex of aphasia. In A. Church (Ed.), Diseases of the nervous system (pp. 265–324). New York: Appleton.

Westman, J. C. (1990). Handbook of learning disabilities. Boston: Allyn and Bacon.

Wiederholt, J. L. (1974). Historical perspectives on the education of the learning disabled. In L. Mann & D. Sabatino (Eds.), The Second Review of Special Education. Philadelphia: Journal of Special Education Press.

Willeford, J. A. & Burleigh, J. M. (1985). Handbook of central auditory processing disorders in children. Orlando, FL: Grune & Stratton.

Winter, S. (1987). Irlen lenses: An appraisal. Australian Educational and Development Psychologist, 4, 1–5.

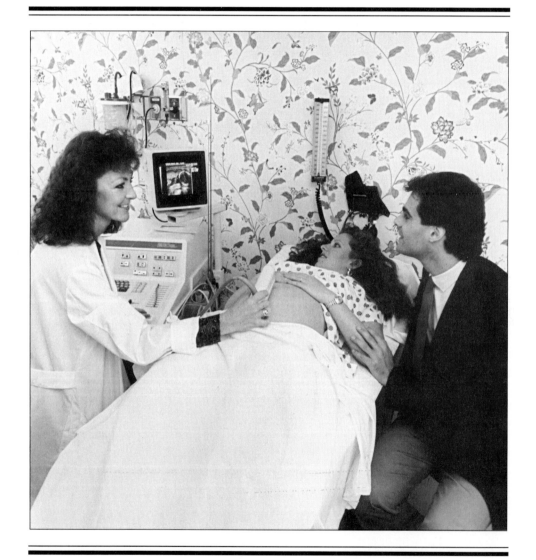

Pertinent prenatal, perinatal, and postnatal events affect a child's learning.

CHAPTER 5

The Biological Model

In this chapter we will discuss . . .

- The historical development of the study of the relationship among genetics, teratogenic agents like drugs and infections, psychostimulants, and toxins on human development and learning.
- The impact of hereditary and familial factors, including genetics and cellular migration.
- Maternal-fetal interactions such as those involving the passage of drugs and infectious diseases through the placenta.
- Fetal factors such as exposure to toxemia and anoxia during birth, and complications during labor.
- The effects of psychostimulant drugs like Ritalin, Dexadrine, and Cylert on hyperactivity and attention.
- Dietary factors such as those presented by Feingold, and their impact on learning.
- The use of megavitamins to overcome metabolic deficiencies.
- The impact of toxins on learning and related skills.

Physicians in the last part of the nineteenth century used their medical knowledge to observe and describe patients experiencing difficulties in communication and adaptive functioning. These physicians wrote of patients' case histories documenting learning problems and medical conditions. (Chapter 4 contains an explanation of how these and many other early- and mid-20th-century physicians began formal medical studies of learning problems and applications to learning processes.) Accordingly, physicians began documenting individuals' disorders of spoken language, written language, and perceptual or motor processes. Wiederholt (1974) suggested that early physicians made concerted efforts to describe patients' behavioral characteristics and to localize specific sensory, perceptual, motor, and language functions to precise brain components. Physicians collected much useful information by describing patients' backgrounds, observing patients' behavioral patterns, and correlating medical and learning data acquired through autopsies at patients' deaths. Professionals continued their search for understanding throughout the mid-20th century, formulating theoretical positions concerning the disorders' etiologies (e.g., Goldstein, 1939, 1942; Strauss & Werner, 1942; Werner & Strauss, 1941).

Importantly, researchers began to associate school-related difficulties with brain damage. Early-20th-century physicians and learning researchers joined forces in associating biological factors with atypical learning and development. Knowledge of the biological link to learning accumulated as the century advanced. Physicians assumed general biological patterns in observable learning problems, as they associated patients' behaviors and developmental skills to general family patterns and learning research (e.g., Fisher, 1905; Hinshelwood, 1911, 1917; Thomas, 1905). By the mid-20th century, studies evolved focusing on neurological and psychoeducational aspects of problem learning and behavior (e.g., Cruickshank, 1972; Frostig, 1965; Kephart, 1960; Strauss & Werner, 1942; Werner & Strauss, 1941). Physicians and medical scientists continued to make important contributions to the fields of biology, chemistry, genetics, and neurology. They found further evidence of aberrant family-learning patterns and offsprings' intraindividual development (e.g., Eustis, 1947; Marshall & Ferguson, 1939). Researchers began documenting familial learning difficulties that purportedly passed down from one generation to the next. Studies focused on genetic and environmental issues relying on families, twins studies, and siblings research (e.g., Hallgren, 1950; Hermann, 1959). These researchers, referred to as *medical behaviorists*, represent learning researchers interested in analyzing specific genetic and genetic-environmental implications of learning processes.

By the latter part of the mid-20th century, *geneticists* (i.e., physicians interested in studying heredity and its variations) and medical behaviorists had gathered more detailed genetic data. Mid-20th-century scientists began associating genetics, prenatal, perinatal and postnatal events (see Figure. 5.1) with attention, memory, retention, motivation, academic performance, ability levels, and social skills (Ladewig, London, & Olds, 1990; McKusick, 1969; Patton, Beime-Smith, & Payne, 1990). They studied congenital word blindness (e.g., Hallgren, 1950), familial patterns in reading disabilities (e.g., Hermann, 1959), and the differential characteristics of twins and their influences on academic achievement gains in language, mathematics, and associated aberrant behaviors (e.g., Jost & Sontag, 1944; Morrison & Stewart, 1973; Nichols & Chen, 1981; Vandenberg, 1966). Some suggested relationships to reading and language problems among relatives of individuals with learning problems;

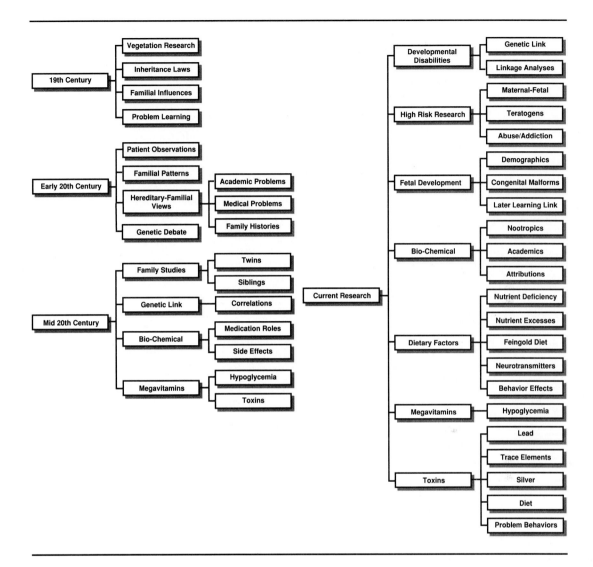

Figure 5.1
Overview of research associated with the biological model

others studied familial associations of mathematical difficulties and family histories of auditory and visual perception problems (e.g., Denckla, 1973; Hallgren, 1950; Hermann, 1959; Jost & Sontag, 1944; Matheny, Dolan, & Wilson, 1976; Morrison & Stewart, 1973; Vandenberg, 1966).

Increased data on intraindividual growth, learning, and development grew from biological discoveries. Geneticists and medical behaviorists suspected maternal-fetal interactions and *teratogenic* factors (i.e., interactive agents affecting a child's prenatal development and posing potential life-long ramifications to exposed individuals). Twentieth-century researchers viewed effects of teratogenic factors as they linked maternal ingestion of toxins (e.g., alcohol, drugs) to later learning or behavioral development (e.g., Greer, 1990; Institute of Medicine, 1985; Ladewig et al., 1990; Westman, 1990). Exposed children were assumed to be at risk for lags in school achievement, attention difficulties, hyperactivity, passive-withdrawal behaviors, extreme variations in ability to get along with others, moral behaviors, or socio-emotional skills. Additionally, researchers reasoned alterations of embryonic development and cerebral malformations (e.g., Geschwind & Bechan, 1982), linking problems in the school, home, and community to children's earliest exposures.

Refinements in genetic-prenatal research by the 1980s and 1990s centered on controversial data regarding fetal development and maternal-fetal interactions (e.g., maternal nutrition, maternal health, fetal diseases, uterine-placenta development, maternal-fetal blood compatibility factors, embryologic development, fetal neural circuitry, fetal neurostructure) (Ladewig et al., 1990; Morrison, 1990). Recently, increased maternal drug use and cocaine addiction set the stage for examining the impact of these risk factors on the developing child (Ladewig et al., 1990; Morrison, 1990; Westman, 1990). Additionally, scientists investigated other factors including the nutrition, health, emotional stability, and safety status of mothers prior to conceiving the fetus.

Further studies on the developing child, such as embryonic studies (e.g., Galaburda, 1989), gestational-neural-behavioral aspects to LD (e.g., Geschwind, 1985; Hynd, Marshall, & Gonzalez, 1991), perinatal demographics (e.g., Abel, 1984; Butler, Goldstein, & Ross, 1972; Hanson, Streissguth, & Smith, 1978; Lovitt, 1989; Smith, 1991; Sparks, 1984; Westman, 1990; Wilson, 1975), biochemical-nutritional influences on learning (e.g., Cott, 1972; Feingold, 1975a; Fishbein & Meduski, 1987), and stimulant medication research (e.g., Allen & Drabman, 1991) all represent modern biological-learning approaches by biologists, neurologists, geneticists, and medical behaviorists viewing risk factors to infants, children, and youth. Most assumed biological connections to learning problems. Importantly then, both fetal and maternal factors, maternal-fetal interactions, and events occurring postnatally to individuals with learning difficulties hold historical significance in understanding the impact of prenatal, perinatal, and postnatal events on learning and development.

EFFECTS OF PRENATAL AND PERINATAL EVENTS ON ATYPICAL LEARNING

Two important research avenues underscore our chronology of the study of pre- and perinatal events on atypical learning. These include data on (a) *individuals hereditary-familial endowments* and (b) *high-risk factors in maternal-fetal interactions*. Researchers suggest a link between genetic and genetic-environmental influences and LD.

Researchers often link biological factors to learning or developmental processes, making two general assumptions (Richardson, 1992; Smith, 1991; Westman, 1990). The first assumption is that biological factors such as genetic makeup hold primary importance to individuals' pathology. Sociocultural factors such as poverty hold secondary importance. For example, brain injury due to asphyxia at birth can be assessed without reference to individuals' sociocultural experiences. Sociocultural factors are critical only when they actually cause the biological symptoms, such as when poverty and ignorance lead to poor diet, smoking, or substance abuse during pregnancy, which in turn causes low birth weight or premature birth (Smith, 1991).

The second assumption concerns interactions of individuals' genetic endowment and prenatal, perinatal, or postnatal events. Events happening within and to individuals have profound effects upon learning and development. There has been great and important controversy over these interactions pertaining to the degree to which genetic and environmental conditions operate to influence individuals' functioning, including LD. Genetics may play important roles in the genesis of some LD, although no one genetic or environmental factor has been proved actually to cause LD.

Individuals' Hereditary-Familial Endowments

Westman (1990) described *gestation* as a period of unequal hazard to human life and health. Gestation is the time when many critical events occur within the developing fetus. Researchers now believe alterations or deviations in critical prenatal events pose life-long ramifications in the form of birth defects, physical deformations, learning difficulties, and/or problem behaviors (Ladewig et al., 1990; Westman, 1990). While not all fetuses will develop abnormalities, such variations may evolve from embryonic-fetal exposure at different, but critical, gestation periods (Morrison, 1990; Sparks, 1984; Westman, 1990). Figure 5.2 illustrates critical prenatal periods and the times when the embryo and fetus are most affected by negative influences.

Additionally, there is substantial evidence to suggest that the prenatal period may influence learning and development as much as, or greater than, the postnatal period (Hynd et al., 1991; Pennington & Smith, 1988; Richardson, 1992; Van Dyke & Fox, 1990; Westman, 1990).

Genetics research involves heredity and its variations, providing historical data on learning and developmental processes. Traditionally, physicians, and medical behaviorists studied *genes* (i.e., the basic biological units carrying inherited physical, mental, or personality traits), *chromosomes* (i.e., the threadlike carriers of genetic material and information-housing genes), and *inheritance patterns* (i.e., familial trends resulting from genetic variations) (Coles, 1987; Kelly, 1975; Ladewig et al., 1990; McKusick, 1969; Morrison, 1990; Patton et al., 1990; Westman, 1990).

Table 5.1 provides basic data on inheritance patterns and genetic aberrations that evolved through historic, genetic research. The study of genes, chromosomes, and inheritance patterns, although complex, has profound influences on associations in hereditary-familial views and learning processes. For example, researchers discovered many inborn errors of metabolism, associated mental disabilities, and assumed problem learning or behaviors resulting from analyses of inheritance patterns (Ladewig et al., 1990; Westman, 1990). Earliest investigators sought to unravel biological foundations of learning, and mid-20th-century researchers attempted to connect genetics and learning research. Late-20th-century researchers continued, with further investigations on learning and refinements in genetic transmissions.

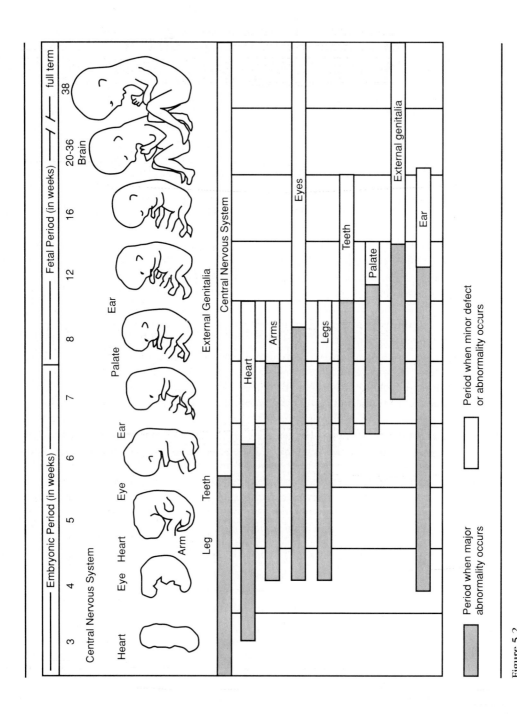

Figure 5.2

Critical prenatal periods and times

Note. From *Before We Are Born* (p. 96), by K. L. Moore and T. V. N. Persaud (Eds.). Copyright 1993 by W. B. Saunders Co., New York.

Table 5.1
Basic Genetic Data on Inheritance Patterns and Genetic Aberrations

Geneticists reported that all hereditary material is carried on tightly coiled strands of DNA known as *chromosomes*. The chromosomes carry the *genes*, the smallest unit of inheritance. Each human cell contains *23 pairs of chromosomes*, with each parent contributing one member of each pair. Human *traits* are transmitted from one generation to the next, according to the makeup of a specific gene pair on a given chromosomal pair. Individuals' many specific characteristics can be traced to the presence or absence of a single gene. Pairs of genes carrying the same trait are called *homozygous*; pairs carrying different traits are called *heterozygous*.

Many inherited diseases are produced by an abnormality in a single gene or pair of genes. Each single-gene trait is determined by a pair of genes working together. These genes are responsible for the observable expression of the trait, referred to as the *phenotype* (e.g., brown eyes, dark skin). The total genetic makeup of an individual is referred to as the *genotype* (i.e., chromosomal structure). One of the genes for a trait is inherited from the mother, the other from the father. An individual who has two indentical genes at a given locus is considered to be *homozygous* for that trait. An individual is considered to be *heterozygous* for a particular trait when he or she has two different *alleles* (i.e., alternate forms of the same gene) at a given locus on a pair of chromosomes. Genetic transmission processes link to familial traits, locations, aberrent genes, and metabolic processes.

Two modes of genetic transmission historically explain major gene effects on problem learning or behaviors. These include *single-gene disorders* and *polygenetic* disorders. The well-known modes of single-gene inheritance are autosomal dominant, autosomal recessive, and X-linked (sex-linked) recessive. There is also an X-linked dominant mode of inheritance that is less common, and a newly identified mode of inheritance, the fragile-X syndrome.

The group of *single-gene disorders* have three basic patterns: autosomal dominant, autosomal recessive, and sex-linked. *Autosomes* represent the 22 matched pairs of chromosomes. *Dominant* implies an inheritance in which an individual gene has control of or can mask the other gene in the pair. *Recessive* are inherited traits that do not express themselves when paired with dominant genes and are influential only when matched with another identical recessive gene. *Sex-linked patterns* relate to the pair of chromosomes determining fetal sex. Although many individuals with sex-linked abnormalities have mental disabilities, some reportedly have LD.

Individuals are born with a clearly established genetic disorder inherited as *dominant* when neither parent has any of the features of that disorder. The individual matures and produces children, some of whom may have the same dominant disorder. If the disorder is to be transmitted from parent to child, the effect of the disorder on the parent is such that it does not preclude that individual from reaching adulthood and reproducing. Dominantly inherited disorders are, therefore, usually milder than recessive or sex-linked disorders. While not specifically associated with LD, dominantly inherited disorders often turn up in students with mild problems. For example, dominantly inherited disorders can result in structural deficits (e.g., cleft lip, club foot, congenital heart disease) rather than more seriously influential metabolic abnormalities (e.g., phenyketonuria: PKU).

Structural defects are usually recognizable at birth or in early infancy. Such defects are congenital as opposed to developing later in life. An example is achondroplasia, a dominantly inherited disorder of skeletal growth characterized by dwarfed legs and arms, large head, and depressed nose. The general health, well-being, and intelligence of individuals with achondroplasia often are unimpaired, although mild problems may result. For example, because the major disability is short stature, the individual may have few learning difficulties. However, the individual may have to face attending social problems as a result of physical appearance. Mental disabilities occurring as part of the dominantly inherited disorder are usually mild, resulting from the structural brain alteration.

(continued)

Table 5.1 *continued*

Recessive inheritance patterns contain a *recessive gene*, one whose presence, as the only member of a gene pair, does not result in a recognizable trait. If both members of the gene pair are similarly involved, a *recessively inherited trait* occurs. Thus, when each parent has one gene of the pair which is abnormal and their child received the defective gene from both parents, a recessive disorder results. However, it is only when both parents have a mutation of the same gene that a disorder may occur in their child. Examples of recessive disorders with familial-ethnic implications are Tay-Sachs, evident in Jewish families; cystic fibrosis, prevalent among northern European families; and sickle cell disease, common to African-American families.

Sex-linked or X-linked inheritance patterns. Sex-linked or X-linked inheritance patterns are associated with *defective genes on the X chromosomes.* The name derives from a variety of recessive traits carried on the X chromosome. Hence, a father passes on his X chromosome to daughters, and his Y to sons, resulting in an X chromosome with a defective gene given to all daughters and to no sons of such a man. This lack of male to male transmission represents X-linked inheritance patterns including conditions such as hemophilia, color blindness, Lesch-Nyhan syndrome, and Duchenne muscular dystrophy. There is no definitive association between these conditions and LD.

Polygenetic is the second mode of transmission. It reflects multifactorial traits: the combined effects of genetic factors acting in concert with prenatal factors. *Multifactorial inheritance problems* result from genes acting on the uterine environment during fetal development. *Traits* appear as a result of the combined influence of genes and environmental factors, and are therefore, multifactorial. Certain birth defects, assuming multifactorial inheritance, include cleft lip and/or cleft palate. When a *birth defect occurs as part of a syndrome* (i.e., associated with other birth defects), it is often caused by a single, mutated, *aberrant gene.* When it occurs as a single event with no other birth defect, then *multifactorial inheritance* has been found to be the likely causation.

Note. Adapted from *Essentials of Maternal-Newborn Nursing*, 2nd edition, by Laedwig, London, & Olds. Copyright © 1990 by Addison-Wesley Nursing. Reprinted by permission. Also adapted from *Handbook of Learning Disabilities*, by J. C. Westman. Copyright © 1990 by Allyn and Bacon, Boston.

Early and Recent Hereditary-Familial Views

Genetic studies initially came into scientific focus around the mid-nineteenth century (McKusick, 1969). George Mendel was the first scientist to describe the basic laws of inheritance based on his work with fruits and vegetables in the 1850s (Kelly, 1975). It wasn't until familial patterns were associated with LD, surfacing around the time of Hinshelwood's work in the 1890s, that many physicians began connecting human genetics, medical problems, and learning patterns (Hinshelwood, 1911). Early-twentieth-century physicians documented written reports on their patients' difficulties, while assuming familial influences passed down from one generation to the next. Mid-twentieth-century geneticists and medical behaviorists also linked genetics and familial problems. Researchers, then, observed and described detailed problems in behavior, language, reading, and mathematics as they documented patients' medical problems and family histories (e.g., Connors, 1970; Finucci, Guthrie, Childs, Abbey, & Childs, 1976; Goody & Reinhold, 1961; Hallgren, 1950; Morrison & Stewart, 1974; Symmes & Rapoport, cited in Coles, 1987).

Today, data are accumulating on the role of learning processes and genetic transmissions, family traits, potential LD chromosomes, and inborn errors of metabolism. Mid-20th-century scientists helped to detect the patterns of inheritance through a process called *karyotyping,* or use of photographic pictures of human chromosomes. This process continues today. Researchers enlarge pictures, cut out chromosomes, and chart from the largest (pair 1) to the smallest (pair 23). In this manner, they can locate a number of chromosomal errors, chromosomal imbalances, and inborn errors of metabolic processes. Associated disabilities traditionally appear through karyotyping (Ladewig et al., 1990; McKusick, 1969). Figure 5.3 illustrates data on human genetics specifying the 46 human chromosomes that evolved from these earliest research attempts.

Additionally, mid-20th-century scientists discovered a number of sex-chromosome abnormalities—that is, cases where individuals have more X or Y chromosomes than usual. Many of the conditions are associated with various impairments, the extent of which is dependent on the type of abnormality and various contributing factors, including familial traits and location of aberrant genes (Ladewig et al., 1990; Westman, 1990). Currently, much is still unknown about the role of hereditary-familial progression. Many of these historical data generate continued controversy in learning research Table 5.2 shows basic data on altered-chromosome genetic defects and incidence, and resulting characteristics in family members.

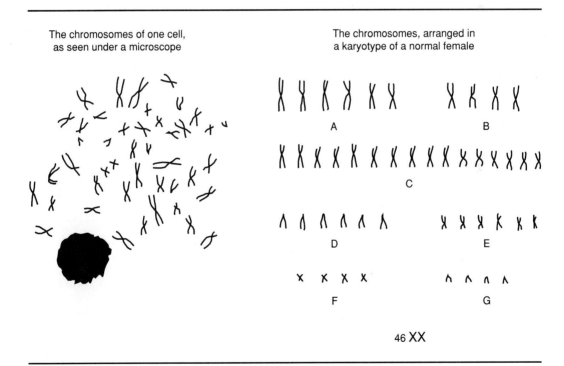

The chromosomes of one cell, as seen under a microscope

The chromosomes, arranged in a karyotype of a normal female

46 XX

Figure 5.3
Data on human genetics specifying the 46 chromosomes
Note. From "The Role of Genetic Mechanisms in Childhood Handicaps," by T. E. Kelly, 1996, in R.H.A. Haslam & P. J. Valletutti (Eds.), *Medical Problems in the Classroom,* 3rd ed. (pp. 193–216). Baltimore: University Park Press.

Table 5.2

Basic Data on Altered-Chromosome Genetic Defects and Incidence, and Resulting Characteristics

Altered Chromosomes	Potential Genetic Defect and Incidence	Characteristics	
21	Trisonomy 21 (Down's syndrome); 1 in 700 lives	Central Nervous System: Mental Retardation	
		Head:	Flattened
			Depressed nasal bridge
			Slant of eyes
			White speckling of the iris (Brushfield spots)
			Protrusion of the tongue
			High, arched palate
			Low-set ears
			Broad, short fingers
		Hands:	Short fingers
			Abnormalities of finger and foot
			Dermal ridge patterns (dermatoglyphics)
			Transverse palmar crease (simian line)
		Other:	Congenital heart disease
21	2 (Down's syndrome); 1%	Classic symptoms as described in trisomy 21 except that the child has normal intelligence	
18	Trisomy 18; 1 in 3000 live births	CNS:	Mental retardation
			Severe hypertonia
		Head:	Low-set ears
			Corneal opacities
			Ptosis (drooping of eyelids)
		Hands:	Third and fourth fingers overlapped by second and fifth fingers
			Abnormal dermatiglyphics
			Webbing of fingers
		Other:	Congenital heart defects
			Renal abnormalities
			Single umbilical artery
			Gastrointestinal tract abnormalities
			Rocker-bottom feet
			Various malformations of other organs
18	Deletion of long arm of chromosomes 18	CNS:	Severe psychomotor retardation
		Head:	Microcephaly
			Stenotic ear canals with conductive hearing loss
		Other:	Various other organ malformations
13	Trisomy 13; 1 in 500 live births	CNS:	Mental Retardation
			Seizures
		Head:	Microcephaly
			Malformed ears

(continued)

Table 5.2   *continued*

Altered Chromosomes	Potential Genetic Defect and Incidence		Characteristics
			Aplasia of external auditory canal
			Cleft lip and palate
		Hands:	Extra digits
			Abnormal posturing of fingers
		Other:	Congenital heart defects
			Gastrointestinal tract defects
			Various malformations of other organs
5	Deletion of short arm of chromosome 5	CNS:	Severe mental retardation
		Head:	Microcephaly
			Low-set ears
		Other:	Failure to thrive
			Various organ malformations
X (sex chromosome)	Only one X chromosome in female (Turner syndrome); 1 in 300 to 7000 live female births	CNS:	No intellectual impairment
			Some perceptual difficulties
		Head:	Low hairline
			Webbed neck
		Trunk:	Short stature
			Increased carrying angle of arm
			Broad shieldlike chest with widely spaced nipples
			Puffy feet
			No toenails
		Other:	Fibrous streaks in ovaries
			Underdeveloped secondary sex characteristics primary amenorrhea
			Usually infertile
			Renal anomalies
			Coarctation of the aorta
X	Extra X in male (Klinefelter syndrome); 1 in 1000 live male births, approx. 1–2% of institutionalized males	CNS:	Mild mental retardation
		Trunk:	Occasional gynecomastia
			Eunchoid body proportions
		Other:	Small, soft testes
			Underdeveloped secondary sex characteristics
			Usually sterile

Note. From *Essentials of Maternal-Newborn Nursing*, 2nd edition, by P. W. Ladewig, M. L. London, & S. B. Olds. (pp. 118–119). Copyright © 1990 by Addison-Wesley Nursing. Reprinted by permission.

Genetic Controversies in LD Research

Coles (1987) argued traditional researchers in family studies had hoped to identify intergenerational patterns of academic problems that would reveal particular modes of genetic transmission. If LD originate from individuals' biology, and if LD also appear often in families, the condition could be expected to originate in the genes. However, the appearance of problem learning also could be due to some unique environmental factors that family members shared (Bijou, 1971). Thus, early controversies in family research centered on the degree of influence and nature of genetic and environmental factors.

The traditional means to explore heredity-environmental questions have been to study twins and siblings in attempts to control for genetic and enviromental influences. If by comparing monozygotic (identical) twins with dizygotic (fraternal) twins who had essentially equal experiences and environmental conditions, a greater concordance of characteristics between monozygotic than between dizygotic twins could be attributed to genetic influences. The rationale evolved because identical twins have identical genes and fraternal twins share roughly 50% of theirs (Coles, 1987; Westman, 1990). Sibling research also followed the rationale of factoring genetic and environmental influences. Table 5.3 describes a chronology of family, twins, and sibling research based on mid-twentieth-century to current research.

Linkage Analyses.   Family involvement patterns and twin studies associating with learning difficulties historically generated controversy between those arguing genetic influences and those favoring environmental basis. Researchers could only assume causal relationships between learning and genetics or genetic-environmental interactions. Applied to atypical learning, the controversy centered on etiological assumptions of observable data patterns in families, and then to predicting or explaining offsprings' academic problems.

While scientists have uncovered many genetic mysteries, current geneticists and medical behaviorists also rely on statistical devices in the form of linkage analyses. In using linkage analyses, scientists attempt to associate genetic factors and specific LD (Pennington & Smith, 1988). The linkage analyses rationale is that the closer two genes on a chromosome are located to each other, the more frequently they are assumed to be inherited together. Genes located further apart on the same or on separate chromosomes are more likely to be transmitted to offspring randomly. Users try to locate LD genes by determining whether or not problem learning coexists with other traits or markers whose genetic origins are known already.

Smith (1991) reported that because genes that lie close together on the same chromosome tend to be inherited as a unit (rather than splitting), individuals with LD sharing a known genetic marker (e.g., blood type, enzyme) may have their LD genes lying on the same chromosome as that marker. However, Coles (1987) suggested traditional flaws in the reasoning of using linkage analyses to determine LD genesis. As in historical family studies, researchers still rely on correlations. Though the correlations are statistically sophisticated, scientists cannot assume causal relationships to etiologies when using such correlational analyses.

Cellular Migration.   Late-twentieth-century researchers continued to link genetics and developmental maturation factors (e.g., Connors, 1970; Finucci et al., 1976; Safer

Table 5.3
A Chronology of Family, Twins, and Sibling Research

Year	Researcher(s)	Finding(s)
1950	Hallgren	Ascertained general learning difficulties in reading, mathematics, and language of fraternal and identical twins. Reported a high prevalence of reading and language problems among relatives of individuals with learning problems: reported 41% related to first-degree relatives.
1959	Hermann	Analyzed dyslexia from medical orientation, viewing "word blindness." Compared nonreading identical twins to fraternal twins in which at least one member displayed problem reading. Reported when problem reading was documented, identical twins were involved more than fraternal twins. Concluded reading, spelling, and writing disabilities have genetic bases.
1961	Goody & Reinhold	Reported on the associations of family history of tone deafness, mirror writing, and mathematical difficulties appearing in various combinations among family members.
1970	Connors	Traced the history of reading disabilities through family analyses. Reviewed shared incidence factors among children with learning difficulties and their family members. Analyzed clinical and genetic assumptions.
1971	Owens	Studied parents and siblings. Parents of students with problem learning had poorer adult reading abilities and high school English grades than did control parents. Siblings shared similar learning difficulties; control siblings tended not to display problem learning.
1972	Symmes & Rapoport	Found "unexpected reading failure" in middle-class children. Assumed genetic basis.
1985	Vogler, DeFries & Decker	Reported that the risk of affected father with LD to son is 40%, while the risk of affected mother to son is 35%.
1985	Finucci, Guthrie, Childs, Abbey, & Childs	Reported that sons tend to be affected by learning problems more than daughters; brothers tend to be affected more than sisters.
1986	Harris	Found fraternal twins' reading levels very similar 20 to 50% of the time. Reported reading achievement of one identical twin can predict that of another about 75 to 85% of the time.
1987	Vellutino	Viewed genetic, sex-linked basis for dyslexia. Found four times as many males as females with problem reading.
1988	Pennington & Smith	Reported twins studies can be used to specify what inheritable LD entails. Underlying deficits relate to difficulties in family members' specific skills that seemingly are genetically transmitted (i.e., reading recognition, spelling, digit span, phonological coding, and phoneme segmentation). A deficit in phonological coding, not orthographic awareness (visual skills) is inherited, occurring through multiple routes.

& Allen, 1973). They focused their attention on analyzing hereditary-familial factors related to developing brains and the maturation process. For example, Geschwind and Behan (1982) advanced the embryological theory linking individuals' handedness, immune system diseases, and LD. These researchers theorized that neurons of the cerebral cortex are not actually formed in that brain area. They argued that before the 21st gestational week, neurons develop in a central area of the brain, then migrate to final positions in the cortex. Geschwind and Behan contended that in the normal brain the right hemisphere develops 1 to 2 weeks earlier than the left. They reasoned that an unusual surge of the hormone testosterone before the 31st gestational week influences the fetal brain of individuals with LD. Due to excess testosterone levels, left hemisphere growth could be delayed, while the right hemisphere remains unaffected (Geschwind & Behan, 1982). The migration of immature neurons in the left hemisphere would be arrested, thus causing abnormalities observed in brains of individuals with LD. In individuals with learning difficulties, the researchers hypothesized that developmental asymmetry causes the right temporal region to develop earlier and the left to become larger.

Hynd and Semrud-Clikeman (1989) reiterated that neurological anomaly patterns of many subjects are most likely due to deviations in the neurodevelopmental process some time during the 5th to 7th month of fetal development. Hynd et al., (1991) reported some unidentified factor appears to be altering both the normal process of cellular migration and neuron placement during fetal development and brain asymmetry. Other researchers also suggested that brain asymmetry occurs prenatally (Witelson & Kigar, 1988; Witelson & Pallie, 1973). While currently there is no evidence suggesting that the brains of individuals with LD are characterized by brain damage or lesions associated with the postnatal period, there appears to be a relationship existing between deviations in neurological development, neurological anomalies, and the specific symptoms shared by divergent behavioral syndromes (Hynd et al., 1991).

Many recent controversies also relate to investigations on gestational migration of neurons to specific brain sites. For example, advocates suggested that during each developmental phase, beginning with fetal development, genetic messages result in chemicals that attach to specific brain receptors, stimulating growth in that particular area (Hynd et al., 1991; Hynd & Semrud-Clikeman, 1989; Pennington & Smith, 1988; Smith, 1991; Westman, 1990). Researchers also suggested that different brain structures, diverse patterns of brain maturation, biochemical irregularities, or susceptibility to diseases impairing brain functioning may be transmitted genetically (e.g., Hynd et al., 1991; Hynd & Semrud-Clikeman, 1989; Smith, 1991; Westman, 1990).

High-Risk Factors in Maternal-Fetal Interactions

Mid-20th-century researchers refined genetic research by studying high-risk factors in maternal-fetal interactions. Earliest attempts, beginning in approximately the 1930s, marked scientific efforts to isolate developmental factors influencing the growing fetus (Westman, 1990). Historically, researchers sought maternal factors and environmental conditions believed to influence infants' chances for survival and healthy diagnoses in later life. Throughout the twentieth century, researchers dis-covered many variables that place prenatal infants (i.e., neonates) at high risk for later development (Scipien, Chard, Howe, & Barnard, 1990). Other factors indicating high-risk status to neonates included the mother's previous obstetrics history and health practices, social factors, and paternal factors (Morrison, 1990; Scipien et al., 1990). Basically, the mother's health and the care afforded to her during her preg-nancy provided the groundwork for many mid-twentieth-century studies. Table 5.4 identifies factors associated with fetal neonatal risks.

Researchers began to single out teratogenic factors as specific agents producing or raising the incidence of congenital malformations in humans, (e.g., including some LD) (Thompson & Thompson, 1980).

Early Teratogenic Research

Professionals began to recognize maternal influences on children's later develop-ment about the time of the Great Depression in the United States. Prenatal and well baby programs throughout the twentieth century provided comprehensive preven-tative and wellness treatment services for families and children experiencing health problems, social behaviors, and school or community difficulties. Program evalua-tion data from these and other projects purportedly linked maternal interactions in prenatal events to neonatal congenital malformations (Connors, 1970; Finucci et al., 1976; Galaburda, 1989; Hynd & Semrud-Clikeman, 1989; Pennington & Smith, 1988; Vogler, DeFries, & Decker, 1985).

Table 5.4 Factors Associated with Fetal Neonatal Risk	I. Exposure to teratogenic substances: Accutane (A popular antiacne drug) Alcohol Amphetamines Aspirin Caffeine Chemicals Diazepam (Valium) Diethylstilbestrol (DES) (counteracts effects of morning sickness) Heroin Nicotine Pesticides Thalidomide (counteracts effects of morning sickness) II. Exposure to radiation III. RH blood incompatibility between mother and child IV. Congenital rubella syndrome V. Inadequate maternal nutrition VI. Inappropriate maternal weight gain

Drugs

While it is now known that nearly all substances taken by the mother during pregnancy transfer across the placenta to the fetus (Sparks, 1984), data into the nature of specific influences has amassed only recently. Originally researchers believed that the placenta acted as a barrier to keep ingested drugs from reaching the fetal system (Westman, 1990). Mid-20th-century researchers began detailing the association between maternal drug abuse, including alcohol and nicotine, and resulting birth defects (e.g., Abel, 1984; Denson et al., 1975; Dunn, McBurney, Ingram, & Hunter, 1977; Ladewig et al., 1990; Sparks, 1984; Wilson, 1975). Researchers began reporting more devastating data including the association of teratogenic agents and physical malformations, growth deficiency, death, and/or functional deficits in learning and behavior (Wilson, 1975). For example, Ladewig et al., (1990) reported on many traditional studies in which scientists determined effects recognizing alcohol as a prime neurobehavioral teratogen.

The degree to which a drug is passed to the fetus depends on the drug's chemical properties, including molecular weight, and on whether it is administered alone or in combination with other drugs (Ladewig et al., 1990; Morrison, 1990). Morrison (1990) suggested that alcohol, amphetamines, aspirin, caffeine, nicotine, and Valium all pose different dangers to the developing child. Greer (1990) suggested significant

Events such as prolonged labor, difficult delivery, induced labor, oxygen deprivation, placenta separation, premature birth, maternal or infant hemorrhage, low birth weight, and low gestational age all reportedly correlate with children's later difficulties.

teratogenic effects on infants exposed prenatally to cocaine and hallucinogens. The exposed fetus is at increased risk for congenital malformations and birthing difficulties. Other researchers suggested that infants exposed to teratogens intrauterinely tend to appear physiologically unable to respond to their care givers. Compared with nonexposed infants, these infants often display depressed interactive abilities. Affected babies reportedly are easily disturbed, difficult to control, and unable to provide positive feedback.

Accumulated data on *alcohol*-related birth defects (Abel, 1984; Hanson et al., 1978; Rosett, 1980) have suggested that elevated correlations can be found for maternal alcohol consumption and perinatal and postnatal growth impairments, later developmental delays, intellectual impairments, and physical deformities. Other perinatal researchers have correlated prenatal exposure to alcohol and brain involvement in the form of infants' decreased cerebellar weight, decreased total brain weight, and functional development of the auditory pathway in the brain stem. Researchers suggesting neurobehavioral effects did find that functional difficulties were usually produced at lower levels of drug exposure than those required to produce physical malformations (Office of Policy Research and Improvement, 1990; Westman, 1990).

Cocaine use in pregnancy also sharply increased during the 1980s (Ladewig et al., 1990). Indiscriminate drug use during pregnancy, particularly in the first trimester, may adversely affect the mother's health and the growth and development of her fetus. Unfortunately, a majority of current drug-abusing women are malnourished. They receive little or no prenatal care (Ladewig et al., 1990; Morrison, 1990; Westman, 1990). Further, cocaine causes maternal circulation problems and increased blood pressure. This has been found to increase a woman's risk of spontaneous abortion in the first or second trimester. It reportedly leads to higher risks in the third trimester including increased uterine contractibility, placenta separation, and increased meconium staining (e.g., fetal ingestion of embryonic fluids and fetal wastes during delivery) (Morrison, 1990; Westman, 1990). Table 5.5 provides possible effects of selected drugs of abuse and addiction on the developing fetus and child.

An important and continuing perinatal consequence of maternal substance abuse during pregnancy is infants' *low birth weight.* Thus, despite recent medical advances, drug-exposed babies are more likely to be born prematurely and have low birth weight, dramatically raising their risk of infant mortality and childhood disability. Many low-birth-weight babies display neurodevelopmental disabilities during or shortly after birth, including cerebral palsy and seizure disorders. These children continue to be susceptible to initial-bonding, feeding, and respiratory problems. Westman (1990) provided continued supporting evidence for perinatal influences and prematurity risks, suggesting that premature infants are particularly at risk for abnormal neurological soft signs, hyperkinetic behaviors, and psychological abnormalities. Finally, perinatal factors put families of babies with low birth weight in emotional and financial crises. As historical studies have confirmed, perinatal factors are significant to the child's learning and development.

Table 5.5
Drugs and Pregnancy

Drug	Potential Effects
Alcohol	Risk of FAS (Fetal Alcohol Syndrome) increases with average daily maternal alcohol intake.
Amphetamines	Excess of oral clefts found in offspring of mothers who took amphetamines in first 56 days from last menstrual period.
Aspirin	Ingestion in late stages of pregnancy is associated with low birth weight, increased incidence of stillbirth and neonatal death, increased length of pregnancy, prolonged labor, increased incidence of antepartum and postpartum bleeding. FDA has issued a strong warning against the use of aspirin during the last three months of pregnancy.
Caffeine	Excessive intake may influence spontaneous abortion or perinatal death.
Nicotine	Increase of early fetal death found due to premature delivery, lower birth weight, lower heart rate, and breathing difficulties.
Diazepam (Valium)	Ingestion in first trimester of pregnancy is associated with frequency of cleft lip with or without cleft palate.

Note. Adapted from *The World of Child Development* by G.S. Morrison, 1990, Albany, NY: Delmar.

Maternal Infections

Ladewig and his peers (1990) found that maternal infections—including urinary tract, vaginal and sexually transmitted—reportedly put pregnancies at risk. Prenatal exposure corroborated traditional observations of perinatal and postnatal functional impairment and offsprings' abnormal behaviors. Table 5.6 illustrates historic infection studies assumed to put the fetus at risk.

Children exposed prenatally to teratogenic influences have increased risks academically, behaviorally, medically, and socially. Maternal abuse and addiction set the stage for children's problems in attention, memory, retention, social skills, and academics. Many children face potential failures in the home, school, and community. Alarming reports continue on attention to pregnant women. For example, women with substance abuse problems who did seek help during pregnancy reportedly could not get it. Two-thirds of the hospitals reporting in the National Select Committee on Children, Youth and Families (NSCCYF) surveyed reported that they had no treatment place to refer substance-abusing, pregnant women (Office of Policy Research and Improvement, 1990). Additionally, many hospitals identified growing numbers of "boarder babies" who remain hospitalized because both parents abandoned or could not care for them. These prenatally exposed children undoubtedly will continue to represent potential candidates for special education or social and health care services. Negative trends must be reversed.

Table 5.6

Infections That Put Pregnancy at Risk

Condition and Etiology	Signs and Symptoms	Intervention	Implications for Pregnancy
URINARY TRACT INFECTIONS Asymptomatic bacteriuria (ASB)	Bacteria present in urine on culture, with no accompanying symptoms.	Drugs: Oral sulfonamides early in pregnancy, ampicillin and nitrofurantoin (Furadantin) in late pregnancy.	Women with ASB in early pregnancy may go on to develop cystitis by third trimester if not treated. Oral sulfonamides taken in the last few weeks of pregnancy may lead to neonatal difficulties.
Cystitis (lower UTI): Causative organisms same as ASB.	Dysuria, urgency, frequency, low-grade fever. Urine culture (clean catch) shows leukocyte increases. More bacteria per mL urine.	Same.	If not treated, infection may ascend and lead to acute problems.
Acute pyelonephritis: causative organisms same as ASB.	Sudden onset. Chills, high fever, flank pain. Nausea, vomiting, malaise. May have decreased urine output, severe colicky pain, dehydration. Marked bacteria in urine culture.	Hospitalization; IV antibiotic therapy. Other antibiotics safe during pregnancy include carbenicillin, methanamine, cephalosporins. Catheterization if output is decreasing. Supportive therapy for comfort. Follow-up urine cultures are necessary.	Increased risk of premature delivery.
VAGINAL INFECTIONS monilial (yeast infection) Candida albicans	Often thick, white, curdy discharge; severe itching. Diagnosis based on presence of spores in a wet-mount preparation of vaginal secretions.	Intravaginal insertion of miconazole or clotrimazole suppositories at bedtime for 1 week. Cream may be prescribed for topical application to the vulva if necessary.	If the infection is present at birth and the fetus is born vaginally, the fetus may contract thrush.
Bacterial vaginosis: Gardnerella vaginalis	Thin, watery, yellow-gray discharge with foul odor often described as "fishy." Wet-mount preparation reveals "clue cells." Application of potassium hydroxide to a specimen of vaginal secretions produces a pronounced fishy odor.	Nonpregnant women treated with metronidazole (Flagyl). Pregnant women treated with ampicillin, at least during first half of pregnancy.	Metronidazole has potential teratogenic effects.
Trichomoniasis: Trichomonais vaginalis	May have frothy greenish gray vaginal discharge, urinary symptoms. Strawberry patches may be visible on vaginal walls or cervix.	During early pregnancy, symptoms may be controlled with clotrimazole vaginal suppositories. Both partners are treated.	Clotrimazole has potential teratogenic effects.

(continued)

Table 5.6 *continued*

Condition and Etiology	Signs and Symptoms	Intervention	Implications for Pregnancy
SEXUALLY TRANSMITTED INFECTIONS Chlamydial infection: Chlamydia trachomatis	Women are often asymptomatic. Symptoms may include thin discharge, burning and frequency with urination, or lower abdominal pain. Lab test available to detect monoclonal antibodies specific for Chlamydia.	Although nonpregnant women are treated with tetracycline, it may permanently discolor fetal teeth. Thus, pregnant women are treated with erythromycin ethyl succinate.	Infant of woman with untreated chlamydial infection may develop newborn conjunctivitis, which can be treated with erythromycin eye ointment (not silver nitrate). Infant may also develop chlamydial pneumonia. May be responsible for premature labor and fetal death.
Syphilis: Treponema pallidum, a spirochete	Primary stage: chancre, slight fever, malaise. Chancre lasts about 4 weeks, then disappears. Secondary stage: occurs 6 weeks to 6 months after infection. Skin eruptions; also symptoms of acute arthritis, liver enlargement, chronic sore throat with hoarseness. Diagnosed by blood tests. Dark field examination for spirochetes may also be done.	For syphilis less than 1 year in duration: 2.4 million U benzathine penicillin G IM. For syphilis of more than 1 year's duration: 2.4 million U benzathine penicillin G once a week for 3 weeks.	Syphilis can be passed transplacentally to the fetus. If untreated, one of the following can occur; second trimester abortion, stillborn infant at term, congenitally infected infant, uninfected live infant.
Gonnorhea: Neisseria gonorrhoeae	Majority of woman are asymptomatic; disease often diagnosed during routine prenatal cervical culture. If symptoms are present they may include vaginal discharge, urinary frequency, inflammation and swelling of the vulva. Cervix may appear eroded.	Nonpregnant women are treated with tetracycline. Pregnant women are treated with penicillin. If the woman is allergic to penicillin, spectinomycin is used. The sexual partner is also treated.	Infection at time of birth may cause ophthalmia neonstorum in the newborn.
Condyloma accuminata: caused by human papiloma virus (HPV)	Soft, grayish-pink lesions on the vulva, vagina, cervix, or anus.	Podophyllin not used during pregnancy. Trichloroacetic acid, liquid nitrogen, or cryocautery; laser therapy done under colposcopy is also successful.	Possible teratogenic effect of podophyllin. Large doses have been associated with fetal death.

Note. Adapted from *Essentials of Maternal-Newborn Nursing*, 2nd edition, by P. W. Ladewig, M. L. London, & S. B. Olds. Copyright © 1990 by Addison-Wesley Nursing. Reprinted by permission.

PERINATAL EVENTS AND ATYPICAL LEARNING

Perinatal events appear to influence individuals' subsequent learning or behavioral development. Perinatal events relate to conditions *during the delivery process*, especially those occurring directly to the infant and/or with maternal interactions, and equally important, *the periods of reactivity immediately following birth*. These include wake and sleep states entailing times of: (a) reactivity (e.g., in which most newborns are alert with periods of vigorous activity, the eyes are open and a strong sucking reflex is present; bonding and breast feeding initiate), (b) inactivity (a quiet phase characterized by sleep), and (c) reactivity (characterized by variability in behavioral responses; bowel sounds increase, feeding initiates). Additionally, at the end of the first 8 hours, most newborns achieve a state of equilibrium after successfully transitioning from the intrauterine to external environments (Morrison, 1990). Historically, scientists did not view perinatal events in learning research. However, infants' demographic data have been collected since the mid-20th century. Table 5.7 shows current vital statistics for the average newborn.

Pasamanick and Knoblock (1960) reviewed newborn records reporting a significantly higher incidence of maternal complications during pregnancy and delivery. They factored variables into maternal demographics. Colligan (1974) later confirmed these perinatal findings in analyzing the effects of toxemia and anoxia (i.e., diminished oxygen supply). Researchers also documented the deleterious effects of prolonged labor, difficult delivery, and/or induced labor on children's later learning problems or potential learning disability (e.g., Birch, 1971; Colligan, 1974; Pasamanick & Knoblock, 1960).

Prematurity

The relationship among gestational age, weight, and mortality is significant for newborns. Since the mid-1970s, prematurity reportedly is a significant cause of infant mortality and/or later problem learning and behaviors (Abel, 1984; Morrison, 1990; Sparks, 1984; Wilson, 1975). Morrison (1990) differentiated newborn birthing terminology suggesting *prematurity* (i.e., born before 37 weeks gestation, conception to

Table 5.7
Average Neonatal Vital Statistics at Birth

Height (length)	
Males	19.9 in.
Females	19.6 in.
Weight	
Males	7.21 lb
Females	7.12 lb
Temperature	97.5–99°F
Heart rate (pulse)	120–160 beats per minute
Head circumference	14 in.
Eye color	Blue or slate gray

Note. Adapted from *The World of Child Development: Conception to Adolescence* p. 193, by G. S. Morrison, 1990. Albany, NY: Delmar.

37 weeks); *term* (born between 38 and 42 weeks gestation—start of week 38 through week 42) and *postterm* (born after 42 weeks gestation). Premature infants have a propensity for: (a) respiratory problems (e.g., inability of the lungs to fill easily with air; increased respiratory effort and higher oxygen use; and apnea, or the cessation of breathing for 20 to 30 seconds); (b) problems with body temperature maintenance (e.g., heat loss due to little insulation from subcutaneous fat developed prenatally); and (c) digestive problems (e.g., inability to ingest and absorb the calories and nutrients needed for growth; poorly developed sucking reflex limiting the ability to intake nutrition orally) (Ladewig et al., 1990). Figure 5.4 illustrates preterm, term, and postterm relationships for weight and mortality.

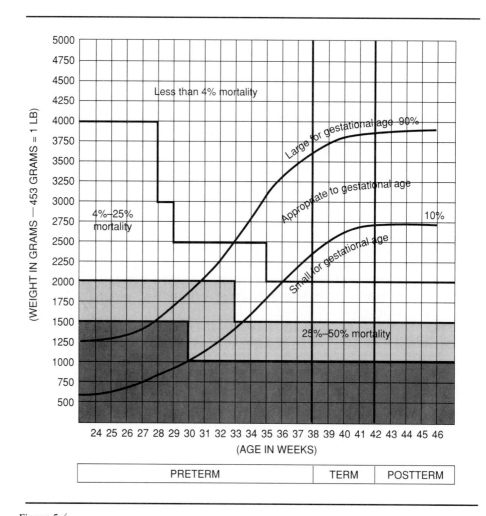

Figure 5.4
Relationship of both weight and mortality.
Note. From *The World of Child Development: Conception to Adolescence*, by C. S. Morrison, 1990, Albany, NY: Delmar.

Table 5.8
The Apgar Scale

Characteristic	0	1	2
Heart rate	Not detectable	Slow—below 100 beats/minute	100-140 beats/minute
Respiratory effort	Infant is apneic	Shallow breathing	Regular breathing; lusty crying
Muscle tone	Completely flaccid infant	Weak, inactive	Flexed arms and legs; resists extension
Reflex irritability: (stimulation of soles of feet)	No reaction	Grimace	Cry
Color	Blue, pale	Body pink, extremities blue	Entirely pink

Source: From "A Proposal for a New Method of Evaluation of the Newborn Infant" by Virginia Apgar, 1953, *Current Research in Anesthesia and Analgesia, 32,* p. 262. Copyright 1953 by the International Anesthesia Research Society. Reprinted by permission.

Newborn Assessment

Scientists interested in infants' demographics studied and refined the assessment of vital statistics. Perinatal events including low Apgar scores (i.e., fetal measurement upon birth and at 3 minutes or 10 minutes after birth, indicating conditions of the uterine environment), reportedly became prime demographic targets in children's later atypical learning patterns. Newborn assessment, developed in 1952 by Virginia Apgar, began as a means of assessing the newborn's physical condition immediately following birth (Morrison, 1990). The rating initiated based on five categories including the infants' heart rate, respiratory effort, muscle tone, reflex irritability, and skin color. A total Apgar score is derived by adding the total number of points available in each of the five categories. A score of nine or ten is excellent and indicates a healthy newborn. A score of seven or below is cause for concern and may indicate potential late problems. The Apgar score historically provided a gross indication of the newborn's chances of survival. Serunian and Broman (cited in Morrison, 1990) associated the Apgar score to mental and motor scores at 8 months, as measured by the Bayley Infant Mental and Motor Scales. These scales purportedly assess young children's psychomotor functions. Newborns with low Apgar scores reportedly had significantly lower 8-month mental and motor scores than newborns with high Apgar scores, indicating even further problems as the child developed. Table 5.8 shows the Apgar scoring system.

POSTNATAL EVENTS AND EFFECTS ON ATYPICAL LEARNING

Biology interacting with postnatal events, occurring *after birth,* entail many processes. Researchers traditionally are of the opinion that postnatal influences are controversial as both tentative causes and effects of LD (Coles, 1987; Silver, 1987; Smith, 1991; Westman, 1990).

Researchers viewed a number of postnatal events associated with individuals' school-related difficulties. These included children's infections and diseases, head or body injuries, and biochemical responses (e.g., effects of psychostimulants, diets, vitamins) (Adler, 1979; Brenner, 1982; Cott, 1972; Feingold, 1975a). Biological and environmental interactions included psychosocial deprivation, sensory deprivation, severe neglect, malnutrition, infections and diseases (e.g., allergies, encephalitis, meningitis, Reye's syndrome, infections, tumors), head or body injuries (e.g., brain insults or trauma, serious concussions, circulation problems, strokes, high fever), or environmental-biological forces (e.g., psychostimulants or biochemicals; dietary influences including vitamins, malnutrition, dehydration; carbon monoxide, or accidents) (Morrison, 1990; Scipien et al., 1990; Ysseldyke & Algozzine, 1990; Westman, 1990). In this section, we analyze, through an historic chronology, prominent postnatal events evolving from: (a) biological-chemical research on children's exposure to psychostimulants or psychotropic medications, (b) dietary studies on food additives and effects of hypoglycemia, (c) vitamin studies entailing megavitamins and nutrient research, and (d) toxic element research.

Biological-Chemical Research: Psychostimulants

Coles (1987) reported on the two-fold function of medications in the LD field: Medications historically have been viewed both to help validate the existence of a biological cause and to treat the LD condition. As early as 1930s, professionals argued that medications not only reduced hyperactivity, but also improved academic achievement. Physicians began prescribing medications purportedly to help children reduce attention problems and to increase their learning potential. Further, during the subsequent years physicians influenced educators' involvement in monitoring the behavior effects of medication.

Recent investigations of the effects of chemical balances and brain alterations on subsequent learning and behavioral school progress provide interesting data. Current researchers have attempted to pinpoint neurotransmitter roles in altering individuals' brain structures, formations, and learning or behavioral developments (Smith, 1991; Westman, 1990).

Early Psychostimulant Studies.   Medication helped to control children's inappropriate behaviors and/or promoted appropriate behaviors and learning. Early medication advocates included Bradley (1937), first describing the positive side effects of the psychostimulant Benzedrine on children with hyperactivity. Since that time, extensive clinical research has pinpointed the most commonly prescribed psychostimulants (e.g., methylphenidate, or *Ritalin;* dextroamphetamine, or *Dexadrine;* pemoline, or *Cylert;* and Imipramine, or *Tofranil)* and their *paradoxical effects;* that is, stimulants reduce activity and distractibility levels and enhance attention and motor responses. Coles (1987) contended that the period from the 1930s to the 1960s entailed growing reports of physicians' increased medical prescriptions aimed at reducing children's brain dysfunction and symptoms, hyperactivity, and learning problems. Some researchers ascribed physicians' increased prescriptions to financial incentives created from the backing and financial support of drug companies promoting the companies' own commercial products (Schrag & Divoky, 1975).

Mid-Century Research.   Mid-20th-century researchers began suggesting many pros and cons to medication consumption. There were potentially beneficial and harmful side effects to prescriptions and dosages. Researchers have generally agreed that stimulant medications result in short-term improvements in a variety of areas including attention, impulsivity, and social behaviors (Bender, 1997). Wender (1971) reported on medication prescription rampages for children, youth, and adults with learning difficulties and problem behaviors. Wender reasoned increased prescriptions and dosages were due to physicians' profound beliefs that drugs helped to calm hyperactivity, improved attention to academic or behavioral tasks, helped to make children more receptive to learning, and actually increased more mature cognitive functioning.

Researchers also began to investigate drug effectiveness measures in school settings, most notably, educators' ability to observe and monitor medication side effects. Connors (1969) categorized educators' medication monitoring of drug effectiveness by developing observation systems for educators' use. He helped educators observe and report on medicated students' behaviors in the identified areas of daydreaming or inattention, defiance or aggression, anxiousness or fear, hyperactivity, and peer relations. Connors (1970), further viewing results of educators' drug monitoring efforts, suggested that improvements of students' control and attention are reasons for school-related drug treatment efforts. He suggested that by improving students' ability in behavioral control, students' cognitions also would be enhanced. Aman (1978) reported that increased prescriptions were available for drugs such as Ritalin, not because researchers supported administering the drug, but because there were laboratory impressions supporting Ritalin's facilitation of students' cognitions. Hinshaw (1995) reported on the effects of Ritalin on the both aggressive and noncompliant behaviors. The medication brought the treated students to performance levels within the range of normal children participating in the study.

Researchers also began viewing specific side effects from stimulant medications. Safer and peers reported growth suppression in children on stimulant medication. They conducted a follow-up study showing students' rebound phenomenon. That is, students displayed accelerated catch-up growth over the summer when the medication was stopped (Safer, Allen, & Barr, 1975). Levine (1987) suggested that side effects (e.g., insomnia and loss of appetite) are usually transient, diminishing as medication tolerance develops. Other reported medication side effects included visual and auditory effects, fine or gross motor difficulties, hair loss, weight changes, drowsiness, depressed affect, irritability, and impulsive behaviors. Table 5.9 illustrates benefits and side effects of stimulant medications evolving from traditional studies on medication.

Current Research.   Current researchers have extended traditional views on medication side effects. For example Levy (1983) and Levine (1987) followed the long term side effects of stimulant medication, concluding negligible medication risks. Wilsher (1986) reported on *nootropic drugs,* a new type of psychoactive compound. These drug types reportedly act on brain functions, that is, they are selective in activating higher brain functions while leaving lower functions largely untouched. Wilsher claimed many investigators using Piracetam, one of the nootropic drugs, have consistently found only a low incidence of adverse effects.

Table 5.9
Benefits and Side Effects of Stimulant Medications

Medication	Length of Action	Controlled Substance?	Potential for Abuse?	Possible Benefits	Possible Side Effects
Ritalin	3–4 hrs	yes	yes	a) Immediate effects	a) Loss of appetite Insomnia Stomach pain Weight loss b) Slowed growth in some children c) Cannot refill/new script monthly
Ritalin-SR	8 hrs	yes	yes	a) Longer duration b) Color and additive free	a) Loss of appetite Insomnia Stomach pain Weight loss b) Slowed growth in some children c) Cannot refill/new script monthly
Dexa-drine (tablets)	4–6 hrs	yes	yes	a) Immediate effects	a) High potential for abuse
(spansule)	8–10 hrs	yes	yes	b) Timed release	
(elixir)	4–6 hrs	yes	yes	c) Easy to swallow	
Cylert	12–18 hrs	no	no	a) Once daily in the morning b) Script can be renewed every 6 months c) Comes in chewable tabs	a) Decrease in appetite b) May cause insomnia c) Two to 6 week and gradual start and stop d) Rare cause of slowed growth in some children e) Rare cause of liver enzyme change
Tricyclics	8–24 hrs	no	no	a) Once daily dose b) Script can be renewed every 6 months c) May also help bedwetting/ some mood problems	a) Dry mouth Constipation Blurry vision Tiredness in some children May take 2–6 weeks to see benefits

Additional research focused on psychostimulants' clinical effectiveness, their mechanism of action, and their relationship to students' problems (e.g., Kavale, 1982; Lovitt, 1989; Silver, 1987). For example, researchers suggested that while controversial, psychostimulants may improve behavioral symptoms of ADD (Gadow, 1983, 1986; Silver, 1987). Some reported on controversies involved in stimulant medications and students' academic performances (e.g., Kavale, 1982; Silver, 1987). Table 5.10 shows research on stimulant medications and students' academic performances.

Researchers also studied stimulant medications and students' attributions to their individual learning abilities. Allen and Drabman (1991) discussed the message value of stimulant medication; that is, students' explanations for behavioral changes in themselves and on other's reactions to them as a result of such medication. The researchers suggested that improvements in students' academic performances result from the students' enhanced willingness to assume responsibility to exert effort.

Table 5.10
Research on Stimulant Medications and Students' Academic Performances

Year	Researcher(s)	Findings
1983	Gadow	Wrote a comprehensive review of the effects of stimulant drugs on students' academic performances, contending the most controversial treatment was dosage.
1987	Silver	Suggested that psychostimulants may improve the symptoms of ADD, that is, lessen the hyperactivity and/or decrease the distractibility, but do not directly alter academic performances. They can, however, make the student more available for learning. Because of the "motor calmness," the student might show improvement in certain fine motor tasks or an increased ability to organize thinking.
1988	Forness & Kavale	Argued that as medical professionals expand their use of child psychopharmacology, professionals involved in educational programming must have increased access to information about both the classroom effects and side effects of such interventions.
1988	Lerner	Reported that the dosage issue is further complicated by a nonexisting ideal cognitive dose—not the same for all children—which somewhat limits the desirability of fixed-dosage studies. The essence of the dosage issue is that it is impractical to reduce dosage gradually with a measure that is not sensitive to short-term effects.
1989	Lovitt	Argued that the optimal dosage to allow some children with hyperactivity to perform cognitive tasks is less than one-half the optimal amount for the suppression of conduct problems. Reported most investigators traditionally relied on standardized achievement tests to determine drug effects on academic performance. However, such tests are given infrequently and are often indirectly related to what students are being taught, rendering the tests insensitive to all but the most profound changes.

However, while stimulant medication has been a major treatment effort for students exhibiting problem behaviors, students receiving medication may report less personal responsibility for academic outcomes. Accordingly, recent attention has focused on the analysis of specific attribution patterns of students with LD, exemplified by comparing their attribution patterns to those of their normally achieving (NA) counterparts (Allen & Drabman, 1991). Researchers used such measures as achievement gains, educator ratings, self-concept scores, and willingness efforts to comply with requested tasks (Cooley & Ayres, 1988; Jacobsen, Lowery, & Ducette, 1986). Many recent researchers contend students can accurately provide their perceptions of biological-chemical effectiveness on achievement and behavior, a noted benefit to stimulant medications. Table 5.11 illustrates research on effects of stimulant medication on attribution patterns.

Dietary Factors

There are historical data on dietary influences and learning. Dietary research has included both nutrient deficiency or excesses (Coles, 1987; Feingold, 1975b). Nutrition in the healthy child historically included consideration of nutritional needs for growth or psychosocial and developmental influences on dietary habits (Scipien et al., 1990). Table 5.12 describes basic nutrients for health, including some major physiological functions in historical studies.

Early Studies.   Feingold (1975a, b) proposed an association between dietary conditions and hyperactivity. He reported that the elimination of certain foods containing artificial colors and flavors, as well as salicylates and certain other additives, could stop hyperactivity. Feingold postulated that hyperkinesis is related to ingested food, with some children experiencing negative reactions to processed food or food additives. He suggested diet control treatment and removal of foods which contain additives, thereby eliminating sources of biochemical imbalances thought to cause problem learning. However, Feingold provided no research support to these claims (Lovitt, 1989; Silver, 1987). While conclusive data were missing on the diets' effectiveness, other investigators followed Feingold's assumptions, using both dietary crossover designs and specific challenge designs (Silver, 1987).

Recent Studies.   Kavale and Forness (1983) conducted a meta-analysis of investigations based on Feingold's claims, reporting that the diet was not an effective intervention for children's hyperactivity. Kavale and Forness found that since treatment effects were only slightly greater than those expected by chance, diet modification should be questioned as a hyperactivity treatment. Silver (1987) reviewed dietary crossover studies, describing the random assignment of children with hyperkinetic behaviors to either the elimination diet or to a control diet. Children were then "crossed over" to another treatment. Behavioral improvements were found in a few children, but only when a control diet was given before the elimination diet. The findings were not noted when the order was reversed (Silver, 1987).

Table 5.11
Effects of Stimulant Drugs on Students' Attribution Patterns

Year	Researcher(s)	Findings
1976	Whalen & Henker	Studied improvements in children's academic performances, from enhanced willingness to assuming responsibility to exerting effort. Found medications convey the message that the solution to a problem lies in targeting biological factors because student is unable to change him/herself. Hence the drug is regarded as the source of eventual change. Such an attribution may decrease student's personal efforts to resolve problematic behaviors.
1980	Pearl	Compared the attribution patterns of students with LD to those of their normally achieving counterparts (NA). Concluded that NA males attribute failure to a lack of effort to a greater extent than do males with LD.
1985	Licht, Kistner, Ozkarago, Shapiro, & Clausen	Found that students with LD who attributed their academic failures to a lack of effort demonstrated greater achievement gains and received better teacher ratings.
1986	Jacobsen, Lowery, & Ducette	Reported that students with LD who attributed their academic failures to a lack of effort evidenced greater achievement gains and received better teacher ratings.
1986	Whalen & Henker	Found that responsibility for a successful change in behavior may be ascribed to the stimulant. Medicating students may influence their self-esteem and/or self-efficacy.
1988	Kistner, Osborne, & le Verier	Reiterated students with LD who attributed their academic failures to a lack of effort evidenced greater achievement gains and received better teacher ratings.
1988	Cooley & Ayres	Reported that attribution of academic failure for students with LD is due to their lack of ability correlated with poorer Piers-Harris Children's Self-Concept Scale scores.
1989	Henker & Whalen	Argued that students whose academic performance is poor may improve if they suppress engaging in alternate activities in order to complete unenjoyable tasks.
1991	Allen & Drabman	Assessed whether students with LD who were taking medication reported less personal responsibility and fewer lack-of-effort attributions in failure situations. Found males with LD who were not treated with medication more often reported that poor academic performance was the result of not having tried hard enough. (i.e., adaptive attribution). Males treated with stimulant drugs, on the other hand, employed such explanations for their academic outcomes as to indicate less personal effort to resolve academic challenges.

Table 5.12

Basic Nutrients and Some Major Physiological Functions

Nutrient	Important Sources of Nutrients	Function as Source of Energy	Function in Cells	Function in Regulating Body Processes
Protein	Meat, poultry, fish Dried beans and peas Eggs Cheese Milk	Supplies 4 cal/g	Constitutes part of the structure of every cell, such as muscle, blood, and bone; supports growth and maintains healthy body cells	Constitutes part of enzymes, some hormones and body fluids, and antibodies that increase resistance to infection
Carbohydrate	Cereal Potatoes Dried Beans Corn Bread Sugar	Supplies 4 cal/g Major source of energy for central nervous system	Supplies energy so protein can be used for growth and maintenance of body cells	Unrefined products supply fiber— complex carbohydrates in fruits, vegetables, and whole grains— for regular elimination; assists in fat utilization
Fat	Shortening, oil Butter, margarine Salad dressing Sausages	Supplies 9 cal/g	Constitutes part of the structure of every cell; supplies essential fatty acids	Provides and carries fat-soluble vitamins (A, D, E, and K)
Vitamin A (retinol)	Liver Carrots Sweet potatoes Greens Butter, margarine	Major source of energy for skin and vision	Assists formation and maintenance of skin and mucous membranes that line body cavities and tracts, such as nasal passages and intestinal tract, thus increasing resistance to infection	Functions in visual processes and forms visual purple, thus promoting healthy eye tissue and eye adaptation in dim light
Vitamin C (Ascorbic acid)	Broccoli Oranges Grapefruit Papaya Mango Strawberries	Major source of energy to fight infections	Forms cementing substances, such as collagen, that holds body cells together, thus strengthening blood vessels, hastening healing of wounds and bones, and increasing resistance to infection	Aids in utilization of iron

(continued)

Table 5.12   *continued*

Nutrient	Important Sources of Nutrients	Function as Source of Energy	Function in Cells	Function in Regulating Body Processes
Thiamin (B$_1$)	Lean pork Nuts Fortified cereal products	Aids in utilization of energy	Helps in nervous system functions	Functions as part of a coenzyme to promote the utilization of carbohydrates; promotes normal appetite; contributes to normal functioning of nervous system
Riboflavin (B$_2$)	Liver Milk Yogurt Cottage cheese	Aids in utilization of energy	Helps in skin formation	Functions as part of a coenzyme in the production of energy within body cells; promotes healthy skin, eyes, and clear vision
Niacin	Liver Meat, poultry, fish Peanuts Fortified cereal products	Aids in utilization of energy	Constitutes digestive tract system	Functions as part of a coenzyme in fat synthesis, tissue respiration, and utilization of carbohydrate; promotes healthy skin, nerves, and digestive tract; aids digestion and fosters normal appetite.
Calcium	Milk, yogurt Cheese Sardines and salmon with bones Collard, kale, mustard and turnip greens	Aids in utilization of energy	Combines with other minerals within a protein framework to give structure and strength to bones and teeth	Assists in blood clotting; functions in normal muscle contraction and relaxation and normal nerve transmission
Iron	Enriched farina Prune juice Liver Dried beans and peas Red meat	Aids in utilization of energy	Combines with protein to form hemoglobin, the red substance in blood that carries oxygen to and carbon dioxide from the heart	Functions as part of enzymes involved in tissue respiration

Note. Adapted from National Dairy Council, *Guide to Good Eating,* 4th ed. Rosemont, IL: (1985)

Silver (1987) also reported on challenge studies in which children were maintained on Feingold's elimination diet throughout the study. Periodically, children were challenged with foods containing artificial food colors. Researchers noted whether the hyperkinetic state was precipitated or aggravated by this challenge (Goyette, Connors, Pette, & Curtis, 1984). Goyette and peers found that, while small, there did appear to be a subset of children with behavioral disturbances who responded to some aspects of Feingold's diet. However, with notable exceptions, the specific dietary elimination of synthetic food colors did not appear to be a major factor in the reported responses of a majority of these children. Mattes and Gittelman (1983) responded to crossover designs and challenge studies, also reporting on the ineffectiveness of Feingold's diet.

However, Fishbein and Meduski (1987) recently added to traditional controversies. They provided examples of dietary behavior effects in their reviews of brain chemicals called *neurotransmitters* (i.e., chemical messengers located in axon terminals providing neurons, or nerve cells, the means by which neurons communicate among themselves). Examples of neurotransmitters include dopamine, norepinephrine, acetylcholine, and glycerine.

Past researchers investigating neurotransmitter messages found that effects could range from the regulation of vegetative or "automatic" functions to the production of overt behavioral responses including environmental or physiological stimulation (e.g., Weiner & Ganong, 1978; Wurtman & Wurtman, 1977). For example, Weiner and Ganong analyzed the nutrient origin of neurotransmitters, revealing that the hypothalamus, a part of the central nervous system responsible for regulating survival mechanisms and behavior, is activated by neurons that release dopamine, norepinephrine, and serotinin. These researchers suggested that neurotransmitters are directly responsible for behaviors, emotions, moods, and cognitions. Earlier, other researchers reported that neurotransmitter deficiencies and excesses can produce profound disruptions in normal physiological processes (e.g., Coppen, Brooksbank, & Peet 1972; Snyder, 1984). Certain behaviors (e.g., depression) frequently are associated with depleted levels of dopamine in the brain; consequently, concentrated forms of the amino acid tyrosine can help to augment brain concentrations of dopamine for the treatment of depression and related disorders.

Fishbein and Meduski (1987) also reported that syntheses of the neurotransmitter acetylcholine (ACh) provide further evidence for diet-behavior effects. They suggested that neurons modify hormone activities produced by nedocrine glands and consequently have a profound impact on human behavior and regulation. They also reported that neurotransmitter examples clearly show that the production of powerful brain neurochemicals depends on the availability to the brain of the specific components of diets, the dietary precursors. The insufficiency of these precursors has detectable effects on behavior and can be manipulated to produce improvements having profound implications for the LD field. Other researchers reported that ACh is largely responsible for memory, learning ability, and motor coordination (Peters & Levine, 1977; Snyder, 1984).

Megavitamin Research

An additional biological-postnatal event affecting atypical learning is hypoglycemia, a condition due to potential deficiencies in individuals' blood sugar levels.
Cott (1972) suggested that LD may result from inabilities to synthesize normal vitamin amounts in the bloodstream. Cott recommended massive vitamin doses, contending megavitamins provide optimal concentrations of normally occurring body
substances. Parents can control children's blood sugar levels by regulating eating
patterns and controlling diet.

Early Studies.   Early studies on megavitamin research began in the 1950s with the
use of massive doses of vitamins to treat emotional or cognitive disorders related
to schizophrenia. Hoffer, Osmond, and Smythies (1954) proposed the use of nicotinic acid and nicotinamide in the treatment of schizophrenia. Initially, they suggested niacin (nicotinic acid); later they added vitamins C and B_6 (pyridoxine) to
their treatment program. Hoffer and Osmond (1960) formulated the hypothesis that
schizophrenia was the result of highly toxic compounds produced by stress-in-
duced anxiety and metabolism failure. According to Silver (1987), the American
Psychiatric Association published a report that there was no valid basis for the use
of megavitamins in the treatment of mental disorders; to date, no biochemical studies on schizophrenic patients have documented Hoffer and Osmond's claims.

Nonetheless, advocates have continued to propose megavitamin treatments for
problem learning (Adler, 1979; Brenner, 1982; Cott, 1972). Some have suggested
that when individuals with problem learning ingest large doses of capsules or liq-
uids with massive doses of vitamins, problem learning can be controlled. For example, Hoffer (1974) suggested that vitamin deficiency may be a cause of learning
and behavioral difficulties, and recommended megavitamins. However, massive vitamin doses do not improve academic and behavioral skills of students with problem learning (Silver, 1987). Brenner (1982) also investigated the effects of megadoses of selected B-complex vitamins on children with hyperkinesis, finding that
children's hyperactivity might result from improper dietary control.

Recent Research.   Professionals should be careful in recommending megavitamin
therapy. Silver (1987) contended that research has not confirmed megavitamin validity to LD treatment. However, despite negative data, a megavitamin approach remains popular in some parts of the country. Adequate vitamins and nutrients can
be obtained for most children when they eat a balanced diet from the basic food
groups (Ladewig et al., 1990; Morrison, 1990; Scipien et al., 1990). Figure 5.5 provides data on the four basic food groups throughout the growing years. These food
sources have been used as the foundation to counter much of the megavitamin research called for by researchers studying hypoglycemia and learning.

Figure 5.5

A nutrition guide for eating from the basic food groups using the food guide pyramid.

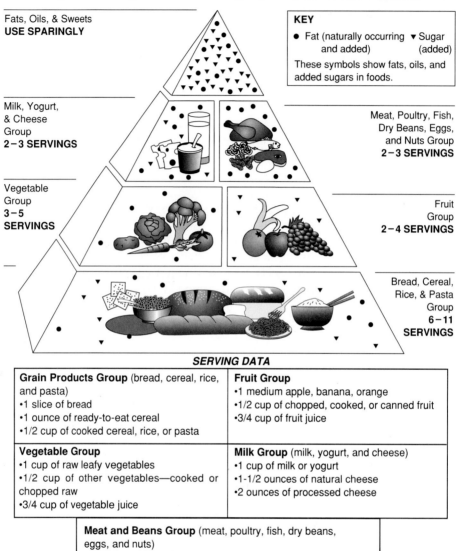

Fats, Oils, & Sweets
USE SPARINGLY

KEY

● Fat (naturally occurring ▼ Sugar
  and added)   (added)

These symbols show fats, oils, and added sugars in foods.

Milk, Yogurt,
& Cheese
Group
2–3 SERVINGS

Meat, Poultry, Fish,
Dry Beans, Eggs,
and Nuts Group
2–3 SERVINGS

Vegetable
Group
**3–5
SERVINGS**

Fruit
Group
2–4 SERVINGS

Bread, Cereal,
Rice, & Pasta
Group
**6–11
SERVINGS**

SERVING DATA

Grain Products Group (bread, cereal, rice, and pasta)	**Fruit Group**
•1 slice of bread	•1 medium apple, banana, orange
•1 ounce of ready-to-eat cereal	•1/2 cup of chopped, cooked, or canned fruit
•1/2 cup of cooked cereal, rice, or pasta	•3/4 cup of fruit juice
Vegetable Group	**Milk Group** (milk, yogurt, and cheese)
•1 cup of raw leafy vegetables	•1 cup of milk or yogurt
•1/2 cup of other vegetables—cooked or chopped raw	•1-1/2 ounces of natural cheese
•3/4 cup of vegetable juice	•2 ounces of processed cheese

Meat and Beans Group (meat, poultry, fish, dry beans, eggs, and nuts)

•2–3 ounces of cooked lean meat, poultry, or fish

•1/2 cup of cooked dry beans or 1 egg counts as 1 ounce of lean meat.

Two tablespoons of peanut butter or 1/3 cup of nuts count as 1 ounce of meat.

Note: *The Food Guide Pyramid illustrates the importance of balance among food groups in a daily eating pattern. Most of the daily servings of food should be selected from the food groups that are the largest in the picture and closest to the base of the Pyramid.*

•*Choose most of your foods from the grain products group (6–11 servings), the vegetable group (3–5 servings), and the fruit group (2–4 servings).*

•*Eat moderate amounts of foods from the milk group (2–3 servings) and the meat and beans group (2–3 servings).*

•*Choose sparingly foods that provide few nutrients and are high in fat and sugars.*

Note: *From Nutrition and Your Health: Dietary Guidelines for Americans (1995). Washington, D.C.: U.S. Department of Agriculture and U.S. Department of Health and Human Services.*

Toxic Influences

Research on toxic influences in the form of lead poisoning (i.e., plumbism) (Scipien et al., 1990) and associated learning difficulties also has an historical following. As with effects of other postnatal events on individuals' learning and development, toxic effects of lead poisoning and trace elements remain controversial (Lovitt, 1989; Silver, 1987; Westman, 1990).

Early Studies.   Earliest studies on toxic influences and lead poisoning effects appeared during the 1940s (Lerner, 1988; Lovitt, 1989). For example, Byers and Lord followed young hospitalized children diagnosed with lead poisoning. The children reportedly lived in old buildings where they were exposed to old lead paint. Many chewed old, lead-painted wood or plaster or ate paint flakes. Byers and Lord (1943) found that many children had difficulties in intelligence, perception, memory, school achievement, and behaviors and reasoned that a relationship may exist between increased exposure to lead and children's problem behaviors. Even low-level chronic exposure to lead during early years may be responsible for children's hyperactivity (Leviton, Bellinger, Allred, Rabinowitz, Needleman, & Schoenbaum, 1993; Minder, Das-Smaal, Brand & Orlebeke, 1994).

Recent Studies.   Needleman (1980) classified children's exposure to lead by measuring the amount of lead in deciduous teeth. Children with high and low lead exposure were then evaluated using a large battery of neuropsychological assessments. Needleman also measured a number of lead covariates known to influence development, revealing that children with high lead levels demonstrated a statistically significant impairment in verbal performance, auditory discrimination, language processing, and attention. These children also demonstrated problem behaviors. Needleman reported there is also evidence that low-level lead exposure can result in attention disorders, emotional disorders, or LD, thus impairing children's school achievement.

Chisolm (1987) estimated 4% of children in the United States have increased blood lead levels with a peak age of occurrence between 2 and 3 years. It is most prevalent in poor, urban Black children and least prevalent in rural White children. Acute symptomatic episodes occur more frequently during the six warmer months of the year (Chisolm, 1987; Scipien et al., 1990). Prevention efforts for undue lead absorption and lead poisoning require early detection and effective intervention. Recommended screening protocol and risk classification of the Centers for Disease Control (1985) as presented in Scipien et al. (1990) are presented in Table 5.13.

Toxic effects of high lead dosages have traditionally elicited followers focusing primarily on severe lead exposure; however, biochemical changes may be brought on by lower lead levels than those associated with clinical symptoms of lead poisoning. Scipien and peers (1990) reported on other lead sources including: dust from lead-painted ceilings and walls; cigarette smoke; drinking water from lead pipes; food cooked in water from lead pipes; food grown in urban plots; eating urban snow and ice; old newspapers with newsprint made from lead pigments; food and juices from lead cans; sucking a contaminated thumb; eating with dirty, lead-dusted hands;

Table 5.13
Interpretation of Blood Lead Test Results and Follow-Up Activities: Class of Child Based on Blood Lead Concentration

Class	Blood Lead Concentration (μg/dL)	Comment
I	≤ 9	A child in Class I is not considered to be lead-poisoned.
IIA	10–14	Many children (or a large proportion of children) with blood lead levels in this range should trigger communitywide childhood lead poisoning prevention activities. Children in this range may need to be rescreened more frequently.
IIB	15–19	A child in Class IIB should receive nutritional and educational interventions and more frequent screening. If the blood lead level persists in this range, environmental investigation and intervention should be done.
III	20–44	A child in Class III should receive environmental evaluation and remediation and a medical evaluation. Such a child may need pharmacologic treatment of lead poisoning.
IV	45–69	A child in Class IV will need both medical and environmental interventions, including chelation therapy.
V	≥ 70	A child with Class V lead poisoning is a medical emergency. Medical and environmental management must begin immediately.

Note. Reprinted from *Preventing Lead Poisoning in Young Children.* Washington, DC: U.S. Department of Health and Human Services/Public Health Service, October 1991.

and inhalation of airborne lead from industrial sources and gasoline. More research on lead poisoning's toxic effects on learning problems is indicated (Leviton et al., 1993; Minder et al., 1994).

Recent toxic-effect investigations have also related to trace elements. For example, Silver (1987) suggested that trace elements, including copper, zinc, magnesium, manganese, and chromium, along with more common elements such as calcium, sodium, and iron are necessary nutrients, although they are controversial in terms of their relationship to atypical learning. Their presence is essential for the maintenance of normal physiological function. No one to date has published data supporting the theory that deficiencies in one or more of these elements is a cause of LD. Yet, Silver reported that in some parts of this country, children are tested for such deficiencies and treated with replacement therapy. There are no research data to support this view or that replacement therapy leads to improvement of LD.

Practical Classroom Applications

This chapter stressed a biological model of learning disabilities. Several key aspects of the applicability of biological theory to the classroom are appropriate and are described below.

1. *All professionals, including teachers, benefit from biological research.* Historical biologists, geneticists, medical behaviorists, and neurologists have advanced the integration of biological and learning knowledge. As in other medical-educational areas, there is an important increasing need between specialists in biology and education to collaborate on research, service, and teaching, in order to increase and improve the quality of medical-behavioral knowledge (Lerner, 1988). Teachers can promote active collaborations in all teaming efforts including to: (a) work cooperatively with families and medical personnel in helping students' adjustments to LD, (b) plan and implement appropriate educational programming considering LD-biological implications, and (c) teach biologically based management skills, such as genetic, drug, or nutritional awareness. Teachers can also assist families and medical personnel in treating biological conditions. For example, teachers may instruct students on needs and benefits of special diets, appropriate exercise regimens, and/or drug influences and potential side effects. They also can provide observational

data to medical professionals to assess the impact of treatments on student behavior.

2. *Teachers can use many biological-medication data, especially in relation to children with Attention Deficit Disorder (ADD).* Today, biological theory plays a vital role in teachers' addressing the recent controversy in special education as it relates to appropriate programming for children and youth identified with ADD or attention deficit disorder with hyperactivity (ADHD).

Importantly, teachers should continue to provide the modifications necessary for students with ADD or ADHD to succeed in general education programs. Teachers should continue with appropriate prereferral and screening methods to discriminate typical student behaviors (e.g., inattention and impulsivity) associated with increased risks of biological-educational impairments.

3. *Teachers can act as liaisons, referring families for consultation with medical clinicians, health care workers, or physicians.* Teachers can help to locate and refer to appropriate medical sources students demonstrating signs of biological high-risk status. Importantly, teachers can value, respect, and/or accept views from other professionals by promoting medical services offered to help students with medical, learning, or behavioral difficulties. Medical and educational data can be shared in IEP planning

(continued)

Practical Classroom Applications (continued)

and development, transition programming, and home, school, and community services.

Importantly, those advocating biological theory have contributed many data, especially genetic knowledge and information on intraindividual differences. For example, as genetic knowledge has increased, biological advocates have held historical significance in diagnosing and treating prenatal and perinatal understandings of mothers and their developing child. These data, in turn, have helped to shape further knowledge on children's later learning and behaviors. Further contributions concerning demographic benefits have evolved from intergenerational family studies and analyses of perinatal variables. Biochemical, dietary, nutritional, and toxic information on learning and behavior continue to contribute many assessment and intervention data related to atypical learning and development. Teachers can continue to monitor students' vital signs for nutritional adequacies, dietary influences, megavitamins, and toxic elements, as well as to observe, assess, and monitor students for signs of

abuse in these areas, a course vital for giving students opportunities to respond appropriately in school settings.

4. *Teachers can use many biological data in their classrooms.* As in psychoneurological research, because many biological and genetic hypotheses may become observable, testable, and supported in the very near future, professionals working in the LD field may structure their future roles around biological influences. As biological knowledge becomes more advanced and usable, teachers' roles may change. Cooperative efforts cannot be overstated. Among other roles, teachers can continue to work cooperatively with families and medical personnel by monitoring students' well-being in all biological aspects. For example, teachers can communicate to families, physicians, and other professionals students' behavioral response data on medications and can also continue to monitor students' individual medication benefits or side effects due to changes in dosages, amounts, or schedules.

SUMMARY

- This chapter introduced readers to historical data on the biological theory of LD, with discussions of biological data and assumed pertinent prenatal, perinatal, and postnatal events on learning.

- Supporters of biological theory have historically influenced the LD field, including data on biological relationships to learning and development. Amassed data concerning hereditary-familial factors, genetics, maternal-fetal interactions, effects of teratogenic agents, perinatal influences, psychostimulants, dietary influences, megavitamins, and toxic elements hold profound significance in current LD knowledge.

- Although often controversial, results from historical, biological research have greatly influenced researchers, physicians, educators, parents, and students.

- Events such as prolonged labor, difficult delivery, induced labor, oxygen deprivation, placenta separation, premature birth, maternal or infant hemorrhage, low birth weight, and low gestational age all reportedly correlate with children's later difficulties.

- Researchers have viewed the interaction of biology and postnatal events including individuals' relationship to biological chemicals, dietary influences, megavitamins, and toxic elements.

- Researchers have focused on the role of psychostimulants such as Ritalin, Dexadrine, and Cylert in controlling students' inappropriate behaviors and providing more appropriate learning opportunities. Recent studies have extended side-effects research, including the relationships between stimulant medications, students' school achievement, and students' attributions to their individual learning abilities.

- Feingold (1975a,b) proposed an association between dietary conditions and hyperactivity, suggesting the elimination of foods containing artificial colors and flavors, as well as salicylates and certain other additives. Investigators responded to studies attempting to corroborate Feingold's findings (i.e., crossover designs and challenge studies), contending the diet's ineffectiveness (e.g., Kavale & Forness, 1983; Mattes & Gittelman, 1983).

- More recently, researchers explored the role of neurotransmitters (e.g., ACh) on brain functioning. Fishbein and Meduski (1987) noted dietary effects involving behavioral control and neurotransmitters, also describing implications to learning and memory problems.

- Researchers viewed megavitamin treatment for suspected hypoglycemia and LD that may result from inabilities to synthesize normal vitamin amounts in the bloodstream (e.g., Cott, 1972; Silver, 1987). Researchers provided controversial evidence on massive vitamin doses and benefits to LD treatments. Lovitt (1989) and Silver (1987) both recommended caution in the use of megavitamin treatment for LD.

DISCUSSION QUESTIONS

We list a number of practitioner discussion questions to generate discussion in tertiary course work. Tertiary instructors and practitioners might address the following:

1. Why has biological theory of LD generated so much historical controversy? What had led to the acceptance and/or denial of basic biological-learning assumptions?

2. How have families with genetic disorders been viewed throughout history? Why have these views been problematic to families? Why not?

3. What are educators' responsibilities in working with families suspected of teratogenic involvement?

4. Why has biological knowledge become a growing concern of school professionals in recent years?

5. As more biological knowledge accumulates, how will educators' roles change in the classroom, school, and community?

6. What are instructional implications for teaching students heavily influenced by postnatal events, such as biological-chemical influences, diet and nutritional variables, megavitamin efforts, or toxic agents?

7. How can professionals adapt instruction to meet these students' needs? What should be done and who should do it?

8. Compare your views of the biological theory of LD to other theories (e.g., psychoneurological theory; holistic theory). How are your views of these theories similar? How are they different?

REFERENCES

Abel, E. L. (1984). *Fetal alcohol syndrome and fetal alcohol effects.* New York: Plenum.

Adler, S. (1979). Megavitamin treatment for behaviorally disturbed and learning disabled children. *Journal of Learning Disabilities, 12,* 678–681.

Allen, J. S., & Drabman, R. S. (1991). Attributions of children with learning disabilities who are treated with psychostimulants. *Learning Disability Quarterly, 14* (1), 75–79.

Aman, M. G. (1978). Drugs, learning, and the psychotherapies. In J. S. Werry (Ed.), *Pediatric psychopharmacology: The use of behavior modifying drugs in children.* New York: Brunner/Mazel.

Bender, W. N. (1997). Medical interventions and school monitoring. In W. N. Bender (Ed.), *Understanding ADHD: A practical guide for teachers and parents* (pp. 107–114). Upper Saddle River, NJ: Prentice Hall/Merrill.

Bijou, S. (1971). Environment and intelligence: A behavioral analysis. In R. Cancro (Ed.), *Intelligence: Genetic and environmental influences.* New York: Grune & Stratton.

Birch, H. G. (1971). Functional effects of fetal malnutrition. *Hospital Practice,* 134–148.

Bradley, C. (1937). The behavior of children receiving benzedrine. *American Journal of Psychiatry, 94,* 577–585.

Brenner, A. (1982). The effects of megadoses of selected B complex vitamins on children with hyperkinesis: Controlled studies with long-term follow-up. *Journal of Learning Disabilities, 15,* 258–264.

Byers, R. K., & Lord, E. E. (1943). Late effects of lead poisoning on mental development. *American Journal of Diseases of Children, 66,* 471–494.

Butler, N. R., Goldstein, H., & Ross, E. M. (1972). Cigarette smoking in pregnancy: Its influence on birth weight and perinatal mortality. *British Medical Journal, 2,* 127–130.

Centers for Disease Control. (1985). *Preventing lead poisoning in young children.* Atlanta: U.S. Department of Health and Human Services.

Chisolm, J. J. (1987). Lead poisoning. In A. M. Rudolph and J. E. Hoffman (Eds.), *Pediatrics.* Norwalk, CT: Appleton-Lange.

Coles, G. S. (1987). *The learning mystique: A critical look at "learning disabilities."* New York: Pantheon.

Colligan, R. C. (1974). Psychometric deficits related to perinatal stress. *Journal of Learning Disabilities, 7,* 154–160.

Connors, C. (1969). A teacher rating scale for use in drug studies with children. *American Journal of Psychiatry, 26,* 884–888.

Connors, C. K. (1970). Symptom patterns in hyperkinetic, neurotic, and normal children. *Child Development, 41,* 667–682.

Cooley, E. J., & Ayres, R. R. (1988). Self-concept and success-failure attributions of nonhandicapped students and students with learning disabilities. *Journal of Learning Disabilities, 21,* 174–178.

Coppen, A., Brooksbank, B. W., & Peet, M. (1972). Tryptophan concentration in the cerebrospinal fluid of depressive patients. *Lancet, 1,* 1393.

Cott, A. (1972). Megavitamins: The orthomolecular approach to behavioral disorders and learning disabilities. *Academic Therapy, 7,* 245–258.

Cowan, W. M. (1979). The development of the brain. *Scientific American 241,* 113–133.

Cruickshank, W. M. (1972). Some issues facing the field of learning disabilities. *Journal of Learning Disabilities, 5,* 380–388.

Denckla, M. B. (1973). Research needs in learning disabilities: A neurologist's point of view. *Journal of Learning Disabilities, 6,* 441–450.

Denson, R., Nanson, J. L. & McWatters, M. A. (1975). Hyperkinesis and maternal smoking. *Canadian Psychiatric Association Journal, 20,* 183–187.

Dunn, H. G., McBurney, A. K., Ingram, S., & Hunter, C. M. (1977). Maternal cigarette smoking during pregnancy and the child's subsequent development: II. Neurological and intellectual maturation to the age of $6\frac{1}{2}$ years. *Canadian Journal of Public Health, 68,* 43–50.

Eustis, R. S. (1947). Specific reading disability: A familial syndrome associated with ambidexterity and speech defects and a frequent cause of problem behavior. *New England Journal of Medicine, 237,* 243–249.

Feingold, B. F. (1975a). *Why your child is hyperactive.* New York: Random House.

Feingold, B. F. (1975b). Hyperkinesis and learning disabilities linked to artificial food flavors and colors. *American Journal of Nursing, 75,* 797–803.

Finucci, J. M., Guthrie, J. T., Childs, A. L., Abbey, H., & Childs, B. (1976). The genetics of specific reading disability. *Annals of Human Genetics, 40,* 1–23.

Fishbein, D. & Meduski, J. (1987). Nutritional biochemistry and behavioral disabilities. *Journal of Learning Disabilities, 20,* 505–512.

Fisher, J. H. (1905). Case of congenital word-blindness (Inability to learn to read). *Ophthalmic Review, 24,* 315–318.

Forness, S. R., & Kavale, K. A. (1988). Psychopharmocological treatment: A note on classroom effects. *Journal of Learning Disabilities, 21,* 144–147.

Frostig, M. (1965). Teaching reading to children with perceptual disturbances. In R. M. Flower, F. Gorfman, & L. I. Lawson (Eds.), *Reading disorders—A multidisciplinary symposium.* Philadelphia: F. A. Davis.

Gadow, K. D. (1983). Effects of stimulant drugs on academic performance in hyperactive and learning disabled children. *Journal of Learning Disabilities, 16,* 290–299.

Gadow, K. D. (1986). Children on medication: Vol 1. Hyperactivity, learning disabilities, and mental retardation. San Diego, CA: College-Hill.

Galaburda, A. M. (1989). Ordinary and extraordinary brain development: Anatomical variation in developmental dyslexia. *Annals of Dyslexia, 39,* 67–80.

Geschwind, N. (1985). Biological foundations of reading. In F. M. Duffy & N. Geschwind (Eds.), *Dyslexia: A neuroscientific approach to clinical evaluation.* Boston: Little, Brown.

Geschwind, N., & Behan, P. (1982). Left-handedness: Association with immune disease, migraine, and developmental learning disorder. *Proceedings of the National Academy of Sciences (USA), 79,* 5097–5100.

Goldstein, K. (1939). *The organism.* New York: American Book.

Goldstein, K. (1942). *Aftereffects of brain injuries in war.* New York: Grune & Stratton.

Goody, W., & Reingold, M. (1961). Congenital dyslexia and asymmetry of cerebral function. *Brain, 84,* 231–242.

Goyette, C. H., Connors, C. K., Pette, T. A., & Curtis, M. (1984). Effects of artificial colors on hyperkinetic children: A double blind challenge study. *Psychopharmacology Bulletin, 13,* 39–40.

Greer, J. V. (1990). The drug babies. *Exceptional Children, 56,* 382–384.

Hallgren, B. (1950). Specific dyslexia (congenital word blindness): A clinical and genetic study. *Acta Psychiatric et Neurologia,* Scandinavica, Suppl. 65-1-287.

Hanson, J. W., Streissguth, A. P., & Smith, D. W. (1978). The effects of moderate alcohol consumption during pregnancy on fetal growth and morphogenesis. *The Journal of Pediatrics, 92,* (3), 457–460.

Harris, J. E. (1986). Clinical neuroscience: From neuroanatomy to psychodynamics. New York: Human Science Press.

Henker, B., & Whalen, C. K. (1989). Hyperactivity and attention deficits. *American Psychologist, 44,* 216–23.

Hermann, K. (1959). *Reading disability: A medical study of word-blindness and related handicaps.* Springfield, IL: Charles C. Thomas.

Hinshaw, S. (1995). An interview with Stephen Hinshaw. *Attention! 1*(4), 9.

Hinshelwood, J. (1911). Two cases of hereditary congenital word-blindness. *British Medical Journal, 1*, 608–609.

Hinshelwood, J. (1917). *Congenital word-blindness.* London: H. K. Lewis & Co.

Hoffer, A. (1974). Hyperactivity, allergy, and megavitamins (letter). *Canadian Medical Association Journal, 111*, 905–907.

Hoffer, A., & Osmond, H. (1960). *The chemical basis of clinical psychiatry.* Springfield, IL: Charles C. Thomas.

Hoffer, A., Osmond, H., & Smythies, J. (1954). Schizophrenia: A new approach: II. Results of a year's research. *Journal of Mental Science, 100*, 29–54.

Hynd, G. W., Marshall, R., & Gonzalez, J. (1991). Learning disabilities and presumed central nervous system dysfunction. *Learning Disability Quarterly, 14*(4), 283–296.

Hynd, G. W., & Semrud-Clikeman, M. (1989). Dyslexia and neurodevelopmental pathology: Relationships to cognition, intelligence, and reading skill acquisition. *Journal of Learning Disabilities, 22*, 204–216.

Institute of Medicine. (1985). *Preventing low birth weight.* Washington, DC: Author.

Jacobsen, B., Lowery, B., & Ducette, J. (1986). Attributions of learning disabled children. *Journal of Educational Psychology, 78*, 59–64.

Jost, H., & Sontag, L. W. (1944). The genetic factor in autonomic nervous system function. *Psychosomatic Medicine, 6*, 308–310.

Kavale, K. A. (1982). The efficacy of stimulant drug treatment for hyperactivity: A meta-analysis. *Journal of Learning Disabilities, 15*, 280–289.

Kavale, K. A., & Forness, S. R. (1983). Hyperactivity and diet-treatment: A meta-analysis of the Feingold hypothesis. *Journal of Learning Disabilities, 16*, 324–330.

Kelly, T. E. (1975). The role of genetic mechanisms in childhood handicaps. In R. H. A. Haslam & P. J. Valletutti (Eds.), *Medical problems in the classroom* (pp. 193–216). New York: Elsevier Science Publishers.

Kephart, N. C. (1960). *The slow learner in the classroom.* Columbus, OH: Merrill.

Kistner, J. A., Osborne, & le Verier, (1988). Causal attributions of learning disabled children: Developmental patterns and relation to academic progress. *Journal of Educational Psychology, 80*, 82–89.

Ladewig, P. W., London, M. L., & Olds, S. B. (1990). *Essentials of maternal-newborn nursing.* Redwood City, CA: Addison-Wesley.

Lerner, J. (1988). *Learning disabilities: Theories, diagnosis and teaching strategies* (5th ed.). Boston: Houghton Mifflin.

Levine, M.D. (1987). *Developmental variation and learning disorders.* Cambridge, MA: Educators Publishing Service.

Leviton, A., Bellinger, D., Allred, E. N., Rabinowitz, M., Needlemann, H., & Schoenbaum, S. (1993). Pre- and postnatal low level lead exposure and children's dysfunction in school. *Environmental Research, 60*, 30–43.

Levy, H. (1983). Developmental dyslexia: A pediatrician's perspective. *Schumpert Medical Quarterly, 1*, 200–207.

Licht, B. A., Kistner, J. A., Ozharago, C., Shapiro, D., & Clausen, S. (1984). Casual attributions of learning disabled children: Individual differences and their implications for persistence. *Journal of Educational Psychology, 77*, 208–216.

Lovitt, T. C. (1989). *Introduction to learning disabilities.* Boston: Allyn and Bacon.

Marshall, W., & Ferguson, J. H. (1939). Hereditary-word-blindness as a defect of selective association. *Journal of Nervous and Mental Diseases, 89*, 164–173.

Matheny, A. P., Dolan, A. B., & Wilson, R. S. (1976). Twins with academic learning problems: Antecedent characteristics. *American Journal of Orthopsychiatry, 46*, 464–469.

Mattes, J. A., & Gittelman, R. (1983). Growth of hyperactive children on maintenance of regimen of methylphenidate. *Archives of General Psychiatry, 40*, 317–321.

McKusick, V. A. (1969). *Human genetics* (2nd ed). Upper Saddle River, NJ: Prentice Hall.

Minder, B., Das-Smaal, E. A., Brand, E. F. J. M., & Orlebeke, J. F. (1994). Exposure to lead and specific attentional problems in school children. *Journal of Learning Disabilities, 27*, 393–399.

Morrison, G. S. (1990). *The world of child development: Conception to adolescence.* Albany, NY: Delmar.

Morrison, J. P., & Stewart, M. A., (1973). The psychiatric status of the legal families of adopted hyperactive children. *Archives of General Psychiatry, 28,* 888–891.

Morrison, J. P., & Stewart, M. A., (1974). Bilateral inheritance as evidence for polygenicity in the hyperactive child syndrome. *Journal of Nervous and Mental Disease, 158,* 226–228.

Needleman, H. L. (1980). Human head exposure: Difficulties and strategies in the assessment of neuropsychological impact. In R. L. Singhal & J. A. Thomas (Eds.), *Lead toxicity.* Baltimore: Urban & Schwarzenberg.

Nichols, P., & Chen, T. (1981), *Minimal brain dysfunction: A prospective study.* Hillsdale, NJ: Erlbaum.

Office of Policy Research and Improvement. (1990). *Cocaine babies: Florida's substance exposed youth.* Tallahassee: Florida Department of Education.

Owen, F. W., Adams, P. A., Forrest, T., Stolz, L. M., & Fisher, S. (1971). Learning disorders in children: Sibling studies. *Monographs of the Society for Research in Child Development, 36* (4, Serial No. 144).

Pasamanick, B., & Knoblock, P. (1960). Brain damage and reproductive causality. *American Journal of Orthopsychiatry, 30,* 298–305.

Patton, J. R., Beirne-Smith, M., & Payne, J. S. (1990). *Mental retardation,* (3rd ed.). New York: Merrill.

Pearl, R. (1982). LD children's attributions for success and failure: A replication with a labeled sample. *Learning Disability Quarterly, 5,* 173–176.

Pennington, B. F. & Smith, S. D. (1988). Genetic influences on learning disabilities: An update. *Journal of Consulting and Clinical Psychology, 56*(6), 817–823.

Peters, B. H., & Levine, H. S. (1977). Memory enhancement after physostigmine in the amnesic syndrome. *Archives of Neurology, 34,* 215–219.

Richardson, S. O. (1992). Historical perspectives on dyslexia. *Journal of Learning Disabilities, 25*(1), 40–47.

Rosett, H. L. (1980). A clinical perspective of the fetal alcohol syndrome. *Alcoholism: Clinical and Experimental Research, 4,* 119.

Safer, D. J. & Allen, R. P. (1973). Factors influencing the suppressant effects of two stimulant drugs on the growth of hyperactive children. *Pediatrics, 51,* 660–667.

Safer, D. J. & Allen, R. P., & Barr, E. (1975). Growth rebound after termination of stimulant drugs. *Journal of Pediatrics, 86,* 113–116.

Schrag, P., & Divoky, D. (1975). *The myth of the hyperactive child.* New York: Pantheon.

Scipien, G. M., Chard, M. A., Howe, J., & Barnard, M. U. (1990). *Pediatric nursing.* St. Louis, MO: Mosby.

Silver, L. B. (1987). The "Magic Cure": A review of the current controversial approaches for treating learning disabilities. *Journal of Learning Disabilities, 20*(8), 498–504.

Smith, C. R. (1991). *Learning disabilities: The interaction of learner, task, and setting* (2nd ed.). Boston: Allyn and Bacon.

Snyder, S. H. (1984). Drug and neurotransmitter receptors in the brain. *Science, 224,* 22–31.

Sparks, S. (1984). *Birth defects and speech-language disorders.* San Diego, CA: College-Hill.

Strauss, A. A., & Werner, H. (1942). Disorders of conceptual thinking in the brain injured child. *Journal of Nervous and Mental Disease, 96,* 153–172.

Thomas, C. J. (1905). Congenital "word blindness" and its treatment. *Ophthalmoscope, 3,* 380–385.

Thompson, J. S., & Thompson, M. W. (1980). *Genetics in medicine* (3rd ed.). Philadelphia: Saunders.

Van Dyke, D. C., & Fox, A. A. (1990). Fetal drug exposure and its possible implications for learning in the preschool and school-age population. *Journal of Learning Disabilities, 23,* 160–163.

Vandenberg, S. G. (1966). Contributions of twin research to psychology. *Psychological Bulletin, 56,* 327–352.

Vellutino, F. R. (1979). *Dyslexia: Theory and research.* Cambridge, MA: MIT Press.

Vogler, G. P., & DeFries, J. C., & Decker, S. (1985). Family history as an indicator of risk for reading disability. *Journal of Learning Disabilities, 17,* 616–618.

Weiner, R. I., & Ganong, W. F. (1978). Role of brain monoamines and histamines in regulation of anterior pituitary secretion. *Physiology Review, 58,* 904–906.

Wender, P., (1971). *Minimal brain dysfunction in children.* New York: Wiley-Interscience.

Werner, H., & Strauss, A. A. (1941). Pathology of figure-background relationship in the child. *Journal of Abnormal and Social Psychology, 36,* 236–248.

Westman, J. C. (1990). *Handbook of learning disabilities.* Boston: Allyn and Bacon.

Whalen, C. K., & Henker, B. (Eds.) (1980). The social ecology of psychostimulant treatment: A model for conceptual and empirical analyses. In Whalen, C. K., & Henker, B., *Hyperactive children: The social ecology of identification and treatment.* New York: Academic Press.

Whalen, C. K. & Henker, B. (1986). Cognitive behavior therapy for hyperactive children: What do we know? *Journal of Children in Contemporary Society, 19,* 123–41.

Wiederholt, J. L. (1974). Historical perspectives on the education of the learning disabled. In L. Mann & D. Sabatino (Eds.), *The second review of special education.* Philadelphia: Journal of Special Education Press.

Wilsher, C. R. (1986). The nootropic concept and dyslexia. *Annals of Dyslexia, 36,* 118–137.

Wilson, E. O. (1975). *Sociobiology: The new synthesis.* Cambridge, MA: Harvard University Press.

Witelson, S. F., & Kigar, D. L. (1988). Asymmetry in brain function follows asymmetry in anatomical form: Gross, microscopic, postmortem and imaging studies. In F. Bollar & J. Grafman (Eds.), *Handbook of neuropsychology (Vol. 1)* (pp. 111–142). New York: Elsevier Science Publishers.

Witelson, S. F., & Pallie, W. (1973). Left hemisphere specialization for language in the newborn, *Brain, 96,* 641–646.

Wurtman, R. J. & Wurtman, J. J. (1977). *Nutrition and the brain.* New York: Basic Books.

Ysseldyke, J., & Algozzine, B. (1990). *Introduction to special education* (2nd ed.). Boston: Houghton Mifflin.

Processing entails a two-step representational mediation process that connects sensory perception of stimuli and motor and verbal responses.

CHAPTER 6

The Psycholinguistic Model

In this chapter we will discuss . . .

- The psychological language-processing system that brings meaning to verbal stimuli.
- Two dimensions of language behavior: processing and organization.
- The representational mediation process which connects sensory and motor behaviors.
- The role of perception in the process of decoding, interpretation, integration, and storage of information.
- Samuel Kirk's pioneering role in the use of the term learning disability and researchers' shift away from a medical model to a psychoeducational explanation of LD.
- The nine subtests of the ITPA including auditory decoding, visual decoding, auditory-vocal association, visual-motor association, vocal encoding, motor encoding, auditory-vocal automatic (later called grammatic closure), auditory-vocal sequencing, and visual-motor sequencing.
- The ITPA's use in diagnosing language processing problems.
- Profile patterns that could be used to help create a diagnostic profile for a specific disability.
- The mixed conclusions by independent researchers regarding the construct validity of the ITPA.
- The underlying belief of psycholinguistic theory that deficits, once identified, could be ameliorated through the process of psycholinguistic training as a precarious assumption.

185

- The psycholinguistic training programs that have been developed including the Peabody Language Development Kit, MWM program for Developing Language Abilities, and GOAL program.

- The lack of consensus by researchers regarding the trainability and the theoretical value of psycholinguistic training programs.

During the 19th century a group of researchers, including Pierre Paul Broca, mentioned earlier, began to systematically hypothesize about the way in which the human brain functions. Broca, a physician/surgeon practicing in France, studied communication and language behaviors of individuals with suspected brain injuries and/or lesions. At the time, conclusive evidence regarding the location and details about suspected lesions or trauma could only be verified upon the patient's death. In 1864, after much debate within the scientific community, Broca put forth an hypothesis regarding laterality of the brain, in which he asserted that speech is a function of the left brain hemisphere. This theory, among the first which led to the recognition that the brain has specific areas dedicated to specific tasks, laid the foundation for the psycholinguistic model of learning which evolved almost a century later.

The research was carried out, for the most part, using adults who had sustained brain injuries and were exhibiting speech impairment. (The idea of speech being part of a greater language process was not yet being studied.) By the late 1860s verbal language studies had progressed to the point of understanding that language was a complex and multifaceted behavior. In 1869, Bastian theorized that language production is supported by the interaction of four specialized centers: the visual-verbal, auditory-verbal, glosso-kinesthetic, and cheiro-kinesthetic (speech) centers. Using this framework as a theoretical starting point, Bastian described four different types of language disorders: *amnesia* (an inability to recall words and/or events), *aphasia* (loss of speech and/or writing ability), *aphemia* (loss of speech ability), and *agraphia* (loss of writing ability).

Over the intervening 75 years, speech studies gradually fell out of the realm of the medical model and into the wider domain of linguists and psychologists. Abnormal and insufficient speech was looked at increasingly as a disturbance of language production. Language theories developed into far-reaching studies that took into account the human need to communicate as a function basic to human behavior across cultures, classes, and intellectual levels. The ability to comprehend and use verbal and written symbols is central to an individual's academic achievement.

MEDIATION MODEL

During the early- to mid-20th century, Charles Osgood (1953, 1957), along with other psychologists including Staats (1971) and linguistic researchers, put forth a psychologically based communication theory using (children's) normal models of language acquisition as a basis for understanding disordered language-acquisition patterns. Previous to this period, adult language disorders (based on models formulated from the data originally obtained during mid-19th-century brain studies) were used to design a model that was applied to children experiencing language delay or disabilities. Osgood noted that it was inappropriate to use brain-injured adults as a theoretical model, because the adults were experiencing *language loss,* whereas the children were undergoing *language acquisition.*

Language, as defined by Osgood, is a complicated behavior, elicited by, and in response to, verbal stimuli. In order for communication to qualify as a human language, specific criteria must be met: Signals must be nonrandom and recurring auditory, visual, or gestural signals; they must be reproducible by the individual receiving the signal; they must have semantic and syntactic meaning, and they must have flexibility, in that they can be recombined to create new combinations of signals to convey meaning (Osgood, 1980).

The theory promoted by Osgood was an outgrowth and refinement of behaviorism, although it went well beyond a simple behavioral stimulus-response relationship and attempted to explain what occurred to mediate the stimulus and response (see Figure 6.1). Lacking empirical evidence for this theory, Osgood made the assumption that learning processes are based in the individual's *central nervous system* (CNS). The *mediational model* (Osgood, 1957) promotes the belief that a number of intervening steps occurring between stimulus and response allow for receiving stimuli, giving it meaning, and responding to it. The abilities to use language functionally and, by extension, to develop cognitive skills, are central to Osgood's premise.

According to this theoretical framework, language behavior has two distinct dimensions: processing and organization. *Processing* entails the decoding (receiving), association (the mediational process an individual employs), and encoding (responding) to stimuli. The individual receives linguistic symbols (stimuli) via a channel (auditory, visual, or kinesthetic path). Once received, these stimuli are mediated and cognitively processed to give them meaning. A normally functioning user can then generate a meaningful response. These processes are mediated by the central nervous system on one of three levels. The lowest level, the projection level, represents those actions that the body carries out almost as a reflex (e.g., salivation). At this level the individual is categorizing and organizing stimuli presented to the central nervous system. Stimuli at this level are channeled to the appropriate areas of the brain for interpretation. The next level of neural organization, integration, is that in which the CNS organizes and sequences both incoming stimuli and responses to it. This level of organization involves physical action such as concurrent regulation of head posture, eye positioning, and speech muscles. The integration level also accounts for an individual's ability to integrate information and seek closure, whether it be visually or auditorily. This level of processing is driven by past and repeated experiences; the frequency in which a stimulus is presented and repeated will have a direct effect on the strength of the individual's response to it. The integration level is directly involved with the individual's ability to organize signals the brain receives. It involves the ability to decode (interpret a stimulus), encode (express a response

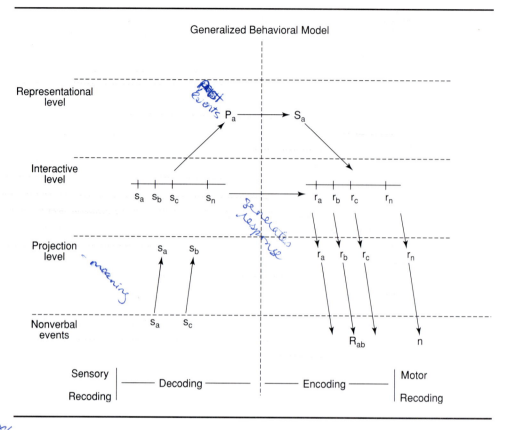

Figure 6.1

Osgood's Generalized Behavioral Model. The organism samples its environment with rapid, sketchy scannings, and its input information (S_a, S_b, etc.) is necessarily complete. However, the sensory signals (s_a, s_b, etc.) generated in the projection system by such scannings activate their sensory correlates in the integrative system (s_a, s_b, —s_n), and these on the basis of past input experience, tend toward completion of the most probable integrations. On the encoding side, self-stimulations from both the representational system (s_m) and from the sensory integration system (s_a, s_b, —s_n) may combine in the selection of those previously learned motor integrations (r_a, r_b, —r_n) which result in vocalization of sequences of words.

Note. Reprinted from the 1957 Nebraska Symposium on Motivation, by permission of the University of Nebraska Press. Copyright, 1957, University of Nebraska Press. Copyright © renewed 1985 University of Nebraska Press.

to a stimulus), form habitual behaviors, and perceive cues. This is also the level of processing where information crosses modalities (e.g., stimuli that are processed via one modality generate a response via another). A familiar example of integration-level processing would be a child lowering his speaking voice to a whisper when he sees an adult holding her index finger vertically in front of her mouth. The third, and most complex level of organization, is the representational level. This is the level at which higher order cognition occurs. Stimuli processed at the representational level give meaning and purpose; it is at this level that learning, integration of new knowledge, and constructs takes place. Perception of stimuli proceeds on one of these three processing levels, depending on the type and purpose of the stimuli, the ability of the individual (assuming intact sense organs), and opportunities for practice.

Osgood believed that these responses, which connect sensory and motor behaviors, developed via a two-step process called a *representational mediation process*. An example of this would be a child seeing something that he or she wants, reaching out for it, and giving a verbalization indicating an understanding of what that thing means to him or her. (The child, in this case has perceived a stimulus visually and responds to it motorically and verbally.) The steps that occur between the stimulus and the appropriate response to it are the mediating steps. Mediation is a complex thought process which is partially memory driven, although Osgood was never as explicit as several other researchers (see Wepman below) regarding the issue of memory.

Learning is also seen as a two-step behavior in which decoding occurs at the representational level and goes through its own mediation process. Decoded perceptions manifest themselves as discrete reactions to particular stimuli. An individual's ability to make decisions regarding decoding and encoding information relies on the individual's ability to select, discriminate familiar from novel, and synthesize new behavioral patterns.

PERCEPTION

Language, according to the theoretical framework, cannot develop without adequate perception and ability to recognize, integrate, and interpret stimuli. Perception is theorized to have a number of steps which interact in a multifaceted and dynamic manner. The process begins with the stimulation of a sense organ, whether it be the eyes (vision), ears (auditory), nose (smell), or a body part (touch). Neural impulses are then sent to the cortex of the brain (input). Supposedly, at this point the brain receives only the impulse; the patterns and intensity of these impulses are controlled by the sense organ itself. These impulses, or stimuli, are then interpreted by the brain; the brain seeks to make sense of these impulses and incorporate them into its existing repertoire (integration). The integration process is presumed to be complicated, in that the brain has to make sense of input stimuli simultaneously from multiple sense organs, as well as draw on memory to synthesize past experiences with the incoming stimuli (Osgood, 1953).

The interplay between these various sources of stimulation (the various sense organs involved and whether or not the input stimuli are novel or old) is thought to help formulate the response (output) that an individual generates. The output also begins as a pattern of neural impulses; however, because it is a response to incoming information, it manifests itself as a stimulation to a muscle, causing movement and/or verbalization. A portion of this response sequence is then recommunicated to the brain as feedback, which then allows an individual to recall a response and, in essence, self-monitor by remaining consistent in the types of responses it generates. An individual's perceptions are constantly undergoing refinement and adjustment due to this feedback mechanism, a process called *equilibrium* (Kephart, 1975). If the system were to break down at any point, and the perception of the input and output information were to become inconsistent, an individual would be said to be experiencing a perceptual disturbance.

WEPMAN AND MYKELBUST

Two contemporaries of Osgood, Joseph Wepman and Helmer Mykelbust, also investigated the issues of language disorders during this time (see Table 6.1). Wepman also believed that language is a function of the CNS. His hypothesis centered on the belief that language is a result of the discrimination and integration of information based on previously learned stimuli. His model involves four dimensions of language: function, processes, memory, and feedback. Stimuli are processed on three levels described as reflex, perceptual, and conceptual. As described by Wepman, the levels have similarities to those postulated by Osgood, with the reflexive level being similar to Osgood's projection level, the perceptual level acting as the mechanism that mediates nonmeaningful language symbols (imitative type behaviors), and the conceptual level being similar to the representational level of Osgood's model. Wepman theorized that only the latter two levels tapped into memory and higher level thinking.

For practical purposes both Osgood and Wepman's theories are similar, if not analogous. The main point of dissension between the two is their orientation, Osgood (1953, 1957, 1980) coming from the perspective of normal language development and Wepman, from that of abnormal language development. Although Osgood's model considers aspects of memory in regard to an individual's ability to differentiate novel from pre-existing knowledge, he did not go into explicit detail regarding the functioning of memory. Wepman's (1967) clinical work, on the other hand, centered on aphasic individuals, thus accounting for his particular interest in the role of memory in language development. In his work, he discussed a construct he called "the memory bank" in which he theorized that individuals receive and store residual images at the perceptual level while integrating these images with previous knowledge at the conceptual level. In Wepman's (1967) model the memory bank interacts with all processes and levels. Wepman's theoretical viewpoint complimented the Osgood model in explaining memory and retention problems.

The work of Mykelbust centered on his work with deaf children (Mykelbust, 1978; Mykelbust & Boshes, 1969). He expanded the language model to include the acquisition of reading and writing skills, which he saw as more complex skills within the hierarchy of developing language skills. According to Mykelbust, language development and subsequent learning takes place in semiautonomous systems within the brain. The systems, which are somewhat analogous to Osgood's channels (e.g., visual and auditory), can act independently (intraneurosensory learning) or in an integrative manner in which two or more systems interact (interneurosensory learning). Although it is improbable that stimuli are acted upon solely by one system,

Table 6.1
Elements of Osgood's, Wepman's, & Mykelbust's Linguistic Theories

	Osgood	Wepman	Mykelbust
Orientation	Theory based on normal language development	Theory based on abnormal language development (research with aphasic individuals)	Theory based on abnormal language development (research with deaf individuals)
Memory and language development	Lacked cohesive explanation on how memory functioned	Particular interest in role of memory. "Memory bank" construct	Theorized how learning style (e.g., visual & auditory) affected ability to learn language (including reading & writing)
Sensory channels	Included intricate interaction between sensory input channels	Included interaction between sensory channels	Included interaction between sensory channels, hypothesized that one channel can interfere with the functioning of another, as well as operate semiautonomously— *"intraneurosensory"*
Stimuli-processing levels	*PROJECTION* (Very basic responses to stimuli) *INTEGRATION* (Organized and sequenced by CNS. Integration of concurrent stimuli received by multiple sensory channels) *REPRESENTATIONAL* (Higher order thinking; integration of new knowledge ideas, constructs; formulation of novel responses)	*REFLEXIVE* (Similar to Osgood's projection) *PERCEPTUAL*** (Imitative, nonoriginal responses; rote responses) *CONCEPTUAL*** Higher thinking skills **Only perceptual and conceptual levels tap into memory functions	Processing takes place through a mediation process, called a *"transducer system."* Breakdown in this system results in disordered language
Language-based responses	Addressed sensory-based responses, verbal and or physical	Addressed issues regarding verbal responses	Expanded language learning theory to include reading and writing as a language-based skill

Mykelbust did hypothesize that one system conceivably could be the primary center responsible for learning specific kinds of concepts. But he conceded that interaction and communication between two or more systems, via a mediation process, called a "transducer system," was probably more common. If all semiautonomous systems are functioning adequately and interdependently, then integrative learning, similar to what Osgood describes as representational mediation, will occur. Language disorders, as well as learning problems, occur should either a semiautonomous system or the transducer system break down. An important point Mykelbust makes in regard to this "system breakdown" is the concept of "overloading," implying that stimuli received (encoded) by one system (channel or path) may interfere with the functioning of another system. This concept has important ramifications for supporters of multisensory approaches. As Kirk and Kirk (1971) later noted, students with LD often do not integrate stimuli from one sensory modality to another.

KIRK AND THE DEVELOPMENT OF A FUNCTIONAL FRAMEWORK FOR PSYCHOLINGUISTICS

The work of Samuel Kirk brought these theoretical frameworks into practice. His early work in the field centered around language training programs with children with mental disabilities. Kirk is credited with operationalizing Osgood's principles with respect to both assessment and remediation.

Moving beyond a medical model, Kirk and his colleagues developed a theory and terminology based on a combination of behavioral and psychological paradigms. The term learning disability was created by Kirk in 1963 at a meeting of what became the Association for Children with Learning Disabilities—ACLD. It was created as a means of moving the focus of the research out of the realm of medicine and into a psychological and educational arena.

Accepting the notion that the CNS is responsible for the receiving and mediation of language processes, Kirk set about to delineate those skills necessary to acquire, process, and produce language. According to Kirk's psycholinguistic model, the senses function as conduits to the brain, where stimuli are perceived, assimilated, and conceptualized. Kirk and Kirk (1971) note that many combinations of input (receiving stimuli) and output (expression or reaction to stimuli) are possible. The extent to which individuals are able to organize and form communication habits from these stimuli affects their ability to use language functionally. Hammill and Larson (1974) define psycholinguistics as

> the study of language, as related to the general or individual characteristics of the user's language. It includes the processes by which a speaker or writer emits signals or symbols and the processes by which these signals are interpreted. In addition, attention is given to the way that the intentions of one individual are transmitted to another and reciprocally, the way that the intentions of another person are received. In short, Psycholinguistics deals with the psychological functions and interactions involved in communication. (p. 5)

Kirk categorized disorders that are perceptually based into three areas: academic, nonsymbolic, and symbolic. The most common academic disabilities are found in reading, writing, and math, all areas with highly loaded language components. Symbolic disabilities are related to linguistic stimuli, that is, to hearing and processing language-related stimuli, even though the individual has normally functioning hearing. Nonsymbolic disorders inhibit the ability to recognize and make use of sensory stimuli on either a receptive or expressive level. One disorder may be basic to another; for instance, a reading disability could be related to a nonsymbolic disorder of perception, which could be related to a neurological deficiency, and so on (Kirk & Kirk, 1971).

Through sensory organs, an individual can understand and produce intelligible language within the scope of three processes: *receptive, organizational, and expressive.* The receptive process allows an individual to recognize and understand what is being communicated. Incoming stimuli (what has been heard or seen) is synthesized with what one already knows within the organizational process, and, on the expressive level, one is able to produce an appropriate verbal or physical response.

The focus of psycholinguistic research was to pinpoint and describe the deficit(s) the child experienced and to formulate remedial programs specific to the skill area displaying weakness. It was believed that although perceptual problems cannot necessarily be corrected, compensatory learning can take place with remedial help. Through a structured program that relies on teaching towards perceptual strengths, a child presented with copious amounts of practice could "compensate" for a deficit by reducing the amount of misperceived input and inaccurate output.

Assessment (and subsequent diagnosis) of perceptual difficulties and linguistically deficient areas is carried out by combining both formal and informal means; however, the essence of psycholinguistic diagnosis has rested with the development of the Illinois Test of Psycholinguistic Abilities (ITPA) by Kirk, McCarthy, and Kirk in 1961 (Kirk, McCarthy, & Kirk, 1968). Indication of a psycholinguistic deficit requires an analysis of specified abilities rather than testing that yields classification information. Mental age, IQ, and grade scores are of little value within this framework, beyond informing a teacher or psychologist that a particular child is experiencing difficulty and is not performing at the same level with peers. However, this intergroup difference is not pivotal to diagnosis; it is the intraindividual differences, including learning style and psycholinguistic strengths and weaknesses that are the essential issues in psycholinguistic training programs.

The theory promotes the idea that the way in which a learning problem (and specifically a language-based one) manifests itself is of much more importance, on a practical level, than is etiologic information. The development of the ITPA was a logical outcome of this belief. Behaviors considered indicative of children affected by these deficits include (but are not limited to): behavior and communication problems, academic troubles, retention problems, and short attention spans. The obvious difficulty underlying diagnosis is that many of these behavioral manifestations can and do describe many children with any number of disabilities other than what are commonly labeled LD.

DEVELOPMENT OF THE ITPA

"One of the greatest contributions of the ITPA is that it has provided a frame of reference which makes it easier to know which behaviors to observe, facilitates the observation, and provides guidelines for planning the modification of those behaviors through remediation". (Bateman, 1968, p. 92)

The original form of the ITPA, published in 1961, was undeniably a great undertaking. The test design sought to include a great age span, including children as young as 2 or 3 up to age 8 or 9. Nine subtests (auditory decoding, visual decoding, auditory-vocal association, visual motor association, vocal encoding, motor encoding, auditory-vocal automatic—later called grammatic closure, auditory-vocal sequencing, and visual-motor sequencing) were designed to test what were believed to be discrete perceptual skills necessary to communicating successfully (see Table 6.2). Kirk did not believe that these were the definitive skills necessary for mastery in order to communicate adequately, but rather these were the skills he believed could be isolated and quantified.

Between 1965 and 1968 the test materials were revised, redesigned, and restandardized with increased ease of administration in mind. The authors sought to keep the test administration under an hour, simplify the recording system, increase objectivity, and to reaffirm the discreteness of each subtest. The functions of each subtest were better geared to reflect real life language skills, and the interest level of the subjects was taken more into consideration. The test packaging was redesigned to be more compact, portable, and durable.

In addition to their physical repackaging of the test, the authors designed and added three new subtests within the auditory closure section: auditory closure, grammatical closure, and sound blending (see Figure 6.2). Grammatic closure and visual sequential memory underwent radical revision. An easier procedure for establishing baseline was put into place, and the norming population was extended to age 10. In other words marketability was improved, making the test attractive not only to the test administrators, but the subjects as well.

Clinical Model of the ITPA

The clinical model of the ITPA is largely based on Osgood's (1957) two-dimensional mediation model. The test's premise, that channels of communication are psychological functions involving sensory input and output, are functionalized and quantified. Osgood's theoretical model outlines three interrelated dimensions to language acquisition: psycholinguistic processes, levels of organization, and channels of communication.

The test was designed to measure these dimensions in children ranging in age from 2 years 4 months to 10 years 3 months. Psycholinguistic processes are described as the means by which an individual acquires and uses habitual language behaviors for normal language production. They are learned and imbedded in the CNS. The habitual behaviors manifest themselves in an individual's ability to receive, express, and organize (associate) stimuli. Language is also organized into two levels of com-

Table 6.2
ITPA Subtests, with Corresponding Channel and Process

Level	Process Accessed	Subtest
Representational	Ability to understand auditory symbols. How well a child understands spoken words. Responses kept to "Yes/No" or head gesture to minimize expressive component	Auditory reception
	Ability to gain meaning from visual symbols. Understanding the concepts of visual symbols and the ability to interpret what one sees	Visual reception
	Ability to manipulate and organize oral stimuli. Use of verbal analogies to test organizational skills	Auditory-vocal association
	Ability to relate visually presented concepts. Stimulus picture is presented along with four optional related and unrelated pictures. Child chooses which optional picture shows a relationship to the stimulus picture	Visual-motor association
	Ability to express concepts verbally	Verbal expression
	Ability to express ideas manually via gestures and movement	Manual expression
Automatic	Ability to make use of repetition in oral language use to acquire or develop automatic habits for handling syntax and inflection	Grammatic closure
	Ability to auditorily comprehend concepts, to recognize when stimuli are incomplete, and to generate or supply the required "closure"	Auditory closure
	Ability to organize and synthesize separate vocalizations into whole words	Sound blending
	Ability to recognize a whole object based on visual representations of its parts	Visual closure
	Ability to remember sequence of auditorily presented stimuli (in this case increasing digit sequences)	Auditory sequential memory
	Ability to remember and reproduce sequences of nonmeaningful visual stimuli	Visual sequential memory

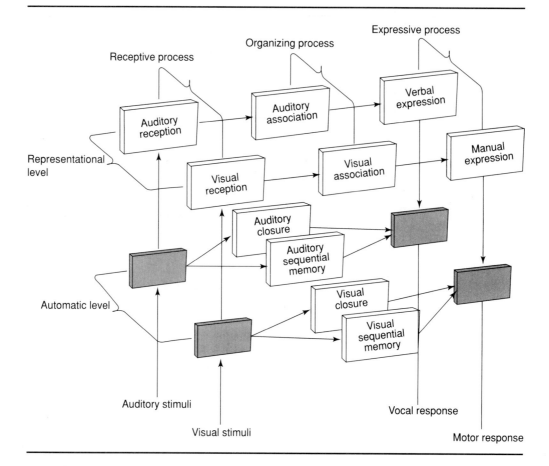

Figure 6.2
Original Subtests of the ITPA.
Note. From *Illinois Test of Psycholinguistic Abilities: Examiner's Manual* by S. A. Kirk, D. J. McCarthy, and W. D. Kirk. Copyright 1968 by the Board of Trustees of the University of Illinois. Used with the permission of the University of Illinois Press.

plexity: automatic and representational. The automatic level allows an individual to recognize and remember linguistic symbols and their sequences, as well as internalize and exhibit habitual language behavior. The representational level enables a person to use language as a meaningful mode of communication, employing grammatical patterns and closure.

The ITPA dealt with only two combinations of sensory channels or paths, auditory-vocal and visual-motor. As responses on the test need to be observed in order to be quantified, the authors made a conscious decision to stick to those channel responses that could be objectively recorded and reviewed, with the knowledge that many potential combinations of responses were not being examined. The authors were also limited by the nature of the test itself, which was highly language loaded, endangering, in a sense, the discrete nature of each of the subskills they were seeking to measure.

The major sensory modes—auditory and visual for reception of stimuli, and vocal and motor for expression—are assessed in regard to the ability to perceive and make sense of the stimuli presented. The auditory and vocal channels allow an individual to receive via the ears and to respond vocally. The visual and motor channels permit perception of stimuli through the eyes and the generation of responses via movements (gestures). Each ITPA subtest pertains to a sensory channel (auditory, visual, vocal, motor, or a combination thereof), level (representational or automatic), and process (receptive, expressive, or organizational). Expressive responses are the favored response patterns because they lend themselves to easy recording and measurement.

Representational level subtests involve decoding, association, and encoding. They were designed to measure a child's skill and ability to understand language, integrate the stimuli with previous knowledge, and to formulate a response. Integration (automatic) level tests examine a child's ability to use rote/habitual kinds of language, with attention to grammatical generalizations and symbols.

The ITPA is designed to yield specific intellectual, perceptual, and/or cognitive information. It is not a test of general cognitive ability, although some of the subtests are believed to be generally linked to cognitive ability. The authors suggested that for obtaining that kind of information one administer a WISC or Stanford-Binet. The ITPA yields several kinds of scores, all of which are envisioned as sources of empirical evidence documenting the presence or absence of a specific psycholinguistic deficit. An examiner can calculate global, partial, and profile scores from the raw data gathered during an ITPA administration. The scores, in conjunction with an analysis of behavioral manifestations, are to be used by the special education teacher to formulate an appropriate remedial intervention for an individual child.

Four *global scores* are derived from the test results: the composite psycholinguistic age (composite PLA), psycholinguistic quotient (PLQ), scaled scores, and an estimated Stanford-Binet mental age. The composite PLA is an overall index derived directly from the test results. The score, a reflection of the overall psycholinguistic development of the child, is expressed in years and months. The PLQ, unlike the composite PLA, is not derived directly from the raw data obtained on an individual, but rather by dividing the composite PLA by the chronological age (CA) of the child (PLA/CA = PLQ). The PLQ indicates the rate of overall psycholinguistic development and is used for classification purposes and comparisons with other children. Scaled scores are transformations of raw scores. A scaled score can be extrapolated for each subtest; a score of 36 with a standard deviation of 6 indicates the mean performance across age groups. The mean scaled score is the average of the scaled scores across the basic subtests; a median scaled score is derived by calculating the median of the basic subtests. The median scaled score is used as a basis for comparisons across age norms. The last global score, an estimated Stanford-Binet mental age is based on data derived from the Stanford-Binet form LM. Mental ages are derived by plotting the mean mental ages against the raw ITPA scores for the appropriate age group.

Part scores, another measure yielded by the ITPA, is a more discriminating method than measurement of global scores. Part scores consider a child's ability on three levels: auditory-vocal versus visual motor, representational level of organization, and automatic level of organization. Comparisons which isolate strengths and weaknesses within the parameter of the psycholinguistic model can be made between tests when looking at part scores.

Finally, the ITPA test protocol provides a graphic representation of the test profile (see Figure 6.3). The format of the graph allows for either psycholinguistic age information or scaled scores. Test patterns are used as anecdotal information in the formulation of a hypothesis regarding an individual's psycholinguistic status.

A lack of understanding regarding what test scores mean and the misuse, whether deliberate or accidental, has been a common problem encountered in educational environments. The ITPA manual states that standard scores and not age scores are the appropriate scores to use when drawing an individual's profile. The use of the standard score rather than the age score allows for the comparison of individuals across subscales with equal variance.

When using the ITPA the test administrator needs to be cautious regarding limitations of the test. The test is designed for children with mental age limits of 2 years 6 months and 9 years 0 months; the test then, would be inappropriate, in any case, with a child having a chronological age of 10 years or greater. Children with mental ages below 3 years are testing the lower end of the test regarding reliability, and those with mental ages of 8 years 6 months, or greater, are nearing the ceiling. The authors have cautioned against using the test on children outside of these limits. The test neither accounts for cultural factors nor is it designed to account for attention difficulties on the part of an individual child. Extraneous factors, such as fatigue, examiner bias, anxiety, rapport, and lack of cooperation, are a concern, as they would be in any testing situation.

Relative success in undertaking the ITPA presupposes that a child has at least minimal skills in certain perceptual areas. Discrimination of auditory, visual, and haptic stimuli at the automatic level are required because there is a memory component involved. The test examines the ability to cross processing lines, which requires that the child who receives input via one modality generate an output via another one (e.g., If communication is initiated verbally, can the child respond with an appropriate facial expression or gesture?)

On the other hand there are certain perceptual areas that the ITPA does not tap. Routine acts of speech and movement that make speech possible are not examined. These types of CNS movements, called nonsymbolic expression, allow for movements such as babbling and sound production.

Recognizing that the ITPA was not definitive in its diagnosis of psycholinguistic abilities, the test authors make suggestions regarding supplementary diagnostic information. Among the diagnostic tests that the authors recommend are the Wepman (1967) for auditory discrimination; Raven Progressive Matrices (1947) and Leiter International Scale (1955), for visual association; the Weschler Intelligence Scale for Children, for verbal expression; and the Peabody Picture Vocabulary Test (1965), for visual and auditory reception.

PROFILE OF ABILITIES

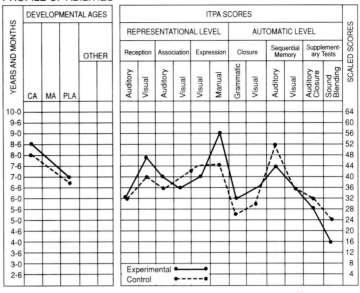

PROFILE OF ABILITIES

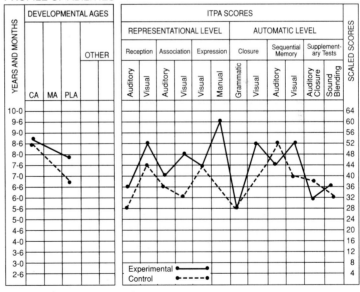

Figure 6.3

ITPA test profiles.

Note. From *Illinois Test of Psycholinguistiic Abilities: Examiner's Manual* by S. A. Kirk, D. J. McCarthy, and W. D. Kirk. Copyright 1968 by the Board of Trustees of the University of Illinois. Used with the permission of the University of Illinois Press.

199

Each ITPA subtest pertains to a sensory channel (auditory, visual, vocal, motor, or a combination thereof), level (representational or automatic), and process (receptive, expressive, or organizational). Expressive responses are the favored response patterns because they lend themselves to easy recording and measurement.

Score interpretation and what one does with the information gained from an ITPA administration is a central theme of Kirk's work. Along with this information and knowledge of a child's functioning, Kirk maintained that administering, scoring, and interpreting the ITPA is only one step in formulating a program for a particular child. In order to get a global picture of a child's status, one needs to carry out a functional analysis of the child's skills and behaviors (e.g., observation) along with administering the ITPA and other formal tests.

Kirk makes a point of differentiating testing and teaching, noting that testing determines a child's weaknesses and that teaching develops skills. In his writing Kirk describes this balance between the need to test and to teach as a "circular relationship" (Kirk & Kirk, 1971), meaning that in order to teach well one must constantly diagnose, remediate, evaluate, carry out a task analysis, and then start all over again. He sees testing as a "discrete experience," an activity that seeks to isolate and evaluate an individual child's level of performance of a particular skill. Successful teaching, on the other hand, should be "integrative," a process in which skills or content are linked to the child's greater body of knowledge (Kirk & Kirk, 1971).

Early Interpretation of the ITPA

Bateman (1968) was among the first researchers who undertook a comprehensive study to examine the diagnostic relevance of the ITPA. She evaluated the ITPA as a tool to help teachers pinpoint specific educational needs of a particular child. Bateman's report included specific findings regarding the ITPA's diagnostic value.

In examining the ITPA subtests, Bateman observed that each subtest had its strengths and weaknesses. The auditory-vocal subtests were culturally biased against nonstandard English speakers. For example, the use of plurals and past tense can differ from that of standard English speakers. The vocabulary presented in the auditory decoding subtest was not well matched to grade level. Consequently, the children often guess at the meaning of words at the upper ranges of the test. Other uncertainties included items on verbal expression, where questions regarding the scoring system were raised. In this subtest, quantity of response—and not quality—was the primary factor taken into account.

Bateman delineated a list of suggested prerequisites for interpreting an ITPA profile. Some of the points were along the lines of common sense (proper administration procedures, examiner becoming familiar with scoring procedures prior to testing, knowledge of area each subtest examines in order to carry out effective probing). Some of the other "pointers" were almost cautionary in nature, reminding the examiner about how language-loaded the test was, including her concerns over subtest independence due to the language factor.

The study also examined the issue of a "test profile," in which profile patterns could be used to help create a diagnostic profile for a specific disability. The general belief at the time was that these kinds of profiles would be helpful in generating curriculum geared to help specific groups of children with disabilities. Bateman recognized, at the time, that the results were tentative. Test profiles, graphically represented, for those with mental disabilities, communication disorders, visual impairments, cerebral palsy, and reading disabilities, as well as the gifted, were included in the study. Bateman's findings were in agreement with Kirk in that they concluded that a definite pattern was exhibited by individuals with specific needs. Children with reading disabilities were found to peak in visual decoding or manual expression. As expected, memory—both visual and auditory—was a weakness, with visual memory showing to be only slightly stronger than auditory. Less significant, but present nonetheless, was a tendency to be deficient in auditory closure. Interestingly, the profile representing mentally handicapped children (IQ of 75 and lower) also indicated a slight preference for the visual channel over the auditory channel. Gifted children, on the other hand, scored higher on auditory-vocal channels. The impact a psycholinguistic approach has regarding curriculum development means the use of stronger visual images and presentations for learners with reading and mental disabilities.

Studies carried out with children experiencing reading difficulties (Kass, 1966; Bateman, 1963, 1967) all confirm that automatic sequential skills are a problem for these children, and that these kinds of deficits are all consistent with Osgood's theoretical model. The children often learn to visually decode, but do not appear to internalize the information at the automatic level. Kass (1966) went on to say that he believed that while children with reading disabilities taking the ITPA were able to decode *pictures* visually, their ability to decode *symbols* visually was not the same skill.

It appeared to these investigators that, in general, performance on the auditory memory portion of the ITPA was a good predictor of reading difficulties. Both visual and auditory memory was viewed as problematical. The use of kinesthetic material (a very common practice at the time) for students with dual deficits had questionable value; there was little to indicate that tactile memory would be any stronger than that of the other two channels. With regard to reading instruction, the teaching of phonetics was linked to children with stronger auditory skills, whereas a sight-word approach was suggested for children with a stronger visual preference.

Construct Validity of the ITPA

In *Standards for Educational and Psychological Tests and Manuals (SEPTM),* French and Michael (1966) suggest the kind of information an educator should be seeking when considering whether or not to give a student a diagnostic test. The degree of validity (how well a test measures what it sets out to measure) and reliability (how consistently the test measures what it sets out to measure) of the particular test being given should add credence to the diagnostic information gained from its administration. For tests like the ITPA that rely heavily on constructs and their intrinsic validity, French and Michael (1966) caution the test administrator on two counts: Construct validity relies on how behavior samples incorporated into the test relate to other outside behaviors, as well as to how well the constructs compliment the internal structure of the test. Simply stated, construct validity is determined by comparing the target test against other tests (Proger, Cross, & Burger, 1973).

The ITPA quickly became one of the standard tests of the typical test battery given to children suspected of having LD (Newcomer, Hare, Hammill, & McGettigan, 1974). Although the test was initially developed in 1961, it was not until 1973 that a comprehensive study examining test validity was undertaken. The two central questions regarding the ITPA were whether or not the subtests actually identified discrete traits, and how consistent the test was with Osgood's model of communication. Some concern was voiced regarding the normalization population; because the test was designed to be used with children exhibiting varying degrees of communication disorders, test validity studies should have concentrated on these subgroups.

Hare, Hammill, & Bartel (1973) examined six subtests of the ITPA battery (Auditory Reception, Visual Reception, Verbal Expression, Manual Expression, Auditory Sequential Memory, and Visual Sequential Memory) and attempted to match them with specifically designed parallel tasks. Each matched task differed from the subtest in question in only one dimension, ". . . for example, in one instance the level of organization, content and process might be held constant while the input or output modality [channel] was changed" (Hare, Hammill, & Bartel, 1973). The authors administered the subtests and tasks to a population similar to that of the original norming group used for the ITPA. Test validity was supported by the study, with some minor contrary findings, as was Osgood's model describing discrete and measurable psycholinguistic traits. The largest discrepancy the study found was on the manual expression subtest, which required both verbal and manual responses.

Although construct validation was viewed positively by Hare, Hammill, and Bartel, they cautioned against universal acceptance of their findings. A general linguistic factor, isolated by some studies, including that of Proger, Cross and Burger (1973), was not isolated by the Hare et al. study. They did, however, isolate seven discrete and measurable factors (graphic language, oral language comprehension, oral language usage, visual sequential memory, auditory sequential memory, visual reception, and expression of function). Since the study dealt with only six subtests within the battery and with a norming population similar to that of the ITPA, making generalization to other populations was difficult at best. In any case, because the study dealt with the theoretical constructs underlying the ITPA, it was of some value for practical application in the classroom.

Descriptive studies that contrasted and compared ITPA profiles with two or more groups tended to show that the test could be used to discriminate, within limitations, between various groups with different attributes. A few of the attributes that the test appeared to be sensitive to were intellect and social and cultural background. It was found that middle-class and White children tended to be stronger at auditory decoding, grammatic closure and auditory association when compared with lower-socioeconomic-status (SES) and non-White children.

In terms of educational significance, the results were not as persuasive as the theoretical rhetoric. Score patterns between reading ability and ITPA scores were not consistent. The research appeared to show a connection between reading and tests measuring auditory-vocal channels more than visual-motor channels, but the results were not conclusive. In comparative studies using children who were labeled Educable Mentally Retarded, the children were subdivided into good and poor readers. The ITPA was not able to differentiate between the two kinds of readers.

Predictive validity of the test was found to be wanting. Correlations with achievement tests was not consistent; some of the subtests were far more predictive than others. It appeared that in studies looking at the levels at which the ITPA could predict overall achievement, it was less able to do so for low ability groups than with average range children.

Later studies using factor analysis methodology to examine the ITPA also unearthed conflicting results. Communication channels (auditory-vocal and visual-motor) loaded (i.e., gravitated toward each other) as the strongest factor. Because factor analysis results can be altered depending on the population one is using for the data, such information is limited in terms of validity.

Another way in which to view the construct validity of an instrument is to look at the convergent patterns, that is, how highly correlated a test is to other similarly structured tests. Such correlations were examined between the ITPA and several other diagnostic and academic achievement tests including the Peabody Picture Vocabulary Test (PPVT), Wide Range Achievement Test (WRAT), Stanford-Binet, California Achievement Test (CAT), New York Achievement Test, and the WISC (vocabulary subtest). Few significant findings were found, with the exception of ITPA total language scores being highly related to CAT mechanics, spelling, and total scores (Proger, Cross, & Burger, 1973).

With so many questions arising regarding the validity, reliability, and appropriate use of the instrument, the fact remained that the ITPA quickly became one of the most widely used, and misused, diagnostic instruments available. Various reasons have been put forth to explain the almost urgent way in which the ITPA was wholeheartedly accepted by the professional community. Historically, the development of the ITPA coincided with Lyndon Johnson's Great Society program and the federal government's plunge into the great experimental preschool program, Headstart. Headstart children as well as the program itself needed an established way in which to measure program outcomes reliably. The ITPA fit the bill almost by default; with the surge of interest in linguistics at the time, it was almost the only psychoeducational published material to be based on linguistic findings. With the increasingly sophisticated way in which psychologists and educators were looking at children, the ITPA offered schools a standardized method to come up with a differential diagnosis. This, along with the number of remedial programs being published with support materials, made use of the ITPA as close to an educational package as one could get at the time.

PSYCHOLINGUISTIC TRAINING

The most precarious aspect of the psycholinguistic theory lay in the belief that deficits, once identified, can be ameliorated through the process of psycholinguistic training. Working under the assumption that language is the necessary antecedent for any subsequent learning, researchers designed compensatory tactics to strengthen a child's stronger learning modes, while also bringing along the weaker ones. Proponents so believed in the uniqueness of each individual's learning patterns and the inherent inability to work with heterogeneous groupings that "individualization" almost became an ideology of its own. Training programs and materials were designed for individual instruction, so much so that group lessons were almost unheard of for a period of time.

Among the goals of a psycholinguistic remedial program is the attempt to ameliorate sensory deficits. Kirk cautioned teachers to evaluate the characteristics of the child before undertaking such a program. Analysis of the child's responses, aside from those recorded by the ITPA is the point at which one should begin. How well the child spontaneously integrates input, formulates output, and is able to cross modalities in informal settings are the learning characteristics one would need to evaluate. The results of the ITPA allow the teacher to measure channel strengths and skills, which are presumed to be discrete within the subtests. This would not give an indication of the manner in which the child crosses back and forth between channels or utilizes his or her abilities in a more natural setting. These patterns should be used as the indicators as to where one would need to start and how content materials should be presented to a student.

As a strategy psycholinguistic training relies on the belief that channel deficits are not innate or unalterable and that remediation of these deficits leads to improved academic performance. Lacking any hard signs of sensory abnormalities (e.g., deafness or blindness), theorists and practitioners proceed on the assumption that soft clinical signs indicate a CNS deficit which explains a child's learning difficulty.

The design of the training programs rely on a philosophy of training toward one's strengths, rather than weaknesses. The child's inherent strengths can thereafter be used to enhance those channels determined to be the weaker ones. A scenario illustrating this might be something akin to the following example in which a child exhibits weak auditory memory, but adequate visual-memory skills. This child would probably encounter less difficulty learning to read via a sight-word approach rather than a phonetic one. Training programs designed for this child would lean toward more activities using visual cues than auditory ones. Exercises whose underlying patterns would be designed to present materials primarily as a visual experience would be implemented. This approach, along with strengthening the visual channels of this particular child would increase the general knowledge base of this child, thus increasing the amount of auditory materials the child would be familiar with through overlapping presentations. Auditory skills would likely increase, even though it may remain the weak "link" regarding sensory input. The danger, however, would be to assume that one modality would automatically strengthen or integrate information into another. Children with learning disabilities often do not automatically transfer and integrate sensory experiences from one sense organ to another.

REMEDIAL PROGRAMS

A number of remedial programs using the ITPA model were developed for classroom use. Basically designed for small self-contained classroom, small-group resource centers, or individual instruction, the programs were designed as kits which are attractive and easy for teachers to use. The most commonly used programs, the MWM Program for Developing Language Abilities (MWM) (Minskoff, Wiseman, & Minskoff, 1972), GOAL Program: Language Development (GOAL) (Karnes, 1972), and the Peabody Language Development Kit (PLDK) (Dunn, Smith, Dunn, Horton, & Smith, 1981) key directly into linguistic constructs as outlined in the ITPA.

All three programs have a number of elements in common; they are prescriptive in nature, flexible in regard to their pace, include a number of suggested structured activities and lessons, and claim to remediate specific linguistic deficits. The MWM had the added feature of a teacher checklist, allowing the teacher to assess problem areas a child may be experiencing informally, without necessarily having to administer a full ITPA battery (Bannatyne, 1974). The programs were designed to be used for both normally developing and language delayed children and in fact were standard components for programming in Headstart classrooms during the program's early years. The authors of these programs, along with other researchers, participated in a lively academic debate through professional journals for a number of years. Over time, researchers (Logan & Colarusso, 1978; Howell Harrison, Stanford, Zahn, & Bracken, 1990) noted mixed results regarding use of these specific programs. Remediation programs employing the MWM and GOAL appear to increase verbal abilities (Logan & Colarusso, 1978), but gains regarding global linguistic abilities remain elusive, even with intervention.

A number of studies (Bateman, 1968; Hammill & Larsen, 1974; Kavale, 1981; Logan & Colarusso, 1978; Lund, Foster, & MCall-Perez, 1978; Saudargas, Madsen, &

Thompson, 1970) seeking to support or discredit the idea of training for these skills ensued over the next 10 years. The results, again, proved to be inconclusive. The reports of successful studies were countered with recalculation of statistics as well as the undertaking of other studies showing divergent results. ITPA results were used as baseline and for measurement of postintervention measures. Although it was clear that through intervention one could raise ITPA subtest scores, it remained unclear how related these discrete numbers were to learning behaviors and overall academic success. Three of the subtests that appeared to be tapping general cognitive abilities were auditory reception, auditory association, and grammatic closure. Some findings indicated that these three subtests were not completely independent of each other, thus weakening confidence in the ITPA's ability to differentially diagnose and predict achievement (Sedlak & Weener, 1973). Subscales from these three subtests yielded the highest predictive coefficients regarding academic achievement in general and reading comprehension in particular. In fact, evidence suggested that reading comprehension measures generally correlated with the auditory-vocal channel activities rather than with those related to visual-motor. (Sedlak & Weener, 1973).

Hammill and Larsen (1974), in one of the earliest reviews of the literature regarding psycholinguistic training, looked at 38 studies carried out between 1964 and 1974 in which the ITPA was used as the criterion for measuring the efficacy of psycholinguistic training. They concluded that the results did not indicate clear support for use of the ITPA. They cautioned against the rapid expansion of programs and materials based on the psycholinguistic model.

Results of studies using the ITPA as the criterion measure for psycholinguistic training is difficult to interpret, as testing was often administered in nonstandardized ways. Several of the studies used only a limited number of subtests and training programs and were unstandardized in both content and measurement. Populations differed from the norming population of the original test as well. The trend appeared to be that the training itself was seen as less beneficial as time went on (Hammill & Larsen, 1974). Many questions arose regarding the feasibility of training discrete psycholinguistic constructs. Verbal expression was collectively seen as the most trainable, with the remaining processes, including memory, reception, and closure, as being largely unchanged by remediation. The area of automatic skills was believed to be most related to a child's ability to read. Unfortunately it was difficult to design materials for this subtest, and so the skill was not presented often enough in most training programs. Even where efficacy of the training was believed to have been significant, the underlying question of how meaningful these tasks were to classroom performance remained an enigma.

In 1981 a meta-analysis, an analysis of an analysis, based on statistical findings of a number of studies assessing the effectiveness of psycholinguistic training, and using the ITPA as the criterion measure, was undertaken by Kenneth Kavale. In his reported results Kavale (1981) questioned Hammill and Larsen's findings. He found that the average child receiving training performed better on psycholinguistic tasks than did 65% of children not receiving the specialized training. Contrary to those who doubted the efficacy of training programs, Kavale concluded that a meta-analysis of such studies yielded positive results, even though he admitted to a great deal of variability in the usefulness of individual subtests.

In the meta-analysis Kavale noted 12 variables that appeared to have a profound effect on how well the training proceeded: approach (individualized vs. nonindividualized instruction), method (direct use of the ITPA and PLDK vs. other materials), subject characteristics (cognitive, behavioral category of children), grade level, IQ, treatment duration (in total hours), internal validity, sample size, outcome measures (total ITPA only versus ITPA plus reports on individual subtests), pupil/teacher ration, and, interestingly, the publication date and forum of the publication. Specific patterns emerged from the study. Some of these patterns from Hammill and Larsen's while other patterns emerged that were not noted previously. Interventions designed for individualized delivery, unsurprisingly, proved more successful than those presented in a small group format.

Kavale's findings were at odds with those of Hammill and Larsen in three ways. The first divergence, as noted, was the level of psycholonguistic skill improvement found through the use of the PLDK versus the ITPA. Although Hammill and Larsen conceded that the information appeared to show results of the PLDK somewhat stronger than that of the ITPA, Kavale found the PLDK results markedly stronger. The second area of contention was in the area of expression, where Hammill and Larsen reported improved manual expression with training, Kavale found that there was significant improvement in both verbal and manual expression. The last significant difference in their findings were in auditory association and visual association. Where Kavale found that all intervention methods improved these channels, Hammill and Larsen did not report any significant findings.

Experimental Remedial Models

Remedial programs were also designed for experimental purposes. In the experimental models discussed here, trends among the findings were distinguished, including the successful training of vocal encoding. Since the ITPA was used as the baseline and criterion readiness measures were not considered, success of psycholinguistic training was not extrapolated to include academic achievement, and indeed several of the authors did not believe that there was an effect on school achievement.

One of the earliest major studies undertaken with special needs children was undertaken by Blessing (1964). Forty children CA ages 8–15, mental age (MA) range from 4yrs 7mos through 8yrs 10mos who exhibited a deficit in vocal encoding were treated for during three 1-hour sessions per week for a period of 4 months. At the same time a control group was given no special language training. Results showed that the experimental group made significantly greater gains in vocal encoding, word count, mean sentence length, and mean for five longest remarks. Stability of these gains was validated by subsequent testing 4 months later. Scores during the later testing remained higher for the experimental group in all areas tested except vocal encoding.

A later study looking at the issue of an LD model was carried out by Minskoff (1967). In this study 15 children, diagnosed as EMR were divided into three groups, with one group receiving what was described as an LD approach, one, a global approach, and a control group. Retest results suggested that the LD remediation had a higher efficacy than either of the other two, and that the control group scored higher than the globally trained group.

One of the few studies that touched on the questions of how psycholinguistic training affects school performance was performed by Lagerman (1970). The study looked at the effectiveness of remediation programs and how they affected reading achievement and psycholinguistic deficits. The children involved showed signs of deficits and were reading a year below expected levels. In this study 22 children, chosen from an original group of 189 third- and fourth-graders, were divided into two groups. One treatment group received training based on the psycholinguistic model; the other group received remedial reading instruction. Treatment was administered twice a week for a total of 50 minutes per week over a 4-month period. Gains made by the two groups were not significant in either reading or 11 of the 12 subtests of the ITPA. Auditory reception, the one exception to the subtest scores did indicate a factor discriminating between the two groups, suggesting a higher efficacy for the group that received remedial reading training.

CONCLUSIONS ON REMEDIAL TRAINING EFFECTS

Although Kavale found that meta-analysis clarified research findings and made them more substantial, there were other researchers at this time who found fault with the findings of Kavale's and Hammill and Larsen's studies. No consensus was ever clearly generated about trainability and the theoretical value of training programs. The practical issue of how these programs improve or enhance academic performance did eventually take over the argument. Since training takes time away from the student's ability to perform on task-content related activities, it has been deemed that although valuable in the general sense of development, psycholinguistic training is not the answer to making children better readers, mathematicians, or scientists. The amount of time a child is on task and is required to respond to that task has decidedly won out over the more theoretical question of which channel is processing the information being presented.

Regarding the issue of multisensory presentations, proponents of psycholinguistic training were not consistent in their message. Many proponents of the theory believed wholeheartredly in the virtue of "the more modalities stimulated the better" in regard to internalizing whatever was being taught. Kirk, however, saw multisensory presentations as a possible confusion to the learner. This form of remediation, according to Kirk has value, "only when the information received from both channels can be integrated ..." (Kirk & Kirk, 1971). Mykelbust also makes the argument that sensory overload can result from such presentations (see Myers & Hammill, 1969).

Making the distinction between what he described as regular teaching versus remedial teaching, Kirk guided instructors to remember that instructional technique is imperative to the presentation of content material. Like an echo of John Dewey in the early part of the century, and as a precursor of the proponents of functional curriculum two decades after his own major contributions, Kirk reminded educators that however we present material to children, the content must be functional. Early identification, developing abilities in the most natural setting possible, while training directly to required performance is the essence of preventing school failure and frustration (Kirk & Kirk, 1971).

Many of the classroom structures familiar today were actually designed in response to the need for an environment friendly to the needs of instructors and students participating in psycholinguistic training programs. The self-contained classroom, where a limited number of similarly labeled children were "contained" with a special education teacher who taught most of their content classes became the most common, although not the sole, service delivery model. With the concern and legal mandates for placement in a less restrictive environment, the itinerant teacher became a more widely accepted notion. The itinerant teacher, who often had no permanent "home" within the school, pulled individuals or small groups of students out of the general classrooms for specific periods of remedial work. These teachers evolved into the resource room teachers, where small numbers of children could be pulled out and be attended to either individually or on a small-group basis for both remediation in specific content or for adaptive help with work being done in the general education classroom. The resource room was originally structured and supplied to support remedial education. As often happens, with tight budgets and understaffed schools the resource room design has been corrupted in many school settings. The least employed model at the time, that of team teaching, with one general and one special education specialist in the same room, is a model that is coming into its own today.

 Practical Classroom Applications

This chapter stressed a psycholinguistic model of learning disabilities. Several key aspects of classroom applicability to this theory are appropriate and are described below.

1.   *By encouraging researchers and practitioners to examine individual learning profiles, proponents of the model provided evidence that LD are not, in fact, a homogeneous disorder, but rather a cluster of ill-defined subtypes of language and learning problems.* The IPTA may have opened a can of worms in that increasingly since the mid-1970s, researchers have been trying to come to some agreement regarding the parameters of the category. Various definitions of LD have in fact more commonly focused on what *does not* characterize LD than what *does* characterize it. This has left these definitions and, by extension, the entire field

open to criticism (Kavale & Forness, 1987; Smith & Luckasson, 1990). The inability to define a common cluster of characteristics has made LD classroom placement suspect, as well as limited the internal and external validity of research studies.

2.   *The psycholinguistic model offers important insights into the language development of children, even though the ITPA itself is no longer in widespread use.* Kirk himself noted on numerous occasions that the ITPA should always be used in conjunction with other formal and informal assessment procedures, in order to develop a more complete picture of a child's language abilities. Documentation of a child's difficulties needs to be part of a *process* involving multiple observations, both formal and informal, in multiple environments. This remains an important point to keep in mind.

(continued)

Practical Classroom Applications (continued)

3.   *Researchers have shown that by teachers teaching directly to the critical task, rather than to the underlying psychological function, children learn to employ both the underlying function, as well as improve in task performance.* Insight into the *mechanisms of language development* are often overlooked in classroom environments overly concerned with surface mechanics of language and reading instruction. This approach may be as misguided as the practice of copious drill work based on the underlying processes involved in language development undertaken by early adherents to the psycholinguistic model. Researchers have shown this approach to be of limited value when the instructional objective is to teach a particular language based skill. Teachers in today's classrooms, therefore, would be well served to understand the underlying processes of language, as they can be used as a reference point for developing students' functional language skills.

4.   *A widely used diagnostic tool, the Peabody Picture Vocabulary Test (PPVT), has survived the often conflicting and somewhat intangible outcomes resulting from* psycholinguistic measures and may be seen as the best legacy of the model. The PPVT and the companion materials developed offer education evaluators and classroom teachers an easy-to-use, easily interpretable diagnostic aid. Again, for teachers relying on information gained from the PPVT, a familiarity with the underlying precepts can only help to strengthen the professional's understanding, and thus ability to guide the processes involved with language—and by extension—reading and writing instruction.

5.   *The overriding legacy of Kirk and other early psycholinguistic theorists is one of making the special educator a diagnostician as well as a technician.* Instructional outcomes cannot, and should not, be guided solely by mass-produced, instructional materials in a "one size fits all" format. If nothing else, the value of *individualized prescriptive drill*, carried out in a balanced program of large- and small-group instruction was well documented during this period. It is important that educational professionals remain students of pedagogical history, as well as practitioners of the latest educational procedures.

SUMMARY

- The nineteenth-century work of Broca led to theories regarding the localization of speech and communication functions within the brain and established the foundations for the psycholinguistic model.

- In the mid-twentieth century Osgood proposed a mediational model that accounts for how verbal information is processed between verbal stimulus presentation and a person's response. Once verbal stimuli are present, an individual decodes (receives information), associates the signal with semantic categories, and then encodes, or responds to the stimuli. Processing entails a two-step representational mediation process that connects sensory preception of stimuli and motor and verbal responses.

- Wepman elaborated on the basic premises of Osgood's model by developing the construct of a "memory bank." Individuals receive and store images at the perceptual level and integrate them with previous knowledge at the conceptual level.

- Mykelbust theorized that stimuli received by one system may interfere with the functioning of another, causing "stimulus overload."

- Samuel Kirk's work on the Illinois Test of Psycholinguistic Abilities (ITPA) moved the focus of the research out of the realm of medicine and into the psychological and educational arenas.

- Psycholinguistic deals with the psychological functions and interactions involved in communication. It includes the processes by which a speaker or writer emits signals or symbols and the processes by which these signals are interpreted.

- The focus of psycholinguistic research was to pinpoint and describe the deficit(s) children experience and to formulate remedial programs specific to the skill area displaying weakness. It was believed that although perceptual problems cannot necessarily be corrected, compensatory learning can take place with remedial help.

- Each ITPA subtest pertains to a sensory channel (auditory, visual, vocal, motor or a combination thereof), level (representational or automatic), and process (receptive, expressive, or organizational). Expressive responses are the favored response patterns because they lend themselves to easy recording and measurement.

- The most precarious aspect of the psycholinguistic theory lay in the belief that deficits, once identified, can be ameliorated through the process of psycholinguistic training. The most commonly used programs, the MWM Program for Developing Language Abilities (MWM) (Minskoff, Wiseman, & Minskoff, 1972), GOAL Program: Language Development (GOAL) (Karnes, 1972), and the Peabody Language Development Kit (PLDK) (Dunn, Smith, Dunn, Horton, & Smith, 1981) key directly into linguistic constructs, as outlined in the ITPA.

- Hammill and Larsen (1974) concluded that the results did not indicate clear support for use of the ITPA. They cautioned against the rapid expansion of programs and materials based on the psycholinguistic model. In a 1981 meta-analysis, Kavale questioned Hammill and Larsen's findings. Contrary to those who doubted the efficacy of training programs, Kavale concluded that studies yielded positive results despite variability in the usefulness of individual subtests.

DISCUSSION QUESTIONS _____

To help extend your understanding, reflect on and discuss the following questions:
1. What is the connection between Broca's early work on human brain functions and more recent findings on the brain and human behavior?

2. What are the connections between Osgood's, Wepman's, Mykelbust's and Kirk's theoretical models?

3. What are some examples of "stimulus overloading" as defined by Mykelbust?

4. Are learning disabilities a psychological and learning-based anomaly, as Kirk proposed, or is there a physiological basis?

5. To what extent should teachers spend instructional time training students in the use of general psychological processes (e.g., auditory-vocal association, visual-motor association, etc.), as compared with time spent training students to use grammar rules (syntax), strategies for deriving meaning (semantics), or social use of language (pragmatics)?

6. What are your beliefs regarding the effectiveness of sensory modality training that was linked to psycholinguistic training, and are those beliefs consistent with research findings?

7. Which instructional approaches or principles (e.g., modality training), although associated with psycholinguistic training, are being used with other models of instruction?

8. After reviewing the articles by Hammill and Larsen (1974) and Kavale (1981), what are your conclusions about the efficacy of psycholinguistic training programs? Were they aborted too early?

REFERENCES

Bannatyne, A. (1974). The MWM program for developing language abilities. *Journal of Learning Disabilities, 7* (5), 6–8.

Bateman, B. D. (1963). *Reading and psycholinguistic processes of partially seeing children.* CEC Research Monograph, Series A, #5.

Bateman, B. D. (1967). Learning disabilities—yesterday, today, and tomorrow. In E. C. Frierson and W. B. Barbe (Eds.), *Educating children with learning disabilities.* New York: Appleton-Century-Crofts.

Bateman, B. D. (1968). *Interpretation of the 1961 Illinois Test of Psycholinguistic Abilities.* Seattle, WA: Special Child Publications.

Blessing, K. R. (1964). *An investigation of a psycholinguistic deficit in educable mentally retarded children: Detection, remediation, and related variables.* (Unpublished doctoral dissertation. University of Wisconsin, Madison. International Dissertations Abstracts, 1964, 25, 2327.)

Dunn, L., Horton, K. B., & Smith, O. J. (1981).

Peabody language development kits. Circle Pines, MN: American Guidance Services.

French, J. W., & Michael, W. B. (1966). *Standards for educational and psychological tests and manuals.* Washington, DC: American Psychological Association.

Hammill, D. D., & Larsen S. (1974). The effectiveness of psycholinguistic training. *Exceptional Children,* 5–14.

Hare, B. A., Hammill, D. D., & Bartel, N. R. (1973). Construct validity of selected subtests of the ITPA. *Exceptional Children, 40,* 13–20.

Howell, K. K., Harrison, T. E., Stanford, L. D., Zahn, B. H., & Bracken, B. A. (1990). An empirical evaluation of three preschool language curricula. *Psychology in the Schools, 27,* 296–302.

Karnes, M. B. (1972). *GOAL Program: Language development.* Springfield, MA: Milton Bradley.

Kass, C. (1966). Psycholinguistic disabilities of children with reading problems. *Exceptional Children,* 533–538.

Kavale, K. (1981). Functions of the ITPA: Are they trainable? *Exceptional Children 47*, 496–510.

Kavale, K. A., & Forness, S. R. (1987). The far side of heterogeneity: A critical analysis of empirical subtyping research in learning disabilities. *Journal of Learning Disabilities, 20*, 23–35.

Kephart, N. (1975). Perceptual-motor problems of children. In S. A. Kirk and J. J. McCarthy (Eds.), *Learning disabilities: Selected papers*. Boston: Houghton Mifflin.

Kirk, S. A. & Kirk, W. D. (1971). *Psycholinguistic learning disabilities: Diagnosis and remediation*. Urbana: University of Illinois Press.

Kirk, S. A., McCarthy, J. J., & Kirk, W. D. (1968). *Illinois Test of Psycholinguistic Abilities* (Rev. ed.). Urbana: University of Illinois Press.

Lagerman, A. P. (1970). *Psycholinguistic characteristics of children with reading disabilities and the effects of remediation on psycholinguistic development and reading achievement*. Unpublished doctoral dissertation. Milwaukee, WI: Marquette University.

Logan, R., & Colarusso, R. (1978). The effectiveness of the MWM and goals programs in developing general language abilities. *Learning Disabilities Quarterly, 1* (3), 32–38.

Lund, K. A., Foster, G. E., & McCall-Perez, F. C. (1978). The effectiveness of psycholinguistic training: A re-evaluation. *Exceptional Children,* 310–319.

Minskoff, J. G. (1967). *A psycholinguistic approach to remediation with retarded-disturbed children*. (Unpublished doctoral dissertation, Yeshiva University, NYC. International Dissertations Abstracts, 1967, 28, 1625-A.)

Minskoff, E., Wiseman, D. E., & Minskoff, G. (1972). *The MWM program for developing language abilities*. Ridgefield, NJ: Educational Performance Associates.

Myers, P. I. & Hammill, D. D. (1969). *Methods for learning disorders*. New York: Wiley.

Mykelbust, H. R. (1978). *Progress in learning disabilities: Volume IV*. New York: Grune & Stratton.

Mykelbust, H. R., & Boshes, B. (1969). *Minimal brain damage in children*. Washington, DC: Neurological and Sensory Disease Control Program, Department of Health, Education, and Welfare.

Newcomer, P., Hare, B., Hammill, D., & McGettigan, J. (1974). Construct validity of the ITPA. *Exceptional Children,* 509–510.

Osgood, C. E. (1953). A behavioralistic analysis of perception and language as cognitive phenomena. In S. J. Bruner (Ed.), *Contemporary approaches to cognition*. Cambridge, MA: Harvard University Press.

Osgood, C. E. (1957). Motivational dynamics of language behavior. In M. R. Jones (Ed.), *Nebraska symposium of motivation* (pp. 348–424). Lincoln: University of Nebraska Press.

Osgood, C. E. (1980). *Lectures on language performance*. New York: Springer-Verlag.

Proger, B. B., Cross, L. H., & Burger, R. M. (1973). Construct validity of standardized tests in special education: A framework of reference and application to ITPA research (1967–71). In L. Mann, & D. A. Sabatino (Eds.), *The first review of special education*. Philadelphia: JSE Press.

Saudargas, R. A., Madsen, Jr., C. H., & Thompson, F. (1970). Prescriptive teaching in language arts remediation for black rural elementary school children. *Journal of Learning Disabilities, 3* (1), 26–32.

Sedlak, R. A. & Weener, P. (1973). Review of research on the Illinois Test of Psycholinguistic Abilities. In L. Mann, & D. A. Sabatino (Eds.), *The first review special education*. Philadelphia: JSE Press.

Smith, D. D. & Luckasson, R. (1990). *Introduction to special education: Teaching in an age of challenge* (2nd ed). Boston: Allyn and Bacon.

Staats, A. (1971). Linguistic-mentalistic theory versus an explanatory S-R learning theory of language development. In D. I. Slobin (Ed.), *The ontogenesis of grammar*. New York: Academic Press.

Wepman, J. (1967). The perceptual basis for learning. In E. C. Frieson & W. B. Barbe (Eds.), *Educating children with learning disabilities*. New York: Appleton-Century-Crofts.

Behaviorists assume that behavior is learned through a history facilitated by associations of antecedents, behaviors, and consequences.

CHAPTER 7

The Behavioral Model

In this chapter we will. . .

- Rationalize the acceptance of behaviorism in education.
- Discuss how behavioral science has influenced the approach to assessment issues and practices, and instructional approaches.
- Describe the effectiveness of behavioral approaches to LD.
- Discuss Pavlov's work on conditioned reflexes and Watson's attention to observable stimuli and responses.
- Describe Thorndike's law of effect, and Skinner's experimental analysis of behavior and application of behavioral principles to education.
- Identify Goldstein's study of soldiers, and Strauss and Werner's investigations of children with brain injuries.
- Discuss Kephart and Lehtinen's educational recommendations for children with brain injuries.
- Examine Cruickshank's highly structured classroom and Whelan, Haring, and Phillips' highly structured approach to learning.
- Discuss Lindsley's precision teaching and Hewett's application of learning and behavioral principles to the management of academic instruction for students with problem behaviors.
- Discuss the principles of animal behavior applied to human behavior.
- Examine the antecedent-behavior-consequence (ABC) model of instruction.
- Define behavior as a function of ineffective interactions between students with disabilities and various instructional antecedents and consequences.

- Examine assessment of students with disabilities.

- Describe direct observation of student academic performance.

- Provide measurement strategies.

- Discuss graphic data display.

- Identify data-based decision making.

- Define curriculum-based assessment, programmed learning, and precision teaching.

- Examine the engineered classroom.

- Describe direct instruction.

- Identify peer tutoring and self-management issues.

- Evaluate how the reduction of inappropriate behaviors does not automatically result in the acceleration or acquisition of positive behaviors.

- Describe a change in research focus from the manipulation of consequences to studies of antecedent treatments.

Early medical- and process-deficit models of LD focused on etiology and led to a variety of medical treatments involving neurological, pharmacological, diet, perceptual, and optometric therapies. Disillusionment with the lack of utility and effectiveness of medical, perceptual-motor, and psycholinguistic models led to interest in the behavioral approaches to LD described in this chapter. The behavioral approach to LD implies no etiology, but examines learners from the perspective of directly observable behavior. In fact, its origins may be traced to a reaction against the prevailing *disease models* that preceded it (Kazdin, 1982). While medical models rely on neurological or biochemical examinations of the internal physiological functions that are presumed to affect academic performance, the behavioral perspective uses both direct behavioral observation of student academic performance and task analysis for identification and assessment of learning problems (Keogh, 1988). Many have criticized the consistent lack of evidence supporting indirect methods of intervention for students with LD. Interventions and treatments such as visual-perceptual, optometric, and psycholinguistic process training, as well as differentiation of instruction according to modality strengths and weaknesses have not reliably enhanced educational performance (Lloyd, 1988). Although these interventions may have some beneficial effects, they are generally no longer considered effective remedies for academic achievement problems.

THE BEHAVIORAL MODEL

Direct academic intervention has become the most widely accepted instructional strategy for students with LD. This chapter traces the development and evolution of behavioral approaches to LD. A rationale for the acceptance of behaviorism into education is presented, beginning with the historical framework for the application of behavioral principles to academic difficulties. This is followed by discussions of how behavioral science has influenced our approach to assessment issues and practices and instructional approaches such as the engineered classroom, programmed learning, direct instruction, precision teaching, peer tutoring, and self-management. We conclude the chapter with a look at the effectiveness of behavioral approaches to LD.

A Change in Focus

Well before the principles of behavioral psychology had been articulated, researchers were laying the ground for such a field. Itard's pioneering work with Victor, the wild boy of Aveyron, in 1800 was one of the earliest documented uses of the principles of positive and negative reinforcement. For example, Itard would reward Victor for reading the word *milk* by giving him a drink of milk. Further, the science of Behavioral Psychology has some of its earliest roots in the work of Ivan P. Pavlov and other Russian physiologists. Pavlov's 1902 to 1936 work on conditioned salivary reflexes in dogs provided an early stepping stone for behaviorists. In Pavlov's laboratory, gastric secretions were measured in drops, thereby quantifying his study of animal behavior. His experimentation in respondent conditioning demonstrated that learning could be reliably predicted. Pavlov advocated objectivity (objectivism) in research and sharply criticized subjective research. Pavlov's work on digestion earned him the Nobel Prize in 1904 and led to an understanding of the importance of learning in accounting for animal behavior. His experiments paved the way for the development of a research paradigm for studying human behavior (Kazdin, 1982).

In America, John Watson, who is generally recognized as the founding father of behavioral psychology, began building on the work of Pavlov and other Russian researchers. Like Pavlov, Watson rejected the assumptions that psychologists needed to study the will, mind, and mental states and focused his attention on clearly observable stimuli and responses. He viewed the study of behavior as an experimental, objective science apart from the mentalism of other areas of psychology, and sought to replace the introspective study of subjective states with an objective study of overt behavior. Watson's highly influential 1913 article "Psychology as the Behaviorist Views It" defined psychology as a purely objective, experimental branch of natural science, with the prediction and control of behavior as its goal (Kazdin, 1978).

The psychology of learning—as distinctive from reflexive behavior—was the focus of research conducted by Edward L. Thorndike. Like Watson, Thorndike rejected mentalistic studies of consciousness as the subject matter of psychology and employed objective experimental methods. During the period from 1911 to 1931, Thorndike investigated learning among diverse animal species and was particularly interested in how animals learn new responses not already in their repertoires. His research with animals who learned to escape from a "puzzle box" in order to obtain food outside the box led him to develop the "laws of learning," which included the law of effect. Thorndike's law of effect stated that consequences can strengthen or weaken the bonds between a stimulus and a response. Pavlov, Watson, and Thorndike were all contemporaries working independently but were greatly influenced by each other. Although Pavlov was a physiologist by training and Watson rejected Thorndike's work as not completely behavioristic, all three made great contributions to our understanding of behavior and learning (Kazdin, 1978).

Skinner further refined and articulated the new science of behavioral psychology in the 1930s, 40s, and 50s (Sloan, 1987). He found that the consequences of our responses determine much of what we learn. Skinner examined the distinction between respondent conditioning, as characterized by the elicited responses studied by Pavlov, and operant conditioning, as characterized by the learned responses studied by Thorndike. Believing that elicited behavior could not account for most of the responses that organisms normally perform, he began the study of what has become known as the experimental analysis of behavior (Kazdin, 1978). He rejected theory, focusing instead on individual organisms, rate or frequency of behavior, and the clinical and social relevance of the science of behavior and its applications. Skinner's experimentation and writings provided the starting point for the application of behavioral principles to other. His description of the principles of reinforcement and operant conditioning opened the doors for the application of behavioral principles to education. Researchers and practitioners began to shift their focus from investigation of brain, internal states, and approaches based on brain deficit theories to investigation of interactions between learners and the learning environment. Observable behavior became the focus of treatment interventions, academic skills were viewed as behavioral chains, and single-subject methodology became the most widely used research strategy (Lloyd, 1988). Variables in the learning environment, including teacher behaviors such as attention, smiling, and physical proximity, were found to serve as reinforcers powerful enough to promote academic gains.

Our knowledge of LD has been traced back to the 1930s. The work of Kurt Goldstein, a behavioral scientist who studied soldiers who had sustained head injuries in World War I (Hallahan & Kauffman, 1976) began the study. In the 1930s, Goldstein identified behavioral characteristics of these soldiers, including hyperactivity, forced responsiveness to stimuli, figure-background confusion, meticulosity, and catastrophic reaction. In the 1940s Alfred Strauss and Heinz Werner followed the work of Goldstein with investigations of children who were believed to be brain injured. Their work led them to the conclusion that individuals could be classified as disabled on the basis of behavior alone, without direct evidence of brain lesions. They further dispelled the notion that there were no individual differences among these "brain-injured" children and, instead, showed great concern for individual differences (Hallahan & Kauffman, 1976). During the period from 1947 to 1955, Strauss, along with Kephart and Lehtinen, developed educational recommendations for the children they worked with that were based on the particular behavioral characteristics of the individual child. They advocated diagnosing strengths and weaknesses and prescribing teaching interventions designed to meet the individual's needs. This work was replicated in the 1950s by Cruickshank, who applied the principles to children having cerebral palsy but normal intelligence in Montgomery County, Maryland. His project utilized both the principles of a highly structured classroom devoid of distracting stimuli and concern for the specific behavioral characteristics of the child with learning problems. Similarly, Richard Whelan in Kansas and Norris Haring and E. Lakin Phillips in Arlington County, Virginia, applied the principles of using a highly structured approach to learning, an environment that was very predictable, and positive consequences for desired behavior in their work with children who had social and emotional disorders. Harring was particularly influenced by Ogden Lindsley and his functional analysis of behavior. Lindsley developed a set of techniques for measurement and analysis which have come to be known as precision teaching and are described in detail later in this chapter. Also influential was the work of Frank Hewett in California in the 1960s. His application of the principles of learning and behavior to the management of academic instruction for students with behavior problems was called the "engineered classroom" and is also discussed later in this chapter. By the time that the term *learning disabilities* was accepted at a meeting of parents in Chicago in 1963, the principles of learning which had been developed from research with animals, soldiers with brain injuries, and children with mental disabilities had evolved to a point where they could be applied to children with normal intelligence and specific learning difficulties.

Assumptions

A belief that behavior is learned and that academic behavior is learned through a history facilitated by associations of antecedents, behaviors, and consequences underlies the behavioral approach to education. Behavioral scientists found early on that the principles of behavior applied to the behavior of humans as well as rats and pigeons, and they applied to the behavior of students with and without learning problems. Antecedent (before the behavior) and consequent (after the behavior) events constitute a majority of what is traditionally referred to as teaching (Koorland, 1986). The presentation of questions, directions, prompts, or cues by the teacher or through instructional materials serves as discriminitive stimuli for student responses which may be reinforced or punished by teachers, peers or others. The ABC model of instruction focuses on antecedent stimuli, learner behavior, and the consequences of that behavior (Bos & Vaughn, 1994).

A Behavioral View of LD

LD may be viewed as a function of ineffective interactions between students with disabilities and various instructional antecedents and consequences (especially those associated with typical instructional strategies). Changes in instructional arrangements are made based on empirical evidence. Public school programs developed by Cruickshank, Bentzen, Ratzburg, and Tannhauser included application of behavioral principles in the manipulation of environmental stimuli such as visual and auditory stimuli, amount of space in which the student works, highly structured daily schedule, and increased stimulus value of the teaching materials (Lerner, 1993). Three characteristics underlie the behavioral approach to academic difficulties: (a) individualization and mastery learning, (b) direct instruction, and (c) an emphasis on measurement (Neeper & Lahey, 1988). The science of human behavior has had a profound effect on the education of students with LD, including assessment issues and approaches, and instructional strategies such as the engineered classroom, programmed learning, direct instruction, peer tutoring, and self-management. Of any of the theoretical models, the behavioral model, although criticized by many, has the strongest empirical research base to support its foundational principles.

ASSESSMENT ISSUES AND APPROACHES

Identification of Students

There are two possible reasons for assessing students with disabilities. The first is to identify a condition for the purpose of program eligibility or placement. The second is to gather the data needed for planning, implementing, and monitoring effective instruction. LD are typically defined and characterized by a discrepancy between achievement and intellectual ability (Mercer, 1987). However, intellectual ability is a concept with little meaning in behavioral science. IQ tests are viewed by behaviorists to measure an individual's performance on such a test, and any inferences beyond that concerning the individual's future potential for learning are seen as dangerous. There is little evidence to suggest that the types of assessments typically performed to identify the presence of a disability provide any useful information for instructional planning. Furthermore, a behavioral approach to LD rejects the notion of labeling children, because labeling implies that the child is not unique and that instruction may not need to be individualized (White & Haring, 1980). From a behavioral perspective, children who are not learning to read may require different methods of instruction whether they are labeled as having LD or not.

Direct Observation of Student Academic Performance

Within the behavioral perspective, behaviors are often referred to as *movements* and are defined by their critical effect or function. They must be defined and described precisely in terms of their beginning and ending points (i.e., discrete behaviors), and they must be repeatable if they are to be changed. Instruction is intricately linked to assessment of student progress on a daily or weekly basis. Instructors are interested in knowing whether a particular academic behavior or movement is accelerating or decelerating. For example, are correct responses to the teacher's mathematics questions increasing, and are incorrect responses decreasing in frequency (White & Haring, 1980)?

Measurement Strategies

The behavioral approach suggests very specific strategies for the measurement of academic movements. The first thing required of instructors is that they "write it down." It is not possible to remember the amount of information that is generated in even a short class during one day. In order to develop an accurate assessment of student progress, the instructor must learn to measure academic behavior in terms of some standard parameters. *Count* refers to the number of times a movement is observed (e.g., Jim raised his hand four times). *Duration* refers to the amount of time elapsed between the beginning of a movement cycle and the end of the cycle (e.g., Sue completed the math problem in 58 seconds). *Latency* refers to the amount of time between the presentation of the stimulus and the learner's response (e.g., Fred began working 2.5 minutes after receiving his directions from the teacher). *Frequency*, or *rate*, is the count per unit time, usually measured in movements per minute (e.g., Anna's rate of single-digit addition is 47 movements per minute). These four dimensions (count, duration, latency, and rate) are the most widely used in measuring academic progress.

Graphic Data Display

The data generated by academic/behavioral assessment strategies is typically displayed as a line or bar graph to develop a picture of the learner's progress. Errors and correct responses are often displayed on the same graph to allow for seeing increasing and decreasing trends (Taylor, 1997; Wolery, Bailey, & Sugai, 1988). The Standard Behavior Chart illustrated in Figure 7.1 (FDLRS Clearinghouse/Information Center, 1983) was originally developed by Lindsley (Pennypacker, Koenig, & Lindsley, 1972) and is used in precision teaching approaches to display rate data (learner movements per minute).

Data-Based Decision Making

Data-based instruction involves the systematic use of student performance data to make decisions regarding instruction (White & Haring, 1980; Wollery et al., 1988). Instructors decide on a minimal amount of change that is acceptable and set goals based on either the learner's previous learning rate, peers' rates, or pre-established standards. Failure to meet the standard for 3 days consecutively is often the criterion suggesting a change in instructional strategies. The instructor must then decide when to make the change, reassess the learner's goals, and avoid placing arbitrary limits on progress or our expectations of the learners. Setting minimum celeration (change per unit time) criteria has been found to affect student progress positively. Teachers must also base their decisions regarding goals and any changes in instructional strategies on the learner's phase of learning (i.e., acquisition, fluency, maintenance, generalization). Fuchs, Fuchs, and Hamlett (1989) have found that setting dynamic, data-based goals within the context of a curriculum-based measurement system results in increased content mastery for students with mild and moderate disabilities. Making instructional decisions based on student performance data avoids the problems associated with students being retaught material they have already learned or attempting to master material they are not ready for (Blankenship, 1985). Data-based decision making provides the link between assessment and instruction that allows teachers to place students into instructional materials, form instructional groups if appropriate, monitor progress, and make instructional modifications for individualization. Bickel and Bickel (1986) suggest that special education be viewed as a decision process driven by data gathered on student performance, and classroom procedures tried.

Curriculum-Based Assessment

Curriculum-based assessment (CBA) is both an assessment and a teaching practice that uses the material to be learned as the basis for evaluating student performance for the purpose of determining the learner's instructional needs (Choate, Enright, Miller, Poteet, & Rakes, 1995). The essential measure of success becomes the learner's progress in the curriculum of the local school (Tucker, 1985). Instead of a new, high-tech assessment procedure, CBA is more appropriately viewed as a return to traditional educational procedures and the ultimate in "teaching to the test." It

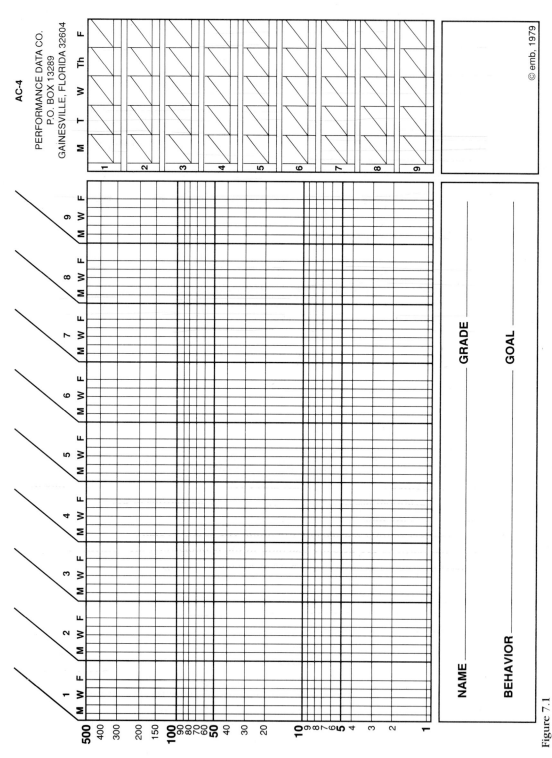

Figure 7.1

Standard behavior chart for charting corrects and errors from probes used in precision teaching.

Note. Reprinted with permission from Behavior Development Co., 5153 S.W. 88 Terrace, Gainesville, FL 32608.

Data-based decision making provides the link between assessment and instruction.

measures the student's level of achievement in terms of the expected curricular outcomes of the school. A first grade student, therefore, is expected to learn the information presented in the school's first grade curriculum or course of study. While traditional educational assessment strategies rely on standardized, psychometric tests,
CBA relies on the materials that will provide the most information regarding the students' mastery of their particular curriculum. The ability of standardized tests to measure what teachers are actually teaching in the schools (i.e., the content validity of
the test) is severely limited because of restricted sampling sizes and modern norming procedures. Therefore, CBA procedures have been researched in areas such as
reading (Deno, Mirkin, & Chang, 1982) and writing (Deno, Marston, & Mirkin, 1982)
and found to be valid measures of student achievement.

   A primary goal of CBA is to provide useful data for instructional planning, data
not readily available from the results of standardized tests (Whinnery & Fuchs, 1992).
Nevertheless, Marston and Magnusson (1985) reported that CBA may also be successfully used for screening, identification, and program planning. CBA's behavioral
flavor comes from the use of direct observation and recording of individual student
performance. Furthermore, the essential comparisons made in CBA are to compare
a learner's performance on one day with his or her performance on a subsequent
day, rather than compare the performance with peers or norms.

An important feature of CBA is its use in identifying the learner's instructional level and avoiding instruction that is either frustrating (too difficult) or boring (too easy). Finding a challenging, but not frustrating, level of instruction is critical because students referred to special education programs are frequently those who have created their own kinds of challenges in the classroom when presented with a curriculum that was either frustrating or boring (Tucker, 1985). Students who, because of disability, disadvantage, or whatever reason, are unable to keep pace with grade level instruction become "curriculum casualties" or "curriculum handicapped," falling further and further behind their peers (Glicking & Thompson, 1985).

CBA includes procedures for the direct observation and analysis of the learning environment, analysis of the processes used by students approaching tasks, examination of student products, and control and arrangement of tasks for the student (Algozzine, 1991). Blankenship (1985) suggests that the essence of CBA is the linking of assessment to curriculum and instruction and recommends the following steps for developing and using CBAs:

1. List the skills presented in the selected materials.
2. Review the list for inclusion of all important skills.
3. Sequence the skills presented in logical order.
4. Write an objective for each skill on the list.
5. Prepare items to assess student skill on each objective.
6. Prepare testing materials for student use.
7. Decide how the assessment will be given.
8. Assess learners with the CBA immediately before beginning instruction.
9. Use results to determine which students have mastered the skills, which students are ready for instruction, and which students lack mastery of prerequisite skills.
10. Readminister the CBA after instruction, to determine which students have mastered the skills, which students require more practice or instruction, and which students are making unsatisfactory progress and require a change in instruction.
11. Readminister the CBA periodically to assess long-term retention.

CBA incorporates the behavioral strategies of direct observation and measurement of student performance and falls within a framework suggested by Ysseldyke and Algozzine (1990) who have suggested that meaningful assessment be guided by the following assumptions: (a) there is no one way to assess students, (b) the primary goal of assessment should be improved instruction, (c) assessment should concentrate on relevant variables and occur often during teaching, and (d) assessment should occur where problem behaviors occur. CBA has been found to be an effective strategy for measuring academic performance. CBA and other data-based assessment strategies allow the teacher to plan individualized instruction based on student needs. The instructional issues and approaches that follow are based on behavioral principles and assume that direct assessment of academic performance has taken place.

INSTRUCTIONAL ISSUES AND APPROACHES

Programmed Learning

The programmed learning approach is based on behavioral principles of providing positive reinforcement for correct responses and withholding positive reinforcement when incorrect responses are made. The reinforcement usually takes the form of feedback informing the students that their answers were correct. Students also are informed immediately when their answers are incorrect and are directed to the materials that will teach them to respond correctly to similar questions or problems. Students are required by the materials to perform a predetermined number of correct responses before moving to subsequent subject matter. A considerable amount of repetition and feedback is thereby built into the program.

The early practice of using a programmed approach originated in 1920 with Pressley's design of a teaching machine (see Skinner, 1958). The student would read a specific question and upon selection of the correct answer, the next question would be supplied. Skinner's (1958) additions to the programmed approach highlighted the influence of behaviorism. The specific skill to be taught was broken into subskills. As each subskill was mastered, the student was provided with frequent and positive reinforcement. Skinner's programmed learning machine provided the model for the development of many programmed learning materials such as workbooks, audiotapes, videotapes, film strip lessons, and computer assisted instruction (CAI).

The materials are specifically designed to be both self-teaching and self-correcting (Mercer, 1983). Students using a programmed learning approach are presented with subject matter which has been broken down into small segments. The materials guide the students through a series of questions or problems and a means to check the correctness of their answers. Workbook materials require learners to check their answers themselves. Teaching machines may provide the answer to the learner and, in a visual display, praise for correct answers. Incorrect responses require the learner to either try again or return to an instructional format. Programmed reading approaches were largely developed in the 1960s (e.g., Buchanan, 1966).

The implementation of programmed instruction enabled the teacher to allow students to proceed at their own learning rates. In addition, the teacher was now able to accommodate more students throughout the day because the teacher was doing less direct instruction and more supervision of instruction. The programmed learning approach was widely used throughout many special education classrooms in the 1960s and 70s.

The premise of the programmed learning approach continues to be utilized throughout special education programs, in the practice of individual seat work as instruction. Teachers design individual programs that allow students to work on different activities and different levels of activities within the same classroom. Each student is given an agenda to follow for the day, which includes a significant amount of independent seat work and often includes a folder of various worksheets. The teacher circulates and assists students as they need help in various aspects of their assigned activities. The practice allows a wide range of students to be assigned to a classroom at the same time. However, it is not to be assumed that a student who is spending the largest percentage of class time in independent seat work is receiving individualized instruction (Stevens & Rosenshine, 1981).

Precision Teaching

Precision teaching (PT) provides a teacher with a quick assessment of a student's progress and assists teachers in making decisions about their students' educational programs. PT practices in the classroom can assist a student in learning new information but its greatest benefit can be derived from the use of PT as a daily assessment of student progress.

PT principles are based on the theory of free operant founded by Skinner in the early 1950s. Ogden Lindsley, considered the founder of PT, developed the principles for PT from procedures he utilized for clients in a state hospital in Kansas while working under B. F. Skinner (Lindsley, 1990). These principles include providing opportunities for frequent correct response, reinforcement of correct response, and recording of correct and incorrect response. For managing behavior problems, the implementation of these practices was readily accepted by educators, but the application of PT principles was not as readily adapted for measuring academic progress. The traditional methods of assessment involve end of the week, end of the chapter, midsemester, end of the semester, and end of the year assessment. Through these traditional evaluation methods, teachers determine mastery only at the end of a learning sequence. PT methods enable a teacher to detect a learning problem early in the learning cycle and to adapt instruction to ensure student mastery of information. The use of percentages as a means for determining student progress does not enable a student to see small amounts of progress and, thus, does not allow for reinforcement of student learning. Deno (1985) concisely describes the advantages of precision teaching versus traditional assessment tools in his analogy of the use of a weight loss program. If a scale only detected a loss of weight after an individual had lost 10 pounds, then an individual losing 8.5 pounds would become frustrated and discontinue the program. PT measures small increments of growth, just as a scale detects small changes in weight, thus enabling changes to be observed before too much time has elapsed and motivation for change, reduced.

The basic principles of PT are stated in the following seven principles:

1. Teachers learn best by studying the behaviors of their students.
2. Rate of response is the universal measure of behaviors.
3. Student performances are charted on a standard celeration chart.
4. Direct and continuous monitoring is emphasized.
5. Behavior and processes are described and functionally defined.
6. Building rather than eliminating behaviors is emphasized.
7. Impact of environmental influences on behaviors is analyzed. (Lovitt, Fister, Freston, Kemp, Moore, Schroeder, & Bauernschmidt, 1990).

To elaborate further:

1. Teachers learn best by studying the behaviors of their students. Through daily

assessment a teacher can analyze whether a learning activity is benefiting the student in mastery of a skill.

2. Rate of response is the universal measure of behaviors. Frequency of response of any behavior is an indicator that a behavior is learned. Continuous, quick, and accurate responding ensures that the response has been learned and that the new response has become part of the student's repertoire.

3. Student performances are charted on a standard celeration chart. A visual display of the learner's performance provides a graphic description of the child's progress in a particular academic skill. The graph enables teachers, professionals, parents, and students to see actual progress being realized in a particular area.

4. Direct and continuous monitoring is emphasized. Direct and continuous measurement of a particular skill selected for mastery assures that the information has been mastered. Often in traditional assessment practices the information learned may or may not be what is assessed on the standardized test at the end of the year. Through continuous daily assessment the progress and mastery of information can be determined early in the learning cycle.

5. Behavior and processes are described and functionally defined. Communication among members involved in the learning process is enhanced because all individuals are clear on the skill to be mastered and the progress that has occurred during the learning cycle. A functional definition of the behavior states how the information to be mastered is received and the response is to be expressed. This assists the teacher in accurately determining what type skills are necessary for learning the new information.

6. Building rather than eliminating behaviors is emphasized. In PT a student learns in a positive environment because new information is built upon information that has been previously mastered in a successful learning situation.

7. Impact of environmental influences on behaviors is analyzed. In daily measurement the effects of variables in the learning situation can be realized due to the close linkage between the learning situation and evaluation.

Procedures of PT.   The five step PT procedure can easily be implemented in a general or exceptional education classroom (Diviaio & Hefferen, 1983) and includes pinpointing the behavior, counting and recording data, setting aims for mastery, graphing daily, and making decisions. The teacher first must *pinpoint* the specific behavior to be mastered. The behavior chosen for mastery is written in functional terms that clearly communicate the receptive and expressive format needed for mastery of the behavior. The following functional descriptions are examples of behaviors that a teacher might select for learning mastery:

oral reading = see/say Dolch Stories Primer

vocabulary words = see/say Dolch Phrases

multiplication facts = see/write mixed multiplication facts 0 through 9

common signs = see/say common signs and label words

metric measurement = see/say metric words

The second step in *PT* is to *count and record* the number of correct answers after a timed probe. Figures 7.2 through 7.6 (FDLRS Clearinghouse/Information Center, 1983) illustrate the probe sheets that would be utilized for the above behaviors.

The timed response for each probe sheet is determined by the teacher with most probes set for 30 seconds to 1 minute. Through a quick 1-minute timing the teacher can be assured that assessment can occur on a daily basis. The number of correct and incorrect responses are recorded on the graph. The type of graph utilized can vary. A semilogarithmic graph, illustrated in Figure 7.1, enables the student to see proportional changes in a skill. This can be especially beneficial when a student is first learning a new skill and may only reach a score of five correct responses. Graphs can be commercially purchased (Figure 7.1) or teacher made with standard graph paper.

The third step of PT is to *set aims for mastery*. A suggested performance standard for mastery of various learning skills is noted below (Diviaio & Hefferan, 1983):

Pinpointed Behavior	Standard
See/Say Sight Words	80–100 words/min.
See/Say Words in Context (oral reading)	200+ words/min.
See/Say Words in Context (silent reading)	400+ words/min.
Think/Say Ideas or Facts	15–30 ideas/min.
See/Write Math Facts	70–90 digits/min.
Think/Say Numbers in Sequence (count bys)	150–200+ min.
See/Say Numbers	80–100/min.

The standards can be used as guidelines for determining mastery for each student. A student may feel more successful if interim goals are selected with the ultimate goal being final mastery of the material.

Graphing daily is the fourth step of PT. Through a clear graphic display of the student's learning progress, the communication between teachers, parents, students, and other professionals is enhanced. In addition, student motivation is high because of the constant visual reminder of progress. Figure 7.7 illustrates a completed chart for see/say Dolch phrases. The sooner a student learns to self-chart, the more efficient the learning process. Part of a successful learning environment is student ownership in the learning process.

The chart enables the teacher and student to complete the final step of the PT program, *making decisions* about educational progress and the student's educational program. Through an examination of the progress on the chart, a clear educational picture is illustrated and decisions can be made about the progress of the student. The amount of progress expected should be based on the individual student. A teacher can determine the level of progress, based on the student's past experiences. An aim is determined and a line drawn to indicate the amount of progress or celeration necessary for the student to reach mastery of the skill. If a teacher cannot determine minimal celeration, the progress rate of peers completing the same skill could be used initially until standards have been determined for the student (White & Haring, 1980). A program needs to be reevaluated and often changed if a student is not making minimal celeration.

	Dolch Stories Primer
THE SEE-SAW	
Jane was going to the store. She went down the street.	11
She saw a boy and a little dog.	19
The boy said, "Come and play with me. You may play with	31
my dog."	33
Jane said, "I will play with you. What can the dog do?	45
He is not very big."	50
"He is a good dog," said the boy. "He can run and jump.	63
And he can ride a see-saw."	70
"Oh, I want to see him ride," said Jane. "Where is it?"	82
"I have it in here," the boy said.	90
He said to the dog. "Go find the see-saw. We will	102
have a ride."	105
The dog ran to the see-saw.	112
"Do you like to ride?" said the boy. "Say 'yes'."	122
The dog said, "Bow-wow."	127
"Look at this," said the boy. "I am up and he is down.	140
He is up and I am down."	147
"What a funny ride for a dog." said Jane.	156
Did you ever see a dog ride a see-saw?	166

Figure 7.2

PT probe of see/say oral reading of Dolch Stories Primer.

				Dolch Phrases Unit 3	
you will like	down here	will read	a pretty picture	about him	12
when I can	with more	if I may	for the baby	if you can	26
you are	must go	too little	it was	on the floor	37
on the chair	we are	his brother	what I want	your mother	49
he is	by the house	all night	the old men	did not go	62
down the hill	he would do	for the baby	about him	he is	75
on the floor	when I can	must go	what I want	on the chair	89
a pretty picture	we are	you will like	it was	all night	101
your mother	did not go	his brother	by the house	will read	113
you are	the old men	down here	he would do	down the hill	126
if I may	too little	with more	if you can	for the baby	139
all night	if I may	you will like	it was	the old men	152
what I want	with more	down here	if you can	you are	164

Figure 7.3

PT probe of see/say Dolch Phrases, Unit 3.

Note. From *A Resource Manual for the Development and Evaluation of Special Programs for Exceptional Students. volume V-0: Techniques of Precision Teaching, Part 1, Part 2, Part 3,* 1983. Tallahassee, FL: Bureau for Exceptional Students, Division of Public Schools, Florida Department of Education.

							see/write							(through x 9s)		
8	3	6	4	4	9	5	2	0	7	6	0	5	5	2	9	
×4	×9	×3	×9	×7	×9	×7	×9	×4	×9	×5	×9	×6	×9	×8	×8	(30)
8	9	2	1	5	9	9	9	2	8	5	9	6	6	1	7	
×2	×7	×3	×9	×9	×2	×3	×0	×3	×9	×8	×5	×2	×9	×3	×3	(57)
9	1	0	3	9	8	7	0	9	9	1	7	9	3	9	4	
×3	×4	×9	×8	×9	×7	×9	×8	×1	×7	×9	×9	×5	×6	×7	×3	(84)
3	9	3	3	3	5	4	4	6	8	5	9	8	2	1	9	
×5	×2	×1	×9	×2	×9	×2	×9	×9	×9	×3	×6	×3	×9	×8	×4	(112)
2	9	7	9	9	3	5	8	6	1	4	6	0	5	8	9	
×5	×0	×6	×7	×5	×9	×4	×9	×8	×9	×7	×9	×4	×9	×5	×0	(140)

Figure 7.4

PT probe of see/write mixed multiplication facts 0 through 9.

Note. From *A Resource Manual for the Development and Evaluation of Special Programs for Exceptional Students. volume V-0: Techniques of Precision Teaching, Part 1, Part 2, Part 3,* 1983. Tallahassee, FL: Bureau for Exceptional Students, Division of Public Schools, Florida Department of Education.

		see/say		Common Signs & Labels, Words Unit 2	
Doctor	Poison	Police	Telephone	Quiet	5
Step Up	Ladies	Step Down	Restrooms	Keep Away	13
Pull—Push	Keep Off the Grass	Bus Stop	Airport	Danger	23
Poison	Restrooms	Keep Away	Keep Off the Grass	Doctor	32
Police	Ladies	Step Up	Danger	Airport	38
Step Down	Bus Stop	Pull—Push	Quiet	Telephone	46
Pull—Push	Poison	Bus Stop	Telephone	Airport	53
Quiet	Danger	Police	Step-Up	Restrooms	59
Doctor	Step-Down	Ladies	Keep Off the Grass	Keep Away	69
Telephone	Airport	Quiet	Doctor	Ladies	74
Police	Keep Away	Danger	Poison	Restrooms	80
Step Down	Keep Off the Grass	Pull—Push	Step Up	Ladies	91
Doctor	Bus Stop	Step Down	Keep Off the Grass	Keep Away	102

Figure 7.5

PT probe of see/say common signs and labels.

Note. From *A Resource Manual for the Development and Evaluation of Special Programs for Exceptional Students. volume V-0: Techniques of Precision Teaching, Part 1, Part 2, Part 3,* 1983. Tallahassee, FL: Bureau for Exceptional Students, Division of Public Schools, Florida Department of Education.

						Metric Words	
			see/say				
hectoliter	gram	millimeter	deciliter	decigram	centiliter	kiloliter	7
meter	kilogram	kilometer	milligram	centigram	milliliter	hectogram	14
centimeter	hectometer	liter	dekameter	decimeter	dekaliter	dekagram	21
liter	milliliter	meter	centiliter	hectoliter	hectogram	kiloliter	28
kilogram	gram	dekaliter	millimeter	centigram	deciliter	kilometer	35
dekameter	milligram	decimeter	hectometer	decigram	centimeter	millimeter	42
centimeter	deciliter	decimeter	hectogram	kilogram	centiliter	dekagram	49
milliliter	dekaliter	milligram	kiloliter	liter	hectoliter	decigram	56
gram	meter	hectometer	dekameter	kilometer	centigram	decimeter	63
gram	centigram	kilogram	decigram	hectometer	hectogram	meter	70
hectoliter	deciliter	dekagram	dekaliter	centimeter	dekameter	milligram	77
centiliter	milliliter	kiloliter	millimeter	kilometer	liter	kiloliter	84
millimeter	kilometer	liter	dekaliter	deciliter	milliliter	meter	91

Figure 7.6

PT probe of see/say metric words.

Note. From *A Resource Manual for the Development and Evaluation of Special Programs for Exceptional Students. volume V-0: Techniques of Precision Teaching, Part 1, Part 2, Part 3,* 1983. Tallahassee, FL: Bureau for Exceptional Students, Division of Public Schools, Florida Department of Education.

The teacher may decide to *slice back* the skill level, or *leap up*. A slice back is made when the teacher develops a new set of materials focusing on the same skill but at a slightly easier level. A leap up in curriculum is made when the teacher jumps a level in the sequence of skills, to motivate and challenge the student. Second graders involved in a leap-up curriculum—from simple addition to mixed addition, subtraction, and multiplication facts—doubled their mastery of skills. The teacher noted that substantially more errors were made in completing the probe sheets, but because of the challenging material, the students were motivated to learn and doubled the amount of material mastered (Lindsley, 1990). If a change is made in the student's program, a clear, dark change line is indicated on the chart, and the new behavior or adapted behavior is noted on the change line. The daily assessment measures collected through the process of PT can be used as mastery for objectives on a student's Individualized Education Program (IEP). The chart can be filed with the student's data sheets as documentation of learning mastery. This documentation is a quick, easy, and reliable method for collecting data that clearly communicates valuable information to other professionals and parents involved with the student (White & Haring, 1980). In addition, the probe sheets are useful communication tools that follow students throughout their educational careers.

PT has been used successfully at all grade levels as a means for monitoring progress and ensuring that specific skills are mastered (Lindsley, 1990). The ease of implementation of PT enables students to be responsible for their own learning, such as graphing their own progress and developing self-initiative in practicing skills to mastery.

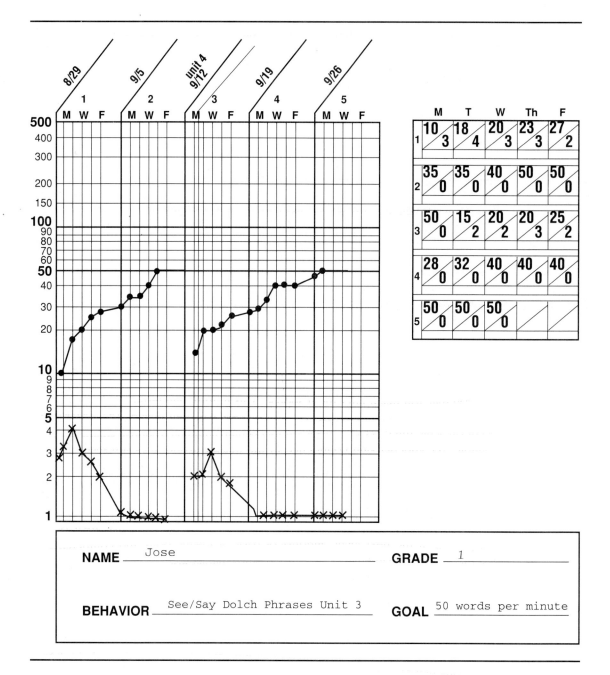

Figure 7.7
Completed PT chart of see/say Dolch Phrases, Unit 3.
Note. From *A Resource Manual for the Development and Evaluation of Special Programs for Exceptional Students. volume V-0: Techniques of Precision Teaching, Part 1, Part 2, Part 3*, 1983. Tallahassee, FL: Bureau for Exceptional Students, Division of Public Schools, Florida Department of Education.

PT enhances the learning of specific skills. The assurance of generalization of these mastered skills to other areas of cognitive development is still an area of concern for many educators. Procedures such as curriculum-based measurement (Fuchs & Fuchs, 1991) may provide the tie to blend both precision teaching and the holistic approach to education.

Engineered Classroom

The engineered classroom was designed by Hewett (1968) in Santa Monica, California, to meet the needs of those students identified as emotionally disturbed. However, the basic behavioral principles underlying the philosophy of the engineered classroom also apply to the environment of students with LD. The premise on which the engineered classroom is designed is based on the inability of exceptional students to adapt to their environments. Hewett (1968) contends that all students progress through the following seven-step academic and social developmental sequence: attention, response, order, exploratory, social, mastery, and achievement.

Stage one is the *attention* level. During this stage students must have the ability to attend to various stimuli to gain knowledge about the environment around them. Students who have difficulty attending will be unable to respond to the surrounding stimuli and unable to progress to the next stage of development, which is the response level. In the *response* stage the student must acknowledge the stimuli and respond to it. Students respond to stimuli through various means, such as writing, talking, or touching. In the response stage, the student is also concerned about the reaction that will occur after the response. This in turn, will result in the motivation to continue to respond, and the learning process has then begun. The *order* stage occurs at stage three, as students learn that certain stimulus response chains are predictable. As students gain confidence in the outside world, they advance to stage four, the *exploratory* stage. In this stage children reach out and examine their environments. As students explore their environments the realization occurs that other individuals are part of that environment. At this level of development students are motivated by the *social* approval and disapproval of peers and significant adults in their lives. This need for approval affects both academic and affective areas of development. At the next level, *mastery* of basic academic skills and competencies, such as reading, mathematics, and good study habits are developed. As students progress toward that final developmental stage, *achievement*, they become more and more aware of their personal achievement and success, without the external variables of peer pressure or grades. At this stage of development students want to learn more because they enjoy learning. Since the exceptional student must have assistance progressing through each developmental stage, the goal of the engineered classroom is to provide the structured environment that assists students through the developmental sequence.

In Hewett's design, the physical structure of the classroom was considered a critical element in the total program. The classroom was divided into three learning centers: the order center, the mastery center, and the exploratory center. Each center provided activities to assist the student in an area of development. The students entered the order center upon arrival to school. During the order-center time of approximately 5 minutes, the students practiced the skills needed to attend to tasks and follow directions. After the order center the students cycled into the mastery center. In the mastery center students worked on academic tasks such as reading and mathematics. In addition, the students continued to receive reinforcement for appropriate behavior, such as attending to tasks. The exploratory center was scheduled for the end of the day and provided the students with simple science activities and crafts. The multisensory emphasis in the exploratory center allowed the students to investigate the environment around them through different avenues. In addition, the science experiments assisted the students in realizing the cause and effect of many events within their environment and to give them confidence in exploring that environment.

A behavioral approach to education was utilized in the classroom, and students learned quickly that certain behaviors would be rewarded. The work record card was the means for establishing the causal relationship between appropriate behavior and reinforcement (Hewett, 1968). Students earned check marks for appropriate social behavior and completion of academic tasks. The completed work record cards were then exchanged for tangible rewards. The emphasis in the engineered classroom was on reinforcing positive behavior, in addition to the use of a sequence of nine hierarchical interventions implemented for those students exhibiting inappropriate behavior. The first seven interventions required adaptations to the environment, such as sending a student to a study carrel or "office," modifying a classroom assignment, use of a verbal cue by the teacher, or changing the student's assignment. If the seven interventions were ineffective, the teacher considered the student a "nonstudent." During the 5- to 10-minute period of isolation the student would be unable to earn positive check marks.

The design of the engineered classroom in the late 1960s became the model for classroom development for many exceptional education classrooms (Hewett & Forness, 1974). The teachers in the engineered classroom determined the starting point for each student in the developmental sequence and guaranteed a positive reward for even small amounts of growth. The consistent structure of the environment assisted students in developing appropriate behaviors, and as the students mastered a particular skill, the teacher would slightly raise the expectations, resulting in continued successful progress.

Hewett set the model for classroom teachers in his design of the engineered classroom. The Santa Monica project was one of the first educational programs which utilized behavioral principles in the design of a structured education program for managing students who cannot adapt to the classroom environment. Hewett (1968) noted substantial improvement in behavior and academic achievement for those students assigned to the engineered classroom model. The difference in achievement gains for students in the structured model were reported to be due to the amount of time spent on tasks. The control group teachers spent significantly more time on discipline and less on academic tasks.

Teachers have continued to use aspects of his model of behavior management and classroom design in developing exceptional education classrooms. Although specifically designed for emotionally disturbed students, the engineered classroom model of structure, task cards, and tangible rewards for appropriate behavior has been implemented in classrooms across all exceptionality areas. Students learn the expectations and rewards for this very structured setting, and positive changes are made in behavior.

Hewett's (1968) original design was for implementation of this very structured approach for one semester, with a transition period to a more traditional learning environment. The need for a program that teaches students to generalize appropriate behavior to other settings and assists students in developing an internal locus of control continues to be a challenge for professionals in all educational settings (Devine & Tomlinson, 1976; Fenitor, Burkholdt, Hamblin, & Smith, 1972; McLaughlin, Dolliver, & Mallady, 1979).

Direct Instruction

Rosenshine's (1976) teacher effectiveness studies and Bereiter and Engelmann's curriculum model laid the foundation for the direct instruction model. Bereiter and Engelmann (1966) developed the DISTAR (Direct Instruction System for Teaching and Remediation) as part of the Follow Through Project for the U.S. Office of Education. This very structured curriculum included teachers spending significant amounts of time in direct instruction, high rates of successful student practice, and a step-by-step sequence of instruction that included mastery learning (Becker, Engelmann, & Thomas, 1971). The DISTAR curriculum was very similar to other behaviorally based education programs (Gersten, 1985) in the implementation of reinforcement for correct responses, breakdown of specific tasks, the practice of modeling and shaping, and the utilization of continual checks for progress.

An independent investigation of the direct instruction model (House, Glass, McLean, & Walker, 1978) through the Follow Through Project revealed students' scores were near or above the national average in three academic areas after academic instruction in the direct instruction model for 4 years (kindergarten through third grade). Advantages of the direct instruction model were also indicated in a long-term investigation of high school students taught in the direct instruction curriculum beginning in 1969 (Darch, Gersten, & Taylor, 1978). Significantly more students graduated from high school, fewer students needed to repeat a grade, and more students were accepted into college than those students instructed in other curricula.

Rosenshine (1976) introduced the term *direct instruction* into the vocabulary of public educators. An analysis of teaching variables used in classrooms where students made substantial academic achievement gains (Rosenshine & Stevens, 1986) revealed certain effective instructional practices:

1. Significant time was spent in active teaching.

2. Students worked on activities, with high rates of success.

3. Teaching was broken down into smaller units of instruction and taught in a sequenced fashion.

4. Immediate feedback was given on student assignments.

5. Frequent interaction between student and teacher about academic activities was noted, with considerable amounts of small-group instruction.

The basis for the model is the belief that all students can improve in academic achievement—no matter what the label—if teachers use "effective instruction" (Englemann, & Carnine, 1982).

Direct instruction refers to high levels of student engagement within academically focused, teacher-directed classrooms using sequenced, structured materials. As developed below, direct instruction refers to teaching activities focused on academic matters where goals are clear to students, time allocated for instruction is sufficient and continuous, content coverage is extensive, student performance is monitored, questions are at a low cognitive level and produce many correct responses, and feedback to students is immediate and academically oriented. In direct instruction, the teacher controls instructional goals, chooses material appropriate for the students' ability level, and paces the instructional episode. Interaction is characterized as structured, but not authoritarian; rather, learning takes place in a convivial academic atmosphere (Rosenshine, 1978, p. 17).

Numerous investigations have been conducted into the value of using such direct instruction strategies as pacing, size of group instruction, and feedback. An investigation of academically below average first graders indicates that fast-paced instruction increases students' attention and appropriate responses. Students taught in small-group instruction learned skills more rapidly than those instructed in one on one settings, and repeated investigations have indicated the importance of immediate feedback, teacher modeling, and student practice of correct response (Neef, Iwata, & Page, 1977; Stromer, 1975).

Teacher Planning in Direct Instruction. In direct instruction the teacher plans lessons that offer high rates of active student engagement time. An investigation by Rosenshine (1978) revealed that in classrooms where only 1 or 2 minutes of the reading period was spent in active student engagement time, little or no academic gains were documented in reading. The goals, objectives, and materials for the lesson are determined by the teacher. The teacher is in charge of the lesson and directly teaches the skills necessary for mastery of information. A child-centered or inquiry approach to learning is often a popular method of instruction for teachers, but these methods have not resulted in the same academic gains for students as has the direct instruction model (Rieth, Polsgrove, & Semmel, 1981).

Teachers need to plan out efficient schedules that reduce the amount of down time within a lesson and to reduce the transition time from one activity to the next. Just a 5-minute delay in beginning to teach and stopping a class 5 minutes early at the end of each period results in a reduction of teaching of approximately 1 hour a day, 5 hours a week, and 1.5 weeks a year. Effective teachers organize their classroom space to enhance efficient classroom instruction. Teaching materials and student materials are readily accessible, thus reducing the amount of student down time.

Delivery of Instruction in a Direct Instruction Model. The delivery of instruction is fast-paced, with considerable amount of time allocated for positive practice of newly learned information and immediate feedback provided to the students. The teacher follows a three-step sequence in teaching new information:

1. **Demonstration.** The teacher introduces new material to be learned and teaches the concept or skill. If applicable, a definition or concept is stated. Well chosen examples and nonexamples are modeled.

2. **Guided Practice.** The students practice the newly learned skill with the guidance and continuous feedback of the teacher. The teacher leads students through responses by providing visual and verbal cues and prompts, when necessary, for the students. The teacher then tests students by finding the level of cues and prompts until the students can make responses accurately and independently. Once the skill is mastered with no errors, the student moves to independent practice.

3. **Independent Practice.** During this stage the student practices the skill until a high degree of fluency is reached. The student must have mastery over the skill or will be continually practicing errors. At this stage the student should be performing the skill without teacher guidance. If a high rate of errors are present the teacher needs to return to step two of guided practice. A significant improvement in academic achievement has been noted when instruction has followed the above three steps (Stevens & Rosenshine, 1981).

Learning Stages.   Another consideration in using direct instruction is the progression of students through the stages of skill development. These stages include concept or skill acquisition, fluency building, maintenance, and generalization. During the *acquisition stage*, the student characteristically makes numerous mistakes, requires cues and prompts, and needs corrective feedback. Teachers provide effective instructional antecedents, which are characterized in this learning stage by giving of extensive direction or guidance, prompts, and cues that assist students in responding accurately.

The acquisition stage can be divided into two levels: *introduction and discrimination.* The differences between these two levels are minimal but significant. The introduction level entails the use of examples only, and the discrimination level entails the use of examples and nonexamples. During the introduction level, the examples-only format helps to establish a pattern of accurate responding. When students respond accurately, those responses are reinforced by the students' sense of success and by teacher praise. During the discrimination level, learning is solidified by having students distinguish between examples and nonexamples (i.e., they are able to determine whether or not the stimulus fits the concept category or fits the situation for using an academic rule).

The second stage of learning, *fluency building*, is characterized by students maintaining high rates of accuracy and increasing the speed with which they make a response. Once students have demonstrated consistent accurate responding, the focus of instruction changes to speed *and* accuracy. Instructional activities at the fluency-building stage involve the student in fast-paced drill. The use of 1-minute timings to measure the student's rate of performance, as done in PT, is an example of a fluency-building activity. Guided and independent practice sessions are scheduled daily to provide concentrated amounts of practice. Once a prescribed level of fast and accurate responding is attained, the skill is considered mastered.

Maintenance is the third stage of learning during which previously acquired concepts or skills are practiced for retention. As in the fluency-building stage, speed and accuracy are emphasized in maintenance activities. However, the practice sessions are spaced apart in intervals ranging from 1 week to 1 month. They may take the form of an end-of-the-week or end-of-the-month review.

The ultimate educational outcome that underlies every instructional activity is to have the students function better in the world outside school, either during or after their school years. This is achieved by fostering *generalization* of what is learned to other situations and times. Exhibiting learned responses in places other than where they were taught is referred to as setting generalization. When responses are made after training conditions have faded completely, then a second form of generalization, time generalization, has occurred.

Lesson Format for Direct Instruction.   An integrated format for applying direct instruction procedures is represented in Table 7.1 as the TEAL model—Teaching: Explicit Activation of Learning (O'Shea & O'Shea, 1997). This integrated format can be used in the development of instruction for students with learning difficulties in a manner that incorporates the critical elements of effective instruction.

1. *Acquisition Stage—Introduction.* As described earlier, this initial stage of learning requires significant amounts of teacher time and attention directed toward planning and monitoring students' responses to target concepts and academic rules (Baker, Simmons, & Kameenui, 1994). The introduction phase of the acquisition stage is characterized by precise demonstrations and guided practice using examples only. The following sequence exemplifies this and other features of lesson development at this stage of learning:

    a. Gain student attention and orient students with an outline of the activities to be completed during the lesson.

    b. Link the present lesson with previous lessons by reviewing related concepts or academic rules previously taught.

    c. During the demonstration, model or induce, through questioning, the target concept or academic rule. Use examples only.

    d. During guided practice, provide extensive opportunities to respond through practice activities involving the target concept or academic rule. Use extensive prompts and cues to solicit responses involving examples only.

        • Lead or induce students in stating definition, attributes, rule, or skill.

        • Lead or induce students in identifying concept examples or applying rules to examples. Use signaling to lead choral responses, when appropriate.

            — Pose a question, wait 3 to 5 seconds, then call on a student for a response.

            — Recognize a student's response by giving academic praise, paraphrasing, amplifying, clarifying, or redirecting to another student.

        • Provide corrective feedback as needed.

    e. For independent practice, provide daily activities involving examples of the target concept or academic rule that students can perform with minimal prompting or cues. Students should be able to perform tasks with 90% accuracy or better.

        • Give directions to complete the activity tasks.

        • Lead students in completing example tasks.

Table 7.1
Teaching: Explicit Activation of Learning (TEAL)

1. **Acquisition Stage—Introduction**
   a. *Advanced Organizer*—outline the activities to be completed during the lesson
   b. *Linkage*—review related concepts, rules, or skills from previous lessons
   c. *Demonstration*—target concept, rule, or skill is demonstrated or induced. *Examples* are demonstrated or induced
   d. *Guided Practice*—target concept, rule, or skill is practiced, with extensive prompting using *examples only*
      1) Lead child in stating definition, attributes, rule, or skill
      2) Lead child in identifying concept examples or applying rules to examples
         a) Use signalling to lead choral responses
         b) Pose question, wait 3–5 seconds, call on reciter
         c) Recognize student response
            1. Give specific praise
            2. Probe, amplify, restate student response
            3. Ask peer for response
         d) Follow corrective feedback steps as needed
      3) Test child's response
   e. *Independent Practice*—target concept, rule, or skill is practiced daily without prompting using *examples only*
      1) Give directions to complete the activity tasks
      2) Lead students in completing example tasks
      3) Indicate deadline for completing activity
      4) Circulate and assist students
      5) Review student responses to activity tasks
   f. *Ending Review*—review target concept, rule, or skill

2. **Acquisition Stage—Discrimination**
   a. *Advanced Organizer*—outline the activities to be completed during the lesson
   b. *Linkage*—review related concepts, rules, or skills from previous lessons
   c. *Demonstration*—target concept, rule, or skill is demonstrated or induced. *Examples and nonexamples* are demonstrated or induced
   d. *Guided Practice*—target concept, rule, or skill is practiced with extensive prompting using *examples and nonexamples*
      1) Lead child in stating definition, attributes, rule, or skill
      2) Lead child in identifying concept examples and nonexamples or applying rules to examples and nonexamples
         a) Use signalling to lead choral responses
         b) Pose question, wait 3–5 seconds, call on reciter
         c) Recognize student response
            1. Give specific praise
            2. Probe, amplify, restate student response
            3. Ask peer for response
         d) Follow corrective feedback steps as needed
      3) Test child's responses
   e. *Independent Practice*—target concept, rule or skill is practiced daily without prompting using *examples and nonexamples*
      1) Give directions to complete the activity tasks
      2) Lead students in completing example tasks
      3) Indicate deadline for completing activity
      4) Circulate and assist students
      5) Review student responses to activity tasks
   f. *Ending Review*—review target concept, rule, or skill

(continued)

Table 7.1 *continued*

---

3. Fluency-Building Stage—target concept, rule, or skill is practiced daily with high rate of speed and accuracy
    1) Review target concept, rule, or skill
    2) Give directions to complete the activity tasks
    3) Lead students in completing example tasks
    4) Indicate deadline for completing activity
    5) Circulate and assist students
    6) Review student responses to activity tasks

---

4. Maintenance Stage—target concept, rule, or skill is practiced weekly or monthly with high rate of speed and accuracy
    1) Review target concept, rule or skill
    2) Give directions to complete the activity tasks
    3) Lead students in completing example tasks
    4) Indicate deadline for completing activity
    5) Circulate and assist students
    6) Review student responses to activity tasks

       • Indicate the deadline for completing activity.

       • Circulate and assist the students as needed.

       • Review students' responses to activity tasks.

    f. Engage students in an ending review to summarize the content covered in the lesson and to signal the transition to the next lesson.

2. *Acquisition Stage—Discrimination.* The acquisition stage continues with the introduction of nonexamples used to teach students to discriminate between the target concept or academic rule and other similar concepts or academic rules. Accurate discrimination responses are indicators that students are solidifying their skills. The steps are identical to those under the acquisition-introduction stage, except that examples and nonexamples are used during instruction.

3. *Fluency-Building Stage.* Lessons at the fluency-building stage entail independent practice activities. Teachers simply introduce the activity and monitor students' responses to a few example stimuli to ensure that they are making responses with relative degrees of speed and accuracy. To ensure that students use their time productively and that fluency is built, teachers follow these steps:

    a. Gain student attention and orient students with an outline of the activities to be completed during the lesson.

    b. Link the present lesson with previous lessons by reviewing related concepts or academic rules previously taught.

    c. Provide daily independent practice activities that engage students in responding to examples and nonexamples of target concept or academic rule. The focus of practice is on high rates of speed and accuracy. Students should be able to perform tasks with 90% accuracy or better.

       • Give directions to complete the activity tasks.

- Lead the students in completing example tasks.
- Indicate the deadline for completing the activity.
- Circulate and assist the students as needed.
- Review students' responses to activity tasks.

   d. Engage students in an ending review to summarize the content covered in the lesson and to signal the transition to the next lesson.

4. *Maintenance Stage*. The primary characteristic of the maintenance stage is that practice schedules are distributed over longer intervals of time. These weekly or monthly practice activities are geared to assist students in retaining appropriate levels of fast and accurate responding. As the interval of time between sessions increases, the need to conduct a brief review of the target concept or academic rule increases. Additionally, instructional antecedents and reinforcement should be thinned. The following steps are guidelines for lesson development:

   a. Gain student attention and orient students with an outline of the activities to be completed during the lesson.

   b. Link the present lesson with previous lessons by reviewing related concepts or academic rules previously taught.

   c. Provide weekly or monthly independent practice activities that engage students in responding to examples and nonexamples of the target concept or academic rule. The focus of practice is on high rates of speed and accuracy. Student should be able to perform tasks with 90% accuracy or better.

- Give directions to complete the activity tasks.
- Lead the students in completing example tasks.
- Indicate the deadline for completing the activity.
- Circulate and assist the students as needed.
- Review students' responses to activity tasks.

   d. Fade out the frequency and intensity of response antecedents and consequences using intermittent schedules.

   e. Engage students in an ending review to summarize the content covered in the lesson and to signal the transition to the next lesson.

5. *Generalization Stage*. Unlike the earlier stages of learning, the steps for teaching generalization outlined below are not taught in separate discrete lessons. Instead, these steps are incorporated, to varying extents, into lessons at all previous learning stages. The primary characteristic of generalization instruction is that students are encouraged to use their skills in other settings and at different times. The following suggestions are means to set the occasion for generalization: (a) use instructional antecedents and consequences that occur in other settings, (b) use materials found in other settings for practicing target concepts or academic rules, (c) use delayed and intermittent reinforcement schedules, (d) teach students to self-reinforce fast and accurate responding, (e) encourage other teachers to reinforce students' use of target concepts and academic rules, and (f) tell students to use concepts and academic rules in other classrooms.

Direct instruction methods are utilized to instruct students with LD efficiently and successfully as they move toward mastery. Direct instruction curricula materials such as DISTAR, Corrective Reading, Corrective Math, and Reading Mastery have been implemented in classrooms across the nation. The curriculum design gives teachers a structured lesson plan that, if followed, practically ensures mastery of specific skills.

Peer Tutoring

A component under the direct instruction practice of teaching to mastery is the practice of peer tutoring. Peer tutoring is one means that allows students to receive a substantial amount of practice of a specific skill without demanding a great deal of individual teacher attention, and to still receive immediate feedback to determine mastery of the skill (Maheady, Mallette, Harper, Sacca, & Pomerantz, 1994).

Once the teacher or student determines the specific skill that needs to be mastered, the peer tutor provides the stimulus and the tutee responds appropriately to that stimulus. The stimulus provided by the peer tutor can be from almost any subject area, but it must be a discreet variable that cues the tutee to respond appropriately. In addition, the peer tutor session can be across many ability levels if the stimulus-response chain has been clearly delineated. Peer tutoring has been used to describe a wide range of student dyads. Peer tutoring in the public schools has been utilized as a means for increasing the socialization of isolated students. The dyads have also allowed students to teach other students new information or to practice a wide range of previously taught skills, both academic and social.

Peer grouping has many benefits beyond the purpose of increasing academic achievement. Peer tutoring has resulted in increased academic performance by the tutee (Greer & Polirstok, 1982; Mathes, Fuchs, Fuchs, Henley, & Sanders, 1994) and is a means for structuring interaction between students who normally do not socialize (Valcante & Stoddard, 1990).

The success of a peer tutoring program relies on a clear understanding of the expectations and procedures for the tutoring session. Therefore, it is critical that peer tutors are trained in the skill of tutoring. Niedermeyer (1970) found increased mastery of content when tutors were given structured training. This training includes teaching the tutor a structured plan for each session, providing practice in appropriate feedback, developing a practical means for evaluating the progress of each session, and teaching the tutor appropriate specific academic and social praise for correct responses. It is imperative that the tutor be knowledgeable of the skill being taught in the tutoring session. This may require preteaching the information to the tutor (Brown, Fenrick, & Klemme, 1971).

The tutor has to be committed to the tutoring session and needs to approach each session with the enthusiasm of a classroom teacher. For this reason tutoring sessions need to be structured with specific tasks to complete. Those programs where a contingency plan was designed for the positive learning and interaction of the tutor-tutee group also report higher success rates (Delquardi, Greenwood, Whorton, Carta, & Hall, 1986). A point system can be implemented for those tutoring groups who finish the daily assignments or reach mastery of material. Evaluative tools, such as precision teaching, that detect daily progress are most effective for providing quick reinforcement for the students' efforts and determining mastery. Through a daily check of progress, on-task behavior is also encouraged. Students visually see progress and realize hard work pays off. In addition, an intermittent bonus point system can be added by the teacher every time *positive phrases* are heard from a tutoring group.

The initial training may delay the start of the tutoring sessions, but it is imperative that the tutor is cognizant of the responsibilities and is capable of completing the task. The teacher models appropriate behaviors throughout the teaching day, but the important teacher behaviors of structuring, demonstrating, prompting, practicing, and reinforcing may need to be demonstrated for the tutor (Stoddard & Valcante, 1991).

The teacher needs to be sure that the content of material to be mastered within the tutor session is appropriate for the members of a particular dyad. Type of presentation of content can be adapted to fit a tutoring session. Heron, Heward, Cook, and Hill (1983) contend that the most successful dyads are those in which there is active participation by both members of the group in a tutor-tutee interaction mode. In addition, those practice areas that have a predeveloped correct answer key enable students of equal abilities to pair, or the key can prevent arguments of overzealous partners who are certain their incorrect answers are correct. The following skills lend themselves to an active presentation and response of both the tutor and tutee:

Tutor Presentation	*Tutee Response*
Orally states spelling word	Writes spelling word; orally states spelling word
Presents a card with vocabulary word from any academic area: science, reading, mathematics, social studies, geography, computers, health, driver's education	Orally defines word
Presents a card with a math fact on front	Mentally computes and orally states the answer
Orally states a numeral	Writes the numeral stated
Presents a color on a card	Orally states the color

Greenwood, Carta, and Maheady (1991) suggest the practice of continually introducing new material to the dyad once the previous information has been mastered. If the expectation of the peer tutoring experience is to increase interaction between two students, the dyad must meet for a consistent period of time. Those peer tutoring sessions resulting in quick mastery of information and then ending of the tutoring session will be successful for teaching content mastery, but the limited interactions of the tutor and tutee will not promote the development of a relationship between partners.

Types of Peer Tutoring Groups.   The traditional tutor groups involves two students: one student less skilled in a particular area being tutored by a more capable student. Tutoring can also involve a team of three members: one tutor and two tutees or a grouping of as many as six students of heterogeneous ability. It is imperative that the groups are heterogeneously grouped by skill ability to ensure that each tutoring group has a student within the group whose ability level of the particular skill being studied will allow for assistance of less capable students when necessary (Maheady, Harper, & Sacca, 1988; Maheady et al., 1994).

Research has clearly demonstrated the effectiveness of peer tutoring (Carlson, Litton, & Zinngraff, 1985; King, 1982; Mathes et al., 1994; Scruggs & Richter, 1985) as a method for teaching specific skills in the general or exceptional education classroom. The practice can improve the academic and social skills of the tutor as well as the tutee (Cohen, Kulik, & Kulik, 1982; Maher, 1984). When students with LD were involved in a peer tutoring experience, they scored significantly higher on a posttutoring social studies test than those students studying independently for the same test. A peer tutoring session for elementary aged LD students resulted in all students reaching mastery for knowledge of capitalization rules. The authors noted additional skill improvement for the peer tutees as a result of teaching the skill to their partners (Campbell, Brady, & Linehan, 1991).

Peer tutoring groups often involve a student with a learning disability in the role of tutee and the general education student as the tutor. However, students with LD have also been used effectively as the tutor as well as the tutee (Dineen, Clark, & Risley, 1977). Peer tutoring has proven to be beneficial for improving academic skills, and as Jenkins and Jenkins (1985) highlight in their study, peer tutoring also allows a student to practice appropriate social skills and can improve a student's social standing within the class.

The academic and social benefits of peer tutoring have been clearly demonstrated in various settings and with a myriad of dyads. Ms. Fracas's classroom illustrates the effectiveness of a peer tutoring program. The students in Ms. Fracas's tenth grade class daily tutor second graders in a nearby elementary school. Ms. Fracas's class is composed of students with a wide range of abilities and disabilities. All 31 of the students walk to a nearby elementary school to tutor second graders who are struggling with their readings. The tutors complete PT timings on oral reading and read a short story each day to the second graders. This has allowed for development of a positive relationship between the high school and elementary students, along with improved oral reading skills for the second graders. The social impact for the high school students has also been evidenced, since it is the first time that some of the high school students have been able to function in the role of tutor rather than tutee, a powerful motivator in and of itself.

Trained peer-tutoring groups are an effective means in which students with learning disabilities can practice mastery of skills previously taught by the teacher. Immediate feedback, increased time on task, and a substantial amount of time engaged in practice are three of the main variables that make peer tutoring such an efficient technique to use with students with LD.

Self-Management

A characteristic of many students with LD is the inability to inherently manage and monitor their own academic and social behavior (Carpenter & Apter, 1988). Through instruction in self-management techniques students can gain the ability to covertly control their own actions (Polsgrove, 1979; Wolery et al., 1988). The basic behavioral principles still apply in teaching self-management, but behavior control is transferred to the student. For example, students are taught self-guiding verbalization that leads them through a set of procedures or behaviors, or students are taught to evaluate their own performance on a task and are to administer self-reinforcement, contingent upon some observable performance criterion. This allows the student to maintain more control over the situation and will enhance the generalization of the behavior to other situations when the teacher or authority figure is not immediately present. Chan (1991), for instance, demonstrated the effectiveness of a self-questioning strategy to enable young readers to improve their comprehension and to do so without prompts and in alternative settings.

In self-management, the students learn to be cognizant of their own behavior and measure progress in the improvement of that particular behavior (Webber, Scheuermann, McCall, & Coleman, 1993). The following example is one means for allowing students to self-manage their own behavior. This example is best suited for a student who is motivated to complete the assignment but who tends to daydream, as is illustrated in the story of Jana.

Jana and her teacher, Ms. Simpkins, decide that Jana needs to stay on task during independent seat work, to finish her assignment. Ms. Simpkins turns on a prerecorded tape that emits a beep every 30 seconds. When the beep goes off, Jana is to put a black pencil check wherever she is on her paper of independent work. Through this simple method Jana can see how much work she completes during the seat work period. This minor adaptation of self-management may assist Jana in increasing her time on task and finishing her assignment.

A student may need a more comprehensive self-management program, such as the one for Steve, a fifth-grade student having trouble with his impulsive call outs during classroom discussions. Steve and his teacher, Ms. Bostick decide that Steve will keep track of his call outs and his hand raises. The following chart (Figure 7.8) could be taped on Steve's desk for data collection. Every time Steve raises his hand he can put a check in the + side of the chart, and every time he calls out, he puts a check in the − side of the chart. For every positive check Steve would move closer to his goal. Upon reaching his goal Steve would receive the pre-agreed upon reward.

The goal of self-management is a decreased need for outside reinforcers even if the reinforcement is self-managed. For this reason it is important to teach the student self-reinforcement as part of the management program. Cognitive behavior modification is one form of self-management that teaches the student to self-reinforce (Meichenbaum, 1977). The students' self-reinforcement of their own positive or correct behavior becomes part of their repertoire in daily problem solving, thus making students more cognizant of the fact that they truly control their decisions and behavior. A five-step process can be taught to students to modify their own behavior (Meichenbaum & Goodman, 1977). Table 7.2 describes the step-by-step procedure and gives examples in both academic and affective areas.

Through self-management of behavior students realize they have control over their actions. In addition, generalization can occur much more readily because the management system is controlled by the student rather than the teacher.

STEVE'S CHART	RAISED HAND	CALLED OUT
8:00–8:30–OPENING		
8:30–9:15–MATH		
9:15–10:15–P.E.		
10:15–11:30–LITERATURE		
12:00–12:30–SCI./S. ST.		
12:30–1:15–CENTERS		
1:15–1:45–LITERATURE		
1:45–2:00–CLOSING		

Figure 7.8
Steve's Chart for self-management of callouts and hand raises.

Table 7.2
Five Steps of a Cognitive Behavioral Model

Steps of the Model	Academic Example	Affective Example
1. Instructor models the task while describing the action.	(Simple subtraction, 3 − 2 = 1, with picture to show calculation) Instructor models: "Let's see what am I supposed to do. I look at the picture and see 3 cats; 2 cats are going away. How many are left? 1 is left. 3 − 2 = 1. Yes, that's right.	Problem: Student continually hits when called names. Instructor models: "That boy is calling me names. What can I do to make him stop without getting myself in more trouble?" Instructor verbalizes possible alternatives: "I can hit him—but I'm not allowed to hit." "I can ignore him—but I can't do it." "I can call him names—but I'll get in trouble." "Out of all these choices ignoring him seems like the best choice. I just have to ignore him. I know I can do it. Good, that's what I'll do."
2. Learner performs the task while the instructor describes how to do it.	The instructor repeats the above procedure while the student performs the calculation along with the instructor.	
3. Learner performs the task once again while talking through it.	The student now performs the calculation and repeats the same procedure the instructor used and verbalizes it out loud.	
4. Learner performs the task once again while only whispering the description.	The student now performs the calculation again but only whispers the procedure he verbalized out loud in Step 3.	Student repeats the same procedure as the instructor in Step 2, verbalizes the procedure in Step 3, and whispers the same procedure in Step 4.
5. Learner performs the task once again with covert self-instruction.	The student performs the calculation again but internalizes the step-by-step procedure.	Student performs the same procedure internally when faced with similar decisions, so as not to act impulsively.

EFFECTIVENESS OF BEHAVIORAL PROGRAMS

The evolution of the science of behavior from Pavlov through the present has had a profound impact on the education of students with disabilities, in general, and those with LD, in particular. Direct assessment of student performance and CBA follow logically from the study of human behavior and learning. The instructional issues and approaches discussed in this chapter, including the engineered classroom, programmed learning, direct instruction, PT, self-management, and peer tutoring have been developed as applications of behavioral principles. Neeper and Lahey (1988) and Koorland (1986) report that behavior-based programs are generally effective for students with LD. They review studies on the effectiveness of remediating handwriting, reading comprehension, letter identification, sight-word vocabulary, arithmetic, silent reading, and oral reading difficulties with direct academic behavioral interventions.

They further discuss early attempts to apply the principles of behavior to inappropriate targets such as impulsivity, attention deficits, and excessive motor activity. These studies were based on the false assumption that it was both necessary and sufficient to decelerate these behaviors, which were assumed to be incompatible with academic progress, to produce academic improvements. It is now generally accepted that the reduction of inappropriate behaviors does not automatically result in the acceleration or acquisition of positive behaviors, academic or otherwise. Now behavioral scientists are more likely to think in terms of replacement instead of reduction.

Behavioral approaches can produce meaningful academic performance improvements without dealing with implied process deficits. Although children with LD may have underlying process deficits, direct treatment of those implied deficits is neither possible nor necessary for academic improvement (Neeper & Lahey, 1988).

 Practical Classroom Applications

Teachers can consider the following implications regarding behavioral models of LD and classroom practices. Application suggestions are presented for teachers' use in behavioral assessment and development of instructional approaches helpful in working with students with LD.

1. *Behavioral models are important in today's classrooms.* Many teachers working with students with LD use teacher-guided instruction directed toward the mastery of specific skills. In this way, teachers can include all students working in small groups with high rates of engagement.

Many teachers continue to rely on effective behavioral principles for classroom instruction. Often, they facilitate student success through the use of fast-paced, structured lessons. They use structured curricula, corrective feedback procedures, and performance monitoring. The critical aspect of behavioral approaches is that teachers control instruction. They determine what and how subject-matter content will be pre-

(continued)

sented (i.e., they observe and evaluate students; they demonstrate target responses and lead students in making responses). As teachers gradually fade cues, students (including those with learning and other disabilities), increasingly are able to respond independently. Teachers give extensive practice so that students have sufficient opportunities to make responses and thus master the target skills. Practice activities are done in a fast-paced mode, for a high density of responses during instructional periods.

During initial learning, teachers work with students in small groups to monitor the accuracy of student responses, ensuring that students engage in academic tasks. When students err, teachers respond to provide corrective feedback that entails taking students through the model, lead, and test sequences. Effective teachers also use a variety of instructional formats; that is, teachers rely on peer tutoring, self-management techniques, and small group instruction.

2. *Direct instruction, based on behavioral principles and effective teaching behaviors, has grown in popularity like no other instructional approach.* There are critical teacher behaviors that correlated positively with student academic gains. Teachers using direct observation and instruction include not only specific teaching procedures, but often use highly structured curriculum materials. The purpose of these popular materials is to help teachers systematically direct students in making accurate responses. Teachers use scripted lesson plans to ensure that precise communication occurs between the teacher and students. During instruction, teachers model target responses, lead students in making the response, and periodically test students' skills in responding without teacher cues.

3. *Teachers are instrumental in ensuring effective instruction.* Students with learning and other disabilities profit from classroom experiences in which teachers execute observation, assessment, and instructional behaviors in a standard, systematic manner. If teachers use predictable steps in lesson development, students are able to participate in activities and perform responses in a more consistent manner. For example, when teachers execute the demonstration step of lesson development, they model target responses for students with LD. The responses relate to the performance of an academic rule (i.e., sets of procedures for performing academic tasks such as solving computations with regrouping) or the formation of concepts (i.e., well-defined categories of information used for classification, such as types of plants). Teachers are then in a better position to observe and assess what is taught directly.

Next, teachers offer supervised guided practice. Guided practice entails teachers using cues and prompts to emit target responses. Teachers first lead groups of students in making the desired response (i.e., the teacher and students perform the response simultaneously). As the students demonstrate accurate responses, the teacher gradually fades the degree of leading. Instead of making the response with the students, the teacher presents the stimulus and has the group of students respond. Unison responding, groups of students making responses simultaneously, allows students more opportunities for responding during a period of time. Teachers must monitor the response of individual students in the group during unison responding, to determine whether all students are responding accurately. In addition, teachers test students by

(continued)

Practical Classroom Applications (continued)

calling on individual students to make responses on their own.

As students become more accurate in their responding, teachers shift the performance criterion to fast and accurate responding. Teachers concentrate on asking for as many responses as possible during a guided practice session. This increases the number of opportunities to respond and helps to ensure skill mastery. Effective teachers ensure that responses are demonstrated and that students have numerous opportunities to practice the responses while the teacher leads.

Finally, once students have performed responses accurately without cues or prompts, teachers using behavioral strategies in direct instruction then provide students the opportunity to independently practice response accuracy and speed. Independent practice, therefore, is minimally supervised practice in which students respond with a 90% or better response accuracy.

Two important and closely related features of independent practice do assist in skill development and efficient management of classroom activities for students with LD. First, teachers can work with other groups of students while one group practices independently. Second, students must be making accurate responses so they can truly work independently of the teacher (i.e., without a constant parade of students moving over to the teacher to ask questions about their seat work). When students engage in independent practice activities, the

teacher should prepare them and monitor their progress in completing the assignment. The following sequence is typical: (a) give directions to complete the activity tasks, (b) lead students in completing example tasks, (c) indicate a deadline for completing the activity, (c) circulate and assist students as needed, and (e) review student responses to activity tasks.

4. *Teachers assist students with learning difficulties by using direct observations, PT, CBA, and data-based decision making.* To ensure appropriate instructional decisions, effective teachers need to know how well students are progressing toward skill mastery. Direct and continuous observing and monitoring of the rate and accuracy of student responses allows teachers to determine the daily instructional needs of each student. Daily observation better ensures that students will not proceed through an extended series of lessons with high error rates before instruction is modified to improve response accuracy. Monitoring can take the form of simply tallying the number of correct and error responses students make during an oral practice session or on a paper-and-pencil seat-work assignment. These frequencies can be kept in a daily log or a bulletin board chart, or can be plotted on a graph. The use of PT can increase the probability that students will make accurate responses. Accordingly, ideal instruction occurs when instructional procedures are so carefully designed that students make no errors; however, students invariably err, regardless of the teaching precision.

SUMMARY

- The behavioral approach to LD uses direct observation of student academic performance and task analysis for identification and assessment of learning problems.
- Behaviorists assume that behavior is learned through a history facilitated by associations of antecedents, behaviors, and consequences.
- Instruction is intricately linked to assessment of student progress and whether a particular academic behavior is accelerating or decelerating.
- Data-based decision making provides the link between assessment and instruction.
- CBA is both an assessment and a teaching practice.
- The programmed learning approach is based on behavioral principles of providing positive reinforcement for correct responses and withholding positive reinforcement for incorrect responses.
- PT provides a quick assessment of a student's progress; CBA links the teacher's evaluation and instruction.
- The premise on which the engineered classroom is designed is based on the provision of a structured environment.
- Direct instruction refers to high levels of student engagement within academically focused, teacher-directed classrooms, using sequenced, structured materials.
- Peer tutoring is one means that allows students to receive a substantial amount of practice of a specific skill.
- Through instruction in self-management techniques students who have LD can gain the ability to covertly control their own actions and maintain more control over the situation.
- Behavioral approaches to assessment and intervention are effective, convenient to classroom practices, and hold empirical value for students and teachers.

DISCUSSION QUESTIONS

To help extend your understanding, reflect on and discuss the following questions:

1. In reflecting on your own beliefs regarding behavioral approaches to instruction, what do you consider their contribution and importance to your own effective instruction?

2. How have behavioral approaches helped teachers assist students having problems in attention during reading and mathematics instruction?

3. Take a position on each of the following issues. The purpose for having students practice learning strategies in controlled materials is to increase: (a) setting generalization, (b) readability of materials, (c) opportunities to use strategies, or (d) skill maintenance. Discuss your responses with peers.

4. Describe at least three advantages of peer tutoring in teachers' work with students with learning difficulties from culturally diverse populations.

5. How have behavioral approaches assisted in the following student variables: memory, attention, verbal mediation, visual imagery, rehearsal, relaxation, and subject-oriented instruction?

6. Consider your own teaching of students with learning and other disabilities. Describe in behavioral terms at least five specific ways you have been an effective teacher who has linked assessment and instructional strategies for your students.

7. Describe whether you have done any of the following: assessed students' academic difficulties; directly observed academic performance; measured student progress; displayed a graphic of student data; conducted a data-based process decision-making; used CBA; applied programmed learning or PT; considered application of the engineered classroom; or used direct instruction, peer tutoring, or self-management techniques.

REFERENCES

Algozzine, B. (1991). Decision making and curriculum-based assessment. In B. Y. L. Wong (Ed.) *Learning about learning disabilities.* San Diego, CA: Academic Press.

Baker, S. C., Simmons, D. C., & Kameenui, E. J. (1994). Making information more memorable for students with learning disabilities through the design of instructional tools. *LD Forum, 19* (3), 14–18.

Becker, W. C., Englemann, S., & Thomas, D. R. (1971). *Teaching: A course in applied psychology.* Chicago: Science Research Associates.

Bereiter, C., & Engelmann, S. (1966). *Teaching disadvantaged children in the preschool.* Upper Saddle River, NJ: Prentice Hall.

Bikel, W. E. & Bickel, D. D. (1986). Effective schools, classrooms, and instruction: Implications for special education. *Exceptional Children, 52,* 489–500.

Blankenship, C. S. (1985). Using curriculum-based assessment data to make instructional decisions. *Exceptional Children, 52,* 233–238.

Bos, C. S., & Vaughn, S. (1994). *Strategies for teaching students with learning and behavior problems.* Boston: Allyn and Bacon.

Brown, L., Fenrick, N., & Klemme, H. (1971). Trainable pupils learn to teach each other. *Teaching Exceptional Children, 4,* 18–24.

Buchannan, C. D. (1966) *Programmed reading.* New York: McGraw-Hill, Sullivan Associates.

Campbell, B. J., Brady, M. P., & Linehan, S. (1991). Effects of peer-mediated instruction on the acquisition and generalization of written capitalization skills. *Journal of Learning Disabilities, 24,* 6–14.

Carpenter, R. L., & Apter, S. J. (1988). Research integration of cognitive-emotional interventions for behavior disordered children and youth. In M. S. Wang, M. C. Reynolds, H. J. Walberg (Eds.), *Handbook of special education: Research and practice* (Vol. 2) New York: Pergamon.

Carlson, M. B., Litton, F. W., & Zinngraff, S. A. (1985). The effects of an intraclass peer tutoring program on the sight word recognition ability of students who are mildly mentally retarded. *Mental Retardation, 23* (2), 74–78.

Chan, L. K. S. (1991). Promoting strategy generalization through self instructional training in students with reading disabilities. *Journal of Learning Disabilities, 24,* 427–433.

Choate, J. S., Enright, B. E., Miller, L. J., Poteet, J. A., & Rakes, T. A. (1995). *Curriculum-based assessment and programming.* Boston: Allyn and Bacon.

Darch, C., Gersten, R., & Taylor, R. (1987). Evaluation of the Williamsburg County Direct Instruction Program: Factors leading to success in rural elementary programs. *Research in Rural Education, 4,* 111–118.

Cohen, P. A., Kulik, J. A., & Kulik, C. C. (1982). Educational outcomes of tutoring: A meta-analysis of findings. *American Educational Research Journal, 19,* 237–248.

Delquardi, J., Greenwood, C. R., Whorton, D., Carta, J. J., & Hall, V. (1986). Classwide peer tutoring. *Exceptional Children, 52,* 535–542.

Deno, S. L. (1985). Curriculum-based measurement: The emerging alternative. *Exceptional Children, 52,* 219–232.

Deno, S. L., Marston, D., & Mirkin, P. (1982). Valid measurement procedures for continuous evaluation of written expression. *Exceptional Children, 48,* 368–371.

Deno, S. L., Mirkin, P., & Chang, B. (1982). Identifying valid measures of reading. *Exceptional Children, 49,* 36–45.

Devine, V., & Tomlinson, J. (1976). The workclock: An alternative to token economies in the management of classroom behaviors. *Psychology in the Schools, 13,* 163–170.

Dineen, J. P., Clark, H. B., & Risley, T. R. (1977). Peer tutoring among elementary students: Educational benefits to the tutor. *Journal of Applied Behavior Analysis, 10,* 231–238.

Diviaio, L. G. & Hefferan, M. P. (1983). *A resource manual for the development and evaluation of special programs for exceptional students, Volume D: Techniques of precision teaching Part 1: Training manual.* Tallahassee: Florida Department of Education.

Englemann, S., & Carnine, D. (1982). *Theory of instruction: Principles and applications,* New York: Irvington.

FDLRS Clearinghouse/Information Center (1983). *A resource manual for the development and evaluation of special programs for exceptional students. Volume V-D: techniques of precision teaching Part 1, Part 2, Part 3.* Tallahassee: Bureau of Education for Exceptional Students, Division of Public Schools, Florida Department of Education.

Fenitor, D., Buckholdt, D., Hamblin, R., & Smith, L. (1972). Noneffects of contingent reinforcement for attending behavior on work accomplished. *Journal of Applied Behavior Analysis, 1,* 1–12.

Fuchs, L. S., & Fuchs, D. (1991). Curriculum-based measurements: Current applications and future directions. *Preventing School Failure, 35* (3), 6–11.

Fuchs, L. S., Fuchs, D., & Hamlett, C. L. (1989). Effects of alternative goal structures within curriculum-based measurement. *Exceptional Children, 55,* 429–438.

Gersten, R. (1985). Direct instruction with special education students: A review of evaluation research. *The Journal of Special Education, 19* (1), 42–58.

Glicking, E. E., & Thompson, V. P. (1985). A personal view of curriculum-based assessment. *Exceptional Children, 52,* 205–218.

Greenwood, C. R., Carta, J. J., & Maheady, L. (1991). Peer tutoring programs in the regular education classroom. In G. Stoner, M. R. Shinn, & H. M. Walker (Eds.), *A school psychologist's interventions for regular education.* Eugene, OR: National Association of School Psychologists.

Greer, R. D., & Polirstok, S. R. (1982). Collateral gains and short-term maintenance in reading and on-task responses by some inner-city adolescents as a function of their use of social reinforcement while tutoring. *Journal of Applied Behavior Analysis, 15,* 123–139.

Hallahan, D. P. & Kauffman, J. H. (1976). *Introduction to learning disabilities: A psycho-behavioral approach.* Upper Saddle River, NJ: Prentice Hall.

Heron, T. E., Heward, W. L., Cook, N. L., & Hill, S. (1983). Evaluation of classwide peer tutoring systems: First graders teach each other sight words. *Education and Treatment of Children, 6,* 137–152.

Hewett, F. M. (1968). *The emotionally disturbed child in the classroom.* Boston: Allyn and Bacon.

Hewett, F. M., & Forness, S. R. (1974). *Education of exceptional learners.* Boston: Allyn and Bacon.

House, E., Glass, G. V., McLean, L., & Walker, D. F. (1978). No simple answer: Critique of the Follow Through education. *Harvard Educational Review, 48,* 128–160.

Jenkins, J. J., & Jenkins, L. M. (1985). Peer tutoring in elementary and secondary programs. *Focus on Exceptional Children, 17* (6), 1–12.

Kazdin, A. E. (1978). *History of behavior modification: Experimental foundations of contemporary research.* Baltimore: University Park.

Kazdin, A. E. (1982). History of behavior modification. In A. S. Bellack, M. Hersen, and A. E. Kazdin

(Eds.), *International handbook of behavior modification and therapy*. New York: Plenum.

Keogh, B. K. (1988). Learning disability: Diversity in search of order. In M. C. Wang, M. Reynolds, & H. J. Walberg (Eds.), *Handbook of special education: Research and practice* (Vol. 2). Elmsford, NY: Paragon.

King, R. T. (1982). Learning from a PAL. *The Reading Teacher, 35*, 682–685.

Koorland, M. (1986). Applied behavior analysis and the correction of learning disabilities. In J. K. Torgesen & B. Y. L. Wong (Eds.), *Psychological and educational perspectives on learning disabilities*. San Diego, CA: Academic Press.

Lerner, J. (1993). *Learning disabilities: Theories, diagnosis, and teaching strategies*. Boston: Houghton Mifflin.

Lindsley, O. R. (1990). Precision teaching: By teachers for children. *Teaching Exceptional Children, 22*, (3), 10–15.

Lloyd, J. W. (1988). Direct academic interventions in learning disabilities. In M. C. Wang, M. Reynolds, & H. J. Walberg (Eds.), *Handbook of special education: Research and practice (Vol. 2)*. Elmsford, NY: Pergamon.

Lovitt, T. C., Fister, S., Freston, J. L., Kemp, K., Moore, R. C., Schroeder, B., & Bauernschmidt, M. (1990). Using precision teaching techniques: Translating research. *Teaching Exceptional Children, 22*, 16–19.

Maheady, L., Harper, G. F., & Sacca, M. K. (1988). Peer-mediated instruction: A promising approach to meeting the diverse needs of LD adolescents. *Learning Disabilities Quarterly, 11*, 108–113.

Maheady, L., Mallette, B., Harper, G. F., Sacca, K., & Pomerantz, D. (1994). Peer-mediated instruction of high-risk students. In K. D. Wood & B. Algozzinne (Eds.), *Teaching reading to high-risk learners*. Boston: Allyn and Bacon.

Maher, C. A. (1984). Handicapped adolescents as cross-age peer tutors: Program description and evaluation. *Exceptional Children, 51*, 56–63.

Marston, D., & Magnusson, D. (1985). Implementing curriculum-based measurement in special and regular education settings. *Exceptional Children, 52*, 266–276.

Mathes, P. G., Fuchs, D., Fuchs, L. S., Henley, A. M., & Sanders, A. (1994). Increasing reading practice with Peabody classwide peer tutoring. *Learning Disabilities Research and Practice, 9*, 44–48.

McLaughlin, T., Dolliver, P., & Mallady, J. (1979). A timer game: Effects on on-task behavior and generalization for academic behavior for an entire special education class. *Contemporary Educational Psychology, 4*, 172–174.

Meichenbaum, D. (1977). *Cognitive behavior-modification: An integrative approach*. New York: Plenum.

Meichenbaum, D. H., & Goodman, J. (1977). Training impulsive children to talk to themselves: A means of developing self-control. *Journal of Abnormal Psychology, 77*, 115–126.

Mercer, C. D. (1983). *Students with learning disabilities* (2nd ed.). Upper Saddle River, NJ: Prentice Hall/Merrill.

Mercer, C. D. (1987). *Students with learning disabilities (2nd ed.)*. Upper Saddle River, NJ: Prentice Hall/Merrill.

Neef, N. A., Iwata, B. A., & Page, T. J. (1977). The effects of known-item interspersal on acquisition and retention of spelling and sight reading words. *Journal of Applied Behavior Analysis, 10*, 738.

Neeper, R. & Lahey, B. B. (1988). Behavioral approaches. In K. A. Kavale, S. R. Forness, & M. Bender (Eds.), *Handbook of learning disabilities, Volume II: Methods and interventions*. Boston: Little, Brown.

Niedermeyer, F. C. (1970). Effects of training on the instructional behaviors of student tutors. *Journal of Educational Research, 64*, 119–123.

O'Shea, L. J., & O'Shea, D. J. (1997). *Teaching: Explicit activation of learning*. Manuscript in preparation.

Pennypacker, H. S., Konig, C. H. & Lindsley, O. R. (1972). *Handbook of the Standard Behavior Chart*, Kansas City, KS: Precision Media.

Polsgrove, L. (1979). Self-control: Methods for training. *Behavior Disorders, 4*, 116–130.

Rieth, H. J., Polsgrove, L., & Semmel, M. I. (1981). Instructional variables that make a difference: Attention to task and beyond. *Exceptional Education Quarterly, 1*, 61–71.

Rosenshine, B. (1976). Classroom instruction. In N. L. Gagne (Ed.), *Psychology of teaching: The 77th yearbook of the National Society for the Study of*

Education. Chicago: National Society for the Study of Education.

Rosenshine, B. (1978). The third cycle of research on teacher effects: Content covered, academic engagement time, and quality of instruction. *In 78th yearbook of the National Society for the Study of Education.* Chicago: University of Chicago Press.

Rosenshine, B., & Stevens, R. (1986). Teaching functions. In M. C. Wittrock (Ed.), *Handbook of Research on Teaching* (3rd ed.) (pp. 376–391). New York: Macmillan.

Scruggs, T. E., & Richter, L. (1985). Tutoring learning disabled students: A critical review. *Learning Disability Quarterly, 8,* 286–289.

Skinner, B. F. (1958). Teaching machines. *Science, 128,* 969–977.

Sloan, J. L. (1987). Behaviorism. In C. R. Reynolds & L. Mann (Eds.), *Encyclopedia of special education.* New York: Wiley.

Stevens, R., & Rosenshine, B. (1981). Advances in research on teaching. *Exceptional Education Quarterly, 1,* 1–9.

Stoddard, K., & Valcante, G. (1991, April). *"Classroom buddies": Methods and effects of mainstreaming on special needs preschoolers and kindergarten regular education students.* Paper presented at the National Council for Exceptional Children Conference, Atlanta, GA.

Stromer, R. (1975). Modifying letter and number reversals in elementary school children. *Journal of Applied Behavioral Analysis, 8,* 211.

Taylor, R. L. (1997). *Assessment of exceptional students: Educational and psychological procedures.* Boston: Allyn and Bacon.

Tucker, J. A. (1985). Curriculum based assessment: An introduction. *Exceptional Children, 52,* 199–204.

Valcante, G., & Stoddard, K. (May, 1990). *Peer tutoring in natural community settings: Strategies for teacher training.* Paper presented at the American Association on Mental Retardation, Atlanta, GA.

Webber, J., Scheuermann, B., McCall, C., & Coleman, M. (1993). Research on self-monitoring as a behavior management technique in special education classrooms: A descriptive review. *Remedial and Special Education, 14* (2), 38–56.

Whinnery, K. W., & Fuchs, L. S. (1992). Implementing effective teaching strategies with learning disabled students through curriculum-based measurement. *Learning Disabilities Research and Practice, 7,* 25–30.

White, O. R. & Haring, N. G. (1980). *Exceptional teaching.* Upper Saddle River, NJ: Prentice Hall/Merrill.

Wolery, M., Bailey, D. B., & Sugai, G. M. (1988). *Effective teaching: Principles and procedures of applied behavior analysis with exceptional students.* Boston: Allyn and Bacon.

Ysseldyke, J. E. & Algozzine, B. (1990). *Introduction to special education* (2nd ed.). Boston: Houghton Mifflin.

Metacognition includes an awareness of what skills, strategies, and resources are needed to carry out an activity.

CHAPTER 8

The Cognitive Model

In this chapter we will discuss...

- The historical development of cognitive approaches to improving thinking skills and learning and performance in academic skill areas.

- Basic tenets of the cognitive model, including memory strategies and their relation to learning.

- Basic applications of the cognitive model as they relate to teaching students to think and use cognitive strategies to improve their learning, including: cognitive behavior modification and self-monitoring, learning strategies, and other approaches such as key-word methods and advance organizers.

- Classroom illustrations of cognitive model approaches for improving written expression, reading comprehension, and mathematics, as well as study and social skills.

E arly pioneers in educational psychology and the study of learning were interested in how thinking, intellectual skills, and inner language influenced knowledge, behavior, and development in children and adults. The field of cognitive psychology can be traced to their work and has bearing on the models used to explain and address LD (Bender, 1995; Lerner, 1994). The cognitive model focuses on knowledge, intellectual skills, and inner language, including simple recall of facts to synthesis and evaluation and their relation to performance. It has bearing on LD since this is a category evidenced by significant difficulties in the acquisition and performance of listening, speaking, reading, writing, reasoning, or mathematical abilities. The cognitive model has been operationalized and adopted in the field primarily in the area of metacognition, an important construct in cognitive psychology.

Metacognition refers to "one's knowledge concerning one's own cognitive processes and products of anything related to them, e.g., the learning-relevant properties of information or data" (Flavell, 1977, p. 232). Knowledge of cognitive processes includes knowledge about them and regulation of them (understanding how you think and doing something about it). Metacognition includes an awareness of the skills, strategies, and resources needed to carry out an activity (Hallahan, Kauffman, & Lloyd, 1986). The term is often interpreted to mean "thinking about thinking," or all self-regulated planning to ensure successful completion of a task (Bender, 1995, p. 273).

Metacognition was given foundation support and applied to academic areas by Flavell and A. L. Brown, who reasoned that metacognition is "awareness and regulation of cognitive activity" (Brown, 1975, p. 3). Students with LD often exhibit difficulties in areas related to knowing what strategies to use to solve problems or produce answers (e.g., mnemonic strategies) and are seen as passive learners (Ryan, Weed, & Short, 1986). Application of the cognitive model and metacognition to the field of LD is evident in the strategies-training work begun by Hallahan, Deshler, and others.

FOUNDATIONS OF THE COGNITIVE MODEL

Flavell (1977) suggested that a person's acquired knowledge influences what the person stores and retrieves from storage, or from memory. Constructive memory stresses the role that a person's general knowledge and cognitive activities play in specific acts of memory (Flavell, 1977). Most of the things remembered in everyday life are meaningful events or important information, unlike those laboratory settings where the subjects are given meaningless lists and information to store in memory and retrieve at a later time. Laboratory settings obtain data from rote memory tasks of memorizing lists of unrelated words or repeating a list of numbers.

Piaget views storage as a construction which, according to Flavell (1977), relates to comprehending and encoding what is to be remembered. When information is taken from memory, this is referred to as retrieval, or Piaget's reconstruction. This process can be "strategic" or "metamnemonic" (Flavell, 1977). Each time information is put into memory, a strategy is also used. According to Flavell (1985) this strategy can be influenced by personal knowledge, task knowledge, or strategy knowledge.

Flavell (1985) describes *personal knowledge* as what one knows about oneself. It is "the ability to recognize and identify experiences of remembering and forgetting when they occur, conceptually differentiating these experiences from such others as thinking, dreaming, and perceiving" (Flavell, 1985, p. 231). What a person knows plays an important role in what that person learns and remembers.

Task knowledge refers to the memory utilized to complete specific tasks (Flavell, 1985). Some tasks may be more difficult than others, depending on the type and amount of information to be remembered. This will also determine the storage and retrieval difficulty level. The more familiar a person is with a task, the easier it will be to store and retrieve the information at a later time.

Strategy knowledge is a wide range of activities a person carries out through mnemonic remembering (Flavell, 1985). Examples of strategies include: verbally rehearsing a telephone number, taking notes, underlining key points, noting important dates on a calendar, and recalling the day's activities to remember where an item was misplaced. Brown (1975) refers to this knowledge as "knowing" and describes strategies as "knowing how to know." A strategy is an activity one uses to remember. Rehearsal, organization, elaboration, and retrieval are components of a strategy. Flavell indicates there may be a production deficiency in strategy usage (see Table 8.1).

Metamemory is a component of strategy knowledge. The focus in metamemory is on verbal knowledge about strategies, as distinguished from using strategies in memory situations (Flavell, 1985). Metamemory is knowledge about anything concerning memory and is needed to understand the variables that effect one's own memory.

As illustrated in Table 8.1, Flavell (1977) describes the development of a memory strategy through three periods. In the first, the strategy is not developed or available for use. Next, during the deficient production period, ability to use the strategy is beginning to develop, and attempts to use the strategy are effective and positive but spontaneous use of the strategy is absent. Finally, in the mature period, ability

Table 8.1
Development of a Memory Strategy

	Major Periods in Strategy Development		
	Strategy Not Available	Production Deficiency	Mature Strategy Use
Basic ability to execute strategy	Absent to poor	Fair to good	Good to excellent
Spontaneous strategy use	Absent	Absent	Present
Attempts to elicit strategy use	Ineffective	Effective	Unnecessary
Effects of strategy use on retrieval	—	Positive	Positive

Note. From *Cognitive Development,* 3/e, (p. 197), by Flawell, Miller, & Miller. © 1993. Reprinted by permission of Prentice-Hall, Inc., Upper Saddle River, NJ.

to use the strategy is well developed and effective, and attempts to elicit the strategy are unnecessary, since spontaneous use of the strategy is present.

Other memory strategies identified by Flavell (1977) include storage strategies such as organization, elaboration, and retrieval. *Organization strategies* are often used by categorizing items or groups. Using this strategy would require grouping similar items. A person trying to remember a list of items (e.g., bread, glue, paper, apples, scissors, milk, and eggs) using an organization strategy would make the task easier by grouping them into foods and school supplies. Someone using an *elaboration strategy* would find a common meaning between two or more things to be remembered, for example, use a visual cue to relate two items or when trying to remember the definition of a word, take a key word from the definition. An association can be made, or a visual picture can be used to relate the two words. *Retrieval strategies* refer to what a person does to pull information out of memory. This could include relating the information to a past experience, using a mnemonic device or visual memory.

Memory studies have concluded that students with LD exhibit difficulties on memory tasks, when compared to their peers without disabilities. This can be attributed to the lack of strategy usage in students with LD. Two common memory strategies taught to students with LD are rehearsal and organization. Rehearsal strategies require the student to repeat the items to be remembered. Organization strategies group items by categories (i.e., animals and plants) and then rehearse the items.

Cognitive theories were first studied when Flavell, Beach, and Chilsky (1966) began asking questions about how children remembered. Changes began taking place in the 1970s, providing the basis for the cognitive development approach, and there was a shift in how researchers viewed what the learner contributed to the learning process. Children were viewed as active learners and were questioned about how they approached a task. Researchers investigated strategies that children employed to attack a problem. It was realized that the material children were asked to learn had an impact on what was learned. Interest also arose in how children acquire prior knowledge.

A. L. Brown (1975) has studied the area of metacognition in depth and has suggested two components that assist in defining metacognition: the knowledge one has about his or her own cognitive processes and the regulation of the cognitive activity.

Early attempts to employ cognitive instructional models with students with LD were those of Hallahan and his colleagues at the University of Virginia's Learning Disabilities Research Institute. They began looking at Meichenbaum's (1977) cognitive behavior modification work with impulsive children and found the technique used to also be beneficial in teaching attention-monitoring strategies and academic routines to children with LD (Hallahan & Reeve, 1980; Kauffman & Hallahan, 1979). The work of the Learning Disabilities Research Institute continued into information-processing laboratory research and the development of classroom techniques. Hallahan, Kneedler, and Lloyd (1983) concluded that cognitive behavior modification (CBM) procedures are most effective when the child is in control of assessment and is continuously working on the task (i.e., using a tape recorder for on/off task behaviors).

Professionals at the Learning Disabilities Research Institute worked with academic strategy training; their approach followed the principles of direct instruction. Academic strategy training is like Meichenbaum's (1977) CBM except that it doesn't rely on self-verbalization to the same degree. Hallahan and his colleagues (1983) found that verbal rehearsal may not be an important component of self-instruction.

A parallel application of metacognitive concepts was developed and extended at the Kansas Learning Disabilities Institute (Clark, Deshler, Schumaker, Alley, & Warner, 1984; Deshler, Alley, Warner, & Schumaker, 1981; Deshler, Schumaker, Lenz, & Ellis, 1984). Using acronyms to structure inner language and facilitate learning, Deshler and his colleagues specified the steps needed to complete common tasks and taught students with LD how to use them. The "learning strategies" approach specified the steps a person would go through when completing a specific task. The steps formed the basis of an inner language the person could use when completing the task. Strategies have been developed and applied to common learning tasks such as reading a paragraph, completing a multiple-choice test, and reading a content-specific chapter.

APPLICATION OF THE COGNITIVE MODEL

Cognition is how we think. Many children with LD need to be taught how to think. They need strategies for tasks such as organization, test taking, and remembering facts. They often do not think about how to approach a task. Some students with LD think they will fail before they attempt a task. If they do perform well, many times these students will attribute it to luck or level of difficulty of the task (e.g., too easy). If they do poorly, they will attribute it to their own lack of ability or effort. Students with LD need to be taught that they are in control. Reid (1988, p. 88) defines *attribution* as "children's explanations for their academic performance." Students with LD need attribution retraining. Some of these students have not been taught how to approach tasks. Because of a lack of strategies, they don't know how to develop solutions to problems or tasks and they shut down. It is assumed that they do not care, but they have not been taught the steps to be successful. Teaching these students strategies helps them to be successful (Bender, 1995).

Once students are taught strategies and how to use them in various settings, they need to begin developing their own strategies for application in other situations. They need to be taught how to think and approach a task. Once they are successful, then they will apply and use new strategies. This approach needs to click for these students. When they are successful, they will attribute this success to effort and continue utilizing strategies.

Some students with LD have developed learned helplessness, a belief that their efforts will not result in desired outcomes (Lerner, 1994). They learn to accept failure, lose motivation, and see themselves as helpless. They do not know how to think for themselves and need to be taught how. They may be dependent on someone telling them how to do everything. Students can be taught how to use appropriate strategies to become more active learners (Ryan et al., 1986).

Generalization is reached when the strategy is applied to various settings and situations. Based on the success of a strategy, students will determine if it is to be used in future situations. They do not always know how to modify a strategy and may need to be taught how to pick and choose pieces of a strategy and then generalize them. This is the ultimate goal for students with LD, who often need to be taught how to learn and how to adapt prior strategies to the task or situation at hand. As students find successes they will begin to generalize strategies to other situations and settings. Many times they need cues to remind them to use the strategies in their classes.

Teachers need to look at how they approach a task themselves and then look at how students with LD approach the same task. They can then question themselves to determine what steps the student with LD may be missing and fill in the gaps. Students with LD have an average IQ, but it is the discrepancy between intelligence and achievement that results in identification and provision of special education services.

Successful applications of metacognitive approaches designed to enhance the use of inner language to foster active approaches to learning, reduce learned helplessness, improve memory and learning, and help students with LD to generalize include CBM and learning strategies instruction.

Cognitive Behavior Modification

CBM was a new educational approach in the 1970s. In this approach, a student attempts to modify unobservable thought processes. The techniques stress providing strategies for both learning and teaching self-instruction and teaching independence and self-control. Meichenbaum's (1977) CBM self-instructional program has influenced current cognitive strategy instruction. There are four steps in Meichenbaum's (1977) CBM approach:

1. Adult model performs a task while talking out loud (cognitive modeling)
2. Children perform same task under direction of model's instruction (self-guidance)
3. Children whisper instructions to themselves as they perform task (faded self-guidance)
4. Children perform task while guiding their own performance via self-speech (self-instruction)

This approach stresses various aspects of self-monitoring and helps students take control of their learning processes. It also gives specific steps for solving problems. Meichenbaum found this technique effective in treating poor attentiveness and impulsivity in children. The basic skills of application of this metacognitive strategy include: (a) predicting consequences, (b) evaluating the results, (c) monitoring the activity, (d) deciding if the strategy makes sense, and (e) using a variety of behaviors to solve problems. Self-monitoring is a broad term used to refer to metacognitive strategies derived from CBM principles and directed at improving classroom behavior (Bender, 1995; Hallahan & Sapona, 1982). In this strategy, students are taught to use inner language to monitor their on-task behavior while doing specific tasks (Bender, 1995). In self-monitoring, students learn to self-instruct, self-evaluate, and self-reinforce.

A self-monitoring approach consists of three components: "(a) strategies, (b) knowledge about the use and significance of those strategies, and (c) explicit self-regulation of strategic performance" (Harris & Pressley, 1991, p. 396). Harris and Pressley (1991) have developed a seven-stage instructional model for strategy development. The stages are general guidelines which can be individualized and reordered if necessary. Stage 1 is preskill development, which requires the student to master all prerequisite skills for the strategy. Stage 2 is a review of the current performance level. Baseline data are collected in this stage, and goals are set for future performance once the strategy is mastered. Stage 3 involves the teacher describing the strategy. This stage explains the steps of the strategy and how and when to use it. Stage 4 is modeling and self-instruction of the strategy. The teacher models through self-instruction as the student observes and writes his or her own self-instructions based on the model. Stage 5 is mastery of the strategy, where the student is to memorize the steps of the strategy. Stage 6 is collaborative practice of the strategy steps and self-instruction. In this stage the student performs the task while implementing the strategy through self-instruction. Stage 7 is independent performance, where the student applies the strategy without guidance or support from the teacher.

Self-monitoring is among the most easily adapted metacognitive approaches for use with students with LD, in general, and those in special education classrooms. For example, Bender provides this illustration (1995):

In self-monitoring strategies, students are taught to use inner language to monitor on-task behavior while doing specific tasks.

> First, a cassette tape is prepared with a bell tone that rings at varying intervals (the intervals should average about 45 seconds in length). At the sound of each bell, the student asks the question, "Was I paying attention?" The student is trained to answer either yes or no and immediately return to the worksheet. (p. 283)

This procedure, which uses simple recording sheets and frequent monitoring of performance, has been found effective in improving on-task behavior in a variety of settings. Harris and Pressley (1991) have found self-monitoring strategy development to be effective with students with LD in improving academic performance and self-efficacy. Other researchers have found this approach to be successful in improving performance in reading comprehension, written language, and mathematical problem-solving classes with these students (Bender, 1995; Graham & Harris, 1989; Lerner, 1994).

Cognitive and metacognitive strategies provide students with LD with a strategy for thinking, planning, monitoring, and performing. The goal in CBM is to teach students how to think and monitor their own behavior. Some students with LD have strategies for doing this, but need to be cued to use them or taught to apply them to other settings and situations. Other students with LD need to be taught the strategies to enable them to become more successful.

Learning Strategies

Difficulties in academic performance are the hallmark of LD. Metacognitive strategies that help students participate more actively in academic tasks have become very popular in recent years. Learning strategies are defined as "techniques, principles, or rules that will facilitate the acquisition, manipulation, integration, storage, and retrieval of academic information across situations and settings" (Alley, & Deshler, 1979, p. 13). A learning strategies model of instruction is designed to teach students "how to learn" rather than to teach students specific content (Alley & Deshler, 1979, p. 13).

The ultimate goal of use of learning strategies is to teach students a skill needed at the present time and to have them generalize the skill across situations and settings at various times. The University of Kansas Learning Strategies Curriculum was designed to assist adolescents with LD in becoming more independent learners. Learning strategies teach the student a step-by-step process for a learning task, which allows the student to become an active part in the learning process. Learning strategies instruction uses an effective teaching model that proceeds from pretest and description to posttest and generalization stages using demonstration, rehearsal, practice, and feedback as primary teaching methods (see Table 8.2).

Initially, strategies are learned in a specific context and are used only in that context. A student more proficient in strategy usage can then think about the strategies and learn to use them for other tasks. This "conscious access to the routines available to the system is the highest form of mature human intelligence" (Brown, Bransford, Ferrara, & Campione, 1983).

Metacognitive strategies can assist students with LD in becoming more efficient academic learners. The importance given to teaching strategies for improving academic performance stems from the underlying academic deficits included in most

Table 8.2

Overview of Learning Strategies Instruction

Step 1: Pretest and Commitment
Step 2: Strategy Description
Step 3: Strategy Demonstration and Modeling
Step 4: Verbal Rehearsal
Step 5: Controlled Practice and Feedback
Step 6: Content-Appropriate Practice and Feedback
Step 7: Posttest and Direction for Generalization
Step 8: Generalization

definitions of LD. Students with LD often are poor in organizational and planning skills needed in learning academic content (Englert & Raphael, 1988). They also do not have a plan of action for organizing their thought processes or performing most academic tasks. As a result they often have negative attitudes towards learning. Ample evidence exists to support the use of learning strategies in the improvement of performance in key academic areas. For example, Welch (1992) indicated that students' attitudes towards paragraph writing improved after instruction and successful use of the PLEASE strategy.

Table 8.3 presents an overview of PLEASE and other effective learning strategies used to assist students in a variety of content areas and which can then be generalized to other situations. This information provides a quick reference of useful strategies found in the research in the areas of written expression, reading, mathematics, study and social skills.

Several researchers have argued that students with LD fail to use age appropriate knowledge-acquisition strategies (Bender, 1995; Deshler & Schumaker, 1986; Lerner, 1994). This problem has been so well documented that its remediation has been the major focus of the University of Kansas Institute for Research in Learning Disabilities (KU-IRLD) (Clark et al., 1984; Deshler et al., 1981; Deshler, et al., 1984).

The KU-IRLD has designed metacognitive interventions to assist students with LD in coping with the demands of secondary school (Deshler & Schumaker, 1986; Deshler et al., 1984). Their model is the Strategies Intervention Model (SIM) and its goal is to "teach students how to learn rather than to teach students specific curriculum content" (Deshler & Schumaker, 1986, p. 583). The goal of learning-strategies instruction as with other methods discussed here, is to teach students a strategy that can be implemented in a specific content area (e.g., social studies, science, English, mathematics) and eventually generalized to other situations and settings.

The learning-strategies approach demands that the student take the major role in his or her learning and requires a commitment on the part of the learner to be responsible. The strategies are designed for adolescents with LD who read above a fourth grade level. The learning-strategies instruction model is divided into three curriculum strands: acquisition, storage, and expression and demonstration of competence (see Table 8.4). It identifies strategies, techniques, and rules that the student can utilize in coping with the demands of secondary school. Although early adolescence is considered the prime time for instruction in learning strategies, younger children have been found able to learn and apply strategies also (Bauwens & Hourcade, 1989; Deshler & Schumaker, 1986; Ellis & Lenz, 1987).

Table 8.3
Overview of Strategies

Strategy	Author(s)	Practical Illustration
Written Expression		
DEFENDS (A strategy for writing positions)	Ellis & Lenz (1987)	**D**ecide on exact position **E**xamine the reasons for the position **F**orm a list of points that explain each reason **E**xpose position in first sentence **N**ote each reason and supporting points **D**rive home the position in the last sentence **S**earch for errors and correct
TREE (A strategy for composing essays)	Graham & Harris (1989)	Note topic sentence Note reasons Examine reasons Note ending
PLEASE (A strategy for writing a paragraph)	Welch, M. (1992)	**P**ick a topic **L**ist your ideas about the topic **E**valuate your list **A**ctivate the paragraph with a topic sentence **S**upply supporting sentences **E**nd with a concluding sentence and **E**valuate your work
Computers & Writing-Instruction Project (CWIP) (Using computers to write)	MacArthur, Schwartz, & Graham (1991)	Think who, what? Use C-SPACE to take notes (**C**haracters, **S**etting, **P**roblem or purpose, **A**ction, **C**onclusion, **E**motion). Write and say more.
Reportive Essay	Wong, Wong, Darlington, & Jones (1991)	Search long-term memory to retrieve events. Mentally relive the event fully through auditory and visual imageries. Reactivate all of the associated emotions.
Reading		
SQ3R (Reading in content areas)	Robinson, F. P., (1961)	**S**urvey. Look at the entire reading assignment for an overview. **Q**uestion. Question self, using the headings. **R**ead. Read to answer the questions. **R**ecite. Answer the questions from memory. **R**eview. Reread the test to clarify.
RARE (Reading for a purpose)	Gearheart, DeRuiter, & Sileo (1986)	**R**eview the questions at the end of the reading selection. **A**nswer all questions you already know. **R**ead the selection. **E**xpress answers to questions that you were unable to answer initially.

(continued)

Table 8.3 *continued*

Strategy	Author(s)	Practical Illustration
Reading		
POSSE (Reading comprehension)	Englert & Mariage (1990)	**P**redict which ideas are in the story. **O**rganize ideas in the story. **S**earch for text structure. **S**ummarize in your words. **E**valuate.
Question-Answer Relationship (QAR) (Four types)	Raphael, T. E. (1986)	1. Right There: Find answers in the story. (literal & detail) 2. Think and Search: Look for the answer in several places. 3. Author and You: Make inferences and conclusions. 4. On Your Own: Answer must come from readers' experience and knowledge.
Critical Thinking Map	Idol, L. (1987)	Include on a story map: 1. Important Events 2. Main Idea/Lesson 3. Other Viewpoints/Opinions 4. Reader's Conclusions 5. Relevance to Today
Five-Step Reading Comprehension Strategy	Schunk & Rice (1987)	What do I have to do? 1. Read the questions. 2. Read the passage to find out what it is mostly about. 3. Think about what the details have in common. 4. Think about what would make a good title. 5. Reread the story if I don't know the answer to a question.
Mathematics		
Eight-Step Solving Strategy for Verbal Math Problems	Montague & Bos (1986)	Read the problem aloud. Paraphrase the problem aloud. Visualize. State the problem. Hypothesize. Estimate. Calculate. Self-check.
Arithmetic Problem Solving	Fleischner, Nuzum, & Marzola (1987)	READ: What is the question? REREAD: What is the necessary information? THINK: Putting together? Add. Taking apart? Subtract. Do I need all the information? Is it a two-step problem? SOLVE: Write the equation. CHECK: Recalculate. Label. Compare.

(continued)

Table 8.3 *continued*

Strategy	Author(s)	Practical Illustration
Mathematics		
Division Facts	Lloyd, Saltzman & Kauffman (1981)	Point to the divisor. Count by the divisor until you get the number of dividend. Make hash marks while counting by. Count the number of hash marks. Write down the number of hash marks.
Multiplication Facts	Lloyd, Saltzman, & Kauffman (1981)	Point to the number you can count by. Make hash marks for other numbers. Count by the number and point once for each hash mark. Write down the last number said.
Solving Word Problems	Karrison & Carroll (1991)	Read the problem. Underline or highlight key words, sentences, or quesitons. Decide what sign to use. Set up the problem. Solve the problem.
Math Problem Solving	Montague (1992)	Read (for understanding). Paraphrase (your own words). Visualize (a picture or a diagram). Hypothesize (a plan to solve the problem). Estimate (predict the answer). Compute (the arithmetic). Check (to make sure everything is right).
Solving Simple Word Problems	Case, Harris, & Graham (1992)	Read the problem out loud. Look for important words, and circle. Draw pictures to help tell what's happening. Write down the math sentence. Write down the answer.
Subtraction using the "4Bs" mnemonic strategy	Frank & Brown (1992)	Begin? In the 1st column. Bigger? Which number is bigger? Borrow? If bottom number is bigger I must borrow. Basic Facts? Remember them. Use Touch Math if needed.

(continued)

Table 8.3 *continued*

Strategy	Author(s)	Practical Illustration
Study Skills		
PARS Study Strategy	Hoover (1989)	**P**review. **A**sk questions. **R**eview. **S**ummarize.
LINCS (A Starter Strategy for Vocabulary Learning)	Ellis (1992)	**L**ist the parts. **I**magine a picture. **N**ote a reminding word. **C**onstruct a LINCing story. **S**elf-test.
Social Skills		
LISTEN	Bauwens & Hourcade (1989)	**L**ook. **I**dle your motor. **S**it up straight. **T**urn to me. **E**ngage your brain. **N**ow
SCORER (A Test-Taking Strategy)	Hoover (1989)	**S**chedule time. **L**ook for **C**lue words. **O**mit difficult questions. **R**ead carefully. **E**stimate answers. **R**eview the work.
SLANT (A Starter Strategy for Class Participation)	Ellis (1991)	**S**it up. **L**ean forward. **A**ctivate your thinking. **N**ame key information. **T**rack the talker.

SELF POWER (A Self-Management Strategy)	Sander, Bott, Hughes, & Ruhl (1991)	Plan to change my behavior:
		  Select and define my goal.
		  Establish my goal and measure.
		  List rewards and choose one.
		  Fix the forms.
		Observe my behavior.
		Write it down.
		Evaluate my performance.
		Reward myself.

I CAN (Personal Commitment strategy)	Swanson (1992)	Independence (work alone) Completion (of work) Accuracy (reach a mastery level) Neatness (write neatly)

Dealing With Anger	McGinnis, Sauerbry, & Nichols (1985)	Stop and count to 10.
		Think of your choices:
		  Tell the person why you are angry.
		  Walk away now.
		  Do a relaxation exercise.
		Act out your best choice.

Table 8.4
Select Strategies from the Learning-Strategies Instruction Model

Strategy	Author(s)	Practical Illustration
Acquisition Strand		
DISSECT (A Word Identification Strategy)	Lenz, Schumaker, Deschler, & Beals (1984)	**D**iscover the context. **I**solate the prefix. **S**eparate the suffix. **S**ay the stem. **E**xamine the stem. **C**heck with someone. **T**ry the dictionary.
Multipass Strategy	Schumaker, Deschler, Alley, Warner, & Denton (1982)	Survey Pass. Read titles, headings, chapter summaries, etc. Size-up Pass. Read chapter questions and skim to locate the answer. Sort-out Pass. Test by checking off questions that can be answered quickly and look in text for other answers.
Paraphrasing Strategy	Schumaker, Denton & Deshler (1984)	Read a paragraph. Ask yourself, "What were the main idea and details in this paragraph? Put the main idea and details into your own words.
Storage Strand		
FIRST-Letter Mnemonic Strategy	Nagel, Schumaker, & Deschler (1986)	**F**orm a word. **I**nsert a letter or letters. **R**earrange the letters. **S**hape a sentence. **T**ry combinations.
LISTS		**L**ook for clues. **I**nvestigate the items. **S**elect a mnemonic device, using FIRST. **T**ransfer the information to a card. **S**elf-test.

(continued)

Table 8.4 *continued*

Strategy	Author(s)	Practical Illustration
Expression and Demonstration of Competence Strand		
PENS (A Sentence-Writing Strategy)	Sheldon & Schumaker (1985)	**P**ick a formula. **E**xplore words to fit the formula. **N**ote the words. **S**earch and check.
COPS (An Error-Monitoring Strategy)	Schumaker, Nolan, & Deshler (1985)	**C**apitalization **O**verall appearance **P**unctuation **S**pelling
WRITER	Schumaker, Nolan & Deshler (1985)	**W**rite on every other line, using PENS. **R**ead your paper for meaning. **I**nterrogate yourself, using COPS questions. **T**ake the paper to someone for help. **E**xecute a final copy. **R**eread your paper.
PIRATES (A Test-Taking Strategy)	Hughes, Schumaker, Deshler, & Mercer (1988)	**P**repare to succeed. **I**nspect the instructions. **R**ead, remember, and reduce. **A**nswer or abandon. **T**urn back. **E**stimate. **S**urvey.
SCRIBE (A Paragraph-Writing Strategy)	Schumaker & Lyerla (1991)	**S**et up a diagram. **C**reate a title. **R**eveal the topic. **I**ron out the details. **B**ind it together with a clincher. **E**dit your work.
Motivational Strategy		
I PLAN (The Education Planning Strategy)	Van Reusen, Bos, Schumaker, & Deshler (1987)	**I**nventory your strengths, weaknesses, goals, and choices for learning. **P**rovide your inventory information. **L**isten and respond. **A**sk questions. **N**ame your goals.
SHARE	Van Reusen, Bos, Schumaker, & Deshler (1987)	**S**it up straight. **H**ave a pleasant tone of voice. **A**ctivate your thinking. **R**elax. **E**ngage in eye contact.

The acquisition strand includes six strategies: (a) the Word Identification Strategy is a word-decoding strategy which utilizes the mnemonic DISSECT to assist students in utilizing the strategy; (b) the Visual Imagery Strategy teaches the student to form a mental picture of the events in a reading passage; (c) the Self-Questioning Strategy assists in forming questions about underlying information in a story and helps to answer comprehension questions at the end of the story; (d) the Paraphrasing Strategy teaches students to paraphrase the main idea and details in each paragraph of the reading passage using the mnemonic RAP; (e) interpreting visual aids assists students in gaining information from tables, charts, graphs, pictures, maps and diagrams; and the Multipass Strategy, used with textbook chapters, requires the student to make three passes over the chapter to survey, find key information, and study the key information.

The storage strand consists of three strategies: (a) The FIRST-Letter Mnemonic Strategy teaches the student to locate and organize important information into lists, with memorization and recall aided by use of the mnemonic device FIRST, which helps students remember the strategy steps; (b) the Paired Associates Strategy teaches pairing or grouping of information to be learned; and (c) the Listening and Note-taking Strategy teaches students to listen for key information in a class and to take notes on the key points. The notetaking involves two columns, one for main ideas and one for details.

The expression and demonstration of competence strand includes six strategies: (a) The Sentence-Writing Strategy is designed to teach students to write simple, compound, complex, and compound-complex sentences, and the mnemonic PENS assists students in remembering the strategy steps; (b) the Paragraph-Writing Strategy SCRIBE teaches students to write organized paragraphs, showing six different steps using the mnemonic; (c) the Error-Monitoring Strategy is designed to assist students in proofreading and locating errors in writing, with COPS and WRITER being two mnemonics utilized in this strategy; (d) the Theme-Writing Strategy teaches students to write themes or essays consisting of five paragraphs; (e) the Assignment-Completion Strategy teaches the students time management and organization to complete homework; and (f) the Test-Taking Strategy teaches students strategies to apply to a testing situation and utilizes the mnemonic PIRATES and four smaller mnemonic steps under PIRATES: PASS, RUN, ACE, and the three Rs (Hughes, Schumaker, Deshler & Mercer, 1988).

The Strategies Intervention Model curriculum also includes a motivational component. The Education Planning Strategy, utilizing the mnemonic I PLAN, teaches students a motivation strategy on how to participate in an Individualized Education Planning conference.

Each of the Kansas Learning Strategies uses a structured technique. As illustrated earlier, there are several stages in teaching a strategy to adolescents with LD. The first includes a pretest and requires the student to make a commitment to learn the strategy. Next the teacher explains the strategy, telling students where to use the strategy and stating the importance of using it. Teacher modeling of the strategy follows, to allow the teacher to show how the strategy should be utilized. In the next stages, verbal practice of the strategy steps, the students need to gain immediate recall of the strategy steps and continue with controlled practice until they are applying the strategy at a level in which they are comfortable working. The next stage involves content-appropriate practice in which the student applies the strategy to grade-level materials. Finally, posttests are used to evaluate competence with the strategy, and procedures for generalization into the content area classroom are provided and used.

Each strategy has cue cards to remind students what to do at each of the stages of the instructional model. A student must master one level before progressing to the next. Management charts are kept in folders or posted in the classroom, and the lessons are carefully scripted for the strategy instructor to follow. Research (Deshler & Schumaker, 1986) has shown marked gains in student progress once strategy instruction has been implemented. Student progress is highly related to the strategy instructor's proficiency in the strategy, and the developers of the model want educational agencies to commit to a staff development program to instruct teachers in the strategy usage (Deschler & Schumaker, 1986).

Other Applications

A number of additional metacognitive strategies have been developed and used with students with LD. Most of these do not rely heavily on self-monitoring or use acronyms to facilitate learning, but each does encourage the use of inner language during the completion of a cognitive task.

Key-word Method. Inefficient memory process plays a vital role in academic performance of students with LD. "It has been hypothesized that these memory problems result from failure to approach memory tasks in a strategic manner reflective of metamemorial awareness" (Palincsar & Brown, 1987, p. 66). The key-word mnemonic method attempts to provide a way of remembering, to facilitate encoding of information for easy retrieval (Matropieri, Scruggs, Bakken, & Brigham, 1992; Mastropieri, Scruggs, & Levin, 1985). The student is taught to recode, relate, and retrieve information to be remembered. Levin (1983) refers to this process as the "three Rs" of associative mnemonic techniques. The key-word technique is a method to remember an unfamiliar item by associating it with a meaningful item in the learner's knowledge base. For example, to learn that *oxalis* is a cloverlike plant, students are taught to think about an ox eating cloverlike plants or to learn that *chiton* means loose garment, they associate a kite made out of loose garments.

Several researchers (Mastropieri, Scruggs, & Fulk, 1990; McLoone, Scruggs, Mastropieri, & Zucker, 1986; Mastropieri et al., 1985; Levin, 1983) have found key-word mnemonics to be successful in promoting learning of vocabulary words in the content areas. Students with LD can benefit from mnemonic strategies if they are taught how to utilize them. Mnemonic instruction is an important technique for the success of students with LD.

Advanced Organizers. Ausubel, in the 1960s, was the first to present the concept of advanced organizers. Use of advanced organizers allows the students to know what can be expected to occur during the class period. Lenz (1983) states that advanced organizers are the activities a teacher uses before teaching, and they include one or more of the following:

  (a) announcement of the benefits of the advanced organizer, (b) topics and subtopics, (c) physical requirements needed for the learner and instructor to accomplish the task,

(d) background information related to new learning, (e) concepts to be learned (specific or general), (f) examples for clarification of concepts to be learned, (g) the organization or sequence in which the new information will be presented, (h) motivational information, (i) relevant vocabulary, (j) goals or outcomes desired. (p. 12)

Students with LD profit from being taught how to utilize advanced organizers. Research has found that advanced organizers can be effective in assisting students with LD in their organizing of information (Lenz, 1983). Classroom teachers using advanced organizers before instruction find themselves generally more effective with students with LD.

PERSPECTIVE ON THE COGNITIVE MODEL

Harris and Pressley (1991) indicate three important points in metacognitive strategy instruction. First, strategy instruction is—and continues to be—a growing area in the field of research. More research is necessary in this instruction and how to apply it to the content areas. Also, strategy instruction needs to be incorporated into the general education classrooms to provide an environment for strategy generalization and also assist students without disabilities.

Second, strategy instruction is not a panacea; there are limitations to using strategies. Strategy instruction does allow teachers to address the needs of students by providing a step-by-step process for approaching tasks, and strategies should be used when they meet the individual needs of the student; that is, they should be used if they assist in remediating the student's problem, appear to be the best solution, and if teachers are able to teach the strategy effectively (Lerner, 1994).

Third, good strategy instruction is not just memorizing the steps. Good strategy instruction incorporates teaching the students why they are learning a strategy, how it will help, when to use the strategy, and the settings appropriate for the use of the strategy. Students need to be actively involved in all stages of the strategy instruction. The teacher's role is to describe the strategy, model the strategy, provide practice, modify the strategy, and reteach when necessary. Effective teachers use the following steps when implementing interventions based on the cognitive model:

Step 1: Assess students' strategy usage for a specified task.

Step 2: Teach students a strategy related to the task.

Step 3: Practice using the strategy, and evaluate proficiency.

Step 4: Apply the strategy in various settings.

Step 5: Evaluate use and modify for application in other settings.

Step 6: Teach students to design their own strategies:
    a. Select a task that needs a strategy.
    b. Break task into component parts.
    c. Devise a mnemonic or other method to remember steps.
    d. Apply the strategy to the task.
    e. Modify steps if necessary (include self-monitoring and self-questioning when appropriate).

Practical Classroom Applications

Cognitive theories have been developed into a variety of practical classroom practices. Applications of these practices have been effective in improving problems of written expression, reading, and mathematics in students with LD, in addition to improving the study skills and prosocial behaviors described below.

1. *Teachers use cognitive applications in teaching written expression.* Effective writing has a goal and involves planning, sentence formulation, and revising (Graham & Harris, 1989). Students with LD often are inefficient in the strategies required for written expression, and adolescents with LD often experience problems on tasks involving written expression (Alley & Deshler, 1979; Graham & Harris, 1989). Educators have started to implement techniques that utilize metacognitive approaches to assist students in improving their written expression skills.

The *PLEASE* strategy (Welch & Link, 1989), using a step-by-step procedure originally researched by Kerrigan (1974), was developed to assist students in planning and writing compositions. A first-letter mnemonic device is used to assist in recalling and cueing the steps of the strategy. Starting with the *P* cues the student to *p*ick a topic, audience, and textual format. The student then is to *l*ist information about the topic to be used in sentence formulation, ongoing evaluation, and organization. *E* step is *e*valuation, which is ongoing throughout the writing process. Students are taught to organize their information list, determine if it is complete, and use this list to formulate sentences. They would then *a*ctivate the paragraph with a topic sentence, *s*upply the supporting sentences using the information on their list, and *e*nd with a concluding sentence and evaluate the paragraph.

The PLEASE strategy has an instructional manual with lessons for each step. Each lesson includes an advanced organizer, vocabulary terms, objectives, and mastery criteria. There are instructional game activities, overhead transparencies, and worksheets. The PLEASE strategy also has a video-assisted instructional program and teacher materials called *Write, PLEASE.* The video includes: learning objectives, lead-in activities, viewing activities, postviewing activities, followthrough activities, and an evaluation. The video models and gives a demonstration of each strategy step which the students can review as often as needed. The video explains each step of the strategy in lessons of 8 minutes in length. There is a video teacher manual that introduces the video and explains how to use the program and activities. The video explains how the teacher is to obtain writing samples and assess them for a topic sentence, supporting sentences, and a conclusion sentence. There are separate instructional activities for controlled practice and small-group and individual activities.

2. *Teachers use cognitive applications in teaching reading comprehension.* POSSE is an instructional procedure designed to increase students' reading comprehension. It can be used at the elementary or secondary level. Using this strategy, students learn to predict ideas from background knowledge, organize ideas, and summarize and evaluate their comprehension (Englert & Mariage, 1990). POSSE can also be helpful in expository texts, as it utilizes a strategy sheet to guide the discussion of such texts. The acronym POSSE is used to cue students of the steps in the strategy. This strategy has three stages: prereading, during-reading, and summarizing.

(continued)

Practical Classroom Applications (continued)

The prereading strategies include predicting and organizing background knowledge. The *predict* step requires the students to use cues from the title, headings, pictures, or beginning paragraphs to predict what the reading will be about. Brainstorming occurs at this stage also. The *organize* step is where the brainstorming ideas are organized into a semantic map.

The during-reading stages include *searching* for text structure, *summarizing*, and *evaluating*. While students are reading they search for text structure to confirm their predictions or generate new ideas. This stage does not require any information to be recorded on the POSSE strategy sheet. In the summarize step, the students name the main idea and identify the details. They then evaluate the text by discussing the main idea, comparing the semantic maps in the prereading and reading stages, clarifying unfamiliar vocabulary and information, and predicting what the next section of the text will be about.

This strategy depends on the participation of students in the discussion process. In the beginning of the strategy instruction the teacher directs the steps through modeling and thinking aloud. As the students learn the strategy, they become discussion leaders. The strategy sheets are gradually faded from the process and are never to be used as independent work sheets.

Question-answer relationship (QAR) strategies are designed to teach students the different types of questions asked in stories. Raphael (1986) describes four types of QARs: Right There, Think and Search, Author and You, and On Your Own (See Table 8.2). The teacher models each type of QAR, using a chart or transparency and reading passages that illustrate each type of QAR. Raphael (1982) said that when teaching QARs give immediate feedback, teach from shorter to longer texts, teach students to be independent, and transition from recognizing an answer to formulating a response. The first two types of QARs are found in the book, and the second two types of QARs are found in the head.

3. *Teachers use cognitive applications in teaching mathematics.* Lloyd, Saltzman, and Kauffman (1981) used "count-bys" to teach *multiplication and division* facts. Count-bys were taught as a preskill for the strategy, through modeling, oral practice, written practice, and work sheets. Using this process, students were taught the counting sequences for 5s, 7s, 2s, 3s, and 4s. The count-bys were then applied to learning multiplication and division facts. Corrective feedback and cue card strips were used to teach the steps of each strategy.

Subtraction using the "4Bs" strategy teaches students to use self-monitoring to solve *subtraction* problems. The mnemonic "4Bs" is used to cue the students to use the strategy, in addition to a checklist, for completing each problem. An explanation of the self-monitoring checklist is given first. Then, the teacher uses examples to model how to use the checklist. The teacher needs to verbalize out loud so that the students can learn the procedure. Students must indicate understanding of the procedure by doing it independently, using a mnemonic device to cue them if necessary. The beginning instruction should include work sheets with the self-monitoring steps written out as a guide and a checklist beside each problem. To fade this, first remove the list of steps from the work sheets, then remove the checklist beside each problem. If needed, a strategy wall chart can be placed in the room for a reference, or individual cue cards can be made. The goal is to gain independence from the checklist.

(continued)

The eight-step solving strategy for verbal math problems is designed to teach students with LD a strategy for solving verbal *math problems*. Materials for this strategy include: a wall chart and outline of the strategy steps, two-step practice problems, and graphs for recording progress. The stages of teaching this strategy consist of: strategy acquisition training, practice, and testing sessions. The steps of most math strategy training follow those of the University of Kansas in the learning strategies model. The steps include: (a) pretest, (b) describe, (c) model, (d) verbal practice, (e) student practice, and (f) corrective feedback (Case, Harris, & Graham, 1992; Fleischner, Nuzum, & Marzola, 1987; Frank & Brown, 1992; Karrison & Carroll, 1991).

4. *Teachers use cognitive applications in teaching study and social skills.* LINCS is a starter strategy for vocabulary learning, that is, strategy to assist students in learning. It can be taught quickly, learned quickly, and used in a variety of settings (Ellis, 1992). LINCS is a mnemonic device used to cue students to apply the vocabulary learning strategy.

The first step, *L*ist the Parts, requires students to list the words they need to know on 3×5 index cards. Samples are illustrated with specific instructions on how to make the card. The second step, *I*magine a Picture, requires the student to create a visual image of the word. The next step, *N*ote a Reminding Word, utilizes the key-word technique to decide on a word that reminds them of the word to be learned. This word is written underneath the word to be learned. For the fourth step, *C*onstruct a LINCing Story, the student uses the learning word, familiar word, and visual image to create a story (short sentence) and writes it on the back of the card under the defini-

tion. And in the fifth step, *S*elf-test, students practice remembering the word and definition.

An instructional manual, required for this strategy, includes specific explanations and directions on how to teach the strategy. The instruction begins with a pretest, which is provided in the manual along with progress charts. The teacher then describes the strategy, using cue cards which can be made into transparencies for instruction. Next is modeling, and model examples are provided for the teacher to use. There is also a practice test for the students that accompanies this stage. Stage 4 is verbal practice, where the students memorize the steps of the strategy before moving to Stage 5, controlled practice and feedback. Practice sets of words and quizzes are included in the manual for this part. Stage 6 is advanced practice and feedback, which uses more difficult words. Stage 7 is posttest and making commitments that ensure mastery of strategy usage, and finally, Stage 8 is generalization of the strategy to other settings.

The *SLANT* strategy is designed to teach students appropriate ways to participate in class (Ellis, 1991). This strategy can be taught in any classroom setting and has an eight-page manual to accompany the strategy. The strategy instruction includes a pretest, where the teacher records behavior with the SLANT steps written across the top of a chart and student names down the side. Next, the teacher describes the purpose of the strategy and the strategy steps and then models how to use the strategy. The students verbally practice the strategy steps and then practice using the steps. For this stage fun activities are suggested in the strategy manual. A posttest is conducted to ensure proper usage of the strategy, and feedback is provided. The last stage of the

(continued)

Practical Classroom Applications (continued)

strategy is generalization of the strategy into other settings.

I CAN is a strategy designed to teach students positive attitudes and thoughts through a personal commitment. Teachers can use the strategy to document change in students, communicate with parents, and incorporate individualized educational planning goals. The I CAN requires a contract to be written with each student. The contract information is taken from the IEP study skill goals or behavioral skill goals. Students goals are reviewed daily using the I CAN statements. This takes approximately 5 minutes. At the end of each lesson the teacher sits with each student and reviews his or her contract. In the beginning this takes about 10 to 15 minutes at the end of each class lesson, but as students become more familiar with the procedure, it takes less time. This strategy utilizes a goal summary sheet and monthly progress chart which, are helpful when reviewing IEP goals with parents.

SUMMARY

- The cognitive model focuses on knowledge, intellectual skills, and inner language and their relation to performance. Metacognition includes an awareness of which skills, strategies, and resources are needed to carry out an activity.

- Students with LD often have difficulties in areas related to knowing which strategies to use to solve problems or produce answers and, as a result, are often seen as passive learners.

- Flavell's research centered on the development of a memory strategy through three periods (i.e., the strategy is not developed or available for use; the strategy is beginning to develop, and attempts to use the strategy are effective and positive, but spontaneous use of the strategy is absent; the strategy is well developed and effective).

- Organization strategies are often used by categorizing items or grouping them into categories. An elaboration strategy refers to a common meaning between two or more things to be remembered. Retrieval strategies refer to what a person does to pull information out of memory. Rehearsal strategies require the student to repeat the items to be remembered.

- Early attempts to employ cognitive instructional models with students with LD were those of Hallahan and his colleagues, who began looking at Meichenbaum's cognitive behavior modification work with impulsive children.

- The learning-strategies approach of Deshler and peers specified steps forming the basis of an inner language a person could use when completing the task. The ultimate goal of using learning strategies is to teach students a skill that is needed at the present time and to generalize the skill across situations and settings at various times.

- The goal in cognitive behavior modification is to teach students how to think and monitor their own behavior. In self-monitoring strategies, students are taught to use inner language to monitor on-task behavior while doing specific tasks.

- In keyword mnemonic strategy, the student is taught to recode, relate, and retrieve an unfamiliar item by associating it with a meaningful item in the learner's knowledge base. Advanced organizers give help in organizing information and point out to the students what can be expected to occur during the class period.

- Cognitive theories have been developed into a variety of practical classroom practices. Applications have been effective in improving problems of students with LD in written expression, reading, and mathematics; they also have been used to improve study skills and social behaviors.

DISCUSSION QUESTIONS

To help extend your understanding of the cognitive model, reflect on and discuss the following questions:

1. What are the fundamental similarities and differences between cognitive approaches to improving learning and approaches based on other theories (e.g., behaviorism, constructivism)?

2. What aspects of the cognitive model would teachers find appealing?

3. How would you develop a metacognitive strategy to teach a friend about the cognitive model?

4. Do you believe learning strategies instruction would be useful for students other than those with LD? Why or why not?

5. Why would a key-word approach be effective in teaching science vocabulary to students with LD?

REFERENCES

Alley, G. & Deshler, D. (1979). *Teaching the learning disabled adolescent strategies and methods.* Denver, CO: Love.

Bauwens, J. & Hourcade, J. J. (1989). Hey, would you just LISTEN. *Teaching Exceptional Children, 21,* 61.

Bender, W. N. (1995). *Learning disabilities* (2nd ed.). Boston: Allyn and Bacon.

Brown, A. L. (1975). The development of memory: Knowing, knowing about knowing, and knowing how to know. As cited in Flavell, J. H. (1985). *Cognitive development.* Upper Saddle River, NJ: Prentice Hall.

Brown, A. L., Bransford, J. D., Ferrara, R. A., & Campione, J. C. (1982). *Learning, remembering, and understanding.* Technical Report No. 244. Champaign, IL: Authors.

Case, L. P., Harris, K. R., & Graham, S. (1992). Improving the mathematical problem-solving skills of students with learning disabilities: Self-regulated strategy development. *The Journal of Special Education, 26* (1), 1–19.

Clark, F. L., Deshler, D. D., Schumaker, J. B., Alley, G. R., & Warner, M. M. (1984). Visual imagery and self-questioning strategies to improve comprehension of written material. *Journal of Learning Disabilities, 17,* 145–149.

Deshler, D. D., Alley, G. R., Warner, M. M., & Schumaker, J. G. (1981). Instructional practices for promoting skill acquisition and generalization in severely learning disabled adolescents. *Learning Disability Quarterly, 4,* 415–421.

Deshler, D., & Schumaker, J. (1986). Learning strategies: An instructional alternative for low-achieving adolescents. *Exceptional Children, 52,* 583–590.

Deshler, D., Schumaker, J. B., Lenz, B. K., & Ellis, E. S. (1984). Academic and cognitive interventions for LD adolescents: Part II. *Journal of Learning Disabilities, 17*, 170–187.

Ellis, E. (1991). *SLANT a starter strategy for class participation.* Lawrence, KS: Edge Enterprises.

Ellis, E. (1992). *LINCS a starter strategy for vocabulary learning.* Lawrence, KS: Edge Enterprises.

Ellis, E. S., & Lenz, B. K. (1987). A component analysis of effective learning strategies for LD students. *Learning Disabilities Focus, 2*, 94–107.

Englert, C. S., & Mariage, T. (1990). Send for the POSSE: Structuring the comprehension dialogue. *Academic Therapy, 25*, 473–487.

Englert, C. S., & Raphael, T. E. (1988). Constructing well-formed prose: process, structure, and metacognitive knowledge. *Exceptional Children, 54*, 513–520.

Flavell, J. H. (1993). *Cognitive development,* 3rd ed. Upper Saddle River, NJ: Prentice Hall.

Flavell, J. H., Beach, D. H., & Chilsky, J. M. (1966). Spontaneous verbal rehearsal in memory tasks as a function of age. *Child Development, 37*, 283–299.

Fleischner, J. E., Nuzum, M. B., & Marzola, E. S. (1987). Devising an instructional program to teach arithmetic problem-solving skills to students with learning disabilities. *Journal of Learning Disabilities, 20*(4), 214–217.

Frank, A. R. & Brown, D. (1992). Self-monitoring strategies in arithmetic. *Teaching Exceptional Children, 24*(2), 52–53.

Graham, S., & Harris, K. R. (1989). Improving learning disabled students' skills at composing essays: Self-instructional strategy training. *Exceptional Children, 56*, 201–214.

Hallahan, D. P., Kauffman, J. M., & Lloyd, J. (1986). *Introduction to learning disabilities.* Boston: Allyn and Bacon.

Hallahan, D. P., Kneedler, R. D., & Lloyd, J. (1983). Cognitive behavior modification techniques for learning-disabled children. In J. D. McKinney & L. Feagans (Eds.), *Current topics in learning disabilities* (Vol. 1). New York: Ablex.

Hallahan, D. P., & Reeve, R. E. (1980). Selective attention and distractability. In B. K. Keogh (Ed.), *Advances in special education* (pp. 32–47). Greenwich, CT: JAI Press.

Hallahan, D. P., & Sapona, R. (1982). Self-monitoring of attention with learning disabled children: Past research and current issues. *Journal of Learning Disabilities, 16*, 616–620.

Harris, K. R. & Pressley, M. (1991). The nature of cognitive strategy instruction: Interactive strategy construction. *Exceptional Children, 57*, 392–404.

Hoover, J. J. (1989). Study skills and the education of students with learning disabilities. *Journal of Learning Disabilities, 22*, 452–455.

Hughes, C. A., Schumaker, J. B., Deshler, D. D., & Mercer, C. D. (1988). *The test taking strategy.* Lawrence, KS: Edge Enterprises.

Idol, L. (1987). A critical thinking map to improve content area comprehension of poor readers. *Remedial and Special Education, 8*, 28–40.

Karrison, J. & Carroll, M. (1991). Solving word problems. *Teaching Exceptional Children, 23*(4), 55–56.

Kauffman, J. M., & Hallahan, D. P. (1979). Learning disability and hyperactivity (with comments on minimal brain dysfunction). As cited in D. K. Reid, *Teaching the learning disabled: A cognitive development approach.* Needham, MA: Allyn and Bacon.

Kerrigan, W. J. (1974). *Writing to the point: Six basic steps.* New York: Harcourt Brace Jovanovich.

Lenz, K. (1983). Using advanced organizers. *The Pointer, 27*, 11–13.

Lenz, B. K., Schumaker, J. B., Deshler, D. D., & Beals, V. L. (1984). *The word identification strategy.* Lawrence: University of Kansas.

Lerner, J. (1994). *Learning disabilities* (6th ed.). Boston: Houghton Mifflin.

Levin, J. R. (1983). Pictorial strategies for school learning: Practical illustrations. In M. Pressley & J. R. Levin (Eds.), *Cognitive strategy research: Educational applications* (pp. 213–237). New York: Springer-Verlag.

Lloyd, J. W., Saltzman, N. J., & Kauffman, J. M. (1981). Predictable generalization in academic learning as a result of preskills and strategy training. *Learning Disability Quarterly, 4*, 203–216.

MacArthur, C. A., Schwartz, S. S., & Graham, S. (1991). A model for writing instruction: Integrating word processing and strategy instruction into a process approach to writing. *Learning Disabilities Research & Practice, 6*, 230–236.

Mastropieri, M. A., Scruggs, T. E., Bakken, J. P., & Brigham, F. J. (1992). A complex mnemonic strategy for teaching states and their capitals: Comparing forward and backward associations. *Learning Disabilities Research & Practice, 7,* 96–103.

Mastropieri, M. A., Scruggs, T. E., & Fulk, B. J. M. (1990). Teaching abstract vocabulary with the keyword method: Effects on recall and comprehension. *Journal of Learning Disabilities, 23,* 92–96.

Mastropieri, M. A., Scruggs, T. E., & Levin, J. R. (1985). Maximizing what exceptional students can learn: A review of research on the keyword method and related mnemonic techniques. *Remedial and Special Education, 6*(2), 39–45.

McGinnis, E., Sauerbry, L., & Nichols, P. (1985). Skillstreaming: Teaching social skills to children with behavioral disorders. *Teaching Exceptional Children, 17,* 160–167.

McLoone, B. B., Scruggs, T. E., Mastropieri, M. A., & Zucker, S. (1986). Memory strategy instruction with LD adolescents. *Learning Disabilities Research, 2,* 45–53.

Meichenbaum, D. (1977). *Cognitive-behavior modification.* New York: Plenum.

Montague, M. (1992). The effects of cognitive and metacognitive strategy instruction on the mathematical problem solving of middle school students with learning disabilities. *Journal of Learning Disabilities, 25*(4), 230–248.

Montague, M., & Bos, C. (1986). The effect of cognitive strategy training on verbal math problem solving performance of learning disabled adolescents. *Journal of Learning Disabilities, 19,* 26–33.

Nagel, D. R., Schumaker, J. B., & Deschler, D. D. (1986). *The FIRST-letter mnemonic strategy.* Lawrence, KS: Excel Enterprises.

Palincsar, A. S., & Brown, D. A. (1987). Enhancing instructional time through attention to metacognition. *Journal of Learning Disabilities, 20,* 66–75.

Raphael, T. E. (1982). Question-answering strategies for children. *The Reading Teacher, 36,* 186–190.

Raphael, T. E. (1986). Teaching question-answering relationships, revisited. *The Reading Teacher, 39,* 516–523.

Reid, D. K. (1988). *Teaching the learning disabled: A cognitive approach.* Needham, MA: Allyn and Bacon.

Robinson, F. P. (1961). *Effective study.* New York: Harper & Row.

Ryan, E. B., Weed, K. A., & Short, E. J. (1986). Cognitive behavior modification: Promoting active, self-regulatory learning styles. In J. K. Torgeson & B. Y. L. Wong (Eds.), *Psychological and educational perspectives on learning disabilities* (pp. 367–397). New York: Academic Press.

Sander, N. W., Bott, D. A., Hughes, C., & Ruhl, K. (1991). Effects of a self-management strategy on task-independent behaviors of adolescents with learning disabilities. *B. C. Journal of Special Education, 15* (1), 65–75.

Schumaker, J. B., Denton, P. H., & Deshler, D. D. (1984). *The paraphrasing strategy.* Lawrence: University of Kansas.

Schumaker, J. B., Deshler, D. D., Alley, G. R., Warner, M. M., & Denton, P. H. (1982). Multipass: A learning strategy for improving reading comprehension. *Learning Disability Quarterly, 5,* 295–304.

Schumaker, J. B. & Lyerla, K. D. (1991). *The paragraph writing strategy.* Lawrence: University of Kansas.

Schumaker, J. B., Nolan, S. M., & Deshler, D. D. (1985). *The error monitoring strategy.* Lawrence: University of Kansas.

Schunk, D. H., & Rice, J. M. (1987). Enhancing comprehension skill and self-efficacy with strategy value information. *Journal of Reading Behavior, 19,* 285–302.

Sheldon, J. & Schumaker, J. B. (1985). *The sentence writing strategy.* Lawrence, KS: Excel Enterprises.

Swanson, D. P. (1992) I CAN. *Teaching Exceptional Children, 24*(2), 22–26.

Van Reusen, A. K., Bos, C. S., Schumaker, J. B., & Deshler, D. D. (1987). *The education planning strategy.* Lawrence, KS: Edge Enterprises.

Welch, M. (1992). The PLEASE strategy: A metacognitive learning strategy for improving the paragraph writing of students with mild learning disabilities. *Learning Disability Quarterly, 15,* 119–128.

Welch, M., & Link, D. (1989). *Write, P.L.E.A.S.E.: A strategy for efficient learning and functioning in written expression* (Videocassette). Salt Lake City: University of Utah, Department of Special Education, Educational Tele-Communications.

Wong, B., Wong, R., Darlington, D., & Jones, W. (1991). Interactive teaching: An effective way to teach revision skills to adolescents with learning disabilities. *Learning Disabilities Research and Practice, 6,* 117–127.

The focus of social constructivistic programs is on functional, genuine, and authentic curriculum and instruction.

CHAPTER 9

The Social Constructivism Model

In this chapter we will discuss. . .

- The historical development of the social constructivistic model in terms of the theoretical base and the grass roots movement for implementing constructivistic practices.
- The use of integrated curricula that couch instruction in the context of authentic, real-life problems across subject areas.
- A child-centered approach that fosters intrinsic motivation.
- The balance between the teacher's control and directedness and the degree of child centeredness that characterize endogenous, dialectical, and exogenous constructivism.
- Instructional procedures guided by Vygotsky's proleptic teaching model and Bruner's expert scaffolding.
- Language development as a key element of learning for students.
- Immersion in reading activities through shared book experiences and other activities.
- The language experience approach and the process conference model.
- Instruction that focuses on concepts, principles, and value judgments.
- The relative value of procedural and declarative information.
- A balance between child-centered discovery learning and more teacher-directed modeling needed for students to construct meaning effectively.

- Concerns over the definition of what is an authentic learning situation and the degree to which school activities are contrived and meaningless.
- The effectiveness of child-centered instruction and the ability of students to guide their own learning.
- The research base of social constructivistic programs.

During the period from 1960 through the mid-1980s, behavioral and cognitive models of learning dominated the field of LD. However, as the limitations of these approaches became evident, a more radical shift began to emerge. Both philosophical and political critiques of these reductionistic models emerged. In the early 1980s, theorists such as Lous Heshusius began attacking the shortcomings of these approaches. Others followed, including Poplin (1988a, 1988b) in two companion articles that critiqued behavioral and cognitive models and offered an alternative view of learning and LD. In the past few years, social constructivism has been featured in topical issues of *Remedial and Special Education, 1995, Volume 16, Issue 3; Learning Disabilities Research and Practice, 1996, Volume 11, Issue 3; The Journal of Special Education, Volume 28, Issue 3.* From an application level, pioneers like Yetta and Ken Goodman, Haliday, and Holdaway advocated for whole language approaches to language arts instruction and Britton, Graves, and Cambourne developed and advocated for the process writing model. These individuals used the foundational work of Vygotsky, Piaget, Dewey, and others as the basis for viewing instruction from a more child-centered orientation. The tenets of Vygotsky's, Piaget's, and Dewey's theories are extended to explaining LD and provide the basis for practical approaches to overcoming learning difficulties. Today the social constructivistic paradigm is being applied to special education in a variety of subject areas such as language arts (Graham & Harris, 1994; Stanovich, 1994), math (Mercer, Jordan, & Miller, 1996), science (Scruggs & Mastropieri, 1994), as well as assessment (Fuchs & Fuchs, 1996; Meltzer & Reid, 1994), and strategic instruction (Collins & Godinho, 1996; MacArthur, Schwartz, Graham, Malloy, & Harris, 1996).

THE THEORETICAL BASIS OF SOCIAL CONSTRUCTIVISM

Social constructivists (Heshusius, 1986, 1989, 1994; Poplin, 1987, 1988a, 1988b; Smith & Heshusius, 1986) argue that positivistic and empiricist traditions underlying earlier theoretical models (i.e., psychoneurological, behavioral, and cognitive) are not adequate to understand human behavior. These reductionistic models are based upon a methodology originally designed in the natural sciences to reduce phenomena to their component parts in isolation from the whole.

The reductionistic approach applied to studying LD is most clearly evident in the use of task analysis and behavioral objectives, especially when academic behaviors are reduced to extremely minute units (e.g., instruction that emphasizes recognition of words-in-isolation tasks). Students are studied as they perform tasks that are completed out of context of anything meaningful to them. Therefore, they lack motivation, and the likelihood of their generalizing a component skill to some meaningful activity (the whole) is low.

Social constructivists, in contrast, argue that the study of human behavior must focus on the complex whole because of the interdependence of the elements of behavior (Dithey, 1923/1988). Human behavior needs to be studied in the context of the social, cognitive, motivational, and pragmatic dimensions of the learning process (Palincsar & Klenk, 1993). The interaction of the dimensions sets the context for behavior. Any attempt to study these dimensions in isolation creates an unnatural and skewed view of behavior. In order to derive a valid interpretation of behavior, observations must be made of naturally occurring behaviors that are *functional, genuine,* and *authentic.* For example, observations of children reading prose while huddled in a corner provide a genuine context for studying their approach to reading. In the context of classroom learning, interpretations based on observations of students completing isolated skill-based tasks (e.g., reading word lists, completing a page of computation problems, etc.) outside of a context that is purposeful, genuine, and authentic to the student do not reflect what students do in real-life contexts. They may read the word lists quickly and accurately, but that does not reflect their reading habits or ability to construct meaning from narrative or expository prose. Likewise in math, they may compute quickly and accurately, but that does not reflect on their ability to solve applied mathematical problems.

The basic tenets of social constructivism are derived from phenomenological thought, which "sets forth the importance of understanding a person's direct experience of her world, irrespective of how she conceptualizes and categorizes it" (Heshusius, 1986, p. 30). Researchers and teachers, therefore, seek to determine how children make their own reality, based on the assumption that students are *self-directed, meaning-constructing, meaning-seeking individuals* who act upon their environments accordingly. Students' knowledge bases are shaped by contextual conditions and meaningfulness as well as by their individual interests and purposes (McPhail, 1995). Self-directed learning is more motivating than teacher-directed learning that imposes the problem and the solution. Academic programs for students with LD (as well as for other students) designed without considering the context of purpose, use, and desired social relations fail to provide motivating and meaningful environments conducive to self-directed learning (Harris & Graham, 1996). Table 9.1 depicts the paradigm shift required to adopt a social constructivistic philosophy.

The whole-language movement, a primary example of the application of social constructivism, is based on the premise that readers construct their own interpretation of the text that authors have written. Meaningfulness and functionality are individualized and there is really no authoritative interpretation. According to Pearson (1989), readers read to construct their own interpretation of discourse that has been written by authors who intend to communicate with their readers for purposes of entertainment, information, or persuasion. It is up to individuals to guide their interpretation based upon their own experiences and what they bring to a task. This prospective on the construction of knowledge implies that a teacher's job is to understand what a child's interpretation is and how it came to be, not one of trying to correct and point the child to some single convergent response or interpretation. In addition, there is a need for an active interpretative community that supports interpretation where we negotiate meaning and share knowledge. For instance, in a social context of talking about an article that was published in the newspaper, meaning is shaped by an individual's discussions with someone else. The individual is

Table 9.1
Paradigm Shift Required of the Whole-Language Philosophy

TRANSMISSION MODEL ←———————————————→ TRANSACTION MODEL

TRANSMISSION MODEL		TRANSACTION MODEL
	What Is Learned	
Defining what we know	*Objective*	Interacting with the unknown
Acquisition of knowledge	*Purpose*	Construction of meaning
Fact orientation	*Outcome*	Thinking process
	How It Is Learned	
Teacher-centered instruction		Student-centered learning
Part to whole	*Strategy*	Whole to part
Skills-based	*Content*	Concept-based
One-dimensional	*Context*	Multidimensional
Dissemination of information	*Teacher role*	Catalyst for problem solving
Passive learning	*Learner role*	Active learning
Mastery	*Assessment*	Demonstrated competence

Source: Monson, R. J., & Pahl, M. M. (1991). Charting a new course with whole language. *Educational Leadership, 48*(6), 51–53. Copyright © 1985 by ASCD. Reprinted by permission. All rights reserved.

influenced by others' interpretations; therefore, there is an authentic social context that helps shape meanings and keep individuals from having extremely divergent interpretations.

THE POLITICAL BASIS: A GRASS ROOTS MOVEMENT

The rise in popularity of social constructivistic models is also associated with a socio-political movement. The basis of the movement has to do with a philosophy of control and empowerment (Goodman, Y., 1989; Pearson, 1989). For students this is accomplished through child-centered approaches to learning. Students work with teachers constructing the direction of their learning. For teachers and school-based administrators, it is accomplished through school-based management approaches that embrace shared decision making by teachers, principals, parents, and students. Proponents are advocating that the power to determine curricula and treatment methodology be placed in the hands of those people who are in the trenches, those who really have to implement curricula. This grass roots movement is designed to empower teachers to develop their own curricula, and with it their own personal views of learning and teaching. It is a rejection of more authoritative, centralized approaches to curricular decision making that follow a top-down approach. Curricula should be designed at the school level in order that teachers have the authority and responsibility to make professional judgments about needs of their students. Centralized school district personnel are not in a position to know or reflect in their decisions the differential needs of students. When decision making is centralized, the emphasis is on consistency across schools and not on meeting the needs of individual students. An example of this desire to control curricula is the rejection of basal readers and other subject area textbooks. Proponents argue that the selection of textbooks dictates the curriculum, and therefore that decision should be left to individual schools.

THE TENETS OF SOCIAL CONSTRUCTIVISTIC INSTRUCTION

Social constructivists preserve the wholeness or integrity of meaningful events through an *integrated curriculum*. They strive to break down artificial barriers that have been created between communicative core subjects of reading, writing, speaking, and listening (e.g., language-experience approach activities). Additionally, the content area curricula are integrated to include problem solving that reflects knowledge structures across social studies, science, literature, art, music, and mathematics. For example, students may study the problem of balanced ecosystems. They may have to read narrative and expository prose, examine scientific principles, and use mathematical algorithms in order to show how an ecosystem works (see Figure 9.1). The integrated curriculum approach is modeled after the British infant school tradition and the project approach of Kilpatrick (1918).

Authenticity, a second key component of social constructivistic approaches, refers to the attempt to have students engage in activities out of some genuine communicative intent rather than some contrived school purpose. Teachers and students focus on real-life situations in the classroom as the basis for communicative intent. Students are involved in real reading, writing, and other language activities that deal with some subject area concept or principle rather than engaging them in readiness activities. Through a supportive learning environment, teachers assist students in processing information through writing, telling, or reading about a concept or principle. Emphasis is on meaning construction and communication and not on the technical elements such as words read correctly, grammar, or recall of isolated facts.

Immersion in authentic tasks is a purposeful deviation from conventional curriculum approaches. In many programs students are seemingly always getting ready to read, solve math problems, and analyze social science or scientific concepts. They are delayed from developing advanced skills and strategies for storing, processing, manipulating, and expressing information. This approach is exemplified in many early readiness programs, including code-emphasis and whole-word basal reading approaches. Students must master sound symbol relationships or a set of sight words before they are exposed to meaningful stories. Primer reading books reflect contrived language forms in order to reflect the limited decoding skills students have. For instance, a code-emphasis book may read, "Nat sat on the mat." Students are delayed until their decoding skills are such that they can begin to read more naturally

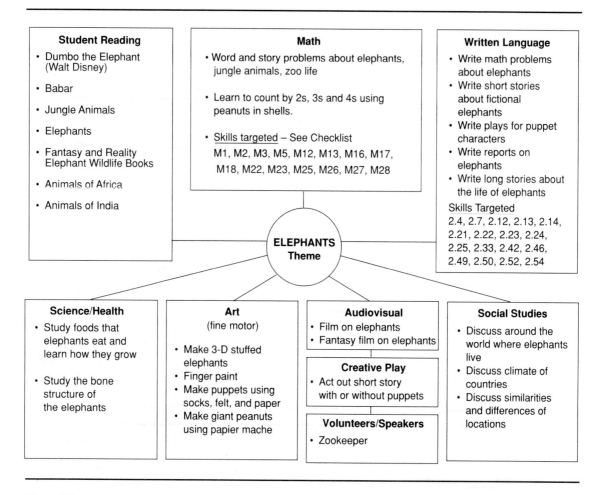

Student Reading
- Dumbo the Elephant (Walt Disney)
- Babar
- Jungle Animals
- Elephants
- Fantasy and Reality Elephant Wildlife Books
- Animals of Africa
- Animals of India

Math
- Word and story problems about elephants, jungle animals, zoo life
- Learn to count by 2s, 3s and 4s using peanuts in shells.
- Skills targeted – See Checklist M1, M2, M3, M5, M12, M13, M16, M17, M18, M22, M23, M25, M26, M27, M28

Written Language
- Write math problems about elephants
- Write short stories about fictional elephants
- Write plays for puppet characters
- Write reports on elephants
- Write long stories about the life of elephants

Skills Targeted
2.4, 2.7, 2.12, 2.13, 2.14, 2.21, 2.22, 2.23, 2.24, 2.25, 2.33, 2.42, 2.46, 2.49, 2.50, 2.52, 2.54

ELEPHANTS Theme

Science/Health
- Study foods that elephants eat and learn how they grow
- Study the bone structure of the elephants

Art
(fine motor)
- Make 3-D stuffed elephants
- Finger paint
- Make puppets using socks, felt, and paper
- Make giant peanuts using papier mache

Audiovisual
- Film on elephants
- Fantasy film on elephants

Creative Play
- Act out short story with or without puppets

Volunteers/Speakers
- Zookeeper

Social Studies
- Discuss around the world where elephants live
- Discuss climate of countries
- Discuss similarities and differences of locations

Figure 9.1
Planning web for integrated curriculum.

written literature. This transition from very contrived discourse to more natural forms does not take place until late second or third grade. In Pearson's (1989) words students are asked to *just hang in there guys as soon as we get these sounds down we'll be able to read real stories on our own.*

Child-Directed Learning

The application of a social constructivistic view can be traced back as early as Comenius' work in 1887 and to the later works of Dewey, Vygotsky, Piaget, and Haliday (Goodman, Y., 1989). Comenius approached learning from the perspective of children exploring their world through real life experiences. He emphasized children using their native language to talk about their experiences. He argued that children should be enticed to learn through motivating activities and materials. Dewey's concept of child-centered learning is a later example of this basic element of social constructivistic approaches (Dewey & Bentley, 1949). Accordingly, learners are viewed as active participants, capable and eager to learn. Their motivation is enhanced by purposeful activities in which the students learn by doing. Purposefulness is defined by the opportunity given to students to have a say in which activities they might engage (Kilpatrick, 1918).

Teachers function to assist learners in directing their explorations and understanding of the world around them. In social constructivistic classrooms, learners are empowered to make decisions about their learning. They take ownership for setting goals and designing ways to reach their goals (Goodman, K., 1989).

Intrinsic Motivation

The pleasure and enjoyment of learning is developed through numerous positive experiences. Young children acquire an intrinsic reinforcement system that is illustrated in the amount of time that they spend engaged in independent learning activities that maintain or extend their knowledge. They enjoy exploring their environment and practicing the skills they have learned.

Children who are emerging self-directed learners have had numerous positive experiences with books and other channels of learning. They've been able to acquire the intrinsic reinforcement system that is illustrated in the amount of time that they spend independently engaging in learning activities. For example, they enjoy being read to and enjoy pretending to be reading or just interacting and telling stories with the aid of a book.

Children use language to guide learning (Vygotsky, 1978). They begin to use different language forms that in essence mimic what is presented in books and communicative interactions with others. So they start to speak with the expression and vocabulary that they would find in books and those they have heard from significant adults and older children. Their intonation is very vigorous and expressive; they tell stories and create and convey information.

Teacher as Facilitator

The degree to which students control and direct their learning and teachers facilitate learning is characterized along a continuum. In the purest form of social constructivism, learning is totally student directed. Students construct knowledge based upon their internal metacognitive analysis and integration of information. Moshman (1982) refers to child-determined exploration and discovery as *endogenous constructivism*. When teachers direct instruction through modeling procedures or explanation of concepts and principles, instruction is characterized as *exogenous constructivism*. Instead of the students depending solely on internal construction of knowledge, they structure their knowledge based upon reciprocal interactions with the environment. Exogenous constructivistic approaches to teacher and student interactions are more akin to behavioral and cognitive models of learning (Harris & Graham, 1994, 1996). The middle ground, *dialectical constructivism*, is characterized as teachers structuring the learning environment in ways that enable students to construct knowledge through guided discovery or less explicit, teacher-led explanation or modeling. Vygotsky's (1978) conceptualization of learning is used most commonly to characterize the social constructivistic view of student and teacher interactions. It exemplifies a form of dialectal constructivism. The instructional procedures that guide teaching are *proleptic teaching* (Vygotsky, 1978), the anticipation of competence, and *expert scaffolding* (Bruner, 1973), support structures for learning. Specifically, the teacher provides a model of a strategy or skill being taught through a natural dialogue with students and gradually allows the students to take over the steps and procedures involved in applying the strategy or skill (Paris & Winograd, 1990; Pressley, Hogan, Wharton-McDonald, Mistretta, & Ettenberger, 1996; Rosenshine & Meister, 1992). The analogy is made to the tutelage that occurs between a master craftsman and an apprentice; the master craftsman provides the support so that the apprentice can carry out some simple aspects of the task with the aid of the tutor (Rogoff, 1990). In the instructional context, neophytes are asked to perform a task before they really have the skills to do it. The parent or a teacher then guides students through a particular activity and gradually relinquishes the responsibilities for completing the activity to students as they become more and more skilled in the task at hand.

This concept is closely related to Y. Goodman's (1989) conceptualization of child-centered learning, whereby teachers *lead from behind*. That is, as students demonstrate needs and seek out assistance, the teacher provides the guidance and support structures to allow the students to learn what they need to complete a particular task. Teachers do not establish and follow a preset curriculum sequence. They follow the sequence dictated by each student's naturally developing needs.

Additionally, there is a reciprocity between teacher and student in what is termed a community of learners. Teachers and students learn from each other and students learn from each other. Approaches to tasks often involve collaboration by groups of learners. Cooperatively, learners study and seek to solve problems. Students and teachers plan and develop curricular activities that are integrated across subject areas in order to facilitate growth and each individual child's emerging repertoire of literary skills. Teachers monitor student progress by *kid watching*, a term popularized by Yetta Goodman. The social aspect of learning is heavily emphasized.

Strategic Learning

Strategies essential for processing language include self-regulating operations that involve self-monitoring of meaning construction, confirmation, and self-correction (Pressley, Harris, & Marks, 1992; Reid & Stone, 1991). In addition, children learn predicative strategies that enable them to use contextual cues and their knowledge of story plot and other structures to form hypotheses about words, events, and relationships in a story.

Six comprehension activities include:

1. Understanding the purposes of language both explicit and implicit;

2. Activating a relevant background knowledge;

3. Allocating attention so that concentration can be focused on the major topics at the expense of trivia;

4. Critical evaluation of content for internal consistency, incompatibility with prior knowledge, and common sense;

5. Monitoring ongoing activities to see whether comprehension is occurring, by engaging in such activities as periodic review and self interrogation; and

6. Drawing and testing inferences of many kinds including interpretations, predictions and conclusions. (Palincsar & Brown, 1984, p. 120).

Four concrete activities that students can use to facilitate the above six are summarizing through self-review, questioning, clarifying, and predicting. One strategy that can be used by students and that has been researched extensively is self-directed summarization, where students monitor their own understanding and determine whether or not they are gaining information, whether comprehension is progressing smoothly. If not, then the process can trigger some remedial actions. Another strategy is self-directed questioning, where students can, in essence, pause and ask questions dealing with clarifying or interpreting information, or predicting events.

Self-directed summarization and self-directed questioning seem to be kind of active indicators that good readers use and poor readers for some reason do not. A number of studies have been conducted to determine the abilities of various groups of individuals to use summarization techniques for instance. Brown, Day, and Jones (1983) found that active summarization of a typical fifth grade academic text did not occur until students were well into their high school years, and those students who were in remedial programs did not master the ability to summarize until they were in junior college.

Reciprocal Teaching.   Studies by Baker (1984) and Martin and Rothery (1981) have noted the need for explicit strategy training for children who are considered slow learners. With the reciprocal teaching model, teachers demonstrate a strategy (e.g., self-questioning or summarization) for students to employ and then gradually encourage students to take over the steps and procedures of applying the particular strategy.

Reciprocal teaching is to some extent based on the reciprocal questioning, but it is much more extensive. Accordingly, the teacher and students take turns not only asking questions about a topic, they also take turns in generating summaries, making predictions about future events, and clarifying misinterpretations or vague information.

Typical procedures used in reciprocal teaching, applied to reading comprehension, entail first starting off with a discussion to draw out the student's prior knowledge. If the passage is new, then the title is read and students are asked to predict what the story might be about. If it is a continuation of a story that was begun the day before, then the teacher might ask students to state the topic of the text and to review several of the important points in the passage. In the early stages of the training, the teacher or adult would take on the role of the model. Then the teacher would have the group read the first segment of the passage. They would model asking a question that a teacher or a test might ask, summarizing what had been read, making clarifications about content read, and finally making predictions of future story events. Another section of the passage is read, followed by students imitating the questioning, summarization, clarification, and prediction. The teacher then takes on the role of a facilitator, providing feedback about the quality of the questions, prompting students to ask questions, or clarifying what a summarization might be.

Positive Teaching and Corrective Feedback

In positive teaching the emphasis is on allowing students to take risks and on teachers accepting more open-ended types of responses or a successive approximation to the actual correct responses. Excessive correction of inaccurate responses is incompatible with positive teaching. Holdaway (1979) is very much concerned with the amount of corrective feedback that is provided to children at early stages of learning and its inhibitions to their desire to take risks and to make predictions.

Unlike followers of behavioral approaches to learning, social constructivists view errors as opportunities for students to determine the extent of their knowledge. Errors indicate the boundaries at which responses are considered inappropriate. Errors represent an opportunity for students to problem solve and self-correct their responses in a very natural way. Students are given responsibility for learning from their mistakes. Power and control of learning reside to a larger degree with the learner. The teacher stays back and acts as a facilitator, allowing the child the opportunity to make mistakes and any necessary corrections. Teachers use errors as windows into students' processing in order to analyze their skill development.

Minilessons

The minilesson is an episode of explicit, teacher-directed instruction (i.e., exogenous constructivism). What trigger the episode are the spontaneous needs of students to learn some technical element that will assist their construction of their knowledge base. Mini lessons are student-generated, "teachable moments." For instance, within a set of guided discovery lessons on the economic principle of supply and demand applied to the citrus industry, students may come to a point where their construction of a meaningful understanding of the cause-and-effect relationship is blocked by a need for information about citrus produce. They need to understand how insects and weather affect the supply of oranges and grapefruit. Therefore, the teacher may then interrupt the guided discovery lesson to explain the effect of frost and insect infestation on oranges. The teacher tells students what happens under frost conditions, and students listen intently. The guided discovery lesson is then resumed as students continue to work in groups, analyzing the relationships that underlie examples of the supply-and-demand principle. A similar situation may arise during a time when students are writing in their journals about a field trip to a dinosaur exhibit at a local museum. Students are trying to write dinosaur names that require the use of the morpheme *saurus*. The teacher may interrupt the writing episode after discovering that a number of students are having difficulty with spelling these dinosaur names and may spend 15 minutes pointing out the morphological commonality in the endings.

APPLICATIONS TO LANGUAGE ARTS CURRICULUM AND LEARNING ACTIVITIES

Language as the Basis for Learning

Both Piaget and Vygotsky have influenced whole-language curricula in terms of how language is used in learning. Piaget's conceptualization of the learner is one that uses language to deal with the *disequilibrium* between a learner's schemata and schemes and application to a particular activity at hand. Language originates within the individual and then is used to communicate thoughts to others. *Egocentric speech* is a step toward greater development of socialized thought and communication processes. For Vygotsky, the social function of language is central. Language functions as a tool to communicate with others and to self-direct an individual through some task. Young children use egocentric speech to guide themselves through activities and are imitative of adults and older siblings in their social environment. For example, children use self-talk to guide themselves through a tea party with a group of dolls by talking out the steps of pouring the tea, wiping up spills, and so on. The *self-guiding verbalizations* are imitations of the steps that have been modeled by others. A child moves from using speech to communicate with others toward the use of speech for self-regulation of behavior (McClaskin, 1989).

In both Piaget's and Vygotsky's conceptualizations, language is a key element of learning. Young learners use language to assist in developing their knowledge structures, in communicating their thoughts with others, and in directing their own behavior. According to Haliday (1975), individuals learn language as they learn through language. As individuals come to know more about language form, meaning, and use, they learn how to use language to gain knowledge from other sources and how to organize their own ideas about the world.

Word Identification through Meaning: Psycholinguistic Basis

In all forms of written and oral language, at least four systems are interdependent: semantics, syntax, morphology, and phonology. Language arts programs differ in the emphasis placed on one system versus the others. However, the systems together represent a set of redundant features that are used for communication. In whole-language approaches the semantic system is used as the primary system for encoding and decoding messages (Smith, 1971). In general, the system deals with referential and relational meaning as the primary system for identifying words and constructing meaning. Syntax and morphology are used as a secondary system to supplement semantic elements (see Figure 9.2). Together these systems are used to help children in decoding and appreciating language.

The third system is the phonological system. In whole-language programs, phonic analysis is taught as a mechanism to analyze words after a set of words has been learned and other contextual strategies are used (i.e., semantic and syntactic relationships between words). Phonics is introduced through contrasts of letters that are different in sound and shape, (i.e., much like the suggestions by Englemann and

Figure 9.2
Psycholinguistic model of reading instruction.

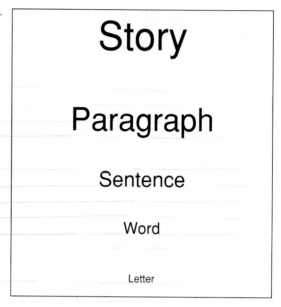

Bruner, 1984, and Stanovich, 1994), but it is done in an incidental and less regimented fashion, usually through mini lessons. For example, students might go through familiar books and search for examples of the initial consonant sounds of /m/ and /f/ and just locate those words and use their knowledge of the story and the words to guess what those words are.

Phonetic features are not discounted but, in fact, are viewed as very important aspects of learning language forms. Phonic systems carry a great deal of information used in the decoding and construction of meaning.

Immersion in Reading Activities

The initial process for developing literacy is to surround students in a setting of books. Adults read to students; students examine and mimic reading of books with other children and adults. They construct stories through language-experience activities, and students are immersed in language activities.

One of the central activities is the **shared book experience**. The shared book experience is an activity during which students gain familiarity with the text, become "book aware," develop motivation, and develop meaning-construction strategies. Additionally, skills in making predictions are developed through closure activities in which students predict events in a story (see photo). In listening tasks, students develop skills in understanding various relationships such as opposites, superlative relationships, sequences, and hierarchical structures of stories. Children begin to learn to construct meaning from metaphors, symbols, and analogies. Over time they be-

Shared book experiences enable students to become "book aware." Activities include students making predictions about story sequence, events, and characters.

gin to recognize some of the visual features of books, such as directionality of print, margins, print layout, bold facing, and so on.

Activities are designed to train students to attend selectively to the different, but interdependent, language systems. They practice using the redundant structure of the systems to make predictions about words, sentences, and ideas that appear in text. In the prediction process students begin to integrate information from the systems. They seek to confirm the accuracy of their predictions and make self-corrections as needed.

Later, students move into experiences that progress through three stages (Holdaway, 1979). The first is the discovery phase and the second is the exploration stage where through rereadings the student becomes familiar with text. Teachers provide some instruction spontaneously as it is applicable to individual situations. This type of participation is on the increase and is a very natural part of this whole process. The third step is the independent experience and expression, where students begin to take books away and individually or in small groups begin to imitate the teacher model in working with books. Although not necessarily recognizing individual words, they go through the motions as if they were actually reading the textbook, moving the pages. They may recount the story either to themselves or to other children or even to their dolls.

Table 9.2
Literacy Development Checklist

Student _____   Teacher _____

	Does not apply	Most of the time	Some-times	Not noticed yet	Comments
I. INTEREST IN BOOKS					
Is willing to read	___	___	___	___	
Shows pleasure in reading	___	___	___	___	
Selects books independently	___	___	___	___	
Chooses books of appropriate difficulty	___	___	___	___	
Samples a variety of genre	___	___	___	___	
II. BOOK KNOWLEDGE					
Beginning of book	___	___	___	___	
End of book	___	___	___	___	
Title	___	___	___	___	
Author	___	___	___	___	
Illustrator	___	___	___	___	
III. READING STRATEGIES					
Uses knowledge of language to understand text	___	___	___	___	
Uses meaning clues in context	___	___	___	___	
Uses meaning clues from prior experience	___	___	___	___	
Uses sentence structure clues	___	___	___	___	
Substitutes a word with similar meaning	___	___	___	___	
Sounds out	___	___	___	___	
Uses word structure clues	___	___	___	___	
Uses story structure clues	___	___	___	___	
Views self as a reader	___	___	___	___	
Notices miscues if they interfere with meaning	___	___	___	___	
Infers words in close-type activities	___	___	___	___	
Takes risks as a reader (guesses)	___	___	___	___	
Summarizes major events in a story	___	___	___	___	
Remembers sequence of events	___	___	___	___	
Demonstrates predicting and confirming	___	___	___	___	
Attends to reading independently	___	___	___	___	

Note. Copyright 1988 by the National Council of Teachers of English. Reprinted with permission.

Eventually, students begin to diverge and subgroups of students evolve. Some students are beginning to read, others are engaging in readinglike and writinglike behaviors, and others are somewhat perplexed by the whole situation. Table 9.2 includes a checklist of characteristics of emerging literacy.

Repeated Exposures to Books

As students begin to diverge because of different rates of reading development, teachers control the difficulty levels of tasks by guiding students to different books and activities. Skill development is a function of the number of repeated exposures to a book that individual students require before they are ready to read a book independently. Repeated exposure is based upon the belief that the more words that pass in front of a child's eyes, the better a reader the child will become (Allington, 1977). With the use of a structured center for listening, the teacher can control the tasks by increasing the number of repetitions for those students who need it. Simultaneously, the teacher can then guide other students who may not need that repetition through use of different activities or books.

Practice Activities

There are a number of other instructional activities associated with a literacy approach that assist students in providing an environment for practicing language skills. Teachers often use forms of *sustained silent reading*. Typically, the entire school, including teachers, administrators, secretaries, custodians, and students, reads for a 10- to 20-minute period. Materials are self-selected. Acronyms such as DEAR (Drop Everything And Read) are used to designate the time period. Teachers also have students engage in *choral reading activities* that may involve the lyrics from a song or stanzas from a poem. Students read together as a chorus. *Reading aloud* is used as students demonstrate mastery of a particular story. The activity is very reinforcing, as students show off their reading skills and share a favorite story in the social atmosphere of a group. In working toward students' reading aloud independently, teachers or other students who can read more fluently may *read along* with particular students. The setting is a social one, with a fluent model that supports the students' acquisition of reading mastery. All of these activities in various ways are used to provide a means for *repeated reading* of specific stories.

Natural Text

In the initial emergent reading program the focus is on getting high-interest types of text, with little regard for the complexity of language. Natural text found in commercially available children's stories is the primary source of reading material (see Photo 9.2). As the students become more conscious of their ability to decode, then graded readers are introduced. These are simpler and easy for students to read so they can work on decoding skills. Linguistically managed texts that introduce words with phonetic elements in some sort of rational progression (i.e., synthetic and analytic phonetic programs) are avoided.

Many commercially available children's story books use naturalistic prose that provides rich and meaningful language experiences.

INTEGRATION OF READING AND WRITING

According to social constructivists, language is a self-regulating, interactive system of communicative behavior. Individuals manipulate and respond to the environment through language and therefore regulate their own language in response to environmental conditions (Englert & Mariage, 1996; Warren and Yoder, 1994).

Traditionally, written language instruction focuses on the structure of language; that is, teaching rules, and the functions of different types of grammatical elements (e.g., word classes, sentence structure, etc.). Little emphasis is placed on the **pragmatics** or **use** of language as a communicative function. For instance, children spend little time attempting to create language through naturalistic activities, such as story or letter writing, without heavy focus on correct spelling, punctuation, and grammar. Consequently, students become more concerned with spelling and grammar than with their effectiveness to convey meaning. According to social constructivists, teachers often inhibit students' creative use and exploration of language such that they become self-conscious and anxious.

Language-Experience Approach

The first associations between social constructivism and methodology are typically made through the language-experience approach. Early use of language-experience approaches involved students and teachers collaborating on story construction. Students unable to use all of the technical conventions of written language (e.g., spelling, punctuation, etc.) dictate to teachers their construction of a story, while the teacher writes down the oral statements. The stories are used as the stimulus for learning language in written and oral forms and to learn about the content communicated within the story. Through constant exposure to their own writing and the writings of others (i.e., books), students begin to use vocabulary that they would find in written discourse they have either written, heard, or read. They tell stories and create and convey information (Holdaway, 1979). As Haliday (1975) postulates, learners learn language, and through language, they learn about the world in which they live.

Although much of what is done in whole-language programs is derived from language-experience approaches to literacy, whole language is more than just the adaptation of the learning-experience approach. It has a broader and deeper theoretical base involving semantics, speech events, psycholinguistics and sociolinguistics. Language experience on the other hand relies on theories of structural linguistics (McGee & Lomax, 1990).

Some methodological experiments that have had a bearing on the literacy movement are:

1. Organic Vocabulary Development, an idea developed by Sylvia Ashton-Warner, a New Zealand novelist and teacher of rural Maori children in New Zealand, is a system for teaching reading based on the combination of a look/say and language-experience approach that lets teachers use the students' own language and motivation and the concepts and ideas that were dearest to them as the core for teaching literacy to them.

2. Grace Fernald provided a basis for the writing to read philosophy in her Multi-Sensory Approaches, where students were involved in writing, from forming letters to writing stories. The use of kinesthetic as well as tactical modalities is believed to reinforce learning.

3. The Individualized Reading Process was promoted by Janet Veatch. Veatch was a strong pioneer in the establishment of an individualized program for children, which flew in the face of the use of basic reading series and sequential programs. Instead, children were to learn from reading a wide range of trade books, which they could self-select and read and enjoy at their own pace.

4. The Initial Teaching Alphabet (ITA) was developed by Sir James Pitman. ITA involves the use of a modified alphabet that makes the relationship between phonemes and graphemes predictable. Children are able to read and write more complex language forms earlier. The predictability of the modified alphabet reduced the number of errors and the frequency with which teachers used error correction procedures. Teachers also have a tendency to be more accepting of successive approximations (Holdaway, 1979).

5. Breakthrough to Literacy is a program derived from the linguistic theory. The program highlights the importance of creative written language from the very beginning of a child's school experience. The developmental literacy approach is based upon the perspective of the beginning literacist expressing personal views through written language. The program begins by circumventing the difficulties with handwriting and written responses by providing a file of sentences. They are used as models for copying and making constructive sentences. Gram-

matical understandings are provided through teaching affixes to words rather than teaching derivations of words.

Process Conferencing Model

Writing instruction has been greatly influenced in the last decade by the social constructivistic model of schooling and learning. There has been a growing interest in the teaching methods for written expression and an emphasis on learning to write through writing, rather than performing writing exercises (Richardson, 1991). Donald Graves and James Britton are two early pioneers in the procedures of process writing. Graves' work (1984) delineates the different steps involved in this process. Cambourne (1988), an academic researcher from Australia, outlined the conditions of learning as a theoretical frame for the process approach to learning.

The process writing paradigm has been described as a series of steps that involve *planning, drafting, conferencing, revising, and publishing.* For students who initially learn to write using process writing, writing drafts and revising is a natural part of writing. Both steps are integrated into the writing process and through repeated practice become ingrained as necessary. Students come to understand the purpose of these steps and accept them as part of this overall process. Through the conferencing and publishing steps, children become very comfortable with sharing their work with others, discussing it with others, and receiving some assistance. Publication also provides them with opportunities to gain skills in proofreading. They must also learn to conform with the formal correctiveness of written discourse (Richardson, 1991).

The conferencing step is the most critical and controversial aspect of this particular approach. The fundamental concern is the difference between *consultation* and *conferencing.* The teacher's interaction with students is much more directive under the consultation mode than it is under the conferencing mode. Walker and Elias (1987) examined 17 writing conferences between students and their writing tutors at a university. They found that:

1. High rated conferences were not necessarily those where students talked the most.

2. What teachers and students talk about is of great importance.

3. In successful conferences, the focus is on the students' work and not on the teacher or teacher's agenda.

4. The agenda for the conference is the formulation and articulation by both participants of the principles of good writing, and evaluation of the student's work against these criteria (Richardson, 1991).

Proponents of process writing instruction initiated the evolution of teaching writing in a very different way than in the past. Conferencing, drafting, revising, and publishing were not being done prior to the powerful movement toward a process, whole-language orientation. The movement to enhance writing instruction has benefited significantly.

Genre-Based Model

A variation of process-oriented writing is the **genre model**. In this context, genre are socially determined and accepted forms or styles of constructing written discourse. According to Martin, Christie, and Rothery (1987) genre is "a staged goal oriented social process . . . genres are referred to as social processes because members of a culture interact with each other to achieve them. It is goal oriented because they have evolved to get things done and is staged because it usually takes more than one step for participants to achieve their goal" (p. 59). To quote Richardson, "Christie and Rothery (1989) have argued that meaning in language 'comes into being in the act of learning language' and that linguistic choices are socially determined by the interaction of the context of culture and the context of the situation" (p. 177).

Christie and Rothery (1989) and others, have identified two sets of genres that are used in schools. *Factual genres* include: *procedure,* how something is done; *description,* what some particular thing is like; *report,* what an entire class of things is like; *explanation,* a reason why a judgment is made; and *argument,* why a thesis has been produced. The second class of genre, called *narrative genre,* includes *recounts,* narrative based on personal experience; *fantasy,* the moral tale, myths, spoofs, and serials; and *thematic* narratives. It is these forms we use in schools and other institutions that help us bring our meanings in some socially acceptable organized fashion. The argument is made that these genre need to be directly taught, and by doing so we are allowing students to use socially constructed form from the textual level to assist them in conveying meaning in a way that is socially acceptable (see Figure 9.3). To quote Richardson (1991) "for children to grasp new knowledge they

Figure 9.3
Language as text.
Note. From P. Richardson (1991). Language as personal resource and as social construct: Competing views of literacy pedagogy in Australia. *Educational Review, 43,* 171–190.

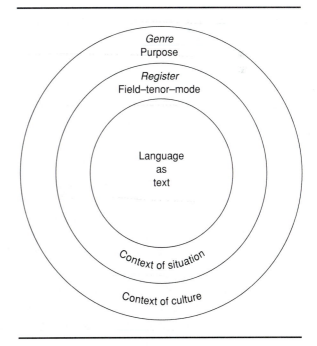

need to have control of the appropriate written genres which need to be explicitly identified and taught" (p. 179).

In descriptions of the genre-based curricula that have been put forth by Christie and Rothery (1989), some individuals have criticized the descriptions as a back-to-basics movement because they deal with teaching writing forms and using teacher-directed instruction, as opposed to a more process-oriented conferencing model. A genre-based curriculum is in opposition to the process orientation. Instead of conferencing, consultation is used. During consultation, a natural interaction occurs between the student and the teacher in which feedback is given based on the individual student's needs. Both the student and the teacher establish agreement about the feedback and the focus of future writing activities. The process is akin to Bruner's scaffold metaphor and Vygotsky's zone of proximal development. That is, the teacher provides enough support and instruction in order to have the student successfully imitate the genre that is being used. As the student acquires new skills and greater sophistication in the use of these genres, then the teacher backs off, becomes more indirect, and allows the student to complete more parts of the process than someone who is more of a novice.

Young writers need to become familiar with genre, but the first place for that to occur may not be in writing. It is often introduced through the reading process, where students are taught to appreciate different genre that are used by other authors.

Invented Spelling

Given the de-emphasis on the mechanics of writing and an emphasis on meaning construction, social constructivistic approaches to spelling instruction focus on more incidental learning (Graham & Harris, 1994; Harris & Graham, 1994, 1996). Students are encouraged to get their ideas down on paper without concern for spelling conventions, especially during early drafts. They are encouraged to use their developing understanding of sound-symbol relationships and memory of words they have encounter in other reading and writing activities to spell words. If their learning is incomplete, they are encouraged to *"invented"* spelling. Students' understanding and use of the conventions of spelling will evolve with experience and incidental learning. Spelling instruction occurs in more naturalistic ways, such as the teacher modeling correct spelling as a natural part of writing, the focus of a minilesson that is an outcome of some teachable moment, or through the process of sharing and editing drafts.

Spelling instruction is guided by analyzing the *invented spelling* of an individual child. It takes place in the context of all spelling. Analysis is used as a qualitative and heuristic tool rather than a quantitative one. Listed below is a set of questions that can be used to provide insights as to how students approach spelling.

1. Is the spelling of a familiar word an unusual one?

Beginning students sometimes create their own spellings for familiar words. These creative uses of language work well in individualized learning environments, but often are less productive when traditional classroom expectations are the norm.

2. Does spelling represent consonants used unconventionally?

Pronunciation—consonants are sometimes spelled differently from how they are pronounced (silent letters—*nife*; students pronounce words incorrectly—*stered* for *started*) Alternative representation—graphemes that represent two or more sounds *c, s, g*-Double consonants.

3. Does the spelling represent vowels used unconventionally?

Letter-name spelling-rounded vowels which usually include /o/ in their spelling are spelled with *o* or *ow*; vowels followed by *r* are spelled with just an *r*. Variable vowel spellings (short vowels) tend to become regularized but other vowel sounds are unpredictable: rode/road, herd/heard, werey/worry. Unstressed vowels—vowels with the schwa sound as *a*bout. When unstressed vowel occurs before consonants *l, m, n,* or *r*, it may be omitted altogether-(treatned/threatened).

4. Does the spelling use suffixes unconventionally (hapend/happened) or use suffix rules that are not known (caryed/carried)?

5. Is the invented spelling a permutation of the intended word—all the right letters but in the wrong order (almots/almost; his slfe/his self[dialectal])?

6. Does the invented spelling differ from the conventional one by only a single letter (mouther/mother; farther/father; of/off; trator/traitor)?

7. Is the invented spelling a real word (rode/road; sons/son's; bring/brang)?

8. Are the invented and conventional spellings punctuated differently (bu't/but)?

A major criticism of whole-language approaches is that there is little explicit instruction given in terms of sound-symbol information (Schickedanz, 1990). In the original language-experience approach, the program depended heavily on children dictating stories to the teacher and the teacher constructing idea charts and narrative stories. Through the interaction with the teacher, students would receive more explicit instruction in the graphic phonemic relationship in spelling and decoding. This is absent in whole-language approaches because that kind of dictation does not take place. It is replaced by a focus on children writing their own stories and using inventive spelling. In such cases, students are allowed to construct words, however they are constructed based on their own knowledge of graphophoneme relationships. Harris and Graham (1994, 1996) express the concern that such incidental instruction is often insufficient and ineffective for students with learning problems or poor language skills. They require more direct instruction in sound-symbol relationships, instruction that follows a more structured curriculum sequence.

APPLICATIONS TO MATH, SCIENCE, AND SOCIAL SCIENCE CURRICULUM AND LEARNING ACTIVITIES

The application of social constructivism to math, science and social sciences is related to the general curricular tenets of integrated content areas and authenticity. Instructional procedures are drawn from cognitivistic models involving learning strategies and inquiry oriented approaches to knowledge construction (Mercer, Jordan, & Miller, 1994, 1996; Scruggs and Mastropieri, 1994).

Curricular Issues

The concepts of integrating content areas and authenticity go hand in hand. The focus of instruction is on applying skills and knowledge to real-life situations. In our everyday situations we deal with problems or situations that involve the integrated use of knowledge and procedures from a variety of content areas. For example, a civil engineer uses knowledge of geology to determine the integrity of rock and soil that will be used as a road bed and must also be able to carry out mathematical algorithms in order to estimate density of the concrete being used to lay the road. In order to utilize existing knowledge and discover other declarative knowledge needed to solve a particular problem, the engineer must have a set of strategies or procedures for acquiring, storing, retrieving, and expressing information. Consequently, integrated content areas are organized around *specific concepts, principles, or values,* rather than around content areas such as science, social science, or math. Students and teachers may engage in a unit of study that focuses on some relevant authentic current event, such as illegal immigration into the United States. The *declarative information* would involve historical information about the United States and the U.S. and world economies, sociology principles that explain cultural differences and immigration patterns, and the geography of the Caribbean basin. The *procedural information* typically focuses on steps for problem solving, making judgments, or hypothesis testing. Other procedures targeted for instruction might include learning strategies that assist students in finding information, such as scanning techniques, self-guided comprehension (e.g., RAP), or storing information, such as note-taking and the use of mnemonics.

In this example, the procedural knowledge is given as much or more attention as the declaration information. The procedural knowledge is viewed as being more enduring because it enables students to undertake various cognitive activities regardless of the declarative information. The procedures are akin to a toolbox that a carpenter takes from job to job. A student likewise takes tools such as problem-solving or note-taking procedures to various sets of declarative information and uses them to construct a better understanding of the associated concepts and principles. The declarative information is still important in a social constructivistic model, but less so than under other curriculum models.

Instructional Procedures

Instruction in math and science emphasizes an inquiry, or Socratic, approach to teaching. Students use a series of questions to direct their construction of meaning. The degree of assistance given by the teacher can vary widely. In its purest form, students are given a concept, principle, or problem, and they construct their own set of questions and procedures to define the concept, identify the principle, or solve the problem (i.e., endogenous constructivism). On the other end of the continuum, the concept, principle, or problem is given and the teacher assists students by posing a series of questions to shape their construction of the concept definition, cause-and-effect relationship of the principle, or the problem solution (i.e., dialectal constructivism).

Through a series of studies, Scruggs and Mastropieri (1994) drew several conclusions regarding the appropriateness of inquiry-oriented techniques for students with LD:

1. Students were able to actively construct scientific knowledge using scientific methods.

2. Positive outcomes in science were associated with implementation of teacher effectiveness variables.

3. Teachers made substantial adaptations in the science curriculum to meet the special needs of learners.

4. Behavioral techniques were useful in promoting appropriate social behavior, attention, and persistence of effort.

5. Highly structured coaching by teachers often seemed necessary and was associated with successful knowledge construction.

6. Peers were helpful in skills applications and social encouragement, but were less helpful in promoting learning outcomes. (pp. 312–317)

Likewise, Mercer et al. (1994, 1996) reported on the effectiveness of techniques that reflect application of constructivistic principles. Their work incorporates the use of explicit modeling of learning strategies to students with disabilities (i.e., exogenous constructivism). A set of techniques associated with cognitive-behavioral theories are used to shape learning activities. The teacher employs advanced organizers, response modeling, guided practice, feedback, mastery learning, and explicit generalization instruction. They conclude that given the learning history of students with disabilities, including problems with automaticity, metacognitive strategies, memory, attention, generalization, proactive learning, and motivation, it is not plausible to expect these students to be successful in using self-guided discovery and learning techniques.

These conclusions reflect a perspective that students with LD can benefit from inquiry-oriented instructional techniques and guided discovery activities, but they may require more teacher assistance in the process than do more skilled learners. Findings of Scruggs and Mastropieri (1994) and Mercer et al. (1994) support a more exogenous constructivism whereby external controls in the learning environment are needed to make instruction effective. Teachers need to manipulate curriculum materials, provide more teacher-led questioning and dialogue, incorporate large quantities of modeling and guided practice, and use externally controlled antecedent and reinforcement techniques to control student behavior. Without teacher-directed instruction, students are unable to construct meaning on their own.

CRITIQUE OF SOCIAL CONSTRUCTIVISTIC MODELS

Authenticity

One of the most nebulous concepts that underlies social constructivism is authenticity. Trying to interpret the differences between authentic, simulated, and contrived types of activities is a difficult task. If a society creates some institution (e.g., school) or some procedure for communicating ideas (e.g., genre), is it authentic? Pearson (1989) pointed out one side of the argument; that is, one could argue that any activity in school is contrived because schools in essence are contrived institutions. This would be consistent with a hard-line view of authenticity by social constructivists.

Gilbert (1990) on the other hand argued that schools and written forms of language are socially constructed, and therefore they are authentic. What social institution is not contrived by society? Schools are social constructs; therefore, they are authentic places or situations. Once we accept tacitly that schools will exist, then the structures used to manage children, time, and materials must be given some recognition as a legitimately socially constructed institution. By doing so, we have to accept them as authentic. Without careful analysis, we should not automatically consider the traditional structures of school as invalid and detrimental to learning. The simulated world of schools may seem pretty exciting to students, given the homes and neighborhoods in which many children and youth live (Pearson, 1989).

Whether we argue either side of the authenticity issue, the fact remains that social constructivists have refocused educators on the fact that schooling is designed to develop a set of skills that can be useful and applied to real-life situations. Schooling does not take place in a void or as an end in and of itself. Curricula and instruction all too often overemphasize fragmented skill development and too frequently have left out the application of skills to real-life situations. Students do need to spend more time reading real things and good, rich literature, writing for real reasons, and solving real or simulated problems in math, science, or social science (Pearson, 1989).

Child-Centered Instruction

Another primary characteristic of social constructivistic models is a child-directed learning approach. Students guide their own learning through the selection of topics and activities, while teachers facilitate learning by "leading from behind." Teachers are more interested in discovery learning rather than expository learning (Pearson, 1989). They assist in managing learning and do not direct learning by standing up and lecturing to students. Consequently, little or no direct instruction by the teacher takes place. Gilbert (1990) suggested that such models create considerable confusion and contradiction regarding instruction, learning, and schooling process. Without having instruction provided, students are confused and do not know what to look for; they wallow around trying to figure out the right ways to do things and what is not an appropriate way to do things. Only those who are of the higher aptitude are able to figure that out and able to then benefit from the schooling process. Others are then left to fend for themselves and, in reality, wind up not learning conventional views of the structure of knowledge, including concept relationships, procedural strategies, and basic techniques for learning. In short, they are doomed to failure.

Gilbert's level of concern may not be warranted because most whole-language teachers *do not* adhere strictly to this lead from behind principle (Pearson, 1989). A number of them do engage in demonstrations, or modeling, and teaching specific tasks during the minilesson in whole-language reading programs. Theorists and proponents of whole language fail consistently to provide any real description of what goes on in those minilessons. It is within these minilessons where direct instruction occurs, yet proponents of whole language fail to describe that process. Another example is the reading recovery program in which there is a lot of one-to-one tutoring. Decoding skills are taught directly, and yet students are still provided the opportunity to develop an abiding love of literature. Students need to be exposed to whatever level of support, from explicit teacher-directed instruction to discovery learning, that enables them to learn from instructional activities (Harris & Graham, 1996).

The same criticism has been lodged regarding process writing. The issues here center on what occurs during the conferencing step. Under the process model, conferencing is very much child directed and child centered; teachers are not supposed to be interjecting or directing the student. They are simply responding to the student, and little or no direct instruction is occurring. Martin (1985) argued that this child centeredness is from "folk psychology" which was an outgrowth of West Coast pop psychology in the United States. This feel-good type of mentality in psychology spawned a lack of concern for any of the conformities that involve writing or any other of life's responsibilities. According to Martin (1985), child-directed writing instruction fails to meet the needs of learners when it overemphasizes ownership, voice, and children selecting their own topics; abrogates responsibility for intervening positively and constructively during conferencing; and mystifies what learners need to learn in order to produce effective written products. As Speigel (1992) advocated, there is a need to build a continuum between whole-language and process writing, and more traditional and explicit forms of writing instruction.

Another inconstancy is the social constructivists' support for learning strategies. The content of learning-strategy curricula is consistent in its emphasis on the process of learning. The way in which students come to learn the process, however, is often teacher directed. A number of models, particularly the University of Kansas model, are based on a very regimented teacher-directed instruction approach.

Social Elitism

There are certain structures of knowledge, forms, and procedures for completing tasks that have been socially constructed and accepted (Richardson, 1991). For example, in written expression there are genre and in literature there are story grammars. Martin (1985) and Delpit (1988) argue that children need to understand those socially agreed upon forms that we use. To fail to do so is not serving the point of view of a social constructivist. Instruction should include a curriculum structure that explicitly treats how structures, forms, and procedures exist, why they exist, and how to use them in learning and communicating. Refusal to teach directly reinforces the educational success of some children through an insidious benevolence, while other children are supportively encouraged to fail (Martin, 1985). Only bright students who can incidentally learn the forms of reading, writing, and learning techniques benefit from such models.

Delpit (1988) looked at this issue in the context of children from different racial, ethnic, and cultural backgrounds. He claimed that White, middle-class children living in a very enriched environment learn the "power code," the spoken and written forms that are used by affluent Whites. They learn that code, White or standard English, within their home lives, and they have a rich, long history of using that code. But, children from disadvantaged, minority homes use a different code system (e.g., Black English). Unless there is direct instruction in this power code, then those children from disadvantaged backgrounds will not learn the power code and, therefore, will be ineffective in trying to integrate themselves into a White, middle-class society.

Stahl and Miller (1989) observed that a number of students do emerge into literature without a great deal of direct instruction. Principally, those students are characterized by coming from middle-class families where they have a very rich literary household, and they have thousands of hours of exposure to various literacy events. For other students who come from disadvantaged homes and who do not have that kind of exposure, there appears to be a need to provide more direct instruction in print recognition and some of the basic fundamental decoding skills necessary for reading. Likewise, Martin (1985) argued that students who do not have the cultural sophistication or the culture congruence and the support from parents at home won't be able to pick up the necessary linguistic or textual forms that are necessary for effective writing.

Polarized Zealots

Some social constructivists argue aggressively for the benefits of their model and have attacked the reductionistic models that have dominated special education (Goodman, K., 1989; Heshusius, 1989, 1994; Poplin, 1987; Smith and Heshusius, 1986). Supporters of reductionism's contributions to education have countered with criticism of social constructivism (Dixon & Carnine, 1994; Phillips, 1976; Simpson, 1992; Ulman & Rosenberg, 1986). Individuals are viewed as either being whole-language or phonics-approach people. They are either for or against one of these approaches. There should be some room for taking the best of different programs, at the risk of being too eclectic, to develop program variations (Harris & Graham, 1996; Speigel, 1992). For example, the level of teacher-directed instruction can be appropriately varied as learners' needs dictate. This approach can be applied to the minilesson format in whole-language programs.

The issue of which models are most effective has been politicized to such a level that the use of certain metaphors creates a whirlwind swell of emotion (Dixon & Carnine, 1994; Pearson, 1989). As soon as terms like *classroom control, manipulation, modeling, guided practice,* or *time on task* are used, social constructivists are enraged. When proponents of more conventional programming models hear things like *authenticity, genuine,* or *leading from behind,* there is an equal and opposite reaction—the conversation ends or a major debate ensues. Little can be gained from the debate until educators get past the metaphors and discuss the similarities and differences in programs.

The often aggressive tone of social constructivists may reflect a zealous attempt to revolutionize education through the use of constructivistic-based education (Pearson, 1989). Revolutionary changes characterized by swiftness and breadth rarely come about. The hard-line stance that proponents of differing views take may only serve to polarize individuals rather than to advance the field of LD. There are many positive attributes of the social constructivistic model, but widespread implementation will be done in an evolutional fashion so that people are allowed the opportunity to accommodate these new methodologies and philosophies (Anderson & Barreara, 1995).

There has to be a realization that constructivistic methodologies are being used in a largely mechanistic world. Proponents of whole language must deal with the reality that teachers and administrators are held accountable to school boards and their constituencies. They are asked to quantify the performance of students through standardized tests and break down the costs of programs into line items. They are asked to maintain the surface behaviors of students so that order is kept in classrooms. These very basic criteria for defining effective programming drive many local educational agencies. Adaptation to a radically different paradigm such as social constructivism, when taken to its extreme, is not easy. As empirical evidence supporting the effective use of social constructivistic models develops, teachers, administrators, and the public they serve will be more likely to push forward with innovative programming.

Research Base

The basic concern surrounding the research base for constructivistic models is the numbers of schools that are adopting these models without sufficient research as to their effectiveness (McGee & Lomax, 1990). Stahl (1990) referred to the movement toward widespread adoption of whole-language programs as riding a pendulum. He cited Slavin's (1989) description of how educational fads develop: "What Slavin has observed is that often in education a program becomes the latest fad and is widely implemented, before being evaluated. Then, when there is dissolution with the total results, the program is discarded, good and bad aspects both, to be replaced with another package" (p. 141).

Ironically, Heshusius, one of the harshest critics of reductionism, lodges the argument that we need to be patient with the development of a research base supportive of the effectiveness of constructivistic or holistic oriented programming. She, in essence, falls into the same trap in pleading for time before evaluations can be made about the effectiveness of social constructivistic programs, yet she vehemently calls for the abandonment of scientific methodology and other mechanistic types of programs and philosophies. In essence, the field is to move blindly using our beliefs structure as the guiding light, rather than empirical evidence. Zeal for change in the absence of supportive data should not replace a more logical and scientific approach. With effectiveness data available to substantiate the beneficial effects, we may cautiously move programs into a social constructivistic framework based on empirical evidence (Anderson & Barreara, 1995).

What is troubling is the widespread adoption of social constructivistic programs and principles without knowing what the long-term effects of these programs are. Without the provision of long-term longitudinal data on the effectiveness of social constructivistic approaches, it is difficult to support them with any degree of zeal. For instance, there is evidence that the effectiveness of whole-language or other approaches washes out by third grade or shortly after third grade. Unless we have really studied the long-term effects of any set of approaches, it is difficult to say which is any better than the other. In the short run, there are periods of time when one appears better than the other. But what is important is to find out what happens over some long span of time. These concerns are evidenced by California students' fall in national ranking on standardized measures of academic achievement, and the state's subsequent rejection of whole-language programming after its statewide adoption.

Another problem area for researchers is delineating the characteristics that define social constructivistic programs from other models. For instance, in the debate over Stahl and Miller's review of the effectiveness of whole-language approaches, McGee and Lomax (1990) criticized the lack of definition that is provided for whole language. Stahl and Miller, according to them, provide little or no mention of the defining concepts of whole-language philosophies—authenticity, risk taking, choice, and empowerment. In the Stahl and Miller (1989) review, a variety of instructional approaches are used either under the basal reading program or the whole-language and language-experience approaches. Another example is the reading recovery program, an often used example of social constructivism that is characterized as involving one-to-one tutoring, whole-language instruction, and systematic decoding instruction.

The difficulty lies in the translation of theory into practice. The same reading or writing activity (e.g., a language experience or process writing activity) may be used in two classrooms, while one classroom espouses a social constructivistic philosophy and the other a cognitive-behavioral view. The lack of a clear delineation at the implementation level may account for the lack of differences between programs found in research.

The issue of similarities in practice may be viewed in terms of research design issues. For instance, in examining the differences between whole-language programs and then those of the basal programs, the better designed studies show lower effect sizes (i.e., differences in program outcome measures). With tighter controls there are more true effects and less contamination. Contaminants, attributes of the programs that do not distinguish one type of program from another, may be creating spurious effect sizes in the less well designed studies. For example, the amount of time spent practicing reading words may be greater for students in reading program A. Without this taken into account, program A appears to produce much greater effects than program B. When the amount of time spent reading words is controlled so that students in both programs A and B spend the same amount of time reading, the difference in effects is negligible. Therefore, the differences between programs A and B are due to time spent reading words and not due to some other characteristic of the program (e.g., phonics training vs. reading meaningful stories).

Practical Classroom Applications

As this chapter has highlighted, the social constructivistic model evolved from concerns regarding the effectiveness of behavioral and cognitive models to develop generalization and the emphasis on external sources of motivation. The movement emanated from a grass roots movement to empower teachers and learners to create and participate actively in curriculum and instructional procedures. Accordingly, functional, genuine, and authentic curriculum and instruction are central to instruction of students with LD. Students can become self-directed, meaning-constructing, and meaning seeking individuals when teachers facilitate information.

Some considerations follow to guide program development emphasizing both the impact of child-centered approaches for students with LD and the research base supporting social constructivistic programs.

1. *Authentic activities make learning more interesting and meaningful.* When learning is set in the context of activities that are meaningful and functional to students, then learners are more apt to participate in the activities, work longer and more diligently, and sustain learning over a longer period of time. When teachers are aware of students' interests, teachers recognize students' needs to select or help select activities that are meaningful to them. For instance, many primary-school-aged children are fascinated by dinosaurs. Teachers can use dinosaurs as a theme and generate a number of activities in which students develop oral and written communication skills encouraging children to talk and write about these curious creatures. With their enthusiasm high, children often find it easier and more meaningful to develop basic skills such as word recognition, spelling, or procedures for finding information in the library or through an on-line computer system. When older students are excited about what they are doing, they, too, are on-task, which allows teachers to lead from behind other students who may require that extra scaffolding, or support.

2. *Learners need assistance and guidance as they develop competence.* Learning is an active process; it does not occur through osmosis. As much as we would like to believe that after we listen to foreign language tapes while sleeping, we will dialogue in Spanish or French at breakfast, it just does not happen. Learning requires effort. And, for learning to occur efficiently, it is often beneficial for others to help guide it. Teacher-directed learning is not always bad (Harris & Graham, 1996), but teachers need to strive to provide the minimum amount of guidance necessary at any point during a student's learning continuum. As described by Moshman (1982), there are various levels of teacher control or directedness that are inversely proportional to the level of child-centeredness. The balance between the two is a function of each learners' needs at any given time.

Social constructivists remind teachers of the need to fade their guidance and allow students the freedom to fail. Then, teachers and students can use errors to help students understand why they failed and what they need to do differently in order to succeed.

3. *Different theories may support the same classroom activities.* Even though the social constructivistic model represents a significant paradigm shift, many of its practical applications are congruent with applications associated with other models. For

(continued)

Practical Classroom Applications (continued)

instance, reciprocal teaching is used to develop procedures or strategies for students to gain meaning from written text. The idea of developing learning strategies for reading comprehension and other skills is also the basis for the learning strategies curriculum that emanates from a cognitive-behavioral model. Proleptic teaching and scaffolding parallel the behavioral procedures of using cues and prompting, then fading. The differences are in explanations of why practices are effective, or the perspective from which practices derive.

As discussed earlier, social constructivists argue that strategy instruction, like reciprocal teaching, is effective because it is done in an authentic, child-centered context. Cognitivists may not disagree that those elements are important, but they would emphasize that students are learning how to regulate their cognitions. Practitioners need to understand both theories and perspectives, but they do not have to be concerned about whether or not their practices are true to one theory or another. They need be more concerned with whether or not applications are effective when applied to students in daily classroom contexts.

4. *Teachers' ultimate instructional goals are to develop students' independence, love of learning, and longevity of learning.* Traditionally, curricula are made so that students learn basic facts structured around academic subject areas (e.g., sciences, social sciences, mathematics, literature, etc.). Social constructivists and others argue for a shift away from an emphasis on factual, content-oriented curricula toward developing students' skills in learning how to learn. They emphasize procedural knowledge,

metacognition, and learning strategies. All entail students learning how to self-regulate their learning. The belief is that students would do better to know how to learn rather than to memorize meaningless facts. Therefore, students need to learn how to encode, decode, store, process, and express information. By doing so, students learn skills that they can use independently, regardless of the specific subject matter. They are preparing to learn on their own. When teachers facilitate procedural knowledge, metacognition, or learning strategies though meaningful activities in which students play active roles, students are more likely to self-motivate, be successful, develop a love of learning, and approach learning as a life-long activity.

5. *An enhanced language-experience approach paired with an integrated curriculum can serve as the basis of a wide range of learning activities.* Information processing is an essential skill in the information age. Using language-experience activities to help students learn strategies for processing and expressing information facilitates their skills in collecting, analyzing, and synthesizing information. The use of the process-conferencing writing model assists students in expressing their ideas. While learning how to process and express information, students are expanding their declarative knowledge. When done through an integrated curriculum that emphasizes real-life problems, they can better see the relevance of their learning. Instruction is less fragmented by skill or content area and is more holistic.

6. *Understanding the structures of knowledge is important.* Although social construc-

(continued)

tivists de-emphasize declarative knowledge, they acknowledge the need to understand the structure of knowledge. There are relationships and categorizations of information reflected in conceptual knowledge. For instance, the botanical and animal classification systems are built upon rules for which plants or animal categories contain essential and nonessential attributes. Students need to know and understand these conventions. They need to define concepts, give examples and nonexamples, state the cause-and-effect relationship of academic laws and principles, be able to state and apply the

steps for completing academic tasks, and be able to make judgments systematically. This is consistent with the arguments posited by supporters of genre-based writing.

Accordingly, students need to learn different structures or principles for writing in different styles and for different purposes. Invented spelling programs, on the surface, may appear untargeted toward spelling rules and conventions. In fact, rules are taught, but without such emphasis that they detract from the primary purpose of writing—expressing ideas.

SUMMARY

- Social constructivism evolved from concerns regarding the effectiveness of behavioral and cognitive models to develop generalization, and the emphasis on external sources of motivation. Heshusius and Poplin, key researchers, argued for social constructivism from a theoretical perspective.

- Social constructivism also emanated from a grass roots movement to empower teachers and learners to determine curriculum and instructional procedures. Yetta, Goodman, Haliday, and Holdaway are proponents of applications of the theoretical model to language arts instruction.

- The focus of social constructivistic programs is on functional, genuine, and authentic curriculum and instruction.

- Students are seen as self-directed, meaning-constructing, and mean-seeking individuals.

- Teachers are seen as facilitators of information; the extent of their control and directedness characterizes different types of constructivism. The extent of teacher control and child-centeredness varies from high teacher control/low child-centeredness (exogenous constructivism) to moderate teacher control/ moderate child-centeredness (dialectal constructivism) to low teacher control/ high child-centeredness (endogenous constructivism).

- Vygotsky's proleptic teaching concept (i.e., in anticipation of competence) and Bruner's expert scaffolding (i.e., support structures for learning) are foundation concepts underlying social constructivistic instruction.

- The literacy movement, or whole-language approach, integrates reading and writing with content-area curricula. This is the primary application of social constructivism to language arts.

- The process conferencing model includes planning, drafting, revising, conferencing, and publishing. It has revolutionized writing instruction.

- Social constructivism characterizes a dramatic paradigm shift that has generated heated discussions regarding learning approaches. Concerns regarding social constructivistic approaches have centered around defining authenticity, the impact of child-centered approaches for students with LD, and a research base supporting social constructivistic programs.

DISCUSSION QUESTIONS

To help extend your understanding, reflect on and discuss the following questions:

1. What are the fundamental similarities and differences between behavioral, cognitivistic, and social constructivistic theories about learning?

2. What impact do theoretical zealots have on moving forward our understanding of learning?

3. In reflecting on your own beliefs regarding instruction, are your practices congruent with your personal theories about learning?

4. Do you believe that students from nondominant cultures are at risk of not learning the conventions of the dominant culture's "power code" in highly child-centered learning environments?

5. What impact do commercial texts and curricula have on what and how teachers teach?

6. If schools are contrived settings, how can teachers ever develop authentic social-constructivistic-oriented programs?

7. Why do you or don't you believe that children are self-motivated, meaning-seeking learners who require only minimal guidance and structure?

8. Will the public at large accept a philosophy and practices that espouse a permissive, child-centered approach without hard evidence of their effectiveness?

REFERENCES

Allington, R. I. (1977). If they don't read much, how they ever gonna get good? *Journal of Reading, 21*, 57–61.

Anderson, G. L., & Barreara, I. (1995). Critical constructivist research and special education. *Remedial and Special Education, 16*, 142–149.

Baker, L. (1984). Children's effective use of multiple standards for evaluating their comprehension. *Journal of Educational Psychology, 76*, 588–597.

Brown, A. L., Day, J. D., & Jones, R. S. (1983). The development of plans for summarizing texts. *Child Development, 54*, 968–979.

Bruner, J. S. (1973). *The relevance of education*. New York: Norton.

Cambourne, B. (1988). *The whole story: Natural learning and the acquisition of literacy in the classroom*. Sydney, Australia: Ashton Scholastic.

Christie, F. & Rothery, J. (1989). Genres and writing: A response to Michael Rosen. *English in Australia, 90,* 3–12.

Collins, J. L., & Godinho, G. V. (1996). Help for struggling writers: Strategic instruction and social identity formation in high school. *Learning Disabilities Research and Practice, 11,* 177–182.

Delpit, L. S. (1988). The silenced dialogue: Power and pedagogy in education of other people's children. *Harvard Educational Review, 58,* 280–298.

Dewey, J., & Bentley, L. (1949). *Knowing the known.* Boston: Beacon.

Dithey, W. (1988). *Introduction to the human sciences.* Detroit, MI: Wayne State University Press. (Original work published 1923.)

Dixon, R., & Carnine, D. (1994). Ideologies, practices and their implications for special education. *Journal of Special Education, 28,* 356–367.

Englemann, S., & Bruner, E. (1984). *DISTAR reading I.* Chicago: Science Research Associates.

Englert, C. S., & Mariage, T. V. (1996). A sociocultural perspective: Teaching ways-of-thinking and ways-of-talking in a literacy community. *Learning Disabilities Research and Practice, 11,* 157–167.

Fuchs, L. S., & Fuchs, D. (1996). Combining performance assessment and curriculum-based assessment to strengthen instructional planning. *Learning Disabilities Research and Practice, 11,* 183–192.

Gilbert, P. (1990). Authorizing disadvantage: Authorship and creativity in the language classroom. In F. Christie (Ed.), *Literacy for a changing world.* Hawthorn, Australia: The Australian Council for Educational Research.

Goodman, K. (1989). Whole-language research: Foundations and development. *The Elementary School Journal, 90,* 207–221.

Goodman, Y., (1989). Roots of the whole-language movement. *The Elementary School Journal, 90,* 113–127.

Graham, S., & Harris, K. R. (1994). Implications of constructivism for teaching writing to students with special needs. *Journal of Special Education, 28,* 275–289.

Graves, D. (1984). The enemy is orthodoxy. In D. Graves, *A researcher learns to write: Selected articles and monographs.* Portsmouth, NH: Heinemann.

Haliday, M. A. K. (1975). *Learning how to mean: Explorations in the development of language.* London: Edward Arnold.

Harris, K. R., & Graham, S. (1994). Constructivism: Principles, paradigms, and integration. *Journal of Special Education, 28,* 233–247.

Harris, K. R., & Graham, S. (1996). Memo to constructivists: Skills count, too. *Educational Leadership, 53*(5), 26–29.

Heshusius, L. (1986). Pedagogy, special education, and the lives of young children: A critical and futuristic perspective. *Journal of Education, 168*(3), 25–38.

Heshusius, L. (1989). The Newtonian mechanistic paradigm, special education, and contours of alternatives: An overview. *Journal of Learning Disabilities, 22,* 403–415.

Heshusius, L. (1994). Freeing ourselves from objectivity: Managing subjectivity or turning toward a participatory mode of consciousness? *Educational Researcher, 23*(3), 15–22.

Holdaway, D. (1979). *The foundations of literacy.* Sydney, Australia: Ashton Scholastic.

Kilpatrick, W. H. (1918). The project method. *Teachers College Record, 19,* 319–335.

MacArthur, C. A., Schwartz, S. S., Graham, S., Malloy, D., & Harris, K. (1996). Integration of strategy instruction into a whole language classroom: A case study. *Learning Disabilities Research and Practice, 11,* 168–176.

Martin, J., (1985). *Factual writing.* Geelong, Australia: Deakin University Press.

Martin, J., Christie, F., & Rothery, J. (1987). Social processes in education: A reply to Sawyer and Watson (and others). In I. Reid (Ed.), *The place of genre in learning: Current debates.* Geelong, Australia: Deakin University Press.

Martin, J., & Rothery, J. (1981). Writing project report no. 2. Working papers in Linguistics No. 1, Linguistics Department, University of Sydney, Australia.

McClaskin, M. M. (1989). Whole language: Theory, instruction, and future implementation. *The Elementary School Journal, 90,* 223–229.

McGee, L. M., & Lomax, R. G. (1990) On combining apples and oranges: A response to Stahl & Miller. *Review of Educational Research, 60,* 133–140.

McPhail, J. C. (1995). Phenomenology as philosophy and method: Applications to ways of doing special education. *Remedial and Special Education, 16*, 159–165.

Meltzer, L., & Reid, D. K. (1994). New directions in the assessment of students with special needs: The shift toward a constructivist perspective. *Journal of Special Education, 28*, 338–355.

Mercer, C. D., Jordan, L., & Miller, S. P. (1994). Implications of constructivism for teaching math to students with moderate to mild disabilities. *Journal of Special Education, 28*, 290–306.

Mercer, C. D., Jordan, L., & Miller, S. P. (1996). Constructivistic math instruction for diverse learners. *Learning Disabilities Research and Practice, 11*, 147–156.

Moshman, D. (1982). Exogenous, endogenous, and dialectical constructivism. *Developmental Review, 2*, 371–384.

Palincsar, A. S., & Klenk, L. (1993). Broader visions encompassing literacy, learners, and contexts. *Remedial and Special Education, 14*(4), 19–25.

Paris, S. G., & Winograd, P. (1990). Promoting metacognition and motivation of exceptional children. *Remedial and Special Education, 11*(6), 7–15.

Pearson, P. D. (1989). Reading the whole language movement. *The Elementary School Journal, 90*, 231–241.

Phillips, D. C. (1976). *Holistic thought in social science*. Stanford, CA: Stanford University Press.

Poplin, M. S. (1987). Self-imposed blindness: The scientific method in education. *Remedial and Special Education, 8*(6), 31–37.

Poplin, M. S. (1988a). The reductionsitic fallacy in learning disabilities: Replicating the past by reducing the present. *Journal of Learning Disabilities, 21*, 389–400.

Poplin, M. S. (1988b). Holistic/constructivist principles of the teaching/learning process: Implications for the field of learning disabilities. *Journal of Learning Disabilities, 21*, 401–416.

Pressley, M., Harris, K. R., & Marks, M. B. (1992). But good strategy instructors are constructivists. *Educational Psychology Review, 4*, 3–31.

Pressley, M., Hogan, K., Wharton-McDonald, R., Mistretta, J., & Ettenberger, S. (1996). The challenges of instructional scaffolding: The challenges of instruction that supports student thinking. *Learning Disabilities Research and Practice, 11*, 138–146.

Reid, D. K. & Stone, C. A. (1991). Why is cognitive instruction effective? Underlying learning mechanisms. *Remedial and Special Education, 2*(3), 8–19.

Richardson, P. (1991). Language as personal resource and as social construct: Competing views of literacy pedagogy in Australia. *Educational Review, 43*(2), 171–190.

Rogoff, B. (1990). *Apprenticeship in thinking: Cognitive development in social context*. New York: Oxford University Press.

Rosenshine, B., & Meister, C. (1992). The use of scaffolds for teaching higher-level cognitive strategies. *Educational Leadership, 49*(7), 26–33.

Schickedanz, J. A. (1990). The jury is still out on the effects of whole language and language experience approaches for beginning reading: A critique of Stahl and Miller's study. *Review of Education Research, 60*, 127–131.

Scruggs, T. E., and Mastropieri, M. A. (1994). The construction of scientific knowledge by students with mild disabilities. *Journal of Special Education, 28*, 307–321.

Simpson, R. G. (1992). Quantitative research methods as the method of choice within a continuum model. In W. Stainback and S. Stainback (Eds.), *Controversial issues confronting special education: Divergent perspectives* (pp. 235–242). Boston: Allyn and Bacon.

Slavin, R. (1989). PET and the pendulum: Faddism in education and how to stop it. *Phi Delta Kappan, 70*, 752–758.

Smith, J. K., & Heshusius, L. (1986). Closing down the conversation: The end of the quantitative-qualitative debate among educational inquirers. *Educational Researcher, 15*, 4–12.

Smith, F. (1971). *Understanding reading: A psycholinguistic analysis of reading and learning to read*. New York: Holt, Rinehart & Winston.

Speigel, D. (1992). Blending whole language and systematic direct instruction. *The Reading Teacher, 46*, 38–44.

Stahl, S. A., & Miller, P. D. (1989). Whole language and language experience approaches for beginning reading: A quantitative synthesis. *Review of Educational Research, 59*, 87–116.

Stahl, S. A. (1990). Riding the pendulum: A rejoinder

to Schickedanz and McGee and Lomax. *Review of Educational Research, 60*, 141–151.

Stanovich, K. E. (1994). Constructivism in reading education. *Journal of Special Education, 28*, 259–274.

Ulman, J. D. & Rosenberg, M. S. (1986). Science and superstition in science education. *Exceptional Children, 52*, 459–460.

Vygotsky, L. S. (1978). *Mind in society: The development of higher psychological processes.* Cambridge, MA: Harvard University Press.

Walker, C. P., & Elias, D. (1987). Writing conference talk: Factors associated with high- and low-rated writing conferences. *Research in Teaching English, 21*, 266–285.

Warren, S. F., & Yoder, P. J. (1994). Communication and language intervention: Why a constructivist approach is insufficient. *Journal of Special Education, 28*, 248–258.

PART THREE

Expansions and Future Directions of the Field

Students with learning disabilities have come to be educated in increasingly integrated settings with their typical peers.

CHAPTER 10

Classroom Inclusion of Students with Learning Disabilities

In this chapter we will . . .

- Discuss changes that have had an impact on special education services and programs.
- Identify the mental health consultation, behavior consultation, and process consultation perspectives.
- Differentiate the expert consultant role and the collaborative consultant role.
- Analyze collaborative structures to facilitate teamwork: collaborative consultation, behavioral consultation, peer collaboration, teacher assistance teams, intervention assistance teams, child study/resource teams, and cooperative teaching.
- Provide brief vignettes to illustrate unique features and overlaps of each collaborative structure.

- Evaluate professional collaboration research.
- Analyze data on collaborative consultation.
- Identify ways of tailoring collaborative efforts.
- Analyze potential barriers limiting collaborative planning and instruction.
- Differentiate characteristics of effective teams.
- Discuss the principles of effective team communication.

Reynolds (1989) has summarized the history of special education service delivery as one of "progressive inclusion" in which students with disabilities have come to be educated in increasingly integrated settings with their typical peers. Special education services for students with LD have also followed this pattern. Although LD services emerged late in the history of special education, compared to services for other categories of exceptionality, the trend toward placing students with LD in mainstream programs has been evident over the past two decades (U.S. Department of Education [USDE] 1995).

FACTORS INFLUENCING CONTEMPORARY SPECIAL EDUCATION

Special education is currently in a serious state of self-examination (W. Stainback & Stainback, 1996). A variety of social, educational, philosophical, and political factors have influenced the rapid evolution of special education programs during the past decade. Significant changes have taken place in America since the first programs for students with LD were introduced in the early 1960s. Changes in society, emerging technology, and decades of educational research have all influenced the development of today's educational goals, program standards, and performance expectations. To understand the growing movement toward more inclusive education, we need to briefly review some of the significant factors that have affected public education during the past 30 years. This chapter examines changes that had an impact on special education services and programs, the evolution of service delivery, and initiatives to support more inclusive educational programming for students with LD.

Changes in the School-Age Population

Many school systems are struggling to meet the expanding needs of students who are vastly different from those served a generation ago. Demographers believe that 30 to 40% of the students in schools today are at risk for academic failure and/or social alienation because of a broad array of social factors such as poverty, drugs, family life stressors, and cultural or language differences. Experts predict significant increases in this population in the coming years (Helge, 1988; Williams, 1992).

Approximately one-fourth of all the children born in this country are born poor (Feistritzer, 1987). Most of these babies are raised in single-parent families headed by young, African-American or Hispanic mothers (Duany & Pittman, 1990). This is a serious concern to public education because factors such as inadequate prenatal and postnatal health care, teenage pregnancy, low birth weight, poor nutrition, abuse and neglect, and limited intellectual stimulation contribute to the subsequent learning problems that many low-income and minority students experience in schools (Congress of the United States, 1987; Hodgkinson, 1993; Stevens & Price, 1992; Wolock & Horowitz, 1984).

It has been clearly established that many school failure predictors correlate with socioeconomic and racial status (Williams, 1992). Educators recognize that at-risk students need intensive academic and/or social support to stay in school. Without broad-based support, these students experience significantly higher rates of grade retention, remedial and special education program enrollment, early school leaving, and teenage pregnancy than their peers (Bempechat & Ginsburg, 1989; Dorfman, 1988; Duany & Pittman, 1990; Hodgkinson, 1993; Orum, 1986; Williams, 1992).

Many of the academic and social classroom problems these students experience are similar to those of students with mild to moderate disabilities (Ornstein & Levine, 1989; Stevens & Price, 1992). Unfortunately, few resources are designed to provide specific help for most at-risk students. This situation has prompted many school systems to re-examine current service delivery and develop new and innovative classroom intervention programs to reach more students (Wiederholt, 1989; Wiederholt & Chamberlin, 1989). In general, most of these programs provide a structured plan of classroom support and performance monitoring for students with identified disabilities. In addition, these programs produce "spillover" benefits that aid other students who do not have access to other support services (Walther-Thomas, in press-a).

Changes in School Standards and Student Performance Expectations

The educational reform movement launched by the Reagan administration called for "excellence" in public education (National Committee on Excellence in Education, 1983). As a result many states enacted legislation creating higher academic standards and performance expectations for students in public schools (Inman, Pribesh, & Salganik, 1990). Today, students complete more rigorous math, science, reading, and foreign language requirements to earn high school diplomas than was the case a decade ago. Advocates for students with disabilities have stressed the need to maintain equity for students, as professionals strive to stimulate educational excellence. Unfortunately, few states have the economic resources to install sufficient academic support programs to help low-achieving students meet these higher goals. As a result, help is generally limited. Where help does exist, it is often provided through the willingness of classroom and support personnel to assume additional instructional responsibilities. Most states expect students with LD to complete the same course work and testing requirements as their peers to earn standard high school diplomas

(Bodner, Clark, & Mellard, 1987; Walther-Thomas, 1990). Higher performance standards, more difficult course work, minimum competency tests, and few remedial instruction resources require educators and families to work together on long-range educational plans. Coordinated planning helps ensure that students with LD develop necessary prerequisite skills and receive appropriate classroom support to perform successfully in mainstream courses needed for graduation.

Changes in Instructional Practices

A number of promising instructional practices and collaborative service-delivery structures have emerged from educational research in recent years. They are receiving increasing support from professionals and families alike. Many of these facilitate teamwork, effective problem solving, and greater educational inclusion of students with identified LD and those at risk for school failure (Idol, 1989; Laycock, Korinek, & Gable, 1991). Some of these arrangements include: cooperative student learning (Johnson & Johnson, 1986; Kagan, 1994; Putnam, 1993; Slavin, Karweit, & Madden, 1989), peer-mediated interventions (Jenkins & Jenkins, 1985; Lloyd, Crowley, Kohler, & Strain, 1988; Thousand, Villa, & Nevin, 1994), curriculum-based measurement (Blankenship, 1985; Fuchs & Deno, 1991; Germann & Tindal, 1985), modified learning environments (Wang & Birch, 1984; Wang, Gennari, & Waxman, 1985) and cognitive learning strategies (Deshler, Ellis, & Lenz, 1996; Deshler & Schumaker, 1986; Palinscar & Brown, 1987). Teacher assistance teams (Chalfant, Pysh, & Moultri, 1979), peer coaching, (Brandt, 1987; Hammond & Foster, 1987) and collaborative teaching arrangements in which educators pool their respective talents and expertise (Bauwens & Hourcade, 1995; Bauwens, Hourcade, & Friend, 1989; Reynolds, 1989; Walther-Thomas, Bryant, & Land, 1996) are additional examples of promising practices to support students in mainstream settings.

The Adaptive Learning Environment Model (ALEM) is an adaptive instruction example from the University of Pittsburgh's Learning Research and Development Center (Friend & Bursuck, 1996). ALEM utilizes various instructional arrangements (e.g., mastery learning, strategies instruction, cooperative teamwork) within the context of the modified general education environment.

The basic components of ALEM include: (a) a well-designed basic skills curriculum that utilizes both highly structured approaches (e.g., peer tutoring, direct instruction) and more open-ended learning activities (e.g., cooperative learning groups); (b) organized classrooms in which the daily instructional sequence and the classroom management plan have been developed to maximize the effectiveness of the learning time and materials (e.g., self-correcting materials, self-monitoring, peer feedback); (c) flexible grouping and instructional team systems to ensure effective and efficient use of student and teacher time (e.g., cooperative groups, partner practice, individual tutoring); (d) regularly scheduled teacher-parent communication to encourage family involvement in children's learning and to integrate school and home experiences effectively; and (e) ongoing staff development and data collection to ensure that teachers develop and employ the skills and strategies needed to create ALEM environments. Research data on the efficacy of the ALEM model in schools suggest that, when conscientiously implemented, the components of the models provide an effective classroom learning environment (Friend & Bursuck, 1996; Wang & Birch, 1984).

Wiederholt (1989) described basic elements that are found in many adaptive learning programs: (a) skill instruction is based on individually assessed learning needs; (b) students help select goals, outcomes, and learning activities; (c) students learn to assess their own instructional needs, plan instructional programs, and evaluate progress; (d) alternative materials and methods are provided to facilitate the learning process; (e) instructional strategies and practice materials allow students to work at their own pace; (f) students are informed about their skill mastery; and (g) students work together in cooperative teams. The development of attractive and effective mainstream instructional arrangements have influenced the thinking of parents and professionals. These models, in addition to other influences previously mentioned, have led a number of advocates to press for more inclusive service delivery in mainstream classrooms (Friend & Bursuck, 1996; W. Stainback & Stainback, 1984, 1996; Villa & Thousand, 1995).

Changes in Service Delivery

Today, most of the special education that students with LD receive is provided through resource programs or in general education classroom settings (Mercer & Mercer, 1996; USDE, 1995; Wiederholt & Chamberlin, 1989). For many years, however, separate self-contained classrooms were the predominant service-delivery option for students with moderate to severe learning and behavior disabilities. In general, these classes were organized categorically and taught by teachers who had specific training in particular disability areas. Only students whose disability label matched a classroom's categorical designation could be served in that particular setting.

Self-contained classrooms, once considered desirable because of the intensive one-on-one help provided, lost popularity during the late 1960s when researchers, practitioners, and parents began to question the educational and social consequences of segregated classrooms for students with disabilities (Carlberg & Kavale, 1980). Concerns surfaced regarding potential negative effects of these environments on student learning and performance, student and teacher expectations, self-esteem, and social skills development. Advocates lost their confidence in self-contained classrooms to meet the long-term social and academic needs of students with disabilities (Dunn, 1968). Parents and professionals had come to believe that greater participation in general education classrooms would socially and academically benefit students with disabilities. Proponents of greater inclusion also championed the inherent right of these students to be educated with their typical peers (Adamson & Van Etten, 1972; Deno, 1970; W. Stainback & Stainback, 1984).

Advocates began to promote a "continuum of services" approach to special education (Adamson & Van Etten, 1972; Deno, 1973; Dunn, 1968; Lilly, 1970). This service-delivery model had two fundamental purposes. The first was to meet the unique learning needs of all students with disabilities by providing more appropriate educational opportunities. A services continuum offered students with disabilities access to intensive special education, supervision, and/or related services (e.g., hospitals, institutions) at one end and full-time general education participation with no special assistance at the other. Systematically arranged along the continuum were various levels of service and support to meet student needs (e.g., weekly speech therapy, daily resource-room instruction, half-day special class placement). Supporters of the continuum envisioned parents and educators working together to identify the most appropriate placements for students with disabilities. These planning teams would select the least restrictive learning environments in which students could succeed. The second purpose of this model was to provide students with disabilities the opportunity to participate actively in the mainstream of schools. These students could receive special education support without experiencing social and/or academic isolation. As a result of advocacy efforts, litigation, and legislation, the continuum of this service-delivery model became a cornerstone in Public Law No. 94–142. During the 1970s and 1980s, less restrictive programs emerged to provide students with disabilities more educational opportunities and a broader menu of support services.

Today, many students with disabilities are served in resource settings (36.3%) (USDE, 1995). These segregated classes comprise a portion of the school day, however, most of the school time is spent in the mainstream with typical peers (West & Cannon, 1988). The primary goal in resource programs is to provide students with disabilities with the skills and support needed to succeed in mainstream classes. Typically, these services include academic and social skills development, remedial instruction, cognitive strategies instruction, content tutoring, and behavior management. School systems find resource programs attractive because they cost less than self-contained programs because resource teachers can maintain larger case loads than self-contained teachers. Many resource programs are cross-categorical in nature (i.e., serving students with various types of disabilities). This organizational structure provides school systems with considerable flexibility in instructional grouping and professional staffing.

While resource programs have provided greater educational inclusion, many concerns have surfaced during the past decade regarding this model. Some of the frequently cited problems include a lack of significant efficacy data (Friend & Bursuck, 1996; Gerber, 1987), problems with reliable classification and placement of students with mild disabilities (Algozzine & Ysseldyke, 1981; Galagan, 1985; Shepard, 1987; Ysseldyke, Algozzine, & Thurlow, 1991), negative effects of labeling students (Reynolds, 1989), continued emphasis on failure rather than prevention (Will, 1986), and growing numbers of students at risk for school failure (Hodgkinson, 1993).

Typical of concerns about the efficacy of resource programs are those reported by Winget (1988):

> Students are unable to generalize or transfer information or skills acquired in a pull-out program to the general classroom setting. Students may miss out on the core curriculum if they are removed from class too often and by multiple resource teachers. Specialists should attempt to ameliorate the specific disabilities rather than focusing on skills and content development. (p. 6)

Resource support has not eliminated basic concerns about the preparation for life (i.e., social, academic, vocational, self-advocacy) that students with disabilities receive (National Center on Educational Outcomes, 1993). Emerging research on young adults with mild disabilities indicates that many secondary special education students do not develop critical skills, leave school early, and do not earn high school diplomas (Edgar, 1987, 1988; USDE, 1995; Zigmond & Thornton, 1985). These students frequently lack basic skills needed to live independently as self-supporting young adults. Consequently, many remain at home long after their age mates have moved out on their own, and are dependent on their families for financial help, companionship, and moral support (Edgar, 1988; Haring, Lovett, & Smith, 1990; Mithaug, Horiuchi, & Fanning, 1985; Sitlington, Frank, & Carson, 1992; USDE, 1995; Wagner & Shaver, 1989).

Many potential benefits of inclusive education have not been realized because few mechanisms exist to facilitate coordinated instructional education planning and programming by general educators and special educators (S. Stainback & Stainback, 1996). At the preservice level, few special education teacher preparation programs prepare future teachers to work collaboratively with their general education counterparts. Few receive adequate opportunities to develop the communication skills, confidence, and philosophical orientation to collaborate successfully with general educators to develop appropriate programming for students (Pugach, 1987; Villa & Thousand, 1995). A notable exception has been the Vermont Consulting Teacher Program (McKenzie, Egner, Knight, Perelman, Schneider, & Garvin, 1970). For more than 25 years, this teacher preparation program has emphasized consultation skills development as a basic teacher education component.

At the in-service level, few opportunities are provided for teachers to work together collaboratively. In most systems, teachers maintain large case loads, have extensive direct service responsibilities, and have very limited time for instructional planning. Few systems provide teachers with opportunities to develop collegial relationships, monitor student progress outside their own classrooms, and explore alternative approaches to instruction, practice, and evaluation (Walther-Thomas, in press-a).

THE REGULAR EDUCATION INITIATIVE (REI) DEBATE

Problems with traditional service delivery and mainstreaming as it was being practiced sparked heated controversy in the early 1980s (O'Shea, O'Shea, & Algozzine, 1989, Ysseldyke et al., 1991). Growing doubts about the efficacy of current practices (Friend & Bursuck, 1996; Will, 1986), coupled with a growing at-risk population (Williams, 1992) and a series of Reagan-era educational reform reports calling for higher academic standards and increased students performance expectations (e.g., *A Nation at Risk*) contributed to this controversy. As a result, in 1986, a major philosophical debate emerged between special education leaders. The debate regarding the REI, as it was known, forced critical examination of the role of special education and its relationship with general education.

Arguments to Support the REI

In 1984, W. Stainback and Stainback proposed a merger of general and special education on moral, ethical, and educational grounds. Many professionals and advocates contended that students with disabilities should be educated exclusively in general education settings to ensure that their long-term educational and social needs were being met effectively (Biklen, 1985; Lilly, 1986; Lipsky & Gartner, 1989).

Madeline Will (1986), then Assistant United States Secretary of Education, supported the REI movement. She contended that general education and special education service providers should share equal responsibility for instructional planning, delivery, and progress monitoring. She noted that broadening the base of professional responsibility would improve the quality of educational services students with disabilities receive.

Proponents based their case for inclusion on four basic concerns about traditional special education service delivery. First, the precedent against educational segregation is well established (e.g., *Brown v. Board of Education, Pennsylvania Association of Retarded Citizens v. Pennsylvania*). This mandate was carried forward in Public Law No. 94–142 and its subsequent amendments (e.g., IDEA). Clearly, IDEA dictates that the first level of educational accommodation and modifications for students with disabilities should take place in general education classrooms. Many school systems, however, ignored this charge and did not use mainstream classroom support as the starting point in special education service delivery. Many systems initiated special education services at a more restrictive level that necessitated use of some type of a "pull out" procedure (Biklen, 1985).

Second, there is a serious lack of data supporting the efficacy of "pull-out" models (e.g., resource rooms, self-contained classes, or separate schools) for students with disabilities. This is particularly true for those with mild disabilities (Carlberg & Kavale, 1980; Gerber, 1987; W. Stainback & Stainback, 1996). There are few well-designed studies that support removing special needs students from the mainstream for academic and/or social skills development (Maheady & Algozzine, 1991; O'Shea & Valcante, 1986).

Third, high costs and unreliable methods used to identify, classify, and place students in special education remain unresolved issues (Brophy, 1986; Lilly, 1988; Ysseldyke et al., 1991). Labor-intensive testing and inaccurate results seriously limit the services many students with disabilities receive (Friend & Bursuck, 1996).

Finally, there are many negative aspects of labeling and educational segregation (e.g., lowered self-esteem, poor academic performance, philosophical emphasis on school failure). It is difficult to justify these procedures when they are contrasted with the positive aspects of educational inclusion (e.g., increases in general knowledge, academic achievement, peer interaction, and failure prevention) (Reynolds, 1989; S. Stainback & Stainback, 1996; Wang & Birch, 1984; Zigmond, 1992).

These concerns have led REI proponents to feel strongly that segregated programming is not a desirable course of action. In addition to these concerns, recent developments in general education have led many REI proponents to believe that the time is right to initiate changes in mainstreaming practices. The emergence of many promising practices such as prereferral interventions, curricular adaptations, learning strategies, cooperative learning, and professional collaboration will enable many general educators to successfully accommodate and maintain "difficult to teach" learners in mainstream classes (Thousand et al, 1994).

Restructuring in general education during the past decade has helped educators and administrators embrace a more inclusive approach to learning (Fernandez, 1991;

Goldring & Rallis, 1993; Joyce, 1990; Walther-Thomas, Bryant, & Land, 1996). These efforts have also helped many general educators develop a broad array of team problem-solving skills, classroom management skills, and instructional strategies to meet the diverse needs of learners in the mainstream (Reynolds, 1989; Salend, 1984; S. Stainback & Stainback, 1996).

Arguments Against the REI

The REI sparked impassioned opposition from some special education professionals (Hallahan, Kaufman, Lloyd, & McKinney, 1988; Kaufman, Gerber, & Semmel, 1988; McKinney & Hocutt, 1988). Opponents still contend that a number of obstacles exist within the current system that will prevent development of an effective integrated service-delivery system. First, the REI debate was almost exclusively a special education event. There has been little input from the general education community and from parents of general and special education students. The views of significant stakeholders in this process have been virtually unexamined.

Second, most special education funding formulas are based on identification of students with disabilities and direct service delivery to them through categorically labeled programs (Hagerty & Abramson, 1987). Typically, more restrictive placements (e.g., special schools) generate more money than do less restrictive placements (e.g., mainstream classroom with special education teacher support). While REI advocates suggest the use of waivers to encourage school systems to explore new service delivery arrangements, few state and federal guidelines have been developed to do so. Consequently, many systems concerned about the potential loss of funds are reluctant to explore new approaches (Hallahan, Kaufman, et al., 1988).

Third, many schools are not presently organized to facilitate the teacher collaboration and coordination needed to implement effective, integrated, service-delivery programs. Teachers have limited scheduling flexibility, heavy direct-service case loads, and minimal planning time. Many worthwhile collaborative endeavors fail in schools because environmental support for new initiatives does not exist (Keogh, 1988; Schumaker & Deshler, 1988).

Fourth, there is a shortage of educators prepared to develop, implement, and monitor inclusive service-delivery programs (Gable, Young, & Hendrickson, 1987; Pugach, 1987; S. Stainback & Stainback, 1996). Few teacher preparation programs emphasize the knowledge and skills needed for successful teaming between general and special educators.

Finally, some researchers have taken issue with claims that current special education programs fail to meet the educational needs of students. They suggest that the methodological weaknesses found in the existing data set make it impossible to draw any definitive conclusions about the actual effectiveness of special education at the present time (Hallahan, Kaufman et al., 1988; Hallahan, Keller, McKinney, Lloyd, & Bryan, 1988; Kaufman, et al., 1988; Keogh, 1988; Wiederholt, 1989).

While the REI debate has waned in the professional literature, the movement toward greater inclusion of students with disabilities has not. Increased concerns about the needs of students at risk for school failure, state and local restructuring efforts, emerging structures for professional collaboration, and growing interest among administrators and teachers have perpetuated field-based efforts to develop more inclusive service-delivery options (W. Stainback & Stainback, 1996; Villa, Thousand, Stainback, & Stainback, 1992).

Because of the move toward more inclusive special education services, it is likely that teachers of students with LD will see their roles as collaborators and consultants expanding in the future. To be effective in these new roles, teachers need to be skilled in both the content and process of effective collaboration. The remainder of this chapter will focus on theoretical perspectives related to collaboration, effective team development, and use of collaborative structures to meet student needs in inclusive settings.

THEORETICAL PERSPECTIVES ON TEAM PROBLEM SOLVING IN SCHOOLS

Larson and LaFasto (1989) defined a team as a group of two or more people who share a common goal that requires coordination among members. When we think about the organizational structure of public schools, we realize how many different teams exists within these systems. Teams are responsible for most of the major decisions that are made in school settings (Goldring & Rallis, 1993). Most educational stakeholders recognize the important roles that such teams play in schools. Team problem solving helps ensure that appropriate action plans are developed to address problems that exist (Fullan, 1993; Joyce, 1990; Senge, 1994). Teams make decisions that affect large numbers of students (e.g., textbook adoption, graduation standards, capital improvements), as well as those that affect individual students' programs (e.g., special education placement, individualized education plan [IEP] development).

Despite respect for teamwork, most school teams learn to work together by a process of trial and error. Team-functioning research has shown that effective groups use fundamental problem-solving tools to increase their productivity (Larson & LaFasto, 1989, Senge, 1994). Little systematic training, however, is provided to help individuals work effectively as team members (Bass & Avloio, 1994; Fullan, 1993; Goldring & Rallis, 1993).

Conoley and Conoley (1988) identified three significant theoretical perspectives related to problem solving within school teams. While the perspectives they present relate primarily to the interactions within dyadic or triadic problem-solving teams, they can be applied to other teams that involve larger numbers of participants. These perspectives represent: mental health consultation, behavioral consultation, and process consultation.

Mental Health Consultation

In mental health settings, the consultant's primary role is to facilitate the consultee's problem solving (Caplan, 1970). Consultees are strongly encouraged to find their own answers to their problems. Consultants focus primarily on the development of positive working relationships with their consultees. They encourage consultee efforts to change attitudes or behaviors that have been targeted. They help consultees recognize their abilities, acknowledge their accomplishments, and take responsibility for progress and/or changes that are made. Consultants avoid taking any credit for ideas that are generated during problem-solving sessions.

Behavior Consultation

Behavioral consultants work with consultees through a highly structured problem-solving process (Babcock & Pryzwansky, 1983). Initially, they develop a mutually acceptable definition of the problem. Next, consultants actively participate in the problem-solving process with consultees. Together they analyze environmental variables that may contribute to the problem (e.g., classroom arrangement, lunchroom rules, teacher responses). A structured intervention plan is developed to eliminate the problem. Finally, clearly defined roles and responsibilities are assigned to group members to ensure successful implementation, evaluation, and follow-up on the proposed intervention plan.

Process Consultation

Process consultants help consultees increase their personal awareness and understanding of problem situations. Together they examine environmental dynamics and explore the ways in which these factors may affect their work (Schein, 1969). Teams frequently use a process consultation approach to improve their team interactions and/or productivity (Conoley & Conoley, 1988). Fundamentals of process consultation are evident in peer coaching, where trained coaches (i.e., consultants) give corrective feedback, communicate new ideas and information in a positive and nonthreatening manner, stimulate reflective thinking, and facilitate the consultees' own problem-solving and decision-making efforts (Joyce & Showers, 1983).

GROUP PROBLEM SOLVING IN SCHOOLS: EXPERT AND COLLABORATIVE MODELS

From these three theoretical perspectives, two distinctly different models of problem solving have emerged. One involves the use of an "expert" consultant to help a consultee solve a problem. The other model utilizes a collaborative consultation approach in which all members of a problem-solving team are viewed as equals. A consultant may find it very useful to be skilled in both of these models. A variety of factors will influence which approach is more appropriate in any given problem-solving situation (e.g., the nature of the presenting problem, previous problem-solving training, the trust level within the problem-solving groups, participant attitudes, available human and/or material resources, and participant skill levels).

The Expert Consultant

In this model, the role of the consultant is defined as that of a master problem solver. The expert model of consultant is frequently used in dyadic relationships. The consultant is perceived as having more knowledge, skills, and/or experience to generate appropriate solutions to presenting problems than is the consultee (Pryzwansky, 1974). Consequently, a hierarchical relationship develops between the consultant

Many service-delivery approaches have emerged that provide students with disabilities and other students at risk for failure with more classroom support. These approaches are all based on professional collaboration and classroom consultation.

and the consultee. Because of unequal distribution of power and status within these relationships, mutual problem solving is not a common feature. Historically, many relationships between service provider and client have been based on this model (e.g., doctor and patient, lawyer and client, and teacher and student).

The Collaborative Consultant

Collaborative consultation is based on a triadic model of problem solving (Tharp, 1975). The first person in the triad is the "target" of concern. In schools, a student whose academic and/or social skills need improvement is usually the designated target for possible intervention. The second person is the "mediator" who is concerned about the target and has influence with him or her. The mediator plays a key role in developing, implementing, and monitoring an appropriate intervention plan. The third person is the collaborative consultant whose knowledge and skills are used to help the mediator develop an appropriate intervention plan. This problem-solving model is used informally or formally among groups. In schools teachers, administrators, ancillary personnel, representatives from community agencies, and parents serve as either mediators or consultants. When possible, the target student is included as a member of the problem-solving group, to enlist his or her input, cooperation, and support for the proposed intervention plan. Mutual problem solving is a key ingredient in this model. Intervention plans reflect the insights and understanding of all participants in this process. Effective collaborative problem solving results in the development of interventions that are appropriate, comprehensive, and supported by those who will be responsible for implementation and monitoring. Research suggests that most teachers prefer consultative relationships built on professional collaboration rather than those that rely heavily on advice from an expert (Pryzwansky & White, 1983).

COLLABORATIVE SERVICE-DELIVERY APPROACHES

During the past 15 years, many service-delivery approaches have emerged that provide more classroom support for students with disabilities and other students at risk for failure. These approaches facilitate the work of school teams as problem solvers, service coordinators, and program developers. They are all based on professional collaboration and classroom consultation. Fuchs and Fuchs (1992) described collaboration as "the current zeitgeist" in educational consultation (p. 94), and they suggested that collaboration is defined in different ways by different people. While variations exist in collaborative service-delivery approaches (e.g., goals, format, organizational structure, interaction skills emphasized) most of the model developers would associate collaboration with a broad array of human interaction skills (e.g., interpersonal problem solving, conflict resolution, resistance management, communication) that are used to facilitate group problem solving and decision making (Walther-Thomas, in press-b). In general, these proponents of classroom service delivery would suggest that effective use of these skills enables school personnel to develop "attitudes and beliefs supportive of a collaborative approach, mutual trust, and a sense of community" (Friend & Cook, 1992, p. 14).

Collaborative Structures to Facilitate Teamwork

Some of the most widely recognized classroom service-delivery structures include: Collaborative Consultation (Idol, Paolucci-Whitcomb, & Nevin, 1986), Behavioral Consultation (Gable, Friend, Laycock, & Hendrickson, 1990), Peer Collaboration (Pugach & Johnson, 1995), Teacher Assistance Teams (Chalfant et al., 1979), Intervention Assistance (Graden, 1989; Graden, Casey, & Christenson, 1985), Child Study/Resource Teams (Hayek, 1987), and Cooperative Teaching (Bauwens & Hourcade, 1995; Walther-Thomas et al., 1996).

Some of these structures are more easily distinguished than others. While there are some differences, most of their major features are not as distinctive as model developers might suggest. In general, these structures are based on the principles of behavioral and/or process consultation. Implicitly or explicitly, they all emphasize active participation by the key stakeholders. All models stress the importance of well-developed professional relationships to ensure that trust and parity exist and that each person's role is valued. Other hallmarks include shared responsibility for problem solving and intervention implementation, intervention monitoring, scheduled follow-up, pooled resources, and professional accountability (Friend & Cook, 1992; Laycock et al., 1991). The structures differ primarily in terms of their specific goals, format for operation, number and roles of participants, and the level of collaborative functioning. Some structures are clearly designed for dyadic relationships, while others are more appropriate for groups of three or more participants. In the descriptions of the various structures that follow, brief vignettes illustrate some of the unique features of each structure. These vignettes also demonstrate that there is considerable overlap between these structures.

Collaborative Consultation.   Collaborative Consultation has been described as "an interactive process that enables professionals with diverse expertise to generate creative solutions to mutually defined problems" (Idol et al., 1986, p. 1). This approach emphasizes professional parity, reciprocity, shared decision making, and use of effective communication skills. Consultants (e.g., special educators, school psychologists, Chapter I teachers, guidance counselors, other specialists) and consultees (e.g., general educators) work together to clarify and solve classroom problems. They explore problems and generate possible alternatives. While this model focuses on dyadic problem solving, the basic process can be easily adapted for use in team contexts (West, 1990).

> Susan, a second-grade teacher, requested help from Bob, her building's "consulting teacher." Bob, elected to this position by his peers for a 1 year period, has a reduced teaching assignment so that he can provide direct and indirect support to teachers requesting his help. Susan is concerned about her students' lack of independent work behavior, low frustration levels, and negative interactions with each other during work periods. Together Bob and Susan discuss these problems and explore possible alternatives. Susan describes strategies she has used and also proposes some new ideas. Bob listens carefully to learn about these problems and to provide Susan with some genuine moral support. After listening to her ideas and experiences, he offers her some additional ideas. After some discussion of the new ideas they have generated, she decides to establish cooperative learning groups for reading and language. Bob agrees to provide indirect classroom help by making some of the student materials she will need and by assisting in developing an effective progress monitoring system. He also gives Susan some direct classroom support during the first week of implementation by supervising students during group work periods.

Behavioral Consultation.   Behavioral Consultation relies heavily on the interaction skills of the participants and on the use of applied behavior analysis (Friend & Bursuck, 1996; S. Stainback & Stainback, 1996; Gable et al., 1990). Consultants guide consultees through a structured interview format to examine the antecedents and consequences of student behavior problems. Together they identify and analyze these problems, develop and implement appropriate behavioral interventions (e.g., contracts, reinforcement systems, self-monitoring programs), and conduct system monitoring to determine the effectiveness of the intervention that is adopted. Modifications are made in the treatment program relative to the student data they collect.

> Cari, an eighth-grade science teacher, requested help from Nan, the resource teacher, because of her concerns about a new student in her class. Jeff, a student with a learning disability, recently enrolled in her fourth-period class. Since that time Jeff has been late for class almost every day, talks out frequently, and rarely brings a pencil or a notebook with him. Cari consults with Nan, the resource teacher, at the end of Jeff's 2nd week, and they discuss his behavior, make a data-collection plan for the following week, and schedule a day when Nan can observe him in class. At the end of the fol-

lowing week they reconvene, discuss their data, and explore alternative intervention strategies. They select a two-pronged approach: They meet with Jeff and his parents to discuss their concerns and institute a behavioral contract with Jeff the following week.

Peer Collaboration.   Peer Collaboration is unique in that it is designed for use by pairs of general educators. They work together in a problem-solving dialogue that leads to problem identification and intervention. One person serves as a peer facilitator for the other. Teachers presenting the problems are encouraged to find their own solutions. Peer collaborators are trained to use self-questioning and reflection procedures to facilitate this process (Pugach & Johnson, 1995).

> Phil, a ninth-grade teacher, is teaching his civics students several metacognitive strategies he learned during a summer institute. Following a month of ongoing instruction and practice of a test-taking strategy, he is disappointed with his students' limited ability to apply this strategy in actual test-taking situations. Maxine, another ninth-grade teacher, is Phil's peer partner. Together they work through a problem-solving session to discuss Phil's concerns. Initially he clarifies the problem his students are experiencing. After some discussion with Maxine, he summarizes the redefined problem. Together they generate possible interventions. Phil selects an appropriate course of action, and they develop an evaluation plan.

Teacher Assistance Teams.   Teacher Assistance Teams (TATs) are larger, school-based, problem-solving groups that help teachers generate intervention strategies for students with academic or behavioral problems (Chalfant & Pysh, 1989; Chalfant et al., 1979). TATs represent a collaborative extension of grade-level teams and high school academic department teams. Generally three classroom teachers serve as the core members of TATs. Some schools include special educators, administrators, or specialists as TAT members; however, Chalfant and his colleagues (1979, 1989) strongly encourage selection of general educators for these roles. They contend that it is important for school personnel to recognize the skills and expertise that many master teachers have in solving social and academic classroom problems effectively. Most TATs meet on a regularly scheduled basis and follow a set of structured meeting procedures to maximize the efficiency of their problem-solving time together (see Table 10.1). Prior to the TAT sessions, individual members meet with teachers requesting to help to clarify the problem and assemble useful data. Working together during the TAT meeting, the team helps the teacher generate possible interventions. The teacher is asked to select the most appropriate solution. Support and follow-up are provided during the intervention phase.

> Helen, a new 11th-grade general math teacher, requested assistance from the TAT team. She was having difficulty controlling the behavior of two girls in the class. They frequently talked back to her, left the room without permission, and often wanted to sleep in class. After submitting a request for assistance form, Helen met with Carl, one of the team members. The purpose of this meeting was to clarify the problems and gather useful information for the TAT meeting, and they scheduled a time for Carl to observe these students firsthand. A week later Helen met with the full TAT team. They discussed the information that she and Carl had gathered. Most of the meeting time was spent brainstorming intervention alternatives. Following brainstorming, the team asked Helen to select the most feasible strategies for her classroom. Together they

Table 10.1
Conducting Problem-Solving Meetings

(First 5 minutes—I through IV)

I. Open meeting, introduce participants, verify attendance
The team facilitator formally initiates the session, welcomes participants, introduces each person by name and position, and ensures all required members are present.

II. Establish role of recorder
The team selects a recorder. The facilitator reminds other team members of their duties: review the student information; be supportive, succinct, and to the point; make recommendations.

III. Clarify purpose of the meeting
The team facilitator states the purpose of the meeting (to assist the referring teacher in designing interventions for her or his general education classroom to meet the needs of the student with learning or behavioral problems).

IV. Present major concerns
Team facilitator begins the discussion by:
A. reviewing reasons why the teacher requested the meeting;
B. summarizing the student's problem areas and data;
C. addressing additional information or concerns and giving the teacher an opportunity to react, state expectations, and/or add information.

V. Establish intervention priorities and goals (3 minutes)
Teacher and team members reach a concensus on the major problem to be targeted for intervention.

VI. Brainstorm possible interventions (5–10 minutes)
Set up a designated time. Record proposed intervention strategies (remedial, alternative, instructional, behavioral) on the Ideas/Suggestions for Interventions form. Encourage diverse responses and building upon others' ideas. Generate as many ideas as possible; do not judge or comment at this point. Avoid "killer phrases" such as "It won't work. I've tried that. How silly . . . . They won't buy that. Yes, but . . . I can't."

VII. Select intervention strategies (2 minutes)
The referring teacher evaluates the brainstormed solutions, may seek clarification from the team, and then selects intervention(s).

VIII. Plan implementation and documentation (5 minutes)
The facilitator leads discussion to plan how intervention will be implemented, evaluated, and documented.

IX. Plan follow-up (5 minutes)
A date for a follow-up meeting is set (recommended within 2–6 weeks, but no longer than one grading period). Content, recommendations, and intervention plan are officially recorded, documented, and submitted for dissemenation.

Source: L. Korineck & V. L. McLaughlin, 1994, Preservice, intervention assistance teaming project. Williamsburg, VA: College of William & Mary, unpublished manuscript.

developed an action plan and scheduled a follow-up meeting to monitor the effectiveness of the plan.

Intervention Assistance Teams (IATs).   These teams were formerly referred to as "prereferral intervention teams" (Graden, 1989; Graden et al., 1985). Now called IATs, this approach offers a multilevel approach to problem solving. It is designed to help reduce special education referrals by providing classroom support for students and teachers. IATs utilize a team approach but begin the problem-solving process with one-to-one consultation. If this level of support does not solve the presenting problem, a larger IAT team reviews the teacher's referral, makes suggestions, and helps the teacher determine whether or not a formal referral for additional testing is appropriate. To accomplish this, a structured six-stage approach is used: (a) a request for consultation is submitted; (b) one-on-one consultation is provided; (c) a classroom observation is conducted by an IAT team member and additional suggestions are provided; (d) a multidisciplinary child review team discusses the student information (e.g., work samples, anecdotal records, test scores, strategies tried), additional interventions may be proposed, and/or the team may elect to proceed to the next level; (e) a referral for a psychoeducational evaluation is submitted and testing is completed; and (f) a formal eligibility meeting is held to review the evaluation results and determine appropriate services.

IATs resemble many other multidisciplinary teams that exist in the schools (e.g., middle school teams comprised of representatives from various academic disciplines: English, math, social studies, and science). Special educators, school psychologists, and administrators may be full-time IAT members or serve on an as-requested basis as the IATs move toward a formal referral for evaluation. IATs are structured to provide direct teacher assistance quickly. This permits greater support for teachers and students when problems develop. It also facilitates closer monitoring of student progress in mainstream settings.

> On the first day of school Scott, a kindergarten teacher, was concerned about Jorge, a young Hispanic student. Jorge was small, shy, and had very limited expressive language skills. Scott's concerns persisted. He tried unsuccessfully to reach Jorge's parents on several occasions. After several weeks of school, Scott submitted a request for IAT team support. Two days later Scott met with Wayne, an IAT member and special educator. They discussed Scott's concerns and reviewed the strategies that he had used to engage Jorge in classroom activities. Wayne provided some additional strategies for Scott to consider. They developed an action plan, and Wayne agreed to observe Jorge in class the following week. Following the observation, Scott and Wayne discussed Jorge. Scott noted that the situation had recently improved. Three days ago a student volunteer had begun working in his classroom five mornings a week. She speaks Spanish and, with Scott's encouragement, she had spent much of the first morning talking to Jorge. After some initial shyness, he spoke fluently with her and explained that he has only lived in America since early summer. Like his parents, he does not speak much English yet. They discussed ways to involve the volunteer actively in Jorge's language instruction. Scott agreed to contact the ESL support services the following day. Wayne agreed to check with Scott weekly to monitor Jorge's classroom performance.

Child Study/Resource Teams (CSRTs).   Another approach to team problem solving involves the CSRT (Hayek, 1987). In the past these teams focused primarily on screening students and making referrals for additional testing. Today they are mandated to provide referring teachers with opportunities to solve problems and develop appropriate classroom intervention strategies. These teams typically consist of principals, special educators, resource specialists, one or more classroom teachers, and referring teachers. CSRT meetings are conducted in much the same way as the previously described TATs. If, however, a student's problem is not resolved after several classroom intervention attempts, the team moves ahead with eligibility proceedings.

> Randy, a seventh-grade health teacher, referred one of his students, James, to the school's CSRT because of his difficulties in keeping up in class. Randy feels certain that James knows more than his grades indicate but feels James isn't performing up to his potential and probably needs special education services.
>
> When Randy meets with the CSRT, they review James's test scores and samples of his work. They also ask Randy to clarify areas of difficulty for James, which include reading the health text, taking notes in class, and passing unit exams. Randy is also asked what he has tried to improve the situation. The team offers additional intervention suggestions to improve James's performance in class. The team asks Randy if he is willing to implement any of these suggestions in an effort to alleviate James's problems. He agrees to try two strategies. First, he will ask another student to make a copy of the daily health notes on carbon paper, to share with James. Second, he will develop a study guide for the unit exams. He mentions that other students will also like the study guide. The CSRT helps Randy develop a way to keep track of James's performance. They also set a date to meet again to discuss his progress.

Cooperative Teaching.   Whereas the previously described collaborative structures represent indirect forms of service delivery, Cooperative Teaching or coteaching extends collaboration to provide direct and indirect classroom support to students with disabilities who are integrated into general education classes (Walther-Thomas, in press-b). This approach is an outgrowth of Collaborative Consultation. Special and general educators jointly plan and instruct heterogeneous groups of students in mainstream classrooms (Bauwens & Hourcade, 1995). Classroom instruction is handled in various ways by coteachers. Both teachers may teach the general content, or the general educator may have responsibility for the content, while the special educator teaches students complementary skills (e.g., learning strategies, study skills) and provides supplemental activities to reinforce learning, such as cooperative learning activities, peer tutoring, or computer activities (Bauwens et al., 1989).

> Pat, a fourth-grade teacher, has several students receiving resource services for their LD mainstreamed into her classroom for social studies. She and Chris, the resource teacher, coteach this subject to the total group three times a week. For their lessons on the Civil War, they jointly decide to take turns covering the causes, major battles, important people, and daily life during the war. Pat will discuss these topics from the perspective of the North, whereas Chris will represent the South's views of events for each topic (team teaching).
>
> When they cover the battles, Pat will be responsible for teaching the major points. Chris will follow up by teaching students to use a key-word mnemonic strategy to help them remember the chronology (complementary instruction).

Chris and Pat also plan a cooperative learning activity, wherein small groups of students will compose "letters to home," describing daily life on the battlefront from the perspective of a northern or southern soldier. Both teachers will monitor the groups and give feedback to the students during this activity (supplemental learning activity).

Pat and Chris meet regularly each week to plan their teaching activities. During these coplanning sessions, they also review students' progress and evaluate the success of their coteaching efforts.

Maintaining a Collaborative Ethic in Alternative Service Delivery

Faithfulness to a collaborative ethic is essential for these service-delivery structures to be effective (Friend & Cook, 1992; Korinek, McLaughlin, & Walther-Thomas, 1995; Laycock et al., 1991). Collaborative approaches can easily become expert systems unless participants consciously work to prevent this from happening. Because of professional role designations (e.g., administrator, school psychologist, special educator), specialty skills certain members may possess, and/or past experiences working together, "experts" within problem-solving groups may emerge. Teams committed to professional collaboration need to remember to: (a) establish a reliable, problem-solving format, (b) utilize effective communication skills, (c) periodically discuss their fundamental assumptions of effective collaboration, and (d) monitor their team's interactions on an ongoing basis to ensure the process is working effectively.

RESEARCH RELATED TO COLLABORATIVE SERVICE DELIVERY

To date, few studies have investigated collaborative relationships between special educators and general educators (Walther-Thomas, in press-a). Most of the studies that have been conducted have examined the relationships between teachers and other school specialists (e.g., school psychologists, behavioral consultants, social workers) (Evans, 1991).

Most of what we believe about the benefits of professional collaboration has come indirectly from research in related areas. Gresham and Kendell (1987) examined eight previous reviews on consultation research. They conducted a meta-analysis of the data, focusing on three key components: (a) outcomes, (b) process, and (c) practitioner utilization. Their analysis of the outcomes information results in two conclusions. First, behavioral consultation produced the largest effect across studies, and second, referral rates for consultation dropped dramatically after 4 or 5 years. Regarding process, the researchers found that consultees were 14 times as likely to identify resources and implement a consultation plan if consultants ask, rather than tell, them how to identify and use resources. Effective consultants were those who possessed strong communication skills (e.g., active listening) and avoided professional jargon. The analysis to practitioner-utilization information studies showed that consultants average approximately 30 consultation requests per year. Approximately 80% of the consultees verbally committed to implementing the consultation plan; however, only 40% actually carried out their plans.

Wegner (1979) examined postconsultation attitudes of teachers. Teachers participated in either expert consultation or collaborative consultation and reported significantly higher ratings for the collaborative approach. Collaborative consultants were viewed as more attentive, more helpful, and offering better suggestions. There were not significant differences, however, in the rate of plan implementation between these two groups. In another study of collaborative consultation, teachers in 10 schools participated in a 14-week study in which consultation support was available to them 2 halfdays per week. Teachers saw the personality traits (e.g., openness, nonthreatening demeanor) of the consultants as important factors in determining whether or not they used the available services.

Pugach and Johnson (1995) examined peer collaboration to determine its effectiveness in the development and implementation of alternative strategies for addressing the learning and behavior problems of students in their classrooms. Forty-eight teachers participated in an in-service training program and selected a partner with whom to work. These teams worked to solve at least four problems together. Following their work, participants reported more tolerance for academic and behavioral problems, and a greater likelihood of trying to solve problems that existed in their classrooms.

In a review of education consultation research, Evans (1991) concluded that the existing research methodology in this area is rudimentary at best. A combination of limiting factors exists: (a) important concepts are frequently poorly defined, (b) few researchers work in this area, (c) existing studies have relied heavily on self-reports (e.g., consumer satisfaction reports), and (d) small samples limit the appropriateness of quantitative methods.

Many research reports on collaborative consultation and other inclusive approaches conclude with statements related to the difficulty of conducting research on these constructs. Researchers frequently note the problems associated with the complexity of topics, and how difficult it is to recommend clear directions for future research (Evans, 1991; Walther-Thomas, in press-a).

Given that small-sample-size problems will continue to hamper quantitative efforts, researchers in this area might need to approach their work from a more qualitative perspective (see Merriam, 1991 for a qualitative research perspective). Maheady, Harper, Mallett, and Sacca (1989) proposed that consultation efforts be evaluated along four dimensions: (a) actual implementation (whether teachers actually use proposed interventions in their classrooms and with what degree of accuracy); (b) effectiveness (whether the proposed interventions make statistically or educationally important differences in students' performance); (c) efficiency (whether the intervention is feasible in terms of time, cost, and material requirements); and (d) social acceptability (whether teachers, pupils, administrators, and parents find the intervention goals, procedures, and outcomes to be acceptable).

While preliminary findings are encouraging, they do not provide conclusive evidence regarding the superiority of collaborative service-delivery approaches in meeting the learning needs of students with disabilities and other at-risk learners. In general, however, they do suggest that professionals, as well as special needs students, benefit from effective collaborative relationships (Evans, 1991; Gresham & Kendell, 1987).

It is important for researchers to investigate these professional relationships over time to see the changes that occur. Evans (1991) notes: "collaborative interaction of any kind is a novel experience. Teachers may feel they are being asked to play a game in which they do not really understand the rules. The creation of a collaborative ethnic in the schools will be a complex process" (p. 13).

STUDENTS PARTICIPATION ON COLLABORATIVE TEAMS FOR ENHANCED INTEGRATION

Students play an important role in implementing school-based changes in service delivery to foster inclusion. Students can be involved in a variety of ways that empower them as primary stakeholders in the educational process. Involvement may range from ongoing participation on teams to periodic involvement in activities addressing special needs or interests (Villa & Thousand, 1995). Student collaboration facilitates relationships and academics through activities such as partner learning, peer tutoring, cooperative learning activities, and/or teacher-student learning teams. Students can assist in determining appropriate accommodations for themselves and/or classmates and provide feedback to professionals regarding learning experiences. Advocacy roles for students include participating on transition planning or IEP teams to help adult collaborators consider student perspectives in planning goals or objectives and integration experiences for other students. Additionally, peer support networks or peer "buddies" in the mainstream can greatly assist inclusion efforts.

Villa and Thousand (1995) suggest students serve as partners in school decision making by being given a voice in developing discipline policies, teacher/administrator practices as they relate to school climate, and representation on school committees. Students with special needs should participate in IEP planning and decision-making experiences to help develop their personal advocacy and decision-making skills. Interest inventories, learning style preferences checklists, and learning profiles can be easily adapted to this same process of student self-assessment and participation.

The advantages of increased involvement of students in collaborative efforts include enhanced motivation; development of problem-solving, teaming, and decision-making skills needed in our complex society; development of a positive sense of community; and improved achievement (Glaser, 1986; Johnson, Holubec, & Roy, 1984; Villa & Thousand, 1995). Students should not be overlooked in collaborative planning and implementation efforts, given the positive outcomes for both students and schools by the integration process.

FAMILY PARTICIPATION ON COLLABORATIVE TEAMS

Families often play key roles in development, implementation, and evaluation of integrated educational services. Increasing demands for higher student performance in schools (e.g., minimum competency tests, increased graduation requirements, high college entrance requirements) necessitate greater involvement by parents in planning and program development (Turnbull, Turnbull, Shank, & Leal, 1995).

Family participation in the design, implementation, and evaluation of special education programs is a powerful tool in student learning (Male, 1991). Home involvement helps ensure that IEP goals address both current and future learning needs of students. Long-range educational planning, beginning at the preschool level, facilitates the development of instructional programs and classroom support that students need to master skills in academic, social, learning strategy, study, and compensatory areas. Shared decision making helps coordinate school and community services and permits smoother transitions from one setting to another. As transitions are made, families can provide valuable information that can help the team build on knowledge and skills acquired in earlier learning experiences as new goals are formulated.

To facilitate involvement, families need to understand their rights and responsibilities as primary decision makers in approving the education programs and placements for their children. Many families, if they understand and support the educational goals designed for their children and youth, can monitor significant dimensions of student performance away from school settings. This information can provide educators with valuable data regarding students' performance at home, in social settings, and on the job. Family involvement facilitates skill development, self-advocacy, and generalization efforts.

Professionals need to recognize that for a variety of legitimate reasons, some families may choose not to be actively involved on educational planning teams. Many factors such as cultural differences, economic demands, family stress, discomfort with school settings, and other competing needs may limit participation (Correa, 1989; Heron & Harris, 1987). Educators must be sensitive to these demands and supportive of family decisions to limit involvement. Despite limited participation, educators need to provide these families with ongoing information about student progress in both written and oral forms, to facilitate relationships and communication (Correa, 1989). Educators should continue to encourage school participation by parents, guardians, and other members of students' immediate and extended families in various ways (e.g., as performance attendees, open house visitors, volunteers, homework supervisors, support group members) (Turnbull et al., 1995).

ADMINISTRATIVE SUPPORT AND PARTICIPATION

Too often building-level program coordination that exists is the result of "teacher deals" (Biklen, 1985). This occurs when specialty teachers (e.g., LD, speech and language, remedial reading) make time to work with classroom teachers because they believe that teacher collaboration and coordination are necessary to ensure appropriate services for the students they serve. These efforts are largely the result of teachers' commitment, personal style, and expertise (S. Stainback & Stainback, 1996). Biklen (1985) noted that this level of curricular coordination often goes unnoticed and/or unrecognized by key building and division administrators and supervisors.

For inclusive service delivery to be effective, administrative leadership is essential (Friend & Bursuck, 1996; Turnbull et al., 1995). As special education teachers and special education administrators begin to explore the possibility of providing more integrated services, building-level administrators must be involved in initial discussions. Without their participation, the redesign of service-delivery programs will be limited and uneven at best (W. Stainback & Stainback, 1996). As Allington and Johnson (1989) note "any resistance by the principal spells doom to the (mainstreaming) effort" (p. 325).

Administrative involvement is needed to ensure that the faculty receives the information and preparation needed to serve as members of collaborating/consulting teams. Collaborators need administrative support to ensure they have time needed to plan and develop appropriate instructional programs and support services (Friend & Bursuck, 1996; Goldring & Rallis, 1993). Principals can facilitate teacher planning by permitting priority scheduling for collaborating teachers, to ensure common planning time. They can also limit or reduce collaborators' existing assignments, to increase planning time. Many teachers may feel that their current responsibilities and case loads are overwhelming. They may be very reluctant to try new approaches to special education service delivery without additional resources and/or modifications in their present assignments. If this process is merely seen as an "add on" to existing services, it will quickly fail.

SELECTING STRUCTURES TO FACILITATE INCLUSION

The forms of collaboration most appropriate for any given school or division depend upon the goals of the program, population served, characteristics of the setting, beliefs regarding responsibility for challenging students, and the nature of existing interactions between teachers, administrators, and specialists. Collaborative efforts should be tailored to the particular setting and involve all key participants in planning, implementation, and modification stages. Endeavors should build upon existing strengths. For example, if a school has a mentoring program for new teachers in the building, peer collaboration or TATs may be logical extensions of existing efforts to support students with learning and other disabilities in inclusive settings. On the other hand, if resource teachers for students with LD already engage in informal consultation with general educators or the CSRT is firmly established, behavioral or collaborative consultation and/or IATs may enhance what is already being done to support students in the mainstream.

Similarly, student and parent collaboration may be incorporated where appropriate. If students are engaging in informal cooperative experiences within the classroom, extending these experiences through some structured form of cooperative learning or peer tutoring may promote more successful integration of students with learning difficulties. Families can lend support and promote collaborative arrangements in their associations with others.

Educators also need to consider potential barriers. Huefner (1988) suggested a number of barriers that often limit teachers' potential for collaborative planning and instruction. Teachers committed to collaboration and integration will find it challenging as they strive to change their current teaching practices (Friend & Bursuck, 1996; S. Stainback & Stainback, 1996). Many teachers may lack instructional strategies for integrating students with disabilities into mainstream settings (e.g., learning strategies, cooperative learning, peer tutoring); however, they may be reluctant to admit this and ask for assistance. Few teachers possess the knowledge and skills needed to work effectively with other adults (Walther-Thomas et al., 1996). Preservice preparation programs seldom focus on topics such as group problem solving, collaborative planning, cooperative instruction, and staff development (Gable et al., 1987). Some professionals may not believe in the appropriateness of educational integration, adhering to a philosophy that learning problems should be handled outside the general education setting.

The organizational structure of schools often inhibits collaborative ventures. Planning time for teachers is very limited (Walther-Thomas, in press-a). Most teacher time at school is spent in direct contact with students. Teachers report the lack of common planning time as a significant barrier to their efforts to plan and teach together (Johnson, Pugach, & Hammittee, 1988; Nevin, Thousand, Paolucci-Whitcomb, & Villa, 1990).

Despite existing constraints, many educators have found ways to work together to provide an array of direct and indirect services to ensure that their students succeed academically and socially in mainstream classes. By combining their respective expertise, educators provide direct and immediate interventions, as well as develop ongoing structural support for students with learning or behavioral disabilities and for other low-achieving students within mainstream settings. Collaborative planning, implementation, and monitoring expands the alternatives professionals use to develop appropriate programs. Positive changes that result from collaborative instructional planning and implementation have been shown to have positive effects on both student and teacher attitudes (Chalfant & Pysh, 1989; Walther-Thomas, in press-a). The generation of new ideas, problem-solving alternatives, and professional support inherent in collaborative approaches make them personally and professionally attractive to participants (Laycock et al., 1991).

PRINCIPLES OF EFFECTIVE COLLABORATION

To provide appropriate special education services for students with LD within mainstream settings, school teams will change both the content of services students receive and the process by which these services are developed, delivered, and evaluated. The content will emphasize use of effective learning strategies, instructional modifications, and curricular adaptations to maximize student performance in these settings. The process by which content decisions are determined will require collaboration by teachers, administrators, ancillary personnel, parents, and students themselves. For collaborating teams to work together in a positive and productive manner, it is important that members understand and apply basic principles related to effective change, team development, and conflict resolution. This section will outline fundamental points related to these topics.

Changes in Educational Settings

As schools make changes to provide more integrated special education services, it is important to remember that institutional change is a slow and difficult process. Research has shown that the individual attitudes of participants involved in adoption of new innovations gradually change over time (Fullan, 1993; Goldring & Rallis, 1993; Senge, 1994). Significant changes in teacher attitude toward new ideas occur after they see improvements in student performance (Guskey, 1986). This will not happen quickly. Educational research has shown that it takes school systems a minimum of 3 to 5 years to make significant and lasting changes in existing programs (Fullan, 1993; Guskey, 1986). Because educational system change occurs so slowly, it is essential for all participants to understand this process to minimize their inevitable feelings of frustration and discouragement.

Fullan (1993) presented 10 basic assumptions about changes that program planners and implementers need to consider as action plans are developed and monitored. Successful implementation is often dependent on thoughtful analysis of these assumptions.

Participants involved in making significant changes in current practices must first recognize that their own personal version of how things should be is not the only version that should or could be implemented. Participants must stay open to new ideas that will naturally occur as a result of their interaction with other team members. Successful innovation implementation involves ongoing transformation and development of initial ideas.

Second, change is a unique experience for each participant. Collective or institutional attitudes evolve out of individual perceptions. Participants will find their own meanings and interpretations of the process. Feelings of ambiguity, ambivalence, frustration, and uncertainty are a natural part of this process.

Third, conflict and disagreement are fundamental parts of successful change. Because each participant has his or her own ideas about the innovations that are taking shape, developing institutional attitudes will inevitably involve conflict. Successful teams utilize effective problem-solving strategies to deal with conflicts that arise. They do not ignore or avoid these situations but work through them to find appropriate solutions.

Fourth, all participants need positive pressure to change established ways of thinking and behaving. This is true for even the most enthusiastic proponents of the process. Participants also need opportunities to react, to interact, to obtain technical assistance, and to formulate their own positions as they implement changes. Unless participants who fail to change are replaced, the heart of successful institutional change involves the ongoing "resocialization" of team members.

Fifth, because significant change is an evolutionary process, it is helpful to consider the institutionalization of new innovations as a model development process. The model is being shaped and refined by the organization as it is being used.

Sixth, lack of innovation implementation by some team members should not be assumed to be resistance or outright rejection of the proposed changes. It may be the result of various factors, such as inadequate resources, limited support, insufficient elapsed time, ineffective training, or differences in personal and/or professional priorities.

Seventh, many people or groups will not change their current behaviors despite committed efforts to help them do so. Lasting implementation (i.e., institutionalization) of complex innovations is especially difficult within large social systems because individual and collective changes must occur on many levels. Implementation breakdowns along the way will impact the network of change that must occur for these innovations to be sustained over time. Incorporating known assumptions (e.g., positive pressure, sufficient preparation, ongoing support) will help stimulate and nurture changes; however, these motivators do not work for all people.

Eighth, a long-range implementation plan (2 to 3 years minimum) needs to be developed. This plan should reflect effective utilization of existing local resources and should address the potential barriers known to exist.

Ninth, knowledge is never used as the sole determiner for important decisions that are made within social systems. Significant change occurs as a result of a combination of factors that include knowledge, on-the-spot decisions, complex political considerations, and group intuition. Ongoing information sharing about the innovation and changes that are occurring is essential to enable participants to use this knowledge resource effectively as subsequent plans and decisions are made.

Finally, change is a frustrating and discouraging process. If the assumptions listed here are not incorporated into the action plan, do not assume significant implementation of the proposed changes will be achieved.

These assumptions about change may lead the reader to wonder how any lasting change can be accomplished, given the potential obstacles. Yet many exciting innovations in integrated service delivery are becoming institutionalized in various settings because of careful consideration of the nature of change and the people affected by it. Change is inevitable; the challenge is to deal with it in a proactive and effective manner (Fullan, 1993).

Characteristics of Effective Teams

The development of integrated service delivery is dependent on the efforts of teams. Team members work together to design, implement, and evaluate services to ensure their effectiveness. While many successful school-based teams have distinctive qualities that make them unique, common characteristics of effective teams have been identified as essential for productive teamwork (Larson & LaFasto, 1989). As school teams are constituted to provide leadership in integrated service delivery, factors that are recognized as fundamental ingredients need to be addressed.

Effective Teams Share Common Goals.   Goals that are clearly stated and elevating help effective teams define their purposes. Common and valued goals also help focus team energy and direct activities to ensure that these aims are achieved.

Effective Teams Are Results-Driven.   Meaningful data are collected related to team interventions and interactions, and this information is analyzed to help teams evaluate their efforts. Team members are committed to making appropriate changes to increase their effectiveness.

Effective Teams Have Competent Members.   Teams respect and value each member's contributions. They share their own knowledge and expertise with others, and they are receptive to the information that others bring to the team. They are willing and eager to develop new skills to enhance the team's functioning.

Effective Teams Have a Unified Commitment to their Work Together.   Members believe in the value of their work together. They feel that their efforts are productive and beneficial for themselves, for those they represent, and for the larger community.

Effective Teams Work Together in a Collaborative Climate.   Effective teams exhibit mutual problem-solving, professional respect and parity, and shared responsibility for decisions that are made.

Effective Teams Hold High Standards of Excellence.   These teams set high expectations for themselves and for those with whom they work. These expectations are clearly defined and openly discussed. Members are proud of their involvement on the team.

Effective Teams Have Principled Leadership.   Many team leadership responsibilities are often shared. Members follow through on assigned responsibilities in an efficient and effective manner. Representing the team well is a high priority for members.

Effective Teams Receive External Support and Recognition.   The accomplishments of effective teams are respected by peers, supervisors, and other significant individuals and groups. Members receive recognition for their contributions. Administrators and supervisors work with teams to provide them with needed resources.

It should also be noted that effective school teams also believe that all students can succeed in school (Olson & Rodman, 1988). Successful schools are led by professionals who believe that regardless of existing barriers, all students have the right to appropriate education and schools have the responsibility to provide these opportunities for students (Goldring & Rallis, 1993).

Morsink, Thomas, and Correa (1991) cited research that has shown effective teams can develop successful programs in schools where serious problems exist (e.g., poverty, low parent involvement, racial or cultural isolation, drug use). They reported that schools generally attribute the success of these programs to the work of local planning teams rather than to administrative or legislative mandates to provide new services.

Principles of Effective Team Communication

Good communication and mutual trust are essential characteristics of effective school-based teams (Friend & Bursuck, 1996; Morsink et al., 1991). Use of proven communication skills (e.g., reflective listening, brainstorming, negotiation) facilitates the exchange of diverse ideas, perspectives, and positions and enables teams to find appropriate solutions to problems they encounter. As participating members work together effectively and trust in each other, their ability to function as a team increases. These characteristics also foster development of a "collaborative ethic" within teams (Phillips & McCullough, 1990, p. 295). Teams that share this ethic respect each other's contributions to the team and value their membership. They recognize the value in collaborative problem solving. They share mutual responsibility for problemsolving, action plan accountability, and group recognition for effective outcomes from their work together (O'Shea & O'Shea, 1992; Phillips & McCullough, 1990). Consequently, effective teams often become more productive over time.

The importance of effective communication skills has been noted by many advocates of collaboration and integrated service-delivery development (e.g., Friend, 1984; West and Cannon, 1988; Zins, Curtis, Graden, & Ponti, 1988). West and Cannon (1988) surveyed nationally recognized leaders in collaboration to target essential teaming skills. In the area of communication the following skills were identified: effective written and oral skills, appropriate nonverbal behaviors, reflective listening skills, confrontation and conflict resolution strategies, questioning and paraphrasing, self-evaluation, positive reinforcement, problem-solving formats, and giving and receiving feedback.

While educators recognize the importance of good communication, few preparation programs provide sufficient instruction and supervised practice to ensure that education professionals develop essential communication skills needed to be effective collaborators (Jellinek, 1990; Price, 1991). School systems interested in developing integrated service-delivery programs for students with LD need to provide appropriate staff development training and ongoing support to help teams develop effective collaborative problem-solving and decision-making skills. Adequate skill preparation will help teams avoid unnecessary communication breakdowns that often limit the effectiveness of teams (O'Shea & O'Shea, in press).

Conflict within teams is often difficult to address appropriately. As differences in philosophy, values, and ideas emerge among team members, conflict is inevitable. Owens (1987) noted that it is important for teams to understand that conflict is a natural part of the team development process. Members are "constantly engaged in the dynamic process of defining and redefining the nature and extent of their interdependence" (p. 246). New collaborators, unfamiliar with team development and unskilled in conflict resolution, may be discouraged when conflict begins to develop within their teams. Understanding conflict as a natural part of team development can help members deal with it more effectively. Providing teams with the basic skills to manage and resolve conflict allows members to communicate more openly with each other. This, in turn, fosters team trust and enables teams to become more effective in their efforts to solve challenging problems together (Owens, 1987).

Table 10.2 outlines the RESOLVE procedures for conflict resolution. This procedure has been used with interdisciplinary assistance teams to facilitate conflict resolution. The RESOLVE mnemonic embodies the fundamental principles required for effective communication and collaboration.

Effective communication within teams is essentially a two-part process. The first part is basic communication skills development. These skills may have been introduced at the preservice. Their development and application, however, may need to be nurtured as a part of ongoing staff development efforts. The second part of the process is more difficult to achieve because it relates to the attitudes of team members. Effective teams share trust and respect for each other. Trust and respect enable

Table 10.2
RESOLVE: Managing Conflict in Team
Situations

Before conflicts develop:
- Cultivate mutual trust, respect, and role parity among team members.
- Use effective problem-solving and communication skills.
- Anticipate others' needs, interests, and positions.
- Develop effective conflict management skills.

When conflicts occur:
- Stay calm, breathe deeply, and listen with an open mind.
- Separate the problem from the person presenting it.
- If the problem can't be adequately discussed at the present time, schedule a convenient time within the next 24 hours to do so.
- Schedule an appropriate location and sufficient time to discuss the issue fully.

In conflict situations use RESOLVE:

Respond verbally and nonverbally to the other person's feelings and ideas. Use the body basics of good communication (e.g., eye contact, body language, attending behaviors, breathing, facial expressions, vocal tone).

Encourage the other person to share her or his perceptions, feelings, and to propose solutions that will be good for all parties.

Stay focused on finding an appropriate solution—don't get sidetracked by other issues.

Organize your thoughts carefully before the meeting. Be prepared.

Listen responsively (e.g., reflecting, clarifying, paraphrasing) to try to understand the other person's position and try to think of the other person's position.

Voice your belief that conflicts are opportunities to increase understanding and improve relationships. Thank the person(s) for his or her willingness to work with you to resolve the conflict.

End on a positive note with a written plan for implementation, monitoring, and follow-up.

After a conflict has been RESOLVEd:
Follow through on commitments that you make during the conflict resolution session.
Self-evaluate your own behaviors in handling the conflict.
Make changes to increase personal and professional effectiveness.

Note. From *Managing Conflict in Team Situations* by C. S. Walter-Thomas, L. Kounek, and V. K. McLaughlin, 1992. Unpublished training materials Williamsburg, VA: College of William and Mary.

participants to contribute to the team's productivity and benefit from the interactive process. In these team environments, members are more willing to share information, listen to each other's ideas, and formulate new perspectives based on team discussions. Morsink and colleagues (1991) suggested two additional attitudinal characteristics that contribute to team effectiveness: confidentiality and sensitivity to cultural differences. Members must also genuinely value the privacy of all participants. As effective sources of support and problem-solving assistance, members must keep team discussions from others who are not directly involved in implementation of intervention plans. Members must also demonstrate their sensitivity to cultural differences. The attitudes and actions of team members must reflect understanding and appreciation of the differences that exist. Team members need to seek out information and multicultural experiences that will enable them to understand these cultures more fully. This will also enhance communication and will increase the likelihood that proposed student, school, and/or family interventions will be appropriate, given these differences.

 ## *Practical Classroom Applications*

As this chapter has highlighted, there is a strong rationale and there are numerous approaches for integrating students with LD into general education classrooms. Various forms of collaboration can serve to provide structure and support for adults serving students in more inclusive programs. Student needs and site characteristics are of critical importance in developing these collaborative structures to ensure the quality and success of these programs. Following are some considerations that emphasize responsible integration and collaboration in guiding program development.

1. *Planning and scheduling for collaborative relationships are critical to their success.* Participants and administrators must work together to secure the time and resources necessary for effective implementation of collaborative alternatives. Time for planning can be carved out of the school day by combining groups of students for designated activities, using volunteers to supervise students for short periods, or using time before or after school. To develop and sustain meaningful communication, this time must be considered an integral part of professional responsibilities.

2. *Program planning efforts should be collaborative.* All parties who will be affected by changes in service delivery should be involved throughout the process of planning, implementing, and evaluating those changes. Teachers, specialists, administrators, parents, and students need to be informed and invited to participate actively as movement is made toward more integrated service delivery. This dialogue may be accomplished through a series of meetings, roundtable discussions, newsletters and other school or community events. At the classroom level, educators can reach out to other teachers, resources specialists, parents, students, and administrators for ideas and assistance in integrating students with LD more effectively.

3. *Changes toward more integrated and collaborative services should build on and be compatible with existing efforts in school settings.* In schools where special education re-

(continued)

source teachers or other specialists already engage in informal consultation, collaborative or behavioral consultation may be a natural extension of their roles. Schools that have established mentoring programs may find peer collaboration and TAT to be helpful enhancements of mentoring efforts. CSRT may spend more of their meeting time assisting teachers with students in the classroom setting. Similarly, departmental or grade-level teams that typically conduct business on an informal basis may decide to follow the more structured format described for the TAT model. Given time constraints, new teams may also be developed to serve in a more assistive and supportive role. General education teachers who already have a solid working relationship with their special education counterparts or resource specialists may wish to try coteaching on a limited basis, as a step toward more integrated and longer-term coteaching relationships.

4. *Alternative structures for collaboration and strategies for integration may be combined to meet a range of student and teacher needs.* Various collaborative structures and classroom integration strategies can be combined to meet a range of student and teacher needs. For example, assistance teams may operate at the school level, as teachers engage in coteaching at the classroom level. In those same classrooms, a variety of peer tutoring and cooperative learning activities may be occurring.

5. *Sufficient preparation and ongoing support are essential to successful collaboration.* Effective communication and problem-solving skills are essential to collaborative service delivery. In addition, adequate staff development in models and processes of collaboration, program planning and evaluation, and instructional techniques provide educators with the tools they need to promote integration. Administrators should work with school personnel to identify priorities and develop a long-range plan to provide them with needed training to be successful in their efforts.

6. *The change process should be considered by innovators as they implement changes toward more integrated service delivery.* Meaningful and lasting changes occur slowly, involve conflicts, and require all participants to work through and have an active voice in shaping the changes. Moving slowly and building on successes help to ensure a firm foundation for further innovation.

SUMMARY

- The trend toward placing students with learning disabilities in mainstream programs has been evident over the past two decades. Many school systems are re-examining current service delivery and developing new and innovative classroom intervention programs to reach more students.

- Promising instructional practices and collaborative service-delivery structures encourage teamwork, effective problem solving, and greater educational inclusion of students with identified LD and those at risk for school failure.

- Few systems provide teachers with opportunities to develop collegial relationships, monitor student progress outside their own classrooms, and explore alternative approaches to instruction, practice, and evaluation.

- The debate regarding the REI forced critical examination of the role of special education and its relationship with general education.

- Because of the move toward more inclusive special education services, it is likely that teachers of students with LD will see their roles as collaborators and consultants expanding in the future. To be effective in these new roles, teachers need to be skilled in both the content and process of effective collaboration.

- Many service-delivery approaches have emerged that provide more classroom support for students with disabilities and other students at risk for failure. These approaches are all based on professional collaboration and classroom consultation.

- Students and families play important roles in implementing school-based service-delivery changes to foster inclusion. Administrative leadership is essential.

- Collaborative efforts should be tailored to the particular setting and involve all key participants in planning, implementation, and modification stages.

- School systems interested in developing integrated service-delivery programs for students with learning disabilities need to provide appropriate staff development training and ongoing support to help teams develop effective collaborative problem-solving and decision-making skills.

- Alternative service-delivery approaches depend on collaboration among general education and special education professionals, parents, and students, as well as related service providers.

DISCUSSION QUESTIONS

To help extend your understanding, reflect on and discuss the following questions:

1. In reflecting on your own beliefs regarding collaboration, are your teamwork, problem solving, and philosophy on educational inclusion of students with identified LD and those at risk for school failure congruent with local, state, and federal recommendations? Why or why not?

2. How did your undergraduate program prepare you in working with other professionals who assist students with LD?

3. What, if any, changes would you suggest in your undergraduate program to prepare you for your current role with students with LD?

4. How are you involved in your local area in re-examining current service delivery and in developing new and innovative classroom intervention programs for students with LD?

5. How will your role, as a teacher of students with LD who will collaborate and consult with parents and administrators, expand in the future?

6. Do inclusion practices occur in your local area? How?

REFERENCES

Adamson, G., & Van Etten, G. (1972). Zero reject model revisited: A workable alternative. *Exceptional Children, 38,* 735–738.

Algozzine, B., & Ysseldyke, J. E. (1981). Special education for normal children: Better safe than sorry? *Exceptional Children, 46,* 238–243.

Allington, R. L., & Johnson, P. (1989). Coordination, collaboration, and consistency: The redesign of compensatory and special education interventions. In R. E. Slavin, N. L. Karweit, & N. A. Maddin (Eds.), *Effective programs for students at-risk.* Needham, MA: Allyn and Bacon.

Babcock, N. L., & Pryzwansky, W. B. (1983). Models of consultation: Preferences of education professionals at five stages of services. *Journal of School Psychology, 21,* 356–359.

Bass, B. M., & Avolio, B. J. (1994). *Improving organizational effectiveness through transformational leadership.* Thousand Oaks, CA: Sage.

Bauwens, J., & Hourcade, J. J. (1995). *Cooperative teaching: Rebuilding the schoolhouse for all students.* Austin, TX: PRO-ED.

Bauwens, J., Hourcade, J. J., & Friend, M. (1989). Cooperative teaching: A model for general and special education integration. *Remedial and Special Education, 10*(2), 17–22.

Bempechat, J., & Ginsburg, H. P. (1989). *Underachievement and educational disadvantage: The home and school experiences of at-risk youth.* Urban Diversity Series No. 99. Washington, DC: Office of Educational Research and Improvement.

Biklen, D. (1985). *Achieving the complete school: Strategies for effective mainstreaming.* New York: Teachers College.

Blankenship, C. S. (1985). Using curriculum-based assessment data to make instructional decisions. *Exceptional Children, 52*(3), 233–238.

Bodner, J. R., Clark, G. M., & Mellard, D. F. (1987). *State graduation practices related to high school special education programs.* Alexandria, VA: ERIC (ERIC Document Reproduction Service No. ED 294–347).

Brandt, R. (1987). Learning with and from one another. *Educational Leadership, 44*(5), 3.

Brophy, J. (1986). Research linking teacher behavior to student achievement: Potential implications for Chapter I students. In B. I. Williams, P. A. Richmond, & B. J. Mason (Eds.), *Designs for compensatory education: Conference proceedings and papers* (pp. 121–179). Washington, DC: Research and Evaluation Associates.

Caplan, G. (1970). *The theory and practice of mental health consultation.* New York: Basic.

Carlberg, C., & Kavale, K. (1980). The efficacy of special versus regular class placement for exceptional children: A meta-analysis. *Journal of Special Education, 14,* 295–309.

Chalfant, J. C., & Pysh, M. (1989). Teacher assistance teams: Five descriptive studies of 96 teams. *Remedial and Special Education, 10*(6), 49–58.

Chalfant, J. C., Pysh, M., & Moultrie, R. (1979). Teacher assistance teams: A model for within-building problem solving. *Learning Disability Quarterly, 2,* 85–96.

Congress of the United States. (1987). *U.S. children and their families: Current conditions and recent trends.* (House Select Committee on Children, Youth, and Families; Stock No. 052–070–06299–1), Washington, DC: U.S. Government Printing Office.

Conoley, J. C., & Conoley, C. W. (1988). *School consultation: A guide to training and practice.* New York: Pergamon.

Correa, V. C. (1989). Involving culturally diverse families in the education of their limited English proficient handicapped and at-risk children. In S. Fradd & M. J. Weismmantel (Eds.), *Bilingual and bilingual special education: An administrator's handbook* (pp. 130–144). San Diego, CA: College-Hill.

Deno, E. (1970). Special education as developmental capital. *Exceptional Children, 37,* 229–237.

Deno, E. (1973). *Instructional alternatives for exceptional children.* Reston, VA: Council for Exceptional Children.

Deshler, D. D., Ellis, E. S., & Lenz, B. K. (1996). *Teaching adolescents with learning disabilities* (2nd ed.). Denver, CO: Love.

Deshler, D., & Schumaker, J. (1986), Learning strategies: An instructional alternative for low-achieving adolescents. *Exceptional Children, 52,* 583–590.

Dorfman, C. (1988). *Youth indicators 1988: Trends in the well-being of American youth.* Washington, DC: U.S. Government Printing Office.

Duany, L., & Pittman, K. (1990). *Latino youths at a crossroads. Adolescent pregnancy prevention clearinghouse report.* Washington, DC: Children's Defense Fund.

Dunn, L. M. (1968). Special education for the mildly retarded—Is much of it justifiable? *Exceptional Children, 35* (1), 5–22.

Edgar, E. (1987). Secondary programs in special education: Are many of them justifiable? *Exceptional Children, 53,* 555–561.

Edgar, E. (1988). Employment as an outcome for mildly handicapped students: Current status and future directions. *Focus on Exceptional Students, 21* (1), 1–8.

Evans, S. B. (1991). A realistic look at the research base for collaboration in special education. *Preventing School Failure, 35* (4), 10–13.

Feistritzer, C. E. (1987). Schools learn a lesson. *American Demographics, 9* (11), 42–43.

Fernandez, J. A. (1991). From the superintendent's perspective. In J. H. Hansen & E. Liftin (Eds.), *School restructuring: A practitioner's guide.* Swampscott, MA: Watersun Publishing.

Friend, M. (1984). Consultation skills for resource teachers. *Learning Disabilities Quarterly, 7,* 246–250.

Friend, M., & Bursuck, W. (1996). *Including students with special needs: A practical guide for classroom teachers.* Boston: Allyn and Bacon.

Friend, M., & Cook, L. (1992). *Interactions: Collaborative skills for school professionals.* New York: Longman.

Fuchs, L. S., & Deno, S. L. (1991). Paradigmatic distinctions between instructionally relevant measurement models. *Exceptional Children, 57,* 488–500.

Fuchs, D., & Fuchs, L. S. (1992). Limitations of a feel-good approach to consultation. *Journal of Educational and Psychological Consultation, 3* (2), 93–97.

Fullan, M. (1993). *Change forces.* London: Falmer Press.

Gable, R. A., Friend, M., Laycock, V. K., & Hendrickson, J. M. (1990). Interview skills for problem identification in school consultation. *Preventing School Failure, 35* (1), 5–10.

Gable, R. A., Young, C. C., & Hendrickson, J. M. (1987). Content of special education teacher preparation: Are we headed in the right direction? *Teacher Education and Special Education, 10,* 135–139.

Galagan, J. E. (1985). Psychological testing: Turn out the lights, the party is over. *Exceptional Children, 52,* 288–299.

Gerber, M. M. (1987). Applications of cognitive-behavioral training methods to teaching basic skills to mildly handicapped elementary school students. In M. C. Wang, M. C. Reynolds, & H. J. Walberg, (Eds.), *Handbook of special education: Research and practice* (Vol. 1, pp. 167–186). Oxford, England: Pergamon.

Germann, G., & Tindal, G. (1985). An application of curriculum-based assessment: The use of direct and repeated measurement. *Exceptional Children, 52* (3), 244–265.

Glaser, W. (1986). *Control theory in the classroom.* New York: Harper & Row.

Goldring, E. B., & Rallis, S. F. (1993). *Principals of dynamic schools: Taking charge of change.* Newbury Park, CA: Corwin.

Graden, J. L. (1989). Redefining "prereferral" intervention assistance: Collaboration between general and special education. *Exceptional Children, 56,* 227–231.

Graden, J. L., Casey, A., & Christenson, S. L. (1985). Implementing a prereferral intervention system, Part I: The model. *Exceptional Children, 51,* 377–384.

Gresham, F. M., & Kendell, G. K. (1987). School consultation research: Methodological critique and future directions. *School Psychology Review, 16* (3), 306–316.

Guskey, T. R. (1986). Staff development and the process of teacher change. *Educational Researcher, 5,* 5–11.

Hagerty, G. J., & Abramson, J. (1987). Impediments to implementing national policy change for mildly handicapped students. *Exceptional Children, 53,* 315–323.

Hallahan, D. P., Kaufman, J. M., Lloyd, J. W., & McKinney, J. D. (1988). Introduction to the series: Questions about the regular education initiative. *Journal of Learning Disabilities, 21* (1), 3–5.

Hallahan, D. P., Keller, C. E., McKinney, J. D., Lloyd, J. W., & Bryan, T. (1988). Examining the research base of the regular education initiative: Efficacy studies and the adaptive learning environments model. *Journal of Learning Disabilities, 21,* 29–35.

Hammond, J., & Foster, K. (1987). Creating a professional learning partnership. *Educational Leadership, 44* (5) 42–44.

Haring, K. A., Lovett, D. L., & Smith, D. D. (1990). A follow-up study of recent special education graduates of learning disabilities programs. *Journal of Learning Disabilities, 23* (2), 108–113.

Hayek, R. A. (1987). The teacher assistance team: A preferral support system. *Focus on Exceptional Children, 20* (1), 1–7.

Helge, D. (1988). Serving at-risk populations in rural America. *Teaching Exceptional Children, 20* (4), 29–31.

Heron, T. E., & Harris, K. C. (1987). *The educational consultant: Helping professionals, parents, and mainstreamed students.* Austin TX: PRO-ED.

Hodgkinson, H. L. (1993). American education: The good, the bad, and the task. *Phi Delta Kappan, 74,* 619–623.

Huefner, D. S. (1988). The consulting teacher model: Risks and opportunities. *Exceptional Children, 54,* 403–414.

Idol, L. (1989). The resource/consulting teacher: An integrated model of service delivery. *Remedial and Special Education, 10* (6), 38–48.

Idol, L., Paolucci-Whitcomb, P., & Nevin, A. (1986). *Collaborative consultation.* Austin, TX: PRO-ED.

Inman, D., Pribesh, S. L., & Salganik, L. H. (1990). *Summary profiles: State education indicators systems.* Paper presented for the Special Study Panel on Educational Indicators. Washington, DC: Pelavin.

Jellinek, M. S. (1990). School consultation: Evolving issues. *Journal of the American Academy of Child and Adolescent Psychiatry, 29,* 311–314.

Jenkins, J., & Jenkins, L. (1985). Peer tutoring in elementary and secondary programs. *Focus on Exceptional Children, 17* (6), 1–12.

Johnson, D. W., & Johnson, R. T. (1986). Mainstreaming and cooperative learning strategies. *Exceptional Children, 52* (6) 553–561.

Johnson, D. W., Johnson, R. T., Holubec, E., & Roy, P. (1984). *Circles of learning.* Arlington, VA: Association of Supervision and Curriculum Development.

Johnson, L. J., Pugach, M. C., & Hammittee, D. J. (1988). Barriers to effective special education consultation. *Remedial Special Education, 9* (6), 41–47.

Joyce, B. R. (1990). *Changing school culture through staff development.* Alexandria, VA.: Association for Supervision and Curriculum Development.

Joyce, B. R., & Showers, B. (1983). *Power in staff development through research on training.* Alexandria, VA: Association for Supervision and Curriculum Development.

Kagan, S. (1994). *Cooperative learning* (2nd ed.). San Juan Capistrano, CA: Kagan Cooperative Learning.

Kaufman, J. M., Gerber, M. M., & Semmel, M. I. (1988). Arguable assumptions underlying the regular education initiative. *Journal of Learning Disabilities, 21* (1), 6–11.

Keogh, B. K. (1988). Improving services for problem learners: Rethinking the restructuring. *Journal of Learning Disabilities, 21* (1), 19–22.

Korinek, L., & McLaughlin, V. L. (1996). *Preservice intervention assistance teaming project.* Unpublished manuscript.

Korinek, L., McLaughlin, V. L., & Walther-Thomas, C. S. (1995). Least restrictive environment and collaboration: A bridge over troubled water. *Preventing School Failure, 39* (3), 6–12.

Larson, C. E., & LaFasto, F. M. J. (1989). *Teamwork.* Beverly Hills, CA: Sage.

Laycock, V. K., Korinek, L., & Gable, R. A. (1991). Alternative structures for collaboration in the delivery of special services. *Preventing School Failure, 35* (4), 15–18.

Lilly, M. S. (1970). Special education: A tempest in a teapot. *Exceptional Children, 37,* 43–49.

Lilly, M. S. (1986). The relationship between general and special education: A new face on an old issue. *Counterpoint, 6* (1), 10.

Lilly, M. S. (1988). The regular education initiative: A force for change in general and special education. *Education and Training of the Mentally Retarded, 23,* 253–260.

Lipsky, D., & Gartner, A. (1989). *Beyond separate education: Quality education for all.* Baltimore: Brookes.

Lloyd, J. W., Crowley, E. P., Kohler, F. W., & Strain,

P. S. (1988). Redefining the applied research agenda: Cooperative learning, prereferral, teacher consultation, and peer-mediated interventions. *Journal of Learning Disabilities, 20* (1), 43–52.

Maheady, L., & Algozzine, B. (1991). The regular education initiative—Can we proceed in an orderly and scientific manner? *Teacher Education and Special Education, 14* (1), 66–73.

Maheady, L., Harper, G. F., Mallet, B., & Sacca, M. K. (1989). *Opportunity to learn prosocial behavior: Its potential role in the assessment and instruction of behavior disordered students.* Paper presented at the CEC/CCBD Topical Conference on Behavior Disordered Youth. Charlotte, NC.

Male, M. (1991). Effective team participation. *Preventing School Failure, 35* (4), 29–36.

McKenzie, H. S., Egner, A. N., Knight, M. F., Perelman, P. F., Schneider, B. M., & Garvin, J. S. (1970). Training consulting teachers in the management and education of handicapped children. *Exceptional Children, 37,* 137–143.

McKinney J. D., & Hocutt, A. M. (1988). The need for policy analysis in evaluating the regular education initiative. *Journal of Learning Disabilities, 21,* 12–18.

Mercer, C. D., & Mercer, A. R. (1996). *Teaching students with learning disabilities* (5th ed.). New York: Macmillan.

Merriam, S. B. (1991). *Case study research in education: A qualitative approach.* San Francisco: Jossey-Bass.

Mithaug, D., Horiuchi, C., & Fanning, P. (1985). A report on the Colorado statewide follow-up survey of special education students. *Exceptional Children, 51,* 397–404.

Morsink, C. V., Thomas, C. C., & Correa, V. I. (1991). *Interactive teaming: Consultation and collaboration in special programs.* New York: Macmillan.

National Center on Educational Outcomes (1993). *Educational outcomes and indicators for students completing school.* Minneapolis, MN: University of Minnesota.

National Committee on Excellence in Education. (1983). *A nation at-risk: The imperative for educational reform.* Washington, DC: U.S. Government Printing Office.

Nevin, A., Thousand, J., Paolucci-Whitcomb, P., & Villa, R. (1990). Collaborative consultation: Empowering public school personnel to provide heterogeneous school for all—or, who rang the bell? *Journal of Educational and Psychological Consulting, 1,* 41–67.

Olson, L., & Rodman, B. (1988, June 22). The unfinished agenda, part II. *Education Week,* 17–33.

Ornstein, A., & Levine, D. (1989). Social class, race, and school achievement: Problems and prospects. *Journal of Teacher Education, 40* (5), 17–23.

Orum, L. S. (1986). *The education of Hispanics: Status and implications.* Washington, DC: National Council of La Raza. (ERIC Document Reproduction Service No. ED 299 266).

O'Shea, D. J., & O'Shea, L. J. (1992). School-based conferences: Types, processes, and content. *Learning Disability Forum, 17,* 17–24.

O'Shea, D. J., & O'Shea, L. J. (in press). Collaboration and school reform: A twenty-first century prospective. *Journal of Learning Disabilities: Special Series: Collaboration and School Reform Practices in the Twenty-First Century.*

O'Shea, L. J., O'Shea, D. J., & Algozzine, B. (1989). The regular education initiative in the U.S.: What is its relevance to the integration movement in Australia? *International Journal of Disability, Development, and Education, 36* (1), 5–14.

O'Shea, L. J., & Valcante, G. (1986). A comparison over time of relative discrepancy scores of low achievers. *Exceptional Children, 53,* 253–259.

Owens, R. B. (1987). *Organizational behavior in education,* (3rd ed.) Upper Saddle River, NJ: Prentice Hall.

Palinscar, A. S., & Brown, D. A. (1987). Enhancing instructional time through attention to metacognition. *Journal of Learning Disabilities, 20,* 66–75.

Phillips, V., & McCullough, L. (1990). Consultation-based programming: Instituting the collaborative ethic in schools. *Exceptional Children, 56,* 291–304.

Price, J. P. (1991). Effective communication: A key to successful collaboration. *Preventing School Failure, 35* (4), 25–28.

Pryzwansky, W. B. (1974). A reconsideration of the consultation model for delivery of school-based psychological services. *American Journal of Orthopsychiatry, 44,* 579–583.

Pryzwansky, W. B., & White, G. W. (1983). The influence of consultee characteristics on preferences for consultation approaches. *Professional Psychology: Research and Practice, 14,* 651–657.

Pugach, M. (1987). The national education reports and special education: Implications for teacher education. *Exceptional Children,53* (4), 308–314.

Pugach, M. C., & Johnson, L. J. (1995). *Collaborative practitioners: Collaborative schools.* Denver, CO: Love.

Putnam, J. (1993). *Cooperative learning and strategies for inclusion.* Baltimore: Brookes.

Reynolds, M. C. (1989). An historical perspective: The delivery of special education to mildly disabled and at-risk students. *Remedial and Special Education, 10* (6), 7–11.

Salend, S. J. (1984). Factors contributing to the development of successful mainstreaming programs. *Exceptional Children, 50,* 409–416.

Schein, E. H. (1969). *Process consultation: Its role in organizational development.* Reading, MA: Addison-Wesley.

Schumaker, J. B., & Deshler, D. D. (1988). Implementing the regular education initiative in secondary schools: A different ball game. *Journal of Learning Disabilities, 21* (1), 36–42.

Senge, P. (1994). *The fifth discipline fieldbook.* New York: Currency.

Shepard, L. A., (1987). The new push for excellence: Widening the schism between regular and special education. *Exceptional Children, 53,* 327–329.

Sitlington, P. L., Frank, A. R., & Carson, R. (1992). Adult adjustment among high school graduates with mild disabilities. *Exceptional Children, 59,* 221–233.

Slavin, R. E., Karweit, N. L., & Madden, N. A. (1989). *Effective programs for students at-risk.* Needham Heights, MA: Allyn and Bacon.

Stainback, S., & Stainback, W. (1996). *Inclusion: A guide to educators.* Baltimore: Brookes.

Stainback, W., & Stainback, S. (1984). A rationale for the merger of special and regular education. *Exceptional Children,* 51, 102–111.

Stainback, W., & Stainback, S. (1996). *Controversial issues confronting special education: Divergent perspectives* (2nd ed.). Boston: Allyn and Bacon.

Stevens, L. J., & Price, M. (1992). Meeting the challenge of educating children at-risk. *Phi Delta Kappan, 74,* 18–23.

Tharp, R. (1975). The triadic model of consultation. In C. Parker (Ed.), *Psychological consultation in the schools: Helping teachers meet special needs* (pp. 131–151). Reston, VA: The Council for Exceptional Children.

Thousand, J. S., Villa, R. A., & Nevin, A. I. (Eds). (1994). *Creativity and collaborative learning: A practical guide to empowering students and teachers.* Baltimore: Brookes.

Turnbull, A. P., Turnbull, H. R., III, Shank, M., & Leal, D. (1995). *Exceptional lives.* Upper Saddle River, NJ: Merrill/Prentice Hall.

U.S. Department of Education (1995). *Seventeenth annual report to Congress on the implementation of the Individuals with Disabilities Education Act.* Washington, DC: Office of Special Education Programs.

Villa, R. A., & Thousand, J. S. (1995). *Creating an inclusive school.* Alexandria, VA: Association for Supervision and Curriculum Development.

Villa, R. A., Thousand, J. S., Stainback, W., & Stainback, S. (1992). *Restructuring for caring and effective education.* Baltimore: Brookes.

Wagner, M. & Shaver, D. M. (1989). *Educational programs and achievements of secondary special education students: Findings from the National Longitudinal Transition Study.* Menlo Park, CA: SRI International.

Walther-Thomas, C. S. (in press-a). Co-teaching teams: Benefits and problems teachers and administrators report over time. *Journal of Learning Disabilities.*

Walther-Thomas, C. S. (in press-b). Inclusion and teaming: Including all students in the mainstream. In T. Dickinson & T. Erb (Eds.), *Interdisciplinary teaming at the middle level.* Columbus, OH: National Middle School Association.

Walther-Thomas, C. S. (1990). *State mandated outcomes assessment of students with mild disabilities.* Unpublished dissertation. Lawrence, KS: University of Kansas.

Walther-Thomas, C. S., Bryant, M., & Land, S. (1996). Co-planning: The key to effective co-teaching. *Remedial and Special Education, 17,* 255–265.

Walther-Thomas, C. S., Korinek, L., & McLaughlin, V. K. (1992). *Managing conflict in team situations: RESOLVE.* Unpublished training materials. Williamsburg, VA: College of William & Mary.

Wang, M. C., & Birch, J. W. (1984). Comparison of a full-time mainstreaming program and a resource room approach. *Exceptional Children, 51*, 33–40.

Wang, M. C., Gennari, P., & Waxman, H. C. (1985). The adaptive learning environments model: Design, implementation, and effects. In M. C. Wang & H. J. Walberg (Eds.), *Adapting instruction to individual differences*. Berkeley, CA: McCutchan.

Wegner, R. D. (1979). Teacher response to collaborative consultation. *Psychology in the Schools, 16*(1), 127–131.

West, J. F. (1990). Educational collaboration in the restructuring of schools. *Journal of Education and Psychological Consultation, 1*(1), 23–40.

West, J. F., & Cannon, G. (1988). Essential collaboration consultation competencies for regular and special educators. *Journal of Learning Disabilities, 21*, 56–63.

Wiederholt, J. L. (1989). Restructuring special education services: The past, the present, the future. *Learning Disability Quarterly, 12*(3), 181–191.

Wiederholt, J. L., & Chamberlin, S. P. (1989). A critical analysis of resource programs. *Remedial and Special Education, 10*(6), 15–37.

Will, M. C. (1986). Educating children with learning problems: A shared responsibility. *Exceptional Children, 52*, 411–415.

Williams, B. F. (1992). Changing demographics: Challenges for Educators. *Intervention in School and Clinic, 27*(3), 157–163.

Winget, P. (1988). Special education/general education is a team effort. *The Special Edge, 2*(5), 1, 6.

Wolock, I., & Horowitz, B. (1984). Child maltreatment as a social problem: The neglect of neglect. *American Journal of Orthopsychiatry, 54*, 530–543.

Ysseldyke, J. E., Algozzine, B., Thurlow, M. L. (1991). *Critical issues in special education*. Boston: Houghton Mifflin.

Zigmond, N. (1992). Keynote address. Annual meeting of the Virginia Council for Learning Disabilities (VCLD), Roanoke, VA.

Zigmond, N. & Thornton, H. (1985). Follow-up of postsecondary-age learning disabled graduates and drop-outs. *Learning Disabilities Research, 1*, 50–55.

Zins, J., Curtis, M., Graden, J., & Ponti, C. (1988). *Helping students succeed in the regular classroom*. San Francisco: Jossey-Bass.

The most important group to students with learning disabilities is the family.

CHAPTER 11

Family Research and Practices

In this chapter we will . . .

- Frame the historical perspective germane to family knowledge, skills, and involvement.

- Provide a chronology of family issues.

- Illustrate the vast diversity and influence families represent.

- Analyze how professionals' family knowledge, skills, and involvement helps children, families, and school personnel.

- Identify family definitions and compositions.

- Compare and contrast family theories, discussing each theory's prominence throughout history.

- Identify practical implications for students with LD.

- Summarize issues related to economical, social, and political variables influencing families historically.

- Identify teachers' roles with families.

- Discuss why family research, policies, and practices hold importance to all professionals involved with students with LD.

- Conclude with a listing of teachers' skills and competencies necessary to work with students' families in advocacy, assessment, collaboration, curriculum, legal procedures, programming, and transition roles.

There are many assumptions that frame the historical perspective provided in this chapter. These assumptions, illustrated in Table 11.1, relate to the importance of family, cross-discipline knowledge and skills, and coadvocacy in the teaching of students with LD.

The most important group to students with LD is the family. All individuals develop initial knowledge of themselves, their communities, and the world by implicit links to individuals who live with them and who will, in most cases, be known to them throughout their lives. Students learn their attitudes, beliefs, and understandings from their parents, siblings, and other family members with whom they interact (Broderick, 1993; Ingoldsby, 1995; Sprey, 1990). Teachers and peers may sway students during critical life points, but students' families carry primary lifetime weight.

Table 11.1
Family Importance, Cross-Discipline Knowledge, and Coadvocacy Links

Family Importance	Cross-Discipline Knowledge and Skills	Professional and Family Coadvocacy Links
Initial Knowledge of Self, Community, and the World:	*Anthropology:*	*Homes:*
Abilities	Family Societies	Parents
Achievement	Historical Families	Siblings
Community Interests	*Biology:*	Grandparents
Community Needs	Biochemical Effects	Aunts
Self-Advocacy	Neurological Variables	Uncles
Self-Esteem	*Genetics:*	Cousins
Self-Strengths	Genetic Influences	Neighbors
Volunteerism	Family Histories	*Schools:*
Attitudes, Beliefs, and Understandings from Parents, Siblings, and Other Members:	Family Trait	Administrators
	Mental Health:	Teachers
	External Family Effect	Counselors
	Internal Families	Family Therapists
	Member's Needs	Paraprofessionals
Cultural Background	*Medicine:*	Psychologists
Empathy for Others	Infant Physical Needs	Social Workers
Ethnic Understandings	Child Physical Needs	School Nurse
Family Traditions	Teen Physical Needs	Vocational Educators
Family Customs	Adult Physical Needs	*Communities:*
Lifetime Influences:	Therapies	Agency Workers
Preschool Years	Medications	Business Leaders
Elementary School	*Psychology:*	Employers
Middle School	Assessments	Lawyers
High School	Treatments	Leisure Therapists
Young Adult	*Teaching:*	Physicians
Middle Adult	Assessments	Social Workers
Aging Adult	Interventions	Religious Leaders
	Sociology:	Politicians
	Community Resources	
	Family Resources	

Family knowledge and skills are important across professions. Various aspects of family life historically have engaged the attention of medical researchers and practitioners, including biologists, geneticists, mental health therapists, pediatricians, and psychiatrists (Paul & Simeonsson, 1993). Further, because of family significance to an individual's psychological and social functioning, family interactions traditionally attracted interest among anthropologists, psychologists, and sociologists (Adams, 1986; Beavers & Hampson, 1990; Paul & Simeonsson, 1993; Strickland, 1993). While there were limitations to family and teacher involvement during the 19th and 20th centuries (e.g., economic necessities forcing long work hours, taking members away from the home), currently, family knowledge, skills, and involvement are teachers' critical priorities when they work with students with LD.

Successful learning requires coadvocacy. School and teacher effectiveness cannot generalize without links to students' homes and communities (Heid & Harris, 1989; Turnbull & Turnbull, 1986, 1990; Shea & Bauer, 1991; Strickland, 1993). Teachers and families assume advocacy roles as they link students' past, current, and future homes, communities, and schools. Cowork of professionals and parents leads to more fruitful outcomes. For example, during the last 40 years, professionals and parents together have spearheaded movements resulting in a number of legislative mandates and regulations emerging from the combined advocacy struggles. Included were the importance of the right to education for all students, family involvement in educational decision making, the need to address technological advances and learning, and opportunities affecting quality of life.

Professionals can help to establish the necessary experiences upon which to build positive programming for their diverse students with LD. One way to begin is by developing an understanding of what families are, of teachers' historic and future roles with families, and of the skills and competencies necessary to assist families.

FAMILIES

Clearly, all professionals in the LD field require updated knowledge and skills, especially as family diversity proliferates. The very nature of diversity implies that families assume many forms (Adams, 1986; Correa, 1989; Hanson, 1993; Smith, 1995). The ethnic backgrounds, cultural heritage, primary and secondary languages, religious preferences, and social histories of students represent this diversity, as do home customs and community practices (e.g., various ways students celebrate birthdays, holiday functions, family habits, or cultural traditions). Diversity is apparent in the many family definitions and compositions comprising home life and households.

Family Definitions and Compositions

Generally speaking, a *family* is two or more individuals who live together and are related to one another by blood or marriage. Included are husband/wife households (with or without children present) and single-parent households (usually the mother and always with children present) (Adams, 1986). A *household* is one or more people who may or may not be related but who maintain a separate living unit together. Households include husband/wife and other family compositions, but also include

Table 11.2
Examples of Diverse Family Households

Household: One or more people who may or may not be related but who maintain a separate living unit.
Husband and Wife
Father-Mother-Child
Persons Related by a Sharing Process
Descent Groups (e.g., Father-Mother-Child-Grandparents)
Adoptive Families
One-Parent Families (e.g., Single Mother; Single Father)
Remarriage Families (e.g., Father-Mother-Step Brothers)
Cohabitant Units (e.g., Female Renters)
Gay Families (e.g., Lesbians-Child)
Roommates
Single Person

individuals living alone or with roommates (Bureau of the Census, 1992). Table 11.2 below summarizes diverse family households.

Historically, the term family has been ambiguous and has had multiple meanings (Aries, 1962; Whall, 1986). For example, before the 18th century no European language had a term for the mother-father-children grouping. The meaning from the Latin cognate *familia*, from a common Indo-European word signifying *house*, persisted from Roman times throughout the Middle Ages into the modern period: the people living in a house, including servants and slaves. Aries (1962) published an historical overview of family life, reporting that family life components, including childhood occurring as a distinct phase of life, received little recognition until the late 17th century. However, after this time, children became the center of the family.

Early Greek philosophers, including Plato and Aristotle, called attention to the importance people's experiences play in personal development. For example, early Greek and Roman parents trained children to be of value to society and tried to walk the fine line between discipline and love (Borstelmann, 1983). However, societal views of families and children's place in families underwent continuing change in the centuries that followed (Stever, 1994).

In the 20th century, social scientists examined various family definitions and compositions. For example, Murdock (1949) defined family as a social group characterized by common residence, economic cooperation, and reproduction. The definition also included adults of both sexes, at least two of whom maintained a socially approved sexual relationship, and one or more children, owned or adopted, of the sexually cohabiting adults. Stephens (1963) viewed the family as a social arrangement based on marriage and a marriage contract, including recognition of the rights and duties of parenthood, common residence for husband, wife, and children, and reciprocal economic obligations between husband and wife. Winch (1979) suggested that the family is a group of related persons in differentiated family positions, such as husband and wife or parent and child. Members fulfill the functions necessary to ensure family survival. Functions include reproduction, child socialization, and emotional gratification. Whall (1986) identified a number of aspects to the family definition, first postulating the family as the environment of a single individual. The second places emphasis on the interaction between individual family members, and the family is thus viewed as a group of interacting dyads, triads, and so forth. Third, a single unit or one group that thinks, feels, and acts in given ways defines a family, and fourth, a unit which interacts and transacts with its exterior environment underscores a family definition.

Lull (1988), further, defined families in terms of composition or type. Thus, persons related by a sharing process (e.g., the same roof, food, culture, money, possessions, or emotions) may constitute a family. Family types, also, may include de-

Table 11.3
Family Definitions and Researchers
Supporting the Definition

Family Definition	Researchers
A family is two or more individuals who live together and are related to one another by blood or marriage.	Adams, 1986
A family is a social group characterized by common residence, economic cooperation, and reproduction.	Murdock, 1949
A family is a social arrangement based on marriage and a marriage contract.	Stephens, 1963
A family is a group of related persons in differentiated family positions and functions.	Winch, 1979
A family is: The environment of a single individual; A group of interacting dyads, triads, etc.; A single unit or one group which thinks, feels, and acts in given ways; and A unit which interacts and transacts with its exterior environment.	Whall, 1986
A family is persons related by a sharing process.	Lull, 1988
A family is a single adult in a household with the presence of a dependent child or adult.	Popenoe, 1993
A family is a view of multiple variations on family expectations and family life.	Doherty, Boss, LaRossa, Schumm, & Steinmetz, 1993; Smith, 1995; Sprey, 1990

scent groups, adoptive families, one-parent families, remarriage families, cohabiting units, and gay and lesbian families. Popenoe (1993) accepted that there may be a single adult leading the household but a family requires the presence of a dependent child or adult. Modern family researchers (Doherty, Boss, LaRossa, Schumm, & Steinmetz, 1993; Smith, 1995; Sprey, 1990) argued there is no single, correct definition of family. Rather, there are multiple definitions formulated from a professional's theoretical perspective shaping observations and expectations of family life. Table 11.3 illustrates various family definitions and the researchers supporting each definition.

Family Theories

There are numerous theories shaping an understanding of what constitutes a family. Smith (1995) described a theory as a set of interconnected ideas that frame the world in a certain way. A theory guides observations and explanations. As such, family theories help to structure family knowledge, observations, interpretations, and use of information in programs and policies affecting family life. Theorists view or contemplate, while explaining general patterns of behavior across families (Osmond & Thorne, 1993). Their theories, then, hold various perspectives and emerging family themes.

FAMILY PERSPECTIVES AND THEMES

Educators, physicians, politicians, psychologists, social reformers, and scientists have described family themes based on family life and societal conditions. Perspectives and resulting themes influenced family knowledge, observations, and interpretations. Table 11.4 illustrates family theories and major themes and their proponents. The section below describes the theory and themes briefly. It offers a short description of the existing theoretical relationship and potential application to students with LD and their families.

Evolution Theory

Darwin was an early professional interested in examining families systematically. In *Origin of Species*, Darwin summarized that the animal species, including humans, evolves through a natural selection of differences in characteristics that increase the organism's ability to survive and reproduce. Accordingly, evolution occurs when changes appear, providing a species or genetic strain some advantage or disadvantage which is significant for survival. Darwin proposed that species change over time through a natural selection process; current organisms descend from earlier, more primitive ones (Darwin, 1859). Darwin's natural selection theme entailed a process by which, through the failure of their carriers to survive, some mutated genes are lost. Because of their relatively highest survival value, other mutated genes form the basis of a new and flourishing strain of species.

The crucial period in the lives of species' members, with respect to the species' survival, is the period through the age of reproduction. Darwin surmised a close similarity between human body structure and function and that of other animals. Darwin's evolution view placed human beings in the same context or in the same continuum with other animals. Hall (1954) suggested that Darwin's view legitimized the scientific study of human beings. Accordingly, behaviors, including learning, are broadly similar throughout the animal world.

Darwin's socioevolutionary theme suggested that a species' family is central to its survival. There is a continuity among animal species, with family representing the continuity. Darwin's terms *phylogeny* (the development of a species over time) and *ontogeny* (the development of the individual organism throughout its lifetime)

Table 11.4
Family Theories and Themes

Family Theory	Family Themes	Relationship to Special Needs Populations
Evolution Theory (Darwin, 1851)	Evolution through natural selection process	Perpetuated the theme of "survival of the fittest"
	Phylogeny (development of a species over time)	Rationalized sterilization attempts on individuals with mental retardation
	Ontogeny (development of the individual organism throughout its lifetime)	
	Current organisms descend from earlier, more primitive ones	
	Crucial species survival period—age of reproduction	
	Survival of the fittest	
Pscyhoanalytical Theory (Freud, 1920, 1923)	Significance of parent-child relationships during the first years of life on an individual's subsequent personality functioning	Did not deal directly with whole family
	Personality is a physical energy system, and at various points within the system the force of energy prompts human behavior	Did not deal directly with family with a special needs member
	Onotgenic growth proceeds through psychosexual development in biologically determined stages	Family problems result from traumatic early childhood and unresolved conflicts of the id, ego, and superego
	Associated personality and psychosexual development	

Table 11.4 *continued*

Family Theory	Family Themes	Relationship to Special Needs Populations
Behavioral Theory (Watson, 1913; Skinner, 1938, 1953; Meichenbaum, 1977)	Classical conditioning: Neutral stimulus pairs with a stimulus to elicit reflex; after repeated pairings, neutral stimulus elicits reflex Operant conditioning: Increase in response frequency if followed by reward or reinforcement and less frequent if followed by punishment Classical conditioning and operant conditioning: Targeted family neuroses, psychoses, mental disabilities, and conduct problems Behavior modification: Applied conditioning principles in therapeutic and educational settings between parents and children	Learning-based approaches in family problems Emphasized structuring the family environment, observational learning, and the family's social behaviors Educational programs evolved into parent training and parent-child behavior modification programs
Exchange Theory (Cheal, 1991; Sabetelli & Shehan, 1993)	Families entail economic relationships Family members act to maximize their profits, rewards, and resources, and to minimize their costs Family members have choices in their exchanges made with other and family members	Neglectful parents are liable to formal sanctions under legislation proscribing child neglect by legal systems
Family Development Theory (Hill & Rodgers, 1964; Broderick, 1993; Mattessich & Hill, 1987)	Families develop and change over time Families have developmental stages Within predictable cyclical stages, families have adjustments and transition periods	Life span needs are important across family developmental stages Families with special needs members have additional tasks and adjustments Individual family factors determine the adaptation that family members make in transitions Families with special needs members often have family stress

Table 11.4   *continued*

Family Theory	Family Themes	Relationship to Special Needs Populations
Family Systems Theory Turnbull & Turnbull 1986, 1990)	Family support and self-advocacy are relevant family variables The family is an integrated system with unique characteristics, strengths, and needs Family members are interdependent	All family members, their transitions, and their ability to cope are important (e.g., not just those of the special needs member) Increasing attention focuses on self-actualizing and empowering all family members
Ecological Model (Hook & Paolucci, 1970; Bubolz & Sontag, 1993)	Families depend on the natural environment for physical sustenance Families depend on the social environment for human contact and meaning A family ecosystem interacts with the environment	Professionals hold responsibility to assist groups lacking resources, social power, and control (e.g., people who are poor, elderly, disabled, or women) A family's ecosystem relates to quality of life issues for families with special needs members
Feminism (Osmond & Thorne, 1993; West & Zimmerman, 1987)	Gender relations are at the core of family life Historically, women have had subordinate roles to men in society and in families The family is a site of oppression and a form for conflict for women	Feminism may offer an advocacy model for family advocates An analogy exists between the historical subordination of women and families with a member with a disability Feminism may help to guide the family empowerment process
Phenomenology Theory and Ways of Knowing (Gubrium & Holstein, 1990, 1993; Lindsey, 1981)	Personal experiences are paramount and hold meaning in everyday life People construct their own social worlds Families hold a variety of meaning to various people	Social and cultural variables affect diverse family members' identities and interactions Social and cultural variables affect interactions and individuals' reactions to interactions

helped to structure a theme of continuity or sameness between children and adults—an important foundation of later themes in developmental theory (Dixon & Lerner, 1992).

Implications for Students with LD.   The socioevolutionary interpretation gained popularity during the latter part of the 19th century, shaping early 20th century researchers (e.g., Thorndike, 1913; Watson, 1928). Social Darwinism, as it became known, characterized family knowledge for approximately 30 years (Adams, 1986). Although there are no direct implications for students with identified LD, Social Darwinism influenced special needs populations by perpetuating the theme of "survival of the fittest." For example, the thinking within the natural selection process, that the fittest survive in the struggle for existence and the weaker perish, helped to rationalize the sterilization attempts on individuals with mental retardation, common occurrences in the eugenics movement of the early 20th century. In order to contain mental retardation, eugenics supporters sought to sterilize individuals with mental retardation in order to curtail their chances of reproductive survival.

Psychoanalytical Theory

Nineteenth century medical researchers and practitioners, also, began studying genetic influences on kinship and the family. By the 20th century, a medical orientation, psychoanalytical theory, emphasized the significance of parent-child relationships during the first years of life on an individual's subsequent personality functioning (Freud, 1920, 1923a, 1923b).

Freud's theory focused on the first 5 years of life, highlighting the importance of childhood, and was instrumental in viewing a person's development over life. Freud suggested that personality is a closed energy system in which psychic energy undergoes changes, ultimately affecting behavior. According to this theory, personality is a physical energy system, and at various points within the system, the force of energy prompts human behavior. Three psychological structures that contain the psychic energy and permit energy to flow and undergo change include the id, ego, and superego. The *id* is the part of an infant's personality seeking immediate satisfaction of biological needs (such as sexual and aggressive motives). A newborn baby receives energy entirely from the id, which is the selfish, pleasure-seeking aspect of personality. In contrast, the *ego* is the part of the personality that is rational and shapes an individual's growing relationship within the family. An infant's biological needs cannot always be met immediately by parents or other caregivers. As such, the child may have to endure discomforts while waiting for others to assist. The ego, derived from the id, develops in response to environmental demands within the family. As an individual gains experience relating to other family members, the ego develops. Finally, the last personality structure, the *superego*, is the part of personality that contains moral standards. Freud suggested that at about age 3, parents communicate standards to their child, praising and punishing behavior. By age 5, the three basic personality structures differentiate one person's personality from anothers.

Five biologically determined stages in Freudian theory relied on the theme of personality development in explaining an individual's id, ego, and superego. That is,

Freud associated personality and psychosexual development in stages including: (a) the oral stage (in which primary gratification of an infant to about age 1 is through oral stimulation); (b) the anal stage (primary gratification from about 1 to 3 years of age is through retention and expulsion of feces); (c) the phallic stage (lasting from about 3 to 5 years of age in which gratification is through the genital region; youngsters rival their same-sex parent for the other parent's affection and resolve Oedipal or Electra anxieties by adopting the qualities of the same-sex parent); (d) the latency stage, (lasting roughly from age 5 until puberty, in which the child concentrates on learning and socializing); and (e) the genital stage (starting at puberty, in which the teen manifests capacity for adult sexuality and productivity).

According to Freudian views (Freud, 1937), a child influenced by the ego, perceives the moral code of the parents. Initially, the child obeys this code in order to gain parental approval. But by the mechanism of identification, the child internalizes parental rules in the conscience (the ego ideal). The conscience encompasses all the moral prohibitions which derive from the actions and statements for which the child receives punishment. Accordingly, parents punish the child for giving expression to sexual and aggressive impulses, and hence the conscience contains prohibitions against such expressions. Freudian theory includes defense mechanisms as general habits which block or distort a psychological process in order to protect the individual against anxiety. A child's defense mechanisms involve the complete blocking out of a psychological process (e.g., denial, repression, and isolation), and secondary defense mechanisms involving distortion of a psychological process (displacement, projection, identification, rationalization, substitution, fantasy, and regression). Defense mechanisms are normal ways of coping with frustration. Psychotherapy procedures and psychoanalysis, based on Freudian manipulation of defense mechanisms, resulted as treatments of choice for individual family members during the early 20th century.

Freudian theory proliferated during the 1920s and 1930s. However, researchers criticized the theory's overemphasis on interpretation of consciousness (Skinner, 1938) and childhood sexuality (Miller, 1993; Stever, 1994).

Implications for Students with LD.   Psychoanalysts never dealt directly with the whole family. Most attached little importance to environmental factors on family problems. For the most part, families comprising members with learning difficulties did not hold prominence in psychoanalytical theory. Instead, family problems were thought to result from traumatic early childhood and unresolved conflicts of the id, ego, and superego.

Using parent-child interactions as a barometer of family relationships, however, Darling (1979) analyzed studies on family member interpretations of the arrival of a child with a disability, and, notably, many studies examined families of children with mental retardation. An assumption was that most parents were likely to reject their child. When parents reacted with acceptance, the theoretical interpretation supported denial or guilt associated with the parental acceptance. The themes of early trauma and unresolved conflicts of the id, ego, or superego were generic to most problems associated with individual affects, behaviors, or beliefs.

Psychosocial Theory

Psychosocial views on parents and the developing child surfaced during the 1950s and 1960s. Erikson relied on Freud's conception of id, ego, and superego and the view that ontogenic growth proceeds through psychosexual development in biologically determined stages. However, Erikson also emphasized the importance of the child's social environment in the developmental process, focusing on development of the reality-oriented ego within the individual's social world (Erikson, 1963).

Thus, psychosocial themes ascertained individual behaviors and varied interactions between parents and child. Interactions included self-help (e.g., feeding, toileting), emotional maturity (e.g., children's independence from parents), and psychological processes (e.g., social development in relation to significant adults and peers). Erikson's (1963) explanation of early psychosocial development to mature adulthood analyzed relationships between the individual child's behaviors and parental interactions. Parental encouragement of the child's movement and orientation, from caregivers, receptive and expressive language development, and the imagination that develops from both locomotion and language, helped to set parameters in child development, physical therapy, and language clinical therapies.

Implications for Students with LD.   Family dysfunction evolving from psychosocial development became paramount to psychiatric understanding of parent-child, parent-parent, and sibling interactions (Erikson, 1963). Although not specific to families containing a member with learning problems, by the 1960s and 1970s considerable attention in family research and theorizing had evolved into the study of psychological patterns of interpersonal home communication. Patterns were indicators of the personality and emotional health of families, including skills of family members in problem solving, communication, and self-control (e.g., some connections to children's learning histories might be hypothesized by analyzing these skills in family members). However, Erikson's views were descriptive in nature and not supported empirically. Miller (1993) reported that because Erikson relied on case study interpretation, psychosocial stages are questionable as explanations of early childhood experiences, family development, and interpersonal home communications indices when families have problems.

Behavioral Theory

Behaviorism and the effects of behavioral interactions of family members developed out of earlier work in stimulus-response learning theories based on the work of Watson and the subsequent work on operant conditioning by Skinner (Skinner, 1938, 1953; Watson, 1913). These latter theories dominated experimental psychology in North America from the 1920s to 1960s. Early work centered on animals but by 1965, efforts supporting classical and operant conditioning techniques were applied toward treatment of many human problems. Classical conditioning entailed a form of learning in which an initially neutral stimulus was paired with a stimulus that elicited a reflex; after repeated pairings, the neutral stimulus alone elicited the reflexive response (Watson, 1913). Operant conditioning, also a form of learning, entailed an increase in the response frequency if followed by a reward or reinforcement and less frequent if followed by punishment (Skinner, 1938, 1953).

Eventually, researchers used themes of classical conditioning and operant conditioning targeting family neuroses, psychoses, mental disabilities, and conduct problems. Behavior modification, the application of conditioning principles in therapeutic and educational settings to shape appropriate behaviors and curb undesirable ones, appeared in research viewing interactions between newborns and parents (Siqueland, 1968), patterns of child rearing (Larrzelere, 1986; Sears, Maccoby, & Levin, 1957), and social learning of parents and children (Bandura, 1960, 1969, 1977). Evolving from behavioral applications were shaping, fading, contingency contracting, and time-out procedures. These procedures highlighted children's behavior modification and parent training applications for children with autism (Lovaas, 1977, 1987; Wing, 1976), delinquency (Milan, 1987), and language problems (Lovaas, Berberich, Perloff, & Schaeffer, 1966). (Chapter 7 details basic tenets of behavioral theory.)

Implications for Students with LD.   Due to a high success rate reported with behavioral procedures (e.g., stimulus control strategies, behavioral contingencies), learning-based approaches began replacing psychoanalytic theory and psychosocial views as treatments of choice for family problems (Stever, 1994). As explained in chapter 7, behavioral theory had much influence on children with learning and other disabilities. In addition to the influence of behavioral science on teachers' assessment issues, practices, and instructional approaches, early documented uses of behavioral principles influenced family researchers. For example, Watson's attention to observable stimuli and responses, and Skinner's experimental analysis of behavior and application of behavioral principles to education greatly influenced educational recommendations in parent training and support classes. Accordingly, many behavioral scientists observed behaviors and collected data on individual and family member dyads or triads (e.g., marital, parental, sibling, extrafamilial). They recorded and charted behavioral effects of courtship practices, marriages and divorce, and family interactions within and outside the home.

Refinements in behavioral approaches led to an emphasis on structuring the family environment, observational learning, and the family's social behaviors (Bandura, 1960, 1969, 1977). Behaviorists began to focus on specific family variables such as parental control of children's behavior, marital conflict, and family resources available in the community. Educational programs for families in the 1970s and early 1980s evolved into specifics of parent training and parent-child behavior modification programs. Professionals began instructing parents successfully on use of clinical, behavioral techniques in the home. Techniques included use of behavioral antecedents and consequences, observations and recordings, behavioral change strategies to increase positive behaviors or decrease negative behaviors, data point plotting, charting and behavioral trends, and using decision-making skills for home data analysis. Researchers also focused on self-assessment and self-instruction, including parents' and children's self-control (Meichenbaum, 1977; Meichenbaum & Goodman, 1971).

Structural-Functional Theory

Structural-functional theorists, operating from a sociological framework, held that society as "an organism" strives to resist change while seeking equilibrium. Social stability and order are positive, natural, and desirable. However, social deviance and disorder are negative and avoidable. When social deviance and disorder occur, they provide evidence of systemic dysfunction. The family structure operates to satisfy member needs for social survival and societal success (Smith, 1995).

Structural-functional advocates suggested that the family is a social component by means of its own internal adaptations and characteristic interactions with other social institutions. The family helps to promote and maintain social balance and stability (Broderick, 1993; Hutter, 1991; Kingsbury & Scanzoni, 1993). A functioning family is a positive contributor to the social order. While the family ensures society's cultural, economical, social, and political well-being, society supports family members who make social contributions. A strong family theme assumes that family relations model power and social relations. Thus, family groups and individual members perform social responsibilities and community tasks.

The structural-functional theory helped to explain family structures and functions with associated social change variables. Interpretations prompted social scientists to construct important global, cross-cultural studies. Comparative studies provided evidence of family composition, roles, and functions across social groups. Structural-functional research described themes important to diverse families, including kinship, marital structures, and universal family functions. The theory provided one of the first formulations of several important systems themes extensively adopted by others, such as those supporting family systems, human ecology, and symbolic interactionism (Smith, 1995).

However, because proponents support rather rigid marital role interpretations and overemphasize stability and change, the theory has critics. For example, critics argue most adherents are too rigid, that their gender role conceptualizations and the tendency to present the nuclear family form as the ideal model negate and discredit other family forms (Broderick, 1993; Epstein, 1988). Some feminists and those supporting the phenomenology view challenge basic assumptions espoused in family structure and function themes (Smith, 1995).

Implications for Students with LD.   Researchers including Farber (1986) and Behr (1990) reported that family research from the 1940s to the 1980s primarily targeted family dysfunction. For example, during the 1950s, family researchers sought variables related to the negative impact of children (particularly children with mental retardation) on the family and risks to the family dysfunction (Ackerman & Behnen, 1956). Attempts at family conceptualization emphasized family pathology and dysfunction. Because the family conceptualization entailed a structured theme among family members, the family roles, responsibilities, and dysfunctional family relationships influenced most family composition descriptions. When a family did not fit the ideal, researchers assumed pathology or disorganization or both.

While structural-functional family theorists did not pinpoint families composed of members with learning or other disabilities, these families were at a disadvantage. Most adherents would argue offspring are in some sense "deviant," "unproductive," or "unable to fulfill" societal expectations. Ackerman and Behnen's (1956) seven deviant family groups and Voiland and Buell's (1961) family psychopathology types exemplified a pathological orientation using a structural-functional family breakdown.

Structural-functional family theorists suggested that healthy families accomplish the task of producing offspring who can function autonomously and enter into long-lasting, external, family relationships (Broderick, 1993; Kingsbury & Scanzoni, 1993). This task is inherent throughout each family member's life and is the basis from which other family tasks surface (e.g., having and raising children, meeting financial obligations, providing religious orientations). Other functional tasks rely on competence in physical survival, family socialization roles, motivation and morale maintenance, social control within the family group and between the family and outsiders, and the social placement of maturing members (Abel, 1986; Broderick, 1993; Hutter, 1981; Kingsbury & Scanzoni, 1993). When families have members with LD, for instance, family tasks cannot be accomplished to the same extent, in the same sequence, or to the same depth as with other families. Families, accordingly, are incompetent because of their implied deviance, productivity level, and lack of meeting social expectations imposed by the member with a learning disability.

Exchange Theory

The exchange theory relied on an economic metaphor (Cheal, 1991). Family members assume gender-differentiated husband/father-wife/mother roles carried out at home (i.e., analogous to the boss-worker relationship in the workplace). At work, as at home, status relations between people of different classes or of different genders underscore family upbringing patterns. For example, a pertinent theme is that the family members act to maximize their profits, rewards, and resources; families, also, seek to minimize their costs. Resources, dependencies, and attractions of family members have an impact on their interactions, intimacy, satisfactions, and stability. Relationships are satisfying when partners equally contribute and receive equal positive outcomes. Relationships are dissatisfying when interactions are not reciprocal. Family themes centering on marital negotiation, power, decision making, reciprocity, and choices exemplify exchange variables (Sabatelli & Shehan, 1993).

Exchange theory supporters suggest that family members have choices in their exchanges made with others: Family members avoid costs and seek rewarding status, relationships, interactions, and feelings. Social norms and kin enforcing sanctions on parents govern child-rearing practices (Cheal, 1991; Sabatelli & Shehan, 1993; Smith, 1995).

Implications for Students with LD.   Exchange themes may attract economists and practitioners in the welfare and juvenile systems. For example, Sabatelli and Shehan (1993) described a "choice and exchange" model in relationship exchanges, whereby norms require that parents feed, clothe, and care for their children. Norms require adequate socialization and supervision so that children will not injure or deprive others of their personal property. Neighbors, relatives, and other reference-group members censure parents not performing these tasks. Neglectful parents are liable to formal legal sanctions under legislation proscribing child neglect. However, the neglected child from a "deviant" family is likely to become a source of embarrassment to parents, may become dependent on parents, or may develop serious health problems (e.g., multiplying parental costs over time). Advocates may argue that parental outcomes are likely to be better if parents accept child care and socialization costs than if they choose not to accept these responsibilities. From this perspective, parents are not exchanging rewards with their children but are choosing the best alternative available. The rationalization is that to neglect their offspring would entail larger costs than would providing adequate care and socialization. Parents of children with learning difficulties or problem behaviors choose the best alternative available to them when they accept the costs involved in caring for their family member with disabilities.

Family Development Theory

A developmental approach centering on family needs and problems at different stages surfaced during the late 1960s and 1970s. Piaget's (1983) cognitive developmental theory in child psychology and other information-processing models in experimental-learning psychology (Case, 1975; Gagne, 1974, 1977; Riegel, 1973) (e.g., problem-solving skills, communication skills, and learning applications) guided professional attention, leading the way for other researchers to expand developmental research.

For example, family development viewed the nuclear family and its patterns of expansion, transition, and contraction (Burr, 1973; Hill & Rodgers, 1964). A relevant theme entailed that a family-change process develops sequentially (Broderick, 1990; Mattessich & Hill, 1987). Families develop predictable cyclical stages (e.g., as a newly established couple; childbearing family; family with school-aged children; family with adolescent members; family with young adults; family in middle years; aging family). Stages provide a framework for family needs such that life tasks (e.g., feeding, clothing, caring for the young child, and supporting the school-aged child economically) and adjustments (e.g., paying for child-care services; "letting go" of the teen-age child) determine the family change process. Emerging family roles vary either by: (a) helping members transition to the next family stage, or (b) creating family crises (Hill & Rodgers, 1964; Mattessich & Hill, 1987). Family crises require role alterations and reorganization through an adjustment and coping process. Disorders accompanying these role changes, for most families, are normal transitions.

Developmental stage themes exemplified the work of prominent family researchers in the 1970s. For example, Tseng and McDermott (1979) suggested a multidimensional family framework in which change helped to classify families as either pathological or dysfunctional. Dysfunctional families appeared categorically along three dimension axes. Axes included family: (a) development, (b) relationships, and (c) systems. The first axis, family development, represented the family's longitudinal stage. In this stage, family members' tasks set parameters for each developmental phase. (Tasks appear from a marriage stage to the family with adult children stage.) A second axis, the cross-sectional, focused on the extent to which individual members influence the family's development. The influence may be either functional or dysfunctional. Classifications included members' risk status to overall family functioning. The third cross-sectional axis considered the family group. Dysfunctional relationships and changing family subsystems comprise family pathology. As such, family classifications entailed functional or dysfunctional relationships influencing internal (e.g., role division) or external processes (e.g., social isolation).

Implications for Students with LD.   Critics report that developmental themes do not capture the enormous variation in family structures and experiences resulting from demographic and social changes. Variations in values, beliefs, and practices of different racial and cultural groups also carry little weight (Broderick, 1993). Nonetheless, some special education researchers have relied on theoretical themes to analyze effects of family stages and transitions when there is a member with a disability, including those with LD (Behr, 1990; Brunk, 1991; Summers, Brotherson, & Turnbull, 1988; Turnbull & Turnbull, 1986). In fact, much of the family data evolving from transition research assumed a stage phase associating tasks and adjustments over a family's life span.

Family researchers often supported the importance of an individual's life-span needs across the family (e.g., Ianacone & Stodden, 1987). They noted additional tasks and adjustments faced by families of students with disabilities (e.g., respite care tasks, increased financial responsibilities, health tasks related to the child's medical needs) (Behr, 1990; Brunk, 1991; Summers et al., 1988; Turnbull & Turnbull, 1986). Factors influencing family's vulnerability were found to determine the adaptation that individual family members make in transitions. For example, Hetherington found that family changes and adaptations often depend on the child's unique characteristics, age and gender, the availability of family resources, subsequent life experiences, and interpersonal relationships between and with family members and neighbors (Hetherington & Baltes, 1988).

Family Stress and Coping Theory

Family-stress and coping theory derived from the work of Hill (1949, 1958) in efforts to understand and assist with family stress reactions in World War II separations and reunions (Behr, 1990). Burr (1973), McCubbin and Patterson (1983), and McCubbin and McCubbin (1987) used the theory themes in 1970s and 1980s family research. Hill's basic tenets (1958) influenced researchers to suggest that a stressor event influences the degree and strength of the family's crisis. Researchers identified Factor A as the stressor event interacting with Factor B, the family's crisis-meeting resources, interacting with Factor C, the definition the family makes of the event, evolving into Factor X, the *crisis*. Burr, and also McCubbin and peers sought the interactions between precrisis variables, their influences on Factor X, and their roles in accounting for differing family abilities to cope with stressor events (e.g., transitions). Precrisis variables influenced whether the crisis evolved, and if so, its extent (Behr, 1990).

Shea and Bauer (1991) reported that family stress may result from changing the child's educational or training opportunities, the families' economic support resources available, or the parents' marital status. Experiences preceding the changing events, also, shaped adaptations that individuals make to specific changes. Important variables included family stage of development, the child's age, other family members' ages, severity of the disability of a member, and family resources available across time (e.g., Behr, 1990; Brunk, 1991; Hetherington & Baltes, 1988; Shea & Bauer, 1991; Summers et al., 1988; Turnbull & Turnbull, 1986). Accordingly, professionals called for long-range planning clarifying specific adjustment supports available to children and families (Bailey, Simeonsson, Winton, Huntington, & Comfort, 1986; Craig & Leonard, 1990; Halpern, 1985; Ianacone & Stodden, 1987; Stewart, 1989; Turnbull & Turnbull, 1986, 1990; Will, 1984).

Behr advocated using family response to stress and coping strategies developed to: (a) increase knowledge on factors associated with the family's response to daily stressful events, (b) investigate cognitive processes associated with individual responses to stressful events, (c) identify values in families in relation to societal norms, (d) create innovative public policies and family practices, (e) clarify family member's perceptions of the individual with a disability, and (f) clarify perceptions of family members with disabilities about themselves, their families, their communities, and the world.

Important in family-stress and coping theory are themes related to response to change, including those of transitions and adversities. Relying on family members' ability to adapt, researchers examined adjustments to negative life events, including an explanation that victims of threatening situations actually benefit from their experience (Taylor, 1983; Taylor, Lichtman, & Wood, 1984). Hence, family members respond to personally threatening events through adjustment processes involving the cognitive themes of: (a) a search for meaning in the event, (b) an attempt to achieve control over the event, and (c) an attempt to enhance self-esteem (Behr, 1990).

Implications for Students with LD.   Stress and coping themes are useful to families with a member with a learning disability. Individual members require support in the many behavioral, economic, legal, psychological, and social stressors common in families. Researchers and practitioners, accordingly, have targeted family understanding of such variables as: (a) reactions of parents toward their children with disabilities and to professional reactions (Crnic, Friedrich, & Greenberg, 1983; Ryckman & Henderson, 1965; Wolfensberger, 1970); (b) the child's effect on the family (Byrne & Cunningham, 1985; Lipsky, 1985), and (c) stress in families (Knafl & Deatrick, 1987; McDonald-Wikler, 1986).

Effective adaptations and coping strategies rely on the family's unique makeup, economic resources, natural supports available, and opportunities in the home, school, and community. These family factors may take on increased teacher prominence as school professionals work in more family-oriented services (Karp, 1993).

Future exploration may help to identify specific family needs, strengths, and useful interventions that can teach coping skills given diverse stressors in the 21st century (e.g., influence of advanced computer technology). Such research efforts may provide meaningful data in family self-help programs and individual self-advocacy services.

Systems Theories

Researchers began to question the labels of deviance, dysfunction, disorder, and negativity associated with many families. Systems theorists evolved based on family interactions and stability (Broderick, 1993; Bubolz & Sontag, 1993; Hill & Rodgers, 1964; Mattessich & Hill, 1987; Simeonsson & Simeonsson, 1981; Smith, 1995). Included in this perspective are several models including the family systems model and the ecological model.

The Family Systems Model.   Family systems themes elaborated on family support and self-advocacy. Clinical psychiatry, family counseling, special education, and social work set the stage for viewing positive family characteristics. Family systems pro-

fessionals postulated the family as an integrated social system with unique characteristics, strengths, and needs (Ianacone & Stodden, 1987; Turnbull & Turnbull, 1986,
1990; Wehman, Moon, & McCarthy, 1986). In the family systems model the family,
as a system, strives to maintain balance while confronting external pressures. Family members are interdependent; each member's behavior affects other members.
Human systems adapt to transitions while establishing permeable boundaries (e.g.,
what distinguishes families are separate residences, family rituals, and customs) (Hill
& Rodgers, 1964). As a system, a family seeks equilibrium, balance, and support during the change process.

A family systems approach in the mid-1980s characterized researchers viewing
the strengths and needs of family members with and without disabilities. Researchers
sought variables related to a family's well-being (Grossman, 1972; Jaffe-Ruiz, 1984;
Knafl, & Dietrich, 1987; Long & Bond, 1984). Behavioral and psychosocial researchers, earlier, had helped to establish training programs, developed along the
lines of parent training and parent-child behavior modification programs. However,
family systems researchers, practitioners, and parents began to urge family support
and family self-advocacy models over these other efforts. The rationalization was to
lessen parent training (e.g., implying a helper-to-helpee model and professional-
over-parents model). New themes surfaced around ideals of family acceptance, advocacy, and self-help without devaluing interdependency (Bailey, Simeonsson, Yoder, & Huntington, 1990; Turnbull & Turnbull, 1986).

In family support and self-advocacy models, the benefits of parent-professional
collaborations and family expertise themes outweighed subordinate roles implied
from "parent training" models. Structural, functional, developmental, social learning,
and behavioral approaches became less prominent in directing families. The family
systems model increased in value as families and professionals tackled home and
community interdependence.

Implications for Students with LD.   The model's usefulness to populations with LD
entails its offering of interaction process descriptions and home, school, and community directions. Themes focus on the whole family's well-being. Increasing attention now focuses on transitions and personal adjustment of all family members—not
just the individual with a disability. Family members, furthermore, are becoming
more self-actualizing and self-empowering during the last decade (with and without
professional help), which, in turn, helps to reinforce their advocacy roles. Professionals and family members empower each other in order to benefit children and
family members. Family systems advocates espouse transition importance and adjustment effects on significant individuals to the family member with a disability
(e.g., including teachers).

Transition research has emanated from a focus on family interactions, stability,
a sense of belonging, each family member's well-being, and on student, family, and
professional interdependence and support. Family systems professionals and families facilitate interactions, stability, and interdependency by: (a) supporting policies
and programs concerned with each family's health and welfare; (b) recognizing individual family resources and avenues for economic stability; (c) examining effects
of parents, siblings, grandparent, neighbors, and so forth on individual family members; (d) analyzing effects of family socialization roles and community responsibil-

ity; and (e) searching for comprehensive school and family policies and programs enhancing families' growth, development, and emotional nurturing (Turnbull & Turnbull, 1986, 1990).

The Ecological Model.   The ecological model focused on the interrelationships between systems and the environment. Themes relate to an individual's family support system and the family's dependency on the natural environment for physical sustenance. The family also depends on the social environment for human contact and meaning (Hook & Paolucci, 1970).

Accordingly, a family ecosystem interacts with environments. Human development occurs in the home through reciprocal interactions with other environments. Families, regardless of their culture, ethnic background, national origin, family development stage, structure, social class, or members' ages, receive energy and information from their ecology. Families rely on their own communication and decision making, as well as on their managing the physical and material resources and technologies available to them.

A pertinent human-ecology theme is that of professional responsibility in assisting groups lacking resources, social power, and control. Human ecologists assist individuals who are poor, elderly, disabled, or women. Advocates emphasize human *quality of life* issues including economic adequacy, justice, freedom, and peace (Smith, 1995). Bubolz and Sontag (1993) suggested that family ecology differs from other family systems models in that all living populations are interdependent with the earth's resources. The world's ecosystem supplements human quality of life. Natural physical-biological environments (e.g., climate, animals, water, plants), the sociocultural environment (e.g., neighbors and community), cultural constructions (e.g., laws, values, and norms), and human-built environments (e.g., farms, cities) hold importance in human ecology.

Implications for Students with LD.   Human ecology may appeal to special educators concerned with the child's ecosystem across learning settings and quality of life issues for children and families. Model adherence may encourage future researchers and practitioners to explore individual families' opportunities for physical, material, and technological advances and resulting children's school success. A family ecosystem has potential to researchers interested in children's achievement and motivation in home, school, or community settings. Understanding parent and children's needs and strengths within the context of the family's learning opportunities may be useful in studies on family decision-making and life-span choices.

Feminism

Recent researchers have underscored personal experiences and subjective definitions in family knowledge, with diversity themes carrying meaning in family knowledge applications. For example, feminism emphasizes understanding differences within and among families, based on social variables including gender, class, race, and ethnicity. Womens' historical, overall societal subordination is paramount in feminism. Feminist scholars purport that culture, not nature, constructs dichotomous role categories including masculine-feminine and woman-man relationships (Osmond & Thorne, 1993; West & Zimmerman, 1987).

Gender relations are at the core of family life. Feminists almost universally accept that women have the main responsibility for family tasks (Abel, 1986; Osmond & Thorne, 1993). Feminists support the importance of women's family work and in other institutions (e.g., occupations, religion, medicine, education), and they move beyond a primary focus on kinship highlighting family dynamics and structural influences on family life.

Supporters contended that feminist theory documents women's subordination in societies worldwide and that family gender roles appear cross-culturally (Smith, 1995). Feminists often suggest that the family is a site of oppression and a forum for conflict. However, the family is also a place offering women a source of strength, solidarity, and comfort. Existing gender relationships (e.g., in the family and society) require correction through social change and political action.

Implications for Students with LD.   While feminism is not applicable directly to students with LD, theory themes may contribute increased information. The theory may offer a rationale for family advocates. It may serve as an advocacy model useful to diverse families with a member having a disability. It may help special needs scholars in comparative studies. Contributions may focus on an analogy between the historical subordination endured by families with a member having a disability and women. Further, feminism themes may help in guiding the family empowerment process. For example, feminism themes may help to clarify the meaning of family life when a member with a disability overcomes adversity and later succeeds. Use of theoretical themes may relate to the feminist emphasis on the cultural, social, and historical influences for family and work roles. Researchers and practitioners interested in family decision making and communications with service agencies may also profit from the theory's application (e.g., it may offer data on domestic abuse factors and young children's imitation.)

Phenomenology Theory and Ways of Knowing

The phenomenology theory also highlighted an understanding of differences within and among families. Personal experiences are paramount themes. Phenomenologists focus on the meaning of everday life, suggesting that because people construct their own social worlds, their possessions, including families, offer a variety of meanings, depending on the observer (Smith, 1995). Those supporting a phenomenological orientation have underscored the importance of family life and interpersonal relationship meaning. Advocates focused on the impact of family beliefs and values on domestic life (Gubrium & Holstein, 1990, 1993; Lindsey, 1981). A recurring theme is that families vary across people (e.g., the father-mother-child relation), or vary by feelings of caring, belonging, and commitment (Gubrium & Holstein, 1990, 1993; Lindsey, 1981).

A phenomenology extension, called symbolic interactionism, supports individualism and autonomy themes. Advocates suggest that the family is a "unit of interacting personalities." Family life is constituted by dyadic and family interactions that maintain marital and parent-child relationships. Each individual's sense of identity derives from social interactions, personal meaning, and individual motivation (Hutter, 1991).

Implications for Students with LD.   McPhail (1995) argued for the support of phenomenology in special education research. He called for alternative approaches (to traditional orientations) in conducting research on human consciousness and meaning. Wansart (1995) suggested researchers should respond to a way of knowing about students' abilities and accomplishments in response to what is learned. Searching for competency and responding to students' evolving learning stories (e.g., often derived from home experiences) can transform many areas of knowledge. Additionally, Reid, Robinson, and Bunsen (1995) described postmodernism and narrative (a way of knowing) as means to expand human boundaries. Knowledge links with interests and ideology in suggesting how the social world has come to be the way it is and how it might be reconstituted to better support the realization of the full potential of human beings.

Discourse analysis, as a means of attaching meaning to experiences, has provided insights on cognitive, social, cultural, affective, and communicative factors influential to knowledge (Forman & McMormick, 1995). The applications of these perspectives to remedial and special education and family diversity may be useful in explaining the social construction of disability, contingent instruction between adults and learners, and communication patterns between parents, children, and professionals.

Finally, symbolic interactionism assumes that cultural symbols and social norms affect interaction. Individuals interpret those interactions. Accordingly, social and cultural variables affect a family member's identity and interactions. The theory's emphasis on meanings individuals assign to interactions adds a phenomenological dimension to family awareness and may be useful in observing and explaining domestic life (Smith, 1995). Symbolic interaction applications may include using social and cultural variables to understand the interplay of family processes. Applications regarding family members' identity and interactions when a member with a disability is present may be targeted in future research efforts.

Family Theories Summary

Professionals began studying the family in the early part of the 20th century. At the time, professionals sought to understand how to observe and explain families more accurately and to influence family life. Accordingly, family perspectives evolved as a result of professionals studying the cultural, economical, historical, legal, political, and social factors relating to families.

In the next section, various family views helped to define historic teacher and family roles. Internal family factors (e.g., family compositions, structures, internal relationships), as well as external factors (e.g., culture, society, and economics) have influenced teachers' interactions with students and their families.

AMERICAN FAMILY HISTORY AND TEACHERS' ROLES

Early Families

The American population was distinctly pioneer from the Revolution until the Civil War. Pioneer families favored early marriage and high fecundity, and members divided their time between home building and home protection. Pioneers brought varied family experiences and expectations from their European homelands, relying on past customs, habits, and life-styles as America expanded westward. Family members often shared experiences, with family traditions evolving through repeated storytelling as a means of transmitting traditions and values (Coontz, 1988).

LePlay of France published a study of the traditional, European family that differentiated European and American families. A stem family represented Europeans, and the ideal family consisted of parents and children. LePlay actually lived with families, taking notes, observing interactions, and participating in family activities. He was a conservative social reformer, underscoring the traditional stem family importance to European life. The stem family was stable, moral, authoritarian, and responsible. Group members gave up individual rights in favor of the larger group's welfare. Family members substituted impersonal, external relationships for intimate kinship feelings. Members usually had late marriage or no marriage, practiced in the family's interest (Adams, 1986; Aries, 1962).

Mid-19th-century American families relied on an extended family model, often with grandparents, both parents, and offspring residing together or nearby. In a nation that discarded hierarchical religion and minimized governmental involvement, the family emerged as the one institution in which the touted ideal of individualism sought expression. Children became the nation's progeny. The "genteel" mode of child rearing dominated (Stannard, 1979). Many families resided in rural areas, the districts outside towns and cities of 4,000 or more inhabitants. Their main concerns centered on basic survival needs. Most families worked as peasant farmers, agricultural workers, or small enterprise employees. Family members worked together to produce foods used for their own consumption. Small goods or cottage industries also serviced many families (Masnick & Bane, 1980).

Changes marked American society by the 1880s. Reasons for the changes were vast: The country moved beyond direct Civil War influences; industrialism increased; free land, available through westward expansion, was running low; electricity brought in the telephone, the incandescent lamp, and the trolley car; and the typewriter facilitated business opportunities. Several socioeconomic factors increased disparities in work and caused a growing schism between public and private realms evolved. Factors included: (a) the fast pace of urban industrialism, (b) the rise of city luxury marked by conspicuous consumption, and (c) the culmination of the slave system. Family life-style changed with marked societal and work changes as well. For example, fathers increasingly became polarized between job and family. In a world slowly witnessing the steady loss of family control and production means, fathers were becoming solely responsible for family income. Many men became more alienated from the work process itself, resulting in social tumult on family life, such that families increasingly suffered the effects of increasing birth rates and divorce (Stannard, 1979).

Social reformers, medical professionals, and politicians began focusing attention on the study of family life. Much credit to family studies evolved from the *National Divorce Reform League* which had its beginnings in the early 1880s, then known as the *New England Divorce Reform League*. This organization hoped to promote public sentiment and family improvement through legislation, (especially in light of increasing divorces). In 1885 the league was made national, and by 1897 the word family was substituted for divorce. The renamed organization became the *National League for the Protection of the Family* (Calhoun, 1918).

Teachers' Roles with Families.   While social advocates began dealing with family issues, however, many school personnel did not participate actively. The main role of teachers was to assess and instruct students in the basics of reading, mathematics, and writing. School rules and classroom etiquette were the main domain of school personnel (Cuban, 1993).

There is evidence that some families did not support school practices. Harpur (1899) examined parents' attitudes and behaviors toward school personnel and found that parents influenced their children's behaviors toward teachers, sometimes negatively. Harpur suggested that student misbehavior and resulting school dropout evolved from lack of cooperation between parents and teachers. In this view, parents served the purpose of modeling student learning by perpetuating family values, sometimes to teacher disadvantage.

Nonetheless, schools, rather than the home, became the center of ingraining conformity. School personnel dealt with the influx of arriving immigrants, and schools became the common forum for diverse students and backgrounds. Ethnic heritage was expressed in a distinctive family life-style, such as through family dress, foods, languages, and traditions. However, assimilation with its domain status, carried with it a presumed superiority on the part of the host culture, in all respects, and an inferiority of the culture of the newly arrived immigrants. That is, migrating families responded to general class, economic, and social pressures, thus giving immigrants of that time a measure of common, low status (Cuban, 1993; Gouldner, 1970; Mindel & Habenstein, 1976).

The "melting pot" metaphor emerged in response to the call for Americanization. The metaphor rationalized that arriving immigrants would fuse together in America, producing a new and better amalgam, combining cultural contributions of each group. Zangwill coined the term in a 1906 play of the same name. On the other hand, avid discussions about the virtues of "cultural pluralism," that is, becoming American while at the same time retaining one's cultural heritage, began in at least 1915, when Kallen first introduced the idea (Cuban, 1993; Gouldner, 1970; Mindel & Habenstein, 1976). Table 11.5 depicts various challenges arriving immigrants faced based on their country of origin and American arrival time.

Early-20th-Century Families

Industrialism characterized early-20th-century society. The study of human social institutions, sociology, was established as an academic discipline. Sociologists associated many social and family problems with widespread industrialism and city expansion. Early-20th-century leaders feared the social impact of growing industrialization, urbanization, and the breakdown of "social order" on family life (Adams, 1986; Lull, 1988; Masnick & Bane, 1980; Stannard, 1979).

Industrialization and Urbanization.   Industrialization and urbanization changed American families. For example, labor division, professional and vocational special-

Table 11.5

Challenges Arriving Immigrant Groups Faced, Based on Origin and Arrival Time to America

Ethnic Origins	Arrival Time	Societal Challenges	School Challenges
Groups representing those of Polish, Japanese, Italian, Irish, and Chinese American families.	Migrated to America in great numbers in pre- and early 19th century periods. Eventually, these families represented the majority population.	The right to express an ethnic heritage in a distinctive family lifestyle, then and now, entailed a societal challenge. General social, economic, and class oppressive pressures included: (a) low status afforded to these ethnic minority groups, (b) limited economic resources, and (c) few opportunities to "get ahead." Other factors included: (a) the influence of the changing frontier, (b) the initiation of urban industrialism, (c) the rise of cities and consumption, and (d) the ascent of industrial capitalism. Many families faced limited economic security, industrial accidents and diseases, unemployment, no health insurance, or poor housing. Poverty and racial discrimination had a negative impact on family life for both adults and children. Religious challenges and the freedom to worship also played an important role in these families' transitions to America.	The extent to which assimilation and acculturation have an impact on ethnic identity and life-style remains one of the key problems by these arriving groups. Nonetheless, schools have become the forum for initiating the assimilation and acculturation process. Administrators and teachers often taught in one-room, ungraded classrooms and ignored the impact of family diversity. Repetition and memorization characterized school challenges, especially to many Southern and Eastern European immigrant students.

Table 11.5   *continued*

Ethnic Origins	Arrival Time	Societal Challenges	School Challenges
Groups representing those of Native American, African American, and Latino families.	Early family members either preceded the arrival of the "White American" or arrived later and were immediately or later placed in some form of bondage: Native Americans were in America prior to the arrival of European families. African American families arrived with the advent of the slave system, occurring approximately from the late-17th-century until the mid- to late-19th century. Many of the Latino immigrant families arrived in the late 19th and early 20th centuries. Many families from the islands south of the United States (e.g., Puerto Rico and Cuba), also arrived in the late 1950s and early 1960s.	Native American, African American, and Latino families were historically subjected to: (a) low status afforded to these ethnic minority groups, (b) limited economic resources, and (c) few opportunities to "get ahead," until the mid- to late-20th century and the arrival of the Civil Rights movement in the mid-1960s. Enslaved to the land, alienated from it, or bound in a latter-day peonage, family members ascribed much status to their family lifestyles. Religious and community leaders in the families' local areas played important roles in helping family members hold onto and build upon their cultural identity and ethnic backgrounds. The role of the truncated or extended family became crucial for cultural and ethnic survival.	Many students from these families faced historical school challenges in the form of discrimination and labeling. Until federal and state legislation in the mid-1970s, expulsions, suspensions, and separate schooling and classes made up the bulk of school experiences. Even after federal and state laws mandated school services, many students from these families often faced a disproportionate amount of labeling and placements in special education services (i.e., relative to the size their ethnic backgrounds presented in schools). Assessment, curriculum, and placement procedures continue to be relevant school challenges to students from these family backgrounds.

ization, movement of families' from rural areas and small towns to cities, and family changes from a production unit to a consumption unit characterized the era (Lull, 1988). Urbanization and modernization also linked to problematic aspects of family, such as poverty, child labor, and illegitimacy. Increasing family consequences to industrialization and urbanization included: (a) family members working long hours (e.g., including work by children under the age of 12), (b) increased parent absence from the home, (c) limited employment wages and virtually no fringe benefits, (d) a

Table 11.5   *continued*

Ethnic Origins	Arrival Time	Societal Challenges	School Challenges
Groups representing those of Arab and Greek families.	Many of these immigrant families arrived in the late 19th and early 20th centuries. Many families also are recent arrivals.	In addition to many of the problems such as limited economic resources and housing opportunities, problems these families faced upon arrival time in the late 19th and early 20th centuries included adjusting to a modern business cycle and a war-plagued industrial society. Family members had to face language and religious barriers imposed upon them by the larger society.	School personnel continued to assume the role of helping students assimilate into the larger culture. Students with language difficulties faced many barriers in school success (e.g., relevant to academics, social skills, and management). In the late 19th and early 20th centuries students faced challenges from school personnel relative to understanding and demonstrating citizenship roles and skills. Other challenges included basics in reading, writing, and arithmetic. Students arriving mid-century, also, faced many language and religious barriers at school.
Groups representing those of Amish, Jewish, Mormon, and French Canadian-American families.	Many family members arrived in the early 18th and 20th centuries.	Socio-religious ethnic factors were relevant to each family member. For example, many sought and continue to seek community and social existence in which religion could be conjoined with all aspects of their family life and livelihood.	For many students from these groups, identity and experiences have been a result of, or strongly influenced by, their respective religious orientations.

paucity of nutritional and family health care, and (e) limited sociocultural opportunities to enhance the family unit (Adams, 1988).

Advances in Children's Welfare and Health.   While helping students assimilate into the American mainstream culture became a major role for many teachers (Cuban 1993), social reformers continued as advocates. For example, the single most important public development available to children was the establishment of the United States Children's Bureau. This agency's 1912 creation signified federal acceptance and responsibility for promoting children's health and welfare (Lathrop, 1912).

Initially, the agency was a research and information center whose function was to investigate and report all matters pertaining to children's welfare and family life. Agency personnel focused on collecting data on infant mortality, birth rates, orphanages, juvenile courts, family desertions, dangerous occupations, children's accidents and diseases, child employment, and legislation affecting children nationwide. Subsequently, the agency assumed administration of the first federal child labor laws and grants-in-aid to states for maternal and child health. Additionally, leaders assumed that children's well-being could best be achieved by fostering the family's economic security through assured compensation for industrial accidents and diseases, unemployment and health insurance, and improved housing. Implementation of most of these programs, however, was still to be achieved during the mid-1930s (Bremner, 1971; Lull, 1988; Stannard, 1979).

Teachers' Roles with Families.   Substantial advances in welfare and health issues affected teachers' roles. For example, much of the philanthropic energy of the early 20th century went into special facility provisions for children who were formerly treated in the same way as adults. Advocates created special hospitals for the treatment of children with physical disabilities or diseases. Among school implications were: (a) public and private institutions intended exclusively for the care of dependent children replaced, or at least supplemented, almshouse care for dependent children (e.g., these institutions came under closer and more stringent state supervision); (b) reform schools increased in size and number to service delinquent youth who would otherwise have been sent to jails and prisons; and (c) the juvenile court movement introduced significant trial differences between youthful and adult offenders (Cuban, 1993; Lull, 1988; Stannard, 1979).

State and federal legislation, accordingly, attempted to safeguard children against premature, excessive, and dangerous labor; sought to protect them against abuse, neglect, immortality, diseases, and unsanitary surroundings; and compelled them to spend increased time in school. These laws, intended to secure all children's better treatment and wider opportunities, advanced governmental authority and diminished parent and guardian power. Usually sponsored by reformers who represented American upper and middle classes, the reforms sometimes met opposition from economic, ethnic, and religious groups who adhered to more traditional parental authority views. Such attitudes manifested themselves in resistance to educational reforms, opposition to regulation of child labor, and hostility to public supervisions of charitable institutions (Morgan, 1981; Stannard, 1979).

However, to many students coming from diverse family backgrounds (e.g., especially diverse students who had learning difficulties, subaverage intellectual func-

The phenomena of increased family diversity, variations in family types and compositions, and more and more individuals
spending less and less time in traditional
family household arrangements have consequences in what students bring to and
take from classrooms.

tioning, or problem behaviors), school remained a difficult setting. Coping with the
school structure and learning requirements acted as a catalyst for problem escala-
tion. Systemic school exclusion and homogenous grouping, in the form of special
classes or separate programs, highlighted many of these students' educational pos-
sibilities (Cuban, 1993).

Mid-20th-Century Families

Society became more mobile during the 1930s and 1940s. Nuclear families began to
expand; mobility increased with more effective transportation systems that affected
family employment, housing, and recreation opportunities. The Great Depression
and World War II further affected American families. For example, men entering the
service resulted in increased responsibilities to other family members on the home
front. Married women in the labor force changed dramatically from 1900 to 1940,
more than quadrupling (Masnick & Bane, 1980; Stannard, 1979).

Important effects evolving from the increases in the mobile nuclear family included: (a) adoption of urban values; (b) the continued employment of women and
children in the nonfamily economy; (c) the beginning of greater freedom in increased
sexual behavior and marital choices; (d) higher expectations in the marital relationship, especially when men came home from the service; (e) more permissive parent-
child relationships; (f) greater emotional involvement of fathers with their children;
and (g) rising survival rates of the very old (Masnick & Bane, 1980; Stannard, 1979).

Teachers' Roles with Families.   Documentation of teacher-family involvement during the period from 1920 until approximately 1960 suggests that teachers often assumed they had to do all for students (Paul & Simeonsson, 1993). Schlossman (1976)
summarized educational trends of American parents reporting that military draft-test
results influenced teachers' family interpretations (e.g., high rates of emotional and

physical unfitness reportedly characterized American students). Cremin (1988) further hinted that teachers found the American family unable to carry out several of its responsibilities as the principal teacher and socializer for young people. This incapacity resulted in increased public institutions to provide care and training outside the family, such as through welfare and public housing (Cremin, 1988; Cuban, 1993; Paul & Simeonsson, 1993; Schlossman, 1976).

School personnel continued their role in promoting conformity. Beliefs about the nature of knowledge, how instructional practices should occur, and how students learn became widespread and deeply Americanized. These beliefs guided policy makers, practitioners, and parents into expecting certain instructional practices. For example, teacher organization and practice of formal schooling continued to socialize and sort students into varied socioeconomic niches. Teachers continued to inculcate in students the dominant social norms, values, and behaviors, preparing students for mainstream entry, and initiated student groupings by age and ability. Over time, administrators and teachers unwittingly distributed dominant cultural knowledge (e.g., English, history, science), inculcated mainstream values (e.g., work ethic, competitiveness), and channeled students into appropriate socioeconomic niches (e.g., some into corporate, professional, and business careers; others into service and low-grade technical jobs) (Bremner, 1971; Cuban, 1993; Morgan, 1981).

Dominant teacher-centered practices enduring during the mid-20th century characterized many 1940s and 1950s classrooms as well. Family members did not question teacher use of standard instructional behaviors: arranging desks in rows to secure uniform behaviors; relying on homework to ascertain parental educational involvement; giving tests and projects to sort students by achievement; having students follow teacher-directed procedures for seat work, recitation, and reports, and segregating or excluding students unable to perform to teacher expectations. Most individuals accepted school practices.

Many students already learning the necessary rules at home met teachers expectations. However, for students where school rules were unfamiliar (e.g., immigrant students; students with learning needs), school adjustment remained difficult. School exclusion, special groups, or separate programs continued to highlight these students' educational assignments.

Parents, school personnel, and social reformers began speaking up, however, such that by the mid-1960s, advocacy groups had evolved for students with special needs. Paul and Simeonsson (1993) reported on teachers and family involvement during this time period. They suggested how perceived family roles, especially in parents of children with disabilities, slowly changed from blame-placing to advocacy. A major historical theme challenged by concerned parents, school personnel, and social reformers entailed that parents held responsibility for their child's learning, ability, or behavior problems. A recurring historical status ascribed to parents and reinforced by professionals indicated parents as scapegoats. Accordingly, parents often assumed blame for their children's disability. In early family theoretical themes, this thinking limited family involvement with schools and helped to create family and school animosity.

However, by the 1960s and 1970s, parents sought legislative mandates and regulations pertaining to the importance of the right to appropriate education for all students and to family involvement in educational decision making. An emphasis in the parental role moved from principal causative factor to principal agent of treatment and change (Paul & Porter, 1981). There was increasing rejection of the parent-as-scapegoat thinking as teachers and other professionals viewed the value of active family involvement. Parents won rights for their children and themselves through state and federal litigation and the development of new laws (e.g., Pub. L. 94–142) that guaranteed appropriate services and participation of parents in decisions about their children. Growing support evolved for positive roles for parents as collaborators with professionals (Turnbull, Summers, & Brotherson, 1984; Turnbull & Turnbull 1986, 1990).

Modern American Families

Demographic analysis reveals that current American families reflect increasing diversity. Changes since the 1960s include: (a) a shift in the age when children leave home; (b) a rise in the proportion of families made up of women living with children or other relatives but not with husbands; (c) a rise in the proportion of single-person households; (d) a decline in husband/wife households as a proportion of all households; (e) a decline in the number of people who live neither alone nor as nuclear family members (i.e., as siblings, parents, or grandparents of the couple or individual heading the household); and (f) an increase in the number of divorced families (Bureau of the Census, 1992; Masnick & Bane, 1980).

For example, Masnick and Bane (1980) found that, far from being abnormal, the low marriage, high divorce, and low fertility rates of the 1960s generation of young adults were consistent with previous long-term trends, though inconsistent with the pattern established by their parents' generation. One of every five marriages ended in divorce by 1960. Masnick and Bane's 1960 figure marked a similar increase over that of 1929—when about one in eight marriages ended in divorce.

While the percentage of single-person households doubled during the period from 1949 until 1979, during the period from 1919 until 1979, it had tripled (Stannard, 1979). Between 1980 and 1990, however, households made up of married couples increased only slightly in number, while other types of households increased dramatically. Fewer and fewer households had children present (Bureau of the Census, 1992).

There were an estimated 94.3 million American households, averaging 2.63 persons per household by 1991. Out-of-wedlock childbearing had increased sharply. Among first births to women 15 to 34 years old in the 1985–89 period, 29% were born out of wedlock, up from 13% in the 1960–64 period. Out-of-wedlock childbearing increased sharply in the past generation for all women. Additionally, single-parenting families were common in African American families as early as the 1960s. (Bureau of the Census, 1992).

Further, family compositions in the form of employed family members and family types underwent change. For example, two-worker families continue to proliferate across families and are becoming an increasing proportion of households overall. In 1990, 53% of women 18 to 44 years old with infants under 1 year old were in the labor force, compared with 38% in 1980. For women with less than a high school education, the rate in 1990 was 30%, not significantly different from the 1980 rate of 28%.

Step-families are also increasing. The divorce ratio, defined as the number of currently divorced persons per 1,000 persons who are married and living with their spouses, rose from 47 in 1970 to 148 in 1991. The higher ratios for women (60 in 1970 and 172 in 1991) than for men (35 in 1970 and 124 in 1991) reflect the higher incidence of remarriage among divorced men than among divorced women (Bureau of the Census, 1992).

Unfortunately, poverty has proliferated such that the number of persons below the poverty level has increased dramatically. The 1990 poverty rate for the White population was 10.7%; for the Hispanic population, 28.1%; and for the African-American population, 31.9%. Further, female-headed families had a median income of just under $17,000 in 1990, less than half the income of two-parent families (Bureau of the Census, 1992).

Family demographics have played an important role in special education populations and services as well. For example, nearly 15 years ago, Kamp and Chinn (1982) found that approximately 30% of all students in special education came from multicultural backgrounds. More recently, Reschley (1989) reported that most special education programs have a disproportionately large number of non-Anglo-American children. The continuing, changing demographics of the United States point to substantive increases in this number. In fact, increases in births of non-White, non-Anglo children have more than doubled over the past 20 years, up from 16% in the 1970s to 36% in 1984 (Research and Policy Committee of the Committee for Economic Development, 1987). Advocates expect these figures to rise, anticipating that by the year 2000, newborns in American families will comprise "2.4 million more Hispanic children; 1.7 million more African-American children; 483,000 more children of other races; and 66,000 more White, non-Hispanic children" than in 1985 (Children's Defense Fund, 1989, p. 116). Table 11.6 summarizes changing family-variable trends.

Teachers' Roles with Families.   Changing American demographics increasingly encourage teachers to consider what they do and how they interact with students and families. The phenomena of increased family diversity, variations in family types and compositions, and more and more individuals spending less and less time in traditional family household arrangements have consequences in what students bring to and take from classrooms.

Current teacher roles with families are vast. Among others, family roles for teachers entail that they: (a) demonstrate knowledge and skills about individual and family needs and strengths; (b) understand and practice life-skills instruction for students with disabilities relevant to independence, community involvement, personal living and employment, and home life of the student; (c) identify diversity and dynamics of families, schools, and communities relative to lifelong instruction for individuals with disabilities and their effective adjustments across the life span; (d) examine instructional techniques and strategies that promote successful change and adaptation for individuals with disabilities and their families; (e) respond to typical concerns of families of individuals with disabilities and develop appropriate strategies to help families deal with these concerns; (f) recognize and program effectively for educational and work support services, including roles of students, parents, and teachers in planning, implementing, and evaluating successful school to work transitions; (g) identify quality of life issues (e.g., leisure time and recreational activities) that provide an important source of pleasure and relaxation for individuals with disabilities; (h) demonstrate successful methods for working with parents, other family mem-

Table 11.6
Changing Family-Variable Trends in America

Time Period	Family-Variable Trends
Mid-19th to Mid-20th Centuries	External forces such as economic pressures and fertility rates governed the actual size and shape of the family, but the "ideal" type, expressed in custom and inheritance law, exerted influence on critical variables including attitudes, relationships, who married and at what age, who stayed home, and who held a position of family authority.
	In the preindustrial era, the family was the principal production unit in agriculture, manufacturing, and commerce. Wealthy aristocratic land-holding families functioned as a managerial unit; members' authority related to its household structure and inheritance customs, with most families governed by paternal authority. The peasant family assigned family tasks according to age and sex variables. Inheritance customs and practices followed property assignments on established bases. In small towns, family roles included various tasks of the clothmaking; trade-spinning; weaving; finishing of leather, wood, and metal goods; and manufacturing. Many families also produced a variety of handi-craft products, with husband and wife usually acting as partners.
	The gradual and comparative aging of the total population, a develop-ment which began to manifest itself early in the 19th century, meant that an increasing share of the American people were available for maintaining and rearing the young.
Mid-20th Century	Family members born prior to 1920 lived through the Great Depres-sion and World Wars I and World War II. Many family members were immigrants or sons and daughters of immigrants, and all were born at a time when over half of the American population was rural. Many spouses married late, had small families, and in their later years, often lived alone.
	Family members born between 1920 and 1940 also lived through World War II. They married early, became increasingly mobile through advances in transportation systems, and produced many children. Many divorced later in life or entered the empty-nest stage during the end of their lives.
	Important midcentury social and cultural influences on the family in-cluded: (a) increased employment of the housewife, beginning approx-imately during World War II and increasing until approximately the be-ginning of the 1950s; (b) an increased standard of living for many; (c) an increase in the size of the nuclear family (from approximately 1945 until 1965); (d) as the struggle for more space in which to live in-creased, an increasing greater dependence on the home, reduction of contact with neighbors, and movement from the city to the suburbs; (e) an increase in family mobility, and consequent lessening of the ties with extended kin; (f) an increase in the disparity in life-style between city and rural dwellers; (g) an increase in the role of the family for emotional interdependence and a decrease in authority of individual family members per se.

Table 11.6   *continued*

Time Period	Family-Variable Trends
Modern	Family members born in the post-World War II period settled in the central cities and in small towns. As they aged, many females sought careers and independence before marriage and childbearing, and both males and females were better educated than earlier generations. Accordingly, recent family trends include: (a) the shrinking size of households; (b) the decline in the proportion of households headed by a married couple; (c) the increase in the number of working mothers; (d) the sharp rise in the number of people who live alone; (d) an increase in divorce and separation; (e) the increase in the number of children living with only one parent; (f) the growing inability of one-earner families to cope with recession and inflation; and (g) the sex and age segregation characterizing American living arrangements.
	Currently, two-worker families and single-parent families continue to proliferate and are becoming an increasing proportion of households overall. Children have increasing numbers of working and divorced parents.

bers, and community personnel; and (i) implement strategies for preparing students to live harmoniously and productively in a multiclass, multiethnic, multicultural, and multinational world.

Unfortunately, a lack of family knowledge and skills can be problematic for educational personnel unfamiliar with different ethnic backgrounds, cultural heritage, and family living arrangements (Correa, 1989; Hanson, 1993; Heid, & Harris, 1989; Hoover & Collier, 1991). All teachers can profit from realistic expectations of families in considering their levels of involvement in community or school programming. Teachers deal with unique family perspectives and personal family expectations for the student's completion of educational goals and objectives. In order to plan, implement, and evaluate effectively, teachers need accurate perceptions of students' family diversity, life-styles, cultures, and the many contributions family diversity can facilitate in classrooms. Teacher understanding of where students live, their homes, and their communities can contribute to effective education.

On a positive note, federal and state mandates now promote active professional participation in family and transition matters. For example, parent and teacher interactions, significantly expanded by passage of Part H of Public Law No. 99–457 (Education of Handicapped Amendments), highlighted recent family-centered intervention services for infants and toddlers with disabilities (Gallagher, 1993). Part H, created to provide comprehensive services, includes multidisciplinary evaluations and intervention services. Development of the Individualized Family Service Plan (IFSP) continues to indicate the degree to which professionals and parents develop appropriate programs. Input from families, professionals, and service-delivery agency personnel helps in the design and implementation of the IFSP.

Germane to all students with diverse learning needs and strengths is federal legislation encouraging their early preparation for adult roles and responsibilities. Public Law No. 102-476 (Individuals with Disabilities Act [IDEA]), passed in 1990, provided a collaboration impetus for interagencies involved in service provision. IDEA highlights family involvement and collaboration by significant individuals important in students' lives. Accordingly, family-centered services became elementary teaching priorities. Family research and practices were found to link to educational accountability, funding provisions, inclusion, participatory school-based management, transitions, and school reform (O'Shea, O'Shea, & Nowocien, 1993).

Family practices proliferated for teachers of school-aged students in the 1990s (O'Shea et al., 1993; Turnbull & Turnbull, 1990). As such, parents participated not only in educational planning for their children with disabilities, but families also participated more fully in the development of home-to-school, within-school, and school-to-community policies. Such involvement included family participation on federal, state, and local interagency coordinating councils; involvement in transition decision making; and involvement in the formation of local and state parent advocacy groups affecting family policy and program decisions. Families of elementary-aged students, in essence, became more of a driving force in the provision of services to their children.

As a result of recent legislation, professional and family involvement also became high school priorities. For example, school-to-work transition services began in the late 1980s with the intent to integrate youth educational and vocational rehabilitation services. Professionals and families concentrated on work-related skills and behaviors as students prepared to exit schools. They began readying students for the adult world, increasingly important at the high school level, such as through the *School to Work Act of 1994*. This act highlighted collaboration and problem solving by the departments of education and labor by encouraging partnership models between the home and school-based and employment-based sites. School and employment personnel, along with parents and students, now seek to plan, implement, and evaluate integrated school-based and work-based learning. These individuals seek outcomes meant to maximize student independence, self-sufficiency, and adult success. Assuming that students with learning disabilities require more assistance than their nondisabled peers do, teachers, families, and community personnel collaborate in response to the need for additional supports linking service settings.

Finally, national advocates called for coadvocacy. Local and state administrators, community personnel, teachers, and parents began to focus more sharply on postschooling, learning outcomes, authentic experiences, and generalization to meaningful tasks. They began voicing a need for more efficient and effective instruction that will prepare all students for life in the next century. National goals called for students to exit school literate and with the knowledge and skills necessary to compete in a global economy. Thus, interagency coordination illustrates intense reform challenges as families and school or community personnel advocate together to prepare students for postschool adult-living objectives. Table 11.7 summarizes historic teacher roles with families.

The next section presents a discussion on family research importance to teachers instructing students with diverse learning strengths and needs. Family knowledge, skills, and involvement are important to all professionals working with students with LD.

Table 11.7
Examples of Teacher Roles with Students and Families

Early Families (Approximately 1775–1900) Examples of Teacher Roles

With students:
1. Instruct students in the basics of reading, mathematics, and writing.
2. Teach students school rules and classroom etiquette.

With families:
1. Have little or no involvement with families.

Early-20th-Century Families Examples of Teacher Roles

With students:
1. Assess and instruct students in the basics of reading, mathematics, and writing.
2. Teach students school rules and classroom etiquette.
3. Begin the assimilation and acculturation process of students' American citizenship.

With families:
1. Communicate about student progress through report cards and homework.

Mid-20th-Century Families Examples of Teacher Roles

With students:
1. Assess and instruct students in the basics of reading, mathematics, writing, Latin, science, history, home economics, music, and art.
2. Teach students school rules and classroom etiquette.
3. Continue the assimilation and acculturation process of students' American citizenship.
4. Sort students by ability, achievement, career choice options, grade levels, and so forth.

With families:
1. Continue to communicate about student progress through report cards and homework.

Modern Families Examples of Teacher Roles

With students:
1. Assess and instruct students in the basics of reading, mathematics, writing, English, biology, chemistry, geology, astronomy, history, home economics, child care, music, art, world cultures, sociology, psychology, industrial arts, geography, science, foreign language, vocational/technical skills, computer technology, physical education, and so forth.
2. Teach students behavior management strategies to increase positive behaviors and decrease negative behaviors, self-management, peer collaboration, and cooperative learning in the home, school, and community.
3. Identify, promote, and facilitate student self-awareness, cultural and family diversity, and interdependence with others—from a community and global perspective.
4. Guide students to other community and school resources, such as counselors, social workers, therapists, and so forth.

With families:
1. Communicate about student progress using report cards, homework, portfolios, rubrics, parent conferences, Individualized Education Programs, and other communication systems used with parents (e.g., parent forms, family newsletters, or parent educational projects), and so forth.

Table 11.7 *continued*

2. Facilitate transitions with parents, other family members, and other care givers within and between students' homes, communities, and schools.
3. Advocate with parents, other family members, and other care givers on behalf of student rights and responsibilities in the home, school, and community.
4. Work with parents, other family members, and other care givers to provide appropriate:
   testing and evaluation of student progress;
   special academic projects in various subject areas developed for individual students;
   special community-based projects developed for individual students and families;
   specially designed bulletin boards, posters, or charts;
   specially designed peer-interaction projects;
   behavior management techniques for individual students or groups;
   collaboration activities with community and other school professionals;
   cultural awareness activities;
   physical-environment and safety projects;
   teacher-made learning materials for individual students;
   teacher-made materials with adaptations or modifications for individual students;
   attendance at district workshops, faculty meetings, PTA meetings, other school groups;
   data-collection and record-keeping systems used in the classroom;
   special use of computers;
   teacher- and student-directed learning centers;
   paraprofessional and classroom volunteer activities;
   videotaping of instructing, management, or collaboration activities.

THE IMPORTANCE OF FAMILY RESEARCH TO TEACHERS INSTRUCTING STUDENTS WITH LD

Historically, families of students and professional knowledge of those families have received little recognition. However, family issues and struggles have shaped the LD field. For example, family researchers and practitioners effectively shifted attention to predominant practices affecting students throughout the life span. Teachers cannot ignore the fact that they must not only have the knowledge and skills to work with students in academic and behavior areas, but, also require familiarity with important issues affecting students outside classrooms. That is, home, school, and community all are relevant learning settings. Each setting contributes to what students bring to and take from school opportunities. Families and communities affect when, where, what, how, and whether diverse students learn.

All professionals working with students with LD can profit from application of the family knowledge shaping and contributing historically to the LD field. The following illustrations examine why knowledge of family research and practices is important.

1. General education services will increase for students with LD. Today's professionals and families face multiple challenges and consider many strategies when they assume that the family and student are central to the service delivery system; effective services revolve around and support families and students (Karp, 1993). Importantly, because students with LD now are receiving more services

in general education classes, there is increased understanding required of every school professional.

For example, there is available a comprehensive picture of integration trends based on national special education statistics. Sawyer, McLaughlin, and Winglee (1994) provided placement data on all children served under the IDEA, Part B, and Chapter 1 of State Operated Programs (SOP). Statistical analyses revealed that placements in the general education classroom show a relatively consistent increase over time for most disability categories and a general national movement to serve more students with disabilities within general education classrooms.

However, for students with LD, interpretation of the trends may be confounded by increases in the number of students identified. While the number of students identified with LD has increased dramatically, every year since 1977–78 (from approximately 1.2 million in 1977–78 to 2 million in 1989–90), percentage increases in general education class placements (since 1985) could be due, in part, to the recent identification of large numbers of students with LD who have less severe disabilities than those identified in earlier years. There is some evidence, for example, that the numerical increase in this disability may be due, in part, to more liberal eligibility criteria resulting in LD identification of "hard to teach," underachieving children (Algozzine & Korinek, 1985). Nonetheless, despite the possibly confounding statistics, the data suggest that students with LD are spending more time in the general education classroom. Roles and responsibilities in family-transition knowledge and skills assume more prominence in educational decision-making as varied professionals serve students with LD.

2. Diversity awareness continues to be a critical component in meeting student needs and strengths. Data reported by Helge (1991) indicated that diverse students fared worse than traditional students in statistical comparisons of at-risk factors for academic and social failure. Diverse students from migrant families who are illiterate or with poor backgrounds face the possibility of dropping out from school. Consequently, students with LD from poor families or those with limited academic opportunities continue to face tremendous risks. Cummins (1986) found that while students with LD compose the largest category of students in special education classrooms, the LD category appears to be favored when diagnosing minority students, particularly students from Hispanic backgrounds.

The number of students with a variety of cultural backgrounds and limited English proficiency placed in programs for students with LD is growing at a disproportionate rate (Jacobs, 1991). Reasons for the placement trend relate to: (a) inability of culturally and linguistically diverse students to perform to teacher expectations for correct academic performance and classroom behavioral standards; (b) inappropriate labels due to poor assessment and evaluation scores which may result from their cultural and linguistic diversity; and (c) teacher expectations and assessment instruments that generally reflect a bias toward the cultural expectations of the majority, White, Anglo-American population in this country.

With such increases in this diverse population added to the historic tendency to identify and place a disproportionate number of children from this population in special education, teachers of students with LD can expect a concurrent rise in the numbers of culturally diverse students receiving their attention. Thus, it becomes imperative for all professionals to understand implications resulting from varied family compositions and households (Correa, 1989; Hanson, 1993; Heid & Harris, 1989; Hoover & Collier, 1991).

3. Understanding various trainings and orientations helps families and professionals. Professionals with whom teachers work have various family conceptualizations and often play a role in school services (e.g., views of administrators, counselors, family legal advocates, family therapists, health care workers, psychologists, teachers, and social workers may clash in IEP meetings). Nonetheless, understanding others' views is vital. As teachers integrate historical family knowledge, they will be in a better position to value, respect, and accept other perspectives. Professionals may bridge the gap between theoretical perspectives and practices in order to integrate family assessment and interventions. For example, teacher use of the governing theoretical concepts and principles can guide them to determine whether espoused professional practices are used to family advantages. Teachers can better select with families and other professionals student assessment and treatment strategies. In turn, more effective family practices may evolve when professionals understand and value each others' orientations.

4. Family knowledge may help to avoid past mistakes. Professional understanding of the historical treatment of families may help to safeguard against past mistakes. Many family policies, procedures, and programs were not available until the late 20th century. It took many years for professionals and society to realize the benefits of active family involvement and contributions families make to education. Procedural safeguards evolving from federal and state mandates have helped. However, family expertise is a valued and recognized variable in school services. Families, as allies, increase resources important to students, schools, and communities.

5. Family knowledge helps in understanding parents' time commitment to educational involvement. Two-worker families are likely to have more money and less time than demographically similar one-worker families (Masnick & Bane, 1980). Teacher perspectives of family involvement may, thus, depend on differences in time allotted by parents to homework tasks, in leisure activities among family members, and in the choice and direction parents want in their child's educational program. Today's decreased size of families, economics, family stressors, and the difficulties in maintaining family ties may increase the importance of friendship, neighborhoods, and organizations as social support systems and personal ties. The point is that as teachers gain information on unique experiences family, they are in better positions to offer realistic programming based on needs and strengths of individual students and families.

6. <u>Long-term family strategies help teachers in transition planning</u>. As a result of recent legislation, student transitions are fast becoming school priorities (Turnbull & Turnbull, 1990; Wehman et al., 1986). Efforts culminate in outcomes maximizing student independence, self-sufficiency, and adult success (Halpern, 1985; Will, 1984). Public Law No. 101–476, the 1990 amendments that include transition services, encouraged students, teachers, and families to coordinate school programming with businesses and transition service agencies, beginning early in students' careers. Student IEPs must now include a statement of transition services needed for students who are 16 or over and when individually appropriate, for students who are 14 or over. The most substantive amendment in Public Law No. 101–476 included transition service plans specifying a statement of interagency responsibilities and linkages. The agency, purpose, contact persons, and time by which the linkage must occur are paramount to professionals and families.

Transition knowledge is vital to all professionals, even teachers of preschoolers. For example, Jones (1991) found that legislative mandates actually increased the number of potential transitions for the preschool years (thus increasing demands placed upon the child, family, and professionals involved in providing services). Dunst, Trivette, and Deal (1988) cautioned teachers that the IFSP may fail due to changing family needs not realistically covered in long-term intentions, methods, and procedures applicable over extended periods of time. When teachers and other professionals work together with families in planning and implementing transitions, they assist long-term student gains.

7. <u>Appreciating family efforts will assist teachers in their own personal effectiveness</u>. Teachers who understand family theories and evolving teaching roles in <u>advocacy</u>, assessment, <u>collaboration</u>, curriculum, <u>legal procedures</u>, programming, and transition roles with family can function as master teachers. They are in a better position to <u>demonstrate effective decision making</u> based on important variables in students' lives. Master teachers distinguish themselves from more narrowly focused technicians. It is not strictly a reflection of the differences between an experienced and a beginning teacher. The distinction also reflects the differences between an experienced teacher who analyzes the social, historical, and theoretical context, and an experienced teacher who can implement assessment or instructional procedures, but without considering why or how implementation affects, and is affected by, variables outside the classroom. Appreciating family efforts, thus, may help many professional, master teachers in individual reflections and their own personal growth and development.

Skills and competencies in assisting students, families, and other service providers in making decisions about, and coping with, family issues help to define the teacher's educational tasks today and for life in the 21st century. Teacher skills and competencies include those listed on Table 11.8. Listings identify <u>teacher skills and competencies in advocacy, assessment, collaboration, curriculum, legal procedures, programming, and transition roles with families</u>.

Table 11.8
Examples of Teacher Skills and Competencies in Family Issues

Area	Skills	Competencies
Advocacy	* Recognition of need for advocacy * Interpersonal skills * Effective communications * Risk-taking abilities * Teaming knowledge * Awareness of student self-directedness encouraged or expected by teachers	Discussing with families expected similarities and differences for students with various disabilities—and degrees of—during home or community experiences. Include discussions on the impact to siblings, grandparents, neighbors, and so forth Encouraging questions and comments. Specifying resources, services, and programs that will help in local advocacy efforts Critiquing, contributing to program changes, and responding to critiques from others Acting on students' behalf Seeking continual changes that promote better outcomes for schools, families, and communities Contributing and providing personal insights to help facilitate self-advocacy Demonstrating recognition of others' advocacy needs and their expertise in behavioral, cultural, economical, educational, ethical, familial, medical, residential, and social factors influencing students with disabilities Teaching students about characteristics of their disabilities, their own strengths and weaknesses, and how they are alike or unalike their peers so that they may increase self-advocacy
Assessment	* Achievement and behavior * Needs of typical and exceptional individuals at home and school * Etiologies of ability, behavior, learning, social skills, and so forth * Theoretical perspectives of ability, behavior, learning, social skills, and so forth * Characteristics of normal, delayed, and disordered patterns of ability, behavior, learning, social skills, and so forth * Effects of student problems in ability, behavior, learning, social skills and so forth on home, school, or community life	Considering assessment variables relative to student integration realities, recreation or leisure skills, financial support, emotional and physical well-being, health awareness, community awareness, and citizenship (guardianship or advocacy) responsibilities Conducting comprehensive assessments including academics; social skills, "follow-along" support needs, home and family variables, student self-help skills, integration setting realities, recreation or leisure skills, financial support, emotional and physical well-being, health awareness, community awareness, citizenship (guardianship or advocacy) rights and responsibilities, and vocational and educational needs

Table 11.8   *continued*

Area	Skills	Competencies
Assessment	* Cultural and environmental milieu of the child and the family * Educational implications of individualized and group assessments * Norm-referenced assessments * Criterion-referenced assessments * Alternative assessments such as portfolios, rubrics, and so forth * Assessment roles of families	Assessing student needs based on settings demands, such as in schools, vocational sites, postsecondary educational training options, careers, or community living sites Using assessments that include indicators of family and student needs, interests, and preferences Using assessment devices that relate to relevant outcome-based adult priorities and family priorities
Collaboration	* Teaming skills * Group process knowledge * Effective communication * Problem solving * Decision making * Strategic planning * Team implementations * Team evaluations * Understanding cross-disciplinary needs * Understanding unique family differences in coping with the demands and challenges of a child with a disability. * Understanding data on other professional roles, academic preparation, clinical experiences, and expertise, and the principles and procedures underlying team building and the group process * Knowledge of family needs across settings, and school or community entrance or exit facilitation * Knowledge on effective cross-disciplinary communication skills, including information on how best to incorporate the basic terminology of other disciplines. * Knowledge of other's backgrounds, experiences, training, philosophical orientations, languages, communication styles, and expectations	Validating others' insights and expertise by demonstrating mutual respect, empathy, openness, congruence, and team decisions Demonstrating respect for family and other service provider contributions in decisions, and working toward a common goal of successful programming When differences arise, facing conflicts and working to resolve them rather than avoiding or letting conflicts escalate. Providing information in a variety of forms (e.g., books, materials) to help students, families, siblings, and other professionals Providing up-to-date information to families on local placement and service options available. Continually sharing resources and information with families Using open communication methods often, such as letters home, shared reports, face-to-face contacts, and home visits Scheduling time to discuss program issues, student progress, parent options, community representative input, or other issues Modifying IEPs, ITPs, or family programs on the basis of student and family needs for a particular service

Table 11.8   *continued*

Area	Skills	Competencies
Curriculum	* Knowledge of normal cognitive and adaptive development and possible deviations relative to specific student's levels of development or degree of disability * Knowledge of age-appropriate curriculum * Knowledge of specific family school-involvement priorities * Knowledge of relevant family data having an impact on curriculum effectiveness (e.g., family backgrounds, cultures, expectations, coping style differences, family support-program needs, parent training desires or accessibility, and teacher influence on home environments)	Coordinating educational service programs with families and adult agencies. Anticipating postschool years including college-bound training, technical schools, vocational training, supported work, or paid employment Planning for a functional curriculum related to student self-advocacy, self-management, awareness of learning strengths and weaknesses, self-instruction, and individual decision making in adult roles. Including students in decision making as much as possible in order to enhance their choices, emphasize their independence, and consider their likes and dislikes. Awareness of changing student needs in less restrictive environments and the accompanying stress related to programming, teacher expectations, and chances for student survival and success Planning, programming, and evaluating for student education and training for work; health and social skills; home and family adjustments; leisure time and recreational pursuits; and community involvement Teaching specific skills that are functional, longitudinal, and based on student self-advocacy and independence Planning, programming, and evaluating, based on realistic resources
Legal Procedures	* Federal, state, and local litigation * Federal, state, and local legislation * Free appropriate public education applications * Educational referrals * Educational assessments * Least restrictive environments * Individual Family Service plans	Demonstrating awareness of relevant local, state, and federal laws having an impact on students, families, and teachers Attending current workshops, in-services, college courses, and so forth to obtain updated legal information Providing information to parents unfamiliar with legal requirements of educational assessment and programming for children

Table 11.8 *continued*

Area	Skills	Competencies
Legal Procedures	* Individualized Education Programs * Parent and student rights * Mediation knowledge * Due process procedures	Explaining the referral processes for formal placement in school programs, assessment procedures, and delivery of services prior to the child's formal entrance to programs Meeting with families, students, and significant professionals often, as part of best practices to avoid legal misunderstandings
Programming	* Knowledge of outcome-oriented programming * Knowledge of content and subject areas * Knowledge of age-appropriate planning * Knowledge of functional curricula * Knowledge of integration of family priorities in programming * Knowledge of future implications of current programming * Recognition of teachers' expectations of parent/family member involvement on the IEP * Recognition of the varied coping styles within the context of the child's level of disability severity, individual needs, family resources, family dynamics, and teacher expectations * Strategic communication between home, community, and school personnel	Seeking plans and programs that include families, are comprehensive, and contain educational curricula that reflect functional outcomes Using flexible planning and recognition of programming variables in family values, goals, and experiences. Seeking students' and families' choices, needs in integration and inclusions, and independence and interdependence. Sharing information such as present student educational or behavioral level, work samples, behavior rating scale results, curriculum-based assessments, or formal testing profiles Defining "functional," based on the unique student and family needs and setting conditions Linking instructional goals and objectives across home and school settings Encouraging families, students, and significant professionals to visit programs Actively soliciting input into goals and objectives from parents, family members, and other professionals Collecting continual data on program effectiveness and for improved program performances. Documenting in writing by signing, dating, and maintaining accurate records and data systems. Making adjustments when changes are required

Table 11.8   *continued*

Area	Skills	Competencies
Transition Roles	Knowledge of: * Transition roles and responsibilities * Characteristics of infants, toddlers, preschoolers, children, youth and adults * Normal stages of family development * Transitions in family development * Coping and adaptations in normal family development * Unique family events and expectations * Family stressors * Family tasks * Family resources and support systems	Anticipating, planning, implementing, and analyzing systematic time-line procedures of critical life events (e.g., coordinating transition needs, beginning years, not months before students leave school) Openly discussing normalization issues with families (e.g., impact of the child on the family; respite care needs; interdependence and independence expectations in various settings) Coordinating referral services with input to family and with cultural expectations provided by parents and family members Making referrals to, and following through on, community services (health, medical, social, advocacy, and so forth) Helping children adjust to the demands of the new environment, including differences in class size, daily schedule, rules and routines, teacher-child ratios, physical arrangement, and expectations Matching the child's current level of performance with the demands and expectations of the future environment Helping parents plan student home responsibilities, respite care arrangements, or family support groups Determining on the IEP, goal specificity, concrete time-line planning, and cross-categorical focus on the students' varied needs and strengths

Practical Classroom Applications

Teachers can consider the following implications regarding their work with the parents, siblings, and other significant family members of students with LD. Application suggestions are presented for teacher use in developing effective family practices.

1. *Knowledge on family diversity, coupled with information on family theories and on the historic roles of school professionals with families, provide the rationale for professional skills and competencies in working with diverse families.* Working with families of students with LD requires many people skills. Effective communication occurs when people listen and respond; share with and empower each other; and demonstrate knowledge of and skills in valuing, respecting, and accepting others whose training, culture, concepts, skills, and values differ. Effective teachers and family members problem solve formats for expressing, sharing, disagreeing, forming partnerships, deciding, and reaching group goals. They use active listening, empathy, positive regard, consensus decision making, others' feedback, recognition of others' knowledge and expertise, display of positive and supportive behaviors, and reflection in agreeing on services and programming for students with LD.

2. *Teachers often help family members during home-to-school contacts. Teachers do such activities as sharing, questioning, clarifying, or problem solving during meetings or activities set up to explain student learning progress.* Teachers share learning resources, clarify student work samples, and explain assessment records. They help parents by lending media, learning aids, and educational materials appropriate to the student's learning skills and abilities. For example, teachers have available reading materials, computer technology, and videos highlight-

ing students using learning strategies. Teachers might offer a lending library for family use. When asked, teachers interpret professional journals and summarize major findings in language appropriate to parents or guardians. They help families by offering choices in meeting times and places conducive to family involvement.

3. *Teachers recognize that families who lack knowledge or are inactive do not necessarily lack interests in their children's education and achievement, but may need alternatives and choices in school involvement.* For example, teachers may send home daily activities to encourage student learning strategies and skill generalization. Teachers want to elicit family help or feedback. However, for families wanting less involvement, teachers may send home class videos, taped sessions, newsletters, or monthly calendars announcing upcoming learning strategies projects that do not require family involvement. Telephone interviews, surveys, formal brainstorming sessions, and informal sessions (e.g., social or community activities tied to school meeting agenda) can address alternative participation arrangements.

4. *School professionals empower families by having parent or sibling experiences and expertise acknowledged by school administrators and faculty.* Teachers can help to ensure that parents are supported in positive, successful interactions with administrators, teachers, and other parents. Teachers help to empower parents by disseminating resources on the legal rights to family involvement guaranteed by state and federal mandates. Teachers of students at risk for or with identified LD can make sure family members get written information on the state system of education, including legal issues related to general education and special education ser-

(continued)

vices; federal and state legislation and litigation important to understanding educational opportunities; statewide or local support initiatives and resources; positive advocacy, collaboration, and consultation; and parent mentor advocacy roles. Teachers can consult with parents regarding parent-to-parent sharing of information, and they can encourage parent participation in training activities and local and state support groups, as well as encourage growth experiences with other parents whose children have participated in special education services. School professionals and parents or families can move in the direction of supporting rather than combating or confronting each other by together planning for, implementing, and evaluating meetings.

5. *Teachers can help family members become better acquainted with their child's educational program and services by assisting families on important topics.* Teachers and families can work together on school services, providing each other written and oral feedback on their expectations and evaluations of group projects. They can often discuss priorities concerning home-school-community partnerships, talking about such activities as the number of acceptable conferences, resources, persons responsible for task completion, potential outcomes, and individual expectations over the course of the year. They can discuss pressing problems such as concerns about increased class enrollments, children's after school options, strains on family economics due to increased medical and therapeutic services, or family roles in carrying out legal mandates in school services.

6. *Teachers can help students with LD by working together with families promoting collaboration, communication, and mutual understanding among parents, special edu-*cation service providers, and parent support groups. Teachers can help to insure that parents understand the scope of educational resources available and assist families in making informed decisions regarding educational opportunities available.

7. *Teachers coadvocate with family members when they work on defining academic knowledge and skills students should have by the time they graduate from public schools.* Teachers can start by asking what the parents believe are appropriate learning outcomes leading to the student's completion of high school graduation requirements. Teachers and families can discuss ways to measure student progress toward learning outcomes and can participate in strategic planning and implementation processes created to help students achieve adulthood success. Professionals and families, together, advocate to prepare students in exercising rights and responsibilities of citizenship, especially the means to productive employment in a modern economy.

8. *Teachers can help parents directly by being aware of increased parent and family needs for knowledge and skills in the changing field of educational services.* Teachers can be the direct support mechanism for parents new to special needs services. They can act as a liaison to support informal and formal mechanisms for information sharing. Teachers can make phone calls, home visits, or set up school-based conferences to ensure family members have opportunities for collaboration with district officials. School professionals can help families view teachers and families as valued partners in the educational process by promoting common training for parents and educators. They can also help families in analysis of local parent needs and family characteristics—the basis of common training.

SUMMARY

- The most important group to students is the family.
- Successful student learning requires coadvocacy by professionals and family members.
- Diversity is apparent in the many family definitions and compositions comprising home life and households. The term *family* has had multiple meanings.
- There are numerous family theories shaping an understanding of what constitutes a family.
- By the mid-20th century, there was increasing rejection of the parent-as-scapegoat thinking, as teachers and other professionals considered the value of active family involvement.
- Growing support evolved for families taking positive roles as collaborators with professionals.
- The phenomena of increased family diversity, variations in family types and compositions, and more and more individuals spending less and less time in traditional family household arrangements have consequences in what students bring to, and take from, classrooms.
- A lack of family knowledge and skills can be problematic for educational personnel unfamiliar with students' ethnic backgrounds, cultural heritage, and family living arrangements.
- Family practices proliferated for teachers of school-aged students in the 1990s.
- Family knowledge, skills, and involvement are important to all professionals working with students with LD.

DISCUSSION QUESTIONS

To help extend your understanding, reflect on and discuss the following questions:

1. What are the cultural, ethnic, and familial backgrounds of students in your classroom?

2. Explore computer programs and other library resources to locate more information related to the influence of the learning, behavioral, linguistic, and cultural characteristics of students, on their home, school and community opportunities. How does this information help you research your own students with LD who are from diverse backgrounds?

3. How has increased family diversity, variations in family types and compositions, and more and more individuals spending less and less time in traditional family household arrangements had consequences for your work with students with LD?

4. In reflecting on your own beliefs regarding family theories, what theoretical contributions do you consider important to your own effective practices for your students' families?

5. What are appropriate family assessment instruments and techniques for identifying and meeting family needs of your students with LD? Target specific ways you can communicate student family needs with parents or guardians.

6. What are specific actions you do to empower your family members of students with LD?

How do you encourage family involvement in your classroom or school?

REFERENCES

Abel, E. (1986). Adult daughters and care to the elderly. *Feminist Studies, 1,* 479–497.

Ackerman, N. W., & Behnen, M. L. (1956). A study of family diagnosis. *American Journal of Orthopsychiatry, 26,* 66–78.

Adams B. N. (1986). *The family. A sociological interpretation* (4th ed.). San Diego, CA: Harcourt Brace Jovanovich.

Algozzine, B., & Korinek, L. (1985). Where is special education for students with high prevalence handicaps going? *Exceptional Children, 51,* 388–394.

Aries, P. (1962). *Centuries of childhood.* New York: Knopf.

Bailey, D. B., Simeonsson, R. J., Yoder, D. E. & Huntington, G. S. (1990). Preparing professionals to serve infants and toddlers with handicaps and their families: An integrative analysis across eight disciplines. *Exceptional Children, 57*(1), 26–35.

Bailey, D. B., Simeonsson, R. J., Winton, P. J., Huntington, G. S., & Comfort, M. (1986). Family-focused intervention: A functional model for planning, implementing, and evaluating individualized family services in early intervention. *Journal of the Division of Early Childhood, 10* (2), 156–171.

Bandura, A. (1960). *Relationship of family patterns to child behavior disorders: A progress report.* Stanford, CA: Stanford University Press.

Bandura, A. (1969). *Principles of behavior modification.* New York: Holt, Rinehart & Winston.

Bandura, A. (1977). Self-efficacy: Toward a unifying theory of behavioral change. *Psychological Review, 84,* 191–215.

Beavers, W. R., & Hampson, R. B. (1990). *Successful families. Assessment and intervention.* New York: Norton.

Behr, S. (1990). *Positive contributions of persons with disabilities to their families.* Lawrence, KS: University of Kansas, Beach Center on Families and Disability.

Borstelmann, L. J. (1983). Children before psychology: Ideas about children from antiquity to the late 1800s. In W. Kessen (Ed.), *Handbook of child psychology: Vol. 1. History, theory, and methods* (pp. 1–40). New York: Wiley.

Bremner, R. H. (1971). *Children and youth in America. A Documentary History. Volume II: 1866–1932.* Cambridge, MA: Harvard University Press.

Broderick, C. B. (1990). Family process theory. In J. Sprey (Ed.), *Fashioning family theory: New Approaches* (pp. 171–206). Newbury Park, CA: Sage.

Broderick, C. B. (1993). *Understanding family processes.* Newbury Park, CA: Sage.

Brunk, G. (1991). *Supporting the growth of the self advocacy movement: What we can learn from its history and activists?* Lawrence, KS: University of Kansas, Beach Family Center on Families and Disability.

Bubolz, M. M., & Sontag, M. S. (1993). Human ecology theory. In P. G. Boss, W. J. Doherty, R. La Rossa, W. R. Schumm, & S. K. Steinmetz (Eds.), *Sourcebook of family theories and methods* (pp. 419–448). New York: Plenum.

Bureau of the Census (1992, February). How we're changing: Demographic state of the nation: 1992. *Current Population Reports, Special Studies Series P-23, No. 177,* Washington, DC: U.S. Department of Commerce.

Burr, W. R. (1973). *Theory, construction, and the sociology of the family.* New York: Wiley.

Byrne, E. A., & Cunningham, C. C. (1985). The effects of mentally handicapped children on families: A conceptual review. *Child Psychology and Psychiatry, 26* (6), 847–864.

Calhoun, A. W. (1918). *A social history of the American family. Volume III: Since the Civil War.* New York: Barnes & Noble.

Case, R. (1975). Gearing the demands of instruction to the developmental capacities of the learner. *Review of Educational Research, 45,* 59–87.

Cheal, D. (1991). *Family and the state of theory.* Toronto: University of Toronto Press.

Children's Defense Fund. (1989). *A vision for America's future.* Washington, DC: Author.

Coontz, S. (1988). *The social origins of private life. A history of American families, 1600–1900.* New York: Verson.

Correa, V. I. (1989). Involving culturally diverse families in the educational process. In S. H. Fradd & M. J. Weismantel (Eds.), *Meeting the needs of culturally and linguistically different students: A handbook for educators* (pp. 130–144). Boston: College-Hill.

Craig, E. R., & Leonard, C. R. (1990). P.L. 99–457: Are speech-language pathologists trained and ready? *ASHA, 32 (April),* 57–61.

Cremin, L. A., (1988). *American education: The metropolitan experience.* New York: Harper & Row.

Crnic, K. A., Friedrich, W., & Greenberg, M. (1983). Adaptation of families with mentally retarded children. A model of stress, coping, and family ecology. *American Journal of Mental Deficiency, 88* (2), 125–138.

Cuban, L. (1993). *How teachers taught. Constancy and change in American classrooms: 1880–1990.* New York. Teachers College Press.

Cummins, J. (1986). Psychological assessment of minority students: Out of context, out of focus, out of control? In A. C. Willig & H. F. Greenberg (Eds.), *Bilingualism and learning disabilities: Policy and practice for teachers and administrators* (pp. 3–11). New York: American Library.

Darling, R. B. (1979). *Families against society: A study of reactions to children with birth defects.* Beverly Hills, CA: Sage.

Darwin, C. (1859). *The origin of species.* New York: Modern Library.

Dewey, E. (1919). *New schools for old.* New York: E. P. Dutton.

Dixon, R. A., & Lerner, R. M. (1992). A history of systems in developmental psychology. In M. H. Bornstein & M. E. Lamb (Eds.), *Developmental psychology: An advanced textbook* (3rd ed., pp. 3–58). Hillsdale, NJ: Erlbaum.

Doherty, W. J., Boss, P. G., LaRossa, R., Schumm, W. R., & Steinmetz, S. K. (1993). Family theories and methods: A contextual approach. In P. G. Boss, W. Doherty, R. LaRossa, W. R. Schumm, & S. K. Steinmetz (Eds.), *Sourcebook of family theories and methods* (pp. 3–30). New York: Plenum.

Epstein, C. F. (1988). *Deceptive distinctions: Sex, gender, and the social order.* New Haven, CT: Yale University Press.

Erikson, E. H. (1963). *Childhood and society* (2nd ed.). New York: Norton.

Farber, B. (1986). Historical context of research on families with mentally retarded members. In J. Gallagher, & P. Vietze (Eds.), *Families of handicapped persons* (pp. 3–24). Baltimore: Brookes.

Forman, E. A., & McMormick, D. E. (1995). Discourse analysis: A sociocultural perspective. *Remedial and Special Education, 16* (3), 150–158.

Freud, S. (1920). Beyond the pleasure principle. In J. Strachey (Ed.), *The standard edition of the complete works of Sigmund Freud.* London: Hogarth Press and the Institute of Psychoanalysis, 1953–1966.

Freud, S. (1923a). *The ego and the id.* New York: Norton.

Freud, S., (1923b). *Origin and development of psychoanalysis.* Chicago: Regenery, Gateway.

Freud, A., (1937). *The ego and mechanisms of defense.* New York: International University Press.

Gagne, R. M. (1974). *Essentials of learning for instruction.* Hinsdale, IL: Dryden Press.

Gagne, R. M. (1977). *The conditions of learning* (3rd ed.), New York: Holt, Rinehart & Winston.

Gallagher, J. (1993). The role of value and facts in policy development for handicapped infants and toddlers and their families. In *Handbook for the development of implementation policies for P. L. 99–457 (Part H).* Chapel Hill, NC: Frank Porter Graham Center.

Gouldner, A. (1970). *The coming crisis in western sociology.* New York: Basic.

Grossman, F. (1972). *Brothers and sisters of retarded children: An exploratory study.* Syracuse, NY: Syracuse University Press.

Gubrium, J. F., & Holstein, J. A. (1990). *What is family?* Mountain View, CA: Mayfield.

Gubrium, J. F., & Holstein, J. A. (1993). Phenomenology, ethnomethodology, and family discourse. In P. G. Boss, W. J. Doherty, R. La Rossa, W. R. Schumm, & S. K. Steinmetz. *Sourcebook of family theories and methods* (pp. 651–672). New York: Plenum.

Hall, C. S. (1954). *A primer of Freudian psychology.* New York: Mentor.

Halpern, A. S. (1985). Transition: A look at the foundations. *Exceptional Children, 51*(6), 479–486.

Hanson, M. J. (1993). Ethnic, cultural, and language diversity in intervention settings. In E. W. Lynch & M. J. Hanson (Eds.), *Developing cross-cultural competence: A guide for working with children and their families* (pp. 3–18). Baltimore: Brookes.

Harpur, U. (1899). *The report of the educational commission of the city of Chicago.* Chicago: Lakeside Press.

Heid, C., & Harris, J. J., III. (1989). Parent involvement: A link between schools and minority communities. *Community Education Journal, 16,* 26–28.

Helge, D. (1991). *Rural, exceptional, at risk.* Reston, VA.: CEC Mini-Library, ERIC Clearinghouse.

Hetherington, E. M., & Baltes, P. B. (1988). Child psychology and life span development. In E. M. Hetherington, R. M. Lerner, & M. Perlmutter (Eds.), *Child development in life-span perspectives* (pp. 1–20). Hillsdale, NJ: Erlbaum.

Hill, R. (1949). *Families under stress: Adjustment to the crisis of war separation and reunion.* New York: Harper.

Hill, R. (1958). Generic features of families under stress. *Social Casework, 49,* 139–150.

Hill, R., & Rodgers, R. (1964). The developmental approach. In H. Christenseon (Ed.), *Handbook of marriage and the family* (pp. 171–211). Chicago: Rand-McNally.

Hook, N., & Paolucci, B. (1970). The family as an ecosystem. *Journal of Home Economics, 62,* 315–318.

Hoover, J. L., & Collier, C. (1991). Teacher preparation for educating culturally and linguistically diverse exceptional learners: Overview of topical issue. *Teacher education and special education, 14*(1), 3–4.

Hutter, M. (1991). *The chinning family: Comparative perspectives.* New York: Wiley.

Ianacone, R. N., & Stodden, R. A. (1987). *Transition issues and directions.* Reston, VA.: Council for Exceptional Children.

Ingoldsby, B. B. (1995). Family origin and universality. In B. B. Ingoldsby & S. Smith (Eds.), *Families in multicultural perspective* (pp. 83–96). New York: Guilford Press.

Jacobs, L. (1991). Assessment concerns: A study of cultural differences, teacher concepts, and inappropriate labeling. *Teacher Education and Special Education, 14*(1), 43–48.

Jaffe-Ruiz, M. (1984). A family systems look at the developmentally disabled. *Perspectives in Psychiatric Care, 22,* 65–71.

Jones, L. (1991). *Strategies for involving parents in their children's education.* Bloomington, IN: Phi Delta Kappa Educational Foundation.

Kamp, S. H., & Chinn, P. C. (1982). *A multiethnic curriculum for special education students.* Reston, VA: Council for Exceptional Children.

Karp, N. (1993). Collaborating with families. In B. Billingsley (Ed.), *Program leadership for serving students with disabilities.* Richmond, VA: Virginia Department of Education, (U.S. DOE, # HO29H10034-93).

Kingsbury, N., & Scanzoni, J. (1993). Structural-functionalism. In P. G. Boss, W. Doherty, R. LaRossa, W. R. Schumm, & S. K. Steinmetz (Eds.), *Sourcebook of family theories and methods* (pp. 195–217). New York: Plenum.

Knafl, K. A., & Deatrick, J. A. (1987). Conceptualizing family response to a child's illness or disability. *Family Relations, 36,* 300–304.

Lathrop, J. C. (1912). The children's bureau. *Proceedings of the National Conference of Charities and Corrections, 1912* (p. 33). Washington, DC: National Conference of Charities and Corrections.

Larrzelere, R. E. (1986). Moderate spanking: Model or deterrent of children's aggression in the family? *Journal of Family Violence, 1,* 27–36.

Lindsey, K. (1981). *Friends as family.* Boston: Beacon Press.

Lipsky, D. K. (1985). A parental perspective on stress and coping. *American Journal of Orthopsychiatry, 55,* 614–617.

Long, D. C., & Bond, L. (1984). Families of the handicapped child: Research and practice. *Family Relations, 33,* 57–65.

Lovaas, O. I. (1977). *The autistic child.* New York: Wiley.

Lovaas, O. I. (1987). Behavioral treatment and normal educational and intellectual functioning in young autistic children. *Journal of Consulting and Clinical Psychology, 55,* 3–9.

Lovaas, O. I., Berberich, J. P., Perloff, B. F., & Schaeffer, B. (1966). Acquisition of imitative speech by schizophrenic children. *Science, 151,* 705–707.

Lull J. (1988). *World families watch television.* Newbury Park: Sage.

Masnick, G. & Bane, M. J. (1980). *The nation's families: 1960–1990.* Boston: Auburn House.

Mattessich, P., & Hill, R. (1987). Life cycle and family development. In M. B. Sussman & S. K. Steinmetz (Eds.), *Handbook of marriage and the family* (pp. 437–469). New York: Plenum.

McCubbin, H. I., & McCubbin, M. A., (1987). Family stress theory and assessment: The T-Double ABCX model of family adjustment and adaptation. In H. I. McCubbin & A. I. Thompson (Eds.), *Family assessment inventories for research and practice* (pp. 3–34). Madison: University of Wisconsin.

McCubbin, H. I., & Patterson, J. M. (1983). Family stress and adaptation to crises: A Double ABCX model of family behavior. In D. Olson & B. Miller (Eds.), *Family studies review yearbook* (pp. 87–106). Beverly Hills, CA: Sage.

McDonald-Wikler, W. (1986). Family stress theory and research on families of children with mental retardation. In J. J. Gallagher & P. M. Vietze (Eds.), *Families of handicapped persons* (pp. 167–196). Baltimore: Brookes.

McPhail, J. C. (1995). Phenomenology as philosophy and method: Applications to ways of doing special education. *Remedial and Special Education, 16* (3), 159–165.

Meichenbaum, D. (1977). *Cognitive-behavior modification. An integrative approach.* New York: Plenum.

Meichenbaum, D. H., & Goodman, J. (1971). Training impulsive children to talk to themselves: A means of developing self-control. *Journal of Abnormal Psychology, 77,* 115–126.

Milan, M. A. (1987). Token economy programs in closed institutions. In E. K. Morris & C. J. Braukmann (Eds.), *Behavioral approaches to crime and delinquency: A handbook of application, research, and concepts* (pp. 195–222). New York: Plenum.

Miller, P. H. (1993). *Theories of developmental psychology* (3rd ed.). New York: Freeman.

Mindel, C. H. & Habenstein, R. W. (1976). *Ethnic families in America. Patterns and variations.* New York: Elsevier.

Morgan, G. D. (1981). *America without ethnicity.* Port Washington, NY: National University Publications.

Murdock, G. P. (1949). *Social structure.* New York: Free Press.

O'Shea, D. J., & O'Shea, L. J., & Nowocien, D. (1993). Parent-teacher relationships in school renewal and educational reform. *Learning Disability Forum, 18* (3), 43–46.

Osmond, M., & Thorne, B. (1993). Feminist theories: the social construction of gender in families and society. In P. G. Boss, W. Doherty, R. LaRossa, W. R. Schumm, & S. K. Steinmetz (Eds.), *Sourcebook of family theories and methods* (pp. 591–622). New York: Plenum.

Paul, J. L., & Simeonsson, R. J., (Eds.). (1993). *Children with special needs: Family, culture, and society* (2nd ed.). Orlando, FL: Harcourt Brace Jovanovich.

Paul, J. L., & Porter, P. B. (1981). Parents of handicapped children. In J. L. Paul (Ed.) *Understanding and working with parents of children with special needs* (pp. 1–22), New York: Holt, Rinehart & Winston.

Piaget, J. (1983). Piaget's theory. In P. H. Mussen (Ed.), *History of child psychology, Volume 1.* (4th ed.). New York: Wiley.

Popenoe, D. (1993). American family decline, 1960–1990: A review and appraisal. *Journal of Marriage and the Family, 55,* 527–541.

Reid, D. M., Robinson, S. J., & Bunsen, T. D. (1995). Empiricism and beyond: Expanding the boundaries of special education. *Remedial and Special Education, 16* (3), 131–141.

Riegel, K. F. (1973). Dialectic operations: The final period of cognitive development. *Human Development, 16,* 346–370.

Reschley, D. (1989). Minority over representation and special education. *Exceptional Children, 54,* 316–323.

Research and Policy Committee of the Committee for Economic Development. (1987). *Children in need: Investment strategies for the educationally disadvantaged.* New York: Committee for Economic Development.

Ryckman, D. B., & Henderson, R. A. (1965, August). The meaning of a retarded child for his parents: A focus for counselors. *Mental Retardation,* 4–11.

Sabatelli, R., & Shehan, C. L. (1993). Exchange and resource theories. In P. G. Boss, W. Doherty, R. LaRossa, W. R. Schumm, & S. K. Steinmetz (Eds.), *Sourcebook of family theories and methods* (pp. 384–411). New York: Plenum.

Sawyer, R. J., McLaughlin, M. J., & Winglee, M. (1994, July). Is integration of students with disabilities happening? An analysis of national data trends over time. *Remedial and Special Education, 15* (4), 204–215.

Schlossman, S. (1976). Before home state: Notes toward a history of parent education in America 1897–1929. *Harvard Educational Review, 46* (3), 436–466.

Sears, R. R., Maccoby, E., & Levin, H. (1957). *Patterns of child rearing.* New York: Harper & Row.

Shea, T. M., & Bauer, A. M. (1991). *Parents and teachers of children with exceptionalities. A Handbook for collaboration* (2nd ed.). Boston: Allyn and Bacon.

Simeonsson, R. J., & Simeonsson, N. E. (1981). Parenting handicapped children: Psychological aspects. In J. L. Paul (Ed.) *Understanding and working with parents of children with special needs* (pp. 51–88), New York: Holt, Rinehart & Winston.

Siqueland, E. R. (1968). Reinforcement patterns and extinction in human newborns. *Journal of Experimental Child Psychology, 6,* 431–442.

Skinner, B. F. (1938). *The behavior of organisms: An experimental analysis.* New York: Appleton-Century-Crofts.

Skinner, B. F. (1953). *Science and human behavior.* New York: Free Press.

Smith, S. (1995). Family theory and multicultural family studies. In B. B. Ingoldsby & S. Smith (Eds.), *Families in multicultural perspective* (pp. 1–29). New York: Guilford Press.

Sprey, J. (1990). Theoretical practice in family studies. In J. Sprey (Ed.), *Fashioning family theory* (pp. 9–33). Newbury Park, CA: Sage.

Stannard, D. E. (1979). Changes in the American family: Fiction and reality. In V. Tufte & B. Myerhoff (Eds.), *Changing images of the family* (pp. 83–96). New Haven, CT: Yale University Press.

Stephens, W. (1963). *The family in cross-cultural perspective.* New York: Holt, Rinehart & Winston.

Stever, F. B. (1994). *The psychological development of children.* Pacific Grove, CA: Brooks/Cole.

Stewart, D. (1989). *A curriculum framework for secondary aged handicapped students designed for use in the state of Georgia under Technical Assistance Activity-03-GA-88-06 (Transition).* Washington, DC: OSERs.

Strickland, B. (1993). Parents and the educational system. In J. L. Paul & R. J. Simeonsson (Eds.), *Children with special needs: Family, culture and society* (2nd ed., pp. 231–255). Orlando, FL: Harcourt Brace Jovanovich.

Summers, J. A., Brotherson, M. J. & Turnbull, A. P. (1988). *The impact of handicapped children on families.* Lawrence, KS: University of Kansas, Beach Center on Families and Disabilities.

Taylor, S. E. (1983). Adjustment to threatening events: A theory of cognitive adaptation. *American Psychologist, 38,* 1161–1173.

Taylor, S. E., Lichtman, R. R., & Wood, J. V. (1984). Attributions, beliefs about control, and adjustment to breast cancer. *Journal of Personality and Social Psychology, 46* (3), 489–502.

Thorndike, E. L. (1913). *Educational psychology: Vol. 2. The psychology of learning.* Westport, CT: Greenwood.

Tseng, W., & McDermott, J. (1979). Triaxial family classification. *Journal of the American Academy of Child Psychiatry, 18,* 22–43.

Turnbull, A. P., & Turnbull, H. R. (1990). *Families, professionals and exceptionality: A special partnership* (2nd ed.). Upper Saddle River, NJ: Prentice Hall/Merrill.

Turnbull, A. P., & Turnbull, H. R. (1986). *Families and professionals: Creating an exceptional partnership.* Upper Saddle River, NJ: Prentice Hall/Merrill.

Turnbull, A. P., Summers, J. A., & Brotherson, M. J. (1984). *Working with families with disabled mem-*

bers: *A family system approach*. Lawrence, KS: University Affiliated Facility.

Voiland, A. L., & Buell, B. (1961). A classification of disordered family types. *Social Work, 6,* 3–11.

Wansart, W. L. (1995). Teaching as a way of knowing: Observing and responding to students' abilities. *Remedial and Special Education, 16* (3), 166–177.

Watson, J. B. (1913). Psychology as the behaviorist views it. *Psychological Review, 20,* 158–177.

Watson, J. B. (1928). *Psychological care of infant and child*. New York: Arno Press.

Wehman, P., Moon, M. S., & McCarthy, P. (1986). Transition from school to adulthood for youth with severe handicaps. *Focus on Exceptional Children, 18* (5), 1–12.

West, C., & Zimmerman, D. H. (1987). Doing gender. *Gender and Society, 1,* 125–151.

Whall, A. L. (1986). *Family therapy theory for nursing*. Norwalk, CT: Appleton-Century-Crofts.

Will, M. (1984). *OSERS programming for the transition of youth with disabilities: Bridges from school to working life*. Washington, DC: Office of Special Education and Rehabilitation Services.

Winch, R. F. (1979). Toward a model of familial organization. In W. R. Burr, R. Hill, F. I. Nye, & I. R. Reiss (Eds.), *Contemporary theories about the family* (vol. 1, pp. 162–179). New York: Free Press.

Wing, L. (1976). A handicapped child in the family. *Developmental Medicine and Child Neurology, 11,* 643–644.

Wolfensberger, W., (1970). Counseling the parents of the retarded. In A. A. Baumeister (Ed.), *Mental retardation: Appraisal, education, and rehabilitation* (pp. 329–400). Chicago: Aldine.

Important changes are taking place in efforts to provide services to students with learning disabilities.

CHAPTER 12

Future Trends and Issues in the Field of Learning Disabilities

In this chapter we will...

- Describe persisting dilemmas and practical concerns that make delivering services a continuing challenge.
- Discuss future practices and continuing issues likely to influence and shape the field of learning disabilities in the next century.

L earning disabilities is one of the newest categories of special education. Its growing pains have been significant and chronic. Continuing issues revolve around definitions, identification and classification practices, and instruction, largely because the edges providing boundaries for the field are blurred. For example, at least five "new and improved" definitions have emerged since LD was first recognized as a special education category, and operationalizations possible for any of them number in the hundreds (Ysseldyke & Algozzine, 1994). Regardless, learning disabilities remains a category for low achievement that cannot be explained by any other diagnostic classification (Ysseldyke, Algozzine, & Thurlow, 1992). Similarly, many of the characteristics associated with LD are common in children and youth with other disabilities (e.g., social problems, inattention, hyperactivity), and behavior rating scales used to make differential diagnoses represent imperfect measures, because no objective markers are available that invariably identify children with LD (Reid, Maag, & Vasa, 1993). Finally, the most effective instructional approaches and interventions for students with LD are also effective with other students with disabilities (i.e., effective instruction works, strategies training works), and interventions and instructional approaches that are not effective with students with LD (e.g., process training) are not effective with other students with disabilities.

As calls for education reform and restructuring continue, the future of special education is uncertain. The movement to educate students with disabilities in natural environments with their neighbors and peers has many worried that hard-fought gains will be lost. Concern for the future has also hit LD. Dealing with efforts to include more and more students with disabilities in classrooms with their neighbors and peers is one area of concern. Dealing with renewed and heightened emphasis on outcomes and performance standards and maintaining identity in the face of burgeoning interest in attention deficit and hyperactivity disorders are others.

CONTINUING DILEMMAS

No field in special education has been subjected to such intense scrutiny or experienced such powerful and continuing controversies as the field of LD (Wong, 1991; Ysseldyke, Algozzine, & Thurlow, 1992). Issues related to definition, identification and classification, and programming have driven professionals' search for truth, justice, and validity since LD were first offered as explanations for low academic achievement and problem behaviors in America's public schools.

The Trouble with Definitions

The definition of LD most widely accepted by professionals in the field is very similar to the definition first formalized in 1967 by the National Advisory Committee on Handicapped Children (Torgesen, 1991). It is the same definition found in Public Law No. 94–142 (The Education of All Handicapped Children Act of 1975, now the Individuals with Disabilities Education Act) and sets LD as a category for students who for a variety of reasons fail to demonstrate mastery of content expected for their age, grade, and mental abilities. The category seems straightforward and appropriate and the federally accepted definition has served the field well, providing a basis for funding instructional and related services programs (Adelman & Taylor, 1983; Lerner, 1994; Torgesen, 1991; Torgesen & Wong, 1986; Wong, 1991).

Despite relatively widespread acceptance, no topic in the area of LD has received more discussion in professional meetings or publications than debate concerning this definition of LD (Myers & Hammill, 1990). For the most part, concern has centered on people, processes, and terms included in, or excluded from, the definition (Lerner, 1994; Myers & Hammill, 1990; Torgesen & Wong, 1986). Wong (1991) points out that different groups of people have placed different demands on the definition, and this has caused problems as well.

Key points of definitional dissatisfaction and dilemma are well articulated by Myers and Hammill (1990). A summary follows:

1. Because LD may be present in individuals of any ages, a definition that refers only to children or literally or figuratively excludes older people is suspect.

2. Reference to basic psychological processes or underlying causes creates difficulties unless it is clear that the intent is to underscore the *intrinsic* nature of LD.

3. Including obsolete terms, such as *perceptual handicaps*, *brain injury*, and *dyslexia* does not clarify or enhance a definition.

4. Including redundant terms (e.g., spelling and writing) and excluding children, youth, and adults with other disabilities or disadvantages creates problems for interpretation and operationalization.

In response to concerns about the status of efforts to define LD, members of the National Joint Committee on Learning Disabilities (NJCLD) set out to solve the problems. The NJCLD is composed of representatives from the American Speech-Language-Hearing Association (ASHA), the Learning Disabilities Association of America (LDA), the Council for Learning Disabilities (CLD), the Division for Learning Disabilities of the Council for Exceptional Children (DLD), the National Association for School Psychologists (NASP), the Division for Children with Communication Disorders of the Council for Exceptional Children (DCCD), the International Reading Association (IRA), and the Orton Dyslexia Society (ODS). After considerable discussion and professional writing (cf. National Joint Committee on Learning Disabilities, 1981), members of the NJCLD agreed to yet another "new definition of learning disabilities" (cf. Hammill, Leigh, McNutt, & Larsen, 1981). And, much like the hype celebrating "new and improved" commercial products, testimonials in professional publications supporting these efforts and justifying sentence structure and word selection are readily available (cf. Hammill, Leigh, McNutt, & Larsen, 1981; Myers & Hammill, 1990). Despite its proposed advantages, the NJCLD definition has not been adopted as federal regulation. We believe this is because key components in any definition of LD continue to be unresolved, and at this problem's base is the fact that defining any category of special education is a process enmeshed in social and political exigencies that make educational integrity a secondary concern at best.

LD Or Not LD?

A disability definition should create a condition with reasonable diagnostic purity. When the definition is applied, a unique group of students should be identified; otherwise the conceptual and practical confusion that results creates significant problems. Put another way, definitions provide conceptual models for understanding the condition created by the act of grouping and separating characteristics. The ultimate goal is to differentiate those who have the condition from those who do not (e.g., deciding whether a student has LD or not).

In conceptual practice, professionals may argue about the appropriateness of calling people with special learning needs "children" or "adults," and they can debate the significance of including or not including spelling as a disorder or the importance of being "disadvantaged" to having a "learning disability." The simple fact remains that without specific criteria for use in identifying students with LD, professionals will operationalize the definitions in different ways, and confusion relative to "who students with learning disabilities are" will remain. This has been the case in the field of LD (Torgesen, 1991; Wong, 1991; Ysseldyke, Algozzine, & Thurlow, 1992).

In work at the Institute for Research on Learning Disabilities, Ysseldyke and his colleagues examined psychoeducational decision-making practices in the area of LD. After five years of research on how professionals screen, diagnose, identify, and place in the area of LD, they identified significant problems in contemporary identification and classification practices. Central to their work was a concern for the lack of universally accepted and applied criteria (*not* definitions) for identifying students with LD. In some of their work, they operationalized LD in more than 40 different, commonly accepted ways. In an article in the *Journal of Learning Disabilities* addressing screening and diagnosis and the "future of the LD field," Algozzine and Ysseldyke (1986) summarized their research related to classification:

> [W]hile many school identified learning disabled students do meet commonly applied criteria (e.g., 15 point difference between ability and achievement, subtest scatter), some do not (Algozzine & Ysseldyke, 1982). Many low-achieving students, never classified as LD, also meet these same criteria (Epps, Ysseldyke, & Algozzine, 1983), and many normal students are classifiable using these criteria (Ysseldyke, Algozzine, & Epps, 1983). In fact, the overlap in scores for many of these students is so great (Algozzine & Ysseldyke, 1983; Ysseldyke & Algozzine, 1982; Ysseldyke, Algozzine, Shinn, & McGue, 1982) that it is difficult for them not to be classified when commonly used criteria are applied to performance estimates on commonly used assessment devices. (p. 396)

These findings are troublesome to professionals in the field of LD because they suggest that public monies are supporting alternative educational programs for students who are not reliably different from many other learners (Torgesen, 1991). They suggest that "current standards for the identification of [students with learning disabilities] in the schools do not reliably identify a group of children whose learning problems are fundamentally different from those of other poor achievers" (Torgesen, 1991, p. 26). And, while the sociopolitical implications of impurities in classification are troublesome, they are somewhat reduced if positive benefits accrue to individuals who *are* classified.

Diagnostic-Prescriptive Dreams Go On

In the early days, when professionals were first becoming concerned about increasing numbers of students failing in school (i.e., the 50's and 60's), diagnostic-prescriptive teaching models were used to justify searching for process disorders in students with LD. The argument went something like this:

> The students have problems processing information. Their process disorders are the basis for their LD. If specific interventions are prescribed to remediate the process disorders, the LD will be effectively treated.

Unfortunately, process training and other diagnostic-prescriptive instructional methods were largely unproductive (cf. Ysseldyke & Algozzine, 1982) and educational approaches recommended for students with LD exemplify the mixture of approaches advocated for other groups of remedial learners (Lerner, 1994; Myers & Hammill, 1990; Torgesen, 1991; Ysseldyke, Algozzine, & Thurlow, 1992). And, it wouldn't really matter if the differential instruction produced important educational gains. However, there is some evidence that this is not the case. For example, O'Shea and Valcante (1986) found that placing students in LD resource rooms over time did not diminish their academic discrepancies (i.e., differences between assessed ability and achievement) as compared to those students with similar discrepancies who remained in mainstreamed settings.

At present, the idea that students with LD will profit from placement in special programs remains largely an undocumented supposition (Torgesen, 1991). Similar problems exist in related areas:

> Until convincing data on such issues as differential response to treatment are provided, the utility of the concept of dyslexia will continue to be challenged because the reading disabilities field will have no rebuttal to assertions that it is more educationally and clinically relevant to define reading disability without reference to IQ discrepancy. . . .
> No amount of clinical evidence, case studies, or anecdotal reports will substitute for the large-scale experimental demonstrations that, compared to other groups of garden-variety poor readers, discrepancy-defined poor readers show differential response to treatment and prognosis—and for further evidence that the reading-related cognitive profile of these two groups are reliably different. (Stanovich, 1989, p. 16)

The continuing criticism has become a driving force for some professionals to argue and search for students with "real" LD, and the beat goes on, the train comes full circle, the generals put mines in the paths of the soldiers.

The history of special education is full of controversy over finding the "right" definition and the "real" students for each of the special education categories. The implications of all this searching are related to finding students with real disabilities. Confusion created by evidence that students with LD and other low-achieving students are psychometric twins with different mothers (cf. Ysseldyke, Algozzine, Shinn & McGue, 1982) has provoked some of the recent searches. Similarly, the continuing conclusion that LD is a heterogeneous, highly variable category has caused problems in generalizing from research (Torgeson, 1991) and has led to efforts to find subgroups of students with pure LD. And, despite statistical machinations that sometime boggle the most well-trained, analytical minds, the most consistent conclusion from all this work is that "we will never identify completely homogeneous subgroups of children" with LD (Torgesen, 1991, p. 30), that doing so would offer little benefit to those concerned with making a difference in the lives of all children who fail to profit from the educational experiences provided in America's schools. The bottom line here is simple: You don't need a name to provide effective intervention for students with learning problems, as long as society (and its agents) will let you provide it without labeling them.

PLANNING FOR THE FUTURE

As the 1980s came to a close, educators wrote, heard, and spoke a language that had taken on a new mission—*reform, restructuring,* and *excellence* were among the terms reflecting the content and direction of this movement. The push for reform arose from a series of reports and public opinion polls that pointed to the presence of significant problems in current educational practice. The mission was given guidelines and direction when in September of 1989, President Bush and the governors from the fifty states met in Charlottesville, Virginia, for a "historic education summit" where, for the first time in the nation's history, a set of national education goals was articulated. The goals focused on school readiness, school completion, student achievement and citizenship, science and mathematics, adult literacy and lifelong learning, and the school environment (safe, disciplined, drug free). For the most part, "school reform efforts [were not] directed toward addressing the special challenges that students with disabilities face" (National Council on Disability, 1989, p. 2); most obviously missing was concern for the diagnostic and intervention needs that are common among students with disabilities, especially those with LD (Ysseldyke, Algozzine, & Thurlow, 1992). The initiative for reform captured LD with continuing controversies created by students with attention deficit/hyperactivity disorder (ADHD), inclusion, and outcomes and accountability.

Categories for the Future

As special education ages, evidence of "hardening of the categories" is not easy to find. In fact, while professionals in some areas (e.g., mental retardation) are proposing more functionally useful definitions in attempts to clean up their definitional problems (Ysseldyke, Algozzine, & Thurlow, 1992), for other conditions, especially LD, current definitions are softer and more lenient than ever before in history. All of which results in more and more students being classified as needing special education (U.S. Department of Education [USDE], 1995) and additional groups begging for assistance for students who still do not fit into existing categories.

At this writing, professional concern for one such group had reached an all-time high and professionals were lobbying to have ADHD included as a new category under the Individuals with Disabilities Education Act (Parker, 1990). The "voluminous body of literature amassed on this topic has evolved into a kind of ADHD paradigm in which a series of unquestioned assumptions [unresolved definitional and diagnostic problems] have become accepted dogma" (Reid, Maag, Vasa, 1993, p. 198), and the American Psychiatric Association now describes a disorder called Attention Deficit Hyperactivity Disorder (ADHD).

People with this disorder are said to show developmentally inappropriate degrees of inattention, impulsiveness, and hyperactivity. Associated features are said to include low self-esteem, mood instability, low frustration tolerance, academic underachievement, problems with social relationships, and temper tantrums. The disorder is said to be common, occurring in as many as 3% of children not currently classified and receiving special education. Because these same characteristics (e.g., attention problems and hyperactivity/impulsivity) are found in students with LD, recent professional concern has turned to differentiating LD from ADHD, and little progress has been made.

There is no federal category or definition for students with attention deficit/hyperactivity disorders. The most widely accepted definition(s) appeared in the Diagnostic and Statistical Manual for Mental Disorders (DSM) of the American Psychiatric Association (APA). The first categorization of characteristics that have become known as ADHD appeared in DSM-II and was called "Hyperkinetic Reaction to Childhood" (American Psychiatric Association [APA], 1968). In DSM-III, 14 characteristics were organized into three groups—inattention, impulsivity, and hyperactivity (APA, 1980)—causing considerable criticism because of the complexity created for professionals trying to differentiate among them. This led to a single list of 14 characteristics being associated with ADHD in DSM-III-R (APA, 1980) and paved the way for the latest efforts to define ADHD in DSM-IV (APA, 1995).

Characteristics associated with ADHD are similar to those associated with LD (see Table 12.1). For example, inattention, hyperactivity, and impulsivity are key behavioral characteristics associated with LD, and "clinically significant distress or impairment in academic functioning" is an analogous phrase for "significant discrepancy between ability and achievement." Moreover, interventions prescribed for students with ADHD are often used with students with LD (e.g., training or shaping appropriate behaviors, reducing inappropriate behaviors, creating stimulating learning tasks, and using varied instructional activities).

Professionals concerned with students with ADHD offer the following "principles of remediation" for improving inattention, excessive activity, and impulsivity (C.H.A.D.D., 1992):

Inattention

- Decrease the length of the task.
  - Break one task into smaller parts, to be completed at different times.
  - Give two tasks, with a preferred task to be completed after the less preferred task.
  - Give fewer spelling words and math problems.
  - Use fewer words in explaining tasks (concise and global verbal directions).
  - Use distributed practice for rote tasks, rather than using mass practice.
- Make tasks interesting.
  - Allow work with partners, in small groups, or in centers.
  - Alternate high- and low-interest tasks.

Table 12.1
Criteria for ADHD

A. Either 1 or 2:
   (1) Six or more of the following symptoms of *inattention* have persisted for at least 6 months to a degree that is maladaptive and inconsistent with developmental level:
   Inattention
      (a) often fails to give close attention to details or makes careless mistakes in schoolwork, work, or other activities
      (b) often has difficulty sustaining attention in tasks or play activities
      (c) often does not seem to listen when spoken to directly
      (d) often does not follow through on instructions and fails to finish schoolwork, chores, or duties in the workplace (not due to oppositional behavior or failure to understand instructions)
      (e) often has difficulty organizing tasks and activities
      (f) often avoids, dislikes, or is reluctant to engage in tasks that require sustained mental effort (such as schoolwork or homework)
      (g) often loses things necessary for tasks or activities (e.g., toys, school assignments, pencils, books, or tools)
      (h) is often easily distracted by extraneous stimuli
      (i) is often forgetful in daily activities
   (2) Six or more of the following symptoms of *hyperactivity-impulsivity* have persisted for at least 6 months to a degree that is maladaptive and inconsistent with developmental level:
   Hyperactivity
      (a) often fidgets with hands or feet or squirms in seat
      (b) often leaves seat in classroom or in other situations in which remaining seated is expected
      (c) often runs about or climbs excessively in situations in which it is inappropriate (in adolescents or adults, may be limited to subjective feelings of restlessness)
      (d) often has difficulty playing or engaging in leisure activities quietly
      (e) is often "on the go" or often acts as if "driven by a motor"
      (f) often talks excessively
   Impulsivity
      (g) often blurts out answers before questions have been completed
      (h) often has difficulty awaiting turn
      (i) often interrupts or intrudes on others (e.g., butts into conversations and games)
B. Some hyperactive-impulsive or inattentive symptoms that caused impairment were present before age 7 years.
C. Some impairment from the symptoms is present in two or more situations (e.g., at school [or work] and at home).
D. There must be evidence of clinically significant impairment in social, academic, or occupational functioning.
E. The symptoms do not occur exclusively during the course of a pervasive developmental disorder, schizophrenia, or other psychotic disorder and are not better accounted for by another mental disorder (e.g., mood disorder, anxiety disorder, dissociative disorder, or a personality disorder).

Note. Reprinted with permission from the *Diagnostic and Statistical Manual of Mental Disorders*, fourth edition. Washington, DC, American Psychiatric Association, 1994.

- Use the overhead projector when lecturing.
- Allow the child to sit closer to the teacher.

- Increase novelty, especially into later time periods of longer tasks.
  - Make a game out of checking work.
  - Use games to overlearn rote material.

Excessive Activity

- Do not attempt to reduce activity, but channel it into acceptable avenues.
  - Encourage nondisruptive, directed movement in classrooms.
  - Allow standing during seat work, especially during the end of the task.
- Use activity as a reward.
  - Give an activity reward (run errand, clean board, organize teacher's desk, arrange chairs) as an individual reward for improvement.
- Use active responses in instruction.
  - Use teaching activities that encourage active responding (talking, moving, organizing, working at the board).
  - Encourage daily writing, painting.
  - Teach child to ask on-topic questions.

Impulsivity

- Give the child substitute verbal or motor responses to make while waiting, and where possible, encourage daydreaming or planning in the interim.
  - Instruct the child on how to continue on easier parts of task (or do a substitute task) while waiting for the teacher's help.
  - Have the child underline or rewrite directions before beginning, or give magic markers or colored pencils for the child to underline directions or relevant information.
  - Encourage doodling or play with clay, paper clips, or pipe cleaners while waiting or listening to instruction.
  - Encourage note taking (even just cue words).

While these are good ideas, clearly there is no diagnostic-prescriptive magic here. Almost any teacher will have at least one student who could profit from interventions as broad and general as those proposed for inattention, excessive activity, and impulsivity. Sometimes the student(s) will be identified with specific LD and sometimes with some other condition (e.g., ADHD). Sometimes the student will not be classified at all. Paying attention, listening, following directions, sitting still, playing quietly, waiting, concentrating, and remembering are difficult for many students, especially when what they are being asked to do competes with other more interesting things to do (as far as they are concerned). Take heart, for while there is plenty of interest and attention provided these students and their problems, again there is not much mystery or magic here. Good teaching is good teaching, and stimulating, active lessons often go a long way in focusing the attention and controlling the activity of *any* students.

What is wrong with creating a new category and providing services for more students? Not much, if done properly with concern for definitional criteria that create a unique group of students with unique needs that can be altered with specific interventions. A key risk is the confusion created when criteria fail to differentiate categories, when assessment practices further embroil a profession in controversy, and when interventions recommended by people who are not teachers fail to bring integrity to the condition (cf. Reid, Maag, & Vasa, 1993).

Inclusion

The belief that more students with disabilities should be educated in the same classrooms as their neighbors and peers is among reform initiatives that have also troubled professionals in LD. Currently known as the inclusion (or inclusive schools) movement, this departure from contemporary practice has its roots in mainstreaming, normalization, and the "regular education initiative" and is given new energy by the large number of students identified with LD each year (currently about half of all students with disabilities are in this category). Educating more students in neighborhood schools and being concerned about the burgeoning masses of students with LD are not new concerns, nor are they particularly radical departures from other future concerns. Regardless, they have generated considerable heat and not much light on how to proceed in reforming special education for students with LD.

Concerns.   Arguments against inclusion are grounded in requirements formulated in federal legislation governing provisions of special education services. Opponents of inclusion for students with LD point to the availability of a continuum of placement options being required by law. They believe special classes provide intensive, highly individualized instruction. They believe also that: (a) resource assistance provides specific skill instruction focused on individual needs; (b) consultation provides support for general education teachers, and accommodations and modification provided in their rooms represent minor support needed by students with LD; and (c) all these instructional options are necessary for students with LD to receive a "free, appropriate public education" guaranteed by Public Law No. 94–142 and its derivatives.

Assumptions Driving Concerns.   The basic problem with inclusion as identified and argued by its opponents is that appropriate services for students with LD cannot be provided in general education settings. Several key assumptions drive this argument (cf. Division for Learning Disabilities, undated):

- A regular classroom setting cannot provide the specific and intensive instructional services appropriate for some students with LD.

- Students with LD who are placed in general education classrooms, to be successful, will need consultation, support services, or direct services—or all—from a specialist at varying points in their school careers.

- The IEP must be formulated prior to determination of the appropriate placement option.
- General education teachers can assist students with LD by using appropriate accommodations and auxillary aids in the classroom.
- Personnel who possess specialized skills in LD must be available to assess learning and guide general education teachers in determining appropriate accommodations, adaptations, and aids.
- Special education and general education professionals must actively work with each family and student to maximize integration with peers, and independence at home, in school, and in the workplace.
- The different professional competencies possessed by LD specialists and general education personnel are both needed to achieve positive educational outcomes for all students with LD.
- The annual IEP review must ensure a free, appropriate public education for each individual student with LD.

Creating policy from such assumptions and beliefs is problematic. First, some of the concepts are not grounded in research, although they may be true, based on what has gone on in the name of education. More important, they represent statements for what should be done to make education for students with LD special, rather than reasons for not doing something else. For example, arguing that personnel who possess specialized skills in LD must be available to assess learning and guide general education teachers in determining appropriate accommodations, adaptations, and aids is a proactive statement of best practice. It is not a reason for avoiding inclusion, and general education teachers will probably welcome such support with open arms. Special educators will have to be sure they prepare people who can provide it and that the people deliver when called upon to do so. Clearly, actions must speak louder than words for inclusion (or traditional special education) to work.

Alternatives.   Typically, when confronted with dissonance and the need for paradigm shifts, professionals meet to identify the problem. They then define the problem, identify the need to change, meet to formulate solutions to the problem, and recommend solutions be adopted. Too often in education, all this action results in a treatise for marching in place, a serious case of paralysis by analysis, another case of the generals putting mines in the paths of the soldiers.

So what is wrong with inclusion? Not much, if done properly, with students placed in general classrooms with consultation, support, and the direct services they need to make their school careers successful. Not much, if done properly with personnel who possess specialized skills in LD being available to assess learning and guide general education teachers in providing appropriate accommodations, adaptations, and aids. Not much, if done properly with special education and general education personnel actively working with each family and student to maximize integration with peers and independence at home, in school, and in the workplace. A key risk in not doing this is perpetuating an "us-them" mentality that is divisive to collaboration and effective teaching.

What Works, Works

In the early days, diagnostic-prescriptive teaching models directed efforts to make special education special. Professionals identified "learning problems" and their "underlying causes" and prescribed interventions to improve them. The logic of the plan was obvious, but the outcomes were disappointing. For the most part, most of the research failed to support the benefits of diagnostic-prescriptive teaching, and professionals began to look elsewhere for solutions to improving instruction (Ysseldyke & Algozzine, 1994).

Today, principles of effective instruction are known, and concern has shifted from evaluating children to evaluating instructional environments (Ysseldyke, Algozzine, & Thurlow, 1992). Now, professionals are concerned with both the extent to which effective teaching is being implemented and the gathering of evidence of it before any special program is created. This means that holding students accountable for achievement in the absence of concern for opportunity to learn, appropriateness and equity of resources, and other "school production" variables simply doesn't make sense (Darling-Hammond, 1993). This also means that student outcomes will be important like never before in history. Concern for high standards will create expectations that will be more difficult to reach, and blaming students for not reaching them probably will no longer be acceptable.

What is wrong with outcomes and accountability? Not much, if done properly, with different professional competencies possessed by specialists in LD and general education brought to bear to achieve positive educational outcomes for all students with LD. The key risks are assuming placement means program and failing to evaluate the extent to which what goes on in the classrooms is truly making a difference in the lives of students being educated there.

LD IN PERSPECTIVE

Having LD as a separate category makes sense if a distinct group of students emerges when definitions are put into practice. This has not been the case. Putting these students together with others with "learning problems" means that the special education rolls will expand to unreasonable levels, and this provides clear support for making inclusion and effective instruction work. The circle is complete and there is no clear-cut simple answer for how to address the problems facing the field of LD. Clearly, a directive for reform can be derived from increased concern with not just doing the right things, but doing things right.

Students with LD are sometimes referred to as having "mild disabilities." The term is not used to imply that these students do not have serious problems learning or that their problems are less important than those of any other students. The term has come to be used for this group of students because many of their characteristics overlap with other conditions, and many of them can be served in general classroom environments or resource rooms with assistance from special education teachers (USDE, 1995; Ysseldyke & Algozzine, 1984, 1990).

For decades, special education existed as a separate, parallel system to general education. With passage of federal legislation and the requirement that students with disabilities be educated in the least restrictive environment, special education began to be seen as part of a continuum of delivering services to them. With passage of federal legislation, a new kind of partnership had to be forged between special and general education. Schools were confronted for the first time with educating in general classrooms new populations of individuals with disabilities. They were also required to provide services to younger (ages 3 to 5) and older (ages 18 to 21) students with disabilities than had previously been served. School systems were required to enter into cooperative arrangements with other agencies for provision of related services (like psychological counseling and physical therapy) and bear the expense of paying for them.

One major area affected by this massive legislation was the training of personnel. To provide services to new populations of students, schools needed appropriately trained teachers. General education teachers, charged with the task of educating any students with disabilities in general classroom settings, need in-service education. Yet schools do not have the financial resources to provide such training. When teachers are faced with the task of providing services they are not trained to provide, they develop considerable job-related stress. Many shift jobs, and others leave the profession. These are continuing problems in special education (Ysseldyke & Algozzine, 1984; Ysseldyke, Algozzine, & Thurlow, 1992).

Important changes taking place to provide services to students with learning disabilities are grounded in the philosophical, moral, ethical, sociological, medical, and educational underpinnings of our society and of models for understanding and treating learning disabilities.

The enrollment of increasing numbers of students with disabilities in public education programs has also placed a large financial burden on the schools. Buildings and equipment must be modified, and new equipment and facilities must be purchased. Because schools must provide education and related services, they end up paying for special curriculum materials and other necessary aides and devices. As the financial burden increases, people begin to question the extent to which provision of services to so many students is worthwhile. Interest in educational outcomes becomes a source of justification for maintaining separate programs.

Major questions also arise regarding limits of responsibility. Even though the mandates appear relatively clear, school personnel have difficulty deciding or defining precisely how services are to be paid for, who should deliver them, and where, how, when, and for how long services will (or should) be provided. As schools are required to serve new age ranges of students with disabilities, there is little provision for enabling school personnel to meet age-related needs. The mandate for service is present, but the technology for provision of service is not. What usually happens is that schools simply expand their curriculum upward or downward in efforts to educate these new populations of students.

We believe there are important changes taking place in efforts to provide services to students with LD. Clearly these efforts are grounded in the philosophical, moral, ethical, sociological, medical, and educational underpinnings of our society, and in the models for understanding and treating LD. We believe understanding the foundations of contemporary practice will go a long way in making special education for students with LD better in the future.

SUMMARY

- Good teaching is good teaching for *any* students.
- Educating more students in neighborhood schools and being concerned about the burgeoning masses of students with LD have generated considerable heat and not much light on how to proceed in reforming special education for students with LD.
- Today, principles of effective instruction are known, and concern has shifted from evaluating children to evaluating instructional environments.
- Holding students accountable for achievement in the absence of concern for opportunity to learn, appropriateness and equity of resources, and other "school production" variables simply does not make sense.
- The enrollment of increasing numbers of students with disabilities in public education programs places a large burden on schools.
- Important changes taking place to provide services to students with LD are grounded in the philosophical, moral, ethical, sociological, medical, and educational underpinnings of our society, and in the models for understanding and treating LD.

DISCUSSION QUESTIONS ────────────────────────────

To help extend your understanding of future and continuing challenges in the field of LD, reflect on and discuss the following questions:

1. Some professionals argue that defining LD is unnecessary; others believe the category does not exist without an accepted definition. What do you think?

2. Do you believe the category of LD adequately represents students having difficulties in school? Why?

3. Some professionals believe that schools create LD. What do you think?

4. What is your philosophy of special education, including its relationship to general education? Compare your views with those of your peers, administrators, local advocacy groups, and parents or guardians of students with LD.

5. Do you believe psychological, behavioral, and cognitive models adequately represent methods appropriate for teaching students with LD?

6. Have services provided to students with LD been successful? Why or why not?

7. In what ways do you think the field of LD should be improved?

REFERENCES ────────────────────────────

Adelman, H. S., & Taylor, L. (1983). *Learning disabilities in perspective.* Glenview, IL: Scott Foresman.

Algozzine, B., & Ysseldyke, J. E. (1982). Classification decisions in learning disabilities. *Educational and Psychological Measurement, 2,* (2), 117–129.

Algozzine, B., & Ysseldyke, J. E. (1983). Learning disabilities as a subset of school failure: The oversophistication of a concept. *Exceptional Children, 50,* 242–246.

Algozzine, B., & Ysseldyke, J. E. (1986). The future of the LD field: Screening and diagnosis. *Journal of Learning Disabilities, 19,* 394–398.

American Psychiatric Association. (1968). *Diagnostic and statistical manual of mental disorders,* second edition. Washington, DC: Author.

American Psychiatric Association. (1980). *Diagnostic and statistical manual of mental disorders,* third edition. Washington, DC: Author.

American Psychiatric Association. (1994). *Diagnostic and statistical manual of mental disorders,* fourth edition. Washington, DC: Author.

C.H.A.D.D. (1992). *Newsletter.* Plantation, FL: Author.

Darling-Hammond, L. (1993). Opportunity to learn is the critical piece of the standards debate. *The Harvard Education Letter, 9* (6), 2.

Division for Learning Disabilities. (undated). *Inclusion: What does it mean for students with learning disabilities?* Reston, VA: Council for Exceptional Children, Author.

Epps, S., Ysseldyke, J. E., & Algozzine, B. (1983). Public policy implications of different definitions of learning disabilities. *Journal of Psychoeducational Assessment, 1,* 341–352.

Hammill, D. D., Leigh, J. E., McNutt, G., & Larsen, S. C. (1981). A new definition of learning disabilities. *Learning Disabilities Quarterly, 4,* 336–342.

Lerner, J. (1994). *Learning disabilities* (6th ed.). Boston, MA: Houghton Mifflin.

Myers, P., & Hammill, D. D. (1990). *Learning disabilities.* Austin, TX: PRO-ED.

National Council on Disability. (1989). *The education of students with disabilities: Where do we stand?* Washington, DC: Author.

National Joint Committee on Learning Disabilities. (1981). *A new definition for learning disabilities.* Washington, DC: Author.

O'Shea, L. J., & Valcante, G. (1986). A comparison over time of relative discrepancy scores of low achievers. *Exceptional Children, 53,* 253–259.

Parker, M. (1990). *Education position paper.* (Available from Children with Attention Deficit Disorders (CHADD), 1859 N. Pine Island Road, Suite 185, Plantation, FL 33322.)

Reid, R., Maag, J. W., & Vasa, S. F. (1993). Attention deficit hyperactivity disorder as a disability category: A critique. *Exceptional Children, 60,* 198–214.

Stanovich, K. E., (1989). *Discrepancy definitions of reading disability: Has intelligence led us astray?* Address presented at the Joint Conference on Learning Disabilities, Ann Arbor, MI, June.

Torgesen, J. K. (1991). Learning disabilities: Historical and conceptual issues. In B. Y. L. Wong (Ed.), *Learning about learning disabilities* (pp. 3–37). San Diego, CA: Academic Press.

Torgesen, J. K, & Wong, B. Y. L. (Eds.). (1986). *Psychological and educational perspectives on learning disabilities.* San Diego, CA: Academic Press.

U.S. Department of Education (1995). *Seventeenth annual report to Congress.* Washington, DC: Author.

Wong, B. Y. L. (Ed.). (1991). *Learning about learning disabilities.* San Diego, CA: Academic Press.

Ysseldyke, J. E., & Algozzine, B. (1982). *Critical issues in special and remedial education.* Boston, MA: Houghton Mifflin.

Ysseldyke, J. E., & Algozzine, B. (1984). *Introduction to special education.* Boston, MA: Houghton Mifflin.

Ysseldyke, J., & Algozzine, B. (1990). *Introduction to special education* (2nd ed.). Boston, MA: Houghton Mifflin.

Ysseldyke, J., & Algozzine, B. (1994). *Special education: A practical approach for teachers* (3rd ed.). Boston, MA: Houghton Mifflin.

Ysseldyke, J., Algozzine, B., & Epps, S. (1983). A logical and empirical analysis of current practices in classifying students as handicapped. *Exceptional Children, 50,* 160–166.

Ysseldyke, J., Algozzine, B., Shinn, M., & McGue, M. (1982). Similarities and differences between underachievers and students classified learning disabled. *Journal of Special Education, 16,* 73–85.

Ysseldyke, J. E., & Algozzine, B., & Thurlow, M. L. (1992). *Critical issues in special education* (2nd ed.) Boston, MA: Houghton Mifflin.

Name Index

Abbey, H., 146, 284
Abel, E.L., 70, 142, 154, 155, 159, 375, 381,
Abramson, J., 329
Ackerman, N.W., 374
Adams, B.N., 363, 370, 383, 384, 388
Adams, J., 5
Adamson, G., 325
Adelman, H.S., 31, 44, 419
Adler, S., 71, 162, 171
Algozzine, B., 4, 6, 11–13, 15, 22, 30, 39, 71, 162, 224, 326–328, 398, 418, 420–422, 428, 429
Allen, J.S., 165, 166
Allen, R.P., 152, 163
Alley, G.R., 42, 46, 76, 77, 261, 264
Allington, R.I., 297
Allington, R.L., 343
Allred, E.N., 173
Aman, M.G., 72, 163
American Academy of Pediatrics, 60, 125
American Printing House for the Blind, 13
American Psychiatric Association, 45
Amiran, M., 62, 77
Anderson, G.L., 58, 66, 309, 310
Anderson, L.M., 64
Anderson, P.L., 44
Apgar, Virginia, 161
Apter, S.J., 244
Aries, P., 364, 383
Aristotle, 364
Armstrong, S., 44
Ashton-Warner, S., 299
Association for Children with Learning Disabilities, 9
Avolio, B.J., 330

Ayres, A.J., 125
Ayres, R.R., 71, 166

Babcock, N.L., 331
Bailey, D.B., 74, 221, 377, 379
Baker, L., 46, 291
Baker, S.C., 238
Bakken, J.P., 273
Bakker, D.J., 115, 118
Baldwin, R.S., 39
Baltes, P.B., 377
Bandura, A., 373
Bane, M.J., 383, 384, 389, 391, 399
Banikowski, A., 44
Bannatyne, A., 205
Barnard, M., 153
Barr, E., 163
Barreara, I., 58, 66, 309, 310
Bartel, N.R., 202
Bass, B.M., 330
Bastian, H.C., 108, 118
Bateman, B., 33, 34, 194, 201, 205
Bauer, A.M., 363, 377
Bauernschmidt, M., 226
Bauwens, J., 265, 324, 333, 338
Beach, D.H., 260
Beavers, W.R., 363
Becker, L.D., 44
Becker, W.C., 235
Behan, P., 70, 142, 152
Behnen, M.L., 374
Behr, S., 374, 377, 378
Beirne-Smith, M., 70, 140
Bellinger, D., 173
Bempechat, J., 323
Bender, L., 100, 102
Bender, W.N., 33, 163, 258, 261, 262, 264, 265

Bentley, L., 289
Berberich, J.P., 373
Bereiter, C., 235
Berlin, 108, 117, 122
Bickel, D.D., 221
Bickel, W.E., 221
Bijou, S., 150
Biklen, D., 328, 342
Billingsley, B.S., 23
Birch, H.G., 159
Birch, J.W., 42, 324, 325, 328
Blalock, G., 42
Blalock, J.W., 46
Blankenship, C.S., 221, 224, 324
Blaskey, P., 125
Blau, A., 114
Blau, H., 67, 68, 116–118
Blenkinsop, J., 44
Blessing, K.R., 207
Bley, N., 44
Bodnar, J.R., 324
Bogdan, R., 80, 82
Bond, L., 379
Bony, E., 84
Borden, K.S., 68, 122, 123
Borg, W.R., 63
Borkowski, J.G., 46
Borstelmann, L.J., 364
Bos, C.S., 219
Boshes, B., 111, 112, 190
Boss, P.G., 366
Bracken, B.A., 205
Bradley, C., 102, 162
Brady, M.P., 244
Brammer, G., 42
Brandt, R., 324
Bransford, J.D., 264

433

Subject Index